The Realization of
Anti-racist Teaching

The Realization of Anti-racist Teaching

Godfrey L. Brandt

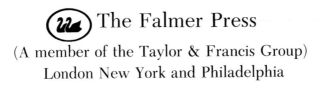

The Falmer Press

(A member of the Taylor & Francis Group)
London New York and Philadelphia

UK The Falmer Press, Falmer House, Barcombe, Lewes, East Sussex, BN8 5DL

USA The Falmer Press, Taylor & Francis Inc., 242 Cherry Street, Philadelphia, PA 19106-1906

First published 1986

Library of Congress Cataloging in Publication Data

Library of Congress Catalog Number: 86-83075

ISBN 1 85000 126 X
ISBN 1 85000 127 8 (pbk.)

Jacket design by Caroline Archer

Typeset in 11/13 Caledonia by
Imago Publishing Ltd, Thame, Oxon

Printed in Great Britain by Taylor & Francis (Printers) Ltd, Basingstoke

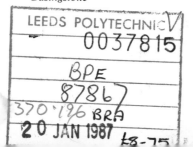

Contents

Acknowledgements

I would like to thank all the teachers and headteachers who let me into their classrooms and schools and cooperated in various ways which contributed to the completion of this book.

Thanks to Roger Hewitt for reading and commenting on chapter 1 and to Chris Mullard for reading the entire manuscript in its 'final draft' stage, knowing that only minor comments could be taken into consideration at that point. Also, thanks for writing the foreword to this book. My students and colleagues also should be credited for providing the stimulating and challenging discussions and debates in which we have engaged.

I should also like to thank those people close to me who provided support and encouragement right up to the completion of the job and special thanks to Pauline for her understanding and care which was generous enough to defer to the typewriter and often motivate her to do my share of the washing-up.

Finally, thanks to Carla Newton for being not only a typist par excellence but for being tremendously efficient, supportive and a friend.

A Contextual Foreword

Any book which consciously claims to address the complex and highly controversial subject of anti-racist education from within a Black and essentially third world perspective is important. This is not merely the case because too few writings of this kind exist or because the field itself is cluttered and in a racist sense dominated by the liberal outpourings of mainly white multiculturalists: but it is so because anti-racist critical work, however well it is argued or written, represents a fundamental challenge to both the edifice of liberal racist 'scholarship' and the racist educational system in which this 'scholarship' is embedded, legitimated, and perpetuated. For this reason alone *The Realization of Anti-Racist Teaching* is as important as it is challenging.

Thus, in crucial opposition to the white multicultural tradition, what is attempted in the chapters that follow is to set the scene, argue the case, and stimulate and engage in the struggle for a new pedagogy — the pedagogy of anti-racism. What this means in theory and practice, practice and theory, cannot, though, be gleaned from the content of the last two chapters on anti-racist teaching and pedagogy. Instead the real meaning is to be found in the context of these two chapters, which in turn is located in the socio-historical context of current debates in race and ethnic relations and more specifically, the actual context of resistance, struggle, and justice which informs and encompasses any notion of anti-racist education developed as an oppositional form of pedagogic theory and practice in a racist society. In other words, the specific as opposed to the general importance of Godfrey Brandt's deliberately accessible book is to be discovered in its contextual backcloth and argument — or in and on the stage of processes as a series of enactments which unravel the conceptual and thematic plot of a new interpretation of a relatively old, frowned upon, and dominated paradigm.

Abstract though they are, it is, however, from these enactments that the book is constructed as a challenge to multicultural ideology and the ethnicism or disconnected cultural form of racism, which permeates multicultural policies and practices. Of the four main contextual pillars around which the detailed enactments occur, the first two are diagnostic. They are concerned with the mapping out and the situating of what might be termed the moral functionalist, Weberian and classical Marxist approaches to the field in order to make space for the book's contribution to new 'theory'. Here the context and anchorage of the analysis heavily draws upon an experientially enacted Black Third World definition of social reality in racist British society and a Black tradition and critique of white European scholarship as exemplified in the work of Robinson and others, including myself. What this perspective provides for the book as a whole, as well as highlighting the connection between racism, capitalism, and colonialism is a context in which it is not only possible to review critically the background to current debates in British race relations, but also a context in which to challenge the racial structure of knowledge, concepts, and paradigms (including Marxism) employed by white academics, policy makers, and practitioners in the field.

Although from within such a perspective the reality of institutionalized racism is historically reconstructed as one of the main warp threads of British history from Elizabeth I's notorious racist proclamation of 1596 to the publication of the Scarman, Rampton and Swann reports in the 1980s, it is, nevertheless, not until the main theoretical premises of the perspective are introduced that Brandt begins to hint at the kind of contribution to 'theory' the book could make. At this point and in my view the correct assertion is made that no understanding of racism in society or in any of its social institutions, such as education, can be attained without employing a theoretical framework which explicitly and structurally recognizes and accounts for the connections between the oppressions, exploitations, and inequalities associated with the notions of race, class, and gender. But to state that this should be so is, of course, a lot easier and quite different from explaining how it is the case. On this latter level a failure has to be registered, although the concept of 'racial gender/genderized race', which emerges from the endeavour to tease out the possible relationships that might exist, secures a gender-race specific presence throughout the book — a presence which distinguishes it from most other books of its kind written by men.

Together these two diagnostic, contextual features, the broadly construed Black Third World perspective and set of theoretical premises on the race-class-gender problematic, pave the way for two other contexts, which are basically prescriptive in nature. That is to say they tend to give rise to a number of possibilities for remedial action, and hence indicate the value of the book's contribution to new 'practice'. The first of these lives in the author's argued-out idea of 'racist education'. What is meant by this idea is not just that schooling or that which mostly occurs in daily classroom life is deemed to be racist, but rather that *education* per se, as institutionalized and non-institutionalized phenomena, process, activity, and practice, is intrinsically racist. Such an idea, which is formed out of a marriage between the creative insights of Bernstein's sociology and the critical work of Black social scientists already alluded to, can only exist if some concept of historical correspondence and lived social connection with the colonial and imperial antecedents of modern British society prevails. For what this adds up to is not just simply the problematization of education as an institution for the realistic attainment of some kind of racial equality or justice: it poses instead the existence of a context, which socially constructed over time, denies even the possibility of any education for Blacks other than that which comes from and through emancipatory struggle.

While such a context of education as being 'racist education' allows for the development of emancipatory, oppositional, and anti-racist education, it does not, however, take the reader too far along the road toward 'the realization of anti-racist teaching'. All it, in fact, does, and this, of course, is much more than is usually found in the literature, is to consolidate the argument and urgency for anti-racist teaching. The context which in a sense bridges the distance between theory and practice, intention and realization is that of a situated pedagogy — the kind of transmission practices developed out of a Black anti-racist definition of educational reality that need to be employed to realize anti-racist teaching.

This pedagogic context, which can only be fully comprehended in terms of the other three contexts already mentioned, is totally dependent upon a view of how transmissions happen, and in a profound way what is the key or social mechanism that regulates the transmissions. At this critical point in the last lap of Brandt's argument some help is received via Bernstein's recent work on 'the pedagogic device'. But despite this, there does, unfortunately, still appear to exist a number of crucial gaps in analysis and argument between the first and last chapters — a problem, which is partially resolved in a proper plea for teachers to link together and with the Black community in the struggle against racism and for a new pedagogy of anti-racism.

This challenge not only constitutes the challenge of Godfrey

Brandt's book, which is commendable because of the four contexts in which it is set and upon which it draws, but, as intended, it also constitutes a challenge to all students, teachers, and other readers, who desire to struggle against racism in education and work towards a pedagogy of anti-racism. For those of use who so desire, *The Realization of Anti-Racist Teaching* is a highly readable and useful beginning.

Chris Mullard
January 1986

Introduction

Within the current climate of debates and counter debates regarding the importance of and the positive need for change in education *vis à vis* race and racism, there has been an increasing amount of literature generated to help highlight the issues for teachers and teacher-trainers.

However, the emphasis has tended to be at the level of theory and policy. This has involved the critique of current theory and the generation of new theory. This theory has tended to both influence and be influenced by policy. The oscillation between concern with theory and concern with policy by educationalists has tended to ignore the impact or lack of same on the actual practice of teaching and the concomitant learning process in British schools and, at present, there are still too few curriculum development projects with a specific anti-racist brief.

This book attempts to address itself to two major issues. The first one is raised by the observations in the previous paragraph. That is, what is the relationship between the educational debate at the level of academic institutions in-service and initial teacher training and LEA policy-makers and the actual practice of teaching? The second question, which is more precisely what the book is about, is how can one link the current theories being promulgated by theorists and activists and the practice of teachers? In other words, is anti-racist teaching practicable or is it simply an academic or political exercise generated by political militants and by academics who are so far removed from the 'chalk face' that they have no sense of the real issues facing teachers and teaching and have little sense of what is operable.

These are the two questions which this book addresses; the first one implicitly, the second, explicitly. In order to do this, I have felt it necessary to provide a socio-historical background to the current debates. This background, the area covered by chapter 1, attempts to briefly outline the history of racism and the parameters of black exploitation and oppression in the European context, especially Britain, and examines the role of the state in this. But in order to make it clear that black people have not simply been passive objects of this racial oppression, I also attempt to briefly chart the ways in which black people have over the years resisted racial discrimination and oppression.

In this first chapter, I also attempt to make the case, both implicitly and explicitly, for looking at racism both historically and contemporaneously through black perspectives. Throughout the book I use Black with a capital 'B' in its contemporary political sense which includes peoples of both the Asian and African Diaspora, because of the reality of their common experience of racism.

In chapter 2 I examine what I have referred to as *The Context of Anti-racist Education* in Britain. By this I am referring to the socio-economic, political and educational climate in which there is an attempt by some to develop an anti-racist pedagogy. This chapter examines certain key concepts like race, racism, education and schooling and also attempts to briefly examine the impact and articulations of the shifting epistemologies in education and their psychological underpinnings. I then introduce the notion of 'racist education' which I argue must be actively, consistently and coherently combatted.

Chapter 3 takes us into an examination of what is involved in the realization of anti-racist teaching. The false division between theory and practice is explored and the notions of deconstruction of 'racist education' is examined alongside its necessary concomitant of the reconstruction of a 'non-racist' education through anti-racism.

Some broad guidelines for anti-racist education are examined as a prelude to chapter 4, in which my observations of teachers at work in both primary and secondary schools are examined and commented upon. *Observing Anti-racist Teaching* is the title of chapter 4 which is divided into a primary section and a secondary section. These observations of teachers who, as I was informed, exposed an anti-racist practice, are by no means exhaustive neither in their remit or in their commentary. Rather, they serve as signals en route to the hopefully widespread development of an anti-racist practice in education. In commenting on these lessons and classes which I have observed, I have attempted to try and evaluate them principally in terms of their own aims and objectives and only secondarily in terms of a set of anti-racist criteria. Yet, a lot is left implicit for the reader to make the connections between the arguments contained within the pages of this book and those observations. Also, I have tried to highlight some of the elements which I consider to be 'good' anti-racist practice. This 'good' anti-racist practice might either be something to do directly with addressing racism itself or it might be to do with contributing to the 'building blocks' of anti-racist practice. These 'building blocks' are those elements which are informed by anti-racism as an ideology and are part of a coherent 'package' called anti-racist education.

The book is written with a shifting modality from the relatively theoretical chapters 1, 2 and 3 to the observational commentary of chapter 4. It is my intention to help make the language and politics of anti-racism accessible to all practitioners and to hold up anti-racist and 'aspiring' anti-racist practice for examination by both practitioners and theorists. Thus, my concern is not simply curriculum planning but, also, curriculum practice, the parameters of which are laid out in chapter 3. It is also my hope that this book will be a useful book for student teachers, practising teachers, educationists, other academics and any-one with some general concern for the future of British education and the specific development of a just, equitable and emancipatory system of education whereby no individual, be they female, Black or working class, or all three, is excluded, marginalized or oppressed simply on the basis of membership of that particular group or on any other basis for that matter.

The reader may want to read the book from beginning to end or to simply 'dip in' at the point of interest. Either approach could be useful. Yet, ultimately, the book will serve best those who are able to make the effort to read all of it because it is crucial in terms of the intentions of the book that the 'practice' recounted in chapter 4 is read through the insights of the previous chapters which are, ultimately, inextricably linked with each other and the final chapter. The assertions of the early chapters are given meaning and weight through the issues raised by the observations of practice.

1   The Socio-historical Background to Current Debates

The History of Racism

The majority of social scientists and educationalists who have looked at the socio-historical background to the current situation have tended to use policy as a focus for understanding the changes that have taken place. Thus people — 'the minorities' — Black people have been cast primarily as reactors to state policy and innovation. The other view (and I think the correct one) is that most Black people who came to this country in the 1950s came with a strong sense of purpose as well as a strong sense of the means of achieving the desired ends. But this sense, this purpose, these ends, were frustrated by racism at various levels (housing, employment, social and educational services). In this light one needs to reread and reinterpret the interactions between state policy and Black people. Understanding of the interaction between race, class, imperialism and nationalism as parameters of the social/racial oppression of Black people is essential. The interface between racial oppression and gender oppression is also significant. Let us then trace the significant historic shifts through looking at the following major epochs which lie at the basis of the current situation in Britain. These epochs are:

(a)   imperialism/colonialism;
(b)   independence and neo-colonialism;
(c)   immigration and nationality;
(d)   the Black British — from immigrant to citizen (the uneasy transition).

The interaction between state policy, practice and political action will run through this analysis.

The History of Racism

The history of racism in the United Kingdom goes back further than the date of the post-war arrival of a significant number of Black people from the colonies. Like the presence of Black people in Britain, racism dates back much further and certainly began to make itself apparent as early as the sixteenth century. In this century, racism was already linked to colour, as it was to other physical features, and to religion/culture. Yet the articulation of contemporary racism tends to be linked primarily to Black people and their presence in this country. This presence is usually treated as though it is a totally contemporary phenomenon and this obsession with the 'presence' as a totally contemporary phenomenon is linked to the debate about numbers and the panic about 'swamping'. As Field and Haikin (1971) write:

> The rapid expansion in the last twenty years of the numbers of coloured people in this country can give the impression that their presence is an entirely contemporary one. Not only does this coloured group remain a very small proportion of the total population, but small numbers of coloured people have been resident here for centuries.

That Black people were the indigenous inhabitants of Africa, Australasia, Asia, etc. is now a widely known and widely accepted fact. That the 'Indians' inhabited the Americas before the arrival of the White man and White woman is also widely known. What is a little known and little publicized fact is that there were Black people in Britain before the Anglo Saxons — the 'English' — arrived.

> Some were soldiers in the Roman Imperial Army that occupied the southern part of our island for three and a half centuries. Others were slaves. Among the troops defending Hadrian's Wall in the third century A.D. was a *division of Moors* (nomerur Maurorum Aurelian-orum) named after Marcus Aurelius or a later emperor known officially by the same name. (Fryer, 1984, I)

Fryer goes on to make the case for the presence, not only of African slaves and soldiers but of officers (praefecti) from North Africa. He cites evidence which suggests that this is indeed the case. For example, the large percentage of skeletons of Black Africans found among the 350 human skeletons excavated in 1951 — nine at York. These fossils dated back to Roman times.

The history of the presence of Black people in Britain is well charted elsewhere.[1] Therefore, it is not particularly useful or necessary to do that in tremendous detail here in this text. What is more important is to deal with the way in which British racism developed and the ways in which Black people have attempted to combat this racism which has affected every area of their lives. Yet since current racist moves are based on the 'numbers' and 'presence' argument, it is a question with which any treatment must deal.

It is clear from the evidence that there has been a continuous Black presence in Britain — notably from the sixteenth century onwards. In his play *Othello* (The Moor of Venice), William Shakespeare reflects to some extent on the Elizabethan attitude to 'aliens' in general, and to Blacks in particular, ranging from sexual stereotypes to social attitudes. While Shakespeare was exposing, through the theatre, the social reality of sixteenth-century England, Elizabeth, the reigning monarch, was herself active in her attempts to rid the country of 'the great number of Negroes and Blackamoors' which (as she is informed) are 'crept into the realm' (File and Power, 1981; also Fryer, 1984, p. 10). This 1596 speech, described as one of the earliest swamping speeches, has resounded over the centuries — the most recent being in the form of speeches made by Enoch Powell and Margaret Thatcher.[2]

It was towards the end of the sixteenth century that Shakespeare was writing or at least thinking of plays such as *The Merchant of Venice* and *Othello*. (*Othello* was published posthumously in the early seventeenth century (1622) and *The Merchant of Venice* in 1600.) It was also towards the end of the sixteenth century that it was becoming fashionable for White propertied and titled families to have one or more Black slaves as a status symbol. This was initiated by Lady Raleigh (wife of Sir Walter). The late sixteenth century and the early seventeenth century can therefore be seen as a crucial moment in the overt articulation of the racialization of relations in Europe as a whole and in Britain in particular. Black people became objectified as property — as status symbols in 'polite' White society and as human capital at the hard end of trade, industry and colonization. As Robinson (1983) puts it:

> The use of slave labour in The New World of the sixteenth century by the Spanish Crown (and soon after the Portuguese) and its Merchant concessionaires was ... a natural step. (pp. 153–4)

He later goes on to argue that:

> ... the British (and French) entrepreneurs — following the models provided by the Portuguese, Spanish and Dutch —

substantially substituted human capital for commodities in the
seventeenth and eighteenth centuries . . . (p. 160)

Despite attempts to substantially reduce it, the Black population
increased in spurts and stalls and by the mid-eighteenth century it was
estimated that there were as many as 14,000 to 20,000 Blacks in London
alone.

In 1772, slavery was declared illegal in England by the ruling of a
judge, Lord Mansfield. Here, I think it is important to note that this
abolition was not the product of a humanitarian conscience or even
because of the philanthropic and liberal campaigns by such as Wilber-
force or even Abe Lincoln. The basis of the change was an economic
one. The slave trade and the upkeep of slaves had become too expensive
for maximum exploitation. It would thus be cheaper to 'buy' the labour
of these people at a fraction of the price and to hand over the
responsibility for their upkeep which for slave owners was in excess of
any 'wages' that they would offer.

> Slaves were expensive to control and developing capitalist
> economies needed a free market in labour and a population
> which could afford to *buy* the goods now being produced in
> factories. Slaves were not a mobile workforce and had no wages
> with which to buy commodities, obviously did not fit the bill and
> thus stood in the way of economic progress. (Gordon and
> Brazier, 1985)

During the nineteenth century people of a range of ethnic groups began
to arrive in Britain — Lascars from the East Indies and Chinese seamen
stranded between ships. At the other end of the social scale, sons of
African chiefs began to come to Britain as students (Field and Haikin,
1971). Most historians seem to agree to a slight break in additions to the
Black British population in the nineteenth century.

What has been described as the 'second phase' of settlement of
Black people in this country began towards the end of the nineteenth
century. This was a settlement mainly of male seamen. However, the
largest influx began after 1914. During World War I there is a record of
demobilization of Black men in this country as well as a requisitioning of
their ships. Of course, some were also recruited to boost the labour force
in chemical and munition factories in various cities. During the Second
World War, Black labour was imported directly from the West Indies to
meet the demands of industry. Some joined the forces but they were
generally encouraged to volunteer for work in the factories.

In the early period of post-war reconstruction Britain, like its

European counterparts, needed labour. This need precipitated mass West Indian recruitment. In this situation of an acute shortage of labour:

> racialism operated on a free market basis — adjusting itself to the ordinary laws of supply and demand. So that in the sphere of employment, where too many jobs were seeking too few workers — as the State itself had acknowledged in the Nationality Act of 1948 — racialism did not debar Black people from work per se. It operated instead to deskill them, to keep their wages down and to segregate them in the dirty, ill-paid jobs that white workers did not want — not on the basis of an avowed racialism but in the habit of an acceptable exploitation. (Sivanandan, 1981/82)

The labour shortage and 'opportunities for advancement' were widely publicized in the Caribbean and by 1951 it was estimated that about 1750 in one year, gradually increasing to between 10,000 and 11,000 in 1954.

Colonialism as a Basis for Immigration

However, before looking further at the specificity of the events and circumstances surrounding Black immigration to this country in the early twentieth century, it is indeed necessary to examine colonialism and the role it played as a bridge between the earlier overt and blatant exploitation of slavery during the period of mercantilist expansion and the later attempt to exploit Black labour centrally (*ie.* in Britain) as the basis of a historical relationship. As argued by the Workers against Racism (WAR):

> In the colonies, nationalism was not a matter of simple rivalries. The imperialist powers asserted their right to colonize by treating the indigenous population as an inferior species. It was in the colonial situation that the vocabulary and culture of racism acquired a systematic form. (WAR, 1985, p. 14)

John Rex (1973) puts it another way:

> Racial discrimination and racial prejudice are phenomena of colonialism. It was as a result of the conquest of poor and relatively under-developed countries by the technologically advanced nations during the nineteenth century, that new kinds

of economy, new forms of social relations of production involving both conqueror and conquered, were brought into being. The inequalities between men of different nations, ethnic groups or religions, or between men of different skin colours, which resulted, were often justified in biological racist theories or some functional equivalent. (p. 75)

The fact is that colonialism in Europe was based on cultural and economic imperialism which was itself an ideology that assumed national, economic and racial superiority of one European nation above the other and of Europe over the rest of the world which was to be 'conquered', 'tamed' and 'claimed' for the crown.

The early phase of colonialism had an emphasis on the extension of the domain of the imperial power. The people who already inhabited those countries were seen as intrinsically inferior. Out of this phase of the British colonizing thrust was born the 'Old' Commonwealth — a term now used as a metaphor for the 'White' Commonwealth and as a major parameter for differential treatment. The second phase of colonial exploitation was more to do with the extraction of wealth from the colonized country.

The aim of this phase was not the establishment of a 'white man's country's, as an extension to the mother country, but rather to introduce into a country in order to extract mineral resources or grow cash crops for export to Europe. (Tierney, 1982, p. 17)

The rhetoric of this phase was one of 'development' and the 'civilizing' of the 'natives'. The reality was the underdeveloping of Asia, Africa and the Caribbean. This process, in terms of the African experience, is well analyzed and discussed by Walter Rodney (1972). The colonies of the latter period of colonization provided Britain not only with raw materials but with a market and a source of cheap labour which was to be exploited not only in the colony but later in the motherland.

Blacks in Post-War Britain

The post-war immigration of Black colonials/British subjects to Britain was a response to a call from the 'Motherland' to come 'home' to mother, to work and to build up a growing industrialized economy. However, besides the exploitation at work in the dirty and ill-paid jobs shunned by White 'indigenous' workers, there was a popular underlying and often blatant call by the White British public for them to 'go home'.

So what was evident in the fifties and sixties was a duality of response to Black workers — an official call to *come* home and a popular cry of 'go home'. Within this contradiction there was a shifting meaning of home. Home meant the 'Motherland' but it also meant the colony from which the Black person had recently come.

The point to be made here is that these Black people were British even before they had ever set foot on the soil of this island. They all came with British passports and had all grown up singing 'Rule Britannia' and asserting that 'Britons never shall be slaves'. But the following years were to prove that this new situation — this bringing together of Black British and of White British, of colonized and colonizer — would be an unhappy marriage. The years to follow have tended to be divided into certain distinct phases which tend to relate to the pre-eminent attitude of the state and the concomitant policy shifts that have characterized these certain relatively distinct periods. The phases are normally referred to as assimilationist, integrationist, and multiculturalist.

Though I would largely accept these broad 'phases', I think it is important to state that these phases are not self-contained, nor did they begin when West Indian and Asian immigrants first entered this country after the war. The fact is that these epochs are interwoven into the history and structure of British racism. Thus the current form and structure of racism in Britain is based on the interrelated, transhistorical and overlapping systems of exploitation: imperialism; capitalism; racialism (see table 1).

As I have suggested earlier, imperialism was both ideological and

Table 1: *Parameters of Black Immigration and Exploitation*

	Racism	**Imperialism**	**Capitalism**
Underpinning ideology	Racial superiority Cultural dominance Xenophobia	Inter national super- iority Cultural dominance Eurocentrism	Ownership Maximization of profits Functional Exploitation
Practices	Racial discrimination Unemployment and low remuneration Racial exploitation Ghettoization	Stratified reward System white black Indigenous immigrant Stratified job allocation Ghettoization	1 Creation of surplus value — underpric- ing labour 2 Use of cheapest labour — Blacks, women, children, migrants
Victims	RACIAL/ETHNIC MINORITY GROUPS	Third world countries COLONIZED PEOPLES	WORKING CLASS Guest workers Blacks Women

economic. The ideological was based on the notion of 'natural' military and maritime superiority. Thus, independent of the financial incentives of colonization in the fifteenth and sixteenth centuries, Britain was active in 'convincing' both her European rivals as well as the 'new world' of her superiority. However, coupled with this ideological intention was the economic intention of exploiting third world countries for the benefit of Europe — exploiting the 'Empire' for the benefit of the imperial power. In return, the colonized peoples received the dubious privilege of the status of 'British subject of Her Majesty's realm'. This appellation later proved to have less of a 'trade in' value than its *prima facie* connotation.

Capitalism, as a system by which the owners of the means of production exploited the labour force for minimal remuneration in the interest of the maximization of profits, provided the impetus and rationale for imperialist expansion. Capitalism combined with imperialism to benefit firstly European society as a whole and, secondly, the upper classes in particular.

Racialism provided a basis for the legitimation of the exploitation of Blacks by Whites. Since Blacks were seen as intrinsically inferior, this exploitation was seen as justifiable. Therefore, in the invitation that went out to the colonies was the implicit intention to exploit an old relationship in a new way.

With the economic boom that came after World War II, there was an accompanying restructuration of the organizational arrangements of exploitation. Britain, because of its access to a broad base of colonial labour, resorted to labour intensive production. The majority of Black people coming to this country in the post-war period found that they had a special place reserved for them in the social/racial status quo and division of labour — at the bottom. In addition they had brought with them a heritage of second classness as 'the colonized' and primarily as working class people. The result within the British social formation was cultural, social and racial domination with the added *de facto* 'alien' status despite the officially designated one. For example, the seamen that landed in Wales in Bute Town found that they had to carry their passbooks (not dissimilar to present-day South Africa) in order to get work. These elements combined to create a more sophisticated form of racism based on a network comprising racialism, imperialism, capitalism, xenophobia, prejudice, ethnocentricity and marginalization, both at the interpersonal *and* institutional levels. The alienation of Blacks in the fifties and early sixties went hand in hand with an educational policy of 'sink or swim'. Thus, no special attention was given to the needs of immigrants from the colonies.

The Assimilationist Phase

State policies in general, and education policies in particular, in the sixties were based on a liberal notion of assimilation. This assimilation was predicated by a liberal racism which implied that though Black people were not as yet equal to White people, if they assimilate and get lost in the fabric of the tapestry of British life they will not be problems and may even become equal.

Thus the focus here — at this point — was largely cultural. There was a culture deficit ideology in operation which implied that if Black people gave up their deficient and inadequate cultures and assimilated into the non-existent 'monolithic' British culture they would in all but colour become White and thereby become acceptable. However, even for those Black people who, as it were, accepted the principle of 'becoming White', the going proved rough if not impossible. They were discriminated against in employment, housing, social benefits and, alas, colour proved to have had much more importance than that with which it had initially been credited. Black people were the victims of racial attacks of both the physical and verbal kinds. The assimilationist thesis was therefore seen to be inadequate in meeting the needs of Black people or even in terms of keeping the peace.

During this period Black people had to find, and found, ways of combating the terrible and often violent and vicious racism experienced in their everyday lives.

The Integrationist Phase

With the proven inadequacy of assimilation as a policy and philosophy, the integrationist phase was begun. This phase was underpinned by a stated belief in the maintenance and protection of the social order. That is, instead of the previously unstated principle of 'get lost in the social fabric or perish', Black people's presence was acknowledged with an accompanying call to the Black community to make an effort to integrate. Thus the key was seen as 'cultural tolerance' (Mullard, 1982a, p. 126) though any adjusting that had to be done was seen to be entirely the responsibility of the Black communities. As Street-Porter (1978) succinctly stated:

> Cultural integration seems to be accepted as a modest tokenism, an acceptance of that which is quaint in minority culture but a worried rejection of those cultural aspects that seem not just

alien but threateningly so. In other words minority groups in practice are allowed complete freedom to define their own cultural identity in so far as this does not conflict with that of the indigenous White community. (pp. 50–1)

Thus the 'innovations' of this phase, though clothed in the rhetoric of harmony through cultural integration, were in fact a restructuring of the racial status quo. As a consequence, the policies and reports can be seen not as simple palliatives but as direct attacks on the resistance of Black people to the continuing oppression facing them within the British social structure.

The Commonwealth Immigrant Advisory Committee was both a part of, and a precipitate to, various initiatives in the government sector. Included among these was the Report *Immigrants and the Youth Service* (HMSO, 1967). In this Report it was unequivocally stated:

We reject the idea of several segregated societies, because this implies that the immigrants should be kept and maintained as separate entities, with social intercourse between them and the host community restricted both by law and by custom. This pattern is unacceptable on moral grounds. A second alternative is the concept of accommodation ... a situation in which immigrants accept the relationships available to them and act on them with some degree of conformity, but do not share the bulk of attitudes which are part of the host society. This too we reject. A third choice is the assimilation of immigrants to the host society ... This concept we also reject ... The aim which we therefore recommend is the *full integration* between immigrants and the host community, and between the various immigrant communities themselves.

Cultural Pluralism

The premise of cultural pluralism is that social relations can be wholly explained through culture and that there is a range of cultures in society which are in themselves homogeneous and have shared interests. Also, that these cultures interact with each other by a system of negotiation thereby coming to a consensus where there is a potential conflict. The state is then seen as a neutral arbiter acting on the behalf of the injured party and against the guilty. Thus class and indeed race could be seen as epiphenominal to the interests of the competing cultural groups.

Yet, beginning in the early seventies, cultural pluralism was being articulated in terms of race. In this articulation race became synonymous with culture. This followed on from and coincided with the two other main formulations of the pluralists — those of 'multiethnicity' and 'multiracialism.'

The dominance of culture as a focus has been premised on the notion of it being all-embracing. That is to say that there are now various races of people living in Britain, that these races are also ethnic groups, that these racial/ethnic groups each has an identifiable culture that is representative of the whole group. In addition, there is the implicit assumption that these cultures are not only equal in value but equal in status and therefore in power. However, at this stage one should state that there are adherents to this position who would vehemently disagree with what is an apparent over-simplification of a relatively wide continuum of practices and beliefs. This will be dealt with in greater detail in my chapter on anti-racist education.

There is one important issue that should be mentioned at this point. That is the tendency to differ (among multiculturalists) over the tendency of 'multuralist' theory and practice to depoliticize culture. The analysis is that there is a social problem which is to do with cultural difference and lack of understanding. Thus in order to bring about positive change one needs to promote cultural exchange and understanding.

In 1985, the position is still largely the same and what is being noted is a reawakening of the rhetoric of cultural pluralism and a reaffirmation of cultural pluralism as the desired goal for British society. The Swann Report, which was in gestation for the five preceding years, is a signifier of this affirmation:

> We consider that a multiracial society such as ours would in fact function most effectively and harmoniously on the basis of pluralism which enables, expects and encourages members of all ethnic groups, both minority and majority, to participate fully in shaping the society as a whole within a framework of commonly accepted values, practices and procedures, whilst also allowing and, where necessary, assisting the ethnic minority communities in maintaining their distinct ethnic identities within this common framework.

It goes on to conclude its remarks on culturalism with the words:

> We would thus regard a democratic pluralist society as seeking to achieve a balance between, on the one hand, the mainten-

ance and active support of the essential elements of the cultures
and lifestyles of all the ethnic groups within it, and, on the other,
the acceptance by all groups of a set of shared values distinctive
of the society as a whole. This then is our view of a genuinely
pluralist society, as both socially cohesive and culturally diverse.

This Report, with which I deal in slightly greater detail in chapter 2, has
been hailed by many as the multiculturalist manifesto. That is, probably
because despite its references to racism and anti-racism, it seems to
assert the primacy of culture as an explanation of social/racial relations.

Anti-racism — An Alternative Focus

Regardless of the shifts in state policy, anti-racism has always been the
essence of Black struggle though only recently has it been articulated as
a specific approach. As Mullard (1983a) argues, in contrast to the other
approaches adumbrated so far:

> Anti-racist education evolved as a racial form of education from
> quite a different starting point and set of tensions, conflicts and
> contradictions. Always present as a form but only recently
> expressed as a specific educational ideology and kind of educa-
> tional politics, it reflects a truly alternative alternative and
> oppositional expression.

Thus it becomes apparent, from looking at the emphases, policies
and practices of the phases outlined, that the shifts represent the
attempts of racism and its structures to maintain the racial status quo and
power relations between Black and White people in Britain. However,
anti-racism is becoming a more widely acceptable ideology and more
acceptable as an educational principle. The fact that it is being taken on
so slowly and so reluctantly is a clear indication of its oppositional
nature. As Mullard emphasizes, the appreciable difference between
anti-racist education and the other racial forms of education is that anti-
racist education is not a White definition but a Black one. It is not a
device of the oppressors but an indication of the resistance of the
oppressed (*ibid*). The goal is social/racial justice.

The Parameters of Black Immigration and Exploitation

The Parameters

At no other point in this book is the issue of the relationship of race and class and race and gender discussed. This is so largely because it would require much more time and a much more thorough treatment than one could afford to offer within the confines of this book. However, it is, I feel, most important to make explicit the position that the book does take in this debate. This is essential in that there are issues underlying all of the current debates, both within the pages of this book as well as in society at large. It is, therefore, a fundamental requirement to consider this phenomenon as an important parameter, alongside the others, of Black immigration and exploitation.

Race, Class and Gender

Since the issue of the interface between race/class/gender is only touched on en passant, I would like to outline, as clearly as possible, my position on this issue. In this sub-section I first of all briefly outline and examine the various major positions taken in this debate and then finally attempt to outline my own position. This position is also implicit in the critique of the limited literature review done in this section of the chapter.

Any full and thorough analysis of the interface between race, class and gender would actually require looking at these phenomena as they interact and as they combine with each in a whole range of permutations. However, the approach in this section is an attempt to briefly look at the issue in terms of the relationship between 'race and class' and between 'race and gender' and between 'race, class and gender'. In other words, it is a look at the ways in which racist structures and processes are amplified and operated in combination and in conjunction with these other major forms of oppression. This is not merely a theoretical or academic exercise but an attempt to examine the social/racial reality of the mass of Black people.

The approaches to the race and class relationship have been referred to in a range of terms but have largely tended to be divided into three main approaches.

These positions — the Marxist, the Weberian, and the moral functionalist — are outlined in Mullard's chapter in *Community Work and Racism* (1982b). In his article, Mullard argues for the need for a relational approach; in his later publications he attempts to further develop and use this relational approach[3] through a complex analysis of the problem. However, it would seem more useful in this book if one should attempt to use not three but five contemporary approaches which include those three approaches plus the Black/radical and the Black/anti-racist feminist approaches which would include explanations such as Mullard, Robinson, Parmar and Carby, who I would argue attempt to redefine the debate in terms of Black and Black feminist perspectives which do not disregard certain useful and influential 'White' traditions but attempt to transcend them in providing a truly alternative and oppositional rationalization and explanation of the dynamic of these equally repressive and exploitative social systems which use different premises and justifications but not dissimilar structures or systems to enact, reproduce and maintain themselves.

These five approaches all can and do include, to some degree, Black participation and enactment, thus 'being Black' does not necessarily place one within the Black radical position; just as being a Black woman does not necessarily mean ideological concurrence with the Black/anti-racist feminist position. Though, as stated earlier, Black radicalism largely applies to those Black people who have been involved in the pursuit of a redefinition of the terrain in politically and ideologically 'Black' terms, White anti-racists may also choose to locate themselves within this position.

Moral functionalists

The moral functionalist position can be simply described as seeing the significance of race as a social category and political reality as minimal. Both race and class are seen in cultural terms and as qualitatively different and unrelated.

Marxists

Marxist approaches to the relationship between race and class are varied and stress different elements but tend to share a subscription to race being epiphenomenal. Certain approaches stress the economic base and Black people as a *'sub-proletariat'*[4], while others stress the 'fact' of Blacks as a 'section' of the working class. According to Mullard (1983a):

> race and class cultures and identities are qualitatively similar,
> related, and historically and biographically prescribed and

ascribed in the capital-accumulation context. The relationship between race and class, class and race is hence *non-autonomous*.

Weberians

Within the Weberian approach race and class are seen as relatively autonomous in that race is used as 'an index of social position and status in the market economy' (*ibid*).

The Black Radical Tradition

What then is the unifying theme or facet of the *Black Radical* approach? The key to this approach is the shared belief in the need to:

(i)   understand the ways in which, historically, White analyses of social/racial relations have at best marginalized Black people and their interest and at worst created, reproduced and maintained the structures and systems of power control and domination;

(ii)   acknowledge that alternative and even 'radical' White approaches tend to directly or indirectly maintain this situation;

(iii)   provide a new oppositional, radical and Black theory and practice of the relationship between race and class that is related to an overall understanding of the ways in which racism operates to maintain itself both as an ideology and as a practice;

(iv)   articulate a position *vis à vis* racism that is not subsumed by or dependent on any other cause or struggle for its validity but that can engage with those causes and struggles in a quest for a more just society;

This Black/anti-racist feminist position comes out of the radical tradition and is informed both by radical feminism as well as Black radicalism.

Two important contributions to this debate are Hazel Carby and Pratibha Parmar, both contributors to the CCCS book, *The Empire Strikes Back*(1982). The words of Carby epitomize the essential ideological position taken by these Black feminists. Carby, in writing about the futility in the relentless pursuit of parallels between racism, sexism and class domination, states:

We would argue that the construction of such parallels is fruitless and often proves to be little more than a mere academic exercise; but there are other reasons for our dismissal of these kinds of debate. The fact that Black women are subject to the simultaneous oppression of patriarchy, class and race is the prime reason for not employing parallels that render their position and experience not only marginal but also invisible. (p. 123)

In discussing the oppressive processes of racism and sexism, Carby suggests that their similarity exists only in that ideologically, they both depend on 'natural' and 'biological' differences for their construction — which is a social one, and therefore both have little internal conceptual coherence. Also in that anti-racist and anti-sexist legislation are equally ineffective.

It seems to me that these five approaches constitute a framework for a genuinely useful analysis of this issue. Let us therefore look at some of the contributions made to this general debate, both to give a 'flavour' as well as to unpick some of the most useful elements for the understanding and rationalization of a truly anti-racist approach to making sense of the parameters of racism.

The contributions selected for examination in this small section of the chapter are not selected as definitive representations of any of the five positions adumbrated earlier but more because they represent positions on the continuum of contemporary contributions to the debate that are currently influential in the thinking of the broad range of people concerned with this field.

Robinson (1983) Black Marxism

Two of the main reasons why Robinson's contribution to this debate is useful is that besides the fact that his book is a richly textured and well researched work, his analysis, as a 'Marxist', of the race/class interface utilizes two crucial premises: the first one is the fact that traditional Marxists use a eurocentric conceptualization of capitalism, social satisfaction and 'class'. The second one is the radical notion of 'racial capitalism'. In this book, Robinson takes a socio-historical and geopolitical look at a range of issues in terms of the interplay between capitalism, nationalism, imperialism, Marxist/socialist theory and the theories and ideology of 'Black radicalism'. He argues that there were at least four distinct moments in the history of European racialism — only two of which are to be found in the dialectic of European development. These four moments he describes as:

(i) The racial ordering of European society from its formative period which extends into the medieval and feudal ages as 'blood' and racial beliefs and legends.

(ii)   The Islamic, therefore Arab, Persian, Turkish and African domination of Mediterranean civilization and the consequent retarding of European social and cultural life: *the dark ages.*

(iii)   The incorporation of African, Asian and peoples of the 'New World' into the world system emerging from late feudalism and merchant capitalism.

(iv)   The dialectic of colonialism, plantocratic slavery and re-sistance from the sixteenth century forwards, and the forma-tion of industrial labour and labour reserves.

However, as observed by Robinson, the tendency has been to begin the analysis of Western racism with the third movement to the almost total neglect of the first and second and with scant attention to the fourth. The results he opines have been 'bizarre'.

This 'bizarre' result, Robinson insists, has led to the reiteration by some students of racism of the premise of a mass psychology of 'chromatic trauma', whereby it is seen as natural that Europeans should react to other people with certain feelings or actions that range from fear and hate to pessimistic caution. Others, he purports, including some Marxists, have argued for 'empiricism', whereby the unavoidable result of slavery and domination is the rationalization of racial superiority and inferiority. For Robinson, the flaws in all the approaches have been the same, the perception that:

(i)   that only the European social and historical processes really matter and that those of the Third World are peripheral if at all important; and

(ii)   that intra-European Racism has tended to be ignored. (p. 84)

Robinson's contribution, I feel, is crucial to the current anti-racist debate in that he makes a point of constructing the debates not around European activity nor with Europe at the centre, but dealing with the issues and historical events as they were influenced by 'other peoples', particularly Africans and the African Diaspora. The existence of the book is itself a challenge to the traditional eurocentric interpretations of history, politics and social relations that have dominated discussions in this field. Robinson's identification of the four 'moments' in the history of European racialism highlights the endemic and institu-tionalized nature of racism in Europe in general and in Britain in particular. It also helps to show up the nonsense of the 'immigrant' number control as a basis for 'good' race relations since European racial exploitation has historically been a part of both home and foreign policy in Britain. By the same token, Robinson is signalling the link between anti-Black and other forms of European racism which challenges the simplistic belief in what he calls the 'mass psychology of chromatic trauma'.

Cashmore and Troyna (1983)

The work of Cashmore and Troyna (p. 42) serves as an example of what Robinson is critical of in terms of the primacy placed on capitalism by European Marxists.

In their chapter on race and capitalism (p. 31), Cashmore and Troyna hang their discussion largely on Cox, O C (1948):

> that people are encouraged to think in terms of race and, therefore, inherent inequality because it benefits 'capitalism'.

They argue that the principal weapon of the capitalist is open racial conflict. That is, when groups divide along racial lines and organize their allegiances on that basis. They maintain that racial antagonism is a fundamental trait of capitalism. Their position comes over as one which sees the concept of 'race' as facilitating the exploitation of Black people in particular and the working class as a whole. This provided the justification for the racial stratification of labour in that Black people were seen as 'degenerate and naturally suited to' menial and degrading work. This phenomenon Cashmore and Troyna purport served to divide the working class and to inhibit a united challenge of the oppressive structures of capitalism (pp. 31–2).

Even though it is difficult, in their brief discussion of the issue, to actually pin down the stance of the authors, there are a few specific positions that come over with relative clarity. The first is that racism is seen as epiphenomenal to class considerations. Secondly, in an attempt to broaden their analysis they reject the idea that 'ethnicity' (which they seem to equate with racism) is a more fundamental source of stratification, but state that;

> we believe that there's material enough to make us recognize that ethnicity and ethnic conflict will be, in the future, at least as significant as class and class conflict. Quite obviously we do not favour some form of 'ethnic analysis' over 'class analysis' nor any similar artificial division. Race relations ... must attempt to integrate both these elements of social stratification and conflict. (pp. 238–9)

This conclusion of Cashmore and Troyna is out of step with their deliberations up to that point and certainly contradicts the point that they later make, simply ascertaining the 'fact' that Black people are a 'splinter group' and 'under class' of the working class in view of their relationship to the means of production. Thus, in short, they see racism as the servant of capitalism, as bolstering capitalism and ultimately as a legacy of capitalism.

Kuper (1974) — Race, Class and Power

For Kuper, there are some societies in which the relationship to the means of production does not define the political struggle and in which class conflict is not the source of revolutionary change. He insists that to interpret the political conflict along racial lines, in terms of class struggle and the relationship to the means of production, confuses the issue.

Kuper uses the case of South Africa to demonstrate the fact that inter-ethnic/racial solidarity fails at the basic level of cooperation. He notes that the sharpest of the racial antagonisms in South Africa has been from White workers towards Black workers. To this reality there can be two reactions Kuper argues: that of seeing races as an epiphenomenon of class struggle or seeing the stratification of labour as an aristocracy of White labour, whereby as in South Africa the privileges of the White working class derive from their political power and franchise as Whites. Kuper seeks to find the independent significance of racial divisions and how this can be reconciled with Marxist theory and notes the various approaches that have been taken to this issue. Having examined these sometimes conflicting theories, especially in relation to revolutionary change, Kuper puts forward an alternative framework for bringing about change based on an understanding of the interrelationship between race and class. He writes:

> The matter is . . . one of offering an alternative emphasis and perspective on revolutionary change in racially and ethnically plural societies to the perspectives derived from class conflict.

Kuper makes the case for a fundamental problem of 'incorporation', (*ie.* incorporation into the capitalist mode of production), whereby the incorporation of races becomes established as a system of domination in that social relations are based on the original differential incorporation of races. (Of course, what is immediately apparent is that Kuper begins his analysis at a very late stage in the history of European racism — one of the main criticisms that would be made by Robinson.) The elaboration of this incorporation, Kuper suggests, is diffuse and institutionalized and therefore the struggle between races is a struggle over the terms of incorporation. This concept of incorporation is pivotal to Kuper's analysis. It enriches as well as impoverishes his argument in that, though it is true in that the 'ruling class' can be seen to have used the differentials in the degree of exploitation to confuse and control working peoples, the concept loses its usefulness when the practice of racism seems to become reduced to a struggle between races over 'incorporation'. In my opinion, the best of Kuper's explanation of the race/class interface is probably best summarized in the following quote on the dynamics of upward social mobility by members of the 'subordinate race' which he argues does not encourage evolutionary change.

> The upwardly mobile are not thereby lost to their original group in contrast to the tendency in class mobility. Race remains an extrinsic point of reference, and upwardly mobile individuals may be readily drawn back into their racial group.
>
> Nevertheless, the cross-cutting relationships between members of different racial groups and upward social mobility by members of the subordinate race, modify the structure of race relations, and may, under conditions of interdependence, provide a basis for evolutionary processes of change. There is no inexorable pre-determination, by the individual incorporation, of the course of race relations.

In conclusion, one can say that Kuper argues that racial conflicts in 'plural' societies are not synonymous with class struggle. Rather classes act within the context of racial conflict and that classes themselves are divided along racial lines. Thus, he argues, classes are subsumed under racial conflict.

Mullard, C. (1985) — Race, Class and Ideology

In his paper, *Race, Class and Ideology: Some Formal Notes* (1985), Mullard argues that it would be best to describe the relationship between race and class as a 'cross-facing transitive relationship'. By 'cross-facing transitive relationship', I take Mullard to mean a relationship or interrelationship whereby the two phenomena act on each other in similar as well as different ways to utilize these elements of its counterpart that best serve its own ends. In this way, oppressions can transfer from one to the other or have a dual reality. So, one can be oppressed both by race and class separately or in combination. Mullard comes to this conclusion on the basis that:

> any outline of the general form of the relationship that might exist between race and class, class and race, cannot be construed

in respect to the autonomy, non-autonomy, or relative autonomy of the two social categories.

This, he argues, is so because the theoretical descriptions of both categories 'exist, live, and manifest themselves in identical processes of expression which in turn give rise to different group formations'. He argues that the basis of their not being autonomous lies in the fact that they depend on the same modes of expression — *ie.* structural, cultural and variable (structural-cultural and cultural-structural), the basis of them being non-autonomous lies in the fact that their modes of expression lead to the formation of different groups and:

> finally, the issue of their relative autonomy has to be discarded because in their identical modes of expression they stand, theoretically, in a compatibly related relationship and, empirically, in an antagonistically related relationship to each other.

One of the apparent problems in Mullard's approach to the issues is the fact that he seems to make a clear distinction between theoreticism and empiricism which disregards the current debates as to whether one could talk about a non-empiricist theory or non-theoretical empiricism. This dichotomous relationship, it seems, is an inadequate explanation of the relationship between approaches to theory and practice. A second problem lies in the fact that though Mullard provides a very useful theoretical tool for analyzing the race/class interface and which he would argue is also appropriate for analyzing the race/gender interface, he does not do it himself and therefore could be seen as falling into the broad church of radical theoreticians that only get as far as nodding in the direction of anti-sexism.

What then is Mullard's contribution to this debate? In this paper, he moves the debate on from articulation of a simplistic causal or parallel relationship between race and class to one that takes more into consideration the dynamic nature of both phenomena.

Feminist Formulations

Jenny Bourne (1983) — Towards an Anti-Racist Feminism

For Bourne, despite the particularity of the struggles against racism and sexism, there is a shared experience of oppression and exploitation even though their origins and developments are unique. In looking at the relationship that has existed between the anti-racist and anti-sexist movements and the broad left, Bourne notes:

In Britain the struggles of feminists and black people have held up in a mirror to the left revealing its inadequacies — its reliance on arid dogma, on economistic formulations, and on its own little hierarchies. Both women and black people have stressed the nature of their oppressions and the need to fight them on their own terms without subsuming their struggle to the class struggle or, indeed, of deferring them till 'after the revolution'. They have emphasized the importance of not viewing racism and sexism purely in terms of their economic function. (p. 3)

In this paper, Bourne takes an internationalist and historical approach to the issue. She examines and highlights the fact that the women's movement got its impetus from the anti-racist Black struggle and notes that one of the primary difficulties of the women's movement has been their failure to understand and to fully take into consideration the role of and function of the state in oppression.

There seems to be no clear overall and central argument in the paper and, thus, what is particularly useful in Bourne's analysis is the different articulation and context of the anti-fascist and the anti-racist movement, which seems only obliquely relevant to her topic. In this examination she provides an invaluable perspective to the history of the struggle of Black women against their oppression as women and as Black people, *vis à vis* the anti-fascist movement. However, in an attempt to position Bourne in relation to the issue under consideration, one can use her own words when she states:

I see anti-racism not as something outside of the women's movement but as intrinsic to the best principles of feminism itself. The extent to which the Women's Movement has failed its own principles is the extent to which it is racist.

Pratibha Parmar — Gender, Race and Class (CCCS, 1982, p. 236)

Parmar starts her analysis from a much stronger position whereby she states categorically that it is inadequate for race to be merely 'tagged on' by a cursory comparison with gender. She maintains in fact that one cannot successfully engage with the issue of race, class and gender with generalized theoretical references. Instead, one must deal with specific instances. She criticizes the way in which the women's movement has, in the past, tended to ignore the struggles of Black women and:

... where visible, to treat them as simply another element of the campaigns in which white women are involved. They have thus failed to accommodate the specificity of black women's experience of racism which have been structured by racially constructed gender roles. (p. 237)

Parmar bases her discussion from the position that the starting point of any analysis of race, class and gender must be the specific historical conditions of the last three decades. She highlights how the specific construction of Black women as workers and (especially in the case of Asian women) as passive. She therefore concludes that, because of the ways in which capital, patriarchy and race structure the exploitation and oppression of Asian women, it is neither desirable nor is it possible to separate out one factor as the primary cause for oppression. However, she articulates the need for separate as well as joint struggle by Black women and White women.

Race, Class and Gender — A Synthesis

What brief conclusions can we therefore draw from the approaches taken, and suggested by, the various contributors to the debate concerning the race/class/gender interface? Historically, contributors to this debate have taken a number of approaches which argue either the paramountcy of class over race and gender or the paramountcy of gender over class and race or the paramountcy of race. Some of the more sophisticated formulations have debated the notion of autonomy, non-autonomy or relative autonomy and have tended to argue for relative autonomy.

Mullard's analysis (Mullard, 1983a) takes this even further by suggesting that the autonomy-relative autonomy formulation is not only insufficient but incorrect. Therefore, as I have described earlier, he rationalizes it in more dynamic terms of a cross-facing transitive relationship. This explanation in my opinion is probably the most useful and accurate one though, as I have stated, Mullard does not go into sufficient detail about gender.

The implicit position being taken in this book is that though there are similarities in the nature, form, structure and processes of oppression through class, gender and race, these ideologies also operate independently. Therefore, depending on the specificity of the historical conjuncture, the socio-political climate and the personal and institutional involvements, race, class and gender can act with, against and/or alongside each other. Thus, the oppositional practice must be dynamic, critical and careful. The gaining of ground against racism at the expense of gender or class discrimination is not only suspect but unacceptable.

British Immigration — Black Exploitation

It should be clear from my analysis so far that the parameters of the network of oppression experienced by Black people are complex and multi-faceted. On this basis, therefore, the socio-historical phenomenon of Black immigration to Britain must be analyzed within the historical and ideological specificity of the combined effects of racism, capitalism and imperialism. The contemporary phenomenon of British institutional racism and the recent phase of post-1914 immigration are inextricably linked to these three phenomena which are themselves linked.

This tripartite typology does not, however, exclude sexism since sexism is represented in each of the ideologies, both separately and as they interact. Thus, Black women experience a 'gendered' racism as a specific reality. In the typology presented in table 1 there is a distinction made between imperialism, racism and capitalism. This typology attempts to acknowledge these different forms of oppression as both distinct and interactive in both transhistorical and contemporary terms.

The general issue of sex and gender is not my major concern here. Yet I would like to reemphasize the importance of the need to combat sexism generally and specifically in terms of the way in which 'gendered' racism has operated to oppress Black women. Thus, this position will remain an implicit consideration which might surface from time to time in reference to specific events or phenomena.

When I refer to 'gendered' racism I am referring to the specific ways in which Black women experience racism that has to do with the combined interactive and dynamic forces of racism and sexism.

Imperialism and Colonialism

As argued in *The Roots of Racism*, (Workers Against Racism (WAR) 1985), when capitalism entered its imperialist phase of development within the last twenty years of the nineteenth century, capitalism became international and the owners became more dependent than before on the nation state. Therefore, as I have stated earlier, the state of play was one of rivalry among imperialist powers coupled by an economic, military and ideological oppression meted out to third world states. Thus:

> The ideology of nationalism legitimized imperialist oppression, the superiority of the colonizers and the inferiority of the colonized. (WAR, 1985, p. 14)

Therefore, it is argued by some that it is in the colonial situation that racism acquired a systematic form. That is, that the institutionalization of a racism that preceded colonization was facilitated by the very existence of the monster that racism itself had created. However, the position of the WAR is that, with the exception of the USA, which had a legacy of internal capitalist slavery:

> In other imperialist countries racism only really emerged as an independent political force with the world-wide movement of labour in the twentieth century. (*ibid*)

For Cashmore and Troyna, also, the whole notion of empire and imperialism are absolutely crucial to any understanding of race relations in Britain in the 1980s. They agree with WAR that the power and control exerted over the colonies was based on, and justified by, the belief in the racial inferiority of Black people. However, they seem to agree with a number of Black commentators, social scientists and historians that though the empire seems to have been dissolved, there is a new empire which continues to operate in the form of certain attitudes, structures and behaviours in British society. This series of reconstructions exists in 1986 in the form of a complex and 'sophisticated' institutional racism which provides the supportive structure for racist attitudes and racist acts.

As Robert Moore (1975) quotes from a Sri Lankan, 'We are over here because you were over there'. This statement is endorsed by Sivanandan (1982) when he expresses the fact that one epoch does not lead tidily into another. 'Each epoch carries with it a burden of the past ... and the longer and more durable the previous epoch, the more halting is the emergence of the new'. With the Second World War came the end of the centre-periphery relationship of British colonialism as well as the 'interimperialist rivalries' of that period. Sivanandan purports that this heralded the start of a new colonialism based on the USA as the centre. Britain, on the other hand, still remained quite attached to its colonial past and so tried 'to seek fresh profit from an old relationship — most notably through the continued exploitation of Colonial labour, but this time at the centre' (*ibid*). Easy access to cheap Black labour, and easy profit from racial exploitation, caused Britain to resort to labour-intensive production. The crucial issue was the fact that because of the colonial relationship (and because of the lack of legal and parliamentary foresight, one might argue), the immigrants came as settlers and not as labourers on contract. This meant that, at least to start with, Britain could not have all the benefits of a migrant labour force. The fact is, as Moore outlines, migrant workers are used largely to fill jobs that local workers will not do, because of either low wages, low esteem or, indeed, both, though usually the jobs are essential for the maintenance of basic public services as well as for bolstering the consumer economy. But he argues further that the important factor is that the migrant labourer is generally disposable (*sic*). He quotes from a German employer who puts it this way:

> The great value of the employment of foreigners lies in the fact
> that we thus have a mobile labour potential at our disposal.

It, therefore, goes without saying that the very fact that it is possible for employers to rid themselves of workers in this manner gives the employer much greater control over the migrant than he would have over a local worker. Concomitant with this lack of power are additional unjust practices such as poor housing, due to little money etc., and poor training since the employer is unlikely to give anything but elementary training and very little promotion, if any. Training and promotion would make the migrant worker less disposable.

It seems that the immigration legislations of successive governments are meant to serve as a way of redressing the balance through oppression (to probably result in voluntary repatriation and to create a situation where the 'privileges' (*sic*) of being members of the Commonwealth are taken away from Black workers), thus beginning the move towards bringing Britain into line with the rest of Europe. In the current crisis, there is additional pressure being put on Black workers as members of the sub-proletariat. An important part of this increasing racist oppression lies in the fact that this large section of the sub-proletariat still have some rights left enshrined in British Law, thus each new immigration act marks yet another step along the continuum of erosion of the rights of Black people.

Moore traces this erosion and sees the 'anti-Black' forces as completely victorious. The problem with Moore's analysis is that he sees the entry of 'fringe' racism into the existing political parties as a result of error in political manoeuvres and also as a result of error in political leaders 'giving in' to extremist views in order to attract votes and to maintain their credibility. Yet he successfully and systematically traces the way in which successive governments repressed and marginalized Black people.

Sivanandan (1982) places a more radical though economistic analysis on this 'erosion'. He articulates it in terms of a shift from immigration control to 'induced repatriation'. At one end of the continuum, the Nationality Act of 1948 conferred British citizenship on 'subjects' of the Commonwealth and colonies, thus, through this settler status, ensuring the continued labour of this new workforce. On the other hand, the 1971 and subsequent immigration acts, in response to the recession, 'terminated all black settler immigration and installed instead a system of contract labour on the lines of the European Gastarbeiter' (p. 131). Thus, Black workers from the Commonwealth now came on a contractual basis at the request of the employer — initially for a year, subject to renewal.

This new system has been wrapped up in the rhetoric of 'race relations' based on the view that 'to improve race relations, to make things better for the coloureds' you must first restrict their numbers (*ibid*). The important difficulty with Sivanandan's approach is that it is probably *too* economistic and tends to see racism mainly in the context of capitalism and economic imperialism. What Moore fails to acknowledge is the fact that the racist policies and acts of the state are based not simply on the reaction or giving in of successive governments to extremist racist groups, but reflects their predisposition not only for the sake of capital but because of their own racism.

Racism and the Role of the State

The role of the state *vis à vis* racism is a continuing debate, both as a universal question as well as in terms of Britain specifically. That South Africa is a racist state does not often provoke much debate in the 'West' or almost anywhere outside South Africa, but when for example the Anti-Racist Teacher Education Network (ARTEN — see appendix) sent out its circular letter — stating that Britain was a racist state and therefore anti-racism was a necessary stance — there was a tremendous defensive response by a lot of individuals and teacher education organizations who were claiming to be concerned about multicultural education. One letter to the *Times Educational Supplement* in 1983 read thus:

> the whole ethos of the letter is wrong ... it represents an extreme statement of the situation and it is conceptually naive to say we're a racist society.

It therefore seems essential that the relationship, role, or involvement of the state in or with racism must be examined to provide a basis for any further discussion about schooling, or any other state institution for that matter, and the nature of its relationship with racism.

The Realization of Anti-racist Teaching

Race and the State — A Typology

Let us therefore look a bit more closely at a range of perspectives on the relationship between the state and racism. Here I am examining four broad positions: the moral functionalist, the Marxist, the Weberian and the anti-racist. All these positions are only markers on a continuum. And, in fact, on closer examination it might be found that these four perspectives/tendencies are not entirely mutually exclusive but might actually borrow from each other some of the conceptualizations and instruments of analysis. Thus, for example, there might be a perceived link between Marxism and anti-racism but, with further analysis, other links become evident. Again, as an example, the anti-racist position may not be functionalist but has been criticized as being 'moralist' since the argument for 'justice' is not only a political and ideological one but ultimately a *moral* one.

Moral functionalists

The moral functionalist position is seen as located within the post-Hegelian conception of the state as an 'organized network of bodies and agencies working in the national and, it is often assumed, moral interests of society' (Mullard, 1982b). This form of explanation is based on a set of propositions about the moral well-being of society, social stability and national security. It is seen as being carried out through the 'regulative' and 'coercive' functions of the state. The implication is that:

> The moral welfare and rights of all citizens can only be protected fully if the state acts positively to regulate and maintain a calculated balance between a society's total stock of social resources and benefits and the actual number of citizens who possess a legal right to these resources and benefits. (*ibid*)

This position recasts otherwise negative immigration policies into positive race relation practices and objectives. For example, the dominant viewpoint of the 1960s which has now become deeply institutionalized today is that, in addition to being an essential prerequisite of harmonious race relations, Black immigration control is a vital component 'in the social armoury required to maintain social security and stability'. This is seen as being achievable only through rigorous Black immigration control and positive encouragement for integration, assimilation or coexistence with the rest of the community at appropriate or even predesignated levels in the class structure.

The state is, therefore, seen as making every attempt to assure this, not only through the successive immigration acts since 1961, but also through the setting up of agencies to ensure a 'fair deal' and to foster and produce harmonious race relations. However, the coercive functions of the state are in a sense symbolized in these same agencies, policies and practices (such as the United Kingdom Immigrant Advisory Service; Councils for Community Relations; the Commission for Racial Equality; the Race Relations Board and the 1965 and 1968 Race Relations Acts). This dialectical and apparently contradictory function of State agencies becomes clearer when we examine concrete examples. Examples such as the case of the Bradford headteacher who can write in the right-wing reactionary journal, *The Salisbury Review*

> The propaganda generated by multi-racial zealots is now augmented by a growing bureaucracy of race in local authorities and this makes freedom of speech difficult to maintain. By exploiting the enormous tolerant tradition in this country, the race lobby has so managed to induce and maintain feelings of guilt in the well disposed majority, that decent people are not only afraid of voicing certain thoughts, they are uncertain of their rights even to think those thoughts. (Honeyford, 1984)

The point to note here is that the rationalization being used by this headteacher is tantamount to the creation of the anti-racist 'bogeyman'. This 'anti-racist bogeyman', one is told, is threatening our (*sic*) British way of life and the freedoms which we enjoy in this society. It is cast in the light of freedom of speech and of thought. What is left unsaid is the fact that this particular brand of 'freedom' which is being extolled is to be enjoyed at the expense of others. The offenders, it is assumed, are those people who would expose this fact, that the racialization of social relations and schooling may be 'functional' in a racist society but it does not make it either right or just. The ultimate coup for the racists was the invitation that was extended to Mr. Honeyford to meet with the Prime Minister along with a number of 'top' educationists (of a particular political and physical colour) to talk about, one supposes, the infiltration of political 'zealots' into schools. Whatever the intention of this move by the Prime Minister was, it can only be read by Black Britons and the country at large as giving a stamp of approval to racist educational practice and practitioners. The target for criticism is perceived as the growing number of anti-racist teachers whose only desire is to improve the quality and equality of educational provision for all pupils.

All such movements are being branded as Left extremist. But as I have implied in this chapter, the ideology of Left is not necessarily synonymous with Black interests, be they Marxist or otherwise. But what would the Marxists say?

The Marxists

The disagreements among Marxists are often as many as those between Marxists and other schools of thought. There are those Marxists who tend to overemphasize the economic base, those who highlight capitalist structures and those 'critical' Marxists who utilize a Marxist approach to test the mettle of the particular social system or political strategy. Therefore, in dealing with this broad approach one needs to emphasize that any discussion here must be in terms of generalities and therefore could be more true of one set of 'Marxists' than another. For, in contemporary Marxism, there are a number of ideological camps. As Bottomore (1984) writes:

> Marxist sociology is now probably best regarded as a very general paradigm within which there exists strong family re-semblances between different specific theoretical formulations, which may also, however, have significant connections with other, non-Marxist theories or models.

Mullard (1982b) places the Marxist explanation in the context of analyzing all so-called state responses, policies and practices as constituting 'at best, a massive deception and, at worst, a banal symphony of social control orchestrated by the state in the post-war phase of late or advanced capitalism'. As an 'executive committee' of the ruling class, the state is seen not as responding to racism *per se*, nor to demands of Black groups. Instead, it is seen as responding to the needs and interests of capital.

This viewpoint tends to be economistic in suggesting that the material and economic foundations of society determine all other aspects of social, political, cultural and ideological life.

> In brief, the whole history of black immigration control legislation from the 1948 Nationality Act to the present 1981 Nationality Bill can be viewed and explained in terms of capital in crisis. (*Ibid*, p. 49)

However, it is apparent that Marxists must find an explanation for the apparent contradiction as articulated by the moral functionalists that the state has established a whole network of agencies and policies with the purpose of improving race relations. Of course, all of these initiatives cost both by their day to day administration and by the sums of money provided for funding research by the Home Office, specialist race units and the like.

For some Marxists, much of this explanation is embodied in the concept of ideology.

The distinctions they normally make between the ideological and repressive state apparatuses are, so to speak, analytically brought together in their explanation of the State's apparently positive response to racism. (*Ibid*)

This viewpoint basically states that the organization and work of the state-sponsored race agencies is ideological work. Urban Aid, community development and inner-city partnership schemes like community relations work and multicultural education are seen as:

(i) transmitting a dominant/ruling class conception of the 'race problem' as opposed to the problem of racism;

(ii) culturally reproducing in a racial form the more general social relations of production;

(iii) reproducing the White power structure but also the social structure of legitimation of capitalist society;

(iv) enabling the state to attract, mobilize and control White or Black liberal opinion and energy.

That Stokely Carmichael was banned from Britain by the Home Secretary in 1967 for advocating the development of 'Black consciousness', self-sufficiency, and self-determination only adds further weight to the assertion that the British state has always been far more concerned with repressing Black resistance than with the promoting of racial justice. (*Ibid*)

That he was again banned in 1984 compounds the case against the British state for its active role against Black resistance and the struggle against racism. What is significant for our analysis is that, with the passage of time, there is considerable evidence of the validity and applicability of certain significant elements of Marxist analysis. For example, with the state's radical move to the right, there is an increase in the repressive activity of the state's main agencies of law and order. In this shift, there is a special and correlating impact on Black people — particularly Black youth — which is borne out in the emergence of police 'liaison' of numerous sorts and numerous documented cases of police brutality and harassment of Black people. The creation of mugging (by police and media) as a 'Black youth' crime and the aggressive police role in the race/class resistance of 1980, 1981 and 1985 with the state's reaction to it, is significant in this context. These examples of Toxteth (1981), Handsworth (1985), Brixton (1981 and

1985) and Tottenham (1985) are perpetual reminders of the role of the state in general and the police in particular as agents of racial oppression and control. As Mullard wrote in 1982:

> All these examples ... illustrate the racial nature of class warfare and the continuous endeavours of the ruling class, through the State, to maintain its power by ideological and repressive means. (Mullard, 1982b)

The Weberians

Along the continuum from the Marxist explanation to the moral functionalist explanation, lies a third category of explanation — that of the Weberians. This school of thought tends to view the state as a:

> rational, bureaucratic entity that seeks rationality to maintain and perpetuate a society through a process of the incorporation of interests, demands and challenges. (*Ibid*)

This seems to be the position taken by Cashmore and Troyna (1983) when, for example, they insist that:

> The state is not simply an instrument of the ruling, dominant classes but reflects patterns in which some groups have power over others, patterns, therefore, of inequality. (p. 119–20)

They argue therefore that since White colonialists have dominated the 'non-White' colonized peoples of their empire, 'it is to be expected' that the state institutions of the United Kingdom would reflect and express White interests — particularly the interests of the ruling class. Though I largely agree with this assertion by Cashmore and Troyna, I part company with them when they assert that these institutions also reflect the interests of Black people — using as an example anti-discrimination laws and the like. This they argue is an explanation of why there are political 'reforms' which accommodate the interests of Black people. Though they make the critical statement that those limited interests will ultimately be subservient to the interests of the 'dominant groups', the analysis of Cashmore and Troyna seems to place them firmly in the camp of analysis that sees the state as responding to and incorporating interests. Cashmore and Troyna's analysis is not without some basis. However, though the state might appear to respond to the interests and demands of the weaker groups in society, it is usually reacting to the range of articulated, overt and covert interests and demands of the powerful and dominant groups in society. Yet, this is not the full picture.

'Weberians' tends to see the state as responding to racism in a negative way. That is, in order to appease a racist working class, the state has responded by being racist.

> In fact, it is hardly an exaggeration to conclude, as the Weberians do, that the immigration laws and rules not only become more racist after each public outburst of working class racism, but that they also began to adopt and convey the same messages, even concepts and arguments, that had previously been used by Powell and deplored as 'alarmist' by many of his senior political colleagues. (Mullard, 1982b)

Though it is evident that each of these three explanations has something to offer to an analysis of the state and racism, all are inadequate as complete explanations. They all emphasize the primary importance of a particular response or interest group. This sort of emphasis, therefore, negates the complexity of social reality and, *ipso facto*, minimizes the complexity of the form, nature and role of the modern state.

Also all three explanations are eurocentric and from a White viewpoint. In all of them, racism is viewed as a phenomenon or condition located outside the state per se. Thus, racism itself becomes peripheral or epiphenomenal to the main focus of their argument.

Mullard offers a relational explanation as an alternative. This, he argues, must do a number of things, for which he provides some guidelines. One of the central demands of this approach, he argues, *inter alia*, would be an acceptance of racism as its central focus. Ultimately, Mullard argues, this explanation will see the state not as responding negatively nor positively to racism, but instead that it has *used* racism to appease the three sets of interest groups. Thus, these appeasements and the contradictions they present, have led to a number of developments over the last twenty years. The three major developments he purports are: 'the organizations, agencies and bodies that constitute the state's race bureaucracy; the policy and ideological structures of control; and Black resistance'.

In agreement with Mullard, I would argue, therefore, that any analysis of the issue must be informed by Black formulations. These would be formulations based on experience — the experience of being on the receiving end of racist structures and practices — which is reflectively and perhaps dispassionately analyzed.

Britain — Racist State?

It would seem to me that any close and thorough analysis of the United Kingdom — united or not — must reveal that it is indeed a racist state although not necessarily in the sense in which South Africa is. It is a racist state in that racism, as described and expounded earlier in this chapter, is an 'endemic' and structural part of British institutions — laws, processes, procedures *and* a part of the cultural assumptions, explanations and 'preference' in terms of allocation of resources and support. However, it is not sufficient to leave it there! One must then attempt to explain the ways in which it operates within the specificity of the British context of central government (national state) and local government (local state) and in terms of the range of quangos and non-governmental organizations (NGO) which have a tremendous impact on the daily lives of people.

The British state is not a monolithic and homogeneous entity but a complex structure of networks, levels, interests and orientations that operate both horizontally as well as vertically. Thus, the national state sometimes stands both alongside and in opposition to the local state — the latter being blatantly exemplified by the Whitehall versus metropolitan town halls contest that has taken place for the best part of the five years (1980–85) ending in the demise of the metropolitan authorities. However, there are also contests within the various levels of government bodies, government agencies and local authorities.

One could analyze to a high degree the interplay within and among state institutions but that would need the space of an entire publication. What is important to note is that the net effect of the state machinery over the last few decades has been the propping up and maintenance of the racial status quo and institutional racism. The nature of the racist state is therefore not to be measured by intentionality (a conspiracy theory) but by a practice and effect which must be understood within an overall ideology of institutional racism.

Racism transcends class and has an existence that precedes the current socio-political formation of the British state. Indeed, it is seen to significantly predetermine current state formulations of theory, policy and practice, both through interactions and institutions.

The stated position throughout this book is that Britain is a racist state in that racism is not only an endemic part of the personal perceptions, attitudes and actions of White people, but it is an institutionalized part of both governmental and non-governmental organizations. The underlying questions of this issue are made explicit in the following section of this chapter which attempts to look at the rationale, implementation and impact of immigration and nationality laws and race relations laws. The position taken is that these laws and 'reforms' must be viewed through the perceptions and experience of

Black people who have been the 'objects' of *both* racism *and* race relations legislation. These laws and reforms, it will be made clear, have a direct impact on the lives of Black people wherever they are located within the British social structure.

Race Relations Legislation

In Britain the concept of race relations legislation must not only include acts and laws designated as such, but those which have 'race relations' as part of their implicit intention or rationale.

It is widely known that the race panic of the British state has been strongly related to the 'numbers game' and thus Britain is probably the only country that makes such a firm and overt link between 'immigration' and 'nationality' laws, conflating them into the single category of 'immigration and nationality' laws. The connection therefore between these laws and race relations acts is that there is a logic that goes thus: The ruptures in race relations are anomalous and are based on two factors. The first is the very presence of Black people in this country — which as I have argued before tends to be seen as an entirely contemporary one and a problem — and, secondly, that if there is a resistance to this 'presence' it is largely due to the fact that people (*ie.* White people) have genuine fears about the excessive presence of Black 'aliens' in their communities.

As a result, the best way to ensure 'good' and harmonious race relations is to restrict the 'numbers' of Black people — *ie.* those groups that are seen as racially different and distinct — and to be seen to be doing it. It is even argued that this approach is ultimately best for the Black people now resident here. Thus, poor 'race' relations, however looked at, in the articulations of the state is a problem created by Black people and by their presence in this country. These are the premises underlying all race relations and 'immigration and nationality' laws and acts.

Immigration and Nationality

Until 1948 anyone born in the empire or dominions of Great Britain was a British subject. The 1948 Nationality Act established United Kingdom and colonies citizens and Commonwealth citizens: anyone born in Britain, a British colony or who had a father born there was a 'British subject', though they could simultaneously be a citizen of another country.

However, the increased immigration of the post-war period created a 'panic' concerning the numbers of Black people coming into the country, what more, as of right. This panic precipitated the initiation of 'measures' to cope with the ensuing situation.

In 1962 the Commonwealth Immigrants Act set into motion, for the first time, immigration controls on British subjects from the colonies and ex-colonies who had gained their independence. The Act also introduced a new system of employment control whereby three grades of vouchers had to be obtained, each voucher being related to a different type of job 'opportunity'. This legislation had the greatest impact where it was intended, in the Third World colonies and ex-colonies — the New Commonwealth countries.

In 1965 there was an Immigration White Paper which abolished the third grade employment voucher and limited the number of 'New Commonwealth' British subjects to be allowed into the country to 8500. About 12 per cent of the places were reserved for the Maltese.

It is apparent that the Race Relations Act of 1966, coming as it did one year after the 1965 Immigration and Nationality Act, was intended not as a genuine measure to deal with racism but was a palliative measure to appease dissent, pacify resistance and to legitimate a very unpopular and unjust decision to restrict the numbers of Black people coming into this country. The justification was that they were a product of the same rationale. That is, both by restricting numbers and passing a Race Relations Act, the state was creating a climate of better race relations. But as Sivanandan (1982) correctly notes, this piece of legislation was:

> a half-hearted affair which merely forbade discrimination in 'places of public resort' and, by default, encouraged discrimination in everything else: housing, employment, etc. (p. 114)

Another panic was created in 1968 when the Labour government anticipated the arrival of a large number of British passport holders from Kenya. Another act was rushed through Parliament limiting the rights of entry of this group of British citizens, who happened to be East African Asians.

By 1971 the Immigration and Nationality Acts were becoming more and more complicated but with a number of construing 'loopholes' which prevented the British state from enacting the degree of control of entry for Black, or to use the bureaucratic euphemism, New Commonwealth, citizens. Thus, the concept of patriality was introduced with the intention it seems of making it clear, once and for all, that true British meant White. For all other 'British subjects' it was an 'honour' conferred by the grace of Her Majesty's government and for its convenience. By this Act, all 'New Commonwealth' citizens were effectively transmogrified into defacto 'aliens'. Some of these 'aliens' however had a 'right of abode' if they were British passport holders born in the UK or born to parents born in the UK. This, however, was a small fraction of those people who initially had this right but had it taken away from them by successive Acts of Parliament.

> The 1981 British Nationality Act was a most logical development of the legal traditions started in 1962: the imperative was to control and preserve. By curbing the numbers coming in, it was thought that the alleged 'way of life' could be retained. (Layton-Henry, 1984)

This Nationality Act created three classes of British citizenships under this new Act. Birth and residence in the UK was no longer an automatic qualifier for British citizenship.

The 1983 Act went one stage further and created five categories of British citizenship:

(a) British Dependent Territories;
(b) British Overseas Citizen;
(c) British Subjects;
(d) British Protected Persons;
(e) Citizenship by Birth.

The period between 1945 and 1964 of parliamentary life in Britain is well charted in Layton-Henry's (1984) book *The Politics of Race in Britain* (pp. 44–58). The panic of this period was a large one generated by the mass of the White British working people, fired by extremists, supported to some extent by the Unions and responded to by the British Parliament — both the Conservative government and the Labour opposition. However, as mentioned earlier in reference to Cashmore and Troyna, it would be reductionist to simply conclude that the racist measures taken by the government of the day were strictly in response to the voting public or to thereby apportion blame regarding racist attitudes or acts to the working class masses.

The dynamic interface between 'public' opinion and governmental action cannot simply be explained in terms of causality. It has more to do with a shared ideology of racism across the spectrum of the White power structure which is challenged by differing perceptions of effective strategies, differing class interests and the opportunistic use of the notion of 'public opinion' in order to justify unacceptable acts by the British state.

> In the early post-war period the immigration from the West Indies and later from the Indian sub-continent was largely seen in the context of colonial policy and relations with the Commonwealth. This was true for all the major parties. (*Ibid*, p. 45)

The alternative reading of the situation is that 'colonial policy and relations with the Commonwealth' was only the overt articulation of a range of hidden intentions and events. My preferred reading is that Britain, in the immediate post-war period, in its need for labour, exploited an old relationship to *new* ends (one might even argue to *old* ends). This is borne out by the fact that the decisions about New Commonwealth immigration controls were unilateral. This was not the action of a state that was particularly interested in a relationship as much as it was indeed interested in exploitation.

What then were the events that characterized this period? It did not take long for White resident British workers and their families to begin to see the 'immigrant workers' from the New Commonwealth as a threat, despite the fact that they had been largely confined to the dirty and ill-paid jobs. Naturally, they were looking to the Labour Party and the Unions to stand beside them in the defence of their rights. But as it was to be proved, the Union was to become another site of struggle against institutionalized racism — sometimes covert and sometimes even overt.

The Race Relations Legislation

The history of race relations legislation is a short one beginning with a few initiatives in the 1950s by way of Private Members' bills. This involved people such as Reginald Sorenson and Fenner Brockway (see Layton-Henry, 1984, for an excellent catalogue of the history of race relations initiatives in Britain).

The significant milestones in race relations legislation are the Race Relations Bills of 1965, 1968 and 1976 and the setting up of the Commonwealth Immigrant Advisory Service in 1962, the Community Relations Council (CRC) in 1968 and the final setting up of the CRE in 1976. One popular assumption behind race relations legislation is that its formulation and organization can *only* be in the interest of Black people as victims of racism in a White dominated society. A second popular assumption is that it was through the altruistic and humanitarian concern of the British state that these changes have been made. A third and crucial assumption is that the bodies which were set up as a result of, or in conjunction with, these legislative moves were set up to serve the interests of Black people.

However, a look at the historical and contemporary reality of the workings of these bodies suggests that the principal purpose of their existence was, in fact, to maintain the status quo and whatever positive changes have been made have been made through the struggle of Black peoples for their rights and for justice. In fact, Black resistance was often able to exploit some of the inherent contradictions in government policy.

One powerful example of the contradictions in these legislations resides in the events following the Race Relations Bills of 1965 and 1968. During this period, the people who were actually prosecuted as a result of the race relations were not White racists but Black activists. This contradiction is thrown into sharp focus by the sentencing of Abdul Malik to twelve months' imprisonment for using insulting words to stir up racial hatred at a Black power meeting in Reading. And in the same month of November 1967, four members of the United Coloured People's Association (UCPA) for the same reason.

On the other hand in March 1968, four members of the Racial Preservation Society were acquitted of a charge of incitement to racial hatred. In April Enoch Powell made his now notorious 'river of blood' speech. But it was not even considered that he should be prosecuted. The fact that Fenner Brockway only made any real headway with his proposed Private Members' bill after the 1958 'riots', is testimony to the fact that it was not humanitarian intentions but enlightened self interest that was the primary factor in race relations legislation. And even these concessions (like much of the subsequent ones) had to be prompted and pushed by the taking to the streets of a disenchanted, dispossessed, demeaned and exploited mass of Black people — mostly youth who have said and are saying 'enough is enough'. As Layton-Henry (1984) writes:

> Brockway was to introduce a further eight bills in the period up to 1964 but all failed to reach the statute book. They did, however, gain increasing support, especially after the 1958 riots when a small number of Conservatives and Liberal MPs added their support, but Brockway was not able to persuade the government to support his Bill. (p. 123)

He goes on to say:

> On the Labour side it was the 1958 riots which precipitated the

development of party policy. The riots persuaded the NEC to oppose immigration controls and to support anti-discrimination legislation. The NEC statement after the riots included the following commitment:

Although we believe that the fundamental and long-term solution of this problem is educational, nonetheless there are public manifestations of racial prejudice so serious that they must be dealt with by legislation. (Labour Party, 1958, p. 4)

In 1984, the CRE published a paper, *1976 RACE RELATIONS ACT: TIME FOR A CHANGE?*, making an argument for a new Race Relations Act which is perhaps needed. Yet one must be realistic about both the limitations and the possibilities of such legislation and the possible impact on the lives of Black people and that of society at large. A new Act may simply serve, like its predecessors, to further maintain and to police the perpetuity of the racial status quo in British society.

Black Resistance to Racism

Black resistance to White oppression in the United Kingdom can be analyzed along two axes; a vertical (historical) one and a horizontal (political/philosophical) one. This resistance can be seen both as a progression of varying responses to increasing and changing modes of oppression and as strengthening and development of strategy. It is a development from what was initially seen as a 'sojourn' to what is now seen as 'standing the ground' by Black youth, as well as parents, strongly affirmed and epitomized in the Black people's march slogan, 'Come what may, we are here to stay'.

The history of Black resistance is a history of action ranging from the organized to the spontaneous and from pacifist to violent. The response to the post-war debarrment from pubs, clubs, and the prejudice of and sometimes exclusion from churches, was the eventual setting up of Black clubs, churches and welfare associations. Historically, these were primarily Afro-Caribbean Black responses since Asian Black people tended to have a social life based on their rural cultural traditions of mosque, temple and cultural associations.

In the workplace, 'resistance to racialism took the form of ad hoc responses to specific situations grounded in tradition. Often, those responses were individualistic and uncoordinated, especially as between the communities' (Sivanandan 1981/82). This was due to the racial division of labour; not only were the communities kept apart but there were also 'ethnic shifts' where there were Black people.

As Sivanandan cites, there were at times attempts to form associations, if not unions on the shop floor. For example, there is the case in 1951 of the skilled West Indian workers who met secretly in washrooms to form an association for taking up cases of racial discrimination. However, the employers soon found out and they were driven to hold their meetings in the local barber shop, which changed the focus of the association from the shop floor to the community.

Discrimination in housing, as a problem larger than the scope of individual action, was met with a community response from the outset. Because Black residents were given the worst housing, if any at all, they took to pooling their resources to provide themselves with housing. However, because of the high rates charged by their sources of loans and because of the high prices asked for the houses, these immigrants were forced into multi-occupation and its concomitants of overcrowding, further racial stereotyping and subsequent public health orders.

> Thus it was around housing, principally, but through traditional cultural and welfare associations and groups, that Black self-organization and self-reliance grew unifying the respective communities. It was a strength that was to stand them in good stead in the struggles to come. (*Ibid*)

Another important factor in the development of organized Black struggle was the 'marriage' between Black students and Black workers. As Sivanandan suggests (1981/82), the 'race riots' of 1919 were a catalyst to the formation of the West African Students' Union in 1925, which was formed for the expressed purpose of 'opposing race prejudice and colonialism'. Now the connections were beginning to be made between colonialism and racialism, imperialism and Black exploitation at the centre, between Black workers and Black students.

The nature of Black struggle has been classified under a number of headings. Three of the main categories of classification are what could be broadly described as integrationist, interventionist and separatist. These approaches to the struggle originate in different philosophical/political positions regarding race, race and class, and imperialism and racism.

By 'integrationist' I refer to the position where Black people accept the White 'norms' and cultural values as their own and struggle within those confines to achieve — overachieve, and be 'whiter than White'. Within this perspective, it is seen as being important to be as 'White' as one can be and to take the 'best' of what is to be offered in education, jobs, housing thus proving the Black person can be an equally 'good' citizen as 'good' White citizens.

By 'Interventionist' I refer to that school of thought that accept the need for struggle. But the struggle is seen as only being possible with an acceptance, or seeming acceptance, of White culture and White structures. Having established oneself as a Black aware person, one is able to fight from within.

Separatism is seen as those who argue for a separate development of Black people. For this group it is a question of gaining/claiming power, the source of Black domination. It would be argued that this power can only come from Blacks organizing themselves separately — separate schools, banks, shops, churches. This being based on Black solidarity or, as was popular in the sixties with such as Malcolm X, Stokely Carmichael, etc., Black nationalism *and* Black power. These three models are by no means closed categories but rather represent the markings along an ideological continuum of Black struggle which has taken place and continues to take place in a number of areas: education, social and civil rights, work and the economy.

The Economy

The struggle within the economy, on the shop floor, has been one of the most arduous and difficult tasks for it is at this juncture that race and class meet. Whereas Black people have been exploited as a part of the working class, they have also been exploited as a race. The struggle as a race within the economy has been at best difficult and at worst almost impossible due to the lack of solidarity on the part of the White counterparts of Black workers, and this includes their White colleagues on the shop floor as well as the Union officials. Thus, not only did Black people have to struggle against the racism of employers, but also against the racism of their White 'comrades' (*sic*). For example, in a series of incidents in a Nottingham textiles firm in 1973, it was notable that 'White workers supported Black workers in their demand for money but opposed them on questions of promotion'. As Moore (1975) writes, 'it was easy for management to divide the workers because the Whites feared loss of privileges'. Another example is the case of the workers at Imperial Typewriters in 1974 mentioned elsewhere in this text and yet another, more recent example, is the protracted battle that John Fernandes fought against the racially-based professional attack which he experienced, without either the help or cooperation of the national executive of his union — even though there was *some* support from his local branch.

The question is, has this situation improved? Is the situation any better at at time when Bill Morris has been appointed as the Assistant General Secretary to the TGWU? If the position of Jim Thakoordin (1984) and the Greater London Council's Anti-Racist Trade Union Working Group is anything to go by? Under the chairpersonship of Thakoordin, this Working Group carried out a survey in which they sent out a questionnaire to trade unions. The Report that emerged from this survey was published with the intention of convincing:

> the existing powerholders within trade unions of both the weight of evidence in support of the contribution that their elective and employment practices are, in effect, racist, and to highlight the necessary steps which must be taken to challenge and redress this very serious situation.

The design of the project was dictated by the need to elicit certain basic and factual information from all of the London-based trade unions — a good measure of the country as a whole — about whether they had a policy regarding race and equality and to measure the degree to which they had acted on that policy, both in terms of time and resources allocated. The method of investigation as stated earlier was that of a letter/questionnaire survey.

The response of Thakoordin was that the data indicated quite clearly the dominance of White males at all levels of the unions. He argues that:

> The evidence suggests that equal opportunities simply do not exist for blacks within the Unions despite all the sympathetic propaganda from the TUC and a number of unions. Their recruitment policies do not take account of the need to recruit Black employees. Race Relations courses and conferences are poorly attended and for most of the time are found boring and irrelevant to the real issues of racism. (GLC ARTUWG, 1984, p. 5)

This is the reality for Black workers in this country not only having to battle against the racism of management or the racism on the shop floor but the racism within the very unions that are meant to be fighting their cause.

These are only some examples of a number of documented and unreported cases, including the case of the Black nurse who failed to get the support of her union.[5] The response to this old situation was an old one — the call for a Black Trade Union to represent the needs of Black people.

Civil Rights

The civil rights struggle of Black people in this country is broadly-based and has roots in a variety of political positions. The two main positions are exemplified by the Campaign Against Racial Discrimination (CARD) tradition and the Racial Action Adjustment Society (RAAS) tradition. CARD was formed in February 1965, largely by the instigation of Martin Luther King, who had passed through England in December 1964 on his way to receive his Nobel Peace Prize. And it was in the wake of the visit of Malcolm X in February 1965, that the RAAS was formed. These two organizations represented the liberal/moderate and radical/militant Black positions respectively. However, with the ever-mounting pressure of domination, repression and race hatred and in the climate of progressively more repressive immigration laws and its concomitant institutionalized racism, came a rise in the activities of the fascists.

> Racial attacks had already begun to mount. In 1965, in the months preceding the White Paper but after Griffiths' victory, 'a Jamaican was shot and killed ... in Islington, a West Indian schoolboy in Notting Hill was nearly killed by White teenagers armed with iron bars, axes and bottles ... a group of Black men outside a cafe in Notting Hill received blasts from a shotgun fired from a moving car', hate leaflets appeared in Newcastle-upon-Tyne, crosses were burnt outside 'coloured citizens' homes in Leamington Spa, Rugby, Coventry, Ilford, Plaistow and Cricklewood and a written warning (allegedly) from the Deputy Wizard of the Klu Klux Klan, was sent to the Indian Secretary of Card: 'You will be burnt alive if you do not leave England by August 31st'. (Sivanandan, *et al*)

But by that time, as Sivanandan argues, Black people were no longer willing to put up with repression. They had made the psychological journey from 'sojourners' to 'settlers'. Thus, state racism as well as the overt racist actions of extremist groups pushed Black people into higher and more militant forms of resistance — a shift as Sivanandan puts it 'From Resistance to Rebellion'.

Despite the years of struggle into which Black people have entered over the years, one may well argue that the civil liberties of Black British people have not appreciably improved. The police now have more power than they have ever had before to stop and search people in the street — a power that, it is argued, is used particularly against Black people, especially Black youth. In addition, there seems to be a growth in the organized harassment and torture and murder of Black people by the racist and racialist extremists. So while the 'Newham Seven' have been released from their charges for defending themselves and their community, there are renewed racist attacks on the homes of Asian Black families which leave them frightened, destitute and sometimes *dead*.

This is the paradox of the improvement of civil liberties for Black people. That while there is a marked improvement in the range of settings and positions in which one could set Black people, there is no significant decrease in the overall level or intensity of racism. In fact, as I argue elsewhere in this book, what one in fact notices is racism restructuring itself in civil rights, immigration and nationality legislation. And though landlords can no longer put up signs that say 'No Blacks Here', they can, and do, enact it on different covert and overt bases, though the hidden reasons are the same.

Education

As argued earlier, educational provision for Black people has ranged from an 'Assimilationist model through an integrationist model to one of cultural pluralism'. Thus, the stresses have been different. These models have been initiated since the early 1960s with the Commonwealth Immigrant Advisory Council recommendation to the Home Secretary that special provision should be made for the education of 'immigrant' children, but as Mullard (1982a) suggests:

> the various multiracial education models developed and employed since the early sixties have attempted to foster the cultural subordination and political neutralization of Blacks, they have started to achieve the very thing many of their advocates attempted to prevent — the social isolation and alienation of Blacks in our society.

These various attempts have not only produced isolation and alienation but failure and, in 1971, Bernard Coard published a book, *How the West Indian Child Is Made Educationally Subnormal in the British School System*, and in his section of recommendations of 'things we can do for ourselves' he outlines a number of strategies. Some of these strategies had been in operation. One of the major strategies is that of supplementary education, which is now a widespread strategy within the Black community.

One such project is the Tooting Youth Project which started in 1969 as a voluntary youth club managed by a group of Jamaicans called the 'Ackee Group'. By 1972, now with WCCR sponsorship and ILEA backing (in the form of seconded workers), they had identified a supplementary educational programme as being paramount in their work with Black youth. Though this work has continued until the present, it has not been without problems of opposition and lack of cooperation from the authorities. This has led to the current situation whereby the project is being set up as an independent voluntary organization.

The Tooting Project, of course, needs to be seen in conjunction with the range of supplementary and Saturday schools in existence all over the country. Their continued existence alongside the moves to make mainstream education anti-racist marks the range of strategies being employed by the Black communities to combat racism in all its forms. However, it is important to highlight here the struggles of Black youth, since their experience of racism is a very sharp and immediate one. The poignancy of this experience lies in the nature of the interface between Black youth and institutionlized racism, especially as enacted through the state.

Repression and Rebellion

In Althusserian terms, the state uses Ideological State Apparatuses (ISA) and Repressive State Apparatuses (RSA) with which to control the working class but as Gramsci stated, 'the power of the state lies ultimately in the use of force'. It is, therefore, evident that in the current crisis British society is that much further along the continuum from the moment of consent to the movement of force. Within this ideal it is important that the state's repressive measures should be coupled with continuing attempts at gaining that consent' — to use those repressive measures being employed; thus the ideological notion of 'policing by consent'.

With regard to youth, Davies (1981) notes the state's response to the crisis in hegemony as a shift 'towards a state youth policy' which can be summarized in terms of a shift from consent to coercion. Davies categorizes it in terms of a shift:

(a) from 'education' to 'training';
(b) from ethical pluralism to moral purity;
(c) from winning consent to coercing compliance;
(d) from professional to bureaucratic models of action.

Under (a) he emphasizes the fact that 'the repeated emphasis on the national interest has the effect of legitimizing policies which narrow or eliminate routes to those young people's personal growth'. Referring to the state's move towards moral purity, Davies speaks of the 'increasing commitment of state youth policy to *induction* rather than self-realization'. This Davies argues is evident, not only in relation to economic and political goals, but 'in more specifically, social and cultural areas the same policy trend is apparent'.

Accepting the notion of the racist state one may summise that similar measures are being employed in the management and demanagement of racism. Therefore, both a repressive racism as well as a more subtle and 'consent-wooing' racism is in operation with regard to Britain's Black population. As Gramsci (1971) wrote:

> The crisis of ruling class hegemony . . . occurs either because the ruling class has failed in some major political undertaking for which it has requested or forcibly extracted the consent of the broad masses . . . have passed suddenly from a state of political passivity to a certain activity and put forward demands which, taken together, albeit not organically formulated, add up to a revolution. A 'crisis of authority' is spoken of: this is precisely the crisis of hegemony, or general crisis of the state.

Today in Britain evidence of the youth crisis hinges on both the failure of the state and the growing militancy of youth precipitated both by this 'failure' and the growing attempts of the state to contain and repress any resistance.

Another part of the general crisis of the State is the race crisis whereby the Black communities realize that, despite the various reports of the various government commissions and special committees, the reality of the everyday lives of Black people is one of repression in all areas of their lives. At the sharp end of this socio-racial repression are Black youth, male *and* female.

Let us then focus on the phenomenon of Black youth, their repression and their resistance to it. As Bunyan (1981) writes:

> Britain, along with other capitalist nations, is set on restructuring its productive base in order to participate in the new industrial revolution — (more specifically, through the use of the micro-processor) . . . For Britain, the political and social costs of such a restructuring, which presumes almost a third of the potential working population being permanently unemployed, require the imposition of a highly authoritarian regime.

The state's response to the riots etc. is a sure indication of the imminent shift from a 'liberal democracy' to an 'authoritarian democracy'. Youth have been made the main target — Black youth especially.

The channels through which the state has sought to achieve its gains are varied and range from the use of and collusion with the media and direct control through its departments. In *Policing the Crisis*, Hall *et al* (1979) examine the creation of the 'moral panic' of the mugger which has come to be equated with Black young males. The authors also trace the role that the media has played and continues to play in this. In fact, it is not just Black *youth* that are under attack but they are being used as a metaphor for the hegemonic crisis in relation to Blacks as a whole. This became clearer when, in 1982, Lord Denning made a statement to the effect that the jury of the 1981 Bristol 'riot' trial was 'packed' and 'overloaded' with 'coloured people' and that 'black, coloured and brown people did not have the same standards of conduct as whites' (Leigh, 1982).

Lord Denning declared that 'British citizens were no longer all qualified to serve on juries', because 'the English are no longer a homogeneous race. They are white and black, coloured and brown ... some of them come from countries where bribery and graft are accepted ... and where stealing is a virtue so long as you are not found out. They no longer share the same code of morals (or) religious beliefs' (*ibid*). Even as he was about to retire Denning, as a member and a 'primary definer' of the ruling class, was heralding the transition from a 'liberal' to an 'authoritarian' regime. Simultaneously, there were moves in Parliament for a statutory crime of riot which would carry a penalty of up to fourteen years' imprisonment, and two other statutory crimes of unlawful assembly and affray (*The Times*, 31 December 1982).

> The process by which the state, through its various instruments of government, seeks to maintain control over the internal situation becomes more stringent when faced with external pressures. In this respect, young people are a prime target for control mechanisms and they represent the means through which future social relationships will be reproduced.

Travers isolates the five government agencies mentioned above as the main ones involved in the 'youth problem'. He highlights the ability of the DHSS to control the living standards and the living situations of people through its highly complex system of benefits which is designed to maintain a labour force at base level until it can effectively be deployed within the economy. 'Benefits are deliberately kept below inflation level and this effect on the young working class is to produce a totally dependent and exploitable workforce, or induce criminal behaviour that is kept in check by other departments' (*ibid*).

The DHSS is made up of an incomprehensible network of cross-references and bureaucratic requirements which serve to discourage, embarrass, annoy, confuse and degrade its prospective recipients. Black youth in particular are alienated by the system and 'signing on' is seen by many of them, anyway, to be degrading. Thus, there is a marked under-registration of Black people, especially youths.

The Home Office's role in the state assembly is most significant in that one of the main instruments of the Home Office is the police force, who have been at the forefront of the conflict.

In his article, 'The police against the people', Bunyan (1981) describes the July riot as 'a watershed in British policing and politics'. Through a historical analysis, he highlights the fact that the choice now offered by the state is cooptation and coercion. But given the running down of industry, the increase of unemployment and the cuts in Welfare expenditure, the shift towards coercion and 'authoritarian democracy' must become more pronounced. Consequently, even while Scarman was deliberating on the April 'riots', the police took the offensive. Hundreds were arrested, thousands physically assaulted and the police used CS gas for the first time on the mainland, in Liverpool.

Bunyan joins many others in placing the cause of the riots in the 'aggressive policing policies'. This, however, seems a natural concomitant of a move towards a more authoritarian regime to help contain growing structural unemployment. He traces how, historically, contrary to popular belief, the police have acted against the people, even though, ideologically, they were and are presented as the neutral arm of the neutral state. This 'neutrality' is further legitimized through reference to the 'fact' they 'uphold the law' and the rulings of the court, all of which, 'of course, are in the *national interest*'. Consequently, any political action or resistance to these agencies is seen as action against this 'common interest'. Therefore, the violence of the state is legitimated and political action by 'rioters' is seen as criminal.

> It is no wonder that black youth lead the fight back, for their oppression has been sharpest. Nor is it surprising that the dispossessed white youth only at one remove . . . should follow this lead. (*Ibid*)

Again, as socio-economic scapegoats, Black youth are made into problems. 'South East Asian young women are seen as too passive or rebelling against their too rigid families; Afro-Caribbean young women as receiving not enough or too much discipline; while Afro-Caribbean young men are seen as "lawless criminals".'

One of the recent strategies of the Home Office offensive, following the summer of 1981, has been the release of the breakdown of the police figures, which 'show' a disproportionate involvement of Black people in street crime. Though, in fact, these figures refer to reported crimes and not convictions and, therefore, are by no means conclusive and probably includes a number of arrests related to the 'riots' and to the 'Notting Hill carnival', where 'Black crime' is sought out whether or not the charges are later substantiated. The fact is, in a Home Office study carried out in three cities — Liverpool, Manchester and Birmingham — it was found that 'people of West Indian origin may be less likely to report muggings to the police. A Home Office survey on Moss Side revealed that significantly more White, as opposed to Black, people were willing to report a bag snatch to the police' (Ramsey, 1982).

In *Policing the Crisis*, Hall *et al* trace the chronology of the creation of the moral panic of the black mugger. This involved the state as (primary definers) — including the Duke of Edinburgh, who, when addressing the Royal College of General Practitioners, declared, 'mugging' as a disease of the community for which a cure had to be found (*The Times*, 1 November 1982), the media who generated it and catalyzed it. The reactionary right wing organizations who used it as a further justification for their fascist and racist views, and above all, the police who were gradually gaining more justification and 'public support' for their harassment of Black youth. It was, therefore, only a matter of time until Black youths reacted against this growing repression and oppression, popularly referred to by Black youth as 'Babylon'. As Hall *et al* (1978) noted, 'the confrontations between the police and Black youth in the Black urban areas are assuming a more open politicized form' (p. 329). They use the Brockwell Park incident of 1974 to exemplify this changing nature in that, firstly, there was now a polarity between the police and the *whole* of the Black community including the adults; secondly, there was now a 'substantial, organized and political form of . . . community resistance' and, thirdly, the incident had the effect of pinpointing the source of trouble and disaffection, specifically in the Black urban localities. This, they argue, served to fuse into a single theme: 'crime, race and the ghetto'.

> Accordingly, from this point onwards, the explanatory paradigms shift, bringing out more explicitly than before the social, economic and structural preconditions of the Black crime problem — and thus contributing the final link in the chain which fused crime and racism with the crisis. (*Ibid*, p. 329)
>
> As is true of every other moment of the long 'crisis in hegemony' . . ., race has come to provide the objective correlative of the crisis. (*Ibid*)

Black Youth and the Police

Robert Renier begins his article, 'Black and blue: Race and the police', with a quote from Margaret Simey, Chairperson of the Merseyside Police Committee of spring 1971 in which she stated that:

> The coloured community is fed up with being hounded. No one is safe on the streets after 10.00 pm. One gang we know has given the police an ultimatum to lay off within two weeks or they fight back. It could lead to civil war in the city.

Renier makes a comparison between the American ghetto riots of 1960 and the 1981 'riots' and makes the observation that:

> In all the societies with significant ethnic tensions, the police — as the most visible, concrete embodiment of the dominant group's power — are at the heart of the conflict. (*Ibid*)

He presents the 'objective' treatment of police/Black relationship which at best presents a 'liberal' superficial analysis based on circumstantial factors — visibility, Black response, police recruitment from a racially prejudiced working class based on a number of observational studies, including Holloway's *Inside the British Police*. The conclusion of most of these studies seems to be that 'the problem' is one of 'normal' policing, not one of police race relations. Yet, on the contrary, he cites contradictory evidence from other research projects, such as the experiment conducted by F. Heuss.

The standard official response both in the US and the UK has been in terms of the premises, firstly, that police/Black conflict rests firstly on lack of communication and, secondly, on the attitude/nature of individual officers, not from the structure and strategy. This also seems to be the assumption of the Scarman Report (1981). Lord Scarman asserts that there is no institutional racism and suggests that the problem lie with the racism and racist practices of individual officers. Scarman makes a huge leap to state that:

> Institutional racism does not exist in Britain: but racial disadvantage and its nasty associate racial discrimination have not yet been eliminated. (9.1)

Though Scarman's Report is viewed by the majority of 'liberal' reformists as excellent and progressive, it can be seen as regressive and a (last) great attempt at re-establishing the hegemony of the state, certainly in terms of the 'Black crisis'. While on the one hand affirming that the majority of Black people are decent law abiding citizens, he reaffirms, on behalf of the ruling class and the state (his sponsors), that 'the direction and policies of the Metropolitan Police are not racist'. He continues:

> I totally and unequivocably reject the attack made upon the integrity and impartiality of the senior direction of the force. The criticisms lie elsewhere — in errors of judgment, in lack of imagination and flexibility, but not in deliberate bias or prejudice. The allegation that the Police are the oppressive arm of a racist State not only displays a complete ignorance of the constitutional arrangements for controlling the police: it is an injustice to the senior officers of the force. (paragraph 4, p. 61)

The Scarman Report, therefore, is involved in upholding the ideology that state agencies act as neutral arbiters. This is not only an attempt to obfuscate the role of the police but also his own function in making an 'objective' enquiry and presenting a Report.

This ideology has an important legitimating function 'since it implies that the state acts for the benefit of society as a whole'. Therefore, criticism of Scarman, like other forms of political action or resistance, is presented as acting against the 'common interest' and is therefore destructive. Consequently, it is not surprising that the Scarman Report was greeted with tremendous enthusiasm by the state and the liberal majority.

The Scarman Enquiry and its resultant report is a perfect example of how the state in crisis attempts to use ideological means to justify aggression, state violence and repression. This becomes most evident when one notes that though William Whitelaw, the then current Secretary of State, accepted the Report as being true and important, the 'progressive' elements have been either disregarded or are 'receiving consideration'. Consequently, there is an affirmation of the continuing need for the Special Patrol Group (SPG) or a similar 'reserve mobile force', but little has been done about improving the system of accountability of the police and concomitantly there is a build up of the 'technology of political control'. As Ackroyd *et al* (1977) argue:

> The aim of these technologies is not primarily the physical elimination of their opponents. Their target is the thoughts of their opponents and potential opponents as much as their bodies.

The authors' analysis in relation to Northern Ireland is equally applicable in the way they show how these technologies operate to maximize repression, coupled with the setting up of official committees which successfully serve the purpose of diffusing public protest. Yet, as Ackroyd *et al* put it, the violence which is being 'put down' is in response to the violence of State repression. Writing as they were in 1977, Ackroyd *et al* note that:

> The awareness of the British public about their (*ie.* the new technologies) nature and use has been blunted by the Northern Ireland conflict, which makes it all the more possible for the army (or police) to use them inside Britain at some future date.

In 1981, William Whitelaw sanctioned the possible use of these new technologies for strengthening the offensive of the police in 'riot control' as a 'last resort'. This seems to mirror the observations of Ackroyd *et al* who noted that the failure of traditional riot control and 'legal measures' in Northern Ireland and the 'stepped up Tory offensive' signalled an escalation of the Catholic struggle with the ensuing growth of the IRA, marking the end of the 'non-violent' stage of resistance. Therefore, the authors argue that the new technologies are introduced by the state not only to meet the needs of the state in times of crisis and to fit the general needs of security national but that these technologies:

> are, in fact, a variable in a political equation. Therefore, most commonly the objective is to maximize repression, subject to a constraint that any political backlash depends not on how harmless the technologies are, but on how harmless they *seem*. Humanitarianism then is not an objective but a propaganda claim. (*Ibid*)

The parallels between the Northern Ireland situation and the English inner cities offers great cause for alarm and foreboding when one examines the escalation of police/state aggression against the people, especially young Blacks.

The implications to be drawn from Ackroyd *et al's* overall evalua- tion and analysis of the Northern Irish situation are tremendous. Black people, as an exploited group — not unlike the Northern Irish Catholics — come at the bottom of the hierarchy of exploitation and are exploited both as a class and as a race. The Black Civil Riots Movement in Britain has already begun to move off from the initial stages of non-violent resistance and one might argue that, with the progressive move (*sic*) towards the strong state, Black resistance has reached the stage of 'rebellion'. At the vanguard are Black youth. This is the light in which the recent uprisings, such as Handsworth, Tottenham and Brixton, have to be seen. Whereas a lot of the popular press would want to, and have indeed tended to, portray the disturbances as Afro-Caribbean Black people against Asian Black people, this proved untrue and a lot more complex than it seemed at first.

One of the major reasons given (or not) for the Handsworth incident tends to be 'unemployment'. As *The Observer* editorial of 15 September 1985 argues, the current government tends to deny the reality of riots because it wants to deny the reality of unemployment, whereas the critics of the government have tended to use social upheavals as proof of the inadequacy and paucity of government policy. Thus, it is argued, 'riot' is made into the 'litmus test' of economics.

Another popular reason given is policing and this again is argued from two opposing positions of either that the police are too 'soft' or too 'hard' and aggressive. However, both camps tend to ignore the fact that whether it is hard line policing or community policing, in the words of a Handsworth rastafarian, 'It's the same policing by a different name' (*The Observer*, September 1985).

The fact is that the problem is much more fundamental and resides in the fact that the reality of the day to day lives of Black young people in Handsworth is that they experience racism at every turn in education, in their social relations and relationships with authority ('Babylon'), in their employment status and in housing. Thus the negative experience of racism underpins the overall quality of their lives. But as young people they also experience the oppression of generational control and exploitation (see Brandt (1986), *Anti Racism, the Economy and Post 16 Education*). Thus, in the disturbances of Handsworth, the protagonists were largely Afro-Caribbean Black youths; but among their number were also Asian Black as well as White youth.

The sum total of the crisis in the British state as experienced by Black youth is probably best epitomized in the words of a Black Handsworth electronics engineer quoted in *The Observer*

> I don't say the riots should have happened. It's just tension. Nobody in his right mind would plan a riot like this when his own house will be burned down. We don't want to be millionaires, we just want to live a good life like you ... (15 September 1985)

Black British youth are not satisfied to sit back and passively accept handouts. They are stepping forward to claim for themselves what is the right of each of us — a decent life. It is, therefore, not surprising that in close proximity to the Handsworth disturbances came Brixton and Tottenham, with other smaller but similar incidents, during which live ammunition was used for the first time on mainland Britain. This is the background to current debates and contemporary analyses.

Summary

In this chapter, I have tried to tease out some of the most significant socio-historical phenomena — both official and unofficial, both policy and practice — which have contributed to the current debates regarding anti-racist education.

This has involved looking at the history of European and British racism as an ideology and as a practice. These practical considerations led to looking at Black immigration and settlement in the light of its ideological, economic and political parameters. Also, it was necessary to look at race relations and race relations legislation through the concept of a racist state.

The final section of the chapter looks at selected moments in the history of Black resistance to racism and argues that Black people were not simply passive victims of institutional and interactional racism but have been active in the struggle against it. In the vanguard, it is argued, have been Black youth. This, therefore, sets the scene for looking at the contemporary context in which anti-racism, as an ideology and practice, is being debated and promulgated.

Notes

1 Accounts of Black presence in Britain:
   (a) Conference Papers 'History of Blacks in Britain', Centre for Multi-Cultural Education, University of London Institute of Education.
   (b) Conference Papers, 'History of Blacks in London', Centre for Multi-Cultural Education, University of London Institute of Education.
   (c) FIELD, F. and HAIKIN, P. (1971) *Black Britons*, Oxford, Oxford University Press.
   (d) FILE, N. and POWER, C. (1981) *Black Settlers in Britain, 1555–1955*, London, Heinemann.
   (e) DABYDEEN, D. (Ed.) (1985) *The Black Presence in English Literature*, Manchester, University of Manchester Press.
   (f) FRYER, P. (1984) '*Staying Power*', London, Pluto Press.
2 In April 1968 Enoch Powell made a speech in Birmingham in which he calls up classical allusions to the River Tiber foaming with blood to make the overall point that the White British were being swamped. This speech, along

with his later comment about the 'breeding habits' of Black people and their prolific reproduction of 'grimy piccaninnies' not only mobilized but gave political respectability to overt racialist acts and words.

At the end of 1978, Margaret Thatcher announced that her party would finally see the end to immigration for the sake of 'race relations', the preservation of the 'British way of life' and allaying the fears of the majority. She argued that this country might be rather swamped by people with a different culture.

Both of these speeches use a prognosis of racial conflict based on the Black presence. It is therefore interesting though not surprising that one of the first reactions of a number of members of the current government to the disturbances of 1985 in Handsworth, Brixton and Tottenham was a renewed call for repatriation.

3 Readers may refer to elements in the following: MULLARD, C. (1982b) 'The state's response to racism', in OHRI, A, MANNING, B. and CURNO, P. (Eds.), *Community Work and Racism*, London, Routledge and Kegan Paul; MULLARD, C. (1984) *Anti Racist Education: the Three O's*, London, National Association for Moral Education; MULLARD, C. (1985a) *Race, Class and Ideology: Some Journal Notes*, London, Race Relations Policy and Practice Research Unit, University of London Institute of Education; MULLARD, C. (1985b) *Race, Power and Resistance*, London, Routledge and Kegan Paul.

4 Cashmore and Troyna's position as laid out in *Introduction to Race Relations* (see bibliography) is only one example of this.

5 The Black district nurse, Ada Bernard, who was assaulted by two male trade unionists, failed to get the assistance of her union COHSE for a number of seemingly manufactured reasons. The main one being that she was not a 'paid-up' member at the time of the incident despite the fact that (even if that was an adequate excuse) her un'-paid-up' state was due to the hospital's maladministration. This incident, naturally, created quite some reaction amongst Black trade unionists. But as the *West Indian World* asserted (Friday 9 July 1982), 'Britain's Black workforce will no longer be appeased with anti-racist stances, statements and public pronouncements'. *The Caribbean Times* of the same period made similar statements.

It is also noteworthy that the case was not taken up by the (White) women's movement, though this was clearly a case of male violence against women — an issue of tremendous importance to the movement.

2   *The Context of Anti-racist Education*

Introduction

In this chapter we make a leap from the historical to examining the contemporary context for the articulation and realization of anti-racist teaching in Britain. In any such analysis it is inevitable and imperative that the current reports, policy documents and institutional changes be taken into account. Therefore, the chapter begins with a look at the whole issue of 'race' and 'racism' in education in the context of the Swann Report.

We then move on to look at the issue of race and education in relation to contemporary and currently influential educational theory (which examines and emphasizes the distinction between education and schooling). This leads into a more 'in-depth' look at the changes in emphasis in educational practice precipitated by the shifting epistemologies of 'racist' education. This notion of 'racist' education is used within the specificity of the theoretical position articulated in this book and does not refer to any sort of blanket charge against individual teachers within the state system (or private sector for that matter). But neither does it totally exculpate individual teachers since, as it is argued, the realization of racist practice exists in, and is signified by, the interactions between and the combination of structural, systematic and interpersonal racism. Within this context, the last section briefly examines the notion of 'racist' education itself.

Education, Race and Racism in the Eighties

For good or for ill, probably the most important document to emerge within the discourse of race and education in Britain is the Swann

Report. This Report is divided into five parts which include some sixteen chapters, and a section on the main conclusions and recommendations. These main conclusions and recommendations cover broadly six elements:

(i)   Achievement and underachievement.
(ii)   The notion of 'Education for All'.
(iii)   'A Strategy for Change'.
(iv)   Language and the role of the School.
(v)   Religion and the role of the school;
(vi)   Teacher education and the education of ethnic minority teachers.

Disregarding the glaring omission of any real consideration of the resources and means of implementing change, the Report suffers by the shifting and varied ideological underpinning of its arguments and recommendations. Thus, it is possible, as some people have done, to go through the document and pull out the anti-racist elements, but it is equally possible to go through and pull out the assimilationist or integrationist elements and to make a case for their implementation.

This Report, *Education for All* (February 1985), was intended to be a response to the recommendation of the Select Committee on Race Relations and Immigration of 1977, that the government should institute as a matter of urgency:

> a high level and independent inquiry into the causes of the under-achievement of children of West Indian origin in main-tained schools and the remedial action required.

This recommendation was broadened by the government of the day to include all 'ethnic minority' children. The resultant brief of the Committee, which was set up in 1979 under the chairpersonship of Anthony Rampton, was that it should primarily analyze and assess the relevant intra and extra curricular factors which impinge on school performance and to consider the value and scope of arrangements to review 'ethnic minority performance'; to consider the optimum deployment of resources; and to make recommendations. Special attention, it was understood, should be given to the educational needs and attainment of children of West Indian background.

The response of the education community, like that of the Black community, to the final report of this Committee, which had Lord Swann as its chairperson for its final stage, has been varied and can be placed into three broad categories:

(i)   broad rejection ('racist rubbish');
(ii)   acceptance ('the best thing since sliced bread');
(iii)   partial acceptance ('can do better — should try harder').

My intention in this section is to examine these categories in order to try and ascertain the possible difference that 'Swann' can or cannot make to the important but difficult interface between racism and education.

'Racist Rubbish'

With this broad position there are a number of major issues which are articulated as a major critique of the whole Report. The following are some of them.

First and foremost it is argued that Swann lets teachers off the hook by failing to attribute to teachers the appropriate degree of culpability for the generation, regeneration, and perpetuation of racism in schooling, both in terms of pedagogy as well as curriculum. Thus, like the way in which Scarman let the police off the hook by stating that there is no institutional racism, only individual racism, which is in fact the exception, *Education for All* is seen as supporting the myth that racism among teachers and in the teaching process is a professional aberration and therefore not a major problem. Secondly, it is argued that the report re-enacts the old colonial strategem of 'divide and rule' in order to neutralize growing strength within the Black community through the increasing common identity based on the acknowledgement of a common oppression of racism. The precise example given is the example of the renewed affirmation that 'Asians' are performing much better than their 'West Indian' counterparts and better even (*sic*) than White pupils. This assertion is criticized on many counts. It is criticized because of its gross generalizations of 'Asian' and 'West Indian', has been criticized for the paucity of its research base, but above all on account of the fact that it is an analysis based on a White norm — thus ethnocentric — and in being ethnocentric is clearly racist. It ultimately begs the question, if both the 'West Indian' and 'Asian' communities are victims of racism, why is it that one group performs better than the other? Thereby what is created is a new racial hierarchy based on a false division among the oppressed.

Thirdly, it has been criticized for its failure to sufficiently 'take on board' the important issue of the wider social context of a racism in which Black youth are being criminalized by the White society at large and ultimately by the courts, the legislative system and the police; the ways in which they are pathologized both in the social as well as clinical sense — whereby more and more Black young people (especially young men) are being committed to mental institutions.

Fourthly, the fact that in his guide to the Report Lord Swann failed to highlight racism as a crucial factor, in fact even failed to mention the word, is severely criticized. The fact is that racism is the major element as considered by the Black community and the 'aware' and 'concerned' members of the teaching profession are ignored. This already bad situation is exacerbated by the fact that this guide was selected to be the major element of consumption by the public at large and by schools in particular. It was distributed (free of charge) to schools while the full report is prohibitively priced.

This general school of thought has seen the Swann Report as 'racist rubbish' which takes the struggle against racism no further, but in fact seeks to further control the racially oppressed by the cooptation of the oppositional persons and tendencies within the educational community as well as within the wider Black community.

The 'Best Thing'

It is important to state here that the tripartite typology being used should not be seen as representing the traditional categories of radical/conservative/liberal. This is so because these three tendencies which I have identified do not include such conservative groupings as would say that the whole Report is too anti-racist and assumes a conflict that is not there at all. Rather, it is a typology specific to the rapidly changing discourse of race relations. Each category has its own, as well as mutually shared, problematics.

Thus, within this 'best thing' category, one is looking at a broad church of 'ethnarchs', liberals, gradualists and even careerists (Black and White). For this 'best thing' school of thought, the Swann Report is not only the best we have but the best achievable. The argument is that for the first time in the history of our education system there is a report that clearly and unequivocally recognizes the negative effect of institutional racism on the schooling of all children. They go further to emphasize the fact that within the gradualist British tradition, we have come as far as is possible at the present time. So their conclusion is that it should be accepted and worked with to the best of its present capacity. The main problem with this position is that it tends largely to depoliticize race, racism and race relations. They also tend to see racism as a static structure which can be slowly, permanently and irreversably unassembled.

'Could Do Better — Should Try Harder'

This group, which could be largely described as the critical rationalist/pragmatist, would argue, in very strong terms, that though we should take on board the positive and anti-racist analyses and recommendations of the Swann Report, a lot more could be done to further the aims of anti-racist education, which at this particular historical conjuncture would be inclusive of any conception of 'education for all'.

The first point to be made here is that the oppressed voices of Black people have been screaming to the powers that be for many, many years but nothing really substantial has been done, nor indeed have their voices been recognized — that is, until an 'official' committee gets set up in the name of providing equal opportunity and promoting social harmony. Of course, never is an official committee set up until there is a crisis of consent between the dominant and the dominated. Then when the report is submitted only those elements which are seen as least likely to upset the status quo or better likely to maintain the status quo are implemented. Thus, both the process, as well as the product of a committee enquiry, operate as legitimating devices for difficult, controversial or even overtly repressive decisions by the state.

Education and Schooling — The Context

It is important in discussions such as these to establish the current climate — the socio-economic, the political, the educational — as a basis as well as a backdrop for discussion and debate.

The fact is that the socio-economic climate of the eighties in the United Kingdom is very much one of crisis. However, the government and its optimistic supporters amongst economists, industrialists, and social scientists (though Sir Keith Joseph would deny the latter group their status as scientists), still maintain that the upturn in the economy is imminent.

The political climate — strongly related to the socio-economic, and inseparable for the current Tory government — is fraught with tensions and the political rivalry between the major political parties is accompanied by a tremendous battle for the minds of the British nation. We have also seen over the last five to ten years a large degree of organization on the part of the Black communities, who have not only been articulating their separate interests, demands, and dissatisfactions but have been engaged in the important and politically crucial act of linking arms in the struggle against racism in all of its forms. This has been marked by the formation of a growing range of local community action groups, professional organizations and educational organizations/interest groups. One of the emergent signifiers has been the organizing around the anti-racist struggle and the identification of a common use of the term of 'Black' as a political term to signify a political category of people who are victims of a racism based on visibility and physical/cultural manifestations. Whether it is acknowledged or not this unification of the struggle against a racist state and a racist society at large now poses a considerable threat to racism as it has been traditionally maintained. Thus, political, economic, social and educational initiatives taken by the state have seen the necessity of taking into consideration not only the general concern but the specific concerns of particular groups including the Black community. The government of the day has power and as the embodiment of this power the racist and oppressive state, needs to maintain that power. The state is therefore seeking and is constantly engaged in the struggle for authority. Even the most repressive state needs to have its power legitimated by 'consent'. The embodiment of this phenomenon is the now notorious Tory advertisement which reads 'Labour says he's Black; Tories say he's British'. Even though this party has shown through its actions that it is no friend of black people.

The educational climate, therefore, both as a consequence as well as a part of the same package, is one of economic constraint, accompanied by an ideological struggle for the hegemonic domination of a White, middle class, monetarist, racist ideology. This ideology is both masked as well as overt and is dressed in the nomenclature of 'quality', 'equality', 'firmness', multi-culturalism, pluralism, harmony and the resurrected notion of 'Education for All'.

The notion of Education for All, despite its stated intention of 'pluralism' (whatever it means in that context), seems doomed to fall into the old formulation of 'colour blindness' as 'fairness' (in both senses of the word). Thus, even the 'new' definition of the concept of 'education for all' based on pluralism fails to come to terms with the fact that the assertion of 'education for all' does not get rid of the structures or the systematic realizations of racism — or indeed its effects. This formulation can therefore lead one up the proverbial garden path of yesteryear. In the spirit of this assertion the teacher may well reaffirm

the old sectarian cliche . . . 'I don't teach girls or Blacks or Greeks etc.,
— I teach children'. Herein lies a resuscitated 'old' utterance of a 'new'
racism.

The New Racism   DEF - RACISM

Racism is not simply a belief system or a set of attitudes. It is an ideology
that is located in and realized through structures of power relations in
the interface between ethnicity and culture; economics and social
processes; individuals and institutions. This racism is multi-faceted and
dynamic and must be seen not only in terms of xenophobia (race
hatred), racial prejudice, bias, ethnocentricity or discrimination, but in
terms of power. This power is itself of a varied nature, ranging from the
ideological to the material. The elements are reflected in an overall
racism that is both overt and covert, hidden and blatant, and is practised
both at the individual and institutional levels, within structures and
within systems. Racism is exhibited both in policies and practices which
could be direct or indirect. Therefore, anti-racist action must be of
matching complexity to be at all effective against this dynamic and
oppressive ideology.

Schools, colleges and universities, as agencies of socialization and
cultural transmission, have played in the past and continue to play a
major role in the generation, regeneration and promulgation of racism.
Thus it made clear that racism is not restricted to one particular level of
schooling nor is it the preserve of any one 'level' or 'section' of society.

Racism has a geographical, social and historical specificity. Therefore, in any country, at any point in time, the realization of racist
practice will be of a specific nature though it might be informed by and
based on some parameters which are universal and relatively 'timeless'.

Racism in the Eighties in Britain

The specific realization of racism in Britain in the 1980s seems to be
based on:

(i)   a series of rearticulations of legitimation procedures;
(ii)   a restructuration of legitimation procedures;
(iii) the cooptation of opposition;
(iv)   the fragmentation of oppressed groups.

This overall restructuration of racist practice is testimony to the dynamic nature of racism per se — to its ability to change in the face of the attempts of the Black communities and the anti-racist lobby to struggle against it and to attempt to overthrow its hegemonic reign.

The rearticulation of covert practice

There are several examples of the rearticulation of covert racist practice in Britain today. These rearticulations mark the attempt of the racist Right (though there are also racists on the left) to counteract the attempts of the Black community in collaboration with the anti-racist lobby, to combat and to end the practice as well as the rationalization of racism.

1984 to 1985 has been a period of a marked attempt by some of the articulators of the 'new racism' to woo and to win 'public' opinion in the acceptance of racist practice. This 'wooing' attacks the language and practice of anti-racism largely on the basis of it being seen as 'divisive', 'political', 'extremist', 'inflammatory' and as militating against social harmony. So, anti-racism, as I have stated in chapter 1, is made synonymous with a perceived extremism of the political Left. The recent examples of the attempt to engage in this practice have varied from an ill-conceived and poorly argued paper by Anthony Flew (1984) to the now infamous article by Ray Honeyford (1984), the Bradford headteacher mentioned earlier who put forward a barrage of racist propositions based on racist assumptions but all in the name of professional concern for the pupils of his schools. These articulations seem to get not only the blessing but the active support of the British media. The articles of Roger Scruton (for example, *Times Educational Supplement*, 30 October 1984) are now a permanent and perpetual part of the onslaught on current efforts to restate an acceptable racism.

While this is going on, and prominent newspapers can have articles published entitled 'Black racists', a report is published called *Education for All*. In this report is an important element which calls for 'multicultural education' in all White areas. From an anti-racist standpoint, this is indeed important in that one of the ways in which racism has reconstructed itself in the past is to racialize schooling so that multicultural education becomes a metaphor for 'Black education' or for education where there are a number of Black people present in the school or community. However, it seems to me that the action of which one needs to be careful is the action proceeding from the recommendations. (Of course, the government is not obliged to follow *any* course of action.) One possible outcome within the current economic climate is for resources which were once earmarked for use in 'Black' areas on (possibly) Black-led projects, to be diverted into White areas on the basis of *Education for All.* Thus the Black, largely impoverished communities will again lose out. So if one is arguing for the development of work in all-White areas — and one is — it is important that existing 'mainstream' funding be allocated or reallocated to provide for curriculum development and a revitalized professional practice in education that is liberating and anti-racist.

Restructuring of legitimation procedures

Another important part of the rearticulation of covert practice is the constant restructuring of legitimation procedures.

Within this restructuring there is an increasing tendency to 'play off' sexism, class disability and racism. So, for example, instead of an argument for the reallocation and rethinking of mainstream provision, there is an attempt to place these systems of oppression alongside each other in competitive relations within a context of marginality.

It is important to state again that anti-racism as a concept acknowledges these other forms of oppression and the need to struggle against their continued existence. However, it is important that these systems of oppression are not pitted against each other as a means of weakening the fight of one.

Nevertheless, there is tremendous scope for collaboration towards mutual liberation and justice. Another facet of this restructuring is the renewed and growing tendency towards involving a few Black people in contentious committees and in difficult posts, in order to diffuse or even nullify dissent. The people recruited are often the least representative of the perspectives of the community. However, the Black community is by and large becoming more aware of the use of 'ethnarchy' (Mullard, 1983a)[1] in the management of racism and, as a result, they are combating this tendency and making those 'erring' members of the community accountable.

Cooptation of opposition

This phenomenon is very closely related to the previous section in that it is largely based on the use of 'ethnarchy' and has the principal functions of both managing as well as legitimating institutional racism. However, though individuals can be passive contributors to racism, this observation does not make people (Black or White) involved in these structures to be necessarily active promulgators of racism. This is because the intentions and purposes of the system do not always coincide with the intentions or actions of these individuals. In fact, some of these people may indeed be operating oppositionally within the structure. Thus what is highlighted is the possibility of being gainfully employed within a dialectic discourse of racial management and institutional racism while at the same time being anti-racist. However, what is being put forward here is that one important facet of racism in the eighties is the mushrooming race and cultural relations industry. This growing field is made up of race relations advisers, community relations officers, multicultural advisers and inspectors, consultative committees and committees of investigation, such as the Scarman Committee and the Swann (previously Rampton) Comittee.

In looking at the Swann Committee, it becomes much clearer what function such a committee serves. The process, as well as the product of that committee, can be seen as an exercise in containment. Thus, the first chairperson, who seemed to be raising the issue of racism as a major issue for the Report, was forced to 'resign'. The investigation was completed by one who fails to recognize racism though the concept is discussed and used in various sections of the 807 pages of the Report.

Fragmentation of oppressed groups

This fragmentation (a policy of 'divide and rule') exists not only at the level of the so-called 'competing' oppressions of racism, sexism, class domination and disability mentioned before, but is in existence within and between the racially oppressed groups. Thus, what is being noticed among the Black oppressed groups is a growing fragmentation which is diverting the attention of Black activists, and other victims of racism, from challenging the oppressors, the source of their racial oppression — to competition with other victims of racism. Thus there is a renewed argument emerging about who are the 'real' Blacks and about how some 'Blacks' (however defined) are being recolonized to control and contain resistance and to act as gatekeepers of racist structures.

This general restructuring which I have so far described is tantamount to a restructuration of institutional racism which operates at a structural as well as a systemic level. By structural I refer to the rules, regulations, policies and procedures that govern the ways in which institutions operate. The systemic element in institutional racism lies in the processes. The 'ethos', the 'atmosphere' and the social and cultural relations of institutions also marks the meeting point of the individual racism which has a context and a reinforcement in the structural racism mentioned earlier. Thus, the battle against racism must be of both a general as well as a specific nature. The racist institutional practices of various organizations have a lot in common but there is also a lot different about them. Thus, there is a need to stress the specificity of the realization of institutional racism. This I attempt to do later in chapter 3.

Racism in Education — Combating It

Racism in education is very complex and far-reaching in its impact and ultimate effects. Thus, the deconstruction of institutional racist practice must be direct and at a conscious level. It is dangerous if not downright racist to concentrate on something else, like culture for example, and hope that the rest will follow and racism will end.

The fight to end racism in education must be concerned with changing the context of education, changing the pedagogy and the curriculum, and must examine the administrative arrangements, including questions of student recruitment in higher education and the relationships within the institutions, etc. This overall attempt must be linked to policy formulation and implementation and to the question of resourcing.

The relationship between what has been discussed so far and the Swann Report resides in the fact that it is a part of the educational process in its broader sense. This process of the investigation as well as the product has operated to some degree to neutralize dissent and resistance. Thus, the report 'contains' many of the issues and questions that are there for the Black community — the answers continue to elude the political decision-makers.

It seems therefore that there are three possible responses/outcomes to this Report:

(i)   Complacency;
(ii) Containment;
(iii) Change.

Complacency

Complacency is a distinct possibility on the part of the state as well as the Black community. And the state is completely at liberty to say: 'we have done our best by the Black community, we have done our investigation, we have come up with findings and recommendations, therefore we have done *our* duty'.

If the Black community and the anti-racist lobby are complacent, the state and the education service at large is then free to act on it as it suits them, and one of the possible benefits for the state is a possible greater degree of containment.

Containment

As I have implied throughout this section, the process as well as the product of the Report *Education for All* can act, and has acted, as a tool for containment. One example is the glaring juxtapositions on pages 769 and 773.

On page 769 of *Education for All*, there are three important actual recommendations — (a), (e) and (f). Paragraph (a) is an argument that the problem facing the education system is not how to educate children of ethnic minorities, but how to educate *all* children. Paragraph (e) argues the need to combat racism and paragraph (f) argues the need for 'multicultural understanding ... to permeate all aspects of a school's work ...' What, however, goes unnoticed is the fact that paragraph (c) bows in the direction of centralization in stating that 'this challenge cannot be left to the separate and independent initiatives of LEAs and schools ...'. Of course, there is no mention of the community (particularly the Black community as victims of racism and) as consumers of education. This recommendation, in the light of the wider debate, is ominous and points to an increasing centralization of decision-making and control by the British state.

The other example of attempts at containment resides in the Swann recommendations of 'separate' schools. This section begins with paragraph 6.4, 'The right of ethnic minority communities to seek to establish their own voluntary aided schools is firmly enshrined in law'.

However, this is swiftly followed up in paragraph 6.5 with 'We believe that the demand to exercise this right would be much diminished if the policies for *Education for All* which we have advocated in this Report are adopted'. Thus the leeway is created for the DES to refuse to provide any support for community-initiated or community-run schools on the basis of having adopted the unclear and indeterminate set of principles called 'education for all'.

Change

The alternative path is one of change. One might argue that whatever is done by the Black community and for the anti-racist lobby, change will take place. It is only a question as to whether it is negative or positive and to what degree. I would therefore argue for a concerted effort for positive change but as specified by the Black community. This change must be a firm attempt to deconstruct institutional racism and not simply superficial and palliative change which acknowledges difference (*sic*) or even celebrates it while maintaining the social and racial status quo of racist structures.

The nature and quality of outcomes of the Swann Report and all such other initiatives depends on the action (as opposed to reaction) of the Black community. The anti-racist lobby must be informed by the intentions and articulations of the Black community. However, it seems to me that any action taken *vis à vis* Swann must have certain ingredients. Firstly, there must be a *critical* appraisal concerning the process as well as the product of 'education for all'. Secondly, there must be a sustained dialogue and lobbying around issues. Thirdly, there must continue to be an independent thought-out programme of action of demands and of means of implementation of positive change to combat and deconstruct the racism of the British state and British institutions at large.

Finally, there must be a realistic view by the Black community and others opposing racism of the scope and the time involved in challenging and combating the multi-faceted diversified and complex reality of British racism. By this, one is not advocating complacency or a deference to gradualism but the need to acknowledge the enormity and formidable nature of the struggle.

Racism in Britain is dynamic and complex. Therefore, anti-racist action must also be dynamic and of a matching complexity. The days for empty rhetoric have flown by, the need now is to fight for our lives, the minds, the liberation and ultimate justice of those ensnared and oppressed by racism. The benefits that accrue belong to society at large.

This book is itself seeking to contribute to that struggle by attempting to provide an analysis of current moves towards 'anti-racist' classroom practice with a view towards highlighting a positive approach to anti-racist teaching.

Race and Education

In engaging in an examination of *Race, Racism and Education* and their interrelationship in the context of Britain in the 1980s, one must, I believe, find the correct vocabulary, the vocabulary which adequately and precisely describes the phenomenon discussed. Behind this vocabulary — these words — lie the theoretical framework and ideology which underpin them. Principally, one must make clear what is the meaning attached to the concept of 'racism' even as one takes care not to take the concept of education for granted — neither its aims nor its process, neither its pedagogy nor product, neither its curriculum content nor its curriculum context, neither its structure nor organization. Above all, one must remember the distinction that can and must be made between education and schooling.

In chapter 1 and in the previous section of this chapter, I have tried to examine not only the history of Black people in this country, or the history of racism and resistance to it, but I have also examined the very concept of racism and the specificity of its realization in contemporary British society.

It therefore seems crucial to do a critical examination of concepts of education and schooling before examining the interface between schooling, race and race relations.

Education and Schooling

The distinction between these two phenomena has been the basis of much theoretical and academic debate for decades yet it is a point of continued misunderstanding and misuse. Thus, schooling becomes seen and referred to as education and, as a direct result of that misconception, someone who has had a lot of schooling is often referred to as 'well educated'. By the same token, the 'educated' person tends popularly to be given the 'respect', social position and often economic benefits as a reward for 'personal' achievement with education that is seen as a fixed undynamic commodity. So, to use an analogy, the educated person comes to be seen as the sponge that has successfully absorbed the water of education. The assumption is that the (education) water constantly maintains its property — thus, the only point of evaluation is the degree of absorbency of the sponges. It is well known that at a certain temperature water freezes and, at a point towards the other extreme, water boils. Yet, I am told by scientists that even those points are not constant.

A more sophisticated but similarly functionalist/rationalist position is that all things being equal, learners will perform in accordance with their innate abilities (whether genetically or socially acquired) and the quality of pedagogy. The allied assumption is that the function of schooling is to transport the knowledge and culture the 'society' wants children to have. In this context, society is used unproblematically to suggest the consensual polity. Thus, it is assumed that schooling serves the needs and intentions of the mass of the population and that schools' curricula and pedagogy are only instruments/tools of transmission. However, a number of the 'products' and 'bi-products' of schooling have precipitated the critical examination of all those assumptions, especially in terms of the ways in which schooling in Western capitalist societies has proven to not only maintain but perpetuate the status quo of an unequal and stratified society.

Jones and Williamson (1979), in what they termed an archaeological method of analysis, attempt to examine English popular education of the nineteenth century 'from the standpoint of how the pedagogy of popular schools is formulated and in terms of how the field of political discourse, in which popular education is stated as a need, is constituted'. They argue that contemporary 'educational' practice derives from this nineteenth century education which emerged out of three different 'unities of political knowledge which formed the three successive fields that gave birth to the schoolroom'. Jones and Williamson use a post-structuralist Foucaldian method of analysis. They argue early nineteenth century education did not come about merely as a means of socialization or social control but as a means of 'securing public morality and preventing crime, as a means of forming a population with useful habits, through the instrument of good principles, in order to secure a moral foundation for governmental and religious authority'. They go further to argue that later on, schooling begins to exist 'specifically as a means for regulating the relations between the classes of the population by forming an instrument which is able to modify a class's moral topography'. Schooling then became, they argue, 'a set of techniques specifically adapted to class characteristics' for reproducing the juvenile members of the classes. These authors reject an epoch-based analysis such as pre/post industrial, pre/post capitalist, etc. but seem more concerned with the historical moment. However, in attempting to reject a causal analysis they tend to become ahistorical, even though early in their paper they assert that 'the functions which particular social practices fulfil are themselves historically defined, that is to say they do not exist independent of historical conditions of possibility; they are not pre-given'.

As asserted by Madan Sarup (1983) in the introduction to his book *Marxism, Structuralism, Education.*

When considering state education and its institutionalization in the nineteenth century, it must not be thought that the English bourgeoisie was in favour of working-class education *in general*, actually it was only interested in teaching specific things in a specific way. Schooling was aimed at changing the attitudes and shaping the conduct of the working class by the provision of bourgeoisie was in favour of working-class education in *general*, actually it was only interested in teaching specific things in a specific way. Schooling was aimed at changing the attitudes the place of 'bad' parental working-class upbringing. Working class people besides being made into a punctual, disciplined labour force, had to be 'uplifted' in order to stabilize the political and social order. (p. 1)

It seems to me that there are, amongst others, four major schools of thought which argue that schooling can be viewed from four broad perspectives:

  (i)   an institution of social and cultural transmission and personal/intellectual development — functionalist;
  (ii) an instrument and device for social and cultural reproduction — Marxist-structuralist;
  (iii) a principal site of oppression/social control — Marxist-essentialist;
  (iv) schooling as discourse — post-structuralist approaches.

However, for all four but primarily two to four, the school is a site for struggle. The view of the nature, urgency and strategy required in that struggle is determined by the ideological perspective to which one adheres.

Functionalist

This perspective is informed by such as Durkheim who would argue that any perceived tensions at school would relate more to a question of the degree to which the discipline of the school which reflects the discipline of society has become internalized by the learners. Resistance at school would therefore be seen as a necessary and functional stage in the development of the 'spirit' of discipline which is the internalization of the accepted norms and values of society. If that shift does not take place, or only partially takes place, it is the fault of the child/learner who is therefore deviant and the exception that establishes the rule.[2]

  Since Durkheim's conception of a social formation was one of a collective conscience of which institutions are mere 'crystallized expressions of the collective sentiments, given this form through habit and repetition', as Demaine (1981) puts it. Demaine argues that:

> The social 'whole' for Durkheim is thus an essentially spiritual whole, the unity of the collective conscience, and its 'parts' or 'phenomena' are manifestations of the nature of the whole. They reflect the action of the collective sentiments. Thus, it is possible to 'know' the essence from the phenomena for they are the mere scene of its actions.

Thus, it is not surprising that Durkheim refers to education as:

The influence exercised by adult generations on those that are not yet ready for social life. Its object is to arouse and to develop in the child a certain number of physical, intellectual and moral states which are demanded of him by both the political society as a whole and the special milieu for which he is specifically destined.

This thinking forms the basis of the popular belief that each person is destined to perform a different and specific function in society, each of which is essential for maintaining balance in the status quo and for maintaining society itself. The role of education, therefore, is seen as one of helping to equip individuals to fit into society and to perform their function effectively and to the benefit not only of themselves, but of society at large.

From this standpoint, diversity is seen as necessary and desirable while at the same time being indicative of an overall unity. The appropriate metaphor, therefore, would be that of a machine or, maybe even more accurately, that of a body as expounded in the Patrician 'parable of the Belly', in Shakespeare's *Coriolanus*. This Durkheim/functionalist position has influenced educational theory over the past four decades and continues to do so. One could argue that it is out of this tradition that comes the now much vaunted notion of pluralism and cultural diversity as positive assets to society and schooling.

Social reproduction theory

Some of the major contributors to this broad church are Althusser, Bourdieu, Bowles and Gintis, and Bernstein.

This school of thought emphasizes the important role played by schooling in socially reproducing the mode of production. The underlying assumption *most* shared is that in the socially differential experience of schooling — in terms of hierarchical structures, class, power relation, etc. — 'learners' not merely equipped with general skills and knowledge (if at all), but are given specific types of skills which slot them into their class positions within the occupational structure. They are also thought to be socialized into an acceptance of the moral order and the socio-economic and political status quo.

Althusser (1972) places the school within the category of Ideological State Apparatus (ISA) as opposed to Repressive State Apparatus (RSA). At the core of Althusser's theory is the notion of 'ideological subjugation'. Thus, the school is seen as reproducing the 'ideological predispositions', the social and technical skills of a workforce geared to wage labour. The 'learners' in the school system therefore are not merely given the necessary skills to make them competent to take their place within the labour force, but are schooled in the ideological acceptance of the social order and of the socio-economic division of labour. In the work of Althusser, ideology is the key and schooling is an instrument for social reproduction. Ideology, he maintains, is not the real relations or conditions of production but, rather, the 'imaginary' relation of individuals to the 'real' situation in which they live and operate. It is through this reality of this interface that the individual is socialized into an acceptance of the socio-economic order.

Bowles and Gintis (1976) stress the school's role in providing certain technical skills and in providing learners with specific moral and social values. They argue that the differential experience of schooling highlights the school's role in preparing pupils for their differential work roles through the creation of various personality types:

> ... personality traits (reinforced at various levels of the school system) required of employees, differ according to the work role in question, those at the base of the hierarchy requiring a heavy emphasis on obedience and rules, and those at the top, where the discretionary scope is considerable, requiring a greater ability to make decisions on the basis of well-internalized norms.

Bowles and Gintis' theory, normally referred to as correspondence theory, argues that there is a 'mirror' relationship between schooling and the workplace and is exemplified through the repetition of certain structural features. Within the approach of Bowles and Gintis there is a stress on the *structure* of school organization rather than on curriculum content. They argue that social reproduction happens mainly through the 'hidden curriculum' and implicit social and moral assumptions of schooling.

Cultural reproduction

Though there is a tremendous overlap between this approach and the social reproduction approach, this approach is distinct in that it begins with the assumption of schooling as a crucial instrument in the reproduction of *culture* as well as the cultural status quo.

The work of Basil Bernstein

The work of Basil Bernstein has contributed some useful insights to the whole question of 'cultural transmission'. Bernstein's early work was concerned with the interrelationship between school structure as it operates in and interacts with the wider social structure which is both produced and reproduced by schooling. Class relationships, he argued, both shaped and are shaped by codes — socio-linguistic and educational codes. These codes are seen as comprising the 'boundary-maintaining procedures of *classification* and *framing* which substantiate the power relationships and basic principles of social control'.

> In this way, principles of power and social control are realized through educational knowledge codes and through codes enter into and shape consciousness.

However, Bernstein mentions that this is not just a passive process but one in which the 'rules' are inferred by the socialized persons on the basis of a range of relations. Thus, the socialized is active in his/her socialization. The rules 'are acquired in the process of exploring the classification and framing relationships' (Bernstein, 1977). The more recent work of Bernstein points more to the pedagogic device itself.[3]

Bourdieu

Pierre Bourdieu makes a case for 'The school as a conservative force'. He emphasizes the structural context of cultural transmission and sees the school as performing the two crucial functions of: (i) the conservation of culture; and (ii) the reproduction of culture. The first refers to the way in which those with power are able to classify and prioritize elements of culture in terms of their preferred social value. The second refers to the systematic 'apprenticeship' which the school organizes and through which it transmits not a *collective* cultural heritage but the culture of the dominant class. Bourdieu's argument is that by legitimating only their own cultural forms the dominant classes exert *symbolic violence* over the dominated. By the same token, the control of schooling ensures the reproduction of their cultural dominance. Schooling as a pedagogic device is seen as exerting symbolic violence, and through its apparent neutrality, legitimating culture and power domination.

Two particularly useful concepts of Bourdieu's are the concepts of *habitus* and *cultural capital*. For Bourdieu, the *habitus* is the set of specific perceptions, habits, propensities, taste, manners and thoughts which ensure the conditions for cultural reproduction. *Cultural capital* on the other hand is the unilateral or symbolic means to acquire the principles of the dominant culture. The school is seen as reproducing and legitimating the distinction between those who already possess this 'cultural capital' and those who do not.

Post-structuralist explanations

This method of analysis used by Jones and Williamson derives from the work of Michael Foucault, whose main emphasis has been on the nature of knowledge. Sarup (1953) suggests that Foucault's work is of great importance to students of the social sciences and education for a number of reasons which he outlines.

Race Relations, Sociology and Education

One of the major problems with the sociology of education is that it has tended to be largely male and White and has confined its discursive practice to debates to do with class but class within an assumed monolithic White social formation. Therefore, women and Black people have tended to be at best, marginal, and at worst, invisible.

The sociology of 'race relations' like the sociology of gender developed from these concerns. The fact that phenotypical differentiation is no longer an acceptable basis for racial categorization, there has been a growing tendency to argue for and pursue the formulation and systemizations of a 'race relations' as a sub-committee within the category of social relations.

The fact is that regardless of the lack of any scientific basis for racial classification, regardless of the fact that the human race is now without doubt one species — the social categorization is real in its implications and the basis of systems of oppression and exploitation that vary in their strength, degree of harshness and complexity from the racially under-pinned immigration laws of Britain to the racially-based Apartheid laws of South Africa.

The sociology of 'race relations' of the last two decades in Britain has been preoccupied with two broad themes as identified by Cashmore (1984):

> First with assessing the extent and effects of racism and discrimination upon those who have been their object, and second with the political struggle against racism and discrimination. (p. 220)

Cashmore, in my opinion, correctly asserts that it has been a sociology of conflict which reflects the everyday conceptions of 'race relations' though it tries to provide different explanations.

The third, more recent, theme has been the theme connected to my earlier point about the fallacious concept of 'race'. This position therefore argues that, since the category 'race' does not exist, therefore race relations are no more than 'social relations'. However, my position in this book is that the concepts of racism or racialism are only dependent on the concept of 'race' for their genesis. Once having become a social reality in terms of an ideology and a practice, racism is a reality (even if race isn't) — a social reality. The term race itself, when used, is a social category. Thus, 'race' becomes defined in terms of the parameters of racialization that is generated by racism.

Therefore, when one considers the history of the presence of Black people in Britain, the history of the relationship between Black peoples of the world and Europe, and when one considers the specificity of the British Black experience, whether at the centre or on the periphery of the sometime British Empire, one is struck by the glaring absence of the race dimension, in sociology in general and the sociology of education in particular. However, the entry of 'race' as a parameter of analysis in the sociology of schooling has not been an entirely positive one. One major factor was the fact that the sociologists and other social scientific researchers were still the same people. They were largely White middle class men researching and becoming experts on class analysis and, subsequently, on race-related issues in education and schooling.

Changing Emphases in Educational Epistemologies

As a result of the racism in education and the racist and biased epistemologies which have been dominant, all or most of the research and publications that have been done and written have been presented in such a way as to make Black pupils a problem for the educational system as opposed to seeing the education system as problematic through being racist, mono-cultural and *ipso facto*, demeaning. Thus producing among Black pupils failure, disenchantment and active resistance.

The preoccupations of these studies and research projects have been *inter alia* intelligence, achievement/under-achievement, culture and racism. Under these four broad headings have fallen many specific phenomena of which language is not the least important. It is therefore important and necessary to examine here how intelligence, achievement/under-achievement and culture have historically been racialized and how 'race' (a problematic concept at best) has been depoliticized and continues to be the object of this depoliticization and political/bureaucratic manipulation.

Intelligence and IQ Tests

The issue of 'intelligence' as a focus and the administering of 'IQ tests' has been fraught with tensions and difficulties from its inception, not only in terms of its relationship to Black people as victims of racism in this country and the United States but in relation to the social stratification and class relations. Studies into the use of 'intelligence' and 'IQ' tests as measures of educational ability and capacity for learning have suggested that these tests have been at best useless and at worst discriminating and insulting. Tests have been criticized for their cultural and class bias. In relation to Black pupils these tests have been used to 'prove' the inferior ability of Black pupils who were always found to be deficient.

As Coard (1971) wrote in his seminal paper:

> IQ tests can only be claimed to measure intellectual functioning at a particular moment in time, without being able to give the reasons why the functioning is at that particular level or say which factors are more important than which for each child tested.

Further, Coard argues that the vocabulary and style of all these IQ tests is White and middle class. As he states:

> Many of the questions are capable of being answered by a White middle class boy who, because of being middle class, has the right background of experiences with which to answer the questions — regardless of his real intelligence. The Black working class child, who has different life-experiences, finds great difficulty in answering many of the questions, even if he is very intelligent.

(Current critique even problematizes the notion of a fixed notion of intelligence.) Writing as he was in 1971, Coard was highlighting one of the main preoccupations in the education of Black children over the last four decades. This also applied considerably to working class children in general in the late sixties and early seventies when the educational preoccupation was how to compensate for deficiency in the working class child and by extension in the Black child.

In their book, *Introduction to Race Relations*, Cashmore and Troyna (1983) emphasize the general debate that informed these considerations, that is, the nature v nurture debate. They give a brief catalogue of the major contributions to this debate (though mainly those who were active promulgators of IQ tests as an adequate and efficient measure of intelligence) such as Jensen and Eysenck and the British academic, Sir Cyril Burt. On the other hand, they make a weak case by quoting the NUT document attacking 'scientific racism'. They quote:

> Racism dressed up in pseudo-scientific clothes, even when it attempts to look respectable by quoting apparent 'scientific authority', remains racism and should be combatted today in schools with significant numbers of ethnic minority children but also those in largely 'white schools' have a particular role and responsibility in this context. (NUT, 1978, p. 15)

After a very unsure, weak and heavily imbalanced discussion of the issue, Cashmore and Troyna come to the conclusion that:

> The reason why blacks do not do well at school may well have something to do with fixed inherited features. (*op cit*, p. 142)

This statement is tempered only by a few reasons why they were 'not convinced'.

The ambivalence of Cashmore and Troyna's argument is not dissimilar to that of commentators, theorists and researchers of the last three decades, whereby the assumptions of reactionary right wing and racist psychologists have not been dismissed but used as a basis for further analyses and examination. What, however, is more surprising is the way in which the issue has been resurrected in the Swann Report and given serious discussion. In chapter 3 of the Report, annex A as well as one-fifth of the major section is dedicated to 'the IQ question'. Within the body of the chapter, it is asserted that: 'Present practice, however, has changed markedly, and the limitations of IQ tests are now more clearly appreciated within the education system' (p. 70). They go on to assert, however, that in 'society at large', meaning *White society*, that there is an incorrectly held view that the 'West Indian under-achievement' is due to low IQ.

In this limited and brief discussion of the issue what comes over is the feeling that though the Committee is dismissing the correlation between IQ scores and performance, they seem to be accepting both the notion of a fixed intelligence and the idea of IQ tests as valid and efficacious measurements of that commodity. In this case, it is a little more subtle but there does seem to be a renewed raising of the question of 'well if not that, what *is* wrong with the Afro-Caribbean black children' (whom the Report insists on calling West Indian, despite the fact that the majority of these children will not have even seen the West Indies).

It is in the appendix that there is some attempt to examine the issue thoroughly. In this paper, based both on research and scholarship, by Mackintosh and Mascie-Taylor, there is an attempt by the authors to examine the issue, using historical and transatlantic information and research 'findings/conclusions'. However, it is important to note that in their conclusions they acknowledge that 'there is no guarantee that such data are relevant to the British case. The only safe conclusion is that few secure conclusions can be drawn — and that many of those most confidently asserted reflect preconception and prejudice rather than sober evaluation of the evidence.'

This important premise of their conclusion is an important assertion but it is also a double edged sword in that, in trying to be objective in their evaluation, the authors actually started out by giving credence to certain aspects of the racist assumptions about intelligence and IQ tests. The principal assumption is that to look at studies about 'Black people' in America is instructive with regard to 'Black people' in Britain. Thus, there is a prima facie assumption that whatever the problem, it is resident in being Black regardless of the specificity or national/ geographical setting. Within this assertion the cross-application of analyses are assumed and 'Black' is seen as a discrete racial category. It seems therefore that not only are social relations racialized but so is intelligence.

The crux of the debate is therefore seen as not having so much to do with what is the social reality of being Black and of living in a racist society but essentially about 'being Black'. The paper also falls into the assimilationist formulation of 'us' and 'them', 'host society' and 'immigrant' and assumes a White norm thus, despite the pupils discussed, both Black and White are by and large born in this country, 'indigenous' is used to refer to White children only and (in common with most of the rest of the report and previous research) children of Caribbean and Asian origin are referred to in terms of their regions of parental origin. With this stark juxtaposition it is difficult to accept that this distinction is merely for making clear distinctions. The point that is being made here is a point that is made even more strongly in the following section which discusses how ideologies generate their own language to perform the tasks required.

It is difficult to divorce this 'framing' from the positive points that are also made in the paper, especially when the authors go on to argue that:

> Although discrimination against West Indian families in this country may have an important indirect effect on their children's IQ scores by ensuring that they live in impoverished circumstances, there is less reason to believe that such discrimination, whether by society as a whole or by teachers and IQ testers in particular, has any *direct* effect on the West Indian child's performance.

It is true that the authors do suggest that maybe teachers should not collude with prejudice (prejudice and discrimination are the only concepts they use and seem to have no conception of racism). However, the furthest they seem to go towards making an anti-racist statement is if it turns out that 'racial prejudice' is not a *direct* cause of low IQ scores, so what? 'There are many things in life substantially more important than IQ'. This statement is the ultimate epitome of paternalistic and benevolent condescension.

I have not recounted the detail of annex D for the single reason that it seems to me that it recounts and describes the limited research and research findings of the last decade or so, but makes a good case for the popular racialized notions of IQ not through argument but through coverage. The counter-arguments are understated and perhaps under researched. In this way, the Mackintosh and Mascie-Taylor paper remains within the tradition of educational and (mainly White) psychological research of the last fifteen to twenty years.

Achievement

Throughout the last twenty-five to thirty-five years, the whole question of achievement has featured highly in educational debate. This still is so, not only in relation to class but latterly in relation to race and gender. Consequently, it has tended to be one of the major issues around which the working class and women's struggle as well as the Black struggle has been organized. It is a moot point as to whether it was the community interest and militancy that generated the interest of researchers and other academics or whether it was the other way round. What is significant, however, is the way in which the under-achievement phenomenon has become reified and racialized. This achievement emphasis has been directed largely towards school-leaving qualifications. Thus, this was a major focus of the Rampton Interim Report of 1981 and of the current Swann Report (1985). The fact that the Rampton Report spoke of the important part played by racism in the under-achievement and marginalization of Black pupils was relatively ignored by the authorities and educationalists for the more convenient 'fact' of the differentials of achievement between sections of the Black community. More specifically, the Report suggested that 'Asians' were over-achieving and 'West Indians' were under-achieving when compared to their White counterparts.

As stated before, these findings have been severely criticized for being under-standardized and imprecise since the 'West Indian' and

'Asian' communities have tended to be treated as an undifferentiated mass — homogeneous wholes. So the figures reveal nothing and are therefore erroneous. In commenting on this issue, Cashmore and Troyna (1983) set up their argument by making the broad, racialized and unqualified statement that:

> ... Black children in the United Kingdom are known for their persistent under-achievement for they tend as a group to score less in examinations relative to White and South Asian pupils. (p. 133)

Despite their subsequent discussion of the issue, the impact of the above statement, in bold type, done in a style that was being used throughout the book for definition and quick reference, is racist. It comes over as racist in that it objectifies Black children and reasserts the self-same unqualified racist assumption which one is meant to believe is being countered in their chapter on 'Education — Culture — Disadvantage'. However, if one can get beyond statements such as 'Black children ... are known for their persistent under-achievement' and the implicit pathologization, Cashmore and Troyna introduce one to some of the major publications and research in this field, including the work of Taylor (1981), Driver (1980), Tomlinson (1980) and Reeves and Chevannes (1981). In fact, two later pieces of work by the latter two publications provide us with a useful catalogue of the research in this area (Tomlinson, 1983) and with a useful analysis of the ideological construction of achievement and its specific relationship to the race debate (Reeves and Chevannes, 1983).

Let us, therefore, have a brief look at these two contributions to the debate before we examine the current state of the debate, through an examination of chapter 3 of Swann which is reserved for dealing with the question of achievement/under-achievement.

In addressing the issue, Tomlinson (1983) provides a very useful log of the research that has been done over the last twenty years or so. The formidable list of research into the educational performance of children of Asian origin (table IV.1, p. 47) is second only to the long list of research into the educational performance of children of West Indian origin (table III.1, p. 28). Tomlinson also extrapolates a list of the research which corroborates the position of Driver (1979/80) that 'West Indian' girls perform better than their male counterparts (table III.2, p. 41). The conclusion that Tomlinson draws *vis à vis* research and children of West Indian background goes along with the 'normal' conclusion that these children 'under-achieve' in relation to their White and Asian peers, although the girls in this group 'out-perform' the boys. Her conclusion regarding 'Asian' pupils is that they have tended to under-perform though their performance has improved with length of stay in this country, when their performance is equal in terms of school leaving qualifications.

Let us therefore turn to an examination of the analysis of Reeves and Chevannes (1983) concerning the ideological construction of a phenomenon that has been, and is still, a crucial parameter of analysis regarding the education of Black pupils. As Reeves and Chevannes argue, the use of the concept of under-achievement/achievement is:

> ... a form of reification necessitated by the inadmissability of alternative and more radical solutions to the presenting problems.

The authors argue that the concept has its origins in its predecessors' deprivation, *Cultural Deprivation*, and disadvantage. They therefore chart the connections that they perceive to exist between these epistemologies and isolate the early American 'deprivation theories as the basis of the early British social problem', theories *vis à vis* Black 'immigrants'. Therefore, they note:

> The first national policy towards 'immigrant' children, there-fore, was based on a popular, non-academic, taken-for-granted association of immigrant concentration with low educational standards and a desire to dilute any negative effects immigrant children might have on White performance. A policy of Anglo-assimilation was pursued ... to weaken 'immigrant' cultural links through dispersal and by the exposure of young children to the supposedly beneficial effects of the mainly white school. (p. 24)

The official rhetoric of the education bureaucracy was that this type of action would help the immigrants to better 'settle in'. The fact was that they were acting in response to their own racism as well as that of certain White members of the community who were expressing panic about the threat to White communities and educational standards through 'swamping'. These officially legitimated racial expressions were impeded by resistance in the Black community. This, therefore, created an impetus for a shift to a more legitimate articulation. The notion of cultural deprivation provided this.

Cultural Deprivation

This particular formulation in Britain is formed by the work of American educationalists of the 1930s and 1940s, say Reeves and Chevannes.

They argue that useful parallels may be drawn between American rural-urban migration and Black colonial immigration to Britain. But as they note, Black immigration to Britain was largely a post-war phenomenon. So, in the 1960s when social and educational policy began to be discussed in relation to Black people, it was formulated in terms of an 'older and more direct pathology theory of the immigrant as a social problem'. Therefore, they imply, it is not surprising that for Britain the American approaches were found to be enlightening since American educational and social policy had already gone through the initial stage of simple pathologization of interracial relations and educational performance.

A corollary to the 'cultural deprivation' thesis, Reeves and Chevannes (p. 26) suggest was the whole notion of 'deprivation' itself which was an interest that arose in Britain in the 1960s following various reports including such as the Milner Holland Report (1965) on London housing, the report by the Plowden Committee on primary education (1965) and the Seebohn Social Services Report (1968). Contiguous to this focus on 'deprivation' was the notion of the 'cycle of deprivation'.

> The attraction of the concept for policy-makers, then, was that it avoided questions about the legitimacy of the educational enterprise as a whole and of the relationship between education and the world of work. It focussed less on economic mechanisms, income and price levels, and more on the epiphenomena of urban blight, housing standards and the quality of school buildings. (*ibid*)

This 'deprivation' model was applied broadly to include first White working class children and then extended to include Black children and, as Reeves and Chevannes maintained, the appropriateness of Black children to this 'culturally deprived' label derived not simply from their ascribed qualities but from a 'reformist imperative, shared by the Centre, Left and Right, to find politically acceptable solutions to the social problems of the age'.

This was the context of the various compensatory measures taken in education. But it was then emphasized by a number of educationists, including Bernstein (1971), that 'education cannot compensate for society'. Instead, Bernstein suggests that:

> We need to distinguish between the principles and operations that teachers transmit and develop in the children and the contexts they create in order to do this . . .

We need to examine the social assumptions underlying the organization, distribution and evaluation of knowledge, for there is not one, and only one, answer. The power relationships created outside the school penetrate the organization, distribution and evaluation of knowledge through the social context. The definition of 'educability' is itself, at any one time, an attenuated consequence of these power relationships. (p. 68).

Bernard Coard posed a similarly strong, if more direct, challenge in his book entitled *How the West Indian Child Is Made Educationally Subnormal in the British School System* (1971).

Reeves and Chevannes (1983) trace a shift towards the adoption of 'disadvantage' as a theoretical focus and as a conceptual tool. They suggest that the initial attraction of this formulation lay in the fact of its potential as a 'non-theoretical substitute for a term whose theoretical embeddedness had now become an academic liability' (p. 31). The 'new' term they argued also had conceptual benefits in terms of its presentation as diffuse and largely individual. The authors note that contributors to the debate worked in the 'anti-theoretical empiricist tradition' with its concomitant stress on immediate and identifiable factors within traditionally 'accepted' categories. Reeves and Chevannes, therefore, argue that:

The term's lack of specificity and weak theoretical placement gave researchers the opportunity of identifying factors which could easily embrace ethnicity and race. (p. 33)

In short, it seems to me, therefore, that what Reeves and Chevannes could be read as saying is that disadvantagement as a conceptual tool and as a term has tended to depoliticize and deracialize analyses of social relations, both in society and in schools. Thus, it operated within a reified and insular vacuum of self-definition and self-validation. This did not change the reality.

The authors argue that 'deprivation' and 'disadvantage' have formed the conceptual seed bed of the theory of under-achievement as applied to contemporary British society. As they state it:

Educationalists had become acutely conscious of the blame the victim syndrome, while the racial minorities themselves sought proudly to assert their various cultural traditions and to avoid the paternalism customarily directed at victims. Explanations for racial minority school performance in terms of deficiency or difference stemming from ethnic or class culture were no longer permissible. New terminology, free of taken-for-granted assumptions and theoretical integration was required and imported from across the Atlantic. (p. 35)

It seems that while making a number of valid and important points, these authors become ensnared by their own framework and therefore make certain interpretations and conclusions to suit this framework. One example of this is the excessive importance attributed to American influence on British perceptions.

One should note that, if anything, the terminology is the only thing that was directly borrowed from the USA since the basis of the 'new' conceptualization was already existent in British educational discourse mainly through the *Early Leaving Report* (1954) and *The Crowther Report* (1959), both of which highlighted the high level of wastage of ability amongst pupils (particularly the best as per IQ measurement) through early leaving. However, in the case of these two reports, 'achievement' was highly individualized (though it was noted that the majority of the wastage occurred amongst children from working class families) and was the basis of concern not necessarily for all children but for those of high IQ.

Where I most vehemently part company with Reeves and Chevannes is where they purport that the transition from the 'disadvantage' thesis to that of under-achievement was simply the result of the 'entrapment' of British educationalists by the 'sophisticated' American theoretical web of the notion of the Black self-concept. This reading seems an all too-simplistic explication of the dynamic restructuring of British institutionalized practices and policy. However, I do agree with the affirmations they make regarding the concept and consequences of the notion of 'under-achievement'. For example, they highlight the fact that under-achievement still carries a number of subtle, or I would argue not-too-subtle, implications about relativism of performance profiles in relation to shared and unitary conceptualizations about the parameters of success and failure and about an implicit belief in the British meritocracy in which it is intended that all should succeed debarring negative factors or influences. What Reeves and Chevannes fail to fully deal with in their conclusion is why this concept of under-achievement/achievement has been created and recreated and is still utilized. Thus they miss the implications of a very important element in their own historical sketch. That is, the restructuration of institutionalized policies and practices to maintain the social/racial status quo. However, they allude to this question to some degree when they ask the question, 'How appropriate is the "achievement" appellation for children of Afro-Caribbean descent?'. Their response to this question is quite illuminating and most significant:

> By stressing the universality of achievement among black and white and by drawing on the naturalistic ideal of 'educational potential' the concept might help to obscure biological racist interpretations of the educational condition. By taking for granted that all are striving for the same success, it camouflages educational divisions and the relationship with the class and economic structure, and avoids the question of whether the existing competitive meritocratic system of education can ever ensure equality of educational opportunity. (p. 40)

This phenomenon of achievement, which is carefully documented in Tomlinson (*op cit*) and well analyzed by Reeves and Chevannes (*op cit*), demonstrates its relevance and continuing perceived importance in the prominence it is given in the Swann Report. However, I must make it quite clear at this point that in criticizing this prominence, I am arguing not for the neglect of how Black children fare within the school system. On the contrary, this is precisely my concern. But this concern must be related to the overall question of the nature and impact of institutional racism as it exists and operates, both in society and schools.

The third chapter of the Swann Report, which deals with the issue of 'achievement and under-achievement', begins by acknowledging its own incompleteness and its contradictory evidence. Yet, importantly, it makes the assertion that both 'achievement' and 'under-achievement' are terms which are indiscriminately used in two 'crucially difference senses' (p. 58). Firstly, 'the comparison between the achievement of particular ethnic minorities and *their school-fellows in the White majority*' (their emphasis), and 'the extent to which individuals or groups are achieving their full potential'. This chapter of Swann was stated as being crucial in that it deals with the issue of 'the educational needs and attainments of children from ethnic minority groups' . . . with special reference to pupils of 'West Indian origin'.

The conceptual approach of the Committee therefore was to first of all attempt to 'clarify its use of the terms 'achievement' and 'under-achievement' which, as I have stated, were both seen to be used in two distinct senses. In their preamble they acknowledge the range of problems existent in their data in terms of the range of scores within the 'ethnic' groups and between gender groups. In fact, they note greater differences within groups than they found between groups (though one could rightly question the validity of the overall conclusions of the data, since the bases of data collection were varied and unstandardized and founded largely on 'teacher-definition' of our so-called ethnic groupings).

The question is, however, what was the implicit intention of this section of the Report. At one level it is about the challenging and examination of the claims and assumptions regarding the debates about Afro-Caribbean Black under-achievement. However, at another level, it can be seen as giving them validity through highlighting the racist assumption and beliefs about Black intellectual inferiority. That is, the very adherence to the under-achievement formulation as a focus for discussion gives validity to the concept. Further, the language generated by that particular conceptualization is counter-productive and inimical to emancipatory practice or anti-racist education.

Chapter 3 of Swann re-examines some of the old and some of the current explanations of 'West Indian' and 'Asian' achievement. Using the DES Statistics Branch's annual school leavers survey, they surmise that:

> West Indian school leavers were doing markedly less well than
> white school leavers . . . than their fellows from other groups on
> all the measures used.

The chapter is divided into the following major sections: introduction; the achievement of West Indian pupils; the achievement of Asian pupils; factors involved in school performance; conclusions and implications of findings.

Having reaffirmed the traditional view and the view endorsed by the interim report that West Indian pupils are doing markedly less well than Asian and White pupils, the Report then moves on to discuss the question of the factors involved in school performance. These factors as outlined in the chapter are broadly-based on the findings, conclusion and basic formulation of Verma's research on 'ethnic minority achievement's in the Bradford/Leeds area of West Yorkshire. Having noted the conclusions of the interim report on racism, disadvantage (material and environmental) and school factors such as 'linguistic interference' and teachers' attitudes and expectations, the section turns to look at the 'range of factors involved in achievement and under-achievement'. This range is based almost entirely on Verma's research and on the premise that:

> Since we presented figures that showed Asians on average to be
> performing very much on a par with whites, and since it was
> argued by our critics that Asians were no less subject to racism
> than West Indians, it was said that the prominence we had given

to this factor must be misplaced and that other factors must therefore be at the root of the problem. Low West Indian IQ scores were mentioned as the real cause, and, as we have noted earlier, the absence of any consideration of socio-economic factors was also criticized. It became clear to us that we must examine these criticisms in detail in the final report, as indeed we had, in our interim report, declared our intention of doing.

Verma's study (Swann, chapter 3, Annex F) engaged in analysis at three levels: (i) cultural factors; (ii) immediate environment of the individual; and (iii) individual factors and addressed *inter alia* questions of IQ, West Indian family structure, material and cultural disadvantagement, racism, the structure and ethos of the school and the mismatch between local education authority (LEA) provision and the needs of 'ethnic minority pupils'.

Verma's study upheld the observations and conclusions of previous work done in this area and came to the conclusion that the 'process of examination achievement is ethnically specific; factors affecting the achievement of one ethnic group may not necessarily affect the achievement of another one'. He argues, therefore, that it would be an error 'to attempt to explain the under-achievement of a particular ethnic minority group from an understanding of the achievement process of the majority group' (p. 170). However, he does not state what the precise difference is. He suggests instead the need for further research.

Similarly, the conclusion of chapter 3 itself is that there is need for further research. In addition, there is a call for the eradication of 'discriminating attitudes' among White people, and the evaluation of our education system which ensures the achievement of full potential by all pupils. Thus, they make a plea for further legislation on the one hand and education for attitudinal change on the other (p. 98).

The contribution of the Swann Report to this long-standing and important debate highlights the difficulty which exists in the formulation of the problems in education in terms of achievement/under-achievement. This formulation, as I have argued at various points in this chapter, individualizes and depoliticizes the debate and forces one into a proverbial corner where there is a terrified reluctance to even mention the word *racism*, let alone deal with the concept. It is significant that anytime something along these lines is mentioned, it tends to have to be referred to as 'prejudice' or 'discrimination'. But as I have argued in chapter 1 (and will explore in greater detail later), racism is much more complex and multi-faceted than those two words would allow.

This achievement/under-achievement formulation generates not simply a point of view but a way of thinking and a (reflexive) vocabulary which locks one into a particular way of seeing. Therefore, as Reeves and Chevannes argue, it carries with it notions of relativity. Beyond that it requires a norm — this norm has been, and continues to be, White. Therefore, the plea by Verma for further research is a pointless one since his articulation is also locked into the achievement/under-achievement formulation. Beyond all that, there is the almost intangible and underlying (though unstated) idea that is implicit in this formulation that really what one is doing in arguing the point is arguing against the evidence that 'Afro' blacks above all others are genetically and patho-logically under-achievers in whichever society one looks at. Behind this unspoken assumption seems to lie an implicit 'memory' of the various American studies which have suggested this. Therefore, what becomes clear is that the removal of the dynamic ideology and mechanism of 'racism' as the crucial factor for understanding Black pupils' experience of schooling and 'credentialization' is to bow to or actively support the processes of institutional racism in education and schooling and ulti-mately in society, since school does not operate within a vacuum but is both a product and a part of the process. It is a generator of social systems of power relations.

Historically in Britain, but particularly over the last four decades, there has been an increase in the racialization of culture in that, with the post-war immigration of a number of British Commonwealth citizens from the Caribbean and the Asian sub-continent, ethnicity, race and culture became almost synonymous in popular as well as official usage. This ambivalent usage of terminology and concepts had been both successive and contiguous in education policy and practice, and has been realized through the 'racial forms of education' (and *ipso facto* of knowledge) mentioned earlier (Mullard, 1983a).

The 1967 DES Report, *Immigrants and the Youth Service*, was a significant marker on the historical landscape in that it highlights the subsequent tendency to interpret social relations in terms of cultural relations. Within this formulation, culture has at times been seen as synonymous with race and ethnicity. This culturalism has underscored all the shifts in social and educational theory/policy, possibly with the exception only of the early 'sink or swim' period whereby the new-comers from the Commonwealth were simply expected to assimilate, though no provision was made to aid this.

This Youth Service Report lay on the margins on the assimilationist phase and, what later became known as, the integrationist phase. This is evident in paragraphs 6.2 and 6.3 of the Report when considering 'the meeting of cultures', that is, the 'host' and 'immigrant' cultures. Paragraphs 6.2 and 6.3:

> 6.2 We have to take into account the culture of the host society, in which we include those attitudes, beliefs and practices which people in the United Kingdom are brought up to consider moral or natural. Important among these are expectations about the way people should behave towards one another in their various roles: in the family, among neighbours, towards authorities. In particular, we have to pay regard to the fact, referred to earlier in this report, that ours is a stratified society. We must therefore consider the local expression of culture in that stratum of society where the immigrants converge and live, and the relation of that stratum to the rest of society in the United Kingdom.

> 6.3 We have also to consider the culture in which the immigrant was brought up: the attitudes, beliefs and practices considered moral or natural in his own country. We have also to consider the transition from an immigrant's environment to his new home.

The paragraph immediately following goes on to attempt to discuss the special implications of this meeting of the cultures.

As we noted earlier, the perceptions of the assimilationist phase dictated that Black people should basically submerge or even forget their culture and recognize their place in British society at the bottom of the socio-economic and occupational ladder. Thus, this official focus on culture in that Black people were expected to assimilate into the structure and realization of 'British culture' (*sic*), at the expense of their own culture. This assimilationist thesis as discussed earlier proved to be not only inadequate but unacceptable. This was so because on the one hand Black people, in the main, were unwilling to deny that significant part of their personal and group identities which resided in their cultural expectations and expressions. And, as stated earlier, even when they did, they found it did not make much difference to the discrimination they faced purely on the basis of 'race'.

The notion of integration suffered a not dissimilar fate to its predecessor of assimilationism in that despite its rhetorical position its effect was one of maintenance of the status quo. Therefore, any failure on the part of social policy was read as the 'failure' of 'immigrants' to integrate, thus making it clear that the onus was on them. There was no acknowledgement of cultural bias, ethnocentrism or the racism that lay beneath all this.

In 1977 the Department of Education and Science published a Green Paper on education, that not only recognized the new composition of British society but appeared to want to go somewhat further. This Report stated that:

> 1.11   ... the education appropriate to our Imperial past cannot meet the needs of modern Britain.
>
> 10.11   Our society is a multicultural, multiracial one and the curriculum should reflect a sympathetic understanding of the different cultures and races that now make up our society ...

Of course, it could well be argued that the education of imperialist Britain was *also* inappropriate in human and anti-racist terms but what this statement in the Green Paper seemed to be saying was that it was time for change. The rationale of the change was 'cultural pluralism' which was then beginning to be in ascendancy and is the major foundation of the 'Swann Report' *Education for All*.

Cultural Pluralism

As I have stated in chapter 1, the cultural pluralism of the late seventies and early eighties is premised on a notion of a range of homogeneous cultures in society with shared interests. These cultures are considered to interact with each other by a system of negotiation, which results in consensus. The state is seen as a neutral arbiter. Class, race and other social phenomena are seen as epiphenomenal to the interests of the competing cultural groups. Yet, beginning in the early seventies, cultural pluralism was being articulated in terms of national origins, religion and above all, in terms of race. In this articulation, as we have seen, race had again become synonymous with culture, the dominance of this 'culture' focus being premised on the fact that it is all-embracing. Implicitly there is another set of assumptions; that there are now various discrete 'races' of people living in Britain, that these races are also ethnic groups, that each ethnic/racial group has an identifiable culture that is representative of the group as a whole.

Within the 'rhetoric' of this pluralist articulation there is an assumption that within the workings of society these cultures may not be equal in value, but they are certainly equal in status and power. This is particularly the view of the moral functionalist form of multi-culturalism/

cultural pluralism. This position is summarized in a paragraph from the section (quoted earlier) on 'The concept of pluralism' in the Swann Report:

> We consider that a multiracial society such as ours would in fact function most effectively and harmoniously on the basis of pluralism which enables, expects and encourages members of all ethnic groups, both minority and majority, to participate fully in shaping the society as a whole within a framework of commonly accepted values, practices and procedures. (p. 5)

Where this statement attempts to go further is in going on to say that these changes should be made:

> ... whilst also allowing and, where necessary, assisting the ethnic minority communities in maintaining their distinct ethnic identity within this common framework. (*Ibid*)

as is evident from looking at the tendencies and articulations of the previous phases. Cultural pluralism seems to move on the debate considerably by asserting that the so-called ethnic minority people are in Britain because they 'had a right to and because they wanted a better life' (Richardson, 1985). It also seems to move the debate on in that it argues for the maintenance of ethnic identity and *ipso facto* culture language, etc. Where it falls short in terms of current anti-racist approaches is in its failure to acknowledge the notion of a racist society that is not neutral, nor is it run on negotiated consensuses but in terms of a power structure that is racist and guided by political, social and cultural values of the dominant and ruling group. From the stance of anti-racism, therefore, culture is socially constructed and thus education has to be seen as a part of the product of racist structures and procedures within the specificity of the contemporary British social formation.

Thus, the tendency of cultural pluralists to depoliticize culture and related phenomena is being criticized by anti-racists; the criticism being that it is a poor and erroneous analysis that states that there is a social problem which is to do with cultural differences and lack of understanding. Thus, in order to bring about positive change, one needs to promote cultural exchange and understanding. The only logical product of this line of thinking is that:

> Schools should recognize and affirm ethnic minority children's background, culture and language ... celebrate festivals, organize international evenings, use and teach mother tongues and community languages, teach about ethnic minority history, art, music, religion, literature. (*Ibid*)

Therefore, in short, what one notices in looking at the British preoccupation with cultural explanations of 'race' relations, is a series of shifts from the explicit area of articulation of cultural inferiority, through notions of cultural assimilation, cultural integration, cultural diversity and cultural pluralism. Underlying all these has been the ideology of 'race' and all that that it implies.

'Racist' Education, Racist Schooling

Throughout chapter 1 and so far in this chapter, I have made a number of implicit and explicit points directing us to a conceptualization of the British education system as a racist one. This statement no doubt sends shivers down the spine of racists and liberals alike. This is because many racialists might argue that there are too many 'liberal' and 'multiculturalist' teachers and education authorities for this to be the case. In fact, they would argue that British education is *too* anti-racist. The liberals might argue that this is erroneous since education and schooling is open to a range of pedagogies, ranging from racist to whatever the other might be. Therefore, from this viewpoint, one could draw the conclusion that though there are racialists among teachers and educationalists, it by no means represents the broad spectrum of the teaching force or the educational community.

However, as I have argued so far in this book, but especially in sections three and six of chapter one, Britain is a 'racist state'. This is so in that racism is not simply an endemic part of personal perceptions and attitudes of British Whites, it is an institutionalized part of the British social structure.

The concept of 'structure' is the key — very seldom is there an adequate understanding of racism expressed — an understanding that expresses the structural as well as the interactional nature of racist practice. My premise is that it is neither a product, a strategy nor an ideological epiphenomenon of capitalism (sexism or any other form of oppression). Rather, it is an independent and parallel force that is sometimes adopted by capitalism to strengthen and consolidate the exploitation of the working class — especially when a considerable percentage of that group is of a perceived 'different' and 'inferior' race. But racism may work in the same way to use capital to perpetuate racial domination. Yet, as I have hinted in chapter 1, there are a number of possible approaches to the question of state institutions and racism, even if one does accept the working of racism as separate to and independent from the workings of capitalism. This is the complex range

Figure 1:

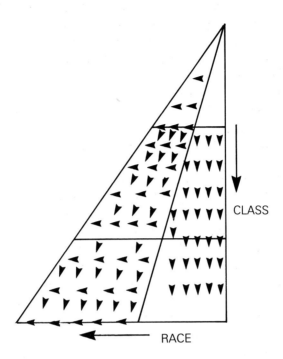

CLASS

RACE

of relations that Mullard (1985) examines in his paper, *Race, Class and Ideology: Some Formal Notes* and summarizes the relationship between race and class as a 'cross-facing transitive' one.

I would refer readers back to my treatment of the race/class/gender question in chapter 1 or to some of the papers and articles examined in that section. What I would like to do here, before going on to look in detail at institutional racism and education, is to present a 'simple' model of the nature of the holism of the oppression of working class Black people — the sum of which is greater than its constituent parts. Racism, as I have stated, is separate and independent from capitalism, yet similar tools of analysis can be applied. Therefore, it is possible to see the state as both a series of agencies dependent, autonomous, semi-autonomous and non-autonomous. At the same time, it is possible to see the state as an initiator as well as an instrument of the 'hegemony' of racism.

The latter position raises some of the same questions that it raises for Marxists; what is the explanation that can be given for the apparent contradictory nature of the state's inter and intra-agency conflicts? That is, how can the racist state accommodate within its official processes oppositional practice? This is one of the major questions for anti-racism.

Institutional Racism and Education

In attempting to unravel the issues tied up in racism and education, one must unpack the fundamental notion of institutional racism — which, despite its general use as a term and concept, is still contentious and often ill-defined. Thus, Lord Scarman in the concluding remarks of his Report, concludes:

> Institutional racism ... does not exist in Britain, but racial disadvantage and its nasty associate racial discrimination have not yet been eliminated. They poison minds and attitudes ...

Thus, racism is reduced to 'disadvantage' which as we have noted tends to blame the victims and the racially discriminatory practices of certain (few implied) individuals. Though on the contrary as well articulated by the anti-racist teacher education network in this open letter:

> In Britain today we live in a profoundly racist society and therefore cannot take a neutral stance towards this ... It is time for those concerned about racism to consider strategies both for practitioners to operate and for establishing this as a priority and mandatory part of teacher education. (*Times Educational Supplement*, 19 September 1983)

The position taken in his book is that what we are dealing with is a racist state and thus the state is actively involved in the generation, reproduction and perpetuation of racism. However, whatever one's analysis of the relationship between the state and race, what is known is that Black people have been *victims* of racism, both at the hand of state institutions as well as at the hands of individuals. Thus, an understanding of the shifts in education is of tremendous significance in the fight against racism in education.

Currently, there is a simple equation being used which states that racism is prejudice plus power. The inadequacy of that statement was shown up most clearly when, following the Tottenham uprising, one police officer accused a Black Council leader of racism on the basis that he was prejudiced about the police and had power. This inversion signalled a number of things; amongst them the way in which 'anti' racist language can be adopted and appropriated for other reasons. This racism as we have shown in chapter 1 is multi-faceted, dynamic and has its base in a whole range of factors which combine to make up the complex ideology of British racism.

Racism is an ideology and set of practices based on the belief in discrete races and in the intrinsic superiority of one group above the

Figure 2:

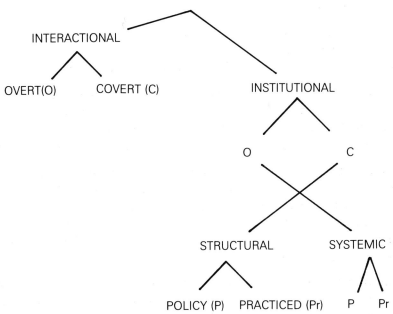

RACISM

POWER PREJUDICE BIAS XENOPHOBIA ETHNO CENTRICITY
DOMINATION MARGINALIZATION

INTERACTIONAL

OVERT(O)   COVERT (C)   INSTITUTIONAL

O   C

STRUCTURAL   SYSTEMIC

POLICY (P)   PRACTICED (Pr)   P   Pr

others. In order to create and maintain a racial hierarchy, the dominant or 'oppressor' group needs power and authority which implies not only a need for tools of 'coercion' but legitimating procedures. These legitimating procedures may include the cooptation of members of the 'oppressed' group through the donning of special privileges or special positions, and through the use of ideological mechanisms to 'convince' the targeted individuals or groups of the validity and wholesomeness of the said racism. This effect I refer to as the 'hegemony' of racism or 'racial hegemony'.

Included in this concept of 'racial hegemony' is the way in which members of the 'oppressor' group rationalize at the level of common-sense the notions and assumptions of racism. Thus, racism can be interactional or institutional, overt or covert. And operated within the specificity of institutions the realization of racism (institutional racism) can be structural or systemic.

Let us, therefore, focus in on the nature and realization 'institutional racism', structural racism is that racism which exists in laws, rules, regulations, hidden (or overt) agendas, procedures and processes which directly or indirectly initiate, promote, propagate and/or maintain racism within that institution and by implication in society. For example, in employment certain jobs in certain White firms might be totally 'out of reach' of Black people simply because of the 'process of recruitment' which is based on family connections and word-of-mouth 'advertising'. Within a system such as this, prospective Black candidates will not be even privy to the mechanism for recruitment. Therefore, they are excluded as a 'racial' group.

Another example is the case of advertising procedures where advertising is done 'generally' but not targetted. Normally, in White institutions, this 'general' advertising is done in the 'White' press which for this purpose is seen as 'general'. The failure to advertise more widely and more specifically in the 'Black' press can be seen here as racist — regardless of the intention. Intentionality does not measure racism, since because of the history of racism in this country racism is not only pervasive but intricately woven into the fabric of British institutions and, to some extent, cultural traditions. However, even if the recruitment practices are improved and more Black people are employed within the institution, that is not the end of the matter. The Black worker, officer, teacher, could be stuck at the bottom of the professional scale for a whole range of reasons, again structural ones.

At this point, there begins an even stronger and dynamic interplay between the hidden, and overt, structures and between those structures and the specific institutional interface between these structures and the structuring structures — the day to day interactions. It is these day-to-day interactions to which I refer as the systemic realization of institutional racism.

Systemic institutional racism may be more difficult to pinpoint since it may be very specific to an institution and has to do with the 'chemistry' of a specific organization. It marks the meeting point between structural and interactional forms of racism, and exists within the specificity of the 'ethos' or socio-cultural environment of the organization. This is not to say that certain generalizations cannot be made. They *can*, on the basis that the *systemic* is also structural — that is, it represents practices which are the structuring structures of institutions. These practices are often intangible and are sometimes vehemently denied by White people because of low level of political perceptiveness, sometimes due to outright racism.

In this case, one of the functions of anti-racism would be to make the covert, overt, the hidden, blatant and to then deal with it. Thus, it is not simply a case of challenging racism but the deconstruction of

Figure 3:

POLICY	PRACTICE
1 Overt	Covert
2 Covert	Covert
3 Covert	Overt
4 Overt	Overt

practices and procedures which generate, regenerate and perpetuate racism and which ultimately reproduce the 'racial' status quo.

The realization of institutional racism is tied to the dynamic interaction between policy and practice whatever the nature of their relationship.

In figure 3 above, one will note four possible combinations of the relationship between policy and practice. The assumption here is that every institution is 'governed' by a policy, whether stated or unstated, and therefore any other permutations are mere theoretical abstractions. For example, in relation to institutional racism it is possible to have an overt racist policy with a covert or overt practice and there are several examples of this in South Africa no doubt. Very few British institutions or organizations have an overt *racist* policy, though there are some such as the National Front and British Movement. However, in Britain it is not difficult to find an organization with a covert racist policy which could be practised covertly or overtly. Of course, there is sometimes a thin line between covert and overt racism since its perception can have a lot to do with the 'awareness' and 'conscientization/politicization' of the perceiver.

The institutional racism in the school system in Britain is not just a reflection of the wider inbuilt oppression and exploitation of certain subordinate categories of the population who are defined as culturally distinct from the dominant ethnic majority. These discriminatory processes are evident in policies and practices which systematically restrict the educational opportunities of racially defined groups. However, in addition, institutional racism also actively engages in the perpetuation of racist attitudes and practices which work against social, educational, as well as economic justice in our society. Thus, it becomes clear that any education that is truly for *all* and for life in this society must address itself directly to the issue of racism.

Let us then examine the ways in which education and schooling operate to enact and perpetuate racism. This racialization of education is diverse and operates through the following processes of marginalization, production, reproduction, repression and regeneration. This racist education is enacted through:

(i) the curriculum: *ie.* what counts as knowledge, from what perspective the teaching takes place, what images are used in teaching, material selected;

(ii) the pedagogy: how the teaching is done, training expectation, teacher pupil relationships;

(iii) the social and cultural environment of the school.

Marginalization

By marginalization I refer to (i) the way in which a sense of 'otherness', and peripherality is perpetuated and encouraged whereby, Black issues, or a Black perspective is seen only relevant if at all, to a school that has a sizeable Black presence. However, even in schools with Black pupils such issues are treated at best as add-on issues. This also relates to (ii), the way in which knowledge is structured, valued and transmitted. Though ethnocentricity is indeed the main characteristic, however, it also relates to access to power as it relates to schooling and ultimately to the outside world. Thirdly, marginalization refers to the process by which Black pupils are denied access to the 'power' within their institutional experience.

Let us briefly examine these three aspects of marginalization, the 'otherness' of a 'racist' education operates at a number of levels which add up to an overall effect. The story is told by Faroukh Dhondy (1982) of the class that was told to bring their flesh-coloured tights and the Black child, who asked 'Whose flesh miss?'. This type of example also applies to the range of situations when teachers make assumptions — on which they act — about hair type, colour of eyes, and so on.

One other powerful example of this is the incident recounted by a Black multicultural adviser visiting a primary school where children were being asked about their favourite foods. On the blackboard the teacher had written a whole range of foods, all examples of Anglo-European cuisine. Therefore, without fail, *all* the children in the class produced combinations that reflected the apparently 'acceptable' dishes. The adviser turned to one Black girl, who had written 'Yorkshire pudding and roast beef' on her book and asked, 'Is this your favourite meal at school or at home?' The child turned with a knowing smile and said, 'At school'. Having been requested by the adviser to write down the favourite foods at home, the child wrote a long and very different list. No doubt, this list might have included Yorkshire pudding and roast beef anyway but there was certainly a lot more to the story. For this child the legitimation given to her social reality by a simple question by an adviser signalled a transition of that reality from peripheral or marginal to her educational experience to being central.

This story is also a good example of how the knowledge that children bring with them to school as a whole can be made marginal to schooling, highlighting the chasm that is created between school knowledge and real life knowledge and, as we have noted, this school knowledge represents certain class, 'race' and gender interests. However, on the theme of marginalization of knowledge, this criticism does not only apply to the Black child's own knowledge but the knowledge that comes from her community, her culture, and the history of her people. So, for example, it is only recently that Black British people like Harriet Tubman, Mary Seacole, Ira Aldridge and Samuel Coleridge-Taylor[4] have crept into the realm of legitimate knowledge in British schools. And still they remain on the margins of acceptability, respectability or focus.

So what of the 'power' within schooling. 'Power' is at the best of times difficult to pinpoint. But this is particularly so in relation to schooling. However, if one is to attempt to locate it within schooling one should say, firstly, that power means that your existence, your knowledge, your history is legitimated by wider society and *ipso facto* by the school. Thereby knowing that at a crunch, there is a back up — a support for you putting into action or putting to the test your feelings and beliefs.

The cultural/'racial' knowledge and ideology of the school provides a context and supportive structure for racist or racialized practice on the behalf of White staff or pupils. The same support is not there for Black pupils unless they acquiesce to the racialized notions of knowledge of society and of relations and ultimately of themselves, implicit in a 'racist' education.

Production

The term 'production' alludes to the way in which schooling itself generates racism. This is done not only at the indirect level of *not* intervening in the transmission of racist concepts or processes but the direct teaching of racist ideology — either wittingly or unwittingly. An example which I have often used is the example of the Surrey middle-school teacher who, in teaching a lesson about the female counterparts and offspring, gave her pupils a list of words.

On this list were the following: Ram, Fox, Negro. In this strange and racist juxtaposition of animals and human, children were asked to respond. The response of one child was Ram: Ewe, Lamb; Fox: Vixen, Cub; Negro: Negress, Child. Child was struck out by the teacher who replaced it with 'piccaninny'.

This sort of practice lies at the base of the ideological construction of Black inferiority. Thus, not only are Black people (Negro is a term Black people now reject as acceptable nomenclature because of its negative, inferior and servile connotations) like animals in social status, they are biologically different and do not reproduce children but an especially different (and inferior by implication) entity called 'piccaninny'.

The whole exercise also has sexist connotations in terms of the female's identity being tied to the male. But more specifically it has 'gendered-racist' implications in terms of the description of the Black woman as *negress*.

Another example is drawn from the well-intentioned practice of a science teacher who, in an attempt to extend the range of the 'knowledge' used in his classroom science, asked pupils to say why it is that people in the tropical third world are less productive. This science teacher then offers an explanation which suggests that it has to do with the fact that they live in hotter climes than we do in Europe. This lesson on 'energy', which had a multicultural intention, had a racist effect again because of the wrong question. What this teacher should have been doing was problematizing the assumption that the third world was less productive. Since a closer examination of this assumption would have highlighted more about modes of production, about production and manufacture, about technology, about the international distribution of wealth, than about human energy or kilojoules.

Reproduction

In terms of what we have noted, the function of 'racist' education to marginalize Black people, their knowledge, experience and social reality and to produce the ideological sustenance of racism, it is also fair to say that the education system serves to reproduce racism. This is so not only in this sense. It can also be argued that the education system serves to reproduce the social/racial division of labour, as Stuart Hall (1979) purports:

> It is the education system which reproduces the wage earner within the class structured division of labour, distributes the cultural skills appropriate to each section within the technical

division of labour, and attempts to construct the collective identity and disposition appropriate to the positions of subordination and secondariness for which the majority are destined.

It is true that there has been much debate around the issue of the role of the education in social reproduction and some of it we have discussed earlier in this chapter. But there is also much evidence to show the ways in which the education system reproduces Black young people as workers at the lower end of the employment market, who are both cheap and expendable. The ways in which the education system does this may change and has changed, but the net effect is the same. The schools have mirrored society in shifting from an overt racist position through an integrationist model to the current multicultural model. This multicultural education is argued by many to operate to the disadvantage of the Black people. Maureen Stone (1981) insists that the objectives of multiracial education are vague and undefined and totally ignore the issues of power and control in the school system. They simplify and idealize the developmental aspects of schooling. They ignore class and treat race and culture as a social psychological abstraction. And, as Hazel Carby (1981) states:

> It is not the opinions of racial and ethnic minorities that are voiced through multiculturalism. Nor are official documents or educational theories about the multicultural curricula addressed to them directly. Rather, racial and ethnic minorities are the object of discussion, predefined as constituting 'the problem'. The audience is the White middle class group of educationalists that have to contain/deal with the 'problem'.

Thus, more and more Black young people are being produced as part of an unemployed reserve army of labour, or as the lowest stratum of labour. Most current reports including the MSC 1982 London Employment Review, tend to show a disproportionate amount of Black people in manual jobs as well as a disproportionately unemployed number, especially Black youth. It is then no wonder that we see a growing and varied amount of Black resistance to the oppression of racist education in a racist state. It is no wonder that the Black community is by and large organizing its own alternative (sometimes called supplementary) education. It is no wonder that more and more teachers and academics, Black and White, are beginning to clearly articulate an anti-racist stance for education. Multicultural education means nothing if it is simply racism showing faces of different colours.

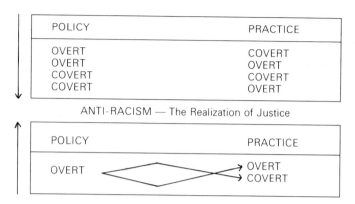

Figure 4:   The Realization of Institutional Racism

Repression and Regeneration

There is a line of argument that puts forward the case for a total withdrawal from the schooling of the state because that schooling is by definition racist and, thus, a major tool for the genocide of Black people. This is not my view.

Though it is true that the overall effect of the education system is, to a large extent, the repression of Black resistance to the oppression of racism, both within and outside the school, it is also true that the school is an important site for the regeneration of racism, both as an ideology and a practice. Yet it is also true that the school can also be a site for oppositional and emancipatory action.

The institutional racism in the school system in Britain is not just a reflection of the wider in-built oppression and exploitation of the distinct subordinate cultural/ethnic/racial groups by the dominant group. Rather, institutional racism is actively engaged in the perpetuation of racist attitudes and practices which systematically restrict the educational opportunities of 'minority' groups while inculcating in the majority continued feelings of superiority. These practices work against justice in our society. Thus, it becomes clear that any education that is truly for all and for life in our diverse and stratified society must be by definition anti-racist.

In chapter 3 we examine the context of anti-racist teaching, its nature as well as the ideological basis.

Notes

1 MULLARD uses the concept of etharchy to refer to the ways in which Black people, having been coopted into the hierarchy of the social structure, operate to compound the oppression of other racially defined oppressed people while being victims of a modified form of oppression themselves. See, for example, MULLARD, C. (1984) *Anti-Racist Education: The Three O's*, London, National Association for Moral Education.

2 See DURKHEIM, E. (1960) *Moral Education*, New York, Free Press.

3 This device, BERNSTEIN argues, has both internal and external orderings and provides the intrinsic grammar of pedagogic discourse through 'distributive' rules, 'recontextualizing' rules and rules of evaluation. As BERNSTEIN purports:

> The pedagogic device is thus a symbolic ruler for consciousness in its selective creation, positioning and oppositioning of pedagogic subjects. It is the condition for the production, reproduction and transformation of culture. The question is whose ruler, what consciousness?'

BERNSTEIN, B. (1985) *On Pedagogic Discourse*, Stencilled Paper, London, Department of Sociology, University of London Institute of Education. Also see ATKINSON, P. (1985) *Language, Structure and Reproduction: An Introduction to the Sociology of Basil Bernstein*, London, Methuen.

4 ALDRIDGE, I.F. (1804–67). The renowned Black American actor who became a naturalized Englishman in 1863. He was immensely popular in Europe, especially Germany, Russia and in Poland, where he died.

SAMUEL COLERIDGE-TAYLOR (1875–1921) was a renowned British Black conductor, musician, and composer of over 100 works, whose contribution to British classical music has passed unnoticed and whose praise has gone unsung. He described himself as Anglo-African and fought strongly against racial prejudice through all his thirty-seven years of life.

MARY SEACOLE (1805–1881) was a British Black nurse (originally from Jamaica), a contemporary of Florence Nightingale, whose selfless caring and resourcefulness for the wounded soldiers of the Crimea brought them much relief from their suffering. Her contribution to Britain has been no less than that of Florence Nightingale yet very few people have actually heard of her. She was the first Black woman to emerge in British public life. After the war she settled in Tavistock Street, Covent Garden. She was buried in the Roman Catholic section of Kensal Green Cemetery.

HARRIET TUBMAN (1820–1913) was an ex-slave who broke free from slavery in America in 1849. She served as a Union Army scout. She was a veritable icon for her fellow oppressed Black Americans and led some 300 of her people to freedom on the underground railroad.

3   Constructing an Anti-racist Pedagogy

Introduction

One of the frequent criticisms levelled at the anti-racist movement (in education particularly) is that it is merely theoretical — mere rhetoric. Therefore, beyond a programme of indoctrination for the children it is seen as impossible to implement.

But 'What do I do in my class tomorrow?' is often the question, not only at primary and secondary school level, but in colleges of further and higher education and universities. Perhaps this is particularly true in those institutions of higher education that see themselves merely in terms of transmission of knowledge. A knowledge which tends to be seen as fixed, objective and value free. Many teachers will say, 'I understand how I can make my teaching multicultural — I can add a wider range of cultural facts and a wider range of cultural examples to my teaching, but anti-racism tells me nothing but the fact that I ought to be against racism.'

This book as a whole deals with some of the major issues implied by these questions and assumptions. However, more precisely, this chapter is intended to be a contribution to the understanding or unravelling of the false dichotomy that is created between theory and practice, especially anti-racist theory and positive educational practice.

In this chapter, first of all, I deal briefly with the broader question of the role of theory in education and argue for a dialectic relationship between educational theory and educational practice. I then examine some of the major aspects of the debate between multiculturalism and anti-racism. Out of this debate, and in the light of the preceding chapter 2, I attempt to outline the 'language' of anti-racism. This is done on the premise, as argued in chapter 2, that language is locked into and a part of the ideological construction of social reality and is therefore tailored to perform and to bolster the ideologies out of which they grow.

The sections that follow deal with anti-racist teaching as praxis and as oppositional pedagogy — they examine the questions of to what extent can an oppositional pedagogy be devised and operationalized within a repressive structure and to what extent is anti-racist teaching not only desirable but realizable within the structure of schooling?

Overall in this chapter, I attempt to provide a possible framework and *modus operandi* for the deconstruction and combating of institutional racism as it operates in schools.

The Role of Theory

The role of theory in education is a much debated and much maligned phenomenon and there are several positions that can and have been taken on it. The three major positions are (i) that theory should precede and determine practice; (ii) that theory should be derived from practice and not vice versa; and (iii) that theory and practice are linked.

It is from the third category that the major permutations arise with regard to this relationship. Such questions can be asked as: Is it an equal relationship? Is one dependent on the other? Which one? Is one valid without the other?

However, whatever the position taken, one could argue that there has been a general shift, over the past two decades at least, towards a theory in education that takes into greater consideration the social context. But as Giroux (1983) argues, any understanding of the nature of theory must begin with some:

> grasp of the relationships that exist in society between the particular and the whole, the specific and the universal.

Giroux attributes the basis of his thinking largely to the work of the Frankfurt School of Sociology's conception of theory which he sees in terms of three premises. Firstly, that in order to understand the significance of 'facts' in society one must have the right social theory (Hookheimer, 1972). Secondly, that theory must ultimately develop the capacity of what he calls 'metatheory', in order to move beyond neutrality. The third and very important aspect of theory is that it ought to unmask. This unmasking function is embodied in the critical spirit of theory itself. This third point he relates to the Frankfurt School's notion of . . . criticism and dialectical thought.

For Held (1980) the notion of dialectics is crucial because it reveals:

> The insufficiencies and imperfections of 'finished' systems of thought . . . It reveals incompleteness where completeness is claimed. It embraces that which is in terms of that which is not, and that which is real in terms of potentialities not yet realized.

Imminent critique, as described by Giroux, is most important in that he describes it as:

> The assertion of difference, the refusal to collapse appearance and essence, the willingness to analyze the reality of the social object against its possibilities. (p. 18)

or as eloquently argued by Adorno *et al* (1976):

> Theory . . . must transform the concepts which it brings, as it were, from outside into those which the object has of itself, into what the object, left to itself seeks to be, and confront it with what it is. It must dissolve the rigidity of temporally and spatially fixed object into a field of tension of the possible and the real: each one in order to exist, is dependent upon the other. In other words, theory is indisputably critical.

Theory and practice are inextricably interrelated. There is currently a reawakened debate about whether theory should be derived from practice or practice from theory. For me, the case is more straight-forward than many would allow. All practice is informed by theory whether acknowledged or not, whether at a conscious level or not. All theory, on the other hand, derives from practice and has its ultimate reality in practice. However, this is not to say that there is or should be a unity between theory and practice because, as Adorno highlights:

> The call for unity of theory and practice has irrisistably degraded theory to the servant's role, removing the very traits it should have brought to that unity. The visa stamp of practice which we demand of all theory became a censor's place. Yet whereas theory succumbed in the vaunted mixture, practice became non-conceptual, a piece of the politics, it was supposed to lead out of it because the prey of power.

One profoundly relevant example is the whole question of anti-racist theory which, as Mullard argues, always existed as a practice but only recently has begun to be expressed as a theory. With regard to theory, Mullard (1984) asserts, 'There can be no anti-racist education without theory'. This statement is the crux of this chapter but the crucial point for the book as a whole goes further. It states that anti-racist theory and anti-racist practice are inextricably linked.

Theory, in this case, should have as its goal emancipatory practice, but at the same time it requires a certain distance from such practice. Theory and practice represent a particular alliance not a unity in which one dissolves the other. (Giroux, 1983, p. 21)

Therefore, Giroux argues further that:

while it is indisputable that experience may provide us with knowledge, it is also indisputable that knowledge may distort rather than illuminate the nature of social reality. The point here is that the value of any experiences 'will depend not on the experience of the subject but on the struggles around the way that experience is interpreted and defined'. (Bennett, 1980, p. 13)

These words to a large extent sum up the conceptual bases of my approach to this question. The purpose therefore of this chapter is to put forward this conceptual basis for the practice of anti-racist teaching within a framework that acknowledges the role, function and interactivity of theory and practice. For this purpose in earlier chapters, I have critically drawn on the work of some people who themselves can be criticized for failing to sufficiently take into consideration the racialization of social relations in Britain as a significant parameter of analysis. However, there are positive elements extrapolated to link with the growing body of thought and theory which falls under the broad label of anti-racist.

In the final analysis, the attempt to put forward an argument and a *modus operandi* for anti-racist practice is mine. This attempt is based on a rereading and reinterpretation of theory and practice based on an autonomous set of principles, aims and intentions and is a part of the move to redefine the terrain in 'Black' terms. My approach is anti-racist. This position, however, draws, to some extent, on radical structuralist traditions for the want of a more precise description. It also attempts to draw its basis not so much from 'Marxism', 'socialism' or 'neo-Marxism', as defined by White European traditions, but from Black experience and Black thought over the last few centuries as clearly adumbrated in works such as Robinson's *Black Marxism* (1983). As Robinson argues:

Black radicalism ... is not a variant of Western radicalism whose proponents happen to be Black. Rather it is a specifically African response to an oppression emergent from the immediate determinants of European development in the modern era and framed by orders of human exploitation of women into the

Figure 5: Perspectives on the relationship between multiculturalism (x) and anti-racism (y)

1	2	3	4	5
(x)	x>y	x:y	y>x	(y)

x = multiculturalism;   y = anti-racism

interstices of European social life from the inception of Western civilisation.

Multicultural Teaching v Anti-racist Teaching

The relationship between multicultural education and anti-racist teaching is currently viewed in a range of ways and not only seen as a simple contest. This observation applies to all of the various levels of educational experience.

In the figure 5, where x represents multiculturalism and y represents anti-racism, we have at one end of the continuum an approach to the issue that would argue for the exclusivity of multiculturalism as the way forward in educational practice. There is a strong 'progressive' argument which makes the case for the need to value 'other people's culture' and to incorporate it into the school curriculum.

This incorporation, the argument goes, would ensure that pupils of 'ethnic minority' backgrounds would have a positive self-image and therefore would be more in sympathy with the school as an institution and with the society at large.

This process and its resultant product works towards better learning and greater social 'harmony'.

This approach to education tends to view society as consensual. Thus it is assumed that there is broad agreement in society about what counts as knowledge, and the basis on which this knowledge is constructed — or at least what it was like until 'they' came. 'They' refers to the 'ethnic minorities' who now live in British society. This is to be the basis of formulations like the titles *Ethnic Minorities in British Schools* (Tomlinson, 1983), and *West Indian Children in British Schools* (Rampton, 1981).

The liberal argument therefore is to make *them* feel a part of *our* society and then we will return to harmony.

The problem with this approach is that it fails to acknowledge the stratification of British society along class, race and gender lines and the oppressive structures that maintain that status quo.

As clearly stated by Carby (1981) it is the 'curious silence about, avoidance of, or inadequacy in, addressing racism'. As Carby suggests, the conflicts and contradictions that are absent from the articulation of multiculturalism lead on to absurd dialogue such as the following:

Schools:	We're all equal here.
Black students:	We *know* we are second-class citizens, in housing, employment and education.
Schools:	Oh, dear. Negative self-image. We must order books with Blacks in them.
Black students:	Can't we talk about the immigration laws or the National Front?
Schools:	No, that's politics. We'll arrange some Asian and West Indian cultural evenings.

Even in its most positive statements and rationalizations this brand of multiculturalism is flawed. For example, in the Green Paper on education, quoted earlier, the argument for change is based on the fact that 'traditional social patterns are *breaking down* (sic)'. This suggests that the social patterns were previously intact and acceptable but are no longer so. This is because *our* community is now 'multicultural' and 'multiracial'. The 'our' refers to British Whites; the 'multicultural' and 'multiracial' is a code for Black people.

If we were in any doubt about this analysis, the Green Paper goes on to state that: 'The education *appropriate* to our imperial past cannot meet the requirements of modern Britain' (my emphasis).

Even if one assumes 'good intentions', what is blatant is that the ideological framework for the problem does not allow for the consideration of racism — especially institutional racism — and starts from the assumption that the 'racist' education of imperialist Britain would be perfect if only there were no Black people here.

Also, in this camp is the work of theorists such as Jeffcoate (1979). Whereas Jeffcoate, on the one hand, argues very strongly for the need to prominently feature and positively represent the cultures of racial minorities in the curriculum, he categorically rejects any argument based on the assumption that:

British society suffers from an endemic malaise, racism, which has acquired the status of a cultural norm and moulds children's attitudes. (p. 26)

In short, he rejects any form of anti-racism. It is in this very vein that one polytechnic professor wrote, in response to the ARTEN letter that:

It is conceptually naive to say that Britain is a racist society. (*Times Educational Supplement* and *Times Higher Education Supplement*, 19 September 1983)

Of course, lying outside this whole debate are those who reject altogether any notion of 'multiculturalism' or, worse, anti-racism. For this school of thought, 'multiculturalism' is itself seen as 'racist' or 'racialist' — using their own meaning of the terms, which could range anything from basically aware to politically active in the defence of their 'race'.

I've already quoted one such example of the Bradford headmaster who openly stated his views about the whole field in these words:

The propaganda generated by multiracial zealots is now augmented by a growing bureaucracy of race in local authorities. And this makes freedom of speech difficult to maintain. By exploiting the enormous tolerance traditional in this country, the race lobby has so managed to induce and maintain feelings of guilt in the well-disposed majority, that *decent* [my emphasis] people are not only afraid of voicing certain thoughts, they are uncertain even of their right to think those thoughts. (Honeyford, 1984, p. 30)

Thus, it seems that 'multiculturalism', however defined, is the target of severe criticism, both by crude *racists* and *anti-racists*, but for totally different reasons. For the racists, multiculturalism is seen as yet another attack on the White status quo. An attack that makes the argument for the inclusion of 'other' cultures into traditional British culture and that creates 'guilt' about the propping up of the racial status quo.

From an anti-racist standpoint, this formulation of multiculturalism acts as a palliative and 'gloss-over' of the real issues of power and injustice.

Multiculturalism Includes Anti-racism — X > Y

From this viewpoint, there is no contest, since multiculturalism is by definition anti-racist. This position is also argued on a number of bases, *inter alia*, that multiculturalism is all inclusive and therefore prevents ghettoization of interests or strategies.

Therefore, multiculturalism is seen as important for all children. Therefore, there is a matching emphasis on the need to revise the curriculum to make it more global and less ethnocentric or eurocentric.

According to view, it is the bulk of 'white' British children who are the most educationally deprived, in an increasingly inter-dependent world, by the mono-cultural and parochial confines of many schools' curriculum and the conventionally Anglo-centric approach to their subject taken by many teachers. (Saunders, 1982)

It seems that this is the position taken by Saunders (1982) in his book, *Multicultural Teaching*. In the book, Saunders begins by recognizing what he refers to as the 'multicultural characteristics' of the school and wider society. He also accepts the 'allegations' of racism in the teaching profession. He also declares his intention to go beyond the 'sensitizing' function in attempting to help teachers to systematically construct, implement and evaluate 'multicultural curricula'.

Whether Saunders was successful in his intention or not is not the point under discussion here. Rather, the point I am addressing is his ideological position which suggests some form of anti-racist action as an implicit part of 'multicultural curricula'.

The problem with Saunders' approach, like that of others operating within this paradigm, is that it fails to realize the way in which the ideological framework and epistemology affects not only the overall rationalization but the specificity of the phenomena — especially the pivotal ones, that proceed out of that way of thinking and of perceiving the world.

Therefore, racism seen through the eyes of the attempt to make education multicultural looks rather different to 'racism' seen through the 'eyes' of an anti-racist discourse.

Yet Green (1982), in his article on this issue, makes a similar case for anti-racism within the multiculturalist framework. He recognizes it as a contested space in which a dynamic and political educational process could be developed. In line with other adherents to this position, he argues that any 'genuine' multicultural education must, by defini-tion, be anti-racist.

So, multiculturalism is seen as the 'spoonful of sugar' which makes the medicine go down. But as is widely known, in scientific terms, not all elements mix and when they do the properties of one or both of those elements can be slightly or even drastically changed, if the elements are not 'sympathetic' to each other. Thus, the 'sugar' could so drastically change the 'medicine' that the latter is made impotent. On the contrary, multicultural education can be seen as the Trojan horse of institutional racism. Within it resides an attempt to renew the structure and processes of racism in education.

This is precisely the point made by the anti-racist critique. Multiculturalism is a racial form of education constructed by the oppressors to maintain the status quo of dominant and dominated, of oppressor and oppressed. An anti-racist critique would indeed cast multiculturalism as a Trojan horse created as a proverbial peace offering but containing within it the backlash of a restructured racism.

If, on the other hand, what is being described by this school of thought does not fit into this explanation, then maybe it should be called by another name.

(x:y) — Multicultural Education: Anti-racist Teaching

This approach to the relationship or the 'contest' between multicultural education or anti-racist education tends to be one of an incorporation of the two concepts. Thus, 'education' is seen as having to be 'multicultural' while the 'teaching' is seen as needing to be 'anti-racist'.

This rationalization has a logic of its own which suggests that, though the context of the curriculum can be changed by multiculturalization, this multicultural curriculum can be taught in a traditional and racist way. The way out of this dilemma is through the important intervention of anti-racist teaching.

In this context, anti-racist teaching is seen as coming about through a teacher with the 'right' attitude, the appropriate knowledge, and the necessary skills to bring about learning that will challenge racism and change the bias of the traditional ethnocentric and biased education to which we have become accustomed in Britain. Positive change and development in this context is seen as coming through dual action. The 'multiculturalizing' of the curriculum content and the consciousness raising of teachers who would then be able to positively use the new material. What tends to get missed out in this approach is the specificity of the construction of the curriculum, both in terms of content and context, and both in terms of inclusions and omissions.

(y>x) — Anti-racist Education Is By Definition Multicultural

There is just a shade of difference between the last position (x:y) and this one (y>x). This difference is that, whereas (x:y) suggests that multiculturalism (x) and anti-racism (y) are different but complimentary, (y>x) suggests that anti-racist education is, by definition, multicultural education and includes it.

Assuming that this approach is informed by anti-racism rather than multiculturalism, the position would be that the school curriculum needs to be multicultural but not merely in content but in context. Therefore, the inclusion of various examples from different cultures would not be sufficient without a changed perspective. Within this framework, it is assumed that there would also be some direct attention paid to the issue of racism, especially in terms of bias, prejudice, ethnocentricity and, to some extent, power.

(y) — Anti-racism

As it must be clear from the foregoing explications, the edges of these approaches, adumbrated here, become fuzzy, especially when posed comparatively with each other. However, the position that seeks to explain the education debate mainly or solely through the discourse of anti-racism would argue that institutionalized multiculturalism is itself a product of institutional racism and a 'racial form' that is itself racist. This is so in that it does not derive directly from Black struggle or the Black experience but rather marks the attempt of racist education to adapt to the challenges posed to it by the transhistorical struggle of Black people in this country against their continued oppression by institutionalized racism.

As Carby (1982) quite succinctly puts it:

> The 'discourse' of multiculturalism is situated within an increasingly racist, social, economic and political climate. It is centrally part of Blacks are a social problem. (p. 13)

In these terms, 'multicultural education' is an expression of the racist education we examined in chapter 2 and, therefore, would need to be challenged, like its predecessors, by a positive anti-racist education which, as I have argued throughout the book, is oppositional. In order to succeed, I have argued, anti-racism must be dynamic and led by the experience and articulations of the Black community as the ongoing victims of rapidly changing ideology and practice of racism.

The Language of Anti-racism

Many of the detractors and critics of anti-racism criticize it for being too polemic, too rhetorical or too political. This is based on an accusation regarding the use of an overtly 'political' language by promulgators of anti-racism. Some of the words usually identified are words such as racism itself, struggle, power and conflict. The use of these words is seen as containing in their very meanings and use an unacceptable degree of politicization.

Among these also is the word 'Black', a term now popularly used by the communities of African, Asian, Afro and Indo-Caribbean origin in Britain as a signal of their identification with each other's separate and common struggle against racism. The term is now in fact being broadened in its use by some, to include other peoples who find themselves victims of, and oppressed by, racism of the institutional and/or interactional kind. So, for example, in his infamous article in the *Salisbury Review* Ray Honeyford does not only attempt to reduce the term racism to sloganism but argues that the word 'Black' has been perverted in the interest of the creation of an 'anti-White' solidarity. This fallacious view is set at the base of a series of further highly charged and racist views about people in general and Black British people in particular.

It, therefore, seems important at this point to be necessary to pause to examine what, indeed, is the language of anti-racism and why it is important to understand the use of certain terms as embodiments of a process of conceptualization. This points us back to that section of chapter 2 that highlights the way in which ideologies generate the vocabularies and language that express, delineate and structure not only *what* is thought about but *how* it is thought about. Let us, for example, juxtapose some examples of the language of multiculturalism and anti-racism (see table 2).

In the table, both the headings describing approach and the words appearing under language represent the language of the discourse. So, both the term racism for example and the accompanying notions of equal human rights, power and justice are part and parcel of anti-racist discourse.

However, given our discussion of the differing conceptualizations of the possible relationship between multiculturalism and anti-racism it is, of course, important to say that one could still be employing the use of the language of one discourse while engaging, from one's point of view, in the other. But the 'bottom line', I would argue, must be to do with the extent to which the approach acknowledges the notion of oppression, institutional racism through both structural and cultural means and the need to consciously combat racism in and through institutions. This approach also operates from a premise that education is a politically defined social process. The only question is in whose interests.

Table 2:   The Language of Multiculturalism/Anti Racism

Phenomenon	Multicultural Approach/Language	Anti-racist Approach/Language
Perception of societal base	Failure in consensus within cultural Pluralism of majority and minority groups	Conflict between racist state and individuals and racially defined oppressed groups
The problem	Institutional and interactional mono-culturalism/ethnicism and ethnocentricity	Institutional and interactional racism
	Non-recognition, marginalizantion, negative image, intercultural misunderstanding	Racial exploitation, oppression, containment, cooptation, fragmentation (divide and rule), power maintenance, marginalization
The key concept	CULTURE Awareness, equality, parity, of esteem, racialism	RACISM Equal human rights, power, justice
The objective	EQUALITY Prejudice, misunderstanding, ignorance	JUSTICE Structure, power, context
The process solution	INTERCULTURALISM	ANTI-RACISM
	Provide information, cultural exchange, cultural/ethnic awareness, permeation, special interest	DISMANTLE, DECONSTRUCT, RECONSTRUCT, the Three O's (Mullard) Observation, Orientation, Operation, struggle

As I have argued before, 'racialism' refers to overt acts of racial aggression based on race hatred and on belief in the racial superiority of the actor. Racism, on the other hand, refers to the complex network of factors which seek to justify and ensure the exclusion of racially-defined oppressed groups from access to the best of the resources in society. It amounts to the relative powerlessness of one or more of these racially-defined oppressed groups through the dominant reign of the oppressor-group. The principal parameters, as I have outlined, are varied and include *inter alia* the economic, socio-cultural, political and military power, marginalization, xenophobia, prejudice and ethnocentricity.

However, it is quite wrong to simply see Black people in Britain quite as mere objects of racist practice since, as I have outlined in chapter 1, this country has a history of Black resistance to racism that is matched only by the history of racism itself. Therefore, within the contemporary education scene, Black people have been and are active in combating racism in society and education.

Community Perspectives and Articulations on Anti-racism

Increasingly in Britain and on the European mainland, there is an emergent and outspoken resistance to racism. This is being identified in direct correlation to the increased activity and militancy of racism in Europe.

In Britain particularly, this action is being articulated more and more clearly in terms of anti-racism in society and in education. The basic premise of this stance, like the premise of this book, is that the relations between the 'races' is a power relationship. The more visible 'racial' groups are, the main objects of the most vicious expressions of racism — this includes both institutional and interactional racism.

Firstly, the Black communities are no longer willing to be marginalized or objectified but insist on the assertion of their existence as equal members of British society. This is exemplified not only by the fight to gain and maintain cultural ground or by the fight to gain and maintain political and other ground within this state. It is demonstrated by a specific fight to change the educational system of this country, so that it not only reflects but promotes their interest and ultimate justice for them and their children. In short, what is sought is justice in education, based on a clear ideology that is neither oppressive, condescending nor patronizing.

Despite the reports to the contrary, the Black communities of Asian as well as Afro/Indo-Caribbean background, have always been concerned about the educational achievement of their children, both in terms of the skills as well as the certification that schooling is seen to have to offer. But whereas in the past they might have been willing to have it at any cost, Black parents are no longer willing to do so. This goes for both the Caribbean as well as Asian communities.

This new wave of energy and 'militancy' in the community is changed by the continuing examples of overt and covert racism which they perceive in their daily lives and the lives of their children. Their position is based on the first or second-hand experience of the street violence, racist laws and educational oppression if not necessarily under-achievement.

The protracted saga of the Honeyford case is an example of this phenomenon in that parents' action and the support given by conscious and concerned members of the wider Black and White community was not based on the simple equation of good exam results equals good education, but on the more important ideological stance that a headmaster who has shown himself to the community as racist, arrogant and contemptuous of his Black pupils, their parents and the Black countries from where these parents originate, cannot possibly offer any children a good education, especially Black children.

The Black communities have demonstrated their dissatisfaction with the content and context and pedagogy of the curriculum of state (and other) mainstream schooling through, *inter alia*, the setting up of various sorts of supplementary schools. The few studies that have been done show that these schools have been set up on a range of bases but all of them, as a matter of course, positively identify and relate the education of the pupils to their own experience, their own culture, their religions and their history. They instill in these young Black people a sense of pride in themselves and in the 'race'. Through this sort of schooling, children encounter Black contemporary and historical figures that they would not have even come across, let alone discuss, in their 'normal' schooling.

This is one of the ways in which the Black community has been providing both a positive experience for the pupils who attend these schools and a positive lead for mainstream educators to follow. Especially those teachers and other educators who would expose an anti-racist stance.

So, first of all, we have noted that the Black community has engaged in anti-racist struggle through political and community action which has an historical resonance; secondly, we have noted the ongoing phenomenon of supplementary schools which addresses the schooling process itself.[1]

Thirdly, another growing phenomenon can be noted which links to both one and two, that of Black parents' associations. These associations and networks operate through community solidarity to fight 'official' expressions of institutional racism which have to do mainly with supporting each other in cases of racism against their own children. In this way, the parent is given the opportunity to lift the issue of a racist incident to do with his/her child from the personal to the community level, thereby broadening the base for struggle and multiplying the chance of a successful outcome to action taken.

There have been certain organizations, such as the Stockwell and Clapham Law Centre in South London, that have, to some extent anyway, through their services, lent support to some such cases but there seems to be scope for much greater action and much wider support from community-based organizations, community workers and educationists at large. It, therefore, seems that in Britain there has been, and continues to be, an ongoing struggle by the Black community at every level to combat racism in education.

Some attempts have been aimed at the level of issues — national or local — at the level of 'cases' and also at the level of the content, context, and pedagogy of school curriculum. The question, it therefore seems, that arises from this observation, is how can anti-racist 'activists' — be they educators or not — support the efforts of this community in the dismantling of a racist education in exchange for a new education for liberation of the people oppressed by current educational practice.

The Aims of Anti-racist Education

As one must be well aware now, if not before, having followed the argument of the book so far, the aims of education are not as simple a question as one might have tended to assume in the past.

Looking back at some of the early articulations of the aims of education, one would be inclined to understand the aims of education in terms of the personal development of the individual, the 'drawing out' of his/her potentials (from the Latin origins of the word meaning to 'draw out' or elicit), the transmission of knowledge from the teacher and the text to the student and the fitting of those abilities, attitudes and knowledge of the student to the society at large.

This rationalization of the function of education, which was largely equated with schooling, has remained at the base of most subsequent theories of the aims of education. This notion has also been servant to a wide range of ideologies which range from education as the exclusive right of the privileged through liberal approaches of education as the major route to upward mobility in an acknowledged, stratified but meritocratic society, to education (or rather schooling) as a 'conservative force' (Bourdieu) and also schooling as an instrument of oppression, repression and the maintenance of the status quo. In the latter analysis, schooling is a construction of the powerful and dominant class for the ideological/intellectual repression of subordinate groups. This repression is seen as aimed to help to maintain the position of the powerful at the expense of the powerless or disenfranchised.

Wrapped up in all these approaches and tendencies have been a range of issues and questions, some of which we have discussed or at least touched on earlier in the book. However, it is from the latter 'broad church', of education as repression, that anti-racism draws its rationalization.

The Aims of Anti-racist Education

Anti-racist education starts from the premise of a racist state and, therefore, acknowledges that the essential aims of education are not necessarily in the interest of the racially defined 'dominated groups', in the same way in which state education is not seen to be constructed for the ultimate benefit of working class pupils.

Therefore, the aims of anti-racist education must be, by definition, oppositional. By oppositional, one is referring to an acknowledged intention to oppose in the education system whatever operates to oppress, repress or disenfranchize one set of pupils on the totally unjustifiable grounds of a perceived 'difference' within which there is an assumption of inherent inferiority. Therefore, what are the aims of anti-racist education? It seems to me that there are three basic aims to anti-racist education which are simply *Equality, Justice* and *Liberation/Emancipation.*

Equality

By equality, in this context, one is referring to an education for all. This aim is not a simple revisit of the old articulations but an assertion of the need to provide an education that is as likely (if not assured) to produce experiences and results that are not 'loaded' and that does not continually disenfranchize any *one* group of people.

Therefore, this notion of equality does not assume a social vacuum or an ahistorical beginning, but a 'fresh start' that begins with the deconstruction of structures and systems which have heretofore operated to generate and perpetuate an inequitable experience of schooling for Black pupils and their oppressed counterparts of White working class pupils and girls.

Within this context, it is therefore not sufficient for teachers to simply state, 'I treat all pupils alike' or 'Black and White are all the same to me' and such like. Rather, it would seem that teachers would have to start by a critical appraisal of the current practice of teaching and the location of their teaching within that.

Thus, this equality aim is an *explicit* not an *implicit* aim, and carries with it a prerequisite. This is that the teacher should acknowledge that schooling, as it operates, is currently not simply 'not working' to provide equal education but is, in fact, on the contrary, working directly and in-directly to perpetuate a system of inequality in schooling and in society.

Justice

For anti-racism, justice carries with it a moral as well as a legal imperative. On the moral level it can be argued that a country, in this case, Britain, has a responsibility to ensure that all its citizens are not only nominally valued equally but are given an equal opportunity to exist, to develop, to partake in what society has to offer and to fully exploit their resources for their benefit, the benefit of their sub-groups and ultimately for the benefit of the country at large.

This intention requires action to ensure that justice does take place. This action needs to happen at a number of levels. In terms of the equal distribution of resources, the equal 'education' and 'training' of the population of how, where and when to tap those resources — also, which resources to tap!

Above all, this justice must be enshrined by law — through legislation, policy-making and monitoring. Built into this legal process must be a system of critical reappraisal to ensure that what was intended is being achieved. When achievement ceases, then change is necessary in order to ensure the ongoing viability of the process and the longevity of the product of justice.

Emancipation

Essential to the ideology of anti-racism is the concept of emancipation — the liberation of both the oppressed and the oppressor from the shackles that bind them both. This is why anti-racism addresses racism itself.

In deconstructing the erroneous notions of racism, the naturalness of discrete racial behavioural characteristics on the basis of phenotypical variation, the natural superiority of the 'White' race over 'Black' people, and the naturalness of the unequal distribution of rights, property and power, the educator is involved in liberating the conscious or unconscious racist from the bondage of ignorance or, worse, ideological mis-education. The results of this are the beginning of a more equitable and just society. More importantly, anti-racism is about the emancipation of the racially defined oppressed groups from the oppressive structures of racist practice and, in some cases, from what I have referred to earlier as the 'hegemony' of racism which affects both the 'racist' and the 'victim'.

This does not assume that Black people, as victims of racism, are sitting and waiting for some mythical ideological liberator to free them from this hegemony. On the contrary, as I have argued throughout this book, Black people in Britain and oppressed peoples throughout the world have always been active in their own emancipation and continue to do so. The role of the educator, therefore, is to aid, facilitate, and possibly catalyze this resistance.

This form of support necessitates a sensitivity to and involvement with the struggles of the Black communities and as articulated by them.

Dismantling and Combating Racism in Education

The deconstruction and challenging of racism is the addressing of the structures and structuring of racism in education. It assumes that the legacy of British racism is enshrined in British law, with regard to wider society and education as a state institution. It addresses the interaction between policy and practice that characterizes institutional racism, and the special and specific way in which this is realized in education and schooling.

It is crucial to re-emphasize that this dismantling of racism happens within the context of national state legislation and policy as well as local state policy and practice. Especially significant for schooling is the climate set by the action or inaction of the local education authority.

The policy development, and infra-structure created by the ILEA (see ILEA (1983) *Race, Sex and Class*), for example, for its schools provided not only a positive and useful context for change but an impetus for schools from both within the outside its boundaries to act against and/or think about the nature and implications of racism for the education of all children.

School Policy

It seems to me that regardless of whether or not an authority has a policy, any school wanting to actively engage with an anti-racist practice should be considering the formulation of an anti-racist policy statement, implementation strategy and monitoring/evaluation procedure.

This is so because whether or not there is a policy statement as we have noted in chapter 2, the school is operating a policy. Therefore, it seems imperative that a school that is serious about realizing the aims of anti-racist education would want to formulate a policy, since one important part of anti-racism is about making explicit the implicit.

However, it must be made clear that the formulation of a policy is not an insurance policy for good practice, or for any practice at all, since that policy may begin and end as an exercise in the management of crisis and may even turn out to be a mechanism for maintaining control.

The formulation of a 'whole school' policy ought to involve all the constituencies that can be and will be affected by the implementation of such a policy. It should involve parents (particularly Black parents), pupils' representatives, support staff and the teaching staff of the school. This initial process is facilitated by a sympathetic and helpful headteacher but cannot be formulated by him or her.

Judging from the informal feedback from schools and other educational institutions where policies were fed down from the top, *ie.* by the headteacher or even a special working party mandated by him or her, they have tended not to work very well, if at all. This is so because teachers often do not identify with it and sometimes do not understand or even care to understand it, since it is seen as yet another intrusion on their tenuous and problematic autonomy.

The second reason they tend not to work is because they tend not to fully take into account the wider context of the school as a part of (rather than apart from) the community. Also, because they tend not to fully take into account the school community comprising not only teachers and pupils, but all the other constituencies which I have mentioned earlier.

Having formulated a policy with this wide involvement, it seems that schools need to then think of how this policy is to be implemented at every level, as well as the way in which the fact of its existence and the nature of its contents is to be communicated to the relevant parties.

In addition, it is necessary that every policy has an 'in-built' system of monitoring with which to help to ensure that the policy is being adequately implemented and that its implementation is having its desired results. The monitoring process has to be an ongoing one, since as one has argued, institutional racism itself is dynamic and can adapt itself to accommodate anti-racist strategies. Therefore, the monitoring process will itself have the responsibility of adapting and readapting strategies to combat a dynamic, changing racism.

Staffing, Recruitment, Training and Development

One crucial part of combating racism in education is the issue of staffing, its recruitment, training and development.

Recruitment

One of the main ways in which institutional racism has worked to perpetuate itself has been through the almost exclusive recruitment of White teachers to the profession. This has operated to largely ensure the perpetuation of White interests, cultural assumptions and the racial status quo of 'White' authority and 'Black' subordination.

Black pupils have been unable to see Black role models and have also failed to see any real positive valuing of themselves or the racially defined groups to which they belong. On the contrary, what they see is the perpetuation of the stereotype of the Black worker in servicing roles both outside and inside the schools, because when there are a few Black workers in the school setting they tend to be in 'support' jobs and not in senior teaching posts.

This phenomenon is a double-edged sword. It also exemplifies the extent to which Black people are excluded from such jobs as teaching through forms of racism which exist not only in schooling but in other areas of social/racial interaction. In fact, two of the main issues attached to the debate around recruitment and the failure of the system to recruit are the inadequate numbers of Black teachers and the failure of training institutions to attract more Black student teachers.

Training

Training is a crucial factor, both for the deconstruction of racism and the reconstruction of non-racism through anti-racism. This refers both to teachers currently in practice, student teachers, including potential teachers among the Black communities, and those who have the responsibility of training teachers.

The in-service training of teachers is paramount if the intention is to have both an immediate and a long-term effect on the teaching profession and, ultimately, the teaching and learning of pupils from all backgrounds. This is so because the current staffing of schools repre-sents the major percentage of teachers that will be in service for the next ten to twenty years and, also, represents the senior teachers and headteachers of the immediate future. So, not only are they the majority but the most powerful within the school system.

Initial Teacher Training (ITT)

The importance placed on in-service training is not to underplay the importance of initial teacher training. Teachers who are to have initial training are in the beneficial position of not having acquired any sort of practice at all. Thus, anti-racist practice could be *the* practice which is learnt — therefore, they would be in the position of having to unlearn very little in terms of their professional practice. Though this is not to suggest that they will not have to unlearn racist expectations, prejudices and behaviours at a personal level.

Training the Trainers

The whole question of both INSET and ITT naturally of necessity raises the issues of who will train the trainers. Since the trainers of teachers in university departments of education (UDEs) and colleges of education are themselves a product of a racist education system and partake both passively and actively in the realization of institutional racism in education. Therefore, trainer training must be of high priority for deconstructing or dismantling racism in education. It is to the precise question that the anti-racist teacher education network addresses itself when it asserted that in Britain we are living in a 'profoundly racist society' and that teacher education must therefore address directly this whole issue.

Staff Development

It is difficult to isolate an area called 'staff development' since everything which I have stated so far in this section relates rather directly to staff development. That is, a formal and/or informal engagement with the staff that prepares them for moving further and faster in their efficiency, and effectiveness efficacy in their job.

This 'staff development' should also be seen as an instrument for facilitating the critical awareness of staff of their own inadequacies and of the various phenomena and issues which impinge on their work. Staff development in terms of staff training that addresses the specificity of the social reality of their own work setting is particularly useful. Its usefulness lies in its scope for uncovering the 'systemic' realizations of racism within the 'ethos' and 'processes' of the institution.

It is this particular realization of racist practice that is addressed by work such as *Through a Hundred Pairs of Eyes* (1985), which is set out with this precise aim in view. This type of work needs to be done in schools, colleges and universities, because piecemeal action is, at best, limited in its effect and, at worst, counterproductive.[2]

The Curriculum

In dealing with the curriculum, it seems that there are three major activities with which one needs to be engaged: (i) the overall critical re-appraisal of the overt curriculum, content, nature of the knowledge of schooling, its omissions, inclusions and orderings; (ii) the materials selected for use within its framework; and (iii) a fundamental challenge of the 'hidden curriculum' which would include questions of perspectives and the hidden agendas of the class and/or the school.

Reappraising the curriculum content

Reappraisal of curriculum content may sometimes mean a challenge to the very basic assumptions of education and schooling, that is, questioning the very topics chosen within secondary curriculum areas and in the primary syllabus. In this questioning some topics will have to go though some will stay. But even for those elements that are left, that is not the end of it. What follows should be an attempt to eradicate the ethnocentrism of both selection and perspective of the various elements of the curriculum.

It will entail the removal of bias, as well as the training of pupils to spot and challenge bias in texts. Above all, it will mean removing all forms of racist content in the curriculum and challenging racism through it, both in schools and society at large.

Curriculum material

It, therefore, becomes clear that curriculum materials are also of enormous significance. What books are selected for teaching? Should certain books be withdrawn because they are racist in their images, their content or in their overt or covert message? What happens to the withdrawn books? These are all questions which need to be answered. Above all, do the materials reflect our diverse society? If so, do they reflect the diversity in a positive light?

It seems clear that materials used in the classroom must reflect our diverse society and in a positive light. They must relate to the experience of the pupils while aiding the transition or extrapolation to a global perspective. They must also be the basis for challenging the stratification and inequitable distribution of society's resources. Therefore, there is a clear shift from any fallacious notion of 'neutral' material to the notion of material which can be useful in challenging inequality, injustice and in challenging racism.

The 'hidden' curriculum

One of the most important functions of anti-racist education is, in fact, to shine a light on the 'hidden' curriculum. Through this illumination comes a liberation of those pupils who have not themselves been issued with the 'torches' of the so-called privileged.

As I have argued, 'racist' education has tended to lock out, marginalize and discriminate against racially defined Black pupils by not validating their knowledge or social reality. In fact, it has operated to actively produce and reproduce racism as an ideology and as a practice. Within this framework of institutional racism, a racial 'code' is enacted, from which Black pupils are largely excluded. It is this racial code that is the harbinger of the hidden curriculum.

Anti-racist education, therefore, must be about making blatant that hidden agenda so that it can be combatted. This can and must be done by moving towards the declaration of perspectives of teachers, of texts and other materials, the declaration of expectations of the school for all its pupils, and the encouragement of the critical awareness of pupils of the form, processes and content of their schooling. Of course, this will have various emphases and forms according to the level of schooling and according to the specific 'ethos' of the school.

Therefore, the 'ethos' of the school must be a target. Instead of viewing the 'ethos' as ethereal, it must be viewed as the social and cultural environment which is constructed out of the covert and/or overt policy, personal attitudes and ideological underpinnings.

It is often through the immaterial and intangible 'ethos' of the school, like any other organization, that the real force and 'hegemony' of racism is experienced through which Black pupils become marginalized, criminalized and ostracized.

However, lest one forgets, it is important to state here that anti-racist education or, more significantly, the deconstruction end of it, is not simply addressed to schools where Black pupils are. Rather, it is addressed to all schools, since it is perhaps in the 'all White' schools that racism thrives best. In this setting it is possible for White teachers to accept and perpetuate unchallenged (even by the mere presence of Black people) racist assumptions, racist 'knowledge' and the matching pedagogy.[3]

Critical Appraisal of Pedagogy

With regard to pedagogy, it is clear that certain pedagogic styles would be inappropriate to anti-racist education and its broad aims of equality, justice, and liberation.

Existing pedagogic practice must be examined to see to what extent it involves exploratory and collaborative learning, which involves not only teachers and pupils but the wider community's perspectives and 'knowledge', especially that of the oppressed groups. There must also be an examination of the quality and nature of relationships between pupils and teachers and pupils and pupils. The role of the teacher in intervening in, or facilitating with, the learning process must also be re-examined in the light of the parameters so far outlined.

Anti-racist Teaching

So far in this book I have argued that, in examining the relationship between racism and education, one has to examine what exactly is meant by these two concepts and sets of practices — both in historical as well as contemporary terms.

I have also argued that these two phenomena must be viewed in relation to the notion of the 'racist state'. I have made the case of the recognition of this notion of the racist state and, by the same token, of 'racist schooling'.

The basis of our discussions has been that racism is multi-faceted and dynamic and must be seen not only in terms of prejudice, 'race hatred', bias, and ethnocentricity but in terms of power and in terms of the legacy of imperialism and colonialism. The power of reality of racism ranges from the ideological to the material and from the institutional to the interactional. The elements of this racism could be either covert or overt, hidden or blatant, and can operate in very specific ways in specific institutions.

Schools, as agencies of 'socialization' and 'cultural transmission' have played and continue to play a major role in the production, reproduction and transmission of racism. But schools must also be seen as sites of struggle. So, it is possible for oppositional discourses to operate within the context of schools but this requires both the 'political' will as well as the professional commitment. Commitment on the part of teachers must be in the three major domains of the discourse of schooling — the domains of curriculum, pedagogy and context.

As I have argued, the education system operates in both indirect and direct ways to transmit racism. This amounts to an 'education for dominance' for White pupils, and for Black pupils, education for failure and domination in school and society. These products of schooling are mediated through these three domains of curriculum, pedagogy and context. These domains, though separable in analysis, are inseparable in practice. Therefore, anti-racist teaching must address all three of them if it is to be effective.

The Basis of Anti-racist Teaching

Before going further, however, it would be useful to try and clarify what I consider to be the basis of anti-racist teaching.

Anti-racism shares with multiculturalism the obvious assertion concerning the 'multiracial' nature and cultural pluralism of British society. But anti-racism goes further in that it does not see the marginalization, exclusion and devaluation of Black culture by White culture as an error of history but as a product of power relations. Within the social/racial status quo the dominant White Anglo-Saxon protestant culture generates and perpetuates its hegemonic reign through a range of devices. Racism, therefore, is an essential and crucial element in the structuring of social relations, particularly those which are racially defined. Fundamental to anti-racism is the concept of the racist state and schooling as a part of the functioning of the state is itself racist. Therefore, we have the notion of 'racist schooling'. In schools, as state institutions, racism operates both overtly and covertly through structural, as well as cultural, mechanisms and processes. This racism is deeply embedded in the very fabric of these processes.

Thus, it becomes clear that racism in education — like any other form of racism — will not disappear with palliative and tokenistic measures, such as depoliticized and decontextualized cultural exchange or cultural exploration. What is required is positive action. Therefore, as long as the education system, like other social and state institutions, is racist, an adequate, appropriate and just education system must be, by definition, anti-racist. That is to say, there is a real need for a coherent and holistic, anti-racist approach, which addresses both directly and indirectly the ways in which the school produces, reproduces and transmits racism, both in the school and in society.

This anti-racist action needs to take place at every level and needs to go beyond the pathologization of the racist individual as if he or she were an aberration, as racism awareness does. This anti-racism must be firmly placed within the structural and cultural contexts of the institution — the school. Indeed, there is a limit to the changes that education itself can make without matching and complementary changes in wider society. That is why anti-racist action in general, and anti-racist teaching in particular, must be located in the wider anti-racist struggle and must take care to ensure that there are links made especially with the Black community. Also, it seems to me that the anti-racist struggle must make room for links with the struggle against other forms of oppression, like sexism and class domination.

Anti-racist Classroom Practice

As succinctly put by Shallice (1984):

> In our role as teachers, we are concerned with the development
> and formation of intellectual ideas and as such we are in a very

different relationship to our work than, for example, car workers. As 'intellectual workers' or 'ideological workers' we have a responsibility to expose the illusions of racism to engage in that fight against it and if we are not prepared to do this, we end up as agents in its perpetuation. We cannot take a neutral stance. (p. 11)

This statement by Shallice pinpoints for us what it is that one is addressing in this discussion. However, like their pupils, teachers are operating simultaneously in a number of arenas. These arenas range from self to universe and are overlaid by various domains, or 'slices', which impinge on them all (see figure 6 below.)

Figure 6:

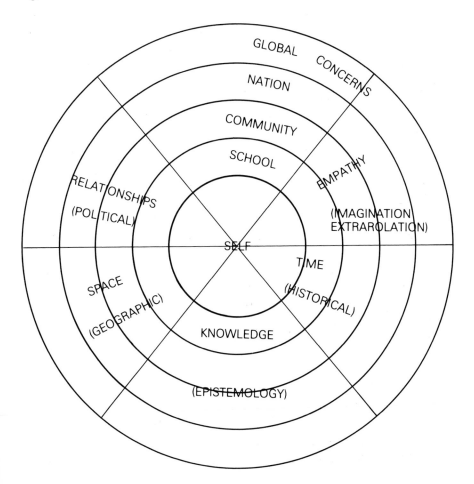

The teacher's practice needs to take into consideration and to be informed by all of these arenas. This should be passed on to the pupils in terms of how their educational experiments are structured.

Pupils' education should therefore be seen as taking place within a context of a series of dynamic interaction between self and the other arenas in figure 6. Thus, their personal education and development is realized through the domains, which relate equally to them as they do to wider society.

In embarking on anti-racist teaching — which all 'good' teaching should be — teachers need to acquire knowledge about the nature and history of the concepts of 'race' and racism in this country. This would include the origins of the fallacious biological conception of 'natural' racial categories and the ways in which it has been used, most specifically in the formulation and articulation of racism. Teachers also need to delve deeper into a true understanding of the so-called cultural pluralism of contemporary Britain. This would require a reappraisal of the whole nation, taking into consideration power and domination which seldom feature as tools for understanding the nature of interactions between cultural/ethnic groups. Teachers need to be actively engaged in a positive development of an understanding of the ways in which White society in general and the education structure in particular operate to marginalize, repress and discriminate against Black pupils and to the benefit of White pupils, purely on the basis of objectifiable 'racial' characteristics. At the same time, teachers need to deal with the observable manifestations of interactional forms of racism through challenging pupils and colleagues alike in their racist behaviours. In doing this, the teacher also needs to be aware of and acknowledge that certain acts on his or her part can have a racist effect, intentionally or unintentionally. By the same token, inaction contributes to the perpetuation of racist practice.

At the level of the school as a whole, the teacher should be concerned about and push for whole school policies which go beyond the rhetoric of multiculturalism. What teachers should be promoting is the formulation of whole-school anti-racist policies which have an inbuilt system of monitoring to ensure that the end product is not simply restructured racism but genuine change. This policy development should be a support, if not the basis, for a new phase of ongoing curriculum development and redevelopment based on anti-racist principles which problematize accepted notions of knowledge as well as the means of dissemination. Anti-racist programme development could also be promoted through year grouping, 'houses', or whatever system of grouping operative in the school's organization. This is what will signal a considered implementation of the policies developed, since it is largely through these structures that the context — including the ethos of the school — is created and maintained. Finally, teachers should try to align themselves to the anti-racist struggle outside the classroom, both at a national and global level. Both Cape Town and Tottenham impinge on the lives of White and Black British children.

With these guidelines and in this context, teachers in both inner city areas as well as rural areas can begin to develop a positive and anti-racist practice, whether their classrooms are perceived as racially mixed or racially homogeneous.

In the Classroom

In the classroom it is important that the teacher bears in mind all the points raised so far. As I have suggested earlier, the three domains under which the teacher ought to consider making changes are the domains of curriculum, pedagogy and context. I have looked at these domains in terms of racist practice and the deconstruction of racist practice. Now, let us briefly examine some of the parameters, the issues and constraints in the reconstruction of non-racist practice through anti-racism.

Context

The context of anti-racist teaching starts at the global level and relates to the national, local and the institutional levels.

At the global level, questions of Third World hunger, famine and liberation struggles all loom large. At the national level, governmental policies, inner city disaffection and disturbances and anti-racist campaigns and struggles are all imperative curriculum material. The disturbances in 1985 in Brixton, Tottenham and other places, the struggles of the Black community against racism in schools in Bradford and other places are all important events.

At the local level, there are a number of things that the teacher can use positively or negatively. For example, many authorities now have some sort of policy relating to this question which might be adequate or inadequate, progressive or retrogressive. Schools operate within the backdrop of these policies which need to be critically assessed on an ongoing basis to see whether the policy itself is adequate, and, if so, whether the method of implementation is also adequate.

Whether the policy of the local education authority is adequate or not, it is an important part of the context in which the teacher is teaching. Therefore, the teacher will need to use the positive elements of the policy, if possible, to support his/her good practice while maintaining critical engagement through whatever avenues are open for making positive change. In some LEAs this is easier to do than others because of the framework provided by the LEA itself for this sort of engagement.

As we enter the school, we are coming closer to an arena substantially in the control and influence of the teacher. It is often said here that the prerequisite of any real change being implemented is the involvement and cooperation of the headteacher. This is so, but it is only *one* of the prerequisites since, as I have stated before, a lot can be and must be done through the institutional structures of the school. (Even though these structures themselves may have to change to accommodate an anti-racist practice.) The other requisites are the school policy mentioned before and a strategy for implementation. The degree to which the context of the classroom itself has to do with all of the aforementioned, plus some of the specific things that the teacher can do in his or her classroom, of course, will have to do with whether one is in a primary classroom or secondary classroom and, in the latter, whether one is a subject teacher only or a form tutor as well.

The Primary Classroom

In my recent visits to some primary schools, I have been reminded of the tremendous potential and responsibility of the primary classroom for a 'good' anti-racist education. The primary classroom presents the teacher and children with the opportunity to create an appropriate and anti-racist context through agreed 'rules' about acceptable and unacceptable names for people, about respect for others, about codes of interpersonal behaviour, about racial, gender or class stereotyping and about bases for challenging unacceptable behaviour. The primary classroom also provides tremendous scope for the creation of a space that is itself anti-racist in its expression, not simply by the use of positive images and messages but messages that challenge injustice and oppression. The display of anti-racist posters, prints, photographs and exemplars of children's work and such like could be particularly effective if they form part of a classroom topic. For example, one of the recent pop tunes in the top twenty is the record *Free Nelson Mandela*, for which there is an accompanying promotional sticker. Both record and sticker could be used in a positive way in the classroom to highlight and raise for discussion issues of racism and the struggle against it. Children could then be encouraged into positive action like letters of support and other forms of support to the family of Mandela, also other people involved in the struggle. They could be encouraged to engage in a whole range of connected activities.

This type of work could also be used as a basis for making the logical links between South African forms of racism and racism in Europe, including Britain. No doubt, similar examples could be found that might point to and start from national and local events and issues.

Primary teachers can also have relevant 'non-racist' and 'anti-racist material available in the classroom as they do with materials on other issues.

The Secondary Classroom

The secondary classroom is different to the primary one but holds similar possibilities in terms of the form rooms, year rooms and/or houserooms. It also carries the possibility of more widely-based displays, artefacts and groundrules.

It becomes obvious that beyond the whole school attempts a large part of the responsibility setting the context would be with year heads, form tutors, pastoral staff and the like, though each teacher must be responsible for context in terms of 'ground rules', for behaviour and for challenging expressions of racism which should be done with the students rather than be handed down. The rest of the work, it would seem, lies in the hands of subject teachers, through the curriculum and pedagogy developed and used.

Curriculum

It should be clear from my argument so far that, alongside the deconstruction of the racist curriculum, teachers have to be engaged in the reconstruction of an anti-racist curriculum. What then should the guidelines be for doing this and what would the product be?

One acknowledges that there are a range of shifting definitions and explanations of what comprises the curriculum. However, suffice it to say that here one is talking about syllabus content, materials and the structured and unstructured/planned and unplanned experiences of pupils. I have already implicitly and, to some degree, explicitly expressed what guidelines the teacher should take to the construction of an anti-racist curriculum, particularly in the section of the chapter 'Dismantling and combating racism in education'. However, it is important to an anti-racist book to make those guidelines explicit, though I am loathe for this book to appear to be prescriptive when its intention is simply to be illuminative.

Syllabus Content

In selecting the new or restructured syllabus content, it would seem that there are a number of questions that teachers need to ask themselves.

(i) Does this syllabus represent a global view? And does it open up opportunities for the development of a global analysis of local and national events?

(ii) Does it relate to the children's experience in any way?

(iii) Does it offer an interactive an dynamic approach to phenomena?

(iv) Does it acknowledge the impact of the 'domains' (figure 6) on the spheres of interaction and influence?

(v) Does it challenge racially defined phenomena and phenomena that seek to perpetuate the dominant power relations within society?

(vi) Does it open up the opportunity for pupils' critical engagement with the subject matter?

(vii) Will it help to further stimulate pupils' critical powers?

(viii) Does it provide the opportunity for pupils to extrapolate ways of challenging bias, racism, sexism, class domination and other forms of oppression?

(ix) Does it address itself specifically to any, all or some of the 'building' blocks of racism and other forms of oppression?

(x) Does it positively acknowledge the history of struggle of Black and other oppressed people against their oppression?

(xi) Does it contribute towards the overall aims of equality, justice and emancipation?

(xii) Does it give validity and legitimacy to the knowledge, experience and language of the learners rather than operating of a predetermined notion of the nature of knowledge?

(xiii) Does it explicity acknowledge and identify the perspectives of the 'authors' of materials?

(xiv)   Does it acknowledge the contribution made by Black people to the country's history, culture and development?

(xv)   Does it leave room for change, adjustment and new questions?

With some more effort, one could probably carry on raising further questions to act as parameters for curriculum selection. However, one feels that these questions could form the basis of an approach to a curriculum development that liberates rather than one that closes off educational 'success' — in its broadest sense — from a large percentage of learners, or one that narrows the perceptions of learners to such an extent that they think that only their limited experience as a 'race', or culture, or ethnic group, is the alpha and omega of existence.[4]

Material

There is now being built up a wide range of anti-racist materials by various projects and groups. In many LEAs, there are curriculum development projects, though most of these are in London and the other Metropolitan areas. There is a need for more of these.

Of note are the ILEA *Primary Curriculum Development Project* and *Anti-Racist Strategies Team*. There are, of course, also other such units and initiatives, such as '*The Promotion of Racial Equality and Justice Project in Secondary Schools*', which is located in Birmingham with similar Department of Education and Science, Educational Support Grant (DES, ESG) projects in other parts of the country, like Manchester and Croydon. Most of these projects and units — some with the multicultural label but attempting to engage in serious anti-racist work — are working with classroom teachers to collaboratively develop new and appropriate material to aid and support a new and developing pedagogy.

These materials are being developed on the basis of their ability to support the aims and objectives of an anti-racist education in terms of their content, perspectives, omissions, ordering and use of positive image to bring about a just and liberating education. Therefore, teachers who are concerned about developing and generating new material should make links with such units. Where they do not exist, teachers need to make links within and outside the school with people working in the same field. In fact, this is a practice which I have observed has already begun to happen. If necessary and useful, these liaisons should be formalized so that they become a part of the 'normal' professional duties of teachers. This is especially useful when it is necessary to meet or plan during school time or to have the occasional day away from school for a collaborative seminar or workshop for materials.

These initiatives will often entail considerable struggle. Therefore, the teacher needs to, when and where appropriate, enlist the aid and support of sympathetic LEA officers, headteachers and other senior teachers.

Structured and Unstructured Experiences

It is difficult to speak in terms of ordering the unstructured experiences of students, except in terms of 'context', which I have discussed at length already. However, lest one should imagine that the unstructured experiences of students are all purely chance happenings, let me emphasize that the school as an experience and institution is, like the classroom, constructed. So, teachers are largely responsible — preferably with the students — for constructing the environment in which they act and with which they interact.

These unstructured experiences will, therefore, equally be influenced by what posters are up in the hallway or classroom and the images seen and the languages in which they are written as by their chance interactions with each other about the latest major event in the neighbourhood or in the national news. It is interesting that when children grow up and become professionals, like teachers, they go to conferences and such like and expect that the major learning will take place in the informal settings of the bar or the television room. Yet, teachers often underplay the importance of children's learning in unstructured and informal settings. In this lies not a criticism but a challenge to the teacher to try to not control, but utilize these settings to positive ends. For example, throwing out a pertinent and provocative question at the end of a lesson relevant to the next lesson, especially but not exclusively in the humanities and social sciences, for prior discussion by students in their free time. The structured experiences of the curriculum are contained within the plan and realization of the lesson. Therefore, it exists in the pedagogy itself.

Anti-racist Teaching as Oppositional Pedagogy

The whole field of pedagogy is itself problematic, but traditional conceptions of the pedagogic device have tended to portray it as *value free* and having to do merely with the 'science' of the best ways of transmitting knowledge. Within this formulation, knowledge was seen as a fixed commodity, which was itself value-free and free for the taking to all those who would accept and have the capacity to receive and retain it. Thus, pedagogy was seen as the system of facilitating the transmission of (or actually transmitting) knowledge to the learner.

More recent theories, while problematizing the nature of knowledge itself, have tended to portray the pedagogic device as value-free, though being capable of being appropriated by the 'oppressor' to maintain the exploitation of the 'oppressed', through assisting and ensuring the management of knowledge and control. Thus, the pedagogic device was seen as value-free but manipulable.

There is a third school of thought that articulates a case for examining the essential pedagogic device. It seems to me that this view ought to be explored further because it may well explain the perpetual reconstructuration of racist pedagogy. However, when I refer to anti-racism as oppositional pedagogy, I am starting from the position that though the experience of schooling is oppressive, it is a contestable space and a site of struggle. As Giroux (1983) puts it:

> While it is crucial to see schools as social sites in which the class, gender, and racial relationships that characterize the dominant society are roughly reproduced, it is equally important to make such an analysis function in the interest of developing alternative, pedagogical practices. The first step in developing such practices would be to focus on the relationship between school culture and the overt and covert dimensions of the curriculum, as well as on the contradictory, lived experiences that teachers and students bring to school on the other. It is in the relationship between school culture and contradictory lived experiences that teachers and students register the imprints and texture of domination and resistance. (p. 63)

Within my use of the concept and within my wider analysis, oppositional pedagogy is a theory and practice that premises itself on the notion of schooling as repressive and as serving to maintain the power structure *vis à vis* the social and racial status quo of schooling as well as in the wider social structure. Schooling, therefore, is seen as principally serving the ends of the powerful in society by maintaining their position of power through ideological induction into dominant norms and values of society, thus, helping to maintain the social/racial status quo. The school is also seen as having a reproductive function, even though the nature of the reproduction is itself a moot point.

Thus, schooling is characterized by conflict. This conflict is not a simple one but diverse and complex. There is a conflict between the ideological aims of schooling and educational goals. There is a conflict between stated 'learning objectives' and the 'learning' that takes place. There is a conflict between the cultural reality of the school, *ie.* the dominant 'school' culture as well as the culture of the teachers — and the cultural knowledge of the students. Above all, there is a conflict between the 'knowledge' of schooling and that of the pupils. In a racist society, these conflicts sharpen. In addition, there is the added conflict of racial myth and the social reality of those oppressed by racist ideology. There is 'built-in' conflict as well as the inevitable overt conflict whereby racially defined groups reject both their pejorative and negative ascription as well as the other realizations of their oppression. The latter constitutes anti-racist action for the racially oppressed pupils.

The tradition in education theory in this country has largely been one based on the depoliticization of schooling, whereby schooling was seen as instrumental, value-free and meritocratic. Thus, schooling was seen as preparing students for their place in society, while imparting to them 'a selection from the culture'. This would make sure that they had not only the knowledge and skills that would prepare them for work and/or further or higher education, but they would have the cultural knowledge which would enable them to fit into society.

In this approach to schooling there were a number of assumptions about both schooling itself and about society at large. Society was perceived as homogeneous and, if not homogeneous, at least showing a consensus of both cultural knowledge and educational aims. However, as I have highlighted, the education in this country has operated almost uniformly to ensure that a certain group 'succeeds' in education whereas other groups have almost consistently 'failed'.

As we have also noted from our earlier deliberations, the privileged group has largely been White middle-class males whereas the 'deprived' groups have tended to be a various cross-section of the oppressed working-class and latterly Black groups. So, extrapolating from our earlier analysis, we note that there has historically been a tradition of disenfranchisement whereby the socially oppressed groups have also been the educationally repressed.

By the same token, and more specifically, the racially oppressed groups in society have also been the educationally repressed. But let us return to the earlier question of the pedagogic device.

It seems to me that certain teaching styles and learning processes lend themselves best to the anti-racist education based on the lines adumbrated in this book. For example, it seems that the didactic/lecturing style has certain inbuilt problems in that it straight off establishes the distinction between the teacher and the taught, from where the knowledge is flowing and to whom, and between who is the expert and who is not.

At the other end of the spectrum there is the learner-centred (child-centred) approach to learning which has also been criticized as inimical to the aims and intentions of anti-racist education. In that for one, it can lock the child firmly into his or her own racist knowledge, acquired outside the classroom which, when passing unchallenged, moves on to further stages of 'fixation'. This high degree of individuation is also criticized for hampering the development of the crucial social education of the child in general and the conceptual and cultural challenges that are posed by these social interchanges.

It seems to me that the teaching style or pedagogic device that recommends itself most strongly, regarding the realization of anti-racist teaching, is collaborative, group-centred learning. This does not deny any usefulness for other devices but rather serves to highlight the numerous benefits obtaining from the latterly mentioned approach to teaching and learning. This group-centred, collaborative approach to learning is, at the very base, a broadly accepted and agreed means of effective mixed ability teaching, whereby members of the group can learn from each other not only the subject matter but of the 'real life' knowledge of themselves and their counterparts as they apply to the lesson in hand. This learning approach also encourages interaction between pupils both in the classroom and outside which opens the door to a cultural education that is done through the lived experiences. Thus, given the right stimulation, pupils can be encouraged to learn respect for each other, which, when extrapolated, can be 'translated' into empathy.

This pedagogic device seems also to be an appropriate base from which to encourage student research — particularly in groups whereby each pupil within the group can research a particular aspect of the subject concerned. This could be tailored to interests and the bed of knowledge pupils might already have on the subject. This process develops in the learners the collaborative and democratic skills of listening, negotiating, compromising. Through this device, the pupil is probably freer to question the teacher and others. Yet this questioning can be refined through interactions with peers. Through the absence of both 'whole class' and 'individual only' pressure, pupils can, in their groups, develop their critical powers crucial to anti-racist education or any other emancipatory education. Within this approach, the teacher is cast more in the role of consultant, arbiter, facilitator, agent provacateur and sometimes archivist or methodologist.

Of course, my own experience and obervations of teaching/learning situations unequivocally suggest that one pedagogic approach throughout the term, or even throughout the lesson, can be ineffective and, therefore, counter-productive. Therefore, it behoves the anti-racist teacher to always bear in mind his/her anti-racist principles alongside the broader educational goals and learning objectives in the preparation of an anti-racist curriculum or in the execution of an anti-racist lesson.

The fourth and final chapter of this book therefore seeks to explore through the observations and, where possible or desired, the participation of the author in a series of anti-racist lessons in some primary and ssecondary schools.

Notes

1 There is, as yet, very little work done on supplementary schooling in Britain. However, there is record of some work being done. Some useful references in TOMLINSON (1983) *Ethnic Minorities in British Schools*, London, Heinemann Educational Books; and in CHRISTIE, (1983) unpublished thesis on supplementary schools, DEAPSIE, University of London Institute of Education.

2 *Through a Hundred Pairs of Eyes* is a programme of trigger incidents, on video, on racism in organizations. This is accompanied by a comprehensive guide on anti-racism in organization. Produced by the Centre for Staff Development in Higher Education, University of London Institute of Education.

3 The work of RUTH BENEDICT, STEVEN ROSE and others form a useful basis for challenging the very concept of race, *vis à vis* phenotypical variation.

4 There is a growing literature, especially in relation to feminist, critique, but also anti-racist critique, which problematizes the whole notion of child/learner-centred education.

4   Observing Anti-racist Teaching

Without much preamble, let us examine a series of lessons which are recounted in the context of certain relevant details about the schools, the education authorities concerned (where relevant), the department concerned, the curriculum, the pedagogic approach, the class teacher and the lesson itself.

All of the teachers and schools were chosen on the recommendation of advisory colleagues who were constantly in touch with schools in the LEAs and, to varying degrees, with individual teachers, especially in connection with the issues being raised in this book. The specifications of the request from me were that all of the teachers recommended should espouse an anti-racist stance in their teaching regardless of the state of development of their practice along these lines and that I should be able to see a 'normal' lesson and be able to speak to them afterwards and discuss it with them. Where possible, informal discussions would be held with the pupils.

From my observations, it would seem that some of the teachers observed were themselves not versed in the theoretical distinctions between multiculturalism and anti-racism. In one case, it is doubtful whether either issue had been raised in the theory or classroom practice of the teacher concerned.

The attempt of this chapter is to evaluate the lessons in terms of the overall aims of the school, the aims of the teacher concerned and in terms of the aims and guidelines discussed in previous chapters of this book. All the schools are identified by 'primary' or 'secondary' plus a letter of the alphabet as a matter of convenience and as a means of maintaining the anonymity of the schools concerned. Similarly, the teachers are given pseudonyms. I begin by looking at two of the primary schools visited and then by looking at the secondary schools.

This chapter signals the pursuit of the development of 'good' anti-racist practice and views all the lessons as giving insights into what this might constitute, given the peculiarities of specific schools and the idiosyncratic styles of individual teachers who draw on a limitless range of teaching styles, skills, materials and insights and use them in a unique way.

However, this privilege of being able to view teachers in action is both useful and essential for the important and difficult task of developing an effective and useful oppositional pedagogy of anti-racism. This is why there was a conscious attempt on my part to try and observe lessons done by teachers who were not necessarily members of prominent or popularly known groups of professed 'anti-racist' teachers. On the contrary, I specifically attempted to find some of the 'ordinary' teachers in 'ordinary' classrooms who had begun to come to the conclusion that the way forward for British education was through anti-racism. Within this attempt to develop a good anti-racist practice, some of the teachers had aligned themselves with other teachers trying to achieve the same goals in their teaching.

The lessons cover a range of subjects/curriculum areas which are by no means exhaustive but go some way towards showing that anti-racism is not confined to certain subject areas but can and must be applied to all curriculum areas in the context of the school as a whole.

Primary Observations

Primary School 'A'

Primary school 'A' is a school situated in a Greater London borough. It was founded in the late nineteenth century to provide a primary education for the residents of the new houses built for people who had moved from London. This school has had a chequered history of name changes and closures and the significant addition of an infant block in the late 1960s. There are some ten classes, including the nursery and reception classes, which cater for about 260 children. The current nursery unit was opened in 1980 and has some forty part-time places, twenty morning places and twenty afternoon places. Some full-time places are possible.

In the school handbook for parents there is an official stated position which includes three important statements for our interest. *Inter alia*, it is asserted that every child would be encouraged to develop to the utmost their own interest and ability. It is also clearly stated that there would be an effort on the part of the school to make sure that the nursery reflects the many different races and cultures represented by the children. Thirdly, there is a clear statement of the welcome awaiting visitors, including parents, child-minders and guardians.

The school is about one-third Black (Asian and Afro-Caribbean) and draws the majority of its pupils from the local housing estates. It has a high proportion of working class pupils, many of whom are from one-parent families.

The curriculum

Primary school 'A' stresses the importance of the acquisition of the basic skills by pupils but not at the expense of the other aspects of the child's education. They also state categorically that: 'In all our work, we try to remember that we are a multiethnic school with children of all colours and many creeds'.

One of the school's attempts to address this issue was the withdrawal of 'racist' and 'sexist' books from the library. All of these books were not removed from the library but placed together on one bookcase in the library. This was due to the fact that the headteacher (and, I suppose, other members of staff as well) felt that it was important that they should be available for reference and for historical record.

Another attempt to address this issue was the school's participation in a bilingual project which aimed to not only orally endorse bilingualism as an asset to children's educational experience, but to implement a programme of the use of bilingualism in the classroom as a vehicle for the education of bilingual pupils. This entailed the appointment of a bilingual (Gujerati/English) teacher whose appointment was preceded by discussions among the staff as a whole as to whether this was an educationally sound and proper idea and as to whether they would all be willing to support the teacher in her/his work. After some deliberation, the project was endorsed by teachers and soon a teacher, Ms. Harry, was appointed and was placed in the reception class with Ms. Lytton — who was already in post. They were appointed as co-workers on an equal basis to engage with each other in a team teaching situation. Children were not going to be withdrawn for language work but all of the language work was to be done in the classroom in the context of 'normal' teaching. Therefore, all children would be somewhat exposed to both English and Gujerati (to varying degrees). The bilingual teacher also had a certain amount of proficiency in Punjabi.

Language policy

The general approach to language in primary school 'A' was that it was of supreme importance in that:

Language not only plays an important part in the social and intellectual development of the young children, but that it also provides for school and adult life the most effective means of communication. (School Handbook)

This is, therefore, the context in which the bilingual project was located. The specific aims and objectives of this project as adumbrated by the two teachers involved were: (i) equality of opportunity; (ii) developing skills and talents that the children bring to school; and (iii) responding positively to a multicultural society.

The project was seen as having certain distinct benefits for all the children, the staff and the school at large, with special and specific benefits for bilingual children. It was seen that the school and staff stood to benefit in terms of the enhanced knowledge of, and relationship with, individual pupils through the positive recognition of the community and pupils' families as a resource. Teachers were also seen as standing to benefit by an increased 'awareness' of linguistic and cultural diversity. Through all these points, a firmer link is forged between school and community.

Bilingual children were seen as benefitting in terms of the 'support' for their learning deriving from the additional aids to their intellectual and cognitive development, and from the support for their own ethnicity. The project was seen as a support to family and community relationships and an extension to their 'vocational and life options'. The benefits in the project for all the children were seen in terms of support for their confidence in their individual language repertoires alongside increased language awareness.

There was also seen to be a complementary increase in the awareness and acceptance of cultural diversity, an increase in inter-group communication. Ultimately, the project was seen as a contribution to combating racism.

The class

In visiting this class, my intention was to find out a number of things. Firstly and foremost, if there was an anti-racist philosophy in operation in the class and/or school, how did it relate to practice?

Proceeding out of that interest were a range of interests. Some of these were: What is the ethos of the classroom? What is the 'ethnic/racial' composition of the class? What is the significance of this? What is the relationship between the teachers and between the teachers and pupils? What is the pedagogic style? How effective does it appear to be? As I have stated earlier, there were two teachers in this

150

reception class who, for the purpose of this book, I have referred to as Ms. Lytton and Ms. Harry. Ms. Lytton was White English; Ms. Harry was a Black teacher of East African Asian background and a fluent speaker of both English and Gujerati.

Having spent a brief initial part of my morning with the head-teacher, I went directly to the classroom of Ms. Lytton and Ms. Harry, who had just completed the very first part of the morning's activities — a story of *The Tiger Who Came to Tea*. The following is the plan of the lesson taught that morning.

Lesson Plan
Age Range: 4–5 years old
Time: 1 hour

Aim of the Lesson

1   To familiarize the pupils with the story *The Tiger Who Came to Tea* by Judith Kerr. Also, to enrich their vocabulary with new words and encourage their oral/aural and written abilities in English, Gujerati and Punjabi.
2   To show that this story could have taken place in any household, *ie.* Indian, Afro Caribbean, etc.
3   To show that in different races, different kinds of foods are eaten, *ie.* plantains, samosas, etc.
4   To talk about the role of mother and father at home: who does the cooking, etc.
5   Sequencing the story.

Materials
Magnetic board and drawn figures, story book, crayons, pencils, tape-recorder, headphones, plastercine, drawing and writing books.

Introduction
Read the story to the pupils *The Tiger Who Came to Tea*. Afterwards by asking questions, to find out what they have understood. Then the story is retold, this time with the help of the pupils and the magnetic board figures. Here pupil-teacher and pupil-pupil interaction should be encouraged.

Development
(four groups)
Integrated classroom organization.
Group 1:   Ask the children to draw a picture from any part of the story. Then they recap the story from the picture which the

teacher writes down. The children trace over and write underneath the teacher's writing.

Group 2: Children retell the story using magnetic figures.
Group 3: Relistening to the story from a tape recorder.
Group 4: Making tigers out of plasticine.

This lesson was located within the context of range of work and activities which were to be derived from the story. The following flow chart (see figure 7) is the flow chart from which the teachers were working.

My point of entry into the activities of the class was the unwinding period following the class, having listened to the story in the listening corner, where they had been seated on the 'big mat'. This 'unwinding' involved standing up and doing a series of exercises with the teachers. The teachers then allocated the children to various areas of the classroom, reminding them at the same time of the activities with which they were to be engaged. During this time, I was taken on a tour of the classroom at least twice (on the suggestion of each of the two teachers). The second tour was given by Gavin, who had had some problems earlier in the morning about not having his own way in the class and had to be taken out as a disciplinary measure.

Before being taken into the hall for the Friday (mid-morning) assembly, the children were recalled to the 'big mat' (the assembly area where they all sit on a large carpet on the floor). This was done in an orderly fashion, table by table, with a high degree of cooperation by the pupils. Pupils were then taken through a series of activities by Ms. Harry which, it would seem, had the intention of effecting a calming down process and the learning or enforcing of the names of the parts of the body. These aims were applicable to all of the pupils but particularly to those pupils who had less of a grasp of English. One example of a relevant bilingual exchange is the following: having led in the identification and naming of parts of the body:

Ms. Harry: OK, you're tapping your shoulders. Now, I'm not going to show you, you're going to show me how to do it. Touch your thighs.
(The teacher then turns and addresses Nazaleen in Gujerati.)
Ms. Harry: 'Ah, head ... eyebrows ... (Nazleen disregards instructions so teacher addresses her) Nazaleen! ... eyebrows ... (Teacher touches her eyebrows. Nazleen responds) You got it ... now cheeks.

Figure 7

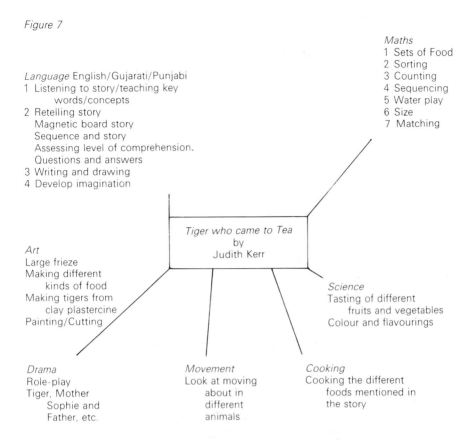

Maths
1 Sets of Food
2 Sorting
3 Counting
4 Sequencing
5 Water play
6 Size
7 Matching

Language English/Gujarati/Punjabi
1 Listening to story/teaching key
   words/concepts
2 Retelling story
   Magnetic board story
   Sequence and story
   Assessing level of comprehension.
   Questions and answers
3 Writing and drawing
4 Develop imagination

Tiger who came to Tea
by
Judith Kerr

Art
Large frieze
Making different
   kinds of food
Making tigers from
   clay plastercine
Painting/Cutting

Science
Tasting of different
   fruits and vegetables
Colour and flavourings

Drama
Role-play
Tiger, Mother
   Sophie and
   Father, etc.

Movement
Look at moving
   about in
   different
   animals

Cooking
Cooking the different
   foods mentioned in
   the story

In this exchange, the teacher, as a class teacher with a 'normal' role in the class, is using her bilingual skill as a 'normal' part of her teaching which the children all take in their stride. (Consequently, there is no strangeness for the rest of the children in hearing other languages, nor is there any feeling of deficiency on the part of Nazleen. In fact, if anything, there is probably a tendency on the part of Nazleen to expect bilingualism of her 'other' contacts within the classroom or school.

In this context, it is also acceptable for the other Gujerati-speaking children to chat with Nazleen and among themselves. Thus, they are not impeded but sped into an acceptable and reasonable level of competence in their heritage language. Alongside this heritage language development is a development of English and the bilingual skills of the pupils.

The pupils are then prepared for the Friday morning assembly and two children are selected to tell the school about their Tiger Book — the book made by the teachers (with the class) about *The Tiger Who Came to Tea* — the story which formed the basis of their current classroom activity. The children were then asked to form a queue by the door that leads into the hall for the Friday morning assembly — which, as I was told, is the assembly where classes share what they have been doing with the rest of the school.

After the assembly was breaktime, during which time I spoke to the teachers in the staff room. When they returned from assembly, the class returned to their activities with which they were engaged before the assembly and breaktime. At lunch-time, they were re-assembled on the big mat and, having received their free lunches, which most of them had where appropriate, they were dismissed one by one as they were collected by various relations and/or friends. This lunch-time collection of pupils and certain other complications were due to the industrial action being taken by the teachers' unions.

Over this period of observation, there were a number of other important points of note, some which I raise in my 'comment' on both primary schools at the end of this section of the chapter.

Primary School 'B'

Primary school 'B' is located in the same borough as secondary school 'C' and is housed in a building that used to cater for some 800 primary pupils but caters now for less than half that amount due largely to the reduction in this age group (4–11) of pupils in the area.

It is a county junior mixed day school and led by a Black headteacher who is now increasingly well-known for his energetic and effervescent commitment to multiculturalism. The school seemed predominantly White, with a percentage of Black pupils. Among the aims of this school are the following:

(i)   to help pupils to understand that we are a part of a multicultural, multiracial society;

(ii)   to give equal curricular opportunity to both boys and girls;

(iii) to extend children's knowledge of themselves and the world in which they live;

(iv) to help children to observe, reason and develop lively and enquiring minds. To foster their ability to question and argue rationally, and then be able to communicate these observations and opinions verbally or in writing to their peers and parents;

(v)   to help children to understand the world in which they live and interdependence of individuals, groups and nations.

The curriculum

The school acknowledges that the content of the curriculum provides both a vehicle for learning as well as a body of knowledge which are considered important for children to acquire. However, they also stress the importance of developing and using skills across the curriculum, despite the convenience of 'subject areas'.

Like primary school 'A', primary school 'B' stresses both the importance of the basics — literacy and numeracy. Again, language is given a position of priority in the curriculum and language support is given by language specialists. With reference to bilingual pupils, the school's handbook for parents states:

> The special needs of these children for whom English is a second language are fostered by a teacher attached to the Language Resource Centre.

The school has a well-resourced library (at least in quantity) from among which the racist and sexist books have been removed. But as the headteacher said, 'I don't throw them away. I like to keep them, so that in in-service staff development training I can say, "Look at these and draw out what is racist or sexist about them".' In some of the communal areas I visited there were some 'multiracial' displays depicting racial harmony, such as White and Black children holding hands and so on.

This school has also become renowned for its marvellous multicultural assemblies. These assemblies are described by the school as moral and religious education (like the rest of the curriculum) which aims to honour and respect the range of customs and beliefs reflected in the community. On the day I went to observe the first year lesson with Mr. Smith, there had been three headteachers from far afield visiting to experience the Diwali assembly of that morning.

The class

The class was made up of predominantly White pupils. Of the twenty-five or so, about four or five were Black-Afro Caribbean and Asian. There was one White pupil, Peter, who was constantly being scolded by the teacher but seemed impervious to the rebukings.

When I arrived in the class I was welcomed by the class teacher and invited to sit in the class and the teacher quickly went back to hearing his pupils read. (As he was to explain later on, there was never enough time to hear all the children read and that this was a class of prolific and quick readers.) The children in the class were welcoming in their manner, which they tried to keep private, some betraying it with a half smile or a giggle. This became obvious when at the end of the lesson, before the break, one Black girl returned after having almost completely left the room to offer me some of her freshly opened bag of crisps and one little White girl having asked whether I was a headmaster, was very interested in finding out who I was, what I did for a living, and whether I was going to return to be with them after the break.

The lesson

The lesson that I observed was a reading and writing lesson in this first year class taught by Mr. Smith. Mr. Smith had been a teacher in that school for some twelve years. He was very experienced, very authoritative and had an efficient air about him. I later found out that Mr. Smith had never taught a first year class up until that academic year and that was his first term. (He had mainly taught the third and fourth years.)

While the children were busy working on their handwriting, working on both lower and upper case letters, Mr. Smith was listening to the individual children read, occasionally disturbed by having to stop to mark and comment on the written work, which was being presented as the children finished.

The class was seated primarily in groups where four or five desks were put together and Mr. Smith was sitting at the back of the class listening to their reading and marking their written work. Occasionally when there was a teaching point, Mr. Smith would call for the attention of the class and would highlight the important point or the recurrent error.

Mr. Smith's pedagogic style was fairly 'traditional' in being stern, apparently unfriendly and authoritative. Therefore, despite the group seating arrangement, there didn't seem to be much encouragement of pupil/pupil interactions beyond the perfunctory. Mr. Smith was a 'good', traditional teacher who had a perpetual sense of how attentive to their work his pupils were being. He picked up very well on general teaching points and delivered his ideas or comments with absolute clarity. Yet the pedagogic style employed in the classroom in this lesson showed little evidence of encouraging critical 'lively and enquiring' minds.

Because of the nature of the lesson, one had ample time to observe more of the context of the learning that was taking place. Besides the fact that there was little apparent rapport between the pupils and the teacher, there was also very little evidence in the reading or the displays of the 'multicultural-multiracial' society mentioned in the aims of the school. The only such evidence was the number of drawings of dragons from a Chinese folk tale which had been done in class earlier in the term.

This class was very regimented and the teacher seemed not to be satisfied with less than near to absolute silence. The expectations of the teacher regarding minimal interactions between pupils seemed to run counter to the seating arrangements. The seating arrangement of the class seemed as if it would be more appropriate to critical engagement and cooperation than the highly individualized ethos being generated in this classroom. In fact, at the start of break time, there was one little lad who just sat there and carried on working. When I asked him why he was not going out, he stated that it was because he had been to the toilet during the lesson. Apparently, if a child had to go to the toilet during classtime, he or she was not allowed out at break time. There was also a very strict rule about re-entering the classroom at break time. This was firmly enforced when one child tried to return to the classroom to the snack she had left in her desk.

Comment: Primary Schools 'A' and 'B'

It seems sensible and useful to look at these two schools alongside each other even though the experiences are not exactly comparable. Both schools were recommended to me by advisers working in the respective areas who were concerned with the issues being raised in this chapter. The advisers and the respective headteachers were asked for teachers who espouse an anti-racist practice and who were considered to be engaged in 'good' practice.

In school 'A', there was a White female headteacher who had been involved in an anti-sexist project as well. She articulated a clear anti-racist standpoint and was seeking the means and the advice of how to implement an anti-racist curriculum while engaging her staff both in the discussion and the practice of anti-racism. School 'B' was the responsibility of a Black male headteacher who did not speak the specific language of anti-racism as such nor did he seem to be seeking actively to implement an explicit anti-racist practice as such. Of course, he had an experience of racism and had a sense of what it was to combat it on a personal or even political level outside the school and, at an administrative level, in the interface between the school and the educational bureaucracy and the wider community. Yet, somehow, this did not seem to translate itself into the process of schooling. Instead, there seemed to be an enthusiastic multicultural approach in operation.

The ethos of both schools were 'parent-friendly' and the relationship between both the headteachers and their staff seemed very good, though qualitatively different. School 'A' described itself as not 'traditional' and not 'progressive'. The children wore uniforms but the teachers all referred to each other by their first names, including the headteacher. In school 'B', there was no clear statement on this specific issue. The children wore no uniforms but their relationship with staff seemed much more formal.

The important issue for this chapter is the fact that, in two very different situations, attempts were being made to develop a new pedagogy. The question is what are the parameters to be used in evaluating the efficacy of the changes in terms of achieving the goal of an anti-racist education? Both schools stress the importance of the acquisition by pupils of the basics in education. Also, both schools seem to rate highly the utmost development of the interests and abilities of pupils. Both of these primary schools also tacitly value the contribution that could be made by parents in general and in their own ways are involved in the attempt to positively include the experiences, cultures and languages of the community at large. In both cases, these aims and objectives are aided by headteachers who, in their own understanding and conceptualization of the issues at stake, are committed to positive action. However, in school 'A', judging simply by my observations, there seems to have been a greater filtering down of commitment and a more closely focussed stance in the work of the classroom. Also, in terms of the broad guidelines adumbrated in chapter 3. The reception class of school 'A' seemed to be more geared up with such building blocks of anti-racism as the collaborative engagement of the pupils in independent, interdependent and critical work which involves not only themselves but their space.

Neither primary school 'A' nor primary school 'B' had a declared anti-racist policy statement. And though there were more explicit statements in the case of school 'A', what we can observe is a case of two schools which are both involved in an attempt to develop a new pedagogy. I would think that the success of these attempts would depend on a range of things, the least of which is not the political will and the professional commitment to positive change along the lines put forward in chapter 3.

Secondary 'Subject' Teaching

Secondary School 'A'

Secondary school 'A' is a mixed comprehensive Church of England school in an Inner London borough. It is located in the midst of a largely working class area and is surrounded by council housing (tower blocks and terraced houses) and a lesser degree of privately-owned homes.

Its student body is made up of a broad mixture of students of varied class and ethnic backgrounds, though the students are primarily working class. About 63 per cent of the student body is Black — the majority of those being Afro Caribbean. At the time of visiting the school it was involved in the process of rethinking its aims and objectives which were still at the discussion stage.

This discussion was being based on the premise of the accepted aims of the school, as agreed by the founding headmaster and the governors. These aims were:

(i)   To establish an accepting community on the model of Christ's teaching and witness for the education of children and young people so as to prepare them for life in society, not only as it is but as it should be.

(ii) To develop this community in order to exploit the personal attitudes, skills and interests of all its members so that each may understand and work in harmony with as great a variety of other people as they may encounter in the community in which they may live.

These two basic aims were seen by the working party (set up to prepare the paper on the aims and objectives of the school) as leading to a variety of objectives under a range of headings. These headings were seen as needing to range from the general to the specific and including headings such as academic, pastoral, general.

The following were the objectives under discussion:

(i)   To ensure that the move from primary to secondary school, from third to fourth year and from fifth to sixth year, further education or a career are as painless as possible and that pupils have adequate counselling on these changes.

(ii)   To consult the pupils about all aspects of school life through the lower and upper school councils.

(iii) To encourage and foster within the pupils a respect for others' opinions on religion, music, art, etc. through the academic work of the school.

(iv)   To encourage pupils to excel at their individual skills, whether this be musical, dramatic, artistic, sporting or academic and to give opportunities throughout the school year for this excellence to be on display for parents, staff, fellow pupils, etc.

(v)   To maintain the system of rewards and punishments that are clear and understood by all (as outlined in the Staff Handbook.)

(vi) To be a school where praise is given fully to pupils and staff where it is felt desirable.

(vii) To make the system of staff consultation as set out in the Staff Handbook work.

(viii) To devise a comprehensive staff development programme which meets the professional and personal needs of all.

(ix) To make sure the special education needs of all pupils are met.

Academic Objectives

(i) To ensure that each pupil in the lower school has equal opportunity to follow the full range of courses available and is thus able to make a reasoned and informed choice at 14+.

(ii) To offer each student the opportunity of following their interests in the upper school whilst ensuring their choice of course does not become too narrow and limit later career and academic choices.

(iii) To provide a broad and adequate set of options for the upper school that allow for entry to further education and that pay tribute to the developments made to the curriculum over recent years.

(iv) To contribute fully to curriculum development in all subject areas.

(v) To increase all pupils' study skills.

Pastoral Objectives

(i) To teach in mixed-ability classes as much as possible while not limiting the brighter pupils and giving as such assistance to the less-able to achieve their full potential.

(ii) To try and keep much of the work-group as a form-group to encourage group identity and responsibility for the actions of one's peers.

(iii) To foster the ideals of Christianity through an organized and structured system of worship. This should, wherever possible, involve the pupils.

(iv) To encourage pupils to help others both outside the school and through work for care committees within the class group.

(v) To develop the social awareness and responsibility of pupils through the structured scheme of active tutorial work throughout the whole school range.

(vi) To ensure that religious education plays a part in the work

throughout the school although it may go by other names.
(vii)   To encourage pupils to respect all other pupils.
(viii) To encourage pupils to respect others' property and to have
a pride in their environment.

Among these aims and objectives, as can be seen, there were no specific references to race or racism. Neither was this so in any other part of this discussion document, though there were general references to respect for others and education for all.

The curriculum

From this context it was clear to see that the emphasis of religious education would be principally and conservatively Christian. And one could have reasonably assumed that this would be so to the exclusion of any consideration of notions of conflict or power in a stratified society. Instead, the emphasis would be harmony and individual righteous living.

Up to that point in the term, pupils had covered topics such as symbols of everyday life, early Christian symbols, symbolic costume, and had just ended in a half-term test of work done. In the second half of the term, these first year pupils were to embark on a project on 'sacred writings', as the syllabus read: 'to coincide with the presentation of *Good News Bibles* to all first years'. (*The Good News Bible* is a modern translation of the *Traditional Christian Bible.*)

The lesson

This lesson had two aims. One, to understand the nature, sequence and context of the books of the Bible and, two, to problematize and examine the creation and presentation of the images of Christ.

The classroom was set up in a formal traditional style of even rows of separate desks, all facing the front, where the teacher's desk was placed. The teacher sat at his desk, took the register and signalled for the lesson to begin. The lesson began with a brief recap of the previous lesson and commendations to some pupils for their work. The teacher then went into a review of the books of the Bible, noting with the children the sequence of the books, where they were located, the nature of the divisions between Old and New Testaments and the bases of the various sub-groupings within the two sections. The teaching style of this first part of the lesson was mainly formal and didactic. The teacher was imparting knowledge to the children who appeared quite keen to listen (having recently received their new Bibles). He did this in as interesting a manner as the particular pedagogic device allowed. Having completed this part of the lesson, the pupils were asked to turn their attention to a set of questions related to the second aim. The first question addressed to the class was: 'What do you think that Jesus looked like?' The responses of the children included statements like, 'A long beard', 'Long robes', 'He had a white robe on', which were all duly compiled on the blackboard and then discussed. The lesson then turned to creating a biographical profile of Jesus. The discussion of some of the names by which he was called produced a diversity of names, including Jah, which produced a little laughter among some in the class. This was noted by the teacher who intervened to endorse the authenticity of the title, both in terms of it being a name for God used by the Rastafarians as well as on the grounds of the Biblical reference to God as Jah in the Old Testament (*Psalm 68*).

There were several other questions about points like his nationality, country of birth and skin colour. One child insisted that Jesus was 'white' or 'pink' (using the teacher's term) in the midst of a class that said that they saw him as brown. This boy's reason was as follows:

Boy (White): Sir, you know those ... when um ... like coloured pictures, you never see him brown or tan.
Girl (Black): But they don't know what colour he is!
Boy I know ...
(general murmuring, including 'he could have been green', which of course provoked laughter)

At this point, the teacher intervenes: 'This is very important, listen please. Listen, please! ... Now! The person who said we don't know ... I think they're quite right. We don't know! Because in those days they hadn't any pictures, they had no videos, they had no TV ...'

In this interaction and the surrounding discussion the teacher takes a stand which challenges the 'normalized' belief of the pupils and presents one suggestion (based on circumstantial evidence) as to why the exact likeness of Jesus could not be known — no record. But it is not left there. He then poses a hypothetical question with which the pupils must engage.

Teacher: Now! if here I am, I'm saying they have new evidence that Jesus Christ had blue eyes, he had blond hair and also the complexion of his skin was white or pink. OK. Now you, as an intelligent RE student, would think that's rather strange.

Amidst hubbub, the teacher asks further questions about climate, geographical location, etc. and the students, with the teacher's help, come to the conclusion that Jesus's skin type had to be dark.

At this stage, four representations of Jesus are introduced. Childen are then asked to identify the country of origin of the artist that drew the pictures and to rate the pictures from one to ten according to how 'good' they thought the picture to be as a representation of Jesus.

Having had some time to engage in this exercise, during which time the teacher walked around the room giving individual attention to some pupils. While talking to some of the pupils myself, it was interesting to note, though not surprising, that most of the pupils found the representations strange. A large percentage of them successfully recognized the origins of the artist but found it difficult to note the drawings, except in terms of how clearly drawn they were.

The drawing the students found most difficult to accept was the Indian drawing which most of them thought to be the least Christ-like.

In summing up this activity, the teacher made the following observation:

> *Teacher*:   Now, if you're an Indian artist and you're going to draw a picture of Christ . . .' (pause to deal with disciplinary matter) 'If I were an Indian artist, that is exactly what I would have done — I'll tell you why. Because being an Indian, I would want to let Jesus be seen to be to looking like myself or my own people . . .'

In this way, the teacher seems to be making a step further on from the issue of the European representation of a European Christ. He in fact is seen to be making the case for alternative representations of Christ in contemporary Britain and the case for the relevance of religion to people not only cerebrally or spiritually but in relation to their social reality.

Observations

In this first year lesson, the teacher can be seen to be doing a number of things. At one level he is challenging the perceptions of the image of Christ into which the pupils had been socialized. But he does not leave it there. He presents a range of alternatives accompanied by an explanation of the rationalization which could be seen as implicit in those specific expressions. He is, therefore, involved in both the deconstruction and the reconstruction of the 'knowledge' to be validated by society and school.

The responses of the children to this series of experiences are characterized by ambivalence. On the one hand, they accept by and large that Jesus could not really be 'White' or 'Pink' but 'Brown', yet they reacted strongly against non-European representations of Christ because they do *not* match up to the representations of Christ to which they had become accustomed. There was a marked difference in the atmosphere in the class between the first half of the lesson and the seccond half. When the teacher was employing a predominantly didactic teaching style which was based on his input and a limited amount of response from them, they were all appreciably quiet and attentive. In fact, the first half of the lesson really challenged nothing for them. It presented them with a set of facts of which they were expected to take note and which they would either commit to memory or forget, as the case might be. Yet they seemed particularly engrossed and committed to this activity. In the second half of the lesson where they were being required to think and answer questions of fact, of deduction and inference as well as of extrapolation, they were both stimulated and distracted. So, at this stage, the teacher had a greater degree of 'discipline' problems. These 'discipline' problems which emerged seemed, to me, to have to do with an apparent lack of familiarity with certain modes of learning and classroom interaction, though my presence as an observer might have also contributed to it.

In fact, these 'discipline' problems, apart from the noise occasionally peaking to unacceptable levels, did not really exist. What seemed to me to be an important omission, at this stage particularly, was the possibility for the pupils to interact and to discuss the questions in smaller groups, rather than sitting in rows as a class facing front. The need for pupils to learn the skills of critical engagement with issues was also highlighted in this lesson.

This was a very positive anti-racist lesson, both in its intentions and realizations. The fact that it was being taught by a Black anti-racist teacher was a positive advantage, because it provided the Black children in the class with some positive support for the vocal questioning they would probably do mentally anyway, but never voice. It also provided the White pupils with a positive teacher/pupil inter-ethnic experience which avoided any tendency towards an 'us looking at them' syndrome. Of course, the 'us' looking at them syndrome does not necessarily have to be a reality, even with a White teacher in a 'White' classroom.

The lesson also left open the important opportunity for a follow-up lesson or follow up lessons which deal with why, in a multiethnic society such as Britain is and why with the multiethnic nature of the Christian church in Britain, are representations of Christ predominantly and erroneously White European.

The further point to be made is the way in which the teacher in secondary school 'A' is attempting to interrupt or intervene into the sets of message and elements of knowledge which are *implicitly* being taught by school and society. However, the question that isn't raised is the question of the dominance of the Christian ethic in a subject area called religious education. No doubt, the raising of this question should be unavoidable in an ordinary state school if it were to have a syllabus and approach such as the one in this school. The issues in school 'A' are, however, quite different and, therefore highlight the need for specificity in the articulation and realization of anti-racist teaching. General principles are useful but ultimately what is important is how these guidelines are used, adopted and adapted to serve the specific context and the specific aims of the school, given that those aims are also anti-racist.

Secondary School 'B'

Secondary school 'B' is in an Inner London borough and, therefore, falls within the jurisdiction of the ILEA guidelines *vis à vis* race, sex and class. Yet, the specific history of this school's attempt to formulate a progressive and liberating school policy goes back a long way, as will become evident.

This secondary school, located in the area it is, draws its students from a wide range of homes in terms of race and class. It is a modern, purpose built school surrounded by lots of green and residential dwellings. Among the principles and aims of this school are the statements that all pupils must experience (not merely have access to) a broad and coherent breadth of curriculum and that this breadth of curriculum should be maintained as far as possible in years four and five and that the curriculum should help all pupils, whatever sex, racial origin, religion or social class 'to develop their talents to the full and to realize that they are equally valued'.

These aims drew attention to the need to address the 'hidden curriculum' and eventually led to a whole restructuring of the organization of the school. Therefore, a faculty system was created to breakdown the fourteen discrete subject departments and their concomitant distinctions, rivalries and compartmentalizations in the schooling and minds of pupils. Thus, three faculties were created alongside a learning support unit. The creation of this new system of faculties happened in the early eighties when the school was in the throes of reorganization and amalgamation and was seen as an asset to the creation and operationalization of the common core curriculum.

The faculty which I visited was the Faculty of Craft, Design and

Technology, Mathematics and Science. The Faculty had seven stated basic aims:

(i)   The pupils' psychological, emotional, moral and social development.

(ii)   The development of pupils' awareness and the awareness of the relevance of areas within the Faculty to society and the historical context of these areas.

(iii) Encouraging pupils to ask questions and search for their own answers.

(iv)   Encouraging and providing conditions through which a child may develop and continue to develop.

(v)   Helping pupils become interdependent and independent in their learning.

(vi)   Encouraging and supporting individual teachers to enable them to work towards the achievement of these aims.

(vii) To develop anti-sexist and anti-racist attitudes by both staff and students.

These aims had come a long way from the previous aims of the Science Department of the school preamalgamation which were nine in number and stressed the following:

(i)   Acquisition of experimental technique and quantifying technique and experience of these.

(ii)   Development of linguistic and numerical skills.

(iii)   Development of the students' natural curiosity and critical analysis with conclusions. Comprehension of the hypothetico-deductive model.

(iv)   Realization of the scope of science.

(v)   Showing the relevance of science to social, political, economical and environmental factors.

(vi)   Development of the ability to utilize sources of information.

(vii)   To enable students both to work confidently as an individual and as a cooperative member of a team.

(viii) To assess whether we are achieving the above aims.

(ix)   The development of science as an integrated study.

Comparing the two sets of aims it is clear to see that as laudable though the earlier aims were (in certain ways), the current aims are a clear improvement and unequivocally anti-racist. The challenge, therefore, that faced the staff of the Faculty, like the rest of the school, was how to implement these aims and the overall anti-racist policy of the school.

It was the intention of the Faculty that the new course offered for students would be integrated (no class subject boundaries), based on small group cooperative learning, will have anti-sexism and anti-racism as an integral part of it and will not be content led but offer students greater control over their own learning.

As part of the new initiative, a lecture theatre was converted into a resources area to which students could go to investigate or collect resources for use in their laboratories. The 'trial' period was seen by the member of staff interviewed to have worked reasonably well, though there had been a lot of doubts expressed by a number of the other teachers who seemed reluctant or afraid to take on the experiment in full. For example, the open door approach to teaching science in the fourth year, where students were able to move from room to room and to freely engage in whatever activity in which they had an interest and for which they could find the resources in the converted resources room, was seen as inappropriate and unacceptable by many teachers, probably because of the relative lack of control of staff over students, because of the additional strain put on materials as well as because of the 'team' approach adopted which many of the staff, apparently, found difficult. Also, it seems that because of insufficient materials, many pupils were reverting to the worksheet syndrome they understood so well.

The lesson which was observed was a fourth year lesson of the year following the initial experimental year. There had been a temporary halt on the practices encouraged in the previous year. It was also understood that the team-based work was not currently in operation.

The Lesson

When I made contact with the teacher in this school, Head of Faculty, and explained my purpose, he was very eager to facilitate the visit and to make links but was slightly reluctant in terms of the material that was currently in use and, due to the fact that what was currently being done was not seen as having arrived at the desired goal. However, we agreed that I would observe a lesson in terms of what it was as well as the curricular changes which were hopefully going to take place in the Faculty in the future. For this particular lesson, no lesson plan had been provided. It was the intention that students would to a large degree decide what their work for that afternoon would be from the range of work possible. Therefore, the teacher spent the first few minutes of the lesson providing the various groups in the classroom with worksheets. Because of the format of this learning situation, it is difficult to give a simple sequential account of the lesson. What is more useful is to give a description of how the learning was structured and the nature of the interaction between students and materials and between teacher and students.

This lesson was taking place in the sometime lecture theatre, sometime resources room, as well as in an adjoining room. The desks were set out in clusters or groups to facilitate independent and interdependent work. The groups of students seated at the desks were all working at different tasks through the use of worksheets. The worksheets within a particular group tended to be related to the same theme like, for example, reproduction. The members of the group in this case had worksheets on elements of that topic, like contraception, cloning, pregnancy, and abortion.

It appeared to me that, in this class, the majority of pupils were generally and genuinely engaging in the work for most of the lesson. In general terms, the girls seemed to be much more industrious than the boys. Overall, the students demonstrated a great deal of independence in their work by more or less 'getting on' with their work. It was also clear to me, from moving around the class, from group to group, that they were not afraid or ashamed to interact with each other about a problem that any of them might face. In fact, this was positively encouraged. The class teacher was also called upon intermittently to explain or give the background to a particular question or statement. There were, however, a few boys — particularly one — who seemed, mentally, relatively 'younger' than his peers; never really getting started and ending up doing something entirely different, like playing with a water tap in the adjoining room for most of the second half of the period. In this lesson there was no whole-class teaching but work with groups and with individuals. This, of course, kept the teacher quite busy for the major part of the lesson.

The teacher taking this class was the Head of Faculty who, as I have stated earlier, was somewhat concerned about a number of things regarding the work of the Faculty which impeded the speedy achievement of an operative anti-racist curriculum. It seemed that, for this teacher, anti-racist and anti-sexist education would be seen to thrive best within a progressive context. And by progressive here I would refer the reader to Bennett's (1976) typology (p. 38) which, with some modifications, applies directly to the approach used by this teacher. The modification would be to number seven on the table of 'Characteristics of progressive and traditional teachers' (p. 38) which in relation to progressive education states: 'Not too concerned with conventional academic standards'. The reason for the modification here is to do with the fact that the Faculty did consider academic success as important if teachers were not to deny their students the type of certification that they had acquired. However, the nature and process of that certification was open to debate.

These characteristics and the aims of the Department would be seen as the essential building blocks of an anti-racist education. There was also concern for the current contents of the curriculum which was largely traditional in that it did not include certain significant issues, like sexual orientation and important contemporary diseases, like Acquired-Immune Deficiency Syndrome (AIDS). And, therefore, was lacking in relevance.

Comment

Having observed this lesson in which a number of students worked consistently and in which a number of students almost consistently opted out, one tends to ask certain questions about the appropriateness of certain approaches or pedagogic devices to an effective anti-racist education.

This progressive pedagogy seemed to offer a number of distinct advantages in that it was geared to validate pupils' experience and to encourage independent thought and action alongside interdependence and cooperation. On the other hand, it seemed as if those students who did not have certain skills — some of which are learnt by middle class White children as part of their home socialization — would actually suffer because the teacher was spending too much time with certain more demanding students. There was also a question of how could the teacher ensure that the 'hidden curriculum' did not take over to the detriment of students from oppressed groups? The dependence of the approach on team involvement and commitment could also be seen as an ongoing impediment in that it is likely that the team, even with a committed head, may not work as a team.

There is also the larger question of to what extent can one Faculty — as big as that one was — work on its own in developing a new pedagogy without the substantial involvement of, and collaboration with, other faculties.

However, it would be very interesting to see the new course as it is developed in the Science and Technology Faculty of this school. If it meets the demands of the aims of this Department, it would be a significant step in the direction of anti-racist education. But a number of issues would have to be taken into consideration. Among these would be the role of the hidden curriculum in the prior adherence to 'progressive' pedagogy and connected to this would be the question whether 'progressive' in this context would necessarily mean oppositional or emancipatory.

Secondary School 'C'

Secondary school 'C' is a split (two) site comprehensive school which serves a wide catchment area. In fact, it has a reputation of drawing students from much further afield than would be expected because of its reputation for welcoming new bilingual students from abroad.

The school prides itself on its relationship with the community. This is exemplified by the headteacher's letter to the staff, which stated:

> Our links with the community have continued to strengthen and our work with primary schools in the neighbourhood will be extended in this coming year.

As stated in the staff handbook, the school sees itself as a major community resource, whose buildings and other resources are used during the day for school and in the evening for community adult education and leisure.

The school seems to operate a clear definition of who constitutes the 'community'. This is seen as the pupils in the first instance, their parents in the second and, then, the wider community of taxpayers to whom the school is also responsible and whose support it also needs.

The handbook makes a number of positive statements. Among them are the following two:

> We have, as a staff, to consider the ways in which we work which inform and involve the various parts of our 'community'.

and

> We are evolving school policies on matters that involve the school and are of great concern to large sections of our community — equal opportunities, bilingualism, curriculum/ community links and primary liaison.

The school has staff with specific responsibility for communication with the community and a community liaison, set up to provide a channel of communication between the wider community, parents and the school.

School policy

As yet, the school has no anti-racist policy though it has a multicultural working party that has been meeting for some time though, among other hiccups, the ongoing industrial action has been having its effect. Nevertheless as implied earlier, there is a positive approach to the 'new arrivals' of children from the Indian sub-continent coming to join their families. The approach of the school is that:

We, as a staff, must do all we can to help those children settle comfortably in their new home and to help them feel secure in what must be a very bewildering, possibly frightening, environment. We must be aware and sensitive to their needs.

Thus, the officially articulated positions of the school positively acknowledge the dietary requirements, dress requirements, religious needs and practices of this large number of largely Sylheti Muslim children from Bangladesh. The school also has a very positive policy on language, especially what they refer to as E2L (*ie*. English as a second language).

The borough in which this school is located has an 'English Language Resources Centre' with a team of specialist E2L teachers and an adviser who acts as the coordinator and overseer of the work of the Centre. Two teachers from this team were to be attached to 'C' school. The work of the E2L Department in the school is seen in terms of withdrawal/separate work and complementary work which involves work with bilingual pupils in the context of their subject-based work. The collaboration between the E2L Department and other departments is seen as of prime importance. In this context, the then currently serving E2L bilingual Bengali/English teacher from the mistitled 'English Language Resource Centre' agreed to contribute to the E2L work of the school on three bases. Firstly, to support the pupils' Bengali; secondly, to help to improve their knowledge, understanding and overall command of English; and, thirdly, that whatever is done would be relevant to the curriculum matter in hand.

But E2L is now not seen as the school's only concern regarding language. On the contrary, the school has had a standing Working Party on Bilingualism for the past two years which involves representatives from the English Department, the E2L Department, modern languages, language across the curriculum and the local English Language Resource Centre. The Curriculum Deputy and the Pastoral Deputy also sit on the Standing Working Party. The attitude that seems to be taken by the Working Party (certainly the member whom I interviewed) is that those concerned people involved in initiatives in this field, like that of anti-racism/multiculturalism, should be one of slow 'chipping away' rather than 'forceful' and 'revolutionary' militancy.

This is the backdrop of the development in the school of a language awareness course for first-year pupils. This development, I was told, was initially a difficult development with which to cope for many teachers in the modern languages department. Yet teachers were beginning to come to terms with it and even enjoy it in some cases as I was told by the teacher whom I interviewed, who also happened to be the teacher of the class I observed as well as the Head of Department. This teacher was somewhat surprised to have been recommended as an anti-racist teacher and certainly seemed not to have any sense of wearing the label, as it were. Yet, he admitted on reflection that what he was attempting to do could be described in those terms.

Having met this teacher at one site, I was driven over to the second site where the lesson I was to observe was taking place. The lesson was one in a unit of fifteen lessons of a 'Language awareness course' which had, as its aim, the intention 'to make pupils aware of the role played by English and other languages in their lives, to show them simply how languages develop and change, and how to go about using and learning them'.

The course, which was intended to last for half a term, had a syllabus of some ten topics but carried a rider which stated that it should be treated as a series of guidelines. This rider also encouraged teachers to be imaginative and encouraging and to capitalize on what the pupils offer. This syllabus included elements such as: What is language?; The history of languages; How languages are mixed together; The languages spoken in Britain, in the borough and in the schools (pupils' surveys included in the appendix); and such like. The lesson observed was a first-year lesson in the beginning of the second half of term. Like all other lessons done, this unit was meant to be informed by the five rules of thumb of the unit:

(i)   We are trying to *legitimize* pupils' languages and cultures, and to make them realize that their skills are acknowledged and valued by us, and can be useful to their educational development.

(ii)   We are trying to make pupils share their skills and, thus, become aware of each other's languages and cultures.

(iii)   We are saying things about the learning process and about the nature of the society in which they live.

(iv)   We are not just teaching facts: we are helping the pupils to think for themselves, to make choices and to develop their own skills and interests. We are also learning from the pupils.

(v)   The course will work if approached with energy and enthusiasm, and if an atmosphere is created in which pupils feel secure enough to share the secrets of their own languages and cultures.

The lesson

The lesson was begun with a call by the teacher for the various written examples of other languages. Very few children had brought any items with them. In fact, only two of the children of the eighteen present had brought something. One item was brought in by the only Afro-Caribbean boy in the class and one by the only Afro-Caribbean/English girl in the class. Their names were, let's say, Charles and Mary.

Mary had brought in an English/French dictionary which was acknowledged but not used. Charles had brought in an 'Instructions for use' leaflet which had some four to five languages on it. The teacher went from language to language on the leaflet which he read out aloud, asking pupils to attempt to identify the respective languages. In doing this, he sought to make the etymological and phonological connections by prompting the pupils to explore the sound and spelling connections between what was before them and what linguistic knowledge they already had. Together with the children, he explored the usefulness of such multilingual instructions and the reasons for the choice of languages on the leaflet. The children were mostly keen and interested and participated in the discussion.

One of the significant questions that was asked was why there was no Hindi, Bengali, Gujarati, etc. on the leaflet. The teacher suggested that it might be that the item was not sold in 'those countries', though he then contradicted himself by saying that maybe there should have been some of these languages on the leaflet. There was then a question from the teacher about one of the languages growing in popularity in commerical use. Eventually, the children came up with the language Arabic, with which there was quite wide concurrence. The explanation was the desire of the English for the Arabs to spend their money in Britain. Further discussion was generated around this topic. However, no direct connection was made between that and possible reasons why Hindi, Urdu and the other languages listed earlier were not getting the same prominence, especially since these languages were seen by the school as being not simply foreign languages but among the languages of multilingual Britain. [Note: The children of school had done a language project which demonstrated the wide range of languages in Britain. The school had also done a survey of the languages in the school (see appendix 2 and 3)]. The lesson then shifted to look at other matters which the teacher had prepared as a back-up in case the pupils had not brought in their examples of languages other than English.

The teacher started the second half of the lesson by projecting the list of statements below on the wall for pupil comment. The statements were exposed one by one (see appendix 4). After getting to number four, the teacher then said:

> *Teacher:* OK, Listen. We will go to one more (. . . Look, I'm
> going to put one more up. And . . . I'm going to ask for
> your reaction, Mr. Brandt, please, to the next one I'm
> going to put up. Just talking through the next one . . .
> OK (to pupils). So, I want you to listen to this.
> Listen what it says, it says.
> Black people are:
> (a) good dancers;
> (b) good at sport;
> (c) muggers;
> (d) happy to be unemployed.

The question was then turned over to me. I agreed to deal with that question only if I could also react to the four preceding statements as well which related to stereotypes about Jews, Americans, Irish and French people. This was agreed. Whilst I was speaking and discussing with the pupils, the teacher went off to find Mrs McNulty, the school secretary, who was Irish.

The teacher, on returning, picked up the notion of stereotype and noted that they may be 'bad' or 'good' but they are, however, still stereotypes which are used to describe and explain all people belonging to the particular group concerned. The Irish secretary was then invited to speak. She gave a very personal account of her experience of anti-Irish racism. This was moving in itself and it provided an example to pupils of how racism is experienced by recipients or victims of that racism. It also encouraged pupils to talk about their experience of racism and the ways in which people are identified as different in terms of colour, dress, religion, language, dialect or accent. The pupils came up with a range of stories about their and other people's experience of racism and with the range of pejorative and negative names by which they and other people had been called. After an informal 'break' in the classwork, pupils were asked to turn their minds to a third activity in which they were asked to listen to a tape that had been made in a similar class a year previous to that lesson.

The tape was introduced by the teacher. On this tape was the work of a pupil who had been asked to write something about her family in her home language. This 'Greek' girl wrote about her grandfather and it was read out in class (and taped), and was later discussed with the pupil, explaining in English what she had said in Greek. This led on to further discussion with the class about the languages spoken in the homes of the pupils. It became clear at this point that in many homes there were not one but two or three languages spoken.

This exercise provided an opening for two Bengali girls who were among the 'new arrivals' to speak aloud in the class about their own languages. This was the first time they had spoken aloud for the whole period of the double lesson. This contribution was encouraged by the teacher and, no doubt, was a positive support and encouragement for their continued attempt to increase the standard of their bilingualism.

Comment

This was an energetic, informally taught, lesson based on the pedagogic principles of participation, enquiry and discovery. The teacher used a range of resources and devices to promote a questioning approach by engaging with the students in a series of questions about what they thought they knew as well as what lay behind that perceived knowledge.

The students demonstrated not only a willingness but the distinct skills required to fully participate in the style of lesson being done.

They seemed to have an awareness of the ground rules of engaging in class discussion in the informal style in which the lesson was conducted. This discipline and attentiveness was by no means military but was adequately and largely considerate of each other and the teacher. There were contributions from a wide range of pupils, though not every single pupil. However, even for those pupils who had nothing to say during the lesson, there was a taciturn involvement. My two points of worry were the apparent invisibility of Caribbean-based creoles and African languages in the class discussions and the apparent exclusion of the two recently arrived Bengali girls, who seemed to be simply left to follow as best as they could in what was going on in the class discussion. Yet, having discussed the latter with the teacher after the lesson, some of my fears were allayed due to the fact of the wider programme of language support that they were receiving in the school. Thus, the conversations that the girls were having from time to time in the lesson were seen as a positive sign that they were using their first language to make sense of the linguistic interactions taking place in the classrooms.

Overall, this lesson demonstrated to me some of the things that could be done in developing an anti-racist practice in language teaching in general but in 'language awareness' type teaching in particular. It was also interesting viewing a teacher that had not concerned himself too much with the label he wore as a teacher *vis à vis* multiculturalism or anti-racism, but in fact was actively engaged in the development of a practice that not only heightened awareness but challenged racism in schooling.

Secondary School 'D'

This school is a voluntary-aided Church of England school, operating in an LEA with a policy on multiculturalism and which also provides some support services, through a multicultural adviser and a multicultural curriculum development team. This school was founded by the amalgamation on one site of two single sex schools — one boys' school and one girls' school — in an outer London borough.

The school covers a catchment that stretches beyond the boundaries of the borough and has the capacity to accommodate the educational needs of some 1100 pupils. In the school's handbook there are two sentences which allude to questions of equality. One sentence states that the school 'strives to serve, equally, the needs of girls and boys from a wide range of backgrounds, races and cultures'. The other sentence, which appears as a corollary to the general aims of the school, states that the school:

> Is committed to multicultural education, to equal opportunities and the eradication of sexism, and the policy statements on these important issues will be incorporated into the school aims when discussions and negotiations are complete.

Generally speaking, the ethos of the school and its handbook suggests a multiculturalist approach to society and education with a slightly more explicit commitment to 'eradicate sexism'. Thus, one of the stated aims of the curriculum is:

> to make pupils aware of the multiplicity of cultures in society and, thus, come to a fuller understanding of the world in which they live.

If the wider practice of the school in any real way reflects the concerns of the school's handbook, including its aims, it would seem that the school is beginning to create space for what I have termed the 'building blocks' of anti-racist teaching. The role of anti-racist teachers in this sort of setting should be to ensure that these 'building blocks' are not 'recolonized' and incorporated by racism but become levers for the development of anti-racist policy and practice.

The school has no anti-racist policy, though there is meant to be a working party which has had some difficulty in meeting due to the industrial action in schools.

Before describing and discussing the lesson which was observed in school 'D', let us look at the two immediately preceding lessons which these third-year students were required to participate in. Let us first look at their learning about *Nanny, A Maroon Leader of the First Part of the Eighteenth Century*, for which the teacher prepared the following handout.

We do not know exactly when Nanny was born, nor whether she was born in Africa or Jamaica. She was born in the late 1600s and died, an old woman, in the 1750s. Her parents were Ashanti, which means that they lived in the country now called Ghana.

Nanny was never a slave. She was a leader of the Maroons, the free black people who lived in Jamaica throughout the era of slavery. The British frequently tried to defeat and enslave the Maroons, but never succeeded.

Nanny was an obeah woman. This means that she was a wise woman who knew how to make medicines and put people into trances to help to cure illnesses. She could also make poisons and cast spells, which could be effective if the person attacked by the spell believed in its power. Nanny is supposed to have kept a huge cauldron boiling, without the use of fire, at the foot of a cliff. When curious British soldiers came to see this miracle, it is said that they fell into the cauldron and were suffocated. Once, to show her power, Nanny told fifty soldiers to load their guns and then to fire on her. Nanny folded back her hands and caught the fifty shots. This was called 'Nantucompong, Nanny takes her back to catch the balls.'

Nanny was the leader of the Maroons who lived at the place named after her, Nanny Town. The British founded Nanny Town in the early 1730s, early in the Maroon War which lasted throughout the 1730s. Nanny did not herself take part in the fighting, but she directed the guerilla campaigns of the Maroon defenders. She used an abeng to communicate with her soldiers from a distance. In 1737 Nanny took a solemn pledge that she and her people would fight the British to the death. Nanny's husband was a respected man, but he was a man of peace and took no part in the war. Nanny had no children but she was regarded as the mother of her people. Nanny always took especial care of the women and children amongst her people. During the war she had the women and children evacuated from Nanny Town, where it was unsafe, to a new settlement that came to be called New Nanny Town (later Moore Town).

The war eventually came to an end when Cudjoe, Nanny's

brother, made a peace treaty with the British in 1739. Nanny was furious when she heard of this, and she ordered the execution of the white soldier who had carried the news to her. But she had to reluctantly accept the terms of the peace treaty for her own people. As the men signed the truce, the women stood by, wearing round their ankles the teeth of white soldiers who had been killed in the war.

In 1740, over a year after the end of the war, the British agreed that 'Nanny and the people now residing with her and their heirs' owned 'a certain parcel of land (Moore Town) containing 500 acres in the parish of Portland'.

Nanny remained the respected leader of her people until her death about fifteen years later. She lies buried on a hill in Moore Town under a great mound marked by boulders, called Bump Grave. (Material prepared by teacher.)

This was followed up by the following work sheet.

NANNY
1 Do you believe the stories in the paragraph about obeah?
2 What do you think were the good and the bad features of Nanny's character?
3 Summarize Cudjoe's treaty with the British on the worksheet provided.
4 What did the Maroons gain by this treaty?
5 What did the Maroons lose by this treaty?
6 Why was Nanny angry that Cudjoe had made the treaty?
7 Why did Nanny agree to abide by the terms of the treaty?
8 Look at the picture illustrating the treaty. This picture was drawn in 1803. Is the picture fair and accurate?

The lesson directly preceding was one on *Cudjoe's Treaty with the British, which ended the First Maroon War, 1st March 1939*.

This lesson was followed by a discussion of the illustration on page 179.

The students all had to respond to the illustration and to say whether, and why, the photograph might be a racist one and how it could be improved or changed. This work had already been done by the pupils on the day of my visit and displayed in the classroom were their various attempts at redoing the illustration in a non-racist way. Their displayed attempts were interesting in terms of the various ways in which the pupils sought to produce a more 'fair' illustration.

A Picture Illustrating Cudjoe's Treaty with The British of 1739

The Picture was Drawn in 1803.

Most of the pupils whose work was displayed on the wall made the two men to be of the same height. A few kept them at the same relative heights but one student had actually reversed the 'height' relations. The comments of the teacher on all of the redone illustrations which kept the relative heights of the men the same as the original were interesting in their uniformity. That is, he questioned in each instance why the White man was so much taller and obviously erect and the Black man short and squat. Most of the pupils dressed the Englishman 'down' rather than dress Cudgoe 'up'. In fact, some of the pupils dressed Cudgoe in very up to date and 'trendy' type dress. In all of these drawings, both men were extending their hands in peace in an apparent attempt to show the event as a bilateral as opposed to a unilateral one. This is a brief sketch of the backdrop to the lesson observed.

The curriculum

The second and third-year history syllabus from which the lesson observed was derived is divided into twelve units, each lasting approximately half a term. For each unit, a common elements sheet, such as the one shown here, is filled out as a result of discussion in a Department meeting before the unit is taught, to establish those elements of the unit that will be explored by all classes. These elements are chosen from those detailed in this syllabus.

COMMON ELEMENTS   1985/1986

THIRD YEAR	UNIT 1	RACISM IN HISTORY
AIMS	1 3 8 2 5 9	
CONTENT	Maroons, Tacky's Rebellion, Map of Triangular Trade, King Pepple, Runaway Servants, The Somerset Case, Abolition of the Slave Trade and Slavery	
PRETEST	None	
KEY CONCEPTS	Negro Maroon Slave	Racism Primary Source Secondary Source
KEY THOUGHT SKILLS	Empathy Causation	Ability to distinguish between primary and secondary sources

KEY	Presentation of Exercise Book
COMMUNICATION	Map
SKILLS	Speech Display

UNIT TEST	Racism

SELF EVALUATION	None
EXERCISE	

The aims of the syllabus were to:

(i)   Give pupils an understanding of how the major forces that have shaped the twentieth century world developed since c.1000.

(ii)   Emphasize resistance by oppressed peoples, the role of women, and the achievements of Black people.

(iii)   Give pupils an understanding of the relationships between local, national and world themes in history.

(iv)   Give pupils the means to understand their own history.

(v)   Enable pupils to use a variety of sources of information.

(vi)   Give pupils an understanding of the nature of facts and of historical evidence.

(vii) To enable pupils to distinguish between fact and opinion and to recognise bias and propaganda.

(viii) Give pupils an understanding of narrative, causation and development over time.

(ix)   Enable pupils to see situations from the point of view of people in radically different circumstances.

(x)   Enable pupils to inform other people of their knowledge and understanding of history in a variety of ways.

(xi)   Enable pupils to assess their own progress in their history course.

(xii) Stimulate interest in history as a leisure pursuit.

Content

These aims were reflected in units that ranged from personal history to the question of the emergence of 'independent nations'. These twelve units spanned the two years and were namely: Personal history; The Normans; Medieval society; Travellers (1095–1550); London to the eighteenth century; Richard Hakluyt and the expansion of Tudor England; Racism in history; The French Revolution; The emergence of independent nations; British economic and social history (1750–1914); The History of the Borough (which was given up to the geography department); and Britain at the time of World War I.

The elements of these units were interesting in their composition. For example, the unit 'World War I' included three elements: (i) World War I; (ii) women in World War I; (iii) Black people in World War I. In this unit, for example, there was a conscious and marked attempt to raise questions here that might have (but should not have) been confined to the unit on racism. This unit is one of the more obvious examples of this.

The unit from which the lesson on Tacky's rebellion was from was the unit on racism in history, which included the following elements: Queen Nzinga; The Atlantic slave trade; The impact of the slave trade on West Africa; The Caribbean in the era of slavery; The end of the slave trade and slavery; Black people in Britain; South Africa. I was told that South Africa was particularly included to help students to examine the links between European and British racism, both historically and currently with the racist regime in South Africa.

Pretests

Some units are prefaced by a pretest, which is intended to establish a yardstick against which pupils' progress can later be measured through and the key features of the unit could be signalled.

Concepts

For each unit a number of key concepts is identified which it is hoped the pupils will understand by the end of the unit. These concepts are tested in the short questions section of the school examination.

Thought skills

The following are some of the 'thought skills' which were considered to be necessary to be developed in the history syllabus of this school: description; narrative; causation; development; change; empathy; nature of facts; evidence; ability to distinguish between primary and secondary sources; ability to distinguish between fact and opinion; recognition of bias and propaganda; analysis; generalization; comparison; relevance; synthesis; categorization; translation; articulation.

The following were the communication skills:

Presentation of exercise book: Contents Page

Page Numbering

Titles

Dates

Written answers to questions in full sentences without writing out questions.

Notes under subheadings
Essays in paragraphs
Pictures
Maps
Diagrams
Graphs
Oral answers to questions
Speech
Discussion
Debate
Display
Booklet
Computer
Project

Most units are concluded with a skills test, designed to assess the extent to which the pupils have mastered a particular skill.

In addition to the unit tests, some units feature a self-evaluation exercise in which pupils assess their own learning. The self-evaluation exercise might be continuous through the unit or discrete at the end of the unit.

The 'test' for the racism in history units was as follows:

1 What is Racism? (3 marks)
2 In what ways was the trans-Atlantic slave trade racist? (5 marks)
3 How can history teaching be racist? (2 marks)

The lesson

The lesson observed in school 'D' was a third year history lesson.

This lesson started with a few questions from teacher to pupils concerning the work from the last lesson. This lead straight into the teacher distributing a handout with the following text of *Tacky's Rebellion in Jamaica, 1760.*

> It arose at the instigation of a Koromantyn Negro of the name of Tacky, who had been a chief in Guinea, and it broke out on the Frontier plantation in St. Mary's parish, belonging to the late Ballard Beckford, and the adjoining estate of Trinity ... On those plantations were upwards of one hundred Gold Coast negroes newly imported, and I do not believe that an individual amongst them had received the least shadow of ill treatment from the time of their arrival there. Concerning those on the Trinity estate, I can pronounce of my own knowlege, that they

were under the government of an overseer of singular tenderness and humanity. His name was Abraham Fletcher; and let it be remembered, in justice even to the rebels, and as a lesson to other overseers, that his life was spared from respect to his virtues. The insurgents had heard of his character from the other Negroes, and suffered him to pass through them unmolested . .

Having collected themselves into a body about one o'clock in the morning, they proceeded to the fort at Port Maria, killed the sentinel, and provided themselves with as great a quantity of arms and ammunition as they could conveniently dispose of. Being by this time joined by a number of their countrymen from the neighbouring plantations, they marched up the high road that led to the interior parts of the country, carrying death and desolation as they went. At Ballard's Valley they surrounded the overseer's house about four in the morning, in which finding all the white servants in bed, they butchered every one of them in the most savage manner, and literally drank their blood mixed with rum. At Esher, and other estates, they exhibited the same tragedy; and then set fire to the buildings and canes. In one morning they murdered between thirty and forty Whites and Mulattoes, not sparing even infants at the breast, before their progress was stopped.

The Maroons were called upon, according to treaty, to co-operate in the suppression [of the rebels]. A party of them accordingly arrived at the scene of action, the second or third day after the rebellion had broken out. The whites had already defeated the insurgents, in a pitched battle, at Heywood Hall, killed eight or nine of their number, and driven the remainder into the woods. The Maroons were ordered to pursue them, and were promised a certain reward for each rebel they might kill or take prisoner. They accordingly pushed into the woods, and after rambling about for a day or two returned with a collection of human ears, which they pretended to have cut off from the heads of rebels which they had slain in battle, the particulars of which were minutely related. Their report was believed, and they received the money stipulated to be paid them; yet it was afterwards found that they had not killed a man; that no engagement had taken place; and that the ears which they had produced had been severed from the dead Negroes which had lain unburied at Heywood Hall.

A party of them, indeed, had afterwards the merit (a merit of which they loudly boasted) of killing the leader of the rebels.

He was a young Negro of the Koromantyn nation, named Tacky, and it was said has been of free condition, and even a chieftain, in Africa. This unfortunate man, having seen most of his companions slaughtered, was discovered wandering in the woods without arms or clothing, and was immediately pursued by the Maroons, in full cry. The chase was of no long duration; he was shot through the head; and it is painful to relate, but unquestionably true, that his savage pursuers, having decollated the body, in order to preserve the head as the trophy of victory, roasted and actually devoured the heart and entrails of the wretched victim.

It was thought necessary to make a few terrible examples of some of the most guilty. Of three who were clearly proved to have been concerned in the murders committed at Ballard's Valley, one was condemned to be burnt, and the other two to be hung up alive in irons, and left to perish in that dreadful situation. The wretch that was burnt was made to sit on the ground and his body, being chained to an iron stake, the fire was applied to his feet. He uttered not a groan, and saw his legs reduced to ashes with firmness and composure; after which, one of his arms by some means getting loose, he snatched a brand from the fire that was consuming him, and flung it in the face of the executioner. The two that were hung up alive were indulged, at their own request, with a hearty meal immediately before they were suspended on the gibbet, which was erected in the parade of the town of Kingston. From that time, until they expired, they never uttered the least complaint, except only of cold in the night, but diverted themselves all day long in discourse with their countrymen, who were permitted, very improperly, to surround the gibbet. On the seventh day a notion prevailed among the spectators, that one of them wished to communicate an important secret to his master, my near relation; who being in St. Mary's parish, the commanding officer sent for me. I endeavoured, by means of an interpreter, to let him know that I was present; but I could not understand what he said in return. I remember that both he and his fellow-sufferer laughed immoderately at something that occurred ... I know not what. The next morning one of them silently expired, as did the other on the morning of the ninth day.

Source: From teacher's own prepared material

The teacher read the text aloud with great clarity and with

explanatory breaks for the benefit of the class who paid rapt attention throughout the reading.

Mr. Porter, the teacher, took great pains to draw the attention of the pupils to the relationship between what they had done so far in the term, especially the last two lessons. Thus, he drew to the attention of the pupils the fact that *Tacky's Rebellion* in 1760 was taking place some twenty-one years after Cudjoe's Treaty and ten years after Nanny's death.

Though on the one hand the teacher's style could be described as didactic, on the other hand he was at pains to encourage criticism and thought. The whole lesson was punctuated with questions such as: 'Do you believe it? Do you think it's true? . . . think about it!' Thus, though on the one hand he was reading the text with great authority, he was *obviously* standing back from the material and inviting or rather encouraging the students to question and evaluate the matter presented. This, as he made clear later, served to help develop the students' ability to critically analyze historical statements and to separate 'fact' from 'fantasy', actual events from vague impressions, and objective truth (inasmuch as it exists) from biased and prejudicial pronouncements. He responded to one child's query about one facet of the story, 'you have to believe *something*, not everything'. No doubt, this might have raised a question for the students as to how does someone know what to believe and what not to. However, it would seem to me that that question was being answered through the very process that the pupils were being taken through in learning to ask themselves certain types of questions about the details of historical events.

During Mr. Porter's presentation of *Tacky's Rebellion*, there were occasional breaks for explanations of words, concepts or events or for highlighting questionable events. One of the questions that came from one of the students was, 'Who might have written the piece they were reading?' This question was deferred by the teacher since this was meant to be one of the questions in the exercise to follow.

It is interesting that afterwards, when Mr. Porter suggested that they should be able to work out who *she* was from the clues in the text, the entire class gasped and almost uniformly (but for a few) retorted, 'She?' I could only suppose that this was a sign of surprise at the gender of the writer in that most of them had been assuming that it had been written by a man.

The final part of the lesson was spent working on the worksheets, during which time the teacher and myself wandered around the class chatting to the pupils about the work that they were doing.

Comment

Judging from the conversation which I had with the teacher following the lesson, I would say that he felt that it had been successful, both in terms of the overall aim of the unit of the course as well as in terms of the specific aims of that particular lesson.

On my own part, I, too, felt it to be a success in a number of ways. At one level, it was dealing with some of the ways in which racism has historically been enacted in the Third World, especially the Caribbean in this case. But the focus of the lesson was not on British conquest or even British defeat, but on the struggles of the oppressed people — so, for example, the lesson observed was on *Tacky's Rebellion*. Of course, it is important to note that this course was begun with African people in their own homelands in pre-slavery society, thus seeking to establish that Black history did not begin in chains.

At the second level, the lesson dealt with the ways in which 'history' is written and transmitted in ways which reflect and often guarantee the prejudices, bias and, in this case (like others), racism.

Thirdly, the teacher managed to successfully combine an apparently didactic approach with group teaching in a mixed ability class. Thus, the interactions during the group-working time, both among the students and between students and teacher, were of crucial value and complementary to the beginning half of the lesson. Various members of groups could help each other and all could be helped by interactions with the teacher. This was done at the pupil's own place of work.

At a fourth level, not only did the pupils seem to enjoy the lesson but they were also making the connections between that lesson and the lessons that preceded. This, among others, was one of the demands of the accompanying worksheet. As can be seen, the range of questions drew on a range of skills and responses of the student, not just skills of comprehension, extrapolation or deduction but skills of critical and reflective analysis: the skills of some of the crucial building blocks of anti-racist teaching.

Of course, one must admit that the specific nature of certain curriculum areas lend to greater possibilities in certain areas and may be less in another. This is why it is subject specialists themselves who need to think about their own subject, their practice and the practice of others in the field in attempting to reevaluate and redevelop an anti-racist curriculum and anti-racist practice.

In this school, secondary school 'D', one has observed a very interesting example of the realization of anti-racist teaching whereby a department with a commitment to developing and enacting an anti-racist practice can within a school that still has not fully worked out its own position, neither in terms of policy or practice, on the issue. In this case, it seemed crucial that the Head of Department was himself committed to anti-racist teaching and an anti-racist curriculum. (It was the Head of Department whose lesson I saw). This made positive change easier. Yet there were elements which needed further work and development, like, to what extent did the teaching of Mr. Porter reflect the quality of teaching of the rest of his Department? To what extent was the work of this Department supported by work in other subject areas and other curriculum departments? To what extent can any single department make a significant difference to pupils' overall experience of schooling?

At the end of the day, it was still felt that the school could do much more. The formulation of an anti-racist policy was also seen as a welcome tool for urging and encouraging curriculum departments in the development of anti-racist curricula and anti-racist teaching.

In this chapter, I have outlined the aims, objectives, content and sequence of events in a series of lessons and classroom interactions observed in primary and secondary schools which have highlighted the difficulties as well as the positive possibilities for the implementation of anti-racist education through curriculum areas. The approach has been to try and locate the report of the observations against a backdrop of the sociogeographic setting and in the context of the education authority's initiatives. Beyond this context there has been no uniform format for looking at these lessons. Each lesson was both planned and executed in a specific and unique way and, therefore, had to be responded to in specific ways.

Some of the questions, however, that structured the observations were questions like — What was the overall aim of the lesson? What was its objective? What was the material used? What was the learning process constructed to achieve the aims and objectives? Was the lesson anti-racist? How did it contribute to the 'building blocks' of anti-racism? If so, how was the lesson challenging racism?

The potentials of both primary and secondary education have been highlighted, through the whole process of schooling and through curriculum subject areas. The curriculum subject areas covered do not necessarily suggest their particular suitability for challenging racism; rather, they are meant to serve as examples of the possibilities within all subject areas.

Conclusion

In this book, I've attempted to weave a simple path through a complicated tapestry of debates, phenomena, theories, policies and practices in the attempt to make clear the link between the theory of anti-racism and the developing practice of anti-racist teaching.

I have argued that in order to engage in the debate in curricula development, and in the development of positive pedagogic practices, teachers and everyone concerned with education must seek to inform themselves about the history, structure and culture of racism. I have suggested that the effective dismantling of racism is dependent on this understanding and this knowledge.

The nature of schooling is examined and it is purported that the education system is a crucial element of the activities of a state that is racist. Thus, the notion of racist education is introduced into the debate. This notion, it is argued, is crucial to the understanding of the remit and the responsibility of educationists to adopt an anti-racist stance in education.

From this backdrop, and in this context, I have observed the work of some 'ordinary' teachers in 'ordinary' classrooms in order to ascertain the nature of the developing pedagogy of anti-racism.

My observations in fact have exposed a very diverse practice in pursuit of diverse goals, all of which in the terms of the practitioners constitute anti-racist practice. This diverse practice and these diverse goals raise a range of questions for the practice and development of the pedagogy of anti-racism.

First of all, it highlights the need for the development of new materials for use in schools as in the case of the history teacher who found that the only way he could adequately do what he wanted to do was to write his own materials (some of which, one hopes, he will make more widely available).

Many of the texts currently used in classrooms are also in question since many of them either actively promote racism or operate to prop up both the ideology and practice of it. It is of positive value that some schools have withdrawn racist material and texts but this action must also be supported by the introduction of new anti-racist and 'non-racist' texts. But, of course, it is difficult, if not impossible, to discuss materials and texts without looking at syllabuses and examinations. Syllabuses and examinations are now too often used as an excuse for not making changes. But even if we assume the legitimacy of this excuse, it seems that it is then necessary for teachers and others involved in education and educational decision-making to begin to work towards and consolidate changes in both syllabuses and examinations.

Overall, the point that is being made is that the way to progress in the development and consolidation of anti-racist education is through action. By the concerted effort by those already committed to combating racism in education to generate new perspectives and new practices in pursuit of the goals of justice, equality of input, process and product, and emancipation. However, the observations suggest that sometimes, even when there is a professional and political will, teachers need the space and stimulation that in-service training provides, in order to clarify their perspectives and sharpen their practice in the attempt to develop and realize anti-racist teaching.

What is also apparent is that there is now an urgent need for extensive research into classroom processes in relation to anti-racist aims and objectives and for more curriculum development projects which engage with both educational practitioners and the community (particularly the Black community). In doing this, curriculum areas should be examined closely to see how they reflect and perpetuate racism. Alongside this new curricula will be developed.

Whatever happens, it seems clear that any change made in the teacher's practice in the classroom must, of necessity, be in the context of the overall policy and practice of the school, in the context of policies and practices of education authorities and in the context of action in the community. This is why it is important for teachers to link arms with each other and with the Black community in the struggle against both the micro and the macro structures of racism in school and society and in the struggle for a new pedagogy — the pedagogy of anti-racism.

Appendices

Appendix 1:

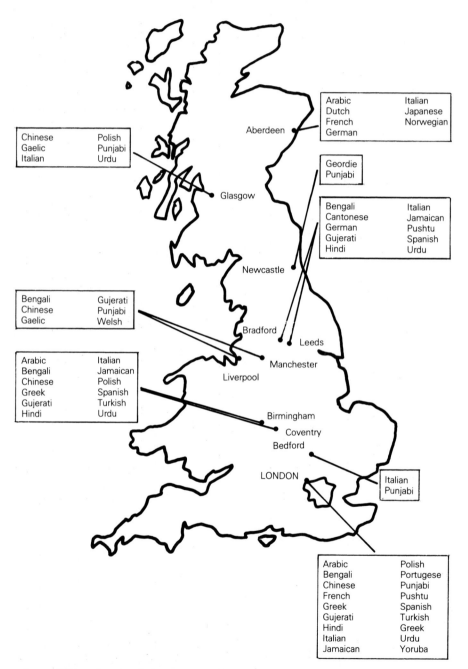

Chinese, Gaelic, Italian, Polish, Punjabi, Urdu

Arabic, Dutch, French, German, Italian, Japanese, Norwegian

Geordie, Punjabi

Bengali, Cantonese, German, Gujerati, Hindi, Italian, Jamaican, Pushtu, Spanish, Urdu

Bengali, Chinese, Gaelic, Gujerati, Punjabi, Welsh

Arabic, Bengali, Chinese, Greek, Gujerati, Hindi, Italian, Jamaican, Polish, Spanish, Turkish, Urdu

Italian, Punjabi

Arabic, Bengali, Chinese, French, Greek, Gujerati, Hindi, Italian, Jamaican, Polish, Portugese, Punjabi, Pushtu, Spanish, Turkish, Greek, Urdu, Yoruba

Aberdeen, Glasgow, Newcastle, Bradford, Leeds, Manchester, Liverpool, Birmingham, Coventry, Bedford, LONDON

Source: Childrens Language Project

Appendix 2

SCHOOL C 1984/5	YEAR 4 RES: 81% NOR: 223 No.	YEAR 4 NR: 180 % NOR	YEAR 3 RES: 82% NOR: 164 No.	YEAR 3 NR: 135 % NOR	YEAR 2 RES: 83% NOR: 132 No.	YEAR 2 NR: 110 % NOR	YEAR 1 RES: 85% NOR: 81 No.	YEAR 1 NR: 69 % NOR
ARABIC	3	1	6	4	6	5	2	2
BENGALI	4	2	11	7	9	7	8	10
BERA	–	–	–	–	–	–	2	2
CREOLE/PATOIS	41	18	30	18	29	22	15	19
CHINESE	4	2	3	2	2	2	4	5
GAELIC/IRISH	2	1	3	2	1	1	1	1
GAR	1	1	–	–	–	–	–	–
GERMAN	1	1	–	–	1	1	–	–
GREEK	35	16	16	10	25	19	8	10
GUJERATI	5	2	3	2	3	2	3	4
HEBREW (CL.)	–	–	–	–	1	1	–	–
HINDI	6	3	4	2	4	3	7	9
HOUSSA	–	–	–	–	–	–	3	4
IBO	1	1	–	–	1	1	1	1
ITALIAN	6	3	–	–	1	1	1	1
NIGERIAN	–	–	–	–	1	1	–	–
PORTUGESE	–	–	1	1	–	–	–	–
PUNJABI	2	1	4	2	1	1	1	1
PUSHTOE	1	1	–	–	–	–	–	–
SPANISH	2	1	2	1	–	–	1	1
SWAHILI	1	1	1	1	1	1	1	1
TURKISH	18	8	13	8	13	10	7	9
TWI	2	1	–	–	2	2	–	–
URDU	4	2	4	2	4	3	3	4
VIETNAMESE	3	1	1	1	–	–	1	1
WELSH	–	–	1	1	–	–	–	–
YORUBA	–	–	2	1	–	–	3	4

Appendix 3

LANGUAGE SURVEY 1984–5				
				[% = NOR]
OF THOSE RESPONDING:	4	3	2	1
BILINGUALS (INC. CREOLE)	115 = 52%	105 = 64%	86 = 65%	47 = 58%
BILINGUALS (NO CREOLE)	74 = 34%	75 = 46%	57 = 43%	32 = 40%
MONOLINGUALS	65 = 29%	59 = 36%	24 = 18%	22 = 27%
1 + LANG. (NOT ENGLISH)	17 = 8%	17 = 10%	16 = 12%	16 = 20%
ATTEND C.L. CLASSESS	43 = 19%	26 = 16%	18 = 14%	10 = 12%
BREAKDOWN OF C.L. CLASSES ATTENDED.				
GREEK (SCHOOL 'C')	11 [TW] + 9 (Op)	4	4	
GREEK (ELSWHERE)	7	6	6	2
TURKISH (SCHOOL 'C')	2	3	3	1
TURKISH (ELSEWHERE)	3	3	3	
GUJERATI	1			2
BENGALI	1			1
URDU	1	2		1
SPANISH	1			1
CHINESE	1	2	2	2
ITALIAN	3			
PUNJABI	1			
ARABIC	2	6		

Appendix 4

(i)   Jews are always rich and mean.
(ii)   Irish people are stupid.
(iii)   French girls are sexy.
(iv)   Americans are rich.
(v)   Black people are:
    (a)   good dancers;
    (b)   good at sport;
    (c)   muggers;
    (d)   happy to be unemployed.
(vi)   All 'Asians' own post-offices.
(vii)   Scottish people are usually:
    (a)   drunk;
    (b)   mean;
    (c)   looking for a fight.
(viii) French people eat frogs and snails.

Bibliography

ACKROYD, D. *et al.* (1977) *The Technology of Political Control*, London, Penguin.

ADORNO, T. *et al.* (1976) 'On logic of the social sciences', in ADORNO, T. *The Positivist Dispute in German Sociology*, Heinemann, London.

ALTHUSSER, L. (1971) 'Ideology and ideological state apparatuses', in COSIN, B.R. (Ed.) (1972) *Education: Structure and Society*, London, Penguin, also in *Lenin and Philosophy and Other Essays*, trans B. Brewster, New York Monthly Review Press.

ATKINSON, P. (1975) *Language Structure and Reproduction: An Introduction to the Sociology of Basil Bernstein*, London, Methuen.

BENNETT, N. (1976) *Teaching Styles and Pupil Progress*, Open Books, London.

BERNSTEIN, B. (1971) 'Education cannot compensate for society', in COSIN, B. *et al.* (Eds.) *School and Society*, London, Routledge and Kegan Paul in association with The Open University.

BERNSTEIN, B. (1973) *Class, Codes and Control*, London, Routledge and Kegan Paul.

BERNSTEIN, B. (1985) *On Pedagogic Discourse*, stencilled paper, London, University of London Institute of Education.

BOTTOMORE, T. (1984) *Sociology and Socialism*, Sussex, Wheatsheaf Books, p. 106.

BOURDIEU, P. (1974) 'The school as a conservative force: Scholastic and cultural inequalities', in EGGLESTON S. (Ed.) *Contemporary Research in the Sociology of Education*, London, Methuen.

BOURNE, J. (1983) 'Towards an anti-racist feminism', *Race and Class*, 15, 1.

BOWLES, S. and GINTIS H. (1976) *Schooling in Capitalist America*, London, Routledge and Kegan Paul.

BRANDT, G.L. (1986) 'Anti-racism: The economy and post-16 education', in GUNDARA, J. JONES, C. and KIMBERLEY, K. (Eds.) *Anti-Racism, Diversity and Education*, London, Hodder and Stoughton.

BUNYAN, P. (1981) 'The police against the people', *Race and Class*, autumn/winter 1981/82, XXIII.

CARBY, H. (1981) *Multicultural Fictions*, stencilled paper, race series SP no. 58, Birmingham, CCCS.

CARBY, H.V. (1982) 'White woman listen! Black feminism and the boundaries of sisterhood', *The Empire Strikes Back*, Hutchinson.

CASHMORE, E.E. (1984) *Dictionary of Race and Ethnic Relations*, London, Routledge and Kegan Paul, pp. 219–20.

CASHMORE, E. and TROYNA, B. (1983) *Introduction to Race Relations*, London, Routledge and Kegan Paul.

CASTLES, S. *et al.* (1984) *Here for Good*, London and Sydney, Pluto.

CENTRE FOR CONTEMPORARY CULTURAL STUDIES (1982) *The Empire Strikes Back*, Birmingham, Hutchinson.

CENTRE FOR STAFF DEVELOPMENT IN HIGHER EDUCATION (1985) *Through a Hundred Pairs of Eyes*, Programme of Triggers and Guide, London, CSDHE University of London Institute of Education.

COARD, B. (1971) *How the West Indian Child is Made Educationally Subnormal by the British School System*, London, New Beacon Books.

COX, O.C. (1948) *Caste, Class and Race: A Study of Social Dynamics*, New York, Doubleday.

CRE (1985) *1976 Race Relations Act: Time for a Change*, London CRE.

DABYDEEN, D. (Ed.) (1985) *The Black Presence in English Literature*, Manchester, University of Manchester Press.

DAVENPORT, M., OSMAN, A. and HARRIS, A. (1985) 'Drugs Crackdown' in *The Sunday Observer*, 15 September.

DAVIES, B. (1981) 'Restructuring youth policies in Britain', *The State We're In*, NYB Occasional Paper 21, November.

DEMAINE, J. (1981) *Contemporary Theories in the Sociology of Education*, London, Macmillan.

DEPARTMENT OF EDUCATION AND SCIENCE (1954) *The Early Leaving* Report, London, HMSO.

DEPARTMENT OF EDUCATION AND SCIENCE (1959) *The Crowther Report*, London, HMSO.

DEPARTMENT OF EDUCATION AND SCIENCE (1977) *Green Paper on Education*, Cmnd 6869, London, HMSO.

DEPARTMENT OF EDUCATION AND SCIENCE (1981) *West Indian Children in British Schools: A Report of the Committee of Enquiry into the Education of Children from Ethnic Minority Groups* (The Rampton Report), London, HMSO.

DEPARTMENT OF EDUCATION AND SCIENCE (1985) *Education for All* (The Swann Report) Cmnd 9453, London, HMSO.

DHONDY, F., BEESE, B. and HASSAN, L. (1982) *The Black Explosion in British Schools*, London, Race Today Publications.

DRIVER, G. (1980) *Beyond Underachievement*, London, CRE.

DURKHEIM, E. (1956) *Education and Sociology*, Glencoe, ILL, The Free Press.

DURKHEIM, E. (1964) *The Rules of Sociological Method*, 8th Ed., New York, The Free Press.

DURKHEIM, E. (1960) *Moral Education*, New York, Free Press.

FIELD, F. and HAIKIN, P. (1971) *Black Britons*, Oxford, Oxford University Press.

FILE, N. and POWER, C. (1981) *Black Settlers in Britain 1555–1955*, London, Heinemann.

FLEW, A. (1984) *Education, Race and Revolution*, London, Centre for Policy Studies.

FRYER, P. (1984) *Staying Power* (The History of Black People in Britain), London, Pluto.

GIROUX, H.A. (1983) *Theory and Resistance in Education*, London, Heinemann Educational Books, p. 17.

GREATER LONDON COUNCIL ANTI-RACIST TRADE UNION WORKING GROUP (1984) *Racism Within the Trade Unions*, London, GLC, November, p. 5.

GORDON, P. and BRAZIER, C. (1985) 'Racism then and now', *The New Internationalist*, 145, March.

GREEN, A. (1982) 'In defence of anti-racist teaching: A reply to recent critiques of multicultural education', *Multiracial Education*, 10, 2.

HALL, S. *et al.* (1978) *Policing the Crisis*, London, Macmillan.

HELD, D. (1980) *Introduction to Critical Theory: Horkheimer to Habermas*, Berkeley, CA, University of California Press.

HMSO, (1967) *Immigrants and The Youth Service*, London, HMSO.

HMSO, (1981) *The Brixton Disorders, 10–12 April, 1981, Report of an Enquiry by the Right Hon. The Lord Scarman, OBE*, Cmnd 8427, London, HMSO.

HOLDAWAY, S. (1977) *Inside the British Police*, London, Blackwell.

HONEYFORD, R. (1984) 'Education and race — An alternative view', *The Salisbury Review*, winter.

HORKHEIMER, M. (1972) *Critical Theory*, New York, Seabury Press.

INNER LONDON EDUCATION AUTHORITY BOOKS (1983) *Race, Sex and Class* (Books 1–4), London, Inner London Education Authority.

JEFFCOATE, R. (1979) *Positive Image — Towards a Multicultural Curriculum*, London, Readers and Writers Publishing Cooperative, Chameleon Press.

JONES, K. and WILLIAMSON, K. (1979) 'The birth of the schoolroom', *Ideology and Consciousness*, 6, autumn.

KUPER, L. (1974) *Race, Class and Power*, London, Duckworth.

LAYTON-HENRY, Z. (1984) *The Politics of Race in Britain*, London, George Allen and Unwin, pp. 122 onwards.

MACKINTOSH, M.J. and MASCIE-TAYLOR (1985) 'The IQ question', ANNEX D. in Department of Education and Science, *Education for All*, Cmnd 9453, London, HMSO.

MOORE, R. (1975) *Racism and Black Resistance in Britain*, London, Pluto Press.

MULLARD, C. (1982a) 'Multiracial education in Britain, from assimilation to cultural pluralism' in TIERNEY, J. (Ed.) *Race Migration and Schooling*, Sussex. Holt.

MULLARD, C. (1982b) 'The state's Response to racism' in OHRI, A., MANNING, B. And CURNO, P. (Eds.) *Community Work and Racism*, London, Routledge and Kegan Paul.

MULLARD, C. (1983a) *Anti-Racist Education — A Theoretical Basis*, stencilled paper, London, Race Relations Unit, Department of Sociology of Education, University of London Institute of Education.

MULLARD, C. (1983b) 'The racial code: Its features, rules and change' in BARTON L. and WALKER, S. (Eds.) *Race, Class and Education*, London, Croom Helm.

MULLARD, C. (1984) *Anti-Racist Education: The Three O's*, London, NAME.

MULLARD, C. (1985) *Race, Class and Ideology, Some Journal Notes*, London, Race Relations Policy and Practice Research Unit, University of London Institute of Education.

NATIONAL UNION OF TEACHERS (1978) *Race, Intelligence and Education: A Teacher's Guide to Facts and the Issues*, London, National Union of Teachers.

(The) Observer, 23rd May 1982, article by D. LEIGH.

(The) Observer, Sunday 15th September 1985, Editorial: *Handsworth: Send for Scarman, Not a Policeman*.

PARMAR, P. (1982) 'Gender, race and class; Asian women in resistance', in Centre for Contemporary Cultural Studies *The Empire Strikes Back*, Birmingham, Hutchinson.

RAMSAY, (1982) 'Mugging: Fears and facts — the law and order debate', *New Society*, 25 March.

REEVES, F. and CHEVANNES, M. (1981) 'The under-achievement of Rampton', *Multiracial Education*, 10, 1.

REEVES, F. and CHEVANNES, M. (1983) 'The ideological construction of Black under-achievement', *Multiracial Education*, 12, 1.

RENIER, R. (1982) 'Black and blue: Race and the police', *New Society*, 17 September.

REX, J. (1973) *Race, Colonialism and the City*, London, Routledge and Kegan Paul.

RICHARDSON, R. (1985) 'Punch and the devil', *The New Internationalist*, 145, March.

ROBINSON, C.J. (1983) *Black Marxism*, London, Zed Press.

RODNEY, W. (1972) *How Europe Under Developed Africa*, Bougle-l'Ouverture Publications.

SARUP, M. (1985) *Marxism, Structuralism, Education*, Lewes, Falmer Press.

SAUNDERS, M. (1982) *Multicultural Teaching — A Guide for the Classroom*, Maidenhead, McGraw Hill.

SCRUTON, R. (1984) *Times Educational Supplement*, 30 October.

SELECT COMMITTEE ON RACE RELATIONS AND IMMIGRATION (1976–77), *Report on the West Indian Community*, London, HMSO.

SHALLICE, J. (1984) *Challenging Racism*, London, Altarf.

SIVANANDAN, A. (1981/82) 'From "resistance to rebellion"', *Race and Class*, autumn/winter, XXIII.

SIVANANDAN, A. (1982) *A Different Hunger*, Pluto.

STONE, M. (1981) *The Education of the Black Child in Britain*, Fontana.

STREET-PORTER, R. (1978) *Race, Children and Cities*, Milton Keynes, Open University Press, pp. 80–7.

TAYLOR, M.J. (1981) *Caught Between — A Review of Research into the Education of Pupils of West Indian origin*, Slough, NFER.

THAKOORDIN, J. (1984) 'Introduction' to *Racism Within the Trade Union*, London GLC.

TIERNEY, J. (1982) 'Race, colonalism and migration', in TIERNEY, J. (Ed.) *Race, Migration and Schooling*, Sussex, Holt.

TIMES EDUCATIONAL SUPPLEMENT (1984) 30 October.

TIMES EDUCATIONAL SUPPLEMENT AND TIMES HIGHER EDUCATION SUPPLEMENT (1983) 19 September.

TIMES EDUCATIONAL SUPPLEMENT AND TIMES HIGHER EDUCATION SUPPLEMENT (1985) 19 August.

THE TIMES (1982) 31 December.

TOMLINSON, S. (1980) 'Ethnic minority parents and education', in CRAFT, M. *et al.* (Eds.) *Linking Home and School*, London, Harper and Row.

TOMLINSON, S. (1983) *Ethnic Minorities in British Schools*, Heinemann Educational Books.

TRAVERS, B. (1982) 'No U-turns on the road to 1984', *Schooling and Culture*, 9, spring.

VERMA, G. (1985) 'Annex F' in Department of Education and Science, *Education for All* (The Swann Report), Cmnd 9453, London, HMSO.

WILLIS, P. (1977a) *Learning to Labour*, Farnborough, Saxon House.

WILLIS, P. (1977b) *How Working Class Kids Get Working Class Jobs*, SP. 43.

WORKERS AGAINST RACISM (1985) *The Roots of Racism*, Junius.

Index

achievement
  see also Asian children, and
    achievement; West Indian
    children, and achievement
  and schooling, 62, 63, 83, 84,
    85–7, 89–94, 122
'Ackee Group', 49
Ackroyd, D. *et al.*, 56–7
Acquired-Immune Deficiency
  Syndrome (AIDS), 169
Adorno, T. *et al.*, 112
advertising
  and racism, 102
Afro-Caribbean children
  see also West Indian children
  and achievement, 91–2
Afro-Caribbean immigrants
  and resistance to racism, 44
Aldridge, I., 105, 109
Althusser, L., 50, 77–8
anti-racism
  see also anti-racist education;
    anti-racist teaching
  and anti-sexism, 25–6
  and Black radicalism, 20, 21
  and classroom practice, 134–7
  community perspectives on, 122–4
  and context of schooling, 133,
    137–9
  and cultural pluralism, 97
  and curriculum, 130–2, 133

  and education, 16, 61–109, 124–6
  and feminism, 25–6
  language of, 119–21
  and moral functionalism, 32–3
  and multiculturalism, 114, 116–18
  and pedagogy, 110–46, 190
  and political Left, 68
  and school policy, 127–8
  and school staffing, 128–30
  and staff development, 130
  and teacher training, 129–30
  teachers and, *see* teachers, and
    anti-racism
  and teaching styles, *see* teaching
    styles
  theory and practice in, 112–13
anti-racist education
  see also anti-racist teaching
  aims of, 124–6
  and emancipation, 126
  and equality, 125
  and justice, 125–6
  and liberation, 126
  as multicultural, *see*
    multiculturalism
  as oppositional, 125
Anti-Racist Strategies Team, 141
Anti-Racist Teacher Education
  Network (ARTEN), 31
anti-racist teaching
  see also anti-racist education

basis of, 133–4
and bilingualism, 149, 150, 151,
    152–3, 155, 171–5
case studies of, 147–88
at classroom level, 134–7, 150–4,
    155–7, 158, 161–3, 167–9,
    172–5, 176–88, 189, 190
context of, 137–9
and curriculum, 139–41, 149, 155,
    161, 169, 180–1
and language, 149–50, 151, 152–3,
    155, 171–5
materials for, 141–2
and multicultural education, 118
as oppositional pedagogy, 142–6
in primary classrooms, 138–9,
    148–58
in secondary classrooms, 139,
    158–88
and syllabus content, 140–1, *see
    also* anti-racist teaching, and
    curriculum
and unstructured experiences, 142
Asian children
and achievement, 63, 85–7, 92
Asian immigrants
cultural traditions of, 44
assimilationist phase, 11, 13, 94–5
'authoritarian democracy', 51–2, 53

Bernard, A., 60n5
Bernstein, B., 77, 78–9, 88–9
bilingualism, 149, 150, 151, 152–3,
    155, 171–5
'Black'
as political term, 66
use of term, 66, 120
Black communities
and anti-racism, 122–4
organization in, 66
Black feminism, 18, 19, 25–6
Black immigration
see United Kingdom, immigration
    to
Black Marxism, 113–14
Black parents' associations, 123

Black people
and employment, 107
and housing, 44–5
marginalization of, 30, 85, 132,
    136
and resistance to racism, 44–59
and sub-proletariat, 18, 30
and trade unions, 46–7, 60n5
and welfare system, 52–3
and working class, 18, 22, 23
Black pupils
see also West Indian children and
    Black workers, 45
and IQ tests, 81–5
marginalization of, 85, 132, 136
Black radicalism, 18, 19–20, 113–14
Black resistance
and civil rights, 47–9
and the economy, 46–7
and education, 49–50
integrationist approach to, 45
interventionist approach to, 45
separatist approach to, 45–6
Black teachers
inadequate numbers of, 129
Black women
see Black feminism; gender
Black workers
and Black students, 45
Black youth
see also Black pupils
and crime, 53–4, 63–4
and police, 55–9
and racism, 55–9
and resistance to repression,
    51–4
and state policy, 50–2
Bourdieu, P., 77, 79
Bourne, J., 25–6
Bowles, S. and Gintis, H., 77, 78
British Movement, 103
Brixton, 57, 58
Brockway, F., 42, 43
Brockwell Park, 54
Bunyan, P., 53
Burt, Sir Cyril, 82

Raleigh, Lady, 7
Rampton, A., 62
Rampton Interim Report (1981), 85
Reeves, F. and Chevannes, M., 86, 87–8, 89, 90–1, 94
religious education, 161–5
Renier, R., 55
repression
and the media, 52
Repressive State Apparatuses (RSA), 50, 77
riots, 45, 52, 53–4, 55, 57, 58
Robinson, C.J., 18, 20–2, 113–14
Roots of Racism, The, 28

Salisbury Review, 120
Sarup, M., 75, 79
Saunders, M., 117
Scarman, Lord, 53, 63, 100
  see also Scarman Committee; Scarman Report
Scarman Committee, 56, 70
  see also Scarman Report
Scarman Report, 55–6
  see also Scarman Committee
school performance
  see achievement
schooling
  see also education
  and conflict, 144
  and conservation of culture, 79
  and cultural capital, 79
  and cultural reproduction, 76, 78–9
  and culture, 78–9
  depoliticization of, 144
  and education, 74–81; *see also* education
  and functionalism, 76–7
  and 'ideological subjugation', 77–8
  in nineteenth century, 74–5
  and power, 105
  and production, 105–6
  as racist, 98–108
  and reproduction of culture, 79
  and social context, 74–5, 76–7,

133–4, 143, 144
  and social reproduction, 77–8, 143
  and symbolic violence, 79
  views of, 75–9
  and the workplace, 78
schools
  see also schooling
  characteristics of case study schools, 148–9, 154, 158–61, 165–7, 170–2, 176–80
  ethos of, 132
  recruitment of teachers to, 128–9
Scruton, R., 68
Seacole, M., 105, 109
secondary schools
  anti-racist teaching in, 158–88
  subject teaching in, 158–88
Seebohm Social Services Report, 88
Select Committee on Race Relations and Immigration (1977), 62
Shakespeare, W., 7
Shallice, J., 134–5
Simey, M., 55
Sivanandan, A., 29, 30–1, 40, 44–5, 48
slavery
  abolition of, 8
  in sixteenth–nineteenth centuries, 7–8
social class
  and education, 77–8
  and gender, 17–20, 25–7
  and intelligence, 82
  and race, 17–27, 46, 99
social relations
  racialization of, 113
social reproduction theory, 77–8
Sorenson, R., 42
South Africa
  Apartheid laws in, 86
  racism in, 23–4, 31, 86, 138–9
Special Patrol Group (SPG), 56
staff development, 130
  see also teachers
state
  and control, 51–4, 56–9, 66, 100–1

IVAN TURGENEV

A Sportsman's Notebook

Translated from the Russian by
Charles and Natasha Hepburn
with an Introduction by Max Egremont

EVERYMAN'S LIBRARY

54

This book is one of 250 volumes in Everyman's Library
which have been distributed to 4500 state schools
throughout the United Kingdom.
The project has been supported by a grant of £4 million
from the Millennium Commission.

First included in Everyman's Library, 1992
Introduction, Bibliography and Chronology © David Campbell
Publishers Ltd., 1992
Typography by Peter B. Willberg

ISBN 1-85715-054-6

A CIP catalogue record for this book is available from the
British Library

Published by David Campbell Publishers Ltd.,
Gloucester Mansions, 140A Shaftesbury Avenue,
London WC2H 8HD

Distributed by Random House (UK) Ltd.,
20 Vauxhall Bridge Road, London SW1V 2SA

CONTENTS

INTRODUCTION

A Sportsman's Notebook, the first of Turgenev's masterpieces, was written in several stages, mostly between 1846 and 1851, with two of the stories in this volume ('The End of Chertopkhanov' and 'The Live Relic') added later for an edition of 1874. Most of the stories appeared first in the Russian literary magazine *The Contemporary* between 1847 and 1851, and were published together in 1852 to the anger of the authorities. These coincided with a happy time in Turgenev's relationship with the Spanish opera singer Pauline Viardot, especially those written in France in 1847 and 1848. Some of the inspiration for the book may have come from the infinitely more dreary *Souvenirs de Chasse* published by Pauline's French husband Louis in 1846. Louis Viardot, a theatrical producer and impresario, was also a keen sportsman. This perhaps contributed to the curious fact that Turgenev and he seemed to have remained friends in spite of the novelist's love for his wife.

Ivan Turgenev came from a landowning family in the Russian province of Oryol. Born in 1818, he grew up on the family estate at Spasskoye in the care of his irascible and tyrannical mother whose behaviour led to his early disgust with serfdom. She appears in several of his stories, most notably 'Mumu', 'Punin and Baburin' and 'The Inn', a forbidding and philistine figure who terrorized her serfs, quite different to her remote philandering husband who died in 1834 without apparently playing a great part in his son's life except to suggest the romantic apartness of the distant parent in 'First Love'. Turgenev attended schools in Moscow and universities in Moscow and St Petersburg before leaving for Berlin. While he was away his mother missed him dreadfully. Later he worked briefly as a civil servant before resigning much against his mother's will to devote himself entirely to writing. He met and fell in love with Pauline Viardot during her visit to St Petersburg in 1843. Turgenev followed her and her husband to Paris and then to wherever she might be in Europe. In 1850, after his mother's death, he inherited

Spasskoye. However his infatuation with Pauline and the hostile reception given to *Fathers and Children* in Russia after its publication in 1862 (particularly by radicals who thought it caricatured their beliefs) made him reluctant to visit his homeland for long.

Like many novelists, Turgenev began as a poet. He was introduced to Pauline Viardot as 'a young Russian landowner, a good shot, an agreeable companion and a writer of bad verses'. These words imply a dilettantism of which Turgenev would be sometimes accused. Dostoevsky caricatured him as the precious and foolish Karamazinov in *The Devils*; Tolstoy condemned his frivolity. Turgenev was not a novelist of belief. In time he follows Pushkin and Lermontov, and early stories such as 'The Duellist', 'Three Portraits', and 'The Jew' show the influence of their Byronic romanticism. He was also the heir to the more naturalistic Gogol, and his first true mentor was the liberal critic Belinsky, a westerner as opposed to a Slavophile. The nearest Turgenev gets to mysticism is in his descriptions of human or natural phenomena, not in some evocation of an unearthly divinity. He has no religion in the sense that Tolstoy or Dostoevsky have.

A Sportsman's Notebook has no backbone of plot or schematic narrative. The episodes are not stories but glimpses of situations or characters, occasionally descriptions of scenery or landscape. For inspiration, Turgenev went back to his youth at Spasskoye, his mother's estate, where hunting expeditions had been a way of escaping briefly from her tyranny. His motive in writing about the countryside must have been at least partly political. The reactionary Tsar Nicholas I was still on the throne and there seemed no prospect of reform. A landowner like Turgenev's mother was the complete mistress of her domain and the serfs who were in bondage to her. Flaubert might remark on how the *Notebook* made him 'want to be shaken alone in a telega through snow-covered fields, to the sound of wolves howling'; for Turgenev, however, there was the added purpose of describing these conditions to readers of influence and education, a very small class in Russia at that time. It is said that a reading of *A Sportsman's Notebook* contributed to Tsar Alexander II's decision to liberate the serfs.

INTRODUCTION

The book is both a work of imagination and of description; Belinsky had advised Turgenev to observe the facts and then filter them through his imagination. *A Sportsman's Notebook* conveys the vastness and beauty of rural Russia. It shows also the eccentricity, cruelty and nobility of many of its inhabitants, a varied collection of peasants, landlords, bailiffs, overseers, horse dealers and merchants. Turgenev observes them from a certain distance; he is a hunter travelling in search of game, often in the company of his faithful guide Ermolai who is probably based on one of his mother's old house serfs, Afanasy Ivanov. It was also from Ivanov that he took down the touching words of the short reminiscence 'About Nightingales'. Descendants of the serf were still living at Spasskoye in 1955.

Ermolai and the narrator wander across the huge landscape of forest and steppe, usually with one or two hunting dogs, travelling sometimes for several days on end, walking or riding in carts, staying in village inns or with hospitable neighbours. Turgenev was fond of dogs. Later he was to write an elegiac memoir of his beloved Pegas, a half-bred retriever who would accompany him on similar shooting expeditions near Baden-Baden. This was the sort of sport which Turgenev enjoyed. No great numbers were killed; the spirit of the countryside and its people were as important as the bag itself, a different concept of pleasure to the great massacres of driven birds which were popular in England and Scotland at this time. Turgenev tried these and seems not to have enjoyed the experience. 'Such expeditions – without dogs – are somewhat monotonous,' he wrote to Tolstoy in 1878. 'In such circumstances one has to shoot very accurately, and I have always been only an average shot.' Louis Viardot, Pauline's husband, was also scornful about shooting in England, disliking the game laws which he said unduly hampered his sport.

Turgenev did not possess what one might call the killer's instinct. Birds and animals could arouse not only his affection but his sentimentality as well. In another reminiscence called 'The Quail' he remembers a hunting trip with his father and an old dog Trezor during which a quail sacrifices itself for her chicks. Later he sees a black-cock do the same; 'after that day,' he writes, 'I found it harder and harder to kill and shed blood'. Indeed, he declares, 'I never became a real sportsman.' Yet Turgenev was a true countryman. During his time of imprisonment in 1852 after the publication of his eulogistic obituary of Gogol he thought longingly of those sporting expeditions of the past. Part of the reason he became so fond of Baden-Baden was because of the woods and forests that encircled the town.

It was the enthusiastic reception accorded to the first sketch of *A Sportsman's Notebook*, 'Khor and Kalinich', that led Turgenev to decide not to abandon literature. Although his poems had been praised initially by Belinsky (whose habit it was to be indulgent towards a writer's first work), they began soon to be met by a certain indifference. In another of his reminiscences Turgenev declares that 'I quite soon realized myself that there was no need for me to carry on with such-like exercises and – made up my mind to give up literature altogether.' However I. I. Panayev, the editor of *The Contemporary*, was looking for articles and Turgenev gave him 'Khor and Kalinich'. Paneyev added the words 'From the sketches of a sportsman'; the piece aroused such interest that Turgenev was encouraged to do another.

He was a careful writer, alive to each nuance of language and subtlety of style. Words fascinated him; he regarded Russian as an exquisite instrument. Constance Garnett, whose translations introduced Turgenev to the English-speaking world, wished later that she had come first to Tolstoy who wrote in a much less artful way. She found *A Sportsman's Notebook* particularly difficult because of the author's use of dialect. Some translators baulk at rendering the idiomatic speech of the peasants or the backwoods landlords into an English equivalent; others attempt what can seem like a version of *The Archers* transposed to the steppes.

Probably much is lost in translation. The Russian critic Zhdanov said he believed it to be impossible to translate Turgenev and retain the effect of the original. Constance Garnett herself declared that 'Turgenev is much the most difficult of the Russians to translate because his style is the most beautiful.' I do not read Russian. Yet to me an atmosphere and

INTRODUCTION

beauty of description come through in English. The book's
extraordinary evocation of the countryside, its life and climate,
the often pathetic condition and struggles of those who live
there: these are there in this version as well.

Rural Russia could be a brutal place. There was poverty
and cruelty, ignorance and disease. Even the narrator's faithful
companion Ermolai is described in 'Ermolai and the Miller's
Wife' as a wife-beater who kills winged birds by biting into
their necks. In 'Raspberry Water' a manor house has burnt
down and been abandoned by its family. Only a pathetic
gardener remains in a hut nearby. It is his job to supply
vegetables for the manorial table a hundred and fifty miles
away; his wife tries vainly to milk a barren cow. Another
peasant tells of the house's previous owner, the wastrel Count
who died bankrupt in a St Petersburg hotel. Once there were
wild parties, decadent extravagance, hounds kept on silver
leads, rapacious mistresses, unthinking severity towards the
serfs. Yet 'the master was everything a master should be,' the
old man says. 'They were good old days, all the same!' Almost
anything can be transformed by memory into human nostalgia
and its longing for a golden age.

Coming as he does from a landowning family, the narrator
cannot escape the occasionally brutal deeds of his forebears.
In 'Ovsyanikov the Freeholder' Ovsyanikov cheerfully relates
how the narrator's grandfather seized some of his family's
land, reacting to their protests by sending his huntsmen and
a gang of ruffians to fetch the freeholder's father and beat him
under the windows of the manor house. The narrator also
shows a Russian vagueness about his ancestral possessions. In
'The Live Relic' he and Ermolai are caught in the rain. The
serf tells him they can shelter at 'a little farm belonging to
your mother; eight versts from here'. Previously he did not
know of the place's existence.

Throughout the book there is this dichotomy: an obvious
distance between the narrator and the country people he
meets, yet also a strong sense of them as individuals. The
distance comes from class and education; the clear characterization from a country upbringing and solitary childhood
during which Turgenev came to rely on the peasants for

company. A youthful affair with a seamstress at Spasskoye resulted in an illegitimate daughter; there may have been other involvements with peasant girls, as was common then on Russian estates. Turgenev could write with sympathy of the landowner Chertopkhanov's love for the peasant girl Masha in 'Chertopkhanov and Nedopyuskin' and 'The End of Chertopkhanov', a precursor of Kirsanov's feelings for Fenechka in *Fathers and Children*. His own affairs were probably not so intense as the one in the story. No woman in Turgenev's life ever matched Pauline Viardot.

A lack of intensity has always been one of the charges laid against Turgenev. It does not diminish his powers of sympathy or feeling. In 'The Live Relic', first published in 1874, long after most of the other stories, the fresh beauty of the sunlit garden after the rain offsets the pathetic predicament of the diseased but once lovely peasant girl who had led the dancing in his mother's household to create one of his most affecting portraits. The blameless Lukerya was doomed before the age of thirty. Turgenev compares her to Joan of Arc and in the context of her suffering the comparison seems apt. Like Tolstoy's Ivan Illyich, she has contracted a mysterious illness after a fall. Her fiancé, the wine butler, grieves for her, then marries someone else. She has been lying in the hut for seven years, looked after by the locals, dreaming and watching the animals and birds, close to the natural beauties around her. There is a sad irony in the local constable's claim that she has been 'smitten by God, for her sins no doubt'.

The theme is that of submission to fate. It is a constant presence in Turgenev's work: in the shocking return of Lavretsky's wife in *The Nest of Gentlefolk*, in Sanin's ill-fated courtship in *The Torrents of Spring*, the death of Insarov in *On the Eve*, the crumbling of Bazarov's strength in *Fathers and Children*. The image of inaction, of the withered body lying on a sick bed, is characteristic as well. At this point all activity can seem to be ultimately futile, even doomed. This, however, does not lessen the moral power or simple strength of the Lukeryas: those who suffer with resignation and even a certain strange joy.

Fate hovers over 'Bezhin Meadow' with an almost supernatural sense of foreboding. On a summer night, peasant boys sit by fires, guarding the horses. They cook potatoes and as the narrator lies near them pretending to sleep he hears their talk of ghostly apparitions and the imaginative world of childhood. Ahead lie the uncertainties and probable hardship of their adult lives; for the moment they are excited innocents. Later the narrator hears of the tragedy that strikes down the most memorable of them. With that characteristic concision of sympathy, Turgenev writes 'A pity, he was a splendid lad!' People and their fate: for Turgenev the elusive link was of ceaseless fascination. In 'King Lear of the Steppes' he writes, 'Everything in the world, good and bad, comes to man, not through his deserts, but in consequence of some as yet unknown but logical laws which I will not take upon myself to indicate, though I sometimes fancy I have a dim perception of them.'

Turgenev's characters live in a way that those of few other writers can. He told Henry James that his stories had their origins not in an idea but a human image; then he would seek a plot or situation in which to place this. The characters in *A Sportsman's Notebook* are precursors of his later often blighted and occasionally heroic inhabitants of rural Russia: the tormented Harlov in 'King Lear of the Steppes', the broken down nobleman in 'The Brigadier', the curious couple in 'Punin and Baburin'. Like these, the people of *A Sportsman's Notebook* convey the sense of their time and position: the way these can bring nobility to some, also lead to frustration or almost absurd stoicism and occasionally create monsters. In 'My Neighbour Radilov' the courteous but preoccupied landowner with whom Turgenev dines is a victim of the Orthodox Church's refusal to allow a man to marry the sister of his dead wife. 'The Bailiff', with its picture of the cruel dandy on his rarely visited property, shows the peasants at the mercy of the landowner's vicious but sycophantic agent; in 'The Estate Office' we see the workings of the capricious bureaucracy of a landed estate. The absurdly pompous Major-General Khvalinsky in 'Two Landowners' is almost as detestable as his neighbour, the bachelor Stegunov who declares 'As I see it, the master is the master, and the peasant is the peasant ... and that's all there is to it.' Stegunov hums as he listens to the sound of his butler being beaten; what makes the incident even more pathetic is that the butler tells Turgenev later that he is sure he deserved his punishment. The serf declares admiringly that 'you won't find another master like him in the whole province'. Turgenev writes simply 'there's the old mother Russia for you, I thought on my way home'.

It is partly through this suffering that Turgenev gives a unique spiritual dimension to the Russian peasant. The dying Lukerya in 'The Live Relic' has it, as does the mysterious dwarf Kasyan in 'Kasyan from Fair Springs' who is said to possess the power of healing. In 'The Bear' it seems as if the giant solitary forester is almost at one with the woods he is protecting on behalf of his master. The death of a man crushed by a tree in 'Death' shows such simple acceptance that Turgenev is moved to write 'Strange how death takes the Russian peasant! His state of mind at his last hour cannot be called indifference or dull-wittedness; he dies as if he were going through a ceremony: coldly, and with simplicity.' By contrast the landowners are usually portrayed in a less attractive light. There is not much spiritual awareness in the arrogant remount officer Prince N. and his toady Lieutenant Khlopakov in 'Lebedyan'.

It is generally the peasants who supply the moments of transcendent beauty. In 'The Singers' the singing competition between Yasha the Turk and the huckster in the 'Snug Nook' pot-house takes place amid squalid and pathetic surroundings but once the music begins each competitor 'climbs out of his skin', the winner attracting 'silent passionate attention' as 'with every note there floated out something noble and immeasurably large, like familiar steppe-country unfolding before you, stretching away into the boundless distance'. The narrator forgets the low pot-house; he thinks of 'a great white gull' slowly stretching its long wings 'towards the familiar sea, towards the low, blood-red sun'. It is a triumph of simplicity, of a skill as natural as the vast countryside itself. At the end another human reality returns; as the narrator leaves he hears a child calling out to one of its siblings to come home to be beaten by their father.

In Turgenev's landscape of forest and steppe lurk those

traits of character which he would develop later in his novels. 'Khor and Kalinich' represent two sides of human nature: the one cautious, reserved and calculating; the other instinctive, talkative and idealistic, a more typical Turgenev hero. The provincial Hamlet of 'Prince Hamlet of Shchigrovo' proves in his dispiriting soliloquy the disastrous effects of self-pity and irresolution, describing his perverse pleasure at having reached 'the extreme limit of misfortune'. It is a study similar to that of the *Diary of a Superfluous Man*, the weakness of will typical also of the main character in *Rudin* and the almost masochistic descent into failure and farce of Nezhdanov in *Virgin Soil*. Turgenev would write later of the contrast between the Hamlets and the Don Quixotes of this world: the men of indecision and introspection and those who are decisive and free from egoism. Objectively he favoured Don Quixote's questing active spirit; he knew, however, that he himself had much more of Hamlet's temperament. This made him understand the failure of the nameless man from Shchigrovo, the thwarted hopeless love of Pyotr Petrovich Karataev for Matrona, of Radilov for Olga in 'My Neighbour Radilov', of Chertopkhanov for Masha. Turgenev believed love to be doomed generally to end in a sense of disappointment or loss.

Turgenev seems at times almost to cherish weakness. Of his central figures, perhaps only Bazarov in *Fathers and Children* and Insarov in *On the Eve* are strong and even they at the end become victims, pathetic in death. One may perhaps look to Turgenev's own life for an echo of this in the follower of the Viardot family around Europe. Turgenev was accepted by Pauline's elderly husband Louis and their children; they were happy even that he should have his own illegitimate daughter by a serf at Spasskoye brought up in their family. But Pauline put her art above all other attachments, whereas Turgenev would have been prepared to give up everything for her. Whether they were ever lovers is doubtful; Turgenev's love for her is not in doubt. It was the strength of her ultimate indifference against the weakness of his devotion. His work seems often to proclaim that lasting mutually satisfying love is unattainable, especially when the passion of one of the lovers is particularly great. The liberal exile Alexander Herzen wrote of the middle-aged Turgenev at Baden-Baden: 'he is in love with the Viardot like an eighteen year old'.

Melancholy, doubt and occasional timidity moulded Turgenev as a writer. He found it more than usually hard to bear the dislike of others; he distrusted the grand solution or the strident campaign. No wonder Tolstoy and Dostoevsky despised him; he could not share their certainties or vigorous determination. In love he was not exactly thwarted but almost certainly unfulfilled. In politics he found himself often cursed by revolutionaries and conservatives alike; perhaps this is always the destiny of the liberal at a time of extremes. Yet the political message of *A Sportsman's Notebook* is simple, if necessarily not too obvious because of the Tsarist censor. The abolition of serfdom was a great radical cause in the 1840s and 1850s. With this, Turgenev was in full agreement. For a few years the book made him immensely admired among educated people in his homeland before the disapproval that followed the publication of *Fathers and Children* in 1862.

He was too subtle a writer to produce a mere political tract. It was partly the Hamlet in him which prevented this, the irresolution his more certain contemporaries castigated and that now seems often a relief from their didactic sermons. His artistry was a barrier to propaganda or preaching. The propagandist or the preacher must put a detailed case; Turgenev wrote once that 'the secret of being tedious was to say everything'. In this book, the first of his masterpieces, he proved the truth of this, impressing others with it as well. Herzen had previously believed Turgenev to be 'educated and clever' but 'superficial and fatuous'. He changed his mind after reading *A Sportsman's Notebook*.

Turgenev once said that 'no matter what I write my work will always take the form of a series of sketches'. In his last novel, *Virgin Soil*, he tried a more ambitious approach, comparable to the grand scale of Tolstoy or Dostoevsky. It did not work although the book has memorable passages, not least the satire of the populist 'back to the people' movement of students and revolutionaries of the late 1860s and the portraits of the 'liberal' noble Sipyagin and his affected wife. His most successful novels are those of character and situation, like

INTRODUCTION

Rudin and *Fathers and Children*. In them his lyrical sympathy
evokes the shades of a wood in autumn, a sense of bitter-sweet
melancholy and regret: hints also of the political and social
turmoil of his homeland, that vast strange landscape of forest
and steppe. Turgenev too had that primitive soul with which
the nineteenth-century Russians captivated Europe.

This makes him a deceptive writer. His books evoke melancholy, disillusion and frustrated romance; they are often chron-
icles of decay, hopelessness and futility. Charm is one of their
chief attributes, together with a beguiling style, a beauty of
description, a deftness of characterization. Yet, as *A Sportsman's
Notebook* shows, he is also profoundly Russian, an exile from a
vast and extraordinary country for which he retained a deep
love in spite of his disapproval of its often brutal and unjust
government. With this love came a profound concern for the
social and political developments of his homeland. Turgenev
refused to shut himself away with his art in the way that his
friend and admirer Flaubert did. He was a stylist but not in
isolation, never apart from his times.

At first glance Turgenev's 'Russianness' is not so obvious as
that of Tolstoy or Dostoevsky. This is partly because his love
of Russia was tempered with respect for western ideas and
institutions about which he knew more than his other great
Russian literary contemporaries. Fluent in several European
languages, he was as at ease in the literary worlds of Paris,
London and Berlin as in those of Moscow and St Petersburg.
Among his friends and admirers were Flaubert, George Sand,
the Goncourt brothers, Carlyle, Monckton Milnes and Henry
James. He attended the Magny dinners and the salon of the
Princess Mathilde. He lived out of Russia for much of his life,
with the Viardots in France or at Baden-Baden and for a brief
time in London during the Franco-Prussian War.

He became a 'westerner' early on, after escaping from his
mother to study in Berlin. It is probable that the scorn of
Potugin in 'Smoke' for simplistic Slavophilism echoes the
views of Turgenev himself and his fears for Russia in the years
of revolutionary turmoil that followed the abolition of serfdom
in 1861. Yet glib 'westerners' such as Panshin in *A Nest of
Gentlefolk* or the old noblemen Ivan Matveitch in 'An Unhappy

Girl' receive rough handling as well. In 1859 Turgenev wrote from the house of his beloved Pauline Viardot in France that 'there is no happiness outside the family – and outside one's native land; everyone should stay in his own nest and put down roots into his native soil. What is the point of clinging on to the edge of someone else's nest?' Turgenev clung to the edge of someone else's nest for much of his life.

To a European reader, he is perhaps the most approachable of the great Russians. He was the first great Russian writer to attain fame in the west and seems to have appealed particularly to the climate of disenchantment and melancholy in England at the end of the nineteenth century. The early translations by Constance Garnett were admired by Arnold Bennett and Galsworthy; Henry James proclaimed him 'the first novelist of the day' although he complained about the Russian's 'atmosphere of unrelieved sadness'. Others have found themselves moved and haunted by the stories of loss and disillusion, of failure and regret, of the often disappointing consequences of enthusiasm, of an almost timeless world where emotion and character draw gentle weak men to an inevitable doom. Most of Turgenev's men are weak, just as many of his women are strong.

Only a Russian could have portrayed such a gallery of fools, eccentrics, brutes and saints; through the great nineteenth-century Russian writers we have come to recognize these characters as typical of only one European country. Turgenev was the polite companion of the Viardots, gentle guest of the Princess Mathilde and cultivated participant in the Magny dinners. Yet he carried with him also those memories of a brutal loveless childhood, the barbarity and arbitrary power that reigned in a huge pitiless landscape where humans were bought and sold like chattels. Against this he felt often quite powerless. The achievement of *A Sportsman's Notebook* is to show how genius can have power enough of its own.

The critical tone of the book annoyed the authorities. Throughout his life they continued to look upon its author with suspicion. After Turgenev's death in France in 1883 his body was taken back to St Petersburg to be buried near Belinsky, his first mentor. The great European writer who had proclaimed himself to be a coward showed his influence in his homeland even from beyond the grave. The Tsar's secret police watched his funeral for signs of political demonstration, a tribute indeed to this man who had been criticized for his weakness and supposed reluctance to take sides.

Max Egremont

SELECT BIBLIOGRAPHY

The biographies of Turgenev that I have found most useful are
Avrahm Yarmolinsky, *Turgenev, the Man, His Art and Age*, Orion Press,
New York, 1959/Deutsch, 1960, and Leonard Schapiro, *Turgenev, His
Life and Times*, Oxford University Press, 1978.

April Fitzlyon's *The Price of Genius*, Calder, 1964, a life of Pauline
Viardot, has much interesting information about the singer's relationship with Turgenev.

Richard Freeborn's *Turgenev: The Novelist's Novelist*, Oxford University Press, 1960, is a thorough guide to the work.

D. S. Mirsky's *A History of Russian Literature*, Routledge, 1927, sets
Turgenev alongside his literary contemporaries, and Isaiah Berlin's
essay on *Fathers and Children* in *Russian Thinkers*, Hogarth Press, 1978,
does the same from a more political point of view.

Turgenev's own letters and autobiographical writings are often
revealing. These have been translated as *Turgenev's Letters*, Athlone,
1983, edited by A. V. Knowles, *Flaubert and Turgenev: A Friendship in
Letters*, Athlone, 1985, edited by Barbara Beaumont, and *Turgenev's
Literary Reminiscences*, Faber & Faber, 1959, edited by David Magar-
shack with an introductory essay by Edmund Wilson.

The biography *Constance Garnett, A Heroic Life*, Sinclair Stevenson,
1991, by Richard Garnett has some material on the difficulties of
translating Turgenev into English.

Henry James's essays on Turgenev reflect his admiration for the
Russian. They can be found in *French Poets and Novelists*, Macmillan,
1878, *Partial Portraits*, Macmillan, 1888, and *The Critical Muse*, Penguin
UK, 1988, edited by Roger Gard. A more recent study by another
novelist is V. S. Pritchett's *The Gentle Barbarian*, Chatto & Windus,
1977.

CHRONOLOGY

DATE	AUTHOR'S LIFE	LITERARY CONTEXT
1818	Born in Oryol, Russia. Childhood spent on family estate at Spasskoye.	Scott: *The Heart of Midlothian*. Keats: *Poems*. Griboedov: *The Student*. Karamzin: *History of the Russian State* (12 vols until 1829).
1819		George Eliot born. Schopenhauer: *The World as Will and Idea*.
1820		Pushkin: *Ruslan and Ludmilla*.
1821		Pushkin: *The Prisoner of the Caucasus*. Dostoevsky and Flaubert born.
1825		Pushkin: *Boris Godunov*.
1827–34	Attends school and university in Moscow.	
1828		Tolstoy born. Mickiewicz: *Konrad Wallenrod*.
1829		Balzac: *Les Chouans* – first volume of *La Comédie humaine*.
1830		Pushkin completes *Eugene Onegin* and writes *The Tales of Belkin*. Stendhal: *Le Rouge et le noir*.
1831		
1832		
1833		
1834–7	Attends St Petersburg university.	
1834	*Steno* (a poetic drama).	Belinsky: *Literary Reveries*. Pushkin: *The Queen of Spades*.
1835		Gogol: *Mirgorod*; *Arabesques*.
1836		Gogol: *The Government Inspector*. Pushkin: *The Captain's Daughter*. Peter Chaadaev's *Philosophical Letter* describes Russia as 'a gap in the intellectual order of things', with no past, present or future.
1837		Death of Pushkin in duel. Dickens: *The Pickwick Papers*.

DATE	AUTHOR'S LIFE	LITERARY CONTEXT
1838–41	Studies at Berlin University. Meets Bakunin, Stankevich and Granovsky, Russian liberal and radical political thinkers.	
1839		Stendhal: *La Chartreuse de Parme*.
1840		Lermontov: *A Hero of Our Time*; *The Novice*.
1841	Returns to St Petersburg. Takes the side of the Westerners in Slavophile v Westerner debate, while remaining on friendly terms with such conservative Slavophiles as the Aksakov brothers.	Death of Lermontov in duel.
1842	Birth of illegitimate daughter by seamstress at Spasskoye.	Gogol: *Dead Souls* and 'The Overcoat'.
1843	*Parasha* – first of his works to attract attention. Meets the critic Belinsky, and Mme Pauline Viardot, with whom he falls in love. Works briefly as a civil servant.	Carlyle: *Past and Present*. Birth of Henry James.
1845	Resolves to devote himself full-time to literature.	Mérimée: 'Carmen'.
1847	Follows Pauline Viardot and her husband to Paris. First visit to England.	Thackeray: *Vanity Fair*. Balzac: *Le Cousin Pons*. Herzen: *Who is to Blame?* Herzen leaves Russia.
1847–50	Lives in France. Most of the stories which later comprised *A Sportsman's Notebook* published in *The Contemporary*.	
1848	Witnesses February revolution in Paris.	George Sand: *La Petite Fadette*. Death of Belinsky. Bakunin: 'An Appeal to the Slavs'.
1849	*The Bachelor* performed (the only one of his plays of this period not to fall foul of the censor).	Dostoevsky arrested as member of socialist Petrashevsky circle. Sentenced to death and reprieved.
1850	Inherits Spasskoye from his mother. *Diary of a Superfluous Man*. Finishes *A Month in the Country*.	Tennyson: *In Memoriam*. Browning: *Men and Women*. Dickens: *David Copperfield*. Herzen: *From the Other Shore*. Death of Balzac.

CHRONOLOGY

1840s and 50s: Slavophile v Westerner debate amongst Russian intellectuals. Westerners advocate progress by assimilating European rationalism and civic freedom. Slavophiles assert spiritual and moral superiority of Russia to the West and argue that future development should be based upon the traditions of the Orthodox Church and the peasant commune or *mir*.

European revolutions. Tsar's manifesto calls upon Russians to arouse themselves for 'faith, Tsar and country'. Russian armies join those of the Habsburgs in suppressing nationalist rebellion in Hungary under Kossuth. *Communist Manifesto* published. Pan-Slav congress in Prague.

DATE	AUTHOR'S LIFE	LITERARY CONTEXT
1851		Melville: *Moby-Dick*.
1852	*A Sportsman's Notebook* published in volume form. Confined to Spasskoye under police surveillance after publishing a eulogistic obituary of Gogol (to 1853).	Death of Gogol. Tolstoy: *Childhood*. Harriet Beecher Stowe: *Uncle Tom's Cabin*.
1854		George Sand: *Histoire de ma vie*.
1855		Trollope: *The Warden*.
1856–63	Returns to France, dividing his time between Paris and the Viardots' estate at Courtavenel.	
1856	*Rudin*.	Aksakov: *Family Chronicles*.
1857		Flaubert: *Madame Bovary*. Herzen's radical journal *The Bell* published in London. Conrad born.
1858	'Asya'.	
1859	*A Nest of Gentlefolk*.	Goncharov: *Oblomov*. Tennyson: *Idylls of the King*. Darwin: *The Origin of Species*.
1860	*On the Eve*. 'First Love'.	George Eliot: *The Mill on the Floss*. Chekhov born.
1861	Working on *Fathers and Children* (largely written on the Isle of Wight, where well-off Russians often went for sea-bathing).	Dostoevsky: *The House of the Dead*. Herzen publishes *My Past and Thoughts* (to 1867).
1862	*Fathers and Children*. Quarrels with Tolstoy during a hunting breakfast in the house of the poet Fet. In spite of this, Turgenev took an active part in getting Tolstoy translated into French, and did much for his reputation in the West.	Hugo: *Les Misérables*. Chernyshevsky imprisoned and exiled to Siberia (to 1883).
1863	Meets Flaubert in Paris. Settles in Baden with the Viardots (to 1871).	Chernyshevsky: *What is to be Done?*
1864	Charged with aiding London expatriate group headed by Herzen. Cleared by senatorial	Dostoevsky: *Notes from Underground*. Trollope: *Can You Forgive Her?*

CHRONOLOGY

HISTORICAL EVENTS

Great Exhibition in London. Opening of St Petersburg to Moscow railway.
Louis Napoleon proclaimed Emperor of France.

Outbreak of Crimean War.

Death of Nicholas I. Accession of Alexander II.

End of Crimean War. By the terms of the Treaty of Paris, Russia forced to
withdraw from the mouth of the Danube, to cease to protect the Orthodox
under Turkish rule and to give up her fleet and fortresses on the Black Sea.
Indian Mutiny: siege and relief of Lucknow.

Russian colonial expansion in South-East Asia.

Garibaldi and 'The Thousand' conquer Sicily. Port of Vladivostock founded
to serve Russia's recent annexations from China.

Emancipation of the serfs (February), the climax of the Tsar's programme of
reform. While his achievement had great moral and symbolic significance,
many peasants felt themselves cheated by the terms of the complex
emancipation statute. Outbreak of American Civil War. Lincoln becomes
President of USA. Victor Emmanuel first King of Italy.
Bismarck becomes chief minister of Prussia. Financial reform in Russia; a
ministry of finance and a state bank created.
1860s and 70s: 'Nihilism' – rationalist philosophy sceptical of all forms of
established authority – becomes widespread amongst young radical
intellectuals in Russia.

Polish rebellion. Poland incorporated in Russian Empire.

The first International. Establishment of the Zemstva, organs of rural self-
government and a significant liberal influence in Tsarist Russia. Reform of
the judiciary; trial by jury instituted and a Russian bar established.

DATE	AUTHOR'S LIFE	LITERARY CONTEXT
1864 cont.	committee in St Petersburg. Beginning of long breach with Herzen.	Tolstoy writes and publishes *War and Peace* (to 1869).
1865		Dickens: *Our Mutual Friend.* Leskov: *Lady Macbeth of Mtensk.* Swinburne: *Atalanta in Calydon.*
1866		Dostoevsky: *Crime and Punishment.*
1867	*Smoke.*	Marx: *Das Kapital,* vol. 1. Zola: *Thérèse Raquin.*
1868		Dostoevsky: *The Idiot.* Browning: *The Ring and the Book.* Lavrov: *Historical Letters.*
1869		Flaubert: *L'Education sentimentale.*
1870	'King Lear of the Steppes'. Lives briefly in London.	Death of Herzen and Dickens. Rossetti: *Poems.*
1871	Settles in Paris with the Viardots.	Dostoevsky: *The Devils.* Zola publishes the *Rougon-Macquart* series of novels (to 1893).
1872	'Spring Torrents'.	George Eliot: *Middlemarch.* Leskov: *Cathedral Folk.*
1873		Bakunin: *Staat en anarchie.* Tolstoy: *Anna Karenina* (to 1877).
1875	Meets Henry James in Paris.	
1876		George Eliot: *Daniel Deronda.* Death of George Sand.
1877	*Virgin Soil.* 'Klara Milich'.	Zola: *L'Assommoir.* Flaubert: *Trois Contes.*
1878	Makes up quarrel with Tolstoy and visits him at Yasnaya Polyana.	Hardy: *The Return of the Native.*
1879	Receives honorary DCL at Oxford for 'advancing the liberation of the Russian serfs'.	Tolstoy: *A Confession* (to 1882). Ibsen: *A Doll's House.*
1880		Dostoevsky: *The Brothers Karamazov.* Death of Dostoevsky, Flaubert and George Eliot.

HISTORICAL EVENTS

Slavery formally abolished in USA. Russian colonial expansion in Central Asia (to 1881).

Dmitri Karakozov, a young nobleman, tries to assassinate the Tsar; he attributes his action to the influence of the radical journal, *The Contemporary*, which is suppressed by the government.
Second Pan-Slav congress in Moscow. Sale of Alaska to USA. Second Reform Act in Britain.

Late 1860s–1870s: Narodnik (Populist) 'going to the people' campaign gathers momentum. Young intellectuals incite peasantry to rebel against autocracy. Lenin born. Franco-Prussian War. End of Second Empire and foundation of Third Republic in France.
Paris Commune set up and suppressed. Fall of Paris ends war. Count Dmitri Tolstoy's reactionary educational reforms.

Three Emperors' League between Germany, Austria and Russia.

'Bulgarian Atrocities' (Bulgarians massacred by Turks). Founding of Land and Freedom, first Russian political party openly to advocate revolution. Russia declares war on Turkey (conflict inspired by Pan-Slavist movement). Queen Victoria proclaimed Empress of India.
Russian forces reach gates of Constantinople. By the Treaty of San Stefano the Turks obliged to recognize independence of Slav nations in the Balkans. Congress of Berlin; with Bismarck acting as 'honest broker' the Great Powers modify the terms of San Stefano, increasing Austrian influence at the expense of Russia. Afghan War. Famous mass trial of Populist agitators ('The Trial of the 193').
Stalin born. Land and Freedom divides into terrorist organization The People's Will, responsible for numerous political assassinations, including that of the Tsar in 1881, and Black Repartition, which continues campaign amongst peasantry and later the urban proletariat.

DATE	AUTHOR'S LIFE	LITERARY CONTEXT
1881	'The Song of Triumphant Love'.	Henry James: *The Portrait of a Lady*. Ibsen: *Ghosts*.
1883	Writes 'Un Incendie en Mer' ('A Fire at Sea'). Sends a letter to Tolstoy from his death-bed, imploring him to return to literary activity from his spiritual writings. Dies in France, 3 September. Buried in St Petersburg.	Maupassant: *Une Vie*. Fet: *Evening Lights*.

CHRONOLOGY

Assassination of Alexander II by Ignatius Grinevitsky. Accession of
Alexander III. Severe repression of revolutionary groups. Alexander III is
much influenced by his former tutor, the extreme conservative Pobedonostsev,
who becomes Chief Procurator of the Holy Synod. Loris-Melikov, architect
of the reforms of Alexander II's reign, resigns. Jewish pogroms.

First Russian Marxist revolutionary organization, the Liberation of Labour,
founded in Geneva by Georgi Plekhanov.

A SPORTMAN'S
NOTEBOOK

Khor and Kalinich

ANYONE WHO has crossed from the district of Bolkhov into that of Zhizdra will probably have been struck by the sharp difference between the natives of the provinces of Orel and Kaluga. The peasant of Orel is short, stooping, sullen; he looks at you from under his brows, lives in flimsy huts of poplar wood, does labour-duty for his master; never goes in for trade; eats badly, wears plaited shoes. In Kaluga the peasant pays rent and lives in spacious cabins of pinewood; he is tall, with a bold gay way of looking at you, and a clean white face; he trades in oil and tar, and on feast-days wears boots. In Orel – I am speaking about the eastern part of the province – the village is usually situated among ploughed fields near a ravine which peters out into a dirty pond. Except for a few willows, which are always ready to oblige, and for two or three lank birches, there is not a tree to be seen for a verst around; one hut huddles against another; the roofs have a rough thatch of rotten straw... In Kaluga, on the other hand, the village is largely surrounded by forest; the huts have a freer, sturdier look and are roofed with planks, the gates are well-fitted, the wicker-work fence round the back-yard is neither tattered nor tumble-down, nor does it offer an open invitation to every pig that may come along... Even the sport is better in the province of Kaluga. In Orel the remaining tracts of forest and bush will have vanished in about five years' time, and there is no question of marshes; but in Kaluga, forests where no timber may be cut stretch for hundreds of versts, and marshes for tens of versts, the blackcock (noble bird) is not yet extinct, the generous snipe abounds, and the fussy partridge cheers and startles both sportsman and dog as he flies violently up from cover.

Once, when I was shooting in the district of Zhizdra, I met in the fields, and got to know, a small landowner from Kaluga, Polutykin by name, an enthusiastic sportsman and

3

proportionately excellent fellow. It's true that he had certain weaknesses: for instance, he had courted all the wealthy marriageable girls in the province and, being rejected and forbidden the house, he would broken-heartedly confide his sorrows to all his friends and continue to send the girls' parents presents of sour peaches and other unripe produce of his garden; he loved to repeat, over and over again, one and the same story, which, notwithstanding Mr. Polutykin's high regard for its excellence, certainly had never made anybody laugh; he admired the works of Akim Nakhimov and the story of Pinna; he stammered; he called his dog 'Astronomer'; he said 'aye' instead of 'yes'; in his house he had introduced a French style of cooking, the secret of which, as understood by his cook, consisted in completely transforming the natural taste of every dish: meat, from the hands of this expert, tasted of fish; fish, of mushrooms; macaroni, of gunpowder; and, with it all, no carrot ever fell into the soup without taking the form of a rhombus or a trapeze. Yet, apart from these rare and unimportant failings, Mr. Polutykin was, as I have already said, an excellent fellow.

On the very first day of my acquaintanceship with him, Mr. Polutykin invited me to stay the night. 'It's about five versts to where I live,' he added. 'It's too far to walk; let's first go and see Khor.' The reader will excuse me from reproducing his stammer.

'And who may Khor be?'

'One of my peasants . . . he lives just here.'

So we went to see Khor. In the middle of the forest, in a cleared and cultivated glade, stood the lonely farm where Khor lived. It consisted of several cabins of pinewood grouped together behind fences; in front of the largest hut was a lean-to roof supported on slender poles. We went in and were met by a young peasant lad of about twenty, tall and good-looking.

'Hallo, Fedya! Is Khor at home?' Mr. Polutykin asked him.

'No, Khor's gone to town,' answered the lad, smiling and showing a row of snow-white teeth. 'Would you like the cart harnessed?'

'Yes, my boy, we would. And bring us some kvass.'

We went into the hut. There were none of your coloured prints stuck to the clean boarding of the walls; in the corner, in front of the heavy icon with its crust of silver, an oil-lamp glimmered; the table of limewood had been freshly scraped and washed; between the timbers and along the jambs of the windows there were no skittish, roving beetles, no lurking, reflective cockroaches. The lad soon appeared with a big white jug full of excellent kvass, a huge hunk of wheaten bread and a dozen salted cucumbers in a wooden bowl. He set all these victuals out on the table, leant in the doorway and began to contemplate us with a smile. Before we had finished eating, a cart rattled up to the door. We went out. A boy of about fifteen, curly-headed and ruddy-cheeked, was sitting with the reins in his hand, with difficulty keeping control of a well-fed roan stallion. Round the cart stood half a dozen gigantic young men, all very much like each other and like Fedya. 'The whole lot are Khor's children,' observed Polutykin. 'Yes, all Khor's litter,'[1] rejoined Fedya, who had followed us out into the porch; 'and not the whole lot, either; Potap is in the forest, and Sidor has gone to town with old Khor ... Look here, Vasya,' he continued, turning to the driver, 'remember you're driving the master, and go at a good pace. Only go easy over the bumps, do you hear, or you'll damage the cart and disturb the master's digestion!'

The rest of Khor's litter chuckled at Fedya's remark. 'Help Astronomer up too,' cried Mr. Polutykin solemnly. Fedya gaily lifted up the dog, which wore a constrained smile, and set him down in the bottom of the cart. Vasya gave the horse its head, and off we went. 'There's my estate office,' said Mr. Polutykin to me suddenly, pointing to a little low house. 'Shall we call in?'

'Certainly.'

'It's disused now,' he explained, getting down from the cart, 'but it's worth looking at all the same.'

1 Khor in Russian means 'polecat', – *Translators*

The office consisted of two empty rooms. The watchman, an old man with one eye, came running out from the back-yard.

'Good day to you, Minyaich,' said Mr. Polutykin, 'and where's the water?'

The one-eyed old man vanished and returned at once with a bottle of water and two glasses. 'Try it,' said Polutykin to me; 'try my excellent spring water.' We drank a glass each, the old man bowing deeply meanwhile.

'Well, now I think we might go on,' observed my new friend. 'In this office I sold ten acres of forest to Alliluyev the merchant, and at a good price, too.'

We took our places in the cart and in half an hour were already driving into the courtyard of Polutykin's house.

'Tell me,' I asked Polutykin at supper, 'why does your Khor live separately from your other peasants?'

'I'll tell you: because he is the clever one among them. About twenty-five years ago his hut got burnt down; so up he comes to my late father and says: "Nikolai Kuzmich, please may I settle on your land, in the forest beside the marsh? I'll pay you good rent." "But why do you want to settle beside the marsh?" "I just do; but you, sir, Nikolai Kuzmich, please don't give me any work to do, but fix any rent you like." "Fifty roubles a year." "Certainly." "And no arrears, mind!" "Of course, no arrears." . . . So he settled beside the marsh. And since then he has been known as Khor.'

'And he's done well out of it?' I asked.

'He has. Now he pays me a hundred roubles rent, and I am going to make him pay more still, I think. I have said to him several times: "Buy your own freedom, Khor, do!" But he, the crafty brute, assures me that he could not manage it; that he has got no money . . . As if he expected me to believe him! . . .'

Next day we went out shooting as soon as we had drunk tea. As we drove through the village Mr. Polutykin told the driver to stop in front of a little low hut and called out loudly: 'Kalinich!'

'Coming, sir, coming,' replied a voice from the yard; 'I'm just tying my shoe.'

We went slowly on: outside the village we were overtaken by a man of about forty – tall, thin, with a small head, carried well in the air. This was Kalinich. His good-natured swarthy face, with pock-marks here and there, appealed to me as soon as I saw it. Kalinich, as I learnt later on, accompanied his master out shooting every day, carried his bag, and sometimes his gun too, marked his birds, brought him water to drink, picked straw-berries, built shelters for him, ran to fetch the drozhky; with-out him Mr. Polutykin could not stir a yard. Kalinich was a man of the gayest and gentlest character imaginable; he was constantly humming below his breath and throwing carefree glances in all directions; he spoke in a slightly nasal voice, smiling and screwing up his pale-blue eyes and often passing his hand over his scanty wedge-shaped beard. He walked slowly but with large strides, leaning slightly on a long thin stick. In the course of the day he and I got talking together several times, and he looked after me without a trace of servility; his attitude to his master was one of fatherly supervision.

When the unbearable midday heat compelled us to seek shelter, he led us to his bee-garden in the very depth of the forest. He opened up for us a little hut, hung with bunches of dried aromatic herbs, gave us some fresh hay to lie on, then himself put a sort of network bag over his head, took a knife, a pot and a piece of burning wood, and went off to the bee-garden to cut us some honeycomb. We washed down the warm translucent honey with spring water, and fell asleep to the monotonous humming of bees and the busy murmur of leaves. A gentle breath of wind awakened me. I opened my eyes and saw Kalinich. He was sitting on the threshold of the half-open door, fashioning a spoon with his knife. I lay and admired his face, which was gentle and serene as the evening sky. Mr. Polutykin also awoke. We did not get up at once. After a long tramp and a deep sleep it is delightful to lie motionless in the hay: a luxurious languor invades the body, the face glows with warmth, a delicious laziness closes the eyes.

At length we rose, went out, and continued our wanderings until nightfall. At supper I spoke again about Khor and also about Kalinich.

'Kalinich is a good fellow,' said Mr. Polutykin: 'a keen, obliging fellow. He's not much good on the land, though; I am always taking him away from it. Every day he comes out shooting with me... What good that does the land, you can well imagine.' I agreed with him, and we went to bed.

Next day Mr. Polutykin was obliged to go into town about some trouble which he had with his neighbour Pichukov. Pichukov had ploughed up some of Polutykin's land and, on this land, had beaten one of Polutykin's peasant women. I went out shooting alone and towards evening I paid a call on Khor. In the doorway of the hut I was met by an old man – bald, short, sturdy and broad-shouldered: Khor himself. I looked at him with curiosity. His cast of face recalled Socrates: the same high bumpy forehead, the same little eyes, the same snub nose. We went together into the hut. My friend Fedya brought me some milk and black bread. Khor sat down on a bench and, tranquilly stroking his curly beard, engaged me in conversation.

He seemed a man conscious of his own worth; slow of speech and movement, with an occasional chuckle from behind his long moustaches. I talked to him about the sowing, the harvest, about the peasant's life... He always seemed to agree with me; only, when he did so, I was conscious of an uneasy feeling that I was not really right after all; our conversation had a certain strangeness about it. Some of Khor's utterances were abstruse – probably the effect of caution. Here is a sample of our conversation for you:

'Tell me, Khor,' I said to him, 'why don't you buy your freedom from the master?'

'And why should I buy it? As things are, I know the master and I know the rent he wants... He is a good master, too.'

'All the same, you would be better off if you were free,' I remarked.

Khor gave me a sidelong glance. 'Certainly,' he said.

'Well, then, why don't you buy your freedom?'

Khor swivelled his head from side to side.

'And what am I to buy it with, sir?'

'Oh, come on, man...'

'Once Khor gets in among people who are free,' he continued below his breath, as if talking to himself, 'any fellow who shaves his beard would be Khor's master.'

'But you could shave your own beard, too.'

'What's a beard? A beard is grass; you can always cut it.'

'Well, then?'

'Of course, Khor might get right in among the merchants; merchants have a good life – and they've got beards too.'

'Well, don't you do a bit of trading, too?' I asked him.

'I trade in a small way, with oil and tar... Now, sir, would you like me to harness the cart?'

You've got your head screwed on the right way, and a firm hold on your tongue, too, I thought. 'No,' I said aloud, 'I don't need the cart; I shall be shooting near your place to-morrow and, if I may, I'll spend the night here in your hay-shed.'

'You'll be welcome. But will you be all right in the shed? I'll tell the women to spread a sheet for you and to put out a pillow. Hey, there, women!' he shouted, rising from his place. 'Come here!... Fedya, you go with them. Women are such fools.'

A quarter of an hour later, Fedya, carrying a lantern, escorted me to the shed. I threw myself down on the sweet-smelling hay, and my dog curled up at my feet; Fedya wished me good night, and the door squeaked and slammed to behind him. For some time I couldn't get to sleep. A cow came up to the door and breathed loudly once or twice; my dog gave a dignified growl at her; a pig went past, grunting reflectively; somewhere nearby a horse began to munch hay and snort...

At length I dropped off to sleep.

At dawn Fedya awoke me. I had taken a great liking to this gay, alert young fellow; he seemed to be a favourite with old Khor too, as far as I could observe. They chaffed each other in the most amiable way. The old man came out to meet me. Whether because I had spent the night under his roof, or for some other reason, at any rate Khor was much more forth-coming towards me than he had been the day before.

'The samovar's waiting for you,' he told me with a smile; 'let's go and have tea.'

We sat down at table. A healthy-looking peasant-woman, one of Khor's daughters-in-law, brought a pot of milk. All his sons came in one after the other.

'What a tall lot you've got!' I observed to the old man.

'Yes,' he replied, biting off a tiny piece of sugar. 'I think that neither I nor the old woman has given them anything to complain about.'

'And do they all live with you?'

'Yes. They all want to live here, so they do.'

'And are they all married?'

'That rascal there won't marry,' he answered, pointing at Fedya, who as before was leaning in the doorway. 'As for Vaska, he's a bit young still, he has time to wait.'

'What should I get married for?' rejoined Fedya. 'I'm all right as I am. What good would a wife be to me? Someone to quarrel with, eh?'

'Well, you . . . I know all about you! You wear silver rings . . . you like sniffing round after servant-girls! Oh, get along with you, now!' continued the old man, imitating the voice of a serving-maid. 'I know all about you, with your white hands and all!'

'But what is there that's good about a peasant-woman?'

'The peasant-woman is a worker,' observed Khor senten-tiously. 'She is a servant to her husband.'

'And what would I want a worker for?'

'Because you like other people to pull your chestnuts out of the fire. Oh, I know you and your sort.'

'Well, marry me off, if you want to. Eh? What? Why don't you say something?'

'Well, that'll do, you joker. You're disturbing the master. I'll marry you off, don't worry. . . . You mustn't mind him, sir; he's only a whipper-snapper, you see, and hasn't had time to learn any sense.'

Fedya shook his head ...

'Is Khor in?' said a well-known voice at the door, and Kalinich came in, holding a bunch of wild strawberries which he had picked for his friend Khor. The old man welcomed him joyfully. I looked with surprise at Kalinich. I must admit, I had not expected that a peasant would be capable of such 'attentions'.

That day I went shooting four hours later than usual, and I spent the next three days at Khor's. I was absorbed by my new acquaintances. I can't say how I deserved their confidence, but they talked to me without constraint. I enjoyed listening to them and observing them. The two friends were not in the least similar. Khor was a positive, practical fellow, an administrator, a rationalist. Kalinich, on the other hand, belonged to the category of idealists, romantics, enthusiasts and dreamers. Khor understood reality, that is to say, he knew how to get on in the world, how to put money aside, and keep on good terms with the master and the other powers that be; Kalinich went about in plaited shoes and lived from hand to mouth. Khor was the father of a large, submissive and united family; Kalinich had once had a wife, of whom he had been afraid, but never any children. Khor saw right through Mr. Polutykin; Kalinich, on the other hand, idolized him. Khor loved Kalinich and gave him his protection; Kalinich loved and revered Khor. Khor spoke little, chuckled, and thought things out for himself; Kalinich expressed himself with warmth, although he was not one of your nightingales of eloquence, like some smart fellows of the artisan class ... But Kalinich was endowed with advantages which even Khor allowed him; for instance, he knew spells to cure fear, frenzy or bleeding; he could drive out worms; his bees did well, he had the right touch with them. Khor asked him, in my presence, to lead a newly-bought horse into the stable, for luck, and Kalinich carried out the request of the old sceptic with conscientious gravity. Kalinich was nearer to nature; Khor, to people, to human society. Kalinich did not like arguing and believed everything blindly; Khor had risen far enough to take an ironic view of life. He had seen a lot, he

knew a lot, he taught me a lot, too. For example, from his
stories I learnt that every summer, just before mowing time,
there appears in the country villages a small cart of unusual
aspect. In the cart there sits a man in a frock-coat with scythes
to sell. In cash he charges one rouble twenty-five copecks; in
notes, a rouble and a half; on credit, four roubles. It goes
without saying that all peasants buy from him on credit. Two
or three weeks later he appears again and demands payment.
The peasant has just cut his oats, and therefore has money to
pay with; he goes with the merchant to the pot-house and there
settles his account. Certain landowners had the idea of buying
scythes themselves for cash and issuing them to their peasants
on credit for the same price; but the peasants showed themselves dissatisfied and even depressed: they were deprived of
the pleasure of tapping on the scythe, listening to it, turning it
in their hands and asking the crafty vendor twenty times or so:
'Well, lad, the scythe is not as good as all that, eh?' The same
tricks take place when it comes to the buying of sickles, the only
difference being that then the women intervene and sometimes
bring the vendor himself to a point where he is obliged to hit
them – for their own good. But for the women the most painful
occasions of all are these. Purveyors of material to the paper-
mills entrust the purchasing of rags to agents of a special type,
who are known in some districts as 'eagles'. An 'eagle' receives
from a merchant two hundred roubles or so in notes and goes in
search of his prey. But, in contrast to the noble bird after which
he is named, he does not practise an open courageous method
of attack: on the contrary, the 'eagle' resorts to cunning and
deception. He halts his cart somewhere in the bushes outside
the village, and makes his way on foot by back-ways and back-
doors, like a casual passer-by or a common tramp. The women
instinctively divine his approach and creep out to meet him. A
business deal is hurriedly completed. For a few copper farth-
ings the woman gives the 'eagle' not only all her unneeded rags,
but often her husband's shirt too and her own petticoat.
Recently the women have found it advantageous to steal from
themselves and to dispose of their hemp in this way, which all

brings more and better business to the 'eagles'. Meanwhile, however, the peasants in their turn have become wise to what goes on, and at the least suspicion, or a single distant rumour, of the appearance of an 'eagle', they take swift and drastic recourse to measures of precaution and correction. And indeed they have good grounds for offence. Selling hemp is *their* business, and sell it they do – not in town, for they would have to go all the way there, but to visiting hucksters, who, having no weights, reckon one pound at forty handfuls – but you know what a handful can be, and what a palm a Russian has, especially when he gives his mind to it!

As an inexperienced man who had not lived much in the country, I listened to a good many stories such as this. But Khor didn't spend all the time telling stories, often it was his turn to question me. He discovered that I had lived abroad and this fired his curiosity... Kalinich kept up with him; but he was more interested in descriptions of nature and mountains, waterfalls, unusual buildings and big cities; Khor was pre-occupied by questions of administration and government. He examined everything in its right order: 'Is it the same way there as it is with us, or otherwise?... Tell us, sir, how is it?' 'Oh, Lord God Almighty!' Kalinich would exclaim as I went on; Khor remained silent, drew his shaggy brows together, and only occasionally remarked: '*This* wouldn't do here, but *that* is good – it's how it ought to be.' I cannot tell you all the questions he asked, and there is no reason why I should; but from our talks I carried away a conviction which will probably surprise my readers, the conviction that Peter the Great was an essentially Russian character, and never more Russian than in his reforms. The Russian is so confident in his strength and steadfastness that he does not mind undergoing change; he cares little about his past, he looks boldly into the future. He likes what is good, he will gladly take what is reasonable, but where it comes from is all the same to him. His sound common sense enjoys a laugh at rigid minds of the German type; but the Germans, in Khor's words, are an interesting lot, and he was quite ready to learn a lesson from them. Thanks to his unusual situation, to his condition of virtual independence, Khor was able to speak to me of many things on which nothing would have extracted a word from another, not even, as peasants say, if you ground him with a grindstone.

He certainly knew where he stood. As I conversed with Khor, I heard for the first time the shrewd simple speech of the Russian peasant. He was a man of fairly wide knowledge, by his own standards, but he could not read; Kalinich, however, could. 'Reading and writing come easy to this lazy rogue,' observed Khor; 'it's like his bees, which never die from the day they are hatched.' 'Haven't you had your children taught to read and write?' Khor was silent for a moment. 'Fedya knows how to.' 'And the others?' 'The others don't.' 'How is that?' The old fellow would not answer and changed the subject. In fact, for all his shrewdness, even he was not without prejudices and preconceived ideas. Women, for instance, he despised from the bottom of his heart, and in moments of hilarity he enjoyed making fun of them. His wife, who was old and shrewish, spent the whole day above the stove, grumbling and scolding incessantly; her sons paid no attention to her, but she kept her daughters-in-law in the fear of God. With reason does the mother-in-law sing in the Russian folk-song:

> *You're a fine one, my son, in your family life,*
> *If you've never a touch of the stick for your wife.*

Once it occurred to me to take the part of the daughters-in-law, and I tried to enlist the sympathy of Khor; but he calmly rejoined: 'Why should you worry your head with such . . . trash? Let 'em squabble among themselves; putting them apart only makes it worse, it's just not worth dirtying your hands.'

Sometimes the old shrew climbed down from the stove, called the dog in out of the passage, saying: 'Here, doggie, here!' then beat it over its thin back with a poker; or else she would stand in the porch and 'yap', as Khor expressed it, at everyone who went by. Nevertheless she stood in awe of her husband and at a word from him would retire to her perch above the stove.

But it was especially entertaining to hear the dispute that arose between Kalinich and Khor when Mr. Polutykin's name came up.

'I won't have you touch him, Khor,' said Kalinich.

'But why doesn't he have some boots made for you?' rejoined Khor.

'Pooh, boots!... What should I want boots for? I'm a peasant...'

'And so am I, but look...' As he spoke Khor lifted his boot and showed Kalinich a boot which looked as if it had been carved out of mammoth-skin.

'Oh – as if you were the same as the rest of us,' answered Kalinich.

'Well, he might give you money for your bast shoes: look, you go out with him when he goes shooting; one day, one pair of shoes.'

'He gives me money to buy them.'

'Yes, last year he was so kind as to give you ten copecks.'

Kalinich turned away indignantly, and Khor burst out laughing until his little eyes completely disappeared.

Kalinich had quite a pleasant voice and accompanied himself on the balalaika. Khor would listen and listen, then suddenly put his head on one side and join in in a plaintive voice. He was particularly fond of the song, 'Oh, my fate, my fate'. Fedya never missed the opportunity for a joke against his father: 'What makes you so sorry for yourself?' But Khor propped his chin on his hand, shut his eyes and went on complaining about his fate... With all this, there could be no one more active at other moments than Khor. He was eternally busy about something or other – mending the cart, fixing the fence, looking over the harness. He was no great stickler for cleanliness, however, and once answered an observation of mine by saying that 'a hut ought to smell lived-in'.

'But,' I rejoined, 'look how clean Kalinich keeps his bee-garden.'

'The bees wouldn't live if he didn't, sir,' he said with a sigh.

Another time he asked me: 'Have you got an estate of your own?'

'Yes.'

'Far from here?'

'A hundred versts.'

'And do you live there, sir?'

'I do.'

'But I expect you spend most of the time shooting?'

'I suppose I do.'

'And quite right, too, sir; shoot blackcock to your heart's content, and change your agent every so often.'

On the evening of the fourth day Mr. Polutykin sent to fetch me. I was sorry to leave the old man. Kalinich and I took our places in the cart. 'Well, good-bye, Khor, look after yourself,' I said. 'Good-bye, Fedya.'

'Good-bye, sir, don't forget us.' We drove off. The sunset was just beginning to blaze. 'It's going to be a glorious day to-morrow,' I remarked, looking at the clear sky. 'No, there is rain coming,' Kalinich rejoined. 'You see how restless those ducks are, and the grass smells too strong, too.'

We drove into the brushwood. Kalinich began to sing under his breath as he bumped up and down on the driver's seat, and stared and stared into the sunset . . .

The following day I left Mr. Polutykin's hospitable roof.

Ermolai and the Miller's Wife

IN THE evening the hunter Ermolai and I went out for the 'flight'... But perhaps there are some of my readers who do not know what I mean by this. So listen, gentlemen.

A quarter of an hour before sunset, in spring, you go into a wood, with a gun, but without a dog. You choose a place somewhere near the skirts of the wood; you have a look round; you inspect the cap; you make a sign to your companion. A quarter of an hour passes. The sun has set, but it is still light in the forest; the air is clear and translucent; the birds are chattering away; the young grass glows with a cheerful emerald brilliance... You wait. Inside the forest it gradually grows dark; the scarlet light of sunset slowly slips along the roots and trunks of the trees, rises higher and higher, passes from the lower branches, still almost bare, to the motionless, sleeping tree-tops... Now even the tree-tops have faded out; the ruddy sky turns to blue. The smell of the forest grows stronger; there is a faint breath of warm dampness; a breeze comes fluttering in to die away beside you. The birds go off to sleep – not all together, but according to their kinds: first the chaffinches fall silent, then, after a few moments, the robins, after them the yellow-hammers. In the forest it grows darker and darker. The trees merge into great masses that loom up ever more blackly; in the blue sky the first small stars make a timid appearance. The birds are all asleep. Only the redstarts and the small woodpeckers still give an occasional sleepy whistle... Soon even they are silent. Once more there rings out above you the clear voice of the chiff-chaff; somewhere an oriole utters its mournful cry, the nightingale chuckles for the first time. Your heart grows tired of waiting, and suddenly – but only sportsmen will understand me – suddenly in the deep stillness there comes a special kind of whirr and swish, you hear the measured stroke of swift wings – and the woodcock, with

17

his long beak drooping gracefully down, comes swimming out from a dark birch-tree to meet your fire.

This is what is meant by 'waiting for the flight'.

So Ermolai and I set out for the 'flight'; but forgive me, gentlemen: I ought first to have presented Ermolai to you.

Imagine a man of about forty-five, tall, thin, with a long sharp nose, a narrow forehead, small grey eyes, tousled hair and a wide mocking mouth. A man who went about winter and summer in a short yellowish nankeen coat of German cut, but with a belt round the waist; who wore baggy blue trousers and a round lambskin cap which had been given to him, as a joke, by a ruined landowner. From the belt hung two bags, one in front, artfully twisted into two halves – for powder and for shot; the other behind – for game; as for wads, Ermolai used to produce them from the apparently inexhaustible resources of his cap. From the money which he received in return for game he could easily have bought himself a bandolier and a game-bag; but such an idea had never even occurred to him, and he continued to load his gun as before, exciting the astonishment of all beholders by the deftness with which he avoided the danger of spilling or mixing his shot and powder. He had a single-barrelled flint-lock gun, with an ugly kick to it, so that his right cheek was permanently swollen out of all proportion to his left. How Ermolai hit the mark with this gun, even the cleverest could not guess – but he did.

He had a pointer called Valetka, a creature of surprises. Ermolai never fed him. 'Why should I?' he argued. 'A dog's a clever beast and ought to be able to find its own food.' And he was right; although Valetka impressed even the most casual passer-by with his extraordinary leanness, he lived – and a long life into the bargain; in spite of his miserable condition, he never ran away or showed the slightest wish to desert his master. Only once, in his youth, he absented himself for two days, under the influence of love; but this was a madness which quickly left him. Valetka's most remarkable quality was his imperturbable indifference to everything in the world . . . If I had not been talking about a dog, I would have used the word 'disenchantment'. His habit was to sit with his short tail tucked under him, frowning, shivering from time to time and never smiling. (It is well known that dogs can smile, and smile very sweetly too.) He had an extremely unprepossessing appearance, and no idle man-servant would ever miss a chance of a spiteful joke about it; but Valetka put up with all these jokes, and a few blows too, with surprising sang-froid. He gave special entertainment to cooks, who immediately dropped what they were doing to rush headlong after him with shouts and curses as soon as, with a weakness not characteristic of dogs alone, he showed his hungry mug through the half-open door of a temptingly warm and succulent-smelling kitchen. In the chase his great qualities were his tirelessness and his very fine nose; but if a wounded hare happened to come his way, then he would eat it up with gusto, to the last bone, in some cool and shady spot underneath a green bush, at a respectful distance from Ermolai, who would be cursing him in all known and unknown dialects.

Ermolai belonged to one of my neighbours, a landowner of the old school – the school which does not fancy wild game and clings to its preference for domestic fowls. It is only on special occasions, such as birthdays, name-days and election days, that cooks in the houses of landowners of this school set about the dressing of long-beaked game, and, working themselves into the frenzy peculiar to the Russian when he does not properly know what he is doing, invent such cunning sauces that the guests for the most part inspect the proffered delicacies with curiosity and attention, but cannot resolve to taste them. It was Ermolai's duty to bring to his master's kitchen once a month two brace of blackcock and two brace of partridge, but otherwise he was allowed to live where and how he pleased. His master had given him up in despair as a fellow who was good for no useful work. It goes without saying that Ermolai received no allowance of powder or shot, in virtue of exactly the same principles as those on which he himself refused to feed his dog. He was a queer fellow: carefree as a bird, talkative enough, absent-minded, and clumsy-looking;

a deep drinker and a rolling stone; when he walked, he shuffled his feet and lurched from one side to the other – yet, with all his shuffling and lurching, he could cover fifty versts in twenty-four hours. He had all sorts of vicissitudes and misadventures; he would spend the night in the marshes, in a tree, on a roof, under a bridge; often he found himself sitting locked up in an attic, a cellar, or a barn, having lost his gun, his dog and the most essential parts of his wardrobe; he would be beaten hard and long – and all the same, after a while, he would return home fully clothed, complete with gun and dog. He was not what you would call of cheerful disposition, although he was almost always in pretty tolerable good spirits. In brief, he was a regular freak.

Ermolai liked a chat with a congenial soul, especially if it was over a glass, but even so it would never be for long; all of a sudden he'd be up and off. 'Where are you going, you rascal – at this hour of the night?' 'To Chaplino.' 'And what takes you to Chaplino, ten versts away?' 'I'd thought of sleeping at Sofron's place there.' 'Why not sleep here?' 'No, no, I can't.' And off goes Ermolai, with Valetka after him, into the pitch-dark night, through bushes, across ravines, only to find that his friend Sofron very likely won't let him in and indeed will take him by the scruff of the neck and throw him out: 'Don't you go bothering honest folk.'

With it all, Ermolai had no rival in the art of catching fish in a flooded stream in spring, tickling for crayfish, smelling out game, enticing quail, training falcons, and catching nightingales with 'the devil's whistle' or 'the cuckoo-passage'[1] ... One thing he could not do was to train dogs; he lacked the patience.

He had a wife, too. He went and saw her once a week. She lived in a miserable half-ruined hut, managed to exist somehow, never knew the day before whether she would have enough to eat on the morrow; altogether hers was a wretched lot. Ermolai, carefree and good-natured as he was, treated her

1 Nightingale fanciers will recognize these terms: they refer to the most beautiful modulations in the bird's song. – *Author*.

roughly and harshly. When at home he took on a grim and threatening appearance – and his poor wife did not know how to please him, trembled at his glance, spent her last copeck buying vodka for him, and covered him obsequiously with her coat when he subsided majestically on the shelf above the stove and fell into an epic slumber. More than once I would observe in him the unwitting display of a sort of sullen cruelty. I did not like the expression on his face when he took a bite out of a wounded bird. But Ermolai never stayed more than a day at home; once away, he again became 'Ermolka', as they called him for a hundred versts around, and as he sometimes called himself. The humblest menial felt his superiority to this vagabond – which, perhaps, was why he would treat him with friendliness: the peasants for their part began by joyfully chasing and catching him, like a hare in a field, but then they would let him go, and wish him luck; once they had got to know the queer fellow, they left him alone, even gave him bread, and enjoyed a talk with him.

This was the man that I took with me as a hunter and with whom I made my way to the 'flight' in a great birch-wood on the bank of the Ista.

Many Russian rivers, like the Volga, have hills on one bank and flat meadows on the other; the Ista follows the same pattern. It is a highly capricious little river, which winds like a snake, and never flows straight for more than half a verst; at some points, from the top of a steep hill, it can be seen for ten versts; with its dams, its pools, its water-mills, and orchards, bowered in willow-thickets and tufted parkland. There are endless fish in the Ista, especially chub (in the heat of the summer the peasants catch them under the bushes in their hands). The little sandpipers whistle up and down the stony banks, which are enlivened here and there with springs of cold and sparkling water; wild duck swim out into the middle of the pools and look cautiously about them; herons perch in shady creeks, under the steep banks...

We waited for the 'flight' for about an hour, shot two brace of woodcock and, wishing to try our luck again before sunrise (for one can wait for the morning flight too), decided to spend the night in the nearest mill. We came out of the wood and went down the slope. Darkly blue, the river was rolling on its way; the air was growing heavy and charged with the vapours of the night. We knocked at the gates of the mill. Dogs began to bark furiously in the courtyard. 'Who's there?' asked a hoarse and sleepy voice. 'We've been out shooting: can we spend the night here?' There was no answer. 'We'll pay for it.' 'I'll go and tell the master ... Shut up, you cursed brutes ... death and destruction on you!' We heard the labourer go into the house, and soon he came back to the gates again. 'No,' he said, 'the master won't let you in.' 'Why not?' 'He's afraid, because you've been out shooting and there's a risk of your setting fire to the mill, what with all your powder and shot.' 'I never heard such nonsense!' 'We had the mill catch fire like that last year: some cattle-dealers spent the night here and somehow or other they set the place on fire.' 'Surely you wouldn't have us spend the night out of doors?' 'That's your affair.' And he went off, stamping his shoes.

Ermolai wished him various evil fates. 'Let's go to the village,' he said at last, with a sigh. But the village was two versts away ... 'Let's spend the night here,' I said. 'It's a warm night out of doors, and if we offer him money the miller will send us out some straw.'

Ermolai agreed without more ado. We started knocking afresh. 'What do you want now?' said the labourer's voice again. 'I told you you can't come in.' We explained to him what we wanted. He went to consult his master and the two of them came back together. The gate opened with a squeak and the miller appeared – a big, fat-faced, bull-necked, pot-bellied fellow. He agreed to my proposition. About a hundred yards from the mill there was a small open shed. Beds of straw and hay were spread for us there; the labourer set up a samovar on the grass beside the stream, squatted down on his haunches and started blowing heartily down the funnel ... The coals burst into flame and brightly lit up his youthful face. The miller went to wake his wife, and finally invited me to spend the night indoors; but I preferred to stay in the open air. The miller's wife brought us milk, eggs, potatoes, bread. Soon the samovar was boiling and we were setting about our tea.

Mists were rising from the river and there was not a breath of wind; corncrakes called nearby; faint sounds came from the mill-wheels: drops falling from the blades, or water running through between the sluices of the dam. We laid a small fire, and while Ermolai baked potatoes in the ashes I dozed off to sleep . . . A low, discreet murmuring woke me again. I lifted my head: in front of the fire, on an up-ended tub, the miller's wife was sitting talking to my hunter. I had already placed her, by her dress, her movements and her accent, as a woman of the servant class, neither peasant nor townswoman; but it was only now that I was able to get a clear view of her features. She seemed to be about thirty; her thin, pale face still showed the traces of a remarkable beauty; I was especially taken with her large, sad eyes. Her elbows were resting on her knees and her face was propped on her hands. Ermolai was sitting with his back to me, throwing twigs on the fire.

'There's cattle disease again in Zheltukhina,' said the miller's wife. 'Old Ivan's cows have both got it . . . God's mercy on us!'

'How are your pigs?' asked Ermolai after a silence.

'Still alive.'

'You might at least give me a sucking-pig.'

The miller's wife said nothing, then heaved a sigh.

'Who's this you are with?' she asked.

'The master from Kostomarov.'

Ermolai threw a few fir-branches on to the fire; they crackled away in unison, and the thick white smoke blew straight into his face.

'Why wouldn't your husband let us come indoors?'

'He's afraid.'

'The great fat lout . . . Arina Timofeyevna, my love, bring me out a little glass of vodka.'

The miller's wife got up and vanished into the darkness. Ermolai began to sing under his breath:

I wear my shoes out, heel and toe,
So oft to see my love I go ...

Arina returned with a small carafe and a glass. Ermolai half-rose, crossed himself, and emptied the glass in one gulp. 'That's what I like,' he added.

The miller's wife sat down again on the tub.

'Well, Arina Timofeyevna – still ailing?'

'Yes.'

'What's the matter?'

'My cough troubles me at night.'

'I think the master's dropped off to sleep,' said Ermolai after a short silence. 'Don't you go to the doctor, Arina: you'll get worse.'

'I wouldn't go anyway.'

'But come and stay with me.'

Arina looked down.

'I'll send my wife away, if you come,' continued Ermolai. 'Really I will.'

'You'd better wake up the master, Ermolai Petrovich: look, the potatoes are done.'

'Let him sleep his head off,' answered my faithful retainer indifferently; 'he's walked enough, and deserves it.'

I turned over in the hay. Ermolai got up and came across to me.

'The potatoes are ready, sir, if you like to start on them.'

I came out from the shed; the miller's wife rose from the tub and made as if to go. I kept her in conversation.

'Have you had this mill for long?'

'A year ago last Trinity.'

'Where does your husband come from?'

Arina paid no heed to my question.

'Where's your husband from?' repeated Ermolai, raising his voice.

'From Belev. He's a townsman from Belev.'

'Are you from Belev, too?'

'No, I'm a serf ... or was, rather.'

'Whose?'

'Mr. Zverkov's. But I'm free now.'

'Which Zverkov?'

'Alexander Silyich.'

'Weren't you his wife's maid?'

'However do you know that? Yes, I was.'

I looked at Arina with redoubled curiosity and sympathy.

'I know your master,' I continued.

'You do?' she answered in a low voice, and looked down.

I must tell the reader why I looked with such sympathy at Arina. While I was in Petersburg, chance made me acquainted with Mr. Zverkov. He held a fairly important position and passed for a man of knowledge and ability. He had a wife who was podgy, sentimental, tearful and ill-natured – a humdrum, boring creature; there was a son, too, a real mother's darling, spoilt and stupid. Mr. Zverkov's appearance was not to his advantage: in a broad, almost square face, his little mousy eyes looked slyly out above a big, sharp, protruding nose with wide-open nostrils; his close-cropped grey hair bristled up from a wrinkled forehead; his thin lips were constantly moving and shaping themselves into a sickly smile. Mr. Zverkov usually stood with his legs apart and his fat hands in his pockets. Once it so happened that I found myself alone with him in a carriage on the way out of town. We fell into conversation. As a man of experience and ability, Mr. Zverkov started to tell me 'what was what'.

'Allow me to observe to you,' he squeaked, after a time: 'All you young people – your views and opinions are all absolutely in the air. You hardly know your own country; Russia, gentlemen, to you is an unknown country – and that's the truth! . . . All you do is read German books. Now, take an instance: you tell me this and that on such and such a subject, well, say, about the servant class . . . all right, I don't dispute it, that's all very fine; but you don't know them, you've no idea what sort of people they really are.' Mr. Zverkov blew his nose loudly and took a pinch of snuff. 'As an instance, let me tell you a little story; it may interest you.' Mr. Zverkov cleared his throat. 'You know what my wife is like: I think you will agree that it would be difficult to find a kinder woman than she. The life her maids lead is no ordinary servant's existence – why, it's heaven itself made visible on earth . . . But my wife has one firm principle: never to keep a married maid – and quite rightly, too, for no good comes of it: she has children, and so on – well, how can you expect her then to look after her mistress as she ought, and pay proper attention to her habits: she can't be bothered any longer, she has other things to think of. You've got to take human nature as you find it. Well, anyway, one day we were driving through our village, about – let me see, when was it exactly? – about fifteen years ago. We notice that the village headman has a daughter, a very pretty girl, and what I call respectful-mannered, into the bargain. My wife says to me: "Koko" – you see, that's what she calls me – "let's take this girl with us to Petersburg . . . I like her, Koko" . . .' I answer: "Let's take her, with pleasure." The headman of course is at our feet, he had never dreamt of such good fortune . . . Well, of course, the girl, like a fool, cries a little. Actually it *must* be rather grim to begin with: leaving home and all that . . . There's nothing surprising about it. However, she soon gets used to us; to begin with they put her in with the housemaids – to train her, of course. Then what do you think happens? . . . The girl makes astonishing progress; my wife takes a regular fancy to her, and over the heads of all the others gives her the privilege of being her own personal maid . . . What d'you say to that! . . . And you've got to give the girl her due. My wife had never had such a maid, definitely not; obliging, modest, obedient – in short, everything you could want. On top of it all, I've got to admit that my wife spoilt her; gave her good clothes, fed her from our own table, let her have tea . . . and everything else you can imagine! So there she was, employed for ten years as my wife's maid. Suddenly, one fine morning, if you please, in comes Arina – that was her name – without asking leave, into my study, and falls at my feet . . . I tell you frankly, that's one thing I can't abide. Human beings should never forget their dignity, don't you agree? "What do

you want?" "Alexander Silyich, sir, please, please..." "What
is it?" "Please let me get married." I confess to you that I was
amazed. "Why, you stupid girl, why, surely you know your
mistress has no other maid?" "I'll serve the mistress the same
as before." "Stuff and nonsense! The mistress never keeps a
married maid." "Malanya can take my place." "I'll thank you
not to argue." "It's as you wish, sir."... I must admit I was
astounded. I should explain that nothing offends me so much,
I'd go so far as to say that nothing offends me so *gravely*, as
ingratitude; that's the kind of man I am...Well, there's
nothing more I can tell you – you know what my wife is, an
angel incarnate, her kindness is beyond description. I think
that even the worst man on earth would have sympathized with
her in this situation. I sent Arina about her business. I thought
she'd be sure to come to her senses; you know, one doesn't like
to believe one's fellow creatures capable of wickedness or black
ingratitude. Well, what d'you think? After six months she has
the impertinence to come to me again with the same request.
This time, I confess, I sent her packing and no mistake.
I threatened her; I swore I'd tell my wife. I was beside
myself...But then, imagine my amazement: some time after,
my wife came to me in tears, in such a state that I got quite a
fright. "Whatever's the matter?" "It's Arina...you understand...I'm ashamed to say more." "It's not possible! Who-
ever...?" "Petrushka, the footman." Then I blew up. I'm the
sort of man that doesn't like half measures...Petrushka was
not to blame. One could always punish him, certainly – but all
the same, he, in my opinion, was not to blame. Arina – h'm –
well – h'm, what more is there to say? Of course I gave orders at
once that her head should be shaved, that she should be put
into sackcloth and sent home to the country. My wife lost an
excellent maid, but there was nothing else to be done. Say what
you like, you can't have laxity in your own home. It's better to
amputate the diseased limb once and for all! Now, judge for
yourself – you know my wife; well, this, this...anyway, this
angel...she had grown fond of Arina, and Arina knew it and
yet wasn't ashamed...Eh? No, honestly...eh? But why talk

about it any more? Anyhow, there was nothing else to be done. For my own part, I felt particularly aggrieved and hurt, for a long time afterwards, by this girl's ingratitude. Whatever you may say . . . don't look for heart or feeling in these people. You can feed a wolf for all you're worth, but he'll still keep an eye on the forest. We live and learn! But I only wanted to prove to you . . .'

And Mr. Zverkov, without finishing the sentence, turned his head away and wrapped himself up more tightly in his cloak, mastering with manly self-control the violence of his feelings.

The reader will now probably understand why I looked so sympathetically at Arina.

'Have you been married to the miller for long?' I asked her eventually.

'Two years.'

'Your master gave his permission?'

'No, they bought my freedom.'

'Who did?'

'Savely Alexeich.'

'Who's he?'

'My husband.' Ermolai smiled to himself. 'But did the master ever speak to you about me?' added Arina after a short silence.

I didn't know how to answer her question. 'Arina!' shouted the miller from the distance. She rose and left us.

'What d'you think of her husband?' I asked Ermolai.

'Nothing.'

'Have they got any children?'

'They had one that died.'

'Did the miller take a fancy to her, or what? . . . Did he pay a lot for her freedom?'

'I don't know. She can read and write; in their business it's . . . well . . . it's useful. Probably he took a fancy to her.'

'Have you known her for long?'

'Yes, I used to go to her master's house before. His place is not far from here.'

'D'you know the footman Petrushka, too?'

'Pyotr Vasilyevich? I knew him, certainly I did.'

'Where is he now?'

'He went for a soldier.'

We were silent.

'It seems she is ailing?' I asked Ermolai at last.

'What else should she be? . . . Well, to-morrow there may be a good "flight". You could do with some sleep now.'

Some wild duck came swishing over us and we heard them dropping down on to the river not far away. By now it was quite dark and growing cold; in the wood a nightingale chuckled loudly. We burrowed into the hay and went to sleep.

Raspberry Water

At the beginning of August the heat often becomes unbearable. At this season, from twelve until three o'clock, even a man of the greatest decision and concentration is unable to go shooting and even the most devoted dog begins to 'clean its master's spurs', which means following him at a walk, screwing up its eyes in pain and hanging out its tongue too far, and, in answer to the reproaches of its master, wagging its tail humbly with an embarrassed expression on its face, but making no move forward. I was out shooting on just such a day as this. For a long time I resisted the temptation to lie down in the shade, even if only for a moment; for a long time my dog searched tirelessly through the bushes, although it was clear that it expected no sensible result from its feverish activity. The stifling heat at length forced me to think of conserving our remaining strength and energy. Somehow or other I dragged myself to the stream of the Ista, with which my indulgent reader is already familiar, made my way down the steep bank, and walked over the wet yellow sand in the direction of a spring which is known in all the country round by the name of Raspberry Water. This spring bursts from a cleft in the bank which has gradually turned into a small but deep ravine, and after twenty yards the water falls with a cheerful babbling rush into the river. Oak-bushes grow in all directions on the slopes of the ravine; near the source is a green patch of short velvety grass; the rays of the sun hardly ever touch its cold silver dewiness. I arrived at the spring; on the grass lay a scoop of birchwood, left there by a passing peasant for the benefit of the world at large. I drank my fill, lay down in the shade and looked around.

Beside the creek where the spring flowed into the river, which for that reason was always a mass of tiny ripples, two old men were sitting with their backs towards me. One of them, tall and fairly thick-set, in a neat dark green coat and a quilted cap, was fishing; the other, who was small and thin and wore a fustian patched jacket and no cap, held on his knees a pot with worms in it and from time to time passed his hand over his small grey head, as if to protect it from the sun. I took a closer look at him and recognized Styopushka from Shumikhino. I ask the reader's permission to introduce this character to him.

A few versts away from my estate lies the big village of Shumikhino, which has a stone church raised in honour of Saints Cosmas and Damian. Opposite this church there used to stand a fine big manor house, surrounded by various dependencies, outbuildings, workshops, stables, coach-houses, bathhouses and temporary kitchens, guest-wings, agents' houses, conservatories, swings for the servants' amusement, and other more or less useful constructions. In this mansion lived a rich landowner's family and everything went swimmingly – when suddenly one fine morning the whole pleasant seat was burnt down to the ground. The owners flitted to another nest and the property fell into neglect. The great expanse of waste ground became a kitchen-garden, cluttered up here and there with piles of bricks, which were all that remained of the old foundations. From the surviving timbers a hut had been hastily knocked together, roofed over with planks which had been bought ten years earlier for the construction of a pavilion in the Gothic manner, and in it were settled the gardener Mitrofan with his wife Axinya and their seven children. Mitrofan had instructions to provide his master's table – one hundred and fifty versts away – with vegetables and garden produce; Axinya was entrusted with the care of the Tyrolean cow which had been bought in Moscow for a large sum, but had unfortunately lacked all capacity for reproduction and had therefore since the time of its purchase given no milk; she was also entrusted with the tufted smoke-coloured drake, the only bird of 'feudal' status; the children were too small to have any special duties assigned to them, which did not prevent them from growing as lazy as could be.

On two occasions I had spent the night in the gardener's hut; whenever I passed by I would collect cucumbers which, God knows why, impressed you even in summer by their size, their unpleasant watery taste, and their thick yellow skin. It was here that I saw Styopushka for the first time. Apart from Mitrofan and his family and Gerasim the deaf old sacristan, who lived on charity in a little cabin belonging to a one-eyed soldier's wife, there was not a single serving-man left in Shumikhino, for Styopushka, with whom I propose to make the reader acquainted, could be regarded neither in general as a man, nor in particular as a servant.

There is no man who does not have some sort of status in society, some sort of human ties; there is no servant who does not receive either his wages or at least some so-called equivalent in kind; whereas Styopushka certainly had no means of subsistence, was related to nobody, and nobody knew how he existed. He didn't even have a past; no one spoke about him; when the census was taken they hardly bothered to count him. There were dark rumours abroad that he had once been employed somewhere as a valet; but who he was, where he came from, whose son he was, how he came to be one of the serfs of Shumikhino, in what manner he acquired the fustian coat which he had worn from time immemorial, where and on what he lived – no one had the slightest idea and, to tell the truth, no one cared either. Even grandfather Trofimich, who knew the family tree of all the Shumikhino retainers as far back as the fourth generation, even he had been known to mention only once that, as he remembered, Styopushka had been related to a Turkish woman whom the late master, Brigadier-General Alexei Romanich, had been pleased to bring back in the baggage-train after one of his campaigns. Even on feast-days, days of universal treating and regaling with bread and salt, with buckwheat pies and green spirits, in the old Russian manner – even on these days Styopushka never appeared when the tables and barrels were set out, never made his bow, never came to kiss his master's hand, never drank a glass in one draught under the master's eye and to the master's health, a glass which had been filled by the greasy hand of the factor; at best, some good-natured soul might run into the poor fellow and give him a half-eaten pie-crust. On Easter Sunday he got the three traditional kisses, but he never turned up his greasy sleeve, never pulled out from his back pocket a red-painted egg, never brought it, panting and blinking, to the master's children or to the lady herself. In summer he lived in a shed behind the chicken-house and in winter in the porch of the bath-house; if the frost was heavy he spent the night in the hay-loft. People were used to seeing him; sometimes they went so far as to give him a friendly kick, but no one ever fell into conversation with him; indeed he seemed never to have opened his mouth from birth. After the great fire this outcast creature took shelter with or, as the Orel people say, 'leant against', the gardener Mitrofan. The gardener left him alone, never offered him a roof, but never drove him out either. And Styopushka in fact did not live at the gardener's; he wandered about the garden and made it his home. His walk and his movements were noiseless: he sneezed and coughed into his hand as if afraid to break the silence; he was for ever hurrying silently about like an ant; and the object of the whole thing was food, just food. And indeed, had he not busied himself from morning to night with matters of subsistence, my friend Styopushka would have died of hunger. It is a sorry fate not to know in the morning how you are going to fill your belly before the day is done. Sometimes Styopushka sits under a fence and gnaws a radish, or sucks a carrot, or scatters round him the shreds of a dirty cabbage stalk; sometimes he groans under the weight of a pail of water which he is carrying away; sometimes he gets a small fire going under a pot, into which he throws black morsels which he brings out from under his coat; sometimes in his little den he can be heard knocking with a piece of wood, driving in a nail, putting up a shelf on which to keep his bread. He does it all in silence, as though peeping round the corner; one look from you and he has vanished. Then suddenly he disappears for a couple of days; it goes without saying that no one notices his absence. Next time you look, he is back again, and somewhere near the fence he has furtively built a fire out of odd splinters. He has a small face, little yellow eyes, hair down to his eyebrows, a sharp nose, enormous transparent ears like a bat's, and what appears to be two weeks' growth of beard, never more nor less. This was Styopushka as I met him on the bank of the Ista sitting beside another old man.

I went up to them, exchanged greetings and sat down beside them. In Styopushka's companion I recognized another acquaintance: this was a liberated serf of Count Pyotr Ilyich ———, by name Mikhailo Savelyev, commonly known as Tuman.[1] He lived in Bolkhovo, with the consumptive inn-keeper with whom I had fairly often stayed. Young officials or other idle travellers passing along the main road to Orel – (merchants, sunk deep inside their striped quilts, never spare the time to look) – can still to this day observe not far from the large village of Troitskoye a huge two-storied wooden house, completely derelict, with its roof fallen in and windows boarded up, thrusting right out on to the roadside. At midday, in clear sunny weather, it is impossible to imagine a sorrier spectacle than this ruin. It was once the home of Count Pyotr Ilyich, a rich magnate of the old days who was famous for his hospitality. The time had been when all the province assembled in his house, danced and made merry in famous style, to the deafening strains of a home-taught orchestra, to the crackling of fireworks and of Roman candles; and, prob-ably, more than one old lady, driving past the now deserted halls of the Boyar, heaves a sigh and recalls times gone by and the days of her youth. For long years the Count continued to give banquets and to walk about with a welcoming smile among the throng of obsequious guests. But, alas, his fortune was not enough to outlast his lifetime. Ruined beyond repair, he went place-hunting in St. Petersburg and died in an hotel bedroom before he knew the result of his quest. Tuman had been his butler and received his freedom while the Count was still alive. He was a man of about seventy, with an agreeable, regular face. He wore an almost constant smile, the sort of smile that is now

1 'Fog'. – *Translators.*

seen only on the faces of survivors from the days of Catherine the Great; a smile that is both benign and stately; when he spoke, his lips parted and came together again slowly, his eyes narrowed amiably and the words came out with a slightly nasal tone. His manner of blowing his nose or taking snuff was equally unhurried, as of a man engrossed in serious business.

'Well, Mikhailo Savelyich,' I began; 'what luck with the fish?'

'Look at my basket, sir, if you will. I've caught two perch, and five roach . . . Show them, Styopushka.'

Styopushka held the basket out to me.

'How are you, Styopushka?' I asked him.

'Oh . . . oh . . . oh . . . all right, sir, not so bad,' answered Styopushka, stammering as though he was rolling weights on his tongue.

'Is Mitrofan well?'

'Well, sir . . . why, yes.'

The poor fellow turned away.

'They're not taking,' said Tuman. 'It's much too hot; the fish are all tucked away under the bushes, fast asleep . . . Put a new worm on, Styopushka.' Styopushka took out a worm, laid it on the palm of his hand, tapped it once or twice, put it on the hook, spat on it and handed it to Tuman. 'Thank you, Styopushka . . . but you, sir,' he continued, addressing himself to me, 'you have been shooting?'

'As you see.'

'Quite so . . . And is that dog that you have with you from England – or from *Fourland*?' The old man enjoyed showing off when he had the chance, as if to say, 'We too have lived in the great world!'

'I don't know what breed he is, but he's a good dog.'

'Quite so . . . and do you hunt with hounds too?'

'Yes, I have two packs.'

Tuman smiled and shook his head. 'That's just how it is. One gentleman is dead keen on hounds and another would not take them as a gift. That's how it is, to my simple way of thinking. A gentleman ought to keep hounds more for the sake of appearances than for anything else, if you take my meaning. And everything ought to be in its proper style: horses in style, whippers-in in style, and everything else too. His late Lordship – may God rest his soul! – was not a born huntsman, it is true, but he kept his hounds, and hunted them about twice a year. The huntsmen would muster in the courtyard, in their red coats trimmed with braid, blowing their horns; out comes his Lordship, his horse is led up; his Lordship mounts, and the head huntsman puts his feet into the stirrups, takes the cap off his head and hands the reins in his cap to his Lordship. His Lordship gives his whip a good crack, the huntsmen cry "halloo", and off they go. A groom rides behind his Lordship, leads his master's two favourite dogs on a silken lead, and keeps a sharp eye on them, too, you may be sure... And there he sits, this groom-fellow, way, way up on a Cossack saddle. A red-cheeked fellow with great big rolling eyes... Well, of course, there were guests there, too, for the occasion. And great fun it was, and everything as it should be... Oh, he's got away, the *Chinaman*!' he added suddenly, giving his rod a twitch.

'They say the Count had quite a time of it in his day?' I asked.

The old man spat on the worm and made a cast.

'He certainly lived like a lord. I dare say that all the leading people from Petersburg came out to see him. There they all were in their blue ribbons, sitting at table feasting. And he was certainly a master-hand at entertaining, too. He used to call me: "Tuman," he says, "I need live sterlets for to-morrow; order them to be sent, do you hear?" "Very good, your Lordship." Embroidered coats, wigs, canes, perfumes, *Lady-Cologne* of the finest quality, snuff-boxes, great big pictures like this – everything ordered straight from Paris. He would give a banquet and, Lord God Almighty! the fireworks, the drives there would be! They would even shoot off cannons. The musicians alone were forty strong. There was a German conductor, but he got too big for his boots; he wanted to eat at the master's table; so his Lordship sent him packing: "Even without him," he says, "my musicians understand their business." Of course, the master's word was law. They would start dancing – and dance until sunrise; they'd mostly dance the *acossaise-matrador* ... Eh ... eh ... our friend is hooked!' The old man drew a small perch out of the water. 'Here you are, Styopushka. – The master was everything a master should be,' continued the old fellow, making another cast. 'And he had a good heart too. He might beat you – but before you could look round he would have forgotten all about it. There was one thing, though: he kept *may-tresses*. Oh, those *may-tresses*, merciful God! It was they who ruined him. For choice, strange to say, he liked a common sort of girl. You would have thought that they would have had all they wanted – but no, they must have everything that's most expensive in the whole of Europe! Of course you can say, why shouldn't the master live as he wants to – it's his own business ... but he shouldn't have gone and ruined himself. There was one of them in particular, by name, Akulina; she is dead now – may she rest in peace! She was a simple sort of girl, daughter of the village policeman at Sitovo, but what a shrew! She used to smack his Lordship in the face. She had him properly bewitched. She had my nephew's head shaven because he had spilt chocolate on her new dress, and he wasn't the only one either. But they were good old days, all the same!' added the old man, with a deep sigh; then he looked down and said no more.

'You had a strict master, I see,' I began, after a few moments of silence.

'That was the fashion then, sir,' rejoined the old man, shaking his head.

'Things are different now,' I observed, looking at him keenly. He gave me a sidelong glance.

'No doubt things are better now,' he muttered, and cast his line far out into the stream.

We were sitting in the shade; but even there the heat was stifling; the heavy sultry air was without a breath; your burning face longed for a breeze, but no breeze came. The sun was fairly beating down from the sombre blue sky; right in front of us on the opposite bank was the yellow blaze of an oatfield, broken here and there by patches of wormwood, and not a single ear was stirring. A little farther downstream a peasant's horse was standing up to its knees in the water, lazily swishing a wet tail; now and then, beneath an overhanging bush, a big fish came to the surface, let off a stream of bubbles and quietly sank again to the bottom, leaving a faint ripple behind. Grasshoppers chirruped in the rust-coloured grass; quails called with a reluctant note; hawks floated smoothly above the fields and often stopped dead, with wings working at full speed and tails fanned out.

We sat there motionless, overcome by the heat. Suddenly we heard a noise behind us in the ravine; someone was coming down to the spring. I looked round and saw a peasant of about fifty, covered in dust, wearing a shirt and plaited shoes, with a basketwork satchel and a coat slung over his shoulders. He came across to the source, drank thirstily and rose to his feet again.

'Hey, Vlas!' exclaimed Tuman, after taking a good look at him. 'Hallo, boy. Where have you come from?'

'Hallo, Mikhailo Savelyich,' said the peasant, walking over to us. 'I've come from miles away.'

'Where have you been all this time?' Tuman asked him.

'I walked to Moscow to see the master.'

'Why?'

'I went to ask him something.'

'What did you want to ask him?'

'To lower my rent, or to move me, or let me work instead of paying ... Since my son died I can't manage on my own any more.'

'Your son died?'

'Yes. He lived in Moscow,' added the peasant, after a silence; 'he was a cabman; he used to pay my rent for me.'

'But *do* you pay rent these days?'

'Yes.'

'And what did your master say?'

'What did he say? He threw me out. He said: "How dare you come straight to me? That's what the factor's for," he says, "and you ought to report to him first . . . and where can I move you to, anyway? You pay your own arrears first," he says. He got very angry.'

'So now you've walked all the way back again?'

'Yes. I went to find out whether my boy hadn't left any belongings behind, but I couldn't make head or tail of it. I told his master that I was Philip's father, but he says to me: "How should I know? Besides, your son left nothing; he still owed me money," he says. So I came back again.'

The peasant told us the whole story with a grin, as if talking about someone else; but in his little shrunken eyes a tear hovered, and his lips twitched.

'What are you doing now – going home?'

'Where else? Of course I'm going home. I expect that by now my wife is whistling in her fist with hunger.'

'But you could . . . well . . .' began Styopushka suddenly, then grew confused, broke off, and began fumbling in his pot.

'Will you go to the factor?' Tuman continued, after a surprised glance at Styopushka.

'What should I go to him for? . . . Even so, I've got my arrears to pay. My son was sick for about a year before he died and could not even pay his own rent . . . but it's all the same to me: there's nothing they can take from me . . . No, my friend, however clever you are, you won't catch me, I haven't got a farthing.' The peasant burst out laughing. 'However sharp he may be, that fellow Kintilyan Semyonich, all the same . . .'

Vlas began to laugh again.

'What? That's bad, Vlas,' said Tuman slowly.

'What's bad? It's not . . .' Vlas's voice broke off. 'What a scorching day,' he went on, wiping his face with his sleeve.

'Who is your master?' I asked.

'Count ——, Valeryan Petrovich.'

'The son of Pyotr Ilyich?'

'Yes,' answered Tuman. 'Pytor Ilyich, his late Lordship, while he was still alive, gave his son the village where Vlas lives.'

'Is he alive and well?'

'Yes, praise be to God,' rejoined Vlas. 'He's got so red in the face, he's all sort of mottled.'

'That's how it is, sir,' continued Tuman, turning to me. 'If it had been near Moscow, it wouldn't have been so bad, but he's been settled *here* and has to pay rent.'

'What are you assessed at?'

'Ninety-five roubles,' muttered Vlas.

'Well, you see how it is: there's very little land, and what there is is under timber for the master.'

'And even that has been sold, they say,' observed the peasant.

'Well, that's how it is...Styopushka, give us a worm... Hey, Styopushka, have you dropped off to sleep, or what?' Styopushka started up. The peasant sat down beside us. We fell silent again. On the other bank someone started singing, but such a melancholy song...My poor friend Vlas grew sadder and sadder.

Half an hour later we parted.

The Country Doctor

ONE AUTUMN, on the way back from an outlying property, I caught a heavy chill. Luckily I was in the local market-town, at the inn, when the fever came on. I sent for the doctor. After half an hour he appeared, a shortish, thinnish man, with black hair. He prescribed the usual sudorific, ordered a mustard-plaster to be applied, deftly tucked my five-rouble note away up his sleeve – meanwhile coughing loudly, it is true, and averting his gaze – and was on the point of going home, when somehow or other he got talking and stayed on. I was oppressed by my fever; I foresaw a sleepless night and was glad to have the chance of a talk with the good man. We had tea served. My friend the doctor let himself go. The little fellow was no fool. He had a lively and rather amusing way of expressing himself. It's strange how things happen in life: you live with someone for a long time, you are on the best of terms, yet you never once speak to them frankly and from the heart; with someone else, you've hardly even got acquainted – and there you are: as if at confession, one or other of you is blurting out all his most intimate secrets. I do not know what I did to deserve the confidence of my new friend – anyway, for no particular reason, he got going, as they say, and told me a rather remarkable story, which I will relate here for the benefit of my courteous reader. I will try to express myself in the doctor's own words.

'You don't happen to know,' he began, in a voice that had grown suddenly faint and trembling (such is the effect of unadulterated 'birch' snuff), 'you don't happen to know our local judge, Pavel Lukich Mylov? You don't? . . . Well, it doesn't matter.' He cleared his throat and wiped his eyes. 'Anyway, this is the story. Let me see, now – to be exact, it was in Lent, at the time of the thaw. I was sitting at the judge's, playing Preference. Our judge is a capital fellow and a great hand at Preference. Suddenly' – this was a word that the doctor often used – 'a message comes that someone is asking for me. I say, "What does he want?" "He's brought a note" – doubtless from a patient. "Give me the note," I say. Yes: it's from a patient... Well, all right – you know, it's our daily bread... The note is from a landowner's widow; she says: "My daughter is dying, for God's sake come, I've sent horses to fetch you." Well, that's all right... but the lady lives twenty versts from town, and night's upon us, and the roads are in such a state, my word! and the lady herself is not so well off as she was; two silver roubles is the most you can expect, and even that is doubtful. Perhaps all that I shall get out of it will be a piece of linen and a little flour... However, duty first, you know: someone's dying. At once I pass my hand to Councillor Kalliopin and return home. I see a small cart standing outside my porch; real peasant's horses – enormous pot-bellies, and woolly hair as thick as felt; and a coachman sitting bareheaded, as a sign of respect. Well, my friend, I think, it's plain that *your* masters don't eat off gold plate... You, sir, may well smile, but I tell you: we are poor men in our profession and we have to notice all these things... If the coachman sits up like a prince and doesn't take off his cap, if he sniggers at you in his beard and toys with his whip – you can rely on a couple of five-rouble notes. But this turn-out here is a very different pair of shoes. Well, I think, it can't be helped: duty first. I grab the essential medicines, and off I go. Believe me, it was all we could do to get there. The road was hellish: streams, snow, mud, ravines, then, suddenly, a burst dam. Chaos! At last I'm there. A little house with a thatched roof. The windows are lit up: they must be waiting for me. A dignified little old lady in a cap comes to meet me. "Save her," she says, "she is dying." I say: "Pray calm yourself... Where is the patient?" "Here, please come this way." I see a small, clean room, an oil-lamp in the corner, on the bed a girl of about twenty, unconscious, heat fairly blazing from her, breathing heavily: a high fever. There are two other girls there, too, her sisters – badly scared, and in tears. "Yesterday," they say, "she was perfectly well and had a good appetite; this morning she complained of a headache, then suddenly in the evening she became like this." I repeat again, "Pray calm yourselves" – it's part of the doctor's job, you know – and I set to work. I bleed her, I order mustard-plasters, I prescribe a mixture. Meanwhile I look at her. I look and look; my goodness, never have I seen such a face before . . . an absolute beauty! I feel so sorry for the girl, it fairly tears me to pieces. Such lovely features, such eyes . . . At last, thank God, she gets more comfortable; she begins to sweat, partly recovers consciousness; looks round, smiles, passes her hand over her face . . . The sisters bend over her and ask: "What's the matter?" "Nothing," she says, and turns her head away . . . I look – she's dropped off to sleep. "Well," I say, "now we must leave the patient in peace." We all tiptoe out; only the maid stays behind in case of emergencies. In the sitting-room the samovar's on the table and a bottle of rum beside it: in our job we can't get along without it. They gave me tea; they asked me to stay the night. I accepted: where else could I go at that hour! The old lady keeps up a steady groaning. "What's the matter?" I ask. "She'll live; calm yourself and go to bed: it's two o'clock." "You'll have me woken up if anything happens?" "Of course I will." The old lady retired and the girls went to their room; a bed was put up for me in the drawing-room. I lay down – but couldn't get to sleep, strangely enough. You'd have thought that I'd worried my head enough already. I couldn't get my patient out of my head. Finally I could stand it no longer and all of a sudden I got up; I thought I'd just go and see how she was. Her bedroom adjoined the drawing-room. Well, I got up, and quietly opened the door, and my heart was fairly beating away. I saw the maid asleep, with her mouth open, snoring away like an animal, and the patient lying with her face towards me, her arms moving restlessly, poor girl! I went up to her . . . and suddenly she opened her eyes and stared at me. "Who are you?" I felt awkward. "Don't be afraid," I said; "I am the doctor; I've come to see how you feel." "You're the doctor?" "Yes, I am . . . your mother sent for me from town; we've bled you, and now, please, you must rest, and in two days, with God's help, we shall have you up and about." "Oh, yes, yes, doctor, don't let me die . . . please, please." "Good heavens, whatever next!" But, I thought to myself, the fever is on her again; I felt her pulse: yes, I was right. She looked at me – and suddenly she took me by the hand. "I'll tell you why I don't want to die, I'll tell you . . . now that we're alone: only not a word, please . . . listen . . ." I bent over her; her lips moved right against my ear, her hair touched my cheek – I admit, my head went round in circles – and she began to whisper . . . I didn't understand a word . . . Oh, of course, she must be delirious. She whispered and whispered, but so quickly, as if in a foreign language, and when she had done she shuddered, dropped her head on the pillow and raised a finger at me. "Listen, doctor, not a word." . . . Somehow or other I calmed her, gave her a drink, woke the maid and went out.'

The doctor took another violent pinch of snuff and sat stock-still for a moment.

'Anyhow,' he continued, 'next day, contrary to my expectations, the patient was no better. I thought and thought and suddenly decided to stay on, although I had other patients waiting for me . . . You know, one shouldn't neglect them: it's bad for one's practice. But, in the first place, the girl was really desperately ill; and secondly, to tell the truth, I felt myself strongly attracted to her. Besides, I liked the whole family. Although they were very hard up, they were extraordinarily cultivated people . . . The father had been a scholar, a writer; he died a poor man, of course, but he'd managed to give his children an excellent education; he left them a lot of books, too. Whether it was because I put my whole heart into looking after the patient, or whether there were other reasons, anyway, I'd go so far as to say that they came to love me in that house like one of the family . . . Meanwhile the thaw got worse and worse: communications were completely broken, I could hardly even get medicines sent out from town . . . The girl got no better . . . day after day, day after day . . . but then . . . well . . .' The doctor paused. 'The truth is that I don't know how to explain to you...' He took another pinch of snuff, sneezed, and swallowed a gulp of tea... 'I'll tell you straight out, my patient... how shall I put it?... fell in love with me, I suppose... or rather, she wasn't exactly in love... but anyway... it's certainly...' The doctor looked down and blushed.

'No,' he continued with some animation, '"Love" is the wrong word. One must see oneself at one's own worth, after all. She was a cultivated, intelligent, well-read girl, and I, well, I'd even forgotten my Latin, more or less completely. My figure, too' – and the doctor looked at himself with a smile – 'is nothing to boast about, I think. But God didn't make me a fool either: I don't call white black; I've got a mind that works at times. For instance, I understood very well that what Alexandra Andreyevna – that was her name – felt towards me was not love, but affection, so to speak, regard, or what not. Although she herself probably misread her feelings towards me, her condition was such, as you can imagine... Anyhow,' added the doctor, who had uttered all these disjointed statements without drawing breath, and with obvious embarrassment, 'I think I've let my tongue run away with me... and the result is that you won't understand what happened... so I'll tell you the story in its proper order.'

He finished his glass of tea and resumed in a calmer voice.

'This is how it was. My patient continued to get worse and worse. You, my good sir, are not a doctor; you have no idea of what goes on inside a doctor's head, especially in his early days, when it dawns on him that a patient's illness is defeating him. All his self-assurance vanishes into thin air. I can't tell you how scared he gets. It seems to him that he's forgotten everything he ever knew, that his patient has no confidence in him, that other people are beginning to notice that he's out of his depth, and don't want to describe the patient's symptoms, that they are looking at him strangely, and whispering... oh, it's terrible! He feels there must be some way of treating the case if only it could be found. Perhaps this is it? He tries – no, wrong after all. He leaves no time for the treatment to take its proper effect...He snatches first at one method, then at another. He takes up his book of prescriptions...here it is, he thinks, this is it! To be quite honest, sometimes he opens the book at random: this, he thinks, must be the hand of fate...Meanwhile there is someone dying; someone whom another doctor would have saved. I must have another opinion, you think; I won't take the whole responsibility myself. But what a fool you look on such occasions! Well, as time goes on, you get used to it, you say to yourself: never mind. The patient has died – it's not your fault; you only followed the rules. But what disturbs you still more is this: when other people have blind confidence in yourself, and all the time you know that you're helpless. It was exactly such confidence that all Alexandra Andreyevna's family felt towards me: they no longer even thought of her as in danger. And I, on my side, was assuring them that there was nothing to worry about, but really my heart was in my boots. To make things even worse, the thaw became so bad that the coachman spent whole days fetching medicines. Meanwhile I never left the patient's room; I simply couldn't tear myself away. I told her all sorts of funny stories; I played cards with her; I spent the nights at her bedside. The old lady would thank me with tears in her eyes; but I thought to myself: I don't deserve your gratitude. I confess to you frankly – there is no reason why I should conceal it now – I was in love with my patient. And Alexandra Andreyevna grew fonder and fonder of me: she would allow no one into her room except me. We would get talking; she would ask me where I studied, what sort of life I led, and about my parents and my friends. And I felt that we shouldn't be talking, but to stop her, stop her really firmly, was more than I could do. I would bury my head in my hands: what are you doing, scoundrel?...And then she would take my hand and hold it, look at me for a long, long time, turn away, sigh and say: "How good you are!" Her hands were so feverish, her eyes so big and languid. "Yes," she would say. "You're a good, kind man. You're not like our neighbours ...you're quite, quite different...To think that I never knew you until now!" "Alexandra Andreyevna, calm yourself," I'd say. "Believe me, I appreciate it; I don't know what I've done to... only calm yourself, for heaven's sake, calm yourself... everything will be all right; you'll get quite well again." By the way, I must tell you,' added the doctor, leaning forward and lifting his eyebrows, 'they had little to do with their neighbours, because the smaller people weren't up to them, and they were too proud to get to know the richer ones. I tell you, it was an extraordinarily cultivated family; so that, for me, it was quite flattering. Alexandra would only take her medicine from my hands... the poor girl would lift herself up, with my help, swallow the medicine and gaze at me... and my heart would fairly turn over. But all the time she was getting worse and worse: she will die, I thought, she will surely die. Believe me or not, I would gladly have lain in the coffin instead of her; but there were her mother and sisters watching me, looking into my eyes, and I could feel their confidence on the wane. "Well, how is she?" "Nothing to worry about, nothing at all" – but what did I mean, "nothing at all"? My head was in a daze. There I was, one night, alone, as usual, sitting at the bedside. The maid was sitting in the room too, snoring for all she was worth... well, one couldn't find fault with the poor girl, she too was quite exhausted. Alexandra had been feeling very bad the whole evening; the fever gave her no rest. Right up to midnight she had been tossing away; at last she seemed to fall asleep; at any rate she stopped moving and lay still. The oil-lamp was burning in the corner in front of the icon. I sat there, my head dropped forward, you know, and I too dozed off. Suddenly it was as if someone had given me a push in the ribs; I looked round... God Almighty! Alexandra was staring at me wide-eyed... her lips parted, her cheeks aflame. "What is it?" "Doctor, am I going to die?" "For heaven's sake!" "No, please, doctor, please, don't tell me that I'm going to live... don't tell me that... if only you knew... listen, for God's sake don't try to hide my condition from me." I noticed how quickly she was breathing. "If I can know for sure that I am going to die... then I can tell you everything I have to say." "Alexandra Andreyevna, for mercy's sake!"

"Listen, I haven't slept a wink, I've been looking and looking at you . . . for God's sake . . . I trust you, you're kind, you're honest, I implore you by everything that's holy on earth – tell me the truth! If only you knew how much it matters to me . . . Doctor, tell me, for God's sake, am I in danger?" "What *can* I tell you, Alexandra Andreyevna?" "For God's sake, I beseech you to tell me." "Alexandra Andreyevna, I can't hide the truth from you – you *are* in danger, but God is merciful . . ." "I'm going to die, I'm going to die . . ." And it was as if she was overjoyed at the thought, her face lit up so; I was fairly terrified. "Never fear, never fear, death has no terror for me." All of a sudden she raised herself on one elbow. "Now . . . well, now I can tell you that I'm grateful to you from all my heart; that you're good and kind; that I love you." . . . I looked at her like a man possessed; I can tell you, I had quite a creepy feeling . . . "Listen to me. I love you." "Alexandra Andreyevna, what have I done to deserve this?" "No, no, you don't understand me, my dear one . . ." And suddenly she reached out, took my head in her hands and kissed me. Believe me or not, it was all I could do not to cry out loud . . . I fell on my knees and hid my head in the pillow. She said nothing; her fingers trembled on my hair; I could hear her crying. I began to comfort her, to assure her . . . I really don't know what I said to her. "You'll wake the maid . . . believe me when I say . . . how grateful I am . . . and calm yourself." "Don't . . . don't," she kept repeating. "Never mind any of them, let them wake, let them come – it doesn't signify: I'm dying anyway . . . Why are you so shy and timid? Lift your head . . . Or can it be that you don't love me, that I was mistaken? . . . If that is so, please forgive me." "What are you saying? . . . I love you, Alexandra Andreyevna." She gazed at me, straight in the eyes, and opened her arms. "Then, put your arms around me." . . . I tell you honestly: I don't understand how I got through that night without going out of my mind. I knew that my patient was killing herself; I saw that she was half-delirious; I also understood that if she had not believed herself on the point of death, she would never have given me a thought; but, say what you like, there must be something appalling about dying at twenty-five without ever having loved; that was the thought that tormented her, that was why, in despair, she seized on me. Now do you see it all? She still held me tightly in her arms. "Have pity on me, Alexandra Andreyevna, have pity on us both," I said. "Why?" she answered, "what is there to pity? Don't you understand that I've got to die?" She kept on repeating this phrase. "If I knew that I was going to live and turn into a well-brought-up young lady again, I should be ashamed, yes, ashamed . . . but, as it is? . . ." "And who told you that you were going to die?" "Oh, no, enough of that, you can't deceive me, you don't know how to lie, just look at yourself." "You will live, Alexandra Andreyevna; I will cure you; we will ask your mother for her blessing . . . nothing will part us; we shall be happy." "No, no, I have your word that I must die . . . you promised me . . . you told me I must . . ." It was a bitter moment for me, bitter for many reasons. You know, sometimes small things can happen: they amount to nothing, but they hurt all the same. It occurred to her to ask me my name, my Christian name, I mean. Of course it would be my ill-luck to be called Trifon.[1] Yes, sir; Trifon, Trifon Ivanich. In the house, all the family called me doctor. Well, there was nothing for it, so I answered: "Trifon." She screwed her eyes up, shook her head and whispered something in French – oh, it was something unflattering, and she laughed unkindly, too. Well, like this, I spent almost the whole night with her. At dawn I went out, like one possessed; it was midday when I returned to her room, after taking tea. God Almighty! You couldn't recognize her: I've seen prettier sights laid out in the coffin. Upon my word, I don't know to this day, I simply don't know how I stood the ordeal. For three days and three nights my patient's life still flickered on . . . and what nights they were! What things she told me! . . . On the last night of the three – just fancy – I was sitting beside her, praying now for one thing only: O, God, take her quickly, and take me

1 'Trifon' is roughly the equivalent of 'Cuthbert'. – *Translators.*

as well . . . when suddenly the old lady, her mother, burst into the room . . . I had already told her the day before that there was little hope, that things were bad, and that it would be as well to send for the priest. As soon as she saw her mother, the sick girl said: "I'm glad that you've come . . . look at us, we love each other, we are pledged to each other." "What's she saying, doctor, what's she saying?" I went pale as death. "She's delirious," I said, "it's the fever." But then, from Alexandra: "Enough of that, just now you spoke to me quite differently and accepted my ring . . . Why pretend? My mother is kind, she will forgive, she will understand, but I am dying – why should I lie? Give me your hand." I jumped up and ran from the room. Of course, the old lady guessed the whole story.

'Anyway, I won't attempt to bore you further, and, what's more, to tell you the truth, it hurts me to remember. The following day my patient passed away. May God rest her soul!" added the doctor hurriedly, with a sigh. 'Before she died, she asked that everyone should go out and leave me alone with her. "Forgive me," she said. "Perhaps I've acted wrongly towards you . . . it's my illness . . . but, believe me, I've never loved anyone more than you . . . don't forget me . . . treasure my ring . . ."'

The doctor turned away; I seized him by the hand.

'Och!' he said, "let's talk about something else, or perhaps you'd like a little game of Preference for low stakes? You know, in our profession we should never give way to such exalted sentiments. In our profession all we should think about is how to stop the children from yelling and the wife from nagging. For, since then, I have gone in for holy matrimony, as they call it . . . with a vengeance . . . I married a merchant's daughter: seven thousand roubles dowry. Her name is Akulina; it's on a par with Trifon. A spiteful hag, I must say, but luckily she sleeps all day . . . What about that game of Preference?'

We got down to Preference for copeck stakes. Trifon Ivanich won two and a half roubles from me – and went home late, very pleased with his victory.

My Neighbour Radilov

I N THE autumn, woodcock are often to be found in the old type of lime-tree plantation. We have quite a number of such plantations in the province of Orel. Our forefathers, when choosing places to live in, never failed to plant five acres of good ground with orchards and avenues of lime. After fifty or often seventy years, these seats, these 'gentle homes', have gradually vanished from the face of the earth. The houses rotted away or were sold for scrap, the stone outbuildings were reduced to heaps of rubble, the apple-trees died and were sawn up into firewood, the hedges and fences were obliterated. Only the limes went on growing in their pristine glory and, now surrounded by ploughed fields, they speak to this feather-headed generation of 'our fathers and forefathers that went before us'. This old lime is a splendid tree . . . It is spared even by the Russian peasant's ruthless axe. Its leaves grow delicately, its mighty branches spread out far and wide and beneath them there is perpetual shade.

One day, roaming the fields with Ermolai after partridges, I found myself beside one of these neglected plantations and made my way towards it. As soon as I came up to the fringe of it, a woodcock rose noisily from a bush, I fired, and at the same moment, from a few paces away, there came a cry, the frightened face of a young girl looked out from behind the trees and immediately disappeared again. Ermolai came running up to me. 'What are you shooting here for? there's a gentleman lives here.' There was not time for me to answer him, nor for my dog, with noble self-importance, to bring me the dead bird, when hurried steps were heard and a tall man with moustaches emerged from the brushwood and came to a halt in front of me, wearing an expression of displeasure. I made such excuses as I could, said who I was, and offered him the bird which had been shot on his property.

'Very well,' he said with a smile, 'I'll accept your bird, but only on condition that you stay and dine with us.'

I confess that I was not overjoyed by his suggestion, but it would have been impossible to refuse. 'This is my land. I am your neighbour Radilov – you may have heard of me,' continued my new acquaintance. 'To-day being Sunday, there ought to be a decent dinner at home, otherwise I wouldn't have invited you.'

I answered as one does on such occasions, and set off at his heels. A path which had recently been cleared soon led us from the lime-grove up to a kitchen-garden. Between ancient apple-trees and overgrown gooseberry-bushes, cabbages displayed their round, pale-green, mottled heads; hop tendrils wound their way round tall stakes; the borders were closely studded with brown stakes, lost in a mass of withered peas; great flat pumpkins lay about on the ground; yellow cucumbers were revealed underneath their dusty angular leaves; along the fence tall nettles waved; in two or three places there grew bushes of tartar, honeysuckle, elder, and dog-rose – remnants of former shrubberies. Close to a small pond, full of slimy reddish water, was a well, surrounded by puddles; ducks were splashing and waddling fussily about in them; in an open space a dog, trembling all over and screwing up its eyes, was gnawing a bone; close at hand a piebald cow was lazily browsing the grass, with an occasional flick of her tail against her bony back. The path took a turning, and behind a thick clump of willows and birches a small, grey old house with a wooden roof and a crooked porch peeped out at us. Radilov halted.

'By the way,' he said, looking me full in the face, with a good-natured expression, 'it's just occurred to me that perhaps you don't feel at all like coming in; in that case . . .'

I didn't let him finish, but assured him that on the contrary I would be delighted to dine with him.

'Well, it's as you wish.'

We went into the house. A young fellow in a long coat of thick blue cloth met us in the porch. Radilov at once told him to give Ermolai a drink of vodka. My hunter bowed respectfully towards the back of the munificent donor. From a hall adorned with various brightly-coloured pictures and hung with check curtains, we went into a small room – Radilov's study. I took off my shooting gear and put my gun in the corner. The boy in the long-skirted coat fussed around brushing me.

'Well, now let's go into the drawing-room,' said Radilov agreeably; 'I want to introduce you to my mother.'

I followed him. In the drawing-room, on a sofa in the middle of the room, sat a little old lady in a brown dress and a white bonnet, with a kind, thin face, and a timid, sad expression.

'Mother, let me introduce our neighbour.'

The old lady half-rose and bowed to me without loosening the grip of her bony hands on her bulging, sack-shaped worsted reticule.

'Have you been in our part of the country for long?' she asked in a low, faint voice, blinking her eyes.

'No, not for long.'

'Do you think of staying here for some time?'

'Until winter, I think.'

The old lady said nothing.

'Now,' interposed Radilov, drawing my attention to a tall thin man whom I hadn't noticed as I came into the drawing-room, 'this is Fyodor Mikheich . . . Well, Fedya, show our guest your skill. Why are you hiding in the corner?'

Fyodor Mikheich at once rose from his chair, took a rickety violin from the window-sill, grasped the bow, not correctly by one end, but by the middle, propped the violin against his chest, shut his eyes, and went off into a dance, humming the tune and scraping away at the strings. He looked about seventy; his long nankeen coat hung sadly on his thin bony limbs. He danced; now he would perform a dashing jig, now sway his little bald head from side to side with a swooning motion and stick out his lean neck; he stood and stamped his feet; sometimes, with obvious difficulty, he flexed his knees; from his toothless mouth came a senile quavering. Radilov must have guessed from my expression that Fedya's 'skill' was giving me no particular satisfaction.

'Thanks, old fellow, that will do,' he said. 'You can go and get your reward.' Fyodor at once put down his violin on the window-sill, bowed, first to me, as a guest, then to the old lady, then to Radilov, and went out of the room.

'He was a landowner, too,' went on my new friend, 'and a rich one, but he ruined himself – and here he is, living with me . . . In his day he was the biggest rake in the province; he ran off with two people's wives, kept his own singers, sang and danced like a master . . . But won't you have some vodka? Dinner's on the table.'

A young girl, the same one I had seen for a flash in the garden, came into the room.

'Ah, and here is Olga!' remarked Radilov, with a slight turn of his head. 'Let me recommend her to your kindness . . . Well, let's go and dine.'

We went into the dining-room and sat down. While we were passing in from the drawing-room and taking our places, Fyodor, whose 'reward' had made his eyes sparkle and his nose slightly red, sang: '*Let Vict'ry's thunder sound!*' A separate place had been laid for him in a corner, on a little table without a napkin. The poor old man couldn't boast of cleanliness, and was therefore always kept at a certain distance from the company. He crossed himself, sighed, and began to eat with a shark-like voracity. The dinner was indeed not a bad one and, the day being Sunday, it didn't fail to include a quivering jelly and the sweet dish known as 'Spanish puffs'. At table Radilov, who had served ten years in an infantry regiment of the line and had campaigned in Turkey, started telling stories; I listened to him with attention and kept a furtive eye on Olga. She was not particularly pretty, but her calm, decisive expression, her broad, white forehead, her thick hair, and especially her brown eyes, which, though small, were clear and full of intelligence and life, would have struck anyone else in my place. She fairly hung on every word of Radilov's; it was not just interest, it was a passionate concentration which expressed itself in her face. In years, Radilov could have been her father. He addressed her in the second person singular, but I guessed at once that she was not his daughter. In the course of conversation he mentioned his late wife. 'Her sister,' he added, indicating Olga. She blushed swiftly and lowered her eyes. Radilov fell silent, then changed the subject. The old lady didn't utter a word all through dinner; she hardly ate at all, and did not press me to do so either. Her features breathed that air of timorous, hopeless expectancy, that senile melancholy, which lays such a painful hand on the heart of the beholder. At the end of dinner, Fyodor was starting to 'toast' his hosts and their guest, but Radilov glanced at me and begged him to be silent; the old man passed his hand over his lips, blinked, bowed, and sat down again, but this time on the very edge of his chair. After dinner, Radilov and I made our way to his study.

In people who are intensely and continuously preoccupied with a single thought or a single passion, one can detect an element in common, a certain external likeness of manner, however much they may differ in qualities, capability, position in the world, or education. The longer I observed Radilov, the more strongly I became convinced that he belonged to this class of people. He spoke about farming, harvesting and haymaking, about war, local gossip, and the approaching elections. He spoke without constraint, and indeed with concern, then suddenly he would sigh, sink back in his chair, like a man exhausted by heavy labour, and pass his hand over his face. His whole good, warm-hearted nature seemed penetrated through and through and saturated by a single feeling. I had already been surprised by my failure to find any passion on his part, either for food, drink, shooting, nightingales from Kursk, epilepsy in pigeons, Russian literature, trotting horses, Hungarian jackets, cards, billiards, *soirées* with dancing, trips to the provincial or national capitals, paper-mills, sugar-beet factories, painted summer-houses, tea, the progress of viciousness in side-horses, or even for fat coachmen, with belts right up under their armpits, those magnificent coachmen with whom,

heaven knows why, every movement of the neck is accompanied by a roll and a bulge of the eyeballs. . . . 'He's a queer sort of
landowner, anyway,' I thought. But, with it all, he made no
pretence of moroseness or dissatisfaction with his lot; on the
contrary, he fairly radiated undiscriminating goodwill, affabil-
ity and an almost irritating disposition to make friends with
anyone and everyone he met. It was true that at the same time
you felt he was incapable of making really close friends with
anyone, not because he never needed other people's society,
but because for a time his whole life had been directed inwards.
As I gazed at Radilov, I couldn't begin to imagine him happy,
either then or at any other time. He was no beauty, either, but
in his glance, in his smile, in his whole being, there lurked –
lurked in the true sense of the word – something extraordinarily seductive. It made you feel that you wanted to get to know
him better and to love him. Of course sometimes the steppe
landowner bobbed up in him, but all the same he was really a
very fine man.

We were beginning to talk about the new Marshal of
Nobility of the district, when suddenly in the doorway we
heard Olga's voice: 'Tea is ready.'

We went into the drawing-room. As before, Fyodor was
sitting in his corner, between the window and the door, with
his legs modestly drawn in beneath him. Radilov's mother was
knitting a stocking. Through the open windows there came
from the garden a breath of autumn freshness and the smell of
apples. Olga was busy pouring out tea. I looked at her now with
closer attention than I had at dinner. She spoke very little, as is
usually the way with girls of provincial society, but at any rate
I failed to detect in her any desire to say something clever,
accompanied with an agonizing sense of emptiness and help-
lessness; with her there were no sighs, as if from an overflow of
indescribable emotions, no upward rolling of the eyes, no
vague and dreamy smiles. Her gaze was calm and equable, as
of someone who rests after great happiness or great anxiety.
Her gait and her movements were free and resolute. I took a
great liking to her.

Radilov and I got talking again. I no longer remember by what path we came to the familiar observation that so often the most insignificant things produce more of an impression on people than the most important ones.

'Yes,' said Radilov, 'I have had that experience myself. I used to be married, as you know. Not for long...three years; my wife died in childbirth. I thought that I would never survive her; I was terribly distressed, broken, but the tears would not come – I just went about as if I were out of my mind. She was duly dressed and laid out on the table – here in this room. The priest came, the deacons came too and began to sing and pray and to burn incense; I bowed right down to the ground, but couldn't shed a single tear. My heart seemed to have turned to stone, my head, too; and my whole body had become a heavy weight. And so the first day went by. Will you believe me? That night I even managed to sleep. The next morning I went in to look at my wife – it was summer, and the sun shone on her from head to foot and so brightly, too. Suddenly I saw' – here Radilov gave an involuntary shudder – 'what do you think? Her eye was not properly closed, and on it a fly was walking...I dropped like a sheaf of corn, and, as soon as I came to myself again, began to weep and weep – there was just no stopping me....'

Radilov paused. I looked at him, then at Olga... Never shall I forget the expression on her face. The old lady put down the stocking on her knee, took a handkerchief out of her bag and furtively wiped away a tear. Fyodor suddenly got up, seized his violin and struck up a song in a strange, hoarse voice. He probably wanted to cheer us up; but we all shuddered at his first note and Radilov begged him to be quiet.

'Anyhow,' he continued, 'what's gone is gone; there is no going back to the past, and, in the end ... everything is for the best in this world, as Voltaire – wasn't it? – observed,' he added hurriedly.

'Yes,' I rejoined, 'of course. What's more, every misfortune can be endured and there's a way out of every bad situation.'

'Do you think so?' said Radilov. 'Who knows, perhaps you are right. I remember, I was lying in hospital in Turkey, more dead than alive, I had marsh-fever. Well, the quarters were nothing to boast about – it was wartime, of course – but, just the same, they might have been worse. And all of a sudden they bring in more patients – and the question is where to put them. The doctor rushes up and down – there's no room. So up he comes to me and asks the dresser: "Is he alive?" The dresser answers: "He was, this morning." The doctor bends down and listens: he hears my breathing. This was more than the good doctor could stand. "Look how stupid nature is," he said. "Look, here is a man dying, dying for certain, but he has still got a squeak in him, he's still dragging on, he's just taking up a place and keeping the others out." Well, I thought to myself, it looks bad for you, Mikhailo Mikhailich . . . But all the same, I got better and am still alive to-day, as you may have been good enough to observe. So you're right.'

'Whatever happened, I would have been right,' I answered. 'Even if you had died, it would have got you out of the fix that you were in.'

'Yes, to be sure,' he rejoined, thumping his hand loudly on the table. 'It's just a question of making up one's mind . . . What's the point of being in a fix? What's the good of lingering, dragging on? . . .'

Olga got up quickly and went out into the garden.

'Well, Fedya, give us a dance!' exclaimed Radilov.

Fyodor jumped up, crossed the room with the special mincing step of the man who plays 'giddy goat' in front of a tame bear, and began to sing: '*While before our gates . . .*'

From the porch we heard the sound of a racing drozhky, and in a few moments there came into the room a tall, burly, broad-shouldered old man. This was Ovsyanikov the freeholder . . . But Ovsyanikov is such a remarkable and original character, that with the reader's permission we will describe him in the next story. For the moment I will only add, on my own account, that on the next day Ermolai and I went out shooting at daybreak, that after shooting we returned home;

that a week later I again called at Radilov's, but found neither him nor Olga at home, and that two weeks later still I learnt that he had suddenly vanished, left his mother and gone off with his sister-in-law. This incident caused much excitement and discussion throughout the province, and it was only then that I finally understood Olga's expression while Radilov was telling us his story. At that moment her face was not just alive with sympathy: it was on fire with jealousy.

Before leaving the country, I visited Radilov's old mother. I found her in the drawing-room; she was playing a game of 'idiots' with Fyodor Mikheich.

'Have you heard from your son?' I asked her eventually.

The old lady burst into tears. I asked her no more questions about Radilov.

Ovsyanikov the Freeholder

PICTURE TO yourself, dear reader, a tall, stout man of about seventy, with a face rather reminiscent of Krylov's,[1] clear intelligent eyes beneath overhanging brows, a dignified bearing, a measured speech, and a deliberate gait: there you have Ovsyanikov. He wore a capacious long-sleeved blue coat, buttoned right up, a lilac-coloured silk handkerchief round his neck, and brilliantly-polished boots with tassels, and in general had something of the look of a well-to-do merchant. His hands were well-shaped, soft and white: often, in the course of conversation, he would play with the buttons of his coat. With his dignity and immobility, his intelligence and indolence, with his straightforwardness and his obstinacy, Ovsyanikov reminded me of the Russian boyars of the period of Peter the Great. The traditional Russian attire would have suited him well. He was one of the last survivors from the good old days.

All his neighbours had an extraordinary respect for him and considered his acquaintance an honour. His fellow-freeholders practically said their prayers to him, started fingering their hats as soon as they caught sight of him in the distance, and regarded him as their pride. Generally speaking it is difficult to distinguish the Russian freeholder from the peasant. His standard of farming is hardly higher than the peasant's, his calves never budge from the buckwheat field, his horses have little life in them, their harness is made of string. Although he was not known as a man of means, Ovsyanikov was an exception to the general rule. He lived alone with his wife in a neat and cosy little house, he kept a few servants, he dressed them in the Russian manner and referred to them as 'hands'. It was in fact they who ploughed his land. He never pretended to be a nobleman, never posed as a landowner, never, as they say, 'forgot himself', never sat down unless invited to do so, and

1 The well-known writer of fables. – *Translators*.

when a new guest arrived would never fail to rise from his place, but with such dignity, such majestic grace that the guest involuntarily bowed to him all the lower for it. Ovsyanikov kept up the old-fashioned ways, not from superstition (for he was a reasonably open-minded man), but from habit. For example, he disliked carriages with springs, because he found them unrestful, and he travelled either in a racing drozhky or in a neat little cart with a leather cushion. He drove his good bay trotting-horse himself. (He kept only bay horses.) His coachman, a red-cheeked peasant-lad, with hair cropped round a basin, in a plush overcoat and a low hat and with a strap round his waist, sat respectfully at his side. Ovsyanikov always slept after dinner, went to the bath-house on Saturdays, read nothing but religious works (for which he would solemnly fix a pair of round silver spectacles on his nose), rose and retired early. He wore no beard, however, and his hair was cut in the German manner. He gave his guests a joyful welcome, but never made them a deep bow, never fussed over them, never pressed preserves or pickles on them. 'Wife!' he would say slowly, not rising from his place, but slightly turning his head in her direction: 'Bring the gentlemen something tasty.' He considered it a sin to sell corn, since it was the gift of God, and in the year '40, at the time of the great famine and the terrible rise in prices, he distributed all his store to the landowners and peasants of the district; in the following year they gratefully repaid him their debt in kind.

Ovsyanikov's neighbours often appealed to him with requests to decide their disputes and make peace between them, and almost always took his advice and bowed to his decision. Thanks to him, many neighbours finally reached agreement on the boundaries of their land. But after two or three encounters with female landowners, he announced his decision never to mediate between disputants of the opposite sex. He could not stand the flurries, the restless bustle, the old-wives' chatter, the fuss.

Once, somehow or other, his house caught fire, and one of his hands rushed up to him at full speed, crying, 'Fire, fire!'

'Well, what are you shouting about?' said Ovsyanikov calmly. 'Give me my hat and stick . . .' He was fond of training horses himself. Once a fiery steed bolted with him downhill into a ravine. 'Well, that will do, that will do, young colt – or you'll kill yourself,' Ovsyanikov said to him good-naturedly and, a moment later, he was flying into the ravine, complete with his racing drozhky, the boy who sat behind him, the horse and all. Luckily there were piles of sand lying at the bottom of the ravine. No one was hurt, only the horse put its leg out. 'Well, you see,' continued Ovsyanikov in a calm voice as he got up from the ground, 'I told you so.'

He had found a wife after his own heart. Tatyana Ilyinichna Ovsyanikova was a tall, dignified, silent woman, with a brown silk handkerchief permanently tied over her head. She had a chilling presence, although no one had ever accused her of severity. On the contrary, many beggars called her 'mother' and 'kind soul'. Her regular features, her big dark eyes, her fine lips, still testified to a once famous beauty. Ovsyanikov had no children.

As the reader already knows, I made his acquaintance at Radilov's, and two days later I went to call on him. I found him at home. He was sitting in a large leather armchair, reading *The Lives of the Saints*. A grey cat was purring on his shoulder. He received me in his usual manner, warmly and with dignity. We fell into conversation.

'Tell me, Luka Petrovich,' I said in the course of our talk, 'things were better, weren't they, in the old days, in your time?'

'Some things were certainly better, I should say,' rejoined Ovsyanikov. 'We had a quieter life; things were easier, certainly . . . but all the same, it is better now; and for your children it will be better still, please God.'

'And I was so expecting you to sing me the praises of the good old days.'

'No, I have no special reason for praising the good old days. Now take yourself, for example. You're a landowner to-day, as your late grandfather was, but you've nothing like the same power, and you're not the same sort of man, either. Even to-day there are other gentlemen who make life difficult for our sort; but evidently that can't be avoided. First you grind the corn and then you get flour. No, I shall never again see the sort of things that I saw when I was young.'

'But what, for example?'

'Well, take your grandfather's case again. A hard man he was. Did much harm to fellows like us! You may know – of course you will, as it is your own land – the wedge-shaped piece of ground between Chepligin and Malinin? . . . You've got it under oats at the moment . . . Well, it's ours – the whole piece, as it stands, is ours. Your grandfather took it away from us; he rode out, pointed with his hand, and said: "My property," and his property it became. My late father (heaven rest his soul!) was a just man, and a hot-tempered one too; he wouldn't take it lying down – indeed who *is* keen on losing his property? – and he made a petition to the court. He did so by himself, as the others wouldn't support him – they were frightened. So they told your grandfather: "Pyotr Ovsyanikov is putting in a complaint against you, sir, on the grounds that you have taken away his land." . . . Your grandfather at once sent his huntsman Bausch to our home with a whole troop of fellows . . . And they took my father and carried him off to your estate. I was a little boy then, I ran after him barefoot. What next? They brought him to your home and flogged him right under the windows. And your grandfather stands on the balcony and looks on; and your grandmother sits in the window and looks, too. My father cries out: "Marya Vasilyevna, gracious lady, save me – *you* at least should have pity on me." But all she does, d'you see, is sit up straight and look on. Well, they made my father promise to give up his claim to the land, and then made him say thank you for having been let off with his life. So the land stayed with you. Go and ask your peasants what the land is called. It's called "cudgel field", because it was taken away with the cudgel. That's the sort of reason why we simple folk don't miss the old ways too badly.'

I didn't know how to answer Ovsyanikov and I didn't dare look him in the face.

'Then we had another neighbour on our hands about that time – Komov, Stefan Niktopolionich. He fairly drove my father to death – first in one way, then in another. He was a drunken fellow and liked entertaining others, but when after a drop or two he would come out in French with "*say bon*" and lick his lips – it was more even than a saint could bear. He'd send out and summon all his neighbours. He'd have a troika standing ready and if you didn't come at once he'd pay you a surprise visit himself... What a strange fellow he was! When he was sober he didn't tell lies but, as soon as he'd had a drink, he'd begin to tell you that he had three houses on the Fontanka in Petersburg: one, red, with one chimney; another, yellow, with two chimneys; the third, blue, with no chimneys; and three sons (and he never so much as married): one in the infantry, one in the cavalry, and the third *all on his own*... And he'd say that he had a son living in each house, and that the eldest entertained admirals, the second entertained generals, and the youngest entertained Englishmen only! Then up he'd get and say: "To the health of my eldest son, he's the best son of the lot!" and he'd begin to cry. And woe betide anyone who wouldn't drink with him. "I'll shoot you!" he'd say, "and I won't let them bury you either!" Then he'd jump up and shout: "Dance, good people, dance for your own entertainment and my consolation!" Well, you'd have to dance, even if it killed you, you'd have to dance. He gave his serf girls terrible trouble. They had to be singing choruses all the livelong night and the one who raised her voice the highest would get a prize. But if they started to get tired he would put his head in his hands and feel sorry for himself: "Oh, fatherless orphan that I am! They're dropping me, like the poor little thing that I am!" The grooms would at once put fresh heart into the girls. He took a liking to my father, and there was nothing to be done about it... he nearly drove him to his grave, and would have done so quite, but luckily he died first himself. He fell down from a dovecote when he was drunk. That's the sort of nice neighbours we used to have.'

'How the times have changed,' I observed.

'Yes, yes,' agreed Ovsyanikov. 'But, there's the other side, too. In the olden days the nobility lived on a grander scale. Not to mention the real magnates; I saw plenty of them in Moscow. I've heard that now they've died out, even there.'

'You have been in Moscow?'

'Yes, long, long ago. I'm now seventy-two, and I went to Moscow when I was fifteen.'

Ovsyanikov sighed.

'Whom did you see there?'

'I saw any number of great magnates – everybody did; they lived openly, in a blaze of glory and admiration. But there was not one of them to touch Count Alexei Grigoryevich Orlov-Chesmensky. I often saw Alexei Grigoryevich; my uncle served as his steward. The Count lived by the Kaluga Gates, on the Shabolovka. There was a real magnate for you! Such presence, such graciousness of manner, not to be imagined or described. His size alone was something extraordinary, and his strength, his expression! Until you knew him, you would be too shy and frightened to enter his house; but once you went in, he would warm you like the sun and all your spirits would rise. He was accessible to everyone, and very open-minded. At the races he drove himself and was ready to take on anybody. And he would never overtake them at once, he'd never hurt their feelings or pull them up short, but he'd just pass them at the very end; and so nice about it, too – he'd console his opponent and praise his horse. He kept tumbler-pigeons of the very best breed. Sometimes he'd go out into the courtyard, sit down in an armchair and order the pigeons to be let out; and all around, on the roof, would be men standing with guns to keep the hawks off. At the Count's feet they'd put a big silver bowl full of water; he'd look into the water, too, to see the pigeons play in it. The poor and needy lived by hundreds on his charity . . . and what fortunes he gave away! When he was angry, it was like a thunderclap. It was terrifying – but nothing really to cry about; you'd look again – and already he'd be smiling. He would give a feast – and make all Moscow drunk . . . And what a brain he had! Look how he beat the Turk. He liked wrestling, too; they brought him champions from Tula, from Kharkov, from Tambov, from all over the place: the ones he threw he'd reward; but if anyone threw him, he'd load him with presents and kiss him on the mouth . . . While I was in Moscow, he gave a party the like of which had never been seen in Russia. He invited to his house all the sportsmen in the whole country, and fixed a day three months ahead. So they all assembled, they brought with them their dogs and huntsmen – why, it was an army, a whole army, that arrived! First of all they feasted in proper style, then they went out to the gates. The people came swarming together! . . . And what d'you think happened? . . . Your grandfather's dog came in first of the lot.'

'Not Milovidka?' I asked.

'Yes, Milovidka . . . So the Count started asking your grandfather to sell him his dog: "Take what you like," says he. "No, Count," says your grandfather, "I am no merchant: I am no seller of unwanted trash; for honour's sake I would be ready even to yield up my wife, only not Milovidka . . . I'd sooner give my own self up into captivity." Alexei Grigoryevich praised him: "That's what I like to hear," he says. Your grandfather took Milovidka back in his carriage; and when Milovidka died, he gave her a funeral with music in his park – he gave the bitch a funeral and set up a headstone with an inscription over her body.'

'Well, your Alexei Grigoryevich certainly gave offence to nobody,' I observed.

'Yes, it's always the same way: it's the small chap that picks the quarrels.'

'And what was this fellow Bausch like?' I asked, after a pause.

'How is it that you've heard of Milovidka and not of Bausch? . . . He was your grandfather's head huntsman and whipper-in. Your grandfather loved him as much as he loved Milovidka. He was a desperate fellow, and whatever your grandfather ordered, he would carry out in the twinkling of an eye – even if it meant climbing on to a knife. And what a halloo he would give: the whole forest would fairly ring with it.

And then he'd suddenly set his jaw, dismount, and lie down...and the moment the hounds no longer heard his voice, the game was up! They'd drop the hottest scent, they'd not run farther for anything in the world. Eh, how angry your grandfather would get! "Don't let me live a moment longer if I can't hang the lazy rascal! I'll turn the devil inside out! I'll drag the scoundrel's heels out through his throat!" But it'd all end by his sending to find out what Bausch wanted and why he wasn't hallooing, and Bausch would then generally ask for a drink, swallow it, get up, and start tallyhoing again for all he was worth.'

'You're fond of hunting, too, Luka Petrovich, I think?'

'I might have been, certainly – but not now: now my day is over – but when I was young...though, you know, it's awkward, because of my standing. It isn't right that fellows like us should ape the nobility. It is true, you may find one of our kind, some drunken idiot who becomes a hanger-on of the gentry ...and what a time he has!...all he does is make a fool of himself. They give him a rotten, stumbling horse; they keep on knocking his cap off on to the ground; they give him a stinging blow with the whip and pretend it was meant for the horse; and all the time it's his job to laugh and make the others laugh too. No, I'll tell you: the humbler your station, the stricter the watch you must keep on yourself if you want to avoid the mud.

'Yes,' continued Ovsyanikov, with a sigh. 'Plenty of water has flowed under the bridges since I've been in the world: the times have changed indeed. I see a specially big change among the nobility. The small landowners have all either gone into the Government service, or else don't stay at home; and as for the bigger fellows, they're not the same men any more. I've seen enough of them, your big landowners, in these boundary cases, and I'm bound to tell you: it delights my heart to see how amiable and obliging they are. The only thing that surprises me is this: they have learnt all the sciences, they talk so eloquently that it fairly melts your heart, but they make no sense out of the business in hand, they're not even conscious of their own interest; any clerk, their own serf, can bend them any way he wants, like so many longbows. You perhaps know Korolev, Alexander Vladimirich. A nobleman through and through, handsome, rich, been to those universities abroad even, I believe, fluent and modest of speech, shakes hands with us all. You know him? . . . Well, listen, then. Last week we all assembled at Berezovka at the invitation of Nikifor Ilyich, the arbitrator. And Nikifor Ilyich the arbitrator says to us: "Gentlemen, we must demarcate our land, it's shameful, our district is so badly behind-hand. Let's get busy." So we did. As usual, there was arguing and quarrelling; our attorney started to be tiresome. But it was Porfyry Ovchinnikov who began the trouble . . . And what about? . . . He himself does not own a square foot of land: he's acting on his brother's behalf. He shouts: "No, you can't cheat *me*! No, you're up against someone of a different kind! Give the plans here! Send the surveyor to me, send the Judas here!" "Well, after all this, what are you claiming?" "D'you think I'm such a fool as that, eh? Do you think that I am going to tell you what my claim is, just like that? . . . No, give the plans here, that's what I say!" and he bangs on the plans with his fists. Marfa Dmitryevna takes mortal offence. She cries: "How dare you defame my reputation?" He answers: "I wouldn't have your reputation even for my bay mare." They had to pour Madeira down her throat. When he calmed down, the others started making trouble instead. Alexander Vladimirovich Korolev, the dear sweet fellow, was sitting in a corner, biting the knob of his cane, and just shaking his head. I felt so ashamed of the whole business, I could stand it no longer, and wanted to run away. What on earth could he be thinking of us? All of a sudden my friend Alexander Vladimirovich gets up and shows that he wants to speak. The arbitrator starts fussing about and says: "Gentlemen, gentlemen, Alexander Vladimirovich wishes to speak." And, to give the gentlemen their due, they all fell silent at once. So Alexander Vladimirovich begins and says: "I think we have forgotten the reason for our assembly: although it's true that demarcation of boundaries is to the advantage of the landowners, what is its real purpose? It is to make things easier for the peasant, to make his work handier for him and his taxes easier to pay; at present he does not know his own land and often walks five miles to do his ploughing – so that you cannot ask too much from him." Then Alexander Vladimirovich said that it was wicked for a landowner not to care about the welfare of his peasants, that, in the long run, if you look at it in the right way, the peasants' interests are exactly the same as ours; if he does well, so do we, if he does badly so do we ... and therefore it is both wicked and ill-considered not to reach agreement because of trifles ... and he went on and on ... and how he spoke! He fairly gripped your heart ... all the gentlemen hung their heads; and as for me, well, I practically burst into tears. Upon my word, you won't find language like his in any old books. But what was the end of it all? He himself refused to give up or sell ten acres of moss-hags. He said: "I am going to drain this marsh with my own labour and I am going to start a cloth factory there, an *improved* cloth factory. I have already chosen the site: I have got my own plans for it. . . ." And had it been fair, it would have been another matter, but the plain truth is that Anton Karasikov, Alexander Vladimirovich's neighbour, had been too mean to give Alexander's agent a bribe of a hundred roubles. So we all went our ways without settling our business. And Alexander Vladimirovich still considers himself in the right and goes on talking about his cloth factory, only he does nothing about draining the marsh.'

'And how does he manage his estate?'

'He's always introducing new methods. His peasants don't like it – but it is no use listening to them. Alexander Vladimirovich is quite right.'

'How is that, Luka Petrovich? I thought you were all for conservatism?'

'My own feelings are a different question. I'm not a nobleman, I'm not a landowner. What do my ideas on farming matter? Anyhow I don't know how to do otherwise. I try to do what is right and just, with God's help. The younger gentry don't like the old ways: I can't blame them ... It's high time people sat down and thought things out. There is only one thing that's a pity: they're all so terribly clever. They treat the peasant like a doll: they turn him this way and that, they break him and throw him away. And the agent, who's a serf, or the bailiff, who's of German origin, gets the peasant into his clutches once more. And if only just one of these young gentlemen would give an example and show how things ought to be done! . . . What will be the end of it? Must I really die without seeing any new system in action? . . . It's a strange thing when the old order passes and there's no new one to take its place!'

I did not know how to answer Ovsyanikov. He looked around, leant closer to me and continued in an undertone: 'Have you heard about Vasily Nikolaich Lyubozvonov?'

'No, I haven't.'

'It's an extraordinary story which you may be able to explain to me. I can't grasp it at all myself. His own peasants told the story but I can't make any sense of what they said. He's a young fellow, you know, and inherited from his mother not long ago. Well, he arrives at his place. The peasants have assembled to have a look at their master. Vasily appears before them. What on earth is it that they see? A master who comes before them in velveteen pantaloons like a coachman, and in boots with trimmings on them: he wears a red shirt, and a coat which is also like a coachman's; he has let his beard grow, and on his head such a queer little hat, and such a queer face too. Not that he is drunk, but just not in his right mind. "Good day to you, my lads; God bless you." The peasants give him a deep bow – but in silence, for he has made them feel shy. And he himself seems to feel shy, too. He begins to make them a speech. "I am Russian," he says, "and you are Russian, too; I love everything that's Russian . . . My soul is Russian and so is my blood." . . . Then suddenly he gives them an order: "Well, my lads, go on, sing me a Russian folk-song." The peasants' knees were all of a tremble; they were knocked quite silly. One stout fellow struck up a song, then dropped down at once and hid behind the others . . . And this is the surprising thing: we have had strange landowners before, gentlemen-desperadoes, regular rakes, certainly: they dressed up as coachmen, I dare say, danced, played the guitar, sang and drank with their own serving-folk, and feasted with the peasants; but this chap Vasily is like a pretty girl: all the time reading books, or writing them, or, if not that, reciting verse aloud – talks to no one, is shyness itself, walks in the garden alone, as if he's bored or sad. The former agent had been quite scared to begin with. Before Vasily's arrival, he ran round the peasants' back-yards, and bowed to them all. Clearly, as they say, the cat had smelt whose meat he had eaten! The peasants were full of hope; they thought to themselves: "No more of your tricks, my friend. Now you'll have to answer for what you've done; now you'll have to dance all right, you mean old rascal! . . ." But instead of that, it turned out – how can I explain it to you? – the Lord himself could not make out what happened! Vasily sends for the agent, talks to him, blushes, you know, and gasps out: "I want you to be just and not to oppress anybody – d'you hear?" And from that day forward he never even sent for him! He lives on his own estate as though he was a stranger there. Well, the agent heaved a sigh of relief, and, as for the peasants, they don't dare to approach Vasily: they're afraid to. And, look, here is another surprising thing: the master bows to them and gives them friendly looks – but their stomachs fairly turn from fear. What an extraordinary story, sir! Eh? . . . Or perhaps I've grown old and stupid or something, and don't understand.'

I answered Ovsyanikov that Mr. Lyubozvonov was probably ill.

'Ill! Why he is fatter across than he is tall, and such a great sprawling face, my word, you'd never think he was a young man . . . But of course, who can tell – except God?' And Ovsyanikov sighed deeply.

'Well, enough of the gentry,' I began. 'What have you got to tell me about the freeholders, Luka Petrovich?'

'No, there I must ask to be excused,' he said hastily. 'It is true, I could tell you . . . But what's the use?' Ovsyanikov waved his hands. 'We'd better have tea. Peasants we are, just ordinary peasants; besides, what else should we be?' He paused. Tea was served. Tatyana Ilyinichna rose from her chair and sat down again closer to us. In the course of the evening she had several times noiselessly gone out and no less quietly returned. Silence reigned in the room. Ovsyanikov, with slow-moving dignity, drank cup after cup.

'Mitya was here to-day,' observed Tatyana Ilyinichna in a low voice.

Ovsyanikov frowned.

'What did he want?'

'He came to beg your pardon.'

Ovsyanikov shook his head.

'There you are,' he went on, turning to me. 'What's a man to do with his relations? He can't just drop them, can he? Take my case: a nice little nephew God has rewarded me with. A head on his shoulders, a smart lad, there's no question of that; quite a scholar – and yet no good's ever likely to come out of him. He was in the Government service – then threw it up: promotion was not fast enough for him, if you please . . . Does he think he is a nobleman, or what? Even *they* don't get promoted to generals at once. Anyway, now he's without a job . . . And as if that wasn't bad enough, he's become a tale-bearer too! He composes petitions for the peasants, writes reports, instructs the village spokesmen, shows up surveyors at their tricks, crawls around the pot-houses, rubs shoulders with townsfolk and yard-sweepers in every tavern. In short, he's heading for a bad end. The police have warned him more than once. Luckily he knows how to crack a joke: he makes them laugh, then gets them into hot water too . . . Why, I bet he's sitting in your little den, isn't he?' he added, turning to his wife. 'I know you, you're so soft-hearted – you've taken him under your wing.'

Tatyana Ilyinichna dropped her head, smiled and blushed.

'So it's like that, is it?' continued Ovsyanikov: 'You molly-coddler! Well, tell him to come in – let it pass. I'll forgive the silly boy for the sake of our dear guest . . . Well, call him, call him . . .'

Tatyana Ilyinichna went to the door and called: 'Mitya!'

Mitya, a lad of about twenty-eight, tall, well-built and curly-headed, came into the room, and, catching sight of me, halted on the threshold. He was dressed in the German fashion, but you'd only to look at the unnaturally high padding of the shoulders to see clearly that his clothes had been cut by the most Russian of tailors.

'Well, come on, come on,' said the old man, 'what are you ashamed about? You must thank your aunt you are forgiven . . . Here, sir, let me introduce him,' he continued, pointing at Mitya, 'my own nephew, but the two of us don't see eye to eye. I've come to the end of my patience!' Mitya and I bowed to each other. 'Well, tell me, what sort of a scrape are you in now? Tell me what they've got against you this time!'

Mitya was clearly reluctant to explain and justify himself in front of me.

'Later on, uncle,' he murmured.

'No, not later on, but now,' persisted the old man. 'I know you're ashamed to speak in front of this gentleman, all the better – it's a punishment for you. Come on, tell us . . . We'll hear what you have to say.'

'I've nothing to be ashamed of,' began Mitya vehemently, and he shook his head; 'please, uncle, judge for yourself. The freeholders of Reshetilovo come and ask for my help. "What is the matter?" I ask. "Here's the matter: our grain-sheds are all in order, they could not be better than they are. Suddenly there comes to us an official and says he's got orders to inspect the sheds. He inspects them and says our sheds are in bad order, seriously neglected, he must report it to his superiors. But how are they neglected, pray? *I* know how, he says. We got together and decided to grease his palm in the usual way, but old Prokhorich prevented us, he said we would only sharpen his appetite; why, hadn't we any means of redress? . . . We took the old man's advice, but the official was annoyed and made a complaint and wrote a report. And now we're called on to answer him." "And are your sheds really in order?" I asked. "Before God, they are indeed; and there's as much grain there as the law prescribes . . ." "Well," I say, "you've nothing to be afraid of, then," and I wrote them out a paper . . . and it's not known yet which way the case has gone . . . But as for the complaint that's been made to you about it all, it's as clear as day: everyone has got his own axe to grind.'

'Everyone except you apparently,' said the old man, in a low voice . . . 'And what are the tricks you have been up to with the peasants of Shutolomovo?'

'How d'you know about that?'

'I just know.'

'There too I was in the right – please judge again for yourself. The peasants of Shutolomovo had ten acres of their land ploughed up by their neighbour Bespandin. "It's my land," he says. The Shutolomovo people pay rent, their master's away abroad – tell me yourself, who is there to help them? But there's no question of it, the land is theirs, they've been serfs on it since time immemorial. So they come to me and ask me to write a petition, and I do. But Bespandin finds out and starts threatening, and says: "I'll take this little Mitya and I'll pull the backs of his shoulder-blades out, or else I'll take his head right off his shoulders." We'll see whether he does. So far my head is safe and sound.'

'Well, don't boast: your head will come to a bad end,' said the old man, 'raving lunatic that you are.'

'But, uncle, didn't you tell me yourself?'

'I know, I know what you are going to say to me,' Ovsyanikov interrupted him. 'Exactly: a man must live justly and ought to help his neighbour. Certainly there are times when a man shouldn't spare himself . . . but do *you* always live up to those principles? Don't they take you to pot-houses, eh? and stand you drinks? and bow to you, eh? and say: "Dmitry Alexeich, sir, help us, and we will prove to you how grateful we are," and don't they slip a silver rouble or a note from under their coat-skirts into your hand? eh? Isn't that what happens? Tell us, isn't it, eh?'

'There I'm certainly guilty,' answered Mitya, lowering his head. 'But I don't accept money from the poor and I don't act against my conscience.'

'You don't accept from them now, but once things go badly for you, then you will. You don't act against your conscience. Get along with you! I suppose you're always on the side of the angels! . . . Why, have you forgotten Boris Perekhodov? Who was it who fussed about him? Who was it who took him under his wing, eh?'

'Perekhodov deserved his fate, certainly . . .'

'He embezzled Government money . . . Nothing more than that!'

'But, uncle, just imagine his poverty, his family . . .'

'Poverty . . . he was a drunkard and a gambler – that's what he was.'

'It was his troubles that started him drinking,' observed Mitya, lowering his voice.

'Troubles, indeed! Well, you could have helped him, if you're so warm-hearted, but without sitting around in pothouses with a drunkard like that, dazzled by his fine words, as though you'd never heard the like.'

'He was the kindest of men . . .'

'According to you, everyone is kind . . . By the way,' continued Ovsyanikov, turning to his wife, 'did you send him . . . well, *you* know?'

Tatyana Ilyinichna nodded.

'Where have you been, these days?' said the old man.

'In town.'

'Playing billiards, I suppose, and drinking tea, and strumming on the guitar, skipping round the offices, writing petitions in back rooms, and prancing about with the sons of merchants? Am I right? . . . Tell us!'

'That's about right,' said Mitya, with a smile. 'Ah yes, I'd almost forgotten: Anton Parfenich Funtikov invites you to dine with him next Sunday.'

'I shan't go to see that pot-belly. He'll give us an expensive fish and then put rancid butter on it. Good luck to him!'

'And then I met Feodosya Mikhailovna.'

'Which Feodosya d'you mean?'

'The one who belongs to Garpenchenko, the landowner, the one who bought Mikulino by auction. This Feodosya is from Mikulino. She lived in Moscow on quit-rent, worked as a sempstress, and paid her rent regularly, $182\frac{1}{2}$ roubles a year. And she knows her job, too; she got good orders in Moscow. But now Garpenchenko has sent for her and just keeps her here, and won't give her any definite duties. She'd be ready to buy herself out, and has told the master so, but he won't let her know his decision. You, uncle, know Garpenchenko – couldn't you have a word with him about it? . . . Feodosya would pay a good price for her freedom.'

'At your expense, eh? Well, all right, I will speak to him, yes. Only I don't know,' continued the old man with an expression of disfavour. 'This Garpenchenko – may the Lord forgive me – is a sharper: he buys up bills of exchange, and lends out money at interest: he acquires properties under the hammer . . . What ill wind brought him to our part of the world, I'd like to know? Oh, I've had enough of these birds of passage! It's no easy matter to get sense out of him – but anyway we'll see.'

'Do your best, uncle.'

'All right, I will. But you look out, look out, there! Don't argue . . . God's mercy on you! . . . But just look out in future. Look out or else, by God, you'll come to no good – by God, you'll come to a bad end. I can't carry you on my shoulders all the time . . . It's not as if I were a man of influence. Well, you can go now, and God bless you.'

Mitya went out. Tatyana Ilyinichna followed behind him.

'Give him a good drink of tea, you mollycoddler,' Ovsyanikov called after her. 'The boy's no fool,' he continued, 'and he's got a good heart, only I'm worried about him . . . But I'm sorry to have bored you for so long with trifles.'

The door from the hall opened. A little grey-haired man in a velvet coat came in. 'Ah, Franz Ivanich!' exclaimed Ovsyanikov; 'good day to you! Is God in his mercy treating you well?'

Allow me, dear reader, to introduce this gentleman to you.

Franz Ivanich Lejeune, a landowner of Orel province and a neighbour of mine, had reached the honourable degree of

Russian nobleman by a somewhat unusual path. He was born of French parents in Orleans and had set out with Napoleon for the conquest of Russia in the capacity of drummer-boy. At first everything went as smoothly as a knife through butter, and our Frenchman entered Moscow with his head held high. But on the way back poor Monsieur Lejeune, half-frozen and without his drum, fell into the hands of the peasants of Smolensk. The peasants of Smolensk shut him up for the night in an empty cloth-mill, and on the next morning brought him to a hole cut in the ice beside the weir, and began to request the drummer *de la Grrrande Armée* to oblige them by diving under the ice. Monsieur Lejeune was unable to agree to their suggestion and, in his turn, began to urge the peasants of Smolensk, in the French tongue, to let him go back to Orleans. '*Messieurs,*' he said, 'I have a mother living there, *une tendre mère.*' But the peasants, probably through ignorance of the geographical situation of the city of Orleans, continued proposing to him an underwater journey down the stream of the sinuous river Gniloterka, and had already begun to urge him forward with gentle blows on the vertebrae of his neck and spine, when suddenly, to Lejeune's indescribable joy, the sound of sleigh-bells was heard, and there drove out across the dam an enormous sledge with the brightest of rugs over its unusually high back-seat and with three roan horses harnessed to it. In the sledge sat a stout, ruddy-faced gentleman in a wolf-skin coat.

'What are you doing there?' he asked the peasants.

'We are drowning a Frenchman, sir.'

'Oh,' replied the gentleman indifferently, and turned away.

'Monsieur! Monsieur!' exclaimed the poor wretch.

'Ah, ah,' said the wolfskin-coat reproachfully. 'You marched on Russia, you and your twelve tongues, you burnt Moscow – damn you – you dragged down the cross from Ivan the Great and now – *monsyor, monsyor!* Now you have got your tail between your legs. The punishment fits the crime . . . Go on, Filka-a!'

The horses started off.

'No, stop!' added the landowner. 'Hey, you, *monsyor*, d'you know *musik*?'

'*Sauvez-moi, sauvez-moi, mon bon monsieur*,' insisted Lejeune.

'There's a fine people for you! Not one of them knows even any Russian. *Musik, musik, savay musik voo? Savay?* Well, answer me! *Comprenay? Savay musik voo? Savay jooay piano?*'

Lejeune at last understood what the landowner was driving at and nodded his head affirmatively: '*Oui, monsieur, oui, oui, je suis musicien, je joue tous les instruments possibles! Oui, monsieur... Sauvez moi, monsieur!*'

'Well, you're a lucky devil,' rejoined the gentleman. 'Let him go, lads, here's twenty copecks to buy yourselves a drink.'

'Thank you, sir, thank you kindly. Take him, by all means.'

Lejeune was installed in the sledge. He choked for joy, wept, trembled, bowed, thanked the gentleman and his driver and the peasants. He was wearing nothing but a green vest with pink ribbons, though it was a day of crackling frost. The gentleman glanced silently at his numb blue limbs, wrapped the poor wretch in his own fur coat and drove him home. There was a scurrying of serving-folk. The Frenchman was soon warmed, fed and dressed. The gentleman took him to see his daughters.

'Here, children,' he told them. 'I have found a teacher for you. You were always nagging at me to have you taught music and French, well here is a Frenchman for you. He plays the piano too. Well, *monsyor*,' he continued, pointing at the cheap little piano he'd bought five years before from a Jew, who was really a seller of eau-de-Cologne, 'show us your skill. *Jooay!*'

Lejeune sat down with a sinking heart; he had never touched a piano in his life.

'Go on, *jooay, jooay*,' repeated the gentleman.

The poor wretch struck the keys in desperation, as he would have done a drum, and played away at random...

'I thought,' he used to say afterwards, 'that my saviour would seize me by the scruff of the neck and throw me out of his house.' But, to the extreme amazement of the reluctant improviser, the gentleman, after waiting a moment, patted him approvingly on the shoulder. 'Good, good,' he said. 'I see you can play; go and have a rest now.'

Two weeks later Lejeune passed on from this gentleman to another, who was rich and cultivated, and took a fancy to him for his gay and gentle ways. Lejeune married his ward, entered the Government service, became a nobleman, married his daughter to a landowner of the Orel province named Lobyzanyev, a retired dragoon and a writer of verses, and came to settle in Orel province himself. This Lejeune, or, as he is now known, Franz Ivanich, was the gentleman I saw arriving to visit his friend Ovsyanikov.

But perhaps the reader is tired of sitting with me at Ovsyanikov's, and I shall therefore lapse into eloquent silence.

Lgov

'LET'S GO to Lgov,' Ermolai, who is already known to the reader, said to me one day. 'We'll shoot all the duck we want there.'

Although wild duck present no special attraction to a real sportsman, the temporary lack of other game (it was the beginning of September: the woodcock had not yet arrived, and I was tired of tramping the fields after partridges) led me to take the advice of my hunter and to make my way to Lgov.

Lgov is a big village in the steppe with a very old single-domed stone church and two mills on the marshy stream of the Rosota. Five versts from Lgov this stream turns into a broad pond with thick rushes covering the banks and growing here and there in the middle. This pool, its creeks and the still depths of its rushes, were the hatching-place and haunt of a countless multitude of duck of every possible kind: mallard, half-mallard, pintail, teal, pochard and so forth. Small flights were continually circling and hovering over the water, but a shot would put up such clouds that the sportsman involuntarily held his hat with his hand and let out a longdrawn 'phew!'

Ermolai and I walked along the pool, but, in the first place, the duck, which is a canny bird, keeps well away from the bank, and secondly, even if some straggling inexperienced teal should expose itself to our fire and fall a victim, our dogs would not have been able to fetch it from the thick rushes: even with the noblest degree of self-denial, they would have been able neither to swim nor to walk on the bottom, but would only have cut their precious noses to no purpose on the sharp edges of the reeds.

'No,' said Ermolai at last. 'It won't work, we must get a boat . . . Let's go back to Lgov.'

We set off. We had gone only a few paces when we were met by a rather mongrelly pointer which came dashing out of a willow-thicket, followed by a man of middle height in a thread-bare blue coat, canary waistcoat and *gris de laine* or *bleu d'amour* trousers, the ends of which were carelessly stuck into a pair of leaky boots, with a red handkerchief round his neck, and a single-barrelled gun over his shoulder.

While our dogs, with the Chinese ceremonial which is the special custom of their kind, exchanged sniffs with their new acquaintance, who in evident alarm had lowered his tail, thrown back his ears, and kept circling rapidly round, with knees stiff and teeth bared, the stranger came up to us and made us an extremely polite bow. He looked about twenty-five; his long reddish hair, which was fairly soaked in kvass, stuck out in solid tufts, his small brown eyes had a friendly twinkle in them, his whole face, which was bound up in a black hand-kerchief as though from toothache, was set in the sweetest of smiles.

'Allow me to introduce myself,' he began in a soft wheedling voice. 'I am Vladimir, a sportsman of these parts . . . Hearing of your arrival, and learning that you were bound for the banks of our pool, I decided that, if you had no objection, I would offer you my services.'

Vladimir's turn of language was exactly that of a young actor who plays the part of leading man in the provinces. I accepted his offer and, while still on the way to Lgov, managed to find out his history. He was a house-serf who had been given his freedom. In tender youth he had learnt music, had then served as a valet, knew his alphabet, had read – so far as I could make out – a few trashy books, and now lived, as so many do in Russia, without a farthing in his pocket, with no steady employment, more or less subsisting on manna from on high. He expressed himself with extreme refinement and was clearly enchanted with his own manners; he was doubtless also a terrible flirt and, in all probability, a successful one, too: Russian girls like fine language. Amongst other things, he gave me to understand that from time to time he visited the neighbouring landowners, went calling in town, played Pre-ference, and had friends in the capital. He was a master of the most different types of smile; what suited him best was the modest, restrained one which played on his lips when he was listening to someone else. He would hear you out, agree with you absolutely, but all the same he would never lose the sense of his own dignity and it was as if he wished to let you know that he too, on occasion, had his own opinion to give. Ermolai, like the none too well-educated and in no way subtle fellow that he was, began to address him in the second person singular. You should have seen the mocking smile with which Vladimir said to him: 'You, sir . . .'

'Why do you wear a handkerchief round your face?' I asked him. 'Have you got toothache?'

'No, sir,' he replied. 'It's something more serious, the result of carelessness. I had a friend, a good man, sir, but, as some people are, he was far from being a sportsman. Well, sir, one day he says to me: "My dear friend, take me out shooting, I'm curious to find out wherein the fun of it lies." As a matter of course, I didn't want to say no to my friend: I myself found him a gun and took him out shooting. Well, sir, we duly had our shooting and finally we decided to take a rest. I sat beneath a tree, but he, on the contrary, started fooling about with his gun and taking aim at myself. I begged him to desist, but he had too little experience to take my advice. A shot rang out, and I lost my chin and the index finger of my right hand.'

We had reached Lgov. Vladimir and Ermolai had both decided that it would be impossible to go shooting without a boat.

'Suchok has a punt,' observed Vladimir; 'but I don't know where he has hidden it. I must run round to see him.'

'Who is he?' I asked.

'A man who lives here, nicknamed Suchok.'

Vladimir and Ermolai set off to find Suchok. I told them that I would wait for them by the church. As I was looking at the gravestones in the churchyard, I came across a square and blackened urn with the following inscriptions: CI-GÎT THÉO-PHILE-HENRI, VICOMTE DE BLANGY; on the second side: BENEATH THIS STONE IS BURIED THE BODY OF A FRENCH

SUBJECT, COUNT BLANGY; BORN 1737, DIED 1799,
AGED 62; on the third side: PEACE TO HIS DUST; and on
the fourth:

> BENEATH THIS STONE LIES A FRENCH ÉMIGRÉ;
> A MAN OF TALENT AND ILLUSTRIOUS BIRTH.
> MOURNING THE MASSACRE OF WIFE AND FAMILY,
> HE FORSOOK HIS COUNTRY, THE PREY OF TYRANTS;
> REACHING THE SHORES OF RUSSIA,
> HE FOUND A HOSPITABLE ROOF FOR HIS OLD AGE:
> HE TAUGHT THE YOUNG AND SOOTHED THE OLD ...
> THE SUPREME JUDGE LAID HIM HERE TO REST.

My reflections were interrupted by the arrival of Ermolai,
Vladimir and the man of the strange nickname, Suchok.

Suchok, a bare-legged, shock-headed tatterdemalion, was,
I thought, probably a retired house-serf, aged about sixty.

'Have you got a boat?' I asked.

'Yes,' he answered in a hoarse and broken voice. 'But it's a
very bad one.'

'How so?'

'It's come unstuck; the bolts have come out of their sockets.'

'That's nothing,' Ermolai put in. 'You should caulk it with
oakum.'

'One could, of course,' agreed Suchok.

'And what do you do?' I asked.

'I am the master-fisherman.'

'How is it that you are a fisherman and have a boat in such
bad repair?'

'Because there are no fish in our river.'

'Fish don't like brackish marsh water,' observed my hunter
importantly.

'Well,' I said to Ermolai. 'Go and find some oakum and
mend the boat for us, only be quick about it.'

Ermolai went off.

'So we are likely to go to the bottom, it seems,' I said to
Vladimir.

'God's mercy on us,' he answered. 'In any event we may presume that the pool is not deep.'

'No, it is not deep,' observed Suchok, who had a strange sleepy way of talking. 'There's slime and grass at the bottom, it's all covered in grass. There are pot-holes, too, of course.'

'But if the grass is so thick,' observed Vladimir, 'it won't be possible to row.'

'And who rows a punt? You have to pole it. I'll go with you, I have got a pole there – or you could use a spade as well.'

'It's awkward with a spade, as I suppose that often you can't reach the bottom,' said Vladimir.

'It's certainly awkward.'

I sat on a tombstone and waited for Ermolai. Vladimir went a little way off, for correctness' sake, and sat down too. Suchok continued to stand where he was, hanging his head, his hands folded behind his back in the traditional attitude.

'Tell me,' I began, 'have you been a fisherman here for long?'

'It will soon be seven years,' he answered, with a start.

'And what was your job before?'

'I was a coachman before.'

'And who reduced you from the rank of coachman?'

'The new lady.'

'What lady?'

'The lady who bought us. You don't know her, sir: Alena Timofeyevna, a stout lady . . . and not young.'

'What gave her the idea of making you into a fisherman?'

'God knows. She came to us from her own estate in Tambov, called the whole staff together and came out to speak to us. First we went and kissed her hand, and she was all right: she didn't get cross . . . Then she began to ask us one after the other what we did and what our jobs were. My turn came, and she asked me what I was. "A coachman," I said. "A coachman? Why, what sort of coachman are you, just look at yourself, what sort of coachman are you? It's not right for you to be a coachman; you must shave your beard and be my fisherman. When I come, you must provide me with fish for my table, do you hear? . . ." So since then I have counted as a fisherman. "And see that you keep my pond in order." . . . But how am I to do that?'

'Whose were you before?'

'We belonged to Sergei Sergeich Pekhterev. He inherited us. He was not our master for long, either, only six years altogether. It was with him that I was a coachman . . . Not in town – he had other coachman there, but in the country.'

'Had you been a coachman since you were young?'

'No, indeed. I became a coachman under Sergei Sergeich. Before that I was a cook – not a town cook, either, but just in the country.'

'Whose cook were you?'

'My former master's, Afanasy Nefeditch, the uncle of Sergei Sergeich. He bought Lgov, Afanasy Nefeditch did, and Sergei Sergeich inherited it from him.'

'From whom did he buy it?'

'From Tatyana Vasilyevna.'

'Which one?'

'The one who died last year near Bolkhovo . . . That's to say, near Karachev. She died an old maid . . . she never married. Did you not know her, sir? We came to her from her father, Vasily Semyonich. She had us for a long time . . . Twenty years or so.'

'You were her cook?'

'Yes, first I was cook, and then I became coffee-server.'

'You became what?'

'Coffee-server.'

'What kind of job is that?'

'I don't know, sir. I stood by the sideboard and was called Anton instead of Kuzma. It was the mistress's order.'

'Your real name is Kuzma?'

'Yes.'

'And you were coffee-server all the time?'

'No, not all the time: I was an *achtyeur* too.'

'Indeed?'

'Certainly I was . . . I acted in the theatre. Our mistress had a private theatre.'

'What sort of parts did you play?'

'I beg your pardon, sir?'

'What did you do in the theatre?'

'Oh, don't you know? They would take me and dress me up; then I would walk, all dressed up, or stand, or sit, as the case might be. They'd tell me what to say – and I'd say it. Once I played the part of a blind man . . . They put a pea under each of my eyelids . . . Yes, that's how it was.'

'And what were you after that?'

'Then I became a cook again.'

'Why did they make you a cook again?'

'Because my brother ran away.'

'And what were you when you were with the father of your first mistress?'

'I had various jobs. First I was a page, then I was a postilion, then a gardener, then a whipper-in.'

'A whipper-in? . . . and you went out hunting, too?'

'Yes, I did, and I hurt myself badly: I was thrown and damaged my horse. Our old master was very strict; he had me beaten, and sent me to a cobbler in Moscow to learn a trade.'

'How was that? You couldn't have been a child when you became a whipper-in?'

'I was twenty-something at the time.'

'Fancy teaching you a trade at that age.'

'It must have been all right, it must have been possible, if the master ordered it. Luckily he soon died and they brought me back to the country.'

'And when did you learn your skill as a cook?'

Suchok raised his thin, yellowish face and chuckled: 'What, lessons for that, too? . . . Why, even women can cook!'

'Well,' I said. 'You've seen a thing or two, Kuzma, in your time. What are you doing now as fisherman, if you haven't got any fish?'

'I don't complain, sir. In fact it's a mercy that they have made me a fisherman. Why, the mistress ordered them to put another old chap like me – Andrei Pupyr – into the paper

factory as a pulper. It's wicked, she says, to eat bread without
working for it. And Pupyr had hoped for some special favour:
he had a young cousin who worked as a clerk in the mistress's
office, and promised to speak to the mistress about him and to
remind her of him. And a fine way he reminded her! . . . And
with my own eyes I had seen Pupyr going down on his knees to
this cousin of his.'

'Have you a family? Did you get married?'

'No, sir, I did not. The late Tatyana Vasilyevna – may God
rest her soul! – allowed none of us to marry. "God forbid," she
used to say. "Don't I live unmarried? What's all the fuss about?
Whatever do they want to get married for?" '

'What d'you live on now? D'you get any wages?'

'Wages? Certainly not, sir . . . they give me food – and I am
quite content, thank God. May God give the mistress a long
life!'

Ermolai returned.

'The boat is mended,' he announced sulkily. 'Go and get the
pole, you! . . .'

Suchok ran off for the pole. Throughout my conversation
with the poor old man, the sportsman Vladimir had been
gazing at him with a contemptuous smile.

'A stupid old man,' he said, when Suchok had left us.
'Completely uneducated, a peasant and nothing more, sir . . .
Not fit to be called a house-serf . . . and yet how he boasted
. . . Just fancy him as an actor! I ask you! You need never have
bothered with him, sir, or troubled to talk to him!'

Within a quarter of an hour we were sitting in Suchok's
punt. (We had left the dogs in a hut in the care of Yegudil the
coachman.) We were not very comfortable, but sportsmen are
an uncomplaining race. Suchok stood in the blunt stern-end
and 'poled'; Vladimir and I sat on the thwart; Ermolai installed
himself forward, right in the bows. In spite of the oakum, water
soon appeared under our feet. Luckily it was a calm day and the
pond lay as if asleep.

We made fairly slow progress. The old man had difficulty in
pulling his long pole out of the sticky mud, as it was all tangled

with green strands of water-grass; masses of round water-lily leaves further hindered the course of our boat. Eventually we reached the rushes, and the fun began. The duck rose noisily and fairly wrenched themselves from the surface, startled by our unexpected appearance in their realm; shots rang out together after them, and it was fun to see the short-tailed fowl turn a somersault in the air and come splashing down heavily on to the water. We did not manage to pick up all the duck we had shot, of course: the lightly-wounded ones dived away; others, killed outright, fell so deep in the rushes that even the lynx eyes of Ermolai could not make them out; but all the same, by dinner-time, our boat was filled to the gunwales with game.

Much to Ermolai's satisfaction, Vladimir shot far from well and, after every miss, expressed astonishment, inspected his gun, blew through it, looked perplexed, and finally explained to us why he had missed. Ermolai, as he always did, shot triumphantly; I, fairly badly, as usual. Suchok looked at us with the eyes of a man who has been in domestic service since his youth, occasionally shouted: 'Look, look, there's another one!' – and constantly scratched his back – not with his hand, but with a wriggle of his shoulders. The weather remained splendid; round white clouds floated quietly past overhead and were clearly mirrored in the water; the reeds rustled around us; here and there the pond glittered like steel in the sun. We were on the point of turning back to the village when suddenly something rather unpleasant happened. For some time we had noticed that the water was slowly rising inside the boat. Vladimir had been given the task of bailing it out with a scoop which my far-sighted hunter had spirited away, against possible emergencies, from an unsuspecting peasant-woman. All went well, so long as Vladimir remembered his duties. But at the end of our shoot, as if by way of farewell, the duck began to rise in such masses that we hardly had time to load. In the heat of the fusillade we paid no attention to the condition of our punt – until suddenly, at a violent movement by Ermolai, who was trying to reach a dead bird and leaning across the gunwale with all the weight of his body, our ancient vessel listed over, took a plunge, and solemnly went to the bottom, luckily not in deep water. We shouted, but it was already too late: within a moment we were standing with water up to our throats, surrounded by the floating bodies of dead duck. To this day I cannot remember without a chuckle the pale, startled faces of my companions (probably my own face was not particularly ruddy at that moment either); but, at the time, I confess that it never occurred to me to laugh. Each of us held his gun over his head, and Suchok, doubtless from a habit of copying his masters, lifted his pole in the air. The first to break the silence was Ermolai.

'The devil and all!' he muttered, spitting into the water. 'That's a fine thing to happen! And you, you old scoundrel!' he added with feeling, turning to Suchok, 'what sort of boat is this of yours?'

'I'm sorry,' whispered the old man.

'And you're a good one, too,' continued my hunter, turning in Vladimir's direction. 'What were you looking at? Why weren't you bailing? . . . you . . .'

But Vladimir was in no state to reply: he was trembling like a leaf, his teeth chattered without meeting, and he wore a completely witless smile. What had become of all his eloquence, his feeling for the finer shades of decency, his sense of his own importance?

The wretched punt wobbled feebly beneath our feet . . . In the moment of shipwreck the water seemed to us extremely cold, but we soon became used to it. When the first shock had passed, I looked round; on all sides, ten paces from us, the reeds began; in the distance, over their tops, the bank could be seen. It looks bad, I thought.

'What shall we do about it?' I asked Ermolai.

'Well, we'll see; this is no place to spend the night,' answered he. 'Here, you, hold the gun,' he said to Vladimir.

Vladimir obeyed without demur.

'I'll go and look for a ford,' continued Ermolai confidently, as if a ford was bound to exist in every lake – took the pole from

Suchok, and set off in the direction of the bank, carefully sounding the bottom as he went.

'Can you swim?' I asked him.

'No, I can't,' came his voice from behind the rushes.

'Very well, then, he'll drown,' observed Suchok indifferently. From the beginning he had been afraid, not of the danger, but of our wrath, and now, completely reassured, simply let out a puff from time to time and, so it seemed, felt in no way impelled to change his situation.

'And will perish to no avail,' added Vladimir mournfully.

Ermolai did not return for more than an hour. That hour seemed to us an eternity. At first we and he exchanged cries with a good heart; then he began to answer our shouts less often, and finally he was completely silent. In the village the bells were ringing for evening service. We didn't talk, and tried not to look at each other. Duck flew over our heads, some prepared to settle beside us, but suddenly shot straight up into the air, quacked and flew away. We began to feel numb. Suchok blinked as though he was getting ready to go to sleep.

Finally, to our indescribable joy, Ermolai returned.

'Well?'

'I got to the bank; I found the ford. Let's go.'

We were all for setting off at once; but first Ermolai put his hand under the water, brought a line out of his pocket, made the dead duck fast to it by the legs, took both ends of the line between his teeth and set off ahead, with Vladimir behind him, and me behind Vladimir. Suchok brought up the rear. It was about two hundred yards to the bank and Ermolai went boldly and unhesitatingly forward (so well had he made out the way), with only an occasional cry of 'Keep to the left – there's a pothole on the right!' or 'Keep to the right, you'll sink in if you go to the left.' . . . At times the water rose to our throats and twice poor Suchok, who was shorter than the rest of us, choked and gave off bubbles. 'Hey, hey, hey!' Ermolai shouted at him menacingly, and Suchok scrambled and floundered and jumped and somehow escaped to a shallower place, but even in these extremities could not make up his mind to take hold of the skirts of my coat. Exhausted, dirty, dripping, we reached the bank at last.

Two hours later, having dried ourselves to the best of our ability, we were all sitting in a big hay-shed preparing to have supper. Yegudil the coachman, an extremely slow, phlegmatic, deliberate, sleepy fellow, stood in the gateway and diligently plied Suchok with snuff. (I have noticed that in Russia coachmen very soon make friends with each other.) Suchok sniffed with frenzy, to vomiting point: he spat and coughed and was clearly enjoying himself. Vladimir looked sad, leant his head on one side, and said little. Ermolai was cleaning our guns. The dogs were wagging their tails at top speed, in anticipation of their groats; the horses were stamping and neighing in the shed ... The sun was setting; its last rays ran out in broad crimson stripes; the sky was full of golden clouds that grew ever more fine-drawn, like a rinsed and combed-out fleece ... From the village came the sound of singing.

Bezhin Meadow

I T WAS a beautiful July day, one of those days which come only after long spells of settled weather. From the earliest morning the sky is clear; the dawn does not blaze and flame, but spreads out in a gentle blush. Instead of the flaming incandescence that goes with sultriness and drought, or the dark crimson that precedes the storm, the sun has a bright and friendly radiance, as it swims peacefully up from behind a long, narrow cloud, shines out briskly, and then veils itself in the lilac-coloured mist. The tenuous upper edge of the spreading cloud sparkles with a serpentine brilliance, like that of beaten silver. But now the dancing beams come shooting out again – and gaily, grandly, as if on wings, the mighty luminary emerges. About midday there usually appears a multitude of high, round clouds, golden-grey, with edges of tender white. Like islands, scattered across a boundless and brimming river, which surrounds them with deep, translucent expanses of an even blueness, they scarcely stir; farther off, towards the horizon, they concentrate, crowd together, there is no more blueness to be seen between them; but the clouds themselves are of the same azure as the heaven, they are penetrated through and through with light and warmth. The colour of the horizon, a pale and floating lilac colour, remains unchanged the whole day, and uniform all around; there is no darkening or deepening to foretell a storm; sometimes, here and there, there are bluish shafts falling down, betokening the passage of a hardly percept- ible shower. Towards evening, these clouds vanish; the last of them, blackish and vague as smoke, lie with a pink curling face turned to the setting sun; over the place where it disappears, as quietly as it rose into the heavens, a scarlet radiance stands for a while over the darkening earth, and, trembling gently, like a carefully-carried taper, the evening star begins to burn. On such days, all colours are softened; they are clear, but not brilliant; they are tinged with a gentleness that is somehow touching. Such days may be scorching-hot, and the steam may rise from the sloping fields; but the wind disperses and breaks up the accumulated sultriness, and whirlwinds – sure sign of settled weather – march in tall white pillars along the tracks across the plough-land. In the dry, clean air there is a smell of wormwood, of rye-harvest, and of buckwheat; even an hour before nightfall you feel no dampness. This is the weather that the husbandman needs to gather in his crop . . .

Once, on just such a day as this, I was shooting blackcock in the district of Chern, in the government of Tula. I had found and shot a fair quantity of game; a bulging game-bag cut mercilessly into my shoulder; but the sunset glow was already dying down, and in the air, still light, although no longer flushed with the rays of the vanished sun, cold shadows were beginning to deepen and to spread, when at last I decided to return home. At a quick pace I passed through a long brake of undergrowth, climbed a hill and, instead of the familiar plateau which I expected, with a clump of oaks to the right and a little white church in the distance, I saw a completely different, unknown landscape. Below my feet ran a narrow valley; immediately opposite, a dense wood of poplar rose in a steep wall. I stopped in perplexity and looked round. . . . Aha! I thought, I've come out in quite the wrong place, I've struck too far to the right; and, amazed at my own mistake, I went swiftly down the hill. I was immediately enveloped in a disagreeable, stagnant dampness, as if I had passed into a cellar; the thick tall grass at the bottom of the valley, dripping wet, made a pale, even tablecloth all round; walking over it was somehow an eerie business. I scrambled out to the other side with all speed and struck off to the left along the poplar-wood. Bats were already flitting above the sleeping tree-tops, wheeling mysteriously and quivering against the dim radiance of the sky; a belated hawk flew briskly past on his straight, high course, hurrying back to his nest. As soon as I come out at that corner, I thought to myself, I shall strike the track at once; but I've gone a good mile out of my way.

Eventually I reached the corner of the wood, but found no sign of any track there: stunted, straggling undergrowth stretched far and wide before me, and behind it, away in the distance, could be seen an empty plain. I halted again. What an extraordinary thing... Where on earth was I? – I began going over again in my mind the course I had taken during the day... 'Oh! This must be Parakhin spinney,' I exclaimed at last. 'Yes! and over there must be Sindeyev wood... However did I manage to get here? So far out of my way?... Very odd! Now I must bear to the right again.'

I went to the right, through brushwood. Meanwhile night approached and grew on me like a storm-cloud; it was as if darkness was welling up from the ground on all sides, with the mists of evening, and streaming down from above at the same time. I fell in with a rough, overgrown path, and went along it, keeping a sharp look-out ahead. Soon it was all dark and still around me – there was only the call of quails from time to time. A small night-bird, flying low on soft and soundless wings, almost knocked into me and shied off to one side. I came to the end of the brushwood and continued along the edge of a field. It was already difficult to distinguish distant objects; the field made a white blur around me; beyond it was a gloomy, towering mass of darkness which looked nearer every moment. My footfalls sounded muffled in the stagnant air. The sky, which had become drained of colour, began to grow blue again – but, this time, with the blue of night. Against it, little stars were stirring and twinkling.

What I had taken for a wood turned out to be a dark, round hillock. 'Then where on earth am I?' I repeated again, aloud, halted for the third time, and looked inquiringly at my piebald-yellow gun-dog Dianka, decidedly the cleverest of all the four-legged creation. But the cleverest of all the four-legged creation only wagged its tail, gave a sad twinkle of its tired eyes and had no sort of practical advice to offer. I felt ashamed in front of it, and set off ahead in desperation, as if I had suddenly guessed which way to go, skirted the hill, and found myself in a gentle hollow in the midst of cultivation. A strange feeling immediately came over me. The hollow was like an almost symmetrical cauldron with sloping sides. At the bottom of it rose, bolt upright, several large white stones, which seemed to have crept down there for a secret conclave, and the whole place had such a deaf-and-dumb feeling, the sky hung so flatly and gloomily above it, that my heart shrank. Some little creature was squeaking faintly and plaintively among the stones. I hastily came out again on to the hillock. Hitherto I had not given up all hope of finding the way home; but here I finally convinced myself that I was completely lost and, no longer attempting to recognize the surrounding landscape, which was almost completely sunk in darkness, boldly set a straight course by the stars ... I went on in this way for about half an hour, plodding forward with difficulty. It seemed to me that I had never been in such a desert in all my life; there was not a twinkle of light to be seen, not a sound to be heard. One sloping hill succeeded another, fields stretched endlessly one after another, bushes fairly started up from the earth under my nose. I was still walking, and already preparing to lie down somewhere until morning came, when suddenly I felt myself on the edge of a fearful precipice.

I quickly withdrew my foot in mid-air, and, through the hardly penetrable darkness of the night, I made out, far below me, an enormous plain. A broad river bounded it in a receding arc; steely gleams of water, flashing faintly here and there, marked its course. The hill on which I was standing dropped sharply in an almost perpendicular cliff; its massive outline showed up blackly against the bluishness of the airy void, and just below me, in the angle of cliff and plain, beside the river, which at this point stood in a dark and motionless mirror, right at the foot of the hill, two fires close beside each other were blazing redly and smoking. Around them, people were stirring, shadows were swaying, and sometimes the front half of a curly head was brightly illuminated ...

At last I recognized where I was. This field rejoices, in our neighbourhood, in the name of Bezhin meadow ... But to return home was quite impossible, especially by night; my legs were foundering beneath me from exhaustion. I decided to go down to the fires and, in company with the people whom I had seen, and took to be drovers, to wait for the dawn. I got safely down, but had not yet let go of the last branch I had seized, when suddenly two big white shaggy dogs hurled themselves at me, barking evilly. The ringing voices of children sounded from around the fires; and two or three boys rose quickly from the ground. I shouted back in answer to their questioning cries. They ran towards me, at once calling off the dogs, who were particularly surprised by the sight of my Dianka, and I went up to them.

I was wrong in taking the people sitting round the fires for drovers. They were just peasant-lads from the neighbouring village, who were minding horses. In the hot summer weather it is the custom in our part of the world to turn the horses out at night to graze in the fields: in daytime the flies and bluebottles would give them no peace. Taking the horses out towards evening time, and driving them back at dawn, is a great treat for the peasant-lads. Sitting bareheaded and in old coats on the liveliest nags, they dash off with gay shouts and cries, waving arms and legs, jumping high in the air and laughing at the tops of their voices. The light dust rises in a yellow pillar and blows along the road; from afar you can hear the jolly clatter of hooves, the horses gallop with ears pricked; in front of them all, with tail up, continuously changing his pace, gallops a shaggy sorrel with his tangled mane full of burrs.

I told the boys that I had lost my way, and sat down beside them. They asked me whence I had come, grew silent and made room for me. We talked for a while. I lay down beneath a bush which had been eaten bare, and began to look around me. It was a marvellous picture: around the fires a circle of reddish, reflected light trembled and seemed to die away into the darkness; at times the flame blazed up and scattered swift gleams beyond the edges of the circle; a thin tongue of light licked the bare willow-twigs and disappeared in a flash – long, sharp shadows, bursting in for a moment in their turn, ran right up to the fires: it was the war of darkness with light. Sometimes, when the flame burnt lower and the circle of light narrowed, from the nearer darkness there would suddenly emerge a horse's head, a bay head with crooked markings, or a plain grey one, and would give us an attentive, dull look, while busily munching the long grass, then would drop back again and immediately vanish. But one could still hear the horse munching and snorting away. From the lighted circle it was difficult to make out what was happening in the shadows, and therefore everything close at hand seemed hidden by a blackish curtain; but farther off, towards the horizon, long shapes could be discerned dimly as hills and woods. The clear, dark sky stood, solemn and immeasurably high above us, in all its mysterious magnificence. It caught one deliciously at the heart to breathe that unmistakable, languorous, cool breath – the breath of a summer night in Russia. Around us there was hardly a sound to be heard . . . only sometimes, from the nearby river, the sudden loud splash of a big fish, and the low murmuring of the rushes on the bank, hardly stirred by the touch of a ripple . . . only the fires crackling away faintly.

The boys sat round them, and with them the two dogs which had so much wanted to eat me up. They were still unable to reconcile themselves to my presence, and, sleepily narrowing their eyes and looking sideways at the fire, gave an occasional growl which had an extraordinary accent of self-importance, began with a growl and finished with a faint whine, as if regretting the impossibility of doing as they wished. The boys were five in all: Fedya, Pavel, Ilyusha, Kostya and Vanya. (I learnt their names as they talked, and propose now to make the reader acquainted with them.)

The first, and eldest of them all, Fedya, seemed to be about fourteen. He was a well-built lad, with handsome, fine, smallish features, fair, curly hair, bright eyes and a permanent smile that was half-jolly, half-absent. By all appearances he came of a well-to-do family and had ridden out to the field, not because he had to, but just for the fun of it. He wore a gay cotton shirt with a yellow pattern; a small, new overcoat, thrown on carelessly, stayed with difficulty on his narrow shoulders; from his blue belt hung a comb. His boots, with very low tops, were really his – not his father's. The second boy, Pavel, had a shock of black hair, grey eyes, broad cheek-bones, a pale, pock-marked face, a large but regular mouth, an enormous pot-head, and an awkward, stocky body. He was an unprepossessing lad, there were no two ways about it, but all the same I liked him: he had an intelligent, direct look, and there was a note of strength in his voice. His dress was nothing to be proud of: it consisted simply of a plain blouse and a patched pair of trousers. The face of the third, Ilyusha, was rather nondescript: hook-nosed, long, short-sighted, it expressed a certain dull, sickly concentration; his tight lips never moved, his contracted brows never parted – he seemed all the time to be keeping his eyes narrowed against the fire. His yellow, almost white, hair stuck out in sharp tufts from beneath a low felt cap, which now and again he took in both hands and rammed down on his ears. He wore a new pair of rope slippers and leggings; a stout cord, wound three times round his waist, elaborately fastened his neat black smock. He and Pavel looked no more than twelve. The fourth lad, Kostya, was about ten, and excited my curiosity by his sad and thoughtful look. His face was small, thin, freckled, sharp-chinned as a squirrel's; I could hardly make out his lips; but a strange impression was produced by his big, black, liquidly brilliant eyes; it was as if they wanted to say something for which no tongue – or at least not his – had any words. He was small and punily built and rather poorly dressed. The last one, Vanya, I had at first not even noticed; he was lying on the ground, quietly curled up under a sheet of matting, and only occasionally stuck out from beneath it his reddish, curly head. This lad was no more than seven.

So I lay under a bush to one side and looked at the boys. A small pot hung over one of the fires; in it potatoes were cooking. Pavel was keeping an eye on them and, on his knees, was prodding with a splinter in the boiling water. Fedya lay propped on his elbow, with the skirts of his coat thrown open. Ilyusha sat beside Kostya, his eyes still narrowed and intense; Kostya, with slightly-drooping head, was gazing far away into the distance. Vanya never stirred beneath his matting. I pretended to be asleep. Gradually the boys got talking again.

At first they chatted of this and that, of to-morrow's duties, of the horses; but suddenly Fedya turned to Ilyusha, and, as if resuming an interrupted conversation, put a question to him.

'Well, so you really did see the ghost?'

'No, I never saw him; you can't see him,' answered Ilyusha, in a low, hoarse voice, the sound of which went to perfection with the expression on his face. 'But I heard him, and I wasn't the only one, either.'

'But where does he walk?' asked Pavel.

'In the old paper-mill.'

'Do you really work in a paper-mill?'

'Certainly we do. My brother Avdyushka and I work in the pulping-rooms.'

'I say! – factory workers! . . .'

'Well, how was it that you heard him?' asked Fedya.

'It was like this. It happened to me and my brother Avdyushka and Fyodor from Mikheyev and Squinting Ivashka and the other Ivashka, the one from Red Hills, and Ivashka from Sukhorukov, too – and other boys were there as well; there were about ten of us boys altogether – the whole shift, all complete. Well, it happened that we spent the night in the paper-mill, that is, it didn't happen just like that, but Nazarov, the foreman, kept us in: "What's the use," he says, "of you trapesing all the way home, my lads? There's plenty of work to-morrow, so you'd better not go home." So we stayed and all lay down together, and Avdyushka started off and said: "Well, boys," he says: "suppose the ghost comes? . . ." and he didn't finish saying it, Avdyushka didn't, when suddenly somebody started walking, over our heads; we were lying downstairs, and he was walking up aloft by the wheel. We listen: he walks, the planks fairly bend and creak beneath him; he passes over our heads; suddenly the water beside the wheel begins to ripple and ripple and knock and knock against the wheel and the wheel begins to turn; and yet the flanges of the water-inlet were closed. We were amazed – who could have lifted them and

let the water through? Anyway the wheel turned and turned
and then stopped. Then *he* walked again, to the door up aloft,
and started coming downstairs, down he came, as if there was
no hurry about it; the treads fairly groaned beneath him, too;
well, he came up to our door, and waited and waited – then
suddenly the door flew wide open. We started up, and stared –
there was nothing there. Suddenly, look, the net on one of the
tubs began to move, came up, dropped and floated and floated
about in the air as if someone was stirring with it, then went
back to its place. Then the hook of another tub came off its nail,
then went back on to the nail again. Then someone seemed to
go to the door and suddenly started coughing and sort of
bleating, like a sheep, and quite loud, too . . . We had all fallen
into a heap together and each of us was trying to get underneath the others . . . Goodness, how scared we were!'

'Just fancy!' said Pavel. 'Why did he start coughing,
though?'

'I don't know; perhaps because of the damp.'

They were all silent for a while.

'Well,' asked Fedya, 'are the potatoes done?'

Pavel felt them.

'No, they're not done yet . . . Do you hear the splash?' he
added, turning his face in the direction of the river. 'Must be a
pike . . . There was a shooting star.'

'Now I'll tell you a story, boys,' said Kostya in his little
tiny voice. 'Listen to the story that I heard father tell the other
day.'

'Well, we're listening,' said Fedya with a protective, condescending look.

'You know Gavrila, the village carpenter?'

'Yes.'

'But d'you know why he is always so glum and silent? This
is why he is so glum; once he went, father said, he went into the
forest, to gather nuts, so he went into the forest to gather nuts,
and lost his way. He walked on and on, boys – but no, he
couldn't find the way; and night was already on him. So he sat
down under a tree; all right, he said, I'll wait for the morning –

he sat down and dozed off to sleep. So he dozed off to sleep, and suddenly he heard someone calling him. He looked – there was nobody. He dozes off to sleep again – and again they call him. He looks again, he looks; and in front of him on a branch sits a water-fairy, swinging, and calling him, and laughing, and dying of laughter, and the moon was shining bright, so bright and clear it shone, that you could see everything. So she called him, and she was so bright as she sat on the branch, and so white, like a dace or a gudgeon – or is it a carp, which is that whitish, silvery colour? And so, boys, Gavrila the carpenter fairly died of fright, but she, why, she just laughed and went on beckoning him to her with her hand. So Gavrila got up and started to do as the water-fairy said, but God must have warned him: he made the sign of the Cross ... But how difficult that was for him to do! It seemed that his hand was just like stone and would not stir ... Oh, it was the devil and all! ... Well, when he made the sign of the Cross, the fairy stopped laughing and suddenly began to cry. She cried, boys, she wiped her eyes with her hair, and her hair was as green as hemp. So Gavrila looked and looked at her and began to ask her: "What are you crying for, you green thing of the forest?" And the water-fairy said to him: "If you hadn't crossed yourself," she says, "you would have lived with me merrily for ever; but I am crying and grieving because you crossed yourself; and I won't grieve alone, either: you too shall grieve for ever." Then she vanished, and Gavrila understood at once how to get out of the forest. And ever since then he has been going about all glum.'

'Well!' said Fedya after a short pause. 'But how could such an evil thing of the forest harm a Christian soul – after all, he didn't obey her?'

'Yes, you well may ask,' said Kostya. 'And Gavrila said that she had a thin, sad little voice, like a toad's.'

'Did your father tell that story himself?' continued Fedya.

'Yes, I was lying on the shelf and heard it all.'

'What a strange thing! Why should he be glum? ... She must have liked him, since she called him.'

'She liked him all right,' agreed Ilyusha. 'Of course, she wanted to tickle him, that's what she wanted. That's their way, these water-fairies.'

'There ought to be water-fairies here, too,' observed Fedya.

'No,' answered Kostya; 'not in a wholesome, open spot like this. The only thing is, though, that the river is near.'

They were all silent. Suddenly, away in the distance, came a drawn-out, ringing, almost plaintive sound, one of those mysterious night-sounds which issue out sometimes from the depth of silence, rise, hang in the air and slowly die away at last. You listen more intently – there is nothing there, but the resonance remains. It seemed that someone had cried out, far, far away, right under the horizon, and that then someone else answered from the forest with a thin, sharp laugh, and that a low whistle went hissing down the river. The boys exchanged glances, and trembled.

'The power of the Cross be with us!' whispered Ilyusha.

'Oh, you lot of crows!' exclaimed Pavel. 'What are you jumping at? Look, the potatoes are done.' They all went up to the pot and began to eat the steaming potatoes. Only Vanya never stirred. 'What's the matter with you?' said Pavel.

Still Vanya never stirred from under his matting. The pot was soon quite empty.

'Have you heard, boys,' began Ilyusha, 'what happened with us the other day at Varnavitsy?'

'At the dam?' asked Fedya.

'Yes, yes, at the broken dam. There's a haunted place for you – haunted, and airless, too. All around it is broken ground, and the ravines are full of snakes.'

'Well, what happened? Tell us . . .'

'This is what happened. You may not know it, Fedya, but there's a drowned man buried there. He was drowned long, long ago, when the pool was still deep; only his grave still shows, and even that, hardly: just a little mound . . . Well, the other day, the agent sends for the kennelman Ermil, and says: "Go to the post office, Ermil." Ermil is always driving to the post; his dogs all starve to death: somehow or other he can't keep them alive – never could, and yet he's a good kennelman, everybody says so. So Ermil went to the post and stayed too long in town and, when he drove back, he was tight. It was night, and bright moonlight... So Ermil rides across the dam: that's how his way took him. He rides across, Ermil the kennelman does, and sees, on the drowned man's grave, a pretty, curly, white lamb, walking. So Ermil thinks: well, I'll take him – why should he be left like that? So he goes down and takes the lamb in his arms. And the lamb doesn't mind a bit. So Ermil comes up to his horse, but the horse shies away from him, and snorts, and shakes his head; but he quietens him down, mounts with the lamb, and rides off holding the lamb in front of him. He looks at the lamb, and the lamb looks him straight in the eyes. Ermil the kennelman feels there is something uncanny about him. Why, he thinks, I don't ever remember a lamb looking a chap in the eyes like that; but never mind; and he begins to stroke the fleece, and say: "Baa-lamb, baa-lamb!" But then the lamb suddenly bares his teeth and answers him back: "Baa-lamb, baa-lamb..."'

The story-teller had hardly uttered this last word, when suddenly both dogs leapt up and with a burst of barking rushed away from the fire and vanished into the darkness. The boys all jumped with fright. Vanya sprang up from under his matting, and Pavel darted off shouting after the dogs. Their barking quickly grew more distant... We could hear the restless hooves of frightened horses. Pavel shouted loudly: 'Grey! Beetle!' After a few moments the barking stopped. Pavel's voice could be heard, already some way off... A little time went by; the boys exchanged puzzled glances as if expecting something to happen... Suddenly came the sound of a galloping horse; it stopped sharp at the very fireside and, holding on by the mane, Pavel jumped nimbly down. The two dogs came darting into the circle of firelight as well, and sat down at once with their red tongues hanging out.

'What was it? What was the matter?' asked the boys.

'Nothing,' answered Pavel, waving his hand at the horse. 'The dogs just scented something. I thought it was a wolf,' he added in an indifferent voice, breathing quickly and full-chestedly.

I found myself involuntarily admiring Pavel. He was splendid at that moment. His ugly face, animated by the gallop, blazed with cool audacity and firm resolution. Without a stick in his hand, at night, he had ridden out alone after a wolf, without turning a hair... That's a fine boy, I thought, as I looked at him.

'Well, did you see them, the wolves?' asked Kostya the coward.

'There are always lots of them about here,' answered Pavel, 'but they're only troublesome in winter.'

He settled down again in front of the fire. Sitting on the ground, he propped his hand on the shaggy neck of one of the dogs and for a while the delighted animal never moved its head, but looked sideways at Pavel with grateful pride.

Vanya huddled up again under the matting.

'But that's a terrible story you told us, Ilyusha,' said Fedya, who, as the son of a well-to-do peasant, was the right one to call the tune (while saying little himself, as if afraid of cheapening his dignity). 'And some evil spirit made the dogs bark like that... I'd certainly heard that the place was haunted.'

'Varnavitsy? ... I should say it is! the old master is supposed to have been seen there more than once – the late master. They say he walks in a coat with long skirts and groans all the time and looks for something on the ground. Grandfather Trofimich met him once, and asked him: "What is it, Ivan Ivanich, sir, that your worship is looking for on the ground?"'

'He asked him?' interrupted Fedya in astonishment.

'Yes, he did.'

'Well, Trofimich is a stout fellow to have done that! And what answer did he get?'

'"I am looking for saxifrage," he says: and he says it in such a flat, flat voice: "saxifrage". "But, Ivan Ivanich, sir, what do you want with saxifrage?" "The grave presses hard on me, Trofimich," he says. "I want to get out and away..."'

'Fancy that!' remarked Fedya. 'As if he hadn't lived enough.'

'That's very strange!' said Kostya. 'I thought you could only see the dead on All-Hallows day.'

'You can see the dead at any hour of the day or night,' asserted Ilyusha with conviction. So far as I could observe, he seemed to know all the village lore better than his fellows ... 'But on All-Hallows day you can see a living man too whose turn it is to die in the same year. All you have to do is to sit at night at the porch of the church and keep on looking at the road. The people who go past you on the road are those who are going to die in the same year. Ulyana in our village sat up like that last year.'

'Well, and did she see anybody?' asked Kostya curiously.

'Certainly she did. First of all she sat for a long, long while and never saw or heard anyone; she only thought she heard a dog barking, barking away somewhere the whole time ... Suddenly she looks, and along the road comes a boy wearing nothing but a shirt; she looks closer, and it's Ivashka Fedoseyev going by ...'

'The one who died in the spring?' Fedya interrupted.

'Yes, that's the one. He was walking along without lifting his head. But Ulyana recognizes him ... And then she looks – a woman is walking past. She looks and looks – and good Lord! – it's she herself, Ulyana herself, walking along the road.'

'Really herself?' asked Fedya.

'Yes, by God, herself.'

'Well, what about it? She still hasn't died.'

'The year isn't up yet. But you just look at her. Her soul only just hangs on to her body.'

They all fell silent again. Pavel threw a handful of dry twigs on the fire. They showed up sharp and black against the sudden blaze of flame, crackled, smoked, and started to shrivel and lift their charred ends. Flickering and trembling, the reflection of the blaze struck out in all directions, especially upwards. Suddenly, out of nowhere, a white pigeon flew straight into this reflection, pulled up in fright, hovered, all suffused with the warm glow, and vanished with a whirr of wings.

'He must have escaped from home,' observed Pavel. 'Now he'll fly until he strikes something, and wherever he does he'll stay until daybreak.'

'Why, Pavel,' said Kostya, 'wasn't that a just soul flying to heaven?'

Pavel threw another handful of twigs on the fire. 'Perhaps,' he said at length.

'But tell me, Pavel,' began Fedya, 'in your village, too, in Shalamovo, did you see the heavenly portent?'[1]

'When the sun hid itself? Of course we did.'

'I suppose you were frightened, too?'

'Yes, and we were not the only ones. Our master, although he told us beforehand that there would be a portent, yet, when it got dark, it seems he got so scared himself, you wouldn't believe it. And in the servants' quarters, as soon as it got dark, the cook went and broke all the pots in the oven with the oven-fork: "Who's going to eat now," she says, "now the end of the world has come?" So the soup was all spilt. And in our village they were saying that white wolves would run about the earth and eat people up, and birds of prey would fly about, and that we would see Trishka[2] himself.'

'Who is Trishka?' asked Kostya.

'Don't you know?' took up Ilyusha excitedly. 'Where do you come from, not to know about Trishka? They must all be stay-at-homes in your village, that's what they must be! Trishka's a marvellous sort of man who's going to come one day; such a marvellous sort of man that you won't be able to take hold of him or do anything to him, such a marvellous man he'll be that some Christian folk will want to get hold of him, they'll go at him with sticks, they'll surround him, but he'll lead their eyes astray, so that they'll start beating each other. Say they put him

[1] This is what the peasants in our part of the country call an eclipse. – *Author*.

[2] The superstition about 'Trishka' probably derives from the legend of Antichrist. – *Author*.

in prison, he'll ask for a drink of water in a bowl; they'll bring him the bowl, and he'll dive into it and vanish right away. They'll throw him in chains, but he'll clap his hands and the chains'll just fall off him. Well, this Trishka will walk in village and town; and this Trishka, the sly fellow that he is, will tempt Christian folk . . . But there'll be nothing that you can do to him. That's the sort of marvellous, sly fellow he'll be.'

'Yes,' continued Pavel in his unhurried voice, 'that's how he'll be. We were expecting him, too. The old people told us that as soon as the heavenly portent started, Trishka would come. Well, the portent started. Everyone went out into the road and into the fields and waited for what would happen next. Round us, you know, the country is clear and open. They looked, and suddenly down from the village on the hill came an odd sort of man with a marvellous sort of head . . . and everybody shouted: "Oy, Trishka is come! Oy, Trishka is come!" And everyone hid where they could. The village elder crept into a ditch; his wife got stuck under the gate and screamed for all she was worth, and gave the dog in her yard such a fright that it snapped its chain and went off through the fence into the forest; and Kuzka's father, Dorofeich, jumped into a field of oats, sat down, and started calling like a quail: "Surely," he thought, "a *bird* ought to be safe from him, fiend and destroyer though he is!" That's how scared we all were! . . . And all the time it was our barrelmaker, Vavila: he'd bought himself a new jug, and had put the empty jug over his head.'

All the boys laughed, and again fell silent for a moment, as often happens when people are talking in the open air. I looked round: night reigned in all the majesty of its empire; the moist freshness of late evening had given place to the dry warmth of midnight, which would lie for some while yet, in a soft veil, over the sleeping fields; we were still a long time from the first murmur, the first rustlings and swishings of dawn, the first dewdrops of daybreak. There was no moon in the heavens; it was the period of late moonrise. The numberless golden stars, twinkling in rivalry, seemed all to be floating gently in the direction of the Milky Way, and, indeed, looking at them, you felt yourself vaguely aware of the earth's purposeful, unceasing course... A strange, sharp, ailing cry sounded, suddenly, twice together, from above the river and, after a few moments, it came again from farther in the distance...

Kostya shuddered... 'What was that?'

'It was a heron calling,' rejoined Pavel calmly.

'A heron,' repeated Kostya. 'But, Pavel, what was it that I heard yesterday evening?' He added after a pause: 'You may know...'

'What did you hear?'

'This is what I heard. I was going from Stone Ridge to Shashkino; first I went right along our hazel-wood, then across the meadow – you know the place where it comes out at the corner of the ravine – well, there, you know, there's a dew-pond; it's all overgrown with reeds; well, I was walking past this dewpond, when suddenly, from out of it, someone sort of groaned, and so sadly, so sadly: "u – u ... u – u ... u – u! ..." Such a fright took hold of me: it was late, and the voice sounded so ill. It was enough to make you cry yourself... What could that have been, eh?'

'In that dewpond, the summer before last, Akim, the forester, was drowned by thieves,' observed Pavel. 'So perhaps it's his soul complaining.'

'Well, there you are, boys,' rejoined Kostya, widening his eyes, which were anyway huge enough. 'I never even knew that Akim was drowned in that dewpond: if I'd known, I'd have been ever so frightened.'

'Or else, there are tiny little frogs, so they say,' continued Pavel, 'which call out sadly like that.'

'Frogs? No, it wasn't frogs ... it wasn't frogs that made that noise.'

A heron called again from over the river: 'Ooh, there he is!' said Kostya involuntarily. 'Like a wood-goblin calling.'

'The wood-goblin doesn't call, he's dumb,' asserted Ilyusha. 'He can only clap his hands and rattle! ...'

'I suppose you've seen him?' Fedya interrupted, in a mocking voice.

'Certainly not, and heaven preserve me from doing so: but others have. Why, the other day, he led one of our peasants astray: took him round and round in the forest, all the way round the same clearing . . . He hardly got home before dawn.'

'Did he see him?'

'Yes, he said he was a great big dark fellow, all muffled up, he seemed to be hiding behind a tree; you couldn't make him out clearly, he seemed to be hiding from the moon, and he looked and looked with his great eyes, and twinkled and twinkled away with them . . .'

'Ugh!' exclaimed Fedya, trembling slightly and shuddering at the shoulders. 'Phew!'

'And what's this pest doing walking the earth?' observed Pavel. 'What does he think he's doing?'

'Don't curse him: look out, or he'll hear you,' said Ilyusha.

Silence fell again. 'Look, look, boys,' came suddenly Vanya's childish voice. 'Look at God's little stars – like bees swarming.' He stuck out his fresh little face from under the matting, leant on his fist and slowly raised his big, calm eyes aloft. All the boys gazed up to the sky and didn't look down for quite a while.

'Well, Vanya,' began Fedya tenderly, 'is your sister Anyutka well?'

'Very well,' answered Vanya, slightly slurring the 'r'.

'Tell her to come and see us; why doesn't she come?'

'I don't know.'

'Tell her to come.'

'I will.'

'Tell her that I'll give her a present.'

'And me too?'

'Yes, you too.'

Vanya sighed.

'Well, no, I don't need one. Better give it to her, she's so good and kind.'

Vanya rested his little head on the ground again. Pavel stood up and took the empty pot in his hands.

'Where are you going?' Fedya asked him.

'To the river, to draw water: I feel like a good drink of water.'

The dogs rose and went after him.

'Mind you don't fall into the river,' Ilyusha called after him.

'Why should he fall?' said Fedya. 'He'll take care.'

'Yes, he'll take care. But anything may happen. Say he bends down and begins to draw water, and the water-goblin takes him by the hand and pulls him under. Afterwards they'll say the lad fell into the water . . . Fell in, indeed! . . . There, he's gone down into the rushes,' he added, listening hard.

There came the rustle of parting reeds.

'Is it true,' asked Kostya, 'that crazy Akulina went off her head when she fell into the water?'

'Yes . . . Just look at her now! . . . But they say that she used to be beautiful. The water-goblin spoilt her. I suppose he didn't expect that they'd pull her out so soon. So he spoilt her, down there at the bottom where he lives.'

(I had met this Akulina more than once. Covered in rags, dreadfully thin, with a face as black as coal, a clouded look and teeth ever-bared, she would stamp for whole hours on the same spot on the road, tightly pressing her bony hands to her breast and slightly shifting her weight from one leg to the other, like a wild creature in a cage. She understood not a word of what was said to her, but only laughed convulsively from time to time.)

'But, they say,' continued Kostya, 'that Akulina threw herself into the river because her lover played her false.'

'Yes, that was why.'

'D'you remember Vasily?' added Kostya suddenly.

'What Vasily?' asked Fedya.

'The one who was drowned,' answered Kostya. 'In this very same river. What a fine chap he was! Oh, what a fine chap! His mother, Feklista, how she loved him! It was as if she felt, Feklista did, that his death would come by water. Vasily used to come with us in summer to bathe in the river – and she'd get all of a fluster. The other mothers didn't care a bit, they'd walk past with their washpails, they'd waddle by, but Feklista would put her pail down and start calling him. "Come back, come back," she'd say, "come back, light of my eyes! Oh, come back, my little eagle!" And how he came to drown, Lord alone knows. He was playing on the bank, and his mother was there too, raking hay, and suddenly she heard what sounded like someone blowing bubbles under water – she looked, and there was only Vasily's cap floating in the water. Well, since then, Feklista, too, hasn't been right in the head. She comes and lies at the place where he drowned; there she lies, boys, and starts to sing – d'you remember, Vasily always used to sing a song – well that's the one she sings, too, and cries and cries, and complains bitterly to God . . .'

'Here comes Pavel,' said Fedya.

Pavel came up to the fire with a full pot in his hand.

'Well, boys,' he began after a silence, 'there's something bad.'

'What?' asked Kostya hurriedly.

'I heard Vasily's voice.'

Everyone shuddered.

'What's that you say?' whispered Kostya.

'So help me God. I'd just begun to bend down to the water, and suddenly I heard my name being called, in Vasily's voice, like it was from under the water: "Pavel, Pavel, come here!" I went away. I got the water, though.'

'Good Lord!' said the boys, crossing themselves.

'That was a water-goblin calling you, Pavel,' added Fedya. 'And we were just talking about Vasily.'

'Oh, that's an evil sign,' said Ilyusha, with deliberation.

'Well, never mind, forget about it!' said Pavel resolutely, and sat down again. 'You can't escape your fate.' The boys became quieter. It was clear that Pavel's story had made a deep impression on them. They began to settle down in front of the fire, as if preparing to sleep.

'What's that?' asked Kostya suddenly, lifting his head.

Pavel listened intently.

'That's curlews flying past and whistling.'

'Where are they flying to?'

'To the country where there's supposed to be no winter.'

'Is there really such a country?'

'Yes, there is.'

'Far away?'

'Far, far away, beyond the warm seas.'

Kostya sighed and closed his eyes. More than three hours had passed since I had been in company with the boys. At last the moon rose; I didn't notice her at once, so small and thin she was. The moonless night seemed still as magnificent as before ... But many stars, which, not long ago, had stood high in the heavens, were now stooping towards the earth's dark rim; everything was perfectly silent all around, with the special silence that usually falls towards daybreak: everything was sunk in the heavy, immobile sleep that precedes the dawn. There was no longer the same strong scent in the air – moisture seemed to be distilled in it afresh. Oh, the short nights of summer! ... The boy's talk had died down with the fires ... Even the dogs were dozing; the horses, as far as I could make out, in the hardly discernible, feebly-pulsing light of the stars, were lying down too, with sunken heads ... A gentle drowsiness came over me and merged into slumber.

A flood of freshness coursed over my face. I opened my eyes – the day was breaking. There was still no flush of dawn, but a growing pallor in the East. I could vaguely make out my surroundings. The pale-grey sky was growing light, and cold, and blue; the stars twinkled feebly or went out; the earth had grown damp, the leaves dripped, from somewhere came sounds of life, and voices, and the damp breath of dawn was already abroad, hovering above the earth. My body answered it with a faint thrill of exhilaration. I rose quickly and went across to the boys. They were all sleeping like the dead around the dying fire; only Pavel half-raised himself and stared fixedly at me. I nodded to him and went my way along the steaming river. I had not gone two versts when, around me in the broad water-meadow and ahead on the deepening green of the hills, from wood to wood, and behind me over the long dusty track, over the flushed sparkling bushes, and along the river, which was of a timid blue below the thinning mist – flowed scarlet,

then red, then golden torrents of youthful, blazing light...
The world began to rustle, awoke, began to sing, to murmur, to
speak. On all sides the heavy dewdrops flashed into blazing
diamonds; to meet me, pure and clear, as if they too had been
washed in the coolness of morning, came the sounds of a
church bell, and suddenly, driven by my friends the boys,
the herd of horses, fresh from sleep, galloped past me...

With sorrow I must add that Pavel died before the year was
out. He was not drowned, but killed by a fall from a horse.
A pity, he was a splendid lad!

Kasyan from Fair Springs

I WAS driving back from shooting in a jolting cart and, overcome by the stifling heat of an overcast day in summer (in
such weather the heat can of course be more unbearable even
than on fine days, and especially so when there is no wind),
I was dozing and swaying, submitting my whole person with a
sullen patience to the nagging attentions of the fine white dust
which rose constantly off the broken track from beneath our
cracked and lurching wheels, when suddenly my notice was
attracted by an unwonted restlessness, a certain fidgety uneasiness on the part of my coachman, who up to that moment had
been dozing away even more soundly than myself. He tightened his reins, began fussing about on his seat and shouting at
the horses, meanwhile gazing somewhere away to one side.
I looked round. We were driving across a wide, cultivated
plain; low hills, also cultivated, merged into it in gentle rolling
undulations; the eye could embrace at least some five versts of
open country: in the distance, small birch-copses were all that
broke the almost straight line of the horizon, with the rounded
tracery of their tree-tops. Narrow paths stretched across the
fields, disappeared into folds in the ground, wound over hil-
locks, and on one of them, which was due to intersect our track
about five hundred yards ahead of us, I could make out some
sort of procession. It was at this that my coachman was gazing.

It was a funeral. In front, in a cart drawn at walking pace by a
single nag, rode the priest; a deacon sat beside him and drove:
behind the cart, four peasants, with heads bared, carried a
coffin covered in a white cloth; two peasant-women walked
behind the coffin. The thin, plaintive voice of one of them
suddenly came to my ears. I listened intently: she was wailing
for the dead. Her song came cheerlessly over the empty fields,
warbling, monotonous, mournful, without hope. My coachman urged on his horses so as to pass ahead of the procession.

To meet a dead man on the road is an evil omen. He was indeed successful in hurrying past before the dead man could reach the track; but we had not gone a hundred yards farther, when suddenly our cart gave a violent jolt, listed to one side and almost overturned. The coachman halted the horses, which had made as if to bolt, threw up his hand and spat.

'What's the matter?' I asked.

My coachman got down in silence and without haste.

'But what is it?'

'The axle's broken – burnt through,' he answered morosely, and suddenly straightened the harness on the side-horse with such indignation that the horse almost toppled right over, managed to stand its ground, snorted, trembled and began tranquilly nibbling its foreleg below the knee. I got down and stood for a while on the track, oppressed by a vague and disagreeable feeling of bewilderment. The right wheel had almost completely collapsed under the cart and now seemed to be lifting its hub aloft in dumb despair.

'What are we going to do now?' I asked at length.

'That's whose fault it is!' said my coachman, pointing with his whip at the procession, which had now turned on to the track and was approaching us. 'I've always noticed that,' he continued; 'it's a sure sign, when you meet a dead man.'

He began again to worry the side-horse, which, sensing his ill-humoured and grim mood, decided to stand motionless, with only an occasional modest flick of its tail. I walked a few paces up and down and halted again in front of the wheel.

Meanwhile the dead man had come up with us. Quietly turning off the track on to the grass, the sad procession made its way past our cart. My coachman and I took off our caps, bowed to the priest and exchanged glances with the coffin-bearers. They were stepping out ponderously, their broad chests bulging. Of the two women following the coffin, one was very old and pale; her motionless features, cruelly disfigured by grief, preserved an expression of dour and solemn dignity. She walked in silence, occasionally raising a bony hand to her thin, sunken lips. The other, a young woman of about twenty-five, had red, tearful eyes and her whole face was swollen with weeping; as she came level with us, she interrupted her wailing and covered her face with her sleeve ... By now the dead man had passed us and had got back on to the track and the woman's plaintive, heart-breaking song burst out again. After silently following with his eyes the measured swaying of the coffin, my driver turned to me:

'That's Martin the carpenter they're burying,' he said: 'the one from Ryaba.'

'How do you know?'

'I recognized the women. The old one's his mother, the young one's his wife.'

'Was he ill, or what?'

'Yes ... the fever ... The day before yesterday the bailiff sent for the doctor, but the doctor was out ... He was a good carpenter; he took a drop now and then, but he was a good carpenter. You can see how badly his wife has taken it .... Well, yes, of course it's true that women's tears don't cost a thing. Women's tears are the same as water ... yes.'

And he bent down, ducked under the side-horse's traces and took hold of the shaft-bow in both hands.

'Anyway,' I remarked, 'what are we going to do?'

My coachman first pressed his knee against the shoulder of the shaft-horse, shook the shaft-bow twice, straightened the strap, then ducked again under the side-horse's trace and, knocking the horse's face as he passed, went up to the wheel; then, without taking his eyes off it, slowly brought out a snuff-box from beneath the skirts of his coat, slowly pulled the top off by its strap, slowly inserted his two thick fingers into the snuff-box (and there was hardly room for both of them, at that), rubbed and rubbed away at the snuff, gave his nose an antici-patory twist, sniffed with deliberation, accompanying every intake with a prolonged grunt; then, screwing up and blinking his tear-filled eyes, as if in pain, he plunged into a profound reverie.

'Well, what about it?' I said at length.

My coachman carefully put the snuff-box away in his pocket, jerked his hat forward on to his forehead, without the help of his hands, just with a flick of his head, and reflectively climbed on to his seat.

'Where are you off to?' I asked him, not without astonishment.

'Please to take your place,' he answered calmly, and picked up the reins.

'But how are we going to go on?'

'We'll go on all right.'

'But the axle . . .'

'Please to take your place.'

'But the axle is broken.'

'It's broken, yes, but we can get as far as the hamlet . . . at a walk, that is. It's over there behind the wood to the right: it's called Yudiny.'

'D'you think we'll get there?'

My coachman did not vouchsafe me a reply.

'I'd better walk,' I said.

'As you please, sir . . .'

He waved his whip and the horses started off.

We did indeed reach the hamlet, although the right forewheel hardly stayed on, and turned in the strangest way. On one hill it practically came off, but my coachman shouted in a furious voice and we got safely down to the bottom.

The hamlet of Yudiny consisted of six little low cabins, which had already managed to take a list to one side, although they had probably not been standing long; some of the backyards were not even fenced-in. As we drove into the hamlet, we met not a single living soul. There was not even a fowl to be seen, not even a dog – or rather only one, a black dog, with a docked tail, which jumped up hurriedly in front of us out of a completely dry trough where it had no doubt been driven by thirst, and at once, without a bark, dashed headlong under a gate. I went up to the first cabin, opened the door, and called for the master and mistress. No one answered me. I called again; the hungry mewing of a cat sounded from behind the inner door. I pushed it with my foot; a thin cat darted past me, with a flash of green eyes in the darkness. I put my head into the room and looked around it. It was dark, smoky and empty. I made my way to the yard and found nobody there either . . . Behind a fence a calf lowed; a lame grey goose limped away to one side. I crossed to the second cabin and there too found not a soul. I went to the yard . . .

Right in the middle of the yard, in broad daylight, in the full blaze of the sun, lay, with his face to the ground and his head covered with a coat, what I took for a boy. A few paces away from him stood a wretched little cart in a thatched lean-to shed, with a bony nag in ragged harness beside it. The sunlight streaming through the narrow interstices of the decrepit roof fell in small pools of light on its shaggy sorrel-brown coat. Up aloft was a boxful of starlings, chattering and looking down with tranquil curiosity from their airy abode. I went up to the sleeper and set about waking him . . .

He raised his head, saw me, and at once jumped to his feet. 'Why, what is it? What's the matter?' he mumbled sleepily.

I didn't answer him at once: such was the impression made on me by his appearance. Imagine a dwarf of about fifty, with a swarthy, wrinkled little face, sharp little nose, brown, hardly perceptible little eyes, and thick curly black hair sticking out on all sides of a tiny head like the hat on top of a mushroom. His whole body was extremely thin and puny and I find it quite impossible to convey in words the utter strangeness of his expression.

'What is it?' he asked me again.

I explained to him what the matter was and he listened to me without taking his slowly blinking eyes off me.

'You couldn't let us have a new axle?' I asked at length. 'I'd be glad to pay for it.'

'But who are you? A sportsman, eh?' he asked, sizing me up from head to foot.

'Yes.'

'You shoot the birds of the heaven, I'll be bound? ... and the creatures of the forest? ... But isn't it a sin to kill God's birds and to shed the blood of the innocent?'

The strange little man spoke with a pronounced drawl. His tone also astonished me. Not only had it no hint of infirmity, but it was surprisingly sweet and young and had an almost feminine tenderness in it.

'I have no axle,' he added, after a slight pause. 'That thing there is no use.' He pointed to his cart. 'I suppose you've got a big cart?'

'Can't I find an axle in the village?'

'Village, indeed! ... No one here has got one. No one is at home either, they're all at work. Be off with you!' he said suddenly, and lay down again on the ground.

I had in no wise expected this conclusion.

'Listen, old fellow,' I said, touching his shoulder, 'be kind, and help me.'

'Be off, and good luck to you! I'm tired; I've been into town,' he told me, and drew his coat over his head.

'But, please help me,' I continued. 'I ... I'll pay you.'

'I don't need your money.'

'Now look here, old fellow ...'

He half got up, and sat with his thin little legs crossed.

'I could take you, if you like, to the clearing. Some merchants have bought our wood – may God be their judge. They're cutting down the wood, and they've built an office. May God be their judge. You could order an axle there, from them, or buy one ready-made.'

'Splendid!' I exclaimed joyfully. 'Splendid! ... Let's go.'

'An oaken axle, a good one,' he continued, not rising from where he sat.

'Is it far to the clearing?'

'Three versts.'

'Oh, well, we could drive there in your cart.'

'Oh, no ...'

'Well, let's go,' I said. 'Let's go, old fellow! My coachman's waiting in the road.'

The old man got up reluctantly and followed me out into the road. My coachman was in a mood of irritation. He had tried to water the horses, but there turned out to be extremely little water in the well, and what there was had a bad taste, which is what matters most, so coachmen say . . . At the sight of the old man, however, he grinned, nodded several times, and exclaimed: 'Ah, Kasyan! Good day!'

'Good day, Erofei, you man of righteousness!' answered Kasyan in a cheerless voice.

I lost no time in conveying his proposal to my coachman; Erofei expressed agreement and drove into the yard. While he was unharnessing the horses, with an air of busy deliberation, the old man stood with his shoulder propped against the gate and looked gloomily first at him, then at me. He seemed perplexed, and, as far as I could make out, not overjoyed by our sudden visitation.

'So they've transferred you, too?' Erofei asked him suddenly, while taking off the shaft-bow.

'Yes.'

'Ugh!' said my coachman through his teeth. 'Martin, you know, the carpenter . . . of course you know Martin from Ryaba?'

'I do.'

'Well, he's dead. We've just passed his coffin.'

Kasyan started.

'Dead?' he said, and looked down.

'Yes, dead. Why didn't you cure him, eh? They say that you can cure people, that you're a healer.'

My coachman was evidently amusing himself at the old man's expense.

'Is that your cart, eh?' he added, indicating it with his finger.

'Yes.'

'Well, it's certainly a cart . . . a cart!' he repeated, and taking it by the shafts he practically overturned it . . . 'A cart, indeed! . . . But what horse are you going to take to the clearing? . . . You'll never manage to harness one of our horses between these shafts: our horses are too big for this sort of a contraption.'

'I don't know,' answered Kasyan. 'No, you'll get there on this beasty here, perhaps,' he added, with a sigh.

'This one?' interjected Erofei, and, going over to Kasyan's nag, he prodded it contemptuously in the neck with the third finger of his right hand. 'Oho,' he added reproachfully, 'the old crow's asleep!'

I asked Erofei to hurry up and harness the horse. I was keen to go myself with Kasyan to the clearing: it ought to be a good place for blackcock. When the cart was ready, and I had somehow installed myself with my dog inside the back of its body, and Kasyan, curled up into a ball, with the same cheerless expression still on his face, had sat down on the raised part in front, Erofei came up to me and whispered, with a mysterious air: 'You're quite right, sir, to go with him. He's one of these cranky fellows; they call him the Flea. I don't know how you got any sense out of him...'

I wanted to remark to Erofei that, so far, Kasyan had struck me as a most judicious fellow, but my coachman at once went on in the same tone: 'But just keep an eye on where he takes you. And please choose the axle yourself, sir; choose the soundest one that you can see. Well, Flea,' he added loudly, 'can I get a crust of bread here?'

'Have a look; maybe you'll find some,' answered Kasyan; he gave a twitch of the reins and off we went.

To my unfeigned surprise, his nag went very tolerably. All the way Kasyan maintained a stubborn silence and answered my questions disjointedly and with reluctance. We soon reached the clearing, and there found the office, a lofty cabin standing by itself at the top of a small ravine, which not far off was blocked by a dam and spread out into a pond. In the office I found two young merchant-clerks, with snow-white teeth, and suavity in their glance, in their ready speech and their shrewd smiles. I compounded with them for my axle, and set off for the clearing. I thought that Kasyan would stay with his horse and await me there, but he suddenly approached me.

'Well, are you going shooting birdies?' he said. 'Eh?'

'Yes, if I find any.'

'I'll go with you . . . may I?'

'Certainly you may.'

So off we went. The clearing stretched for about a verst. I confess that I paid more attention to Kasyan than to my dog. He was not called the Flea for nothing. His black capless noddle (for that matter his hair was the equal of any cap) fairly bobbed up and down among the bushes. He walked extremely fast, hopped as he went, and kept stooping down to pick herbs, stuffing them in his bosom, mumbling something to himself and looking at me and my dog with a strange questioning glance. In the brushwood, in the small scrub, and in clearings, you will often find little grey fowl constantly flitting from one tree to another and whistling and suddenly swooping as they fly. Kasyan imitated them and conversed with them; a young quail flew up chirruping from under his feet, and he chirruped back at it. A lark dropped towards him, singing loudly, with wings a-quiver – Kasyan took up its song. He still avoided conversation with myself . . .

The weather was magnificent, even better than earlier on; there was no break in the sweltering heat. In a clear sky, there floated a few high, almost motionless, clouds, yellowish-white, like remnants of snow in springtime, with a long, flattened shape, like lowered sails. The patternwork of their edges, which were soft and downy as cotton-wool, altered slowly but perceptibly as the moments went by: they were dissolving, these clouds, and they cast no shadow. For a long while Kasyan and I tramped around the clearing. Young saplings, not more than two feet high, surrounded the low and blackened tree-trunks with their slender, smooth stems; round, jagged, grey-bordered growths, the sort from which touchwood is made, clung to these trunks, and the wild strawberry stretched its pink tendrils over them. Close at hand mushrooms sat tightly in families. Our feet kept getting caught and tangled in the long grass, which was wilting under the blazing sun; on all sides our eyes were dazzled by the sharp, metallic flickering of young, reddish leaves on the trees; on every hand were the gleaming blue berries of enchanter's nightshade, the celandine's bright golden bells, and the purple and yellow flowers of the wild pansy; here and there, beside overgrown tracks, on which wheel marks showed up as stripes of fine red grass, stood piles of timber, blackened by wind and rain, and stacked in lengths; slanting rectangles of faint shadow fell from them, otherwise there was not a shadow to be found. The light breeze rose and fell: a sudden burst of it blows straight into your face, and all around there is a cheerful rustling and nodding and movement, a gracious swaying of the supple fern-tops, and your heart rejoices . . . then suddenly it dies away again and all grows still. Only the grasshoppers chatter away together like mad – and how oppressive is their interminable, harsh, dry sound. It goes well with the nagging heat of noon; it seems born of the heat, evoked by it from the incandescent earth.

Without having put up a single bird, we came at length to a new clearing. Here, lately-felled poplars lay sadly on the ground, crushing the grass and undergrowth beneath them; on some of them, dead but still green leaves drooped limply from the rigid branches; on others, the leaves were already dried up and shrivelled. Fresh, golden-white splinters, lying in piles beside the damp, bright-coloured trunks, gave out their special, strong, bitter-sweet scent. From farther off, near the edge of the wood, came the dull thudding of axes, and from time to time, solemnly and serenely, as if bowing and opening its arms, down fell a leafy-headed tree . . . For a long time I found no sport; at last, from a spreading oak-bush densely entwined with wormwood, a corncrake flew up. I hit him; he turned a somersault in the air and dropped. Hearing the shot, Kasyan quickly covered his eyes with his hand and never stirred until I had reloaded my gun and picked up the bird. When I had set off again, he went up to the spot where the dead bird had dropped, bent over the grass, which was spattered with a few drops of blood, shook his head, and gave me a frightened look . . . Afterwards I heard him whispering: 'Sinful! . . . That's what it is – sinful! . . .'

At length the heat compelled us to go into the wood. I threw myself down under a lofty hazel-bush, above which a slender

young maple graciously extended its floating branches. Kasyan
sat down on the stout butt-end of a sawn-down birch. I looked
across at him. High above us, leaves were faintly trembling, and
their liquid green shadows slipped gently backwards and forwards over his frail body, muffled up in its dark coat, and over
his little face. He never lifted his head. Bored by his taciturnity,
I lay on my back and began to admire the peaceful play of the
intricate leafage against the bright, distant sky. It is a strangely
enjoyable occupation to lie on one's back in the forest and look
upwards. You seem to be looking into a bottomless sea, extending far and wide beneath you; the trees seem not to rise from the
ground, but, like the roots of huge plants, to drop perpendicu-
larly down into those glass-clear waves, and the leaves on the
trees are now translucent as emeralds, now opaque with a
goldish, almost blackish, green. Somewhere far, far away, at
the end of its slender twig, a single leaf stands motionless
against a blue patch of pellucid sky, and beside it another one
sways with a movement like the play of a fish on a line, a
movement that seems spontaneous and not produced by the
wind. Like fairy islands under the sea, round wide clouds float
quietly up and quietly away – and suddenly the whole sea, the
radiant air, the sun-drenched branches and leaves, all begin to
ripple and tremble with a transitory brilliance, and there comes
a fresh, thrilling murmur, like the interminable faint splashing
that follows the rising of a sudden swell. You gaze without
stirring, and no words can express the gladness and peace and
sweetness that catch at your heart. You look – and that deep,
clear azure calls to your lips a smile as innocent as itself; like the
clouds in the sky, and as it were in company with them, happy
memories pass before you in slow procession, and you feel your
gaze passing farther and farther into the distance, drawing you
after it into that peaceful, radiant gulf, and you have no power
to tear yourself away from its height, from its depth . . .

'Master, I say, master!' said Kasyan suddenly, in his tuneful
voice.

I half-rose, in surprise; hitherto he had hardly answered my
questions and now he had suddenly addressed me himself.

'What is it?' I asked.

'Why did you kill that birdie?' he began, looking me straight in the face.

'How do you mean, why? ... A corncrake is game: you can eat him.'

'That's not why you killed him, master, as if you were going to eat him! You killed him for your sport.'

'But I'll warrant that you yourself eat goose, or chicken, for example.'

'Those are fowls set apart by God for man; but a corncrake is a free fowl, a fowl of the woods. And he is not the only one; there are many of them – every kind of creature of the woods and the fields and the rivers and the marshes and the meadows and the air and the earth – that it's a sin to kill; you should let them live their allotted span on earth. Other food is reserved for man: other food, other drink; bread, which is God's blessing, and the waters of the heaven, and the creatures that were tamed by our forefathers before us.'

I looked at Kasyan in surprise. His words flowed freely; he did not search for them, he spoke with quiet inspiration and gentle dignity, occasionally closing his eyes.

'Then you think it sinful to kill fish, too?'

'The fish is a cold-blooded creature,' he rejoined, with conviction, 'the fish is a dumb creature. He knows not fear or joy; he is a speechless creature. He has no feeling. Even his blood is not alive. Blood,' he continued after a pause, 'a sacred thing is blood! Blood sees not God's sun, blood hides away from the light ... A deadly sin it is, to show blood to the light – a deadly sin and horror ... deadly indeed!'

He sighed and sank his head. I confess that I looked at the strange old fellow in complete amazement. His speech was not that of a peasant. No simple folk talk like that, not even those with the gift of speech. This language, of such a deliberate solemnity and strangeness ... I had never heard anything like it.

'Tell me, Kasyan,' I began, not moving my gaze from his slightly-flushed face: 'What do you live by?'

He did not at once answer my question. His gaze travelled restlessly round for a moment.

'I live as the Lord ordains,' he said at last; 'but as for what I live by – why, by nothing. I have been a feckless creature, ever since I was a boy; I work when I can – but I am a bad workman. So there I am! My health is bad, and my hands are clumsy. Well, in spring I trap nightingales.'

'You trap nightingales! . . . Then how is it that you just said that we ought not to touch any creature of the woods and fields, and so forth?'

'We ought not to kill them, certainly. Death takes his due without that. Take Martin the carpenter: Martin lived, lived a while, and died; now his wife is weeping for her husband and her little children . . . There is no man, no creature that can cheat death. Death runs not, nor is there any running from him; but neither should we help him . . . I kill no nightingales – God forbid! I trap them, not to torment them, or to do them to death, but for man's pleasure, for his joy and his delight.'

'Do you go to Kursk to trap them?'

'I go to Kursk, and farther, too, if need be. I spend my nights in the marshes and in the woods, alone in the fields, in the solitary places: where the sandpiper whistles, the hare calls, the drake quacks . . . At evening-time I'm on the look-out, in the morning I listen, in the twilight I spread my net over the bushes . . . There are some nightingales that sing so sadly, so sweetly . . . so sadly, too.'

'And you sell them?'

'I give them away to good folk.'

'And what else do you do?'

'How d'you mean, do?'

'How do you occupy yourself?'

The old man was silent.

'I have no occupation . . . I'm a bad worker. I can read and write, though.'

'You can?'

'Yes. Thanks to the help of God, and of some good folk, too.'

'Have you got a family?'

'No.'

'Why . . . are they all dead?'

'No; but that was not the answer that life gave. It's all under Providence, we all move under Providence; man must be righteous – that's all! as God would have us, that's to say.'

'And have you no kin?'

'Yes . . . I have . . . but . . .' The old man became confused.

'Tell me,' I began, 'I overheard my coachman asking you why you didn't heal Martin; are you a healer, too?'

'Your coachman is a righteous man,' Kasyan replied reflectively, 'but he too is not without sin. They call me a healer . . . a fine healer indeed! Why, who can heal? All that comes from God. Healing is only possible as a gift from God. But there are . . . there are grasses and flowers that help, certainly. Take the marigold, for instance – there is a herb that is good for man; there is plantain, too; there is no shame in speaking of that: they are wholesome herbs, herbs of God. There is another sort as well: they help, too, but it is sinful; it is sinful even to speak of them, except may be with prayer . . . And, of course, there are also certain words . . . But he who believes shall be saved,' he added, lowering his voice.

'Did you give Martin nothing?' I asked.

'I heard of it too late,' answered the old man. 'But what of it? It's foreordained for us all at birth. Martin the carpenter was not meant to live, not meant to live on earth; that's how it was. No, if a man is not meant to live on earth, the sun does not warm him as it does his fellow, and bread gives him no sustenance – it is as if something was calling him away . . . yes; Lord rest his soul!'

'Is it long since you were transferred to these parts?' I asked, after a short silence.

Kasyan gave a start.

'No, not long; four years. In the old master's time we all lived in our former homes, but then his executors transferred us. Our old master was a gentle soul, a man of peace – may the kingdom of heaven be his! Of course, the executors decided rightly; it clearly had to be so.'

'Where did you live before?'

'We come from Fair Springs.'

'Is that far from here?'

'A hundred versts.'

'Were you better off there?'

'Yes ... better off. It's open country there, a country of rivers, our own home-country; but here it is all cramped and dried up ... we are like orphans here. At home, at Fair Springs, you go up a hill, you go up – and, good Lord, what is it that you see, eh? ... River and meadow and forest; here a church, over there, meadows again. You can see far, far away. You look, and look, and there's no end to it. Well, the land is certainly better here, it is clay, good clay soil, so the peasants say; anyway, there is corn growing for me in plenty everywhere.'

'But tell me, I dare say you'd like to visit your home-country?'

'Yes, to have a look at it. All the same, I'm well off any-where. I have got no family, I'm a rolling stone. Why! you cannot sit at home for ever, eh? So when you go off, when you go off,' he repeated, raising his voice, 'your heart grows lighter, indeed it does. And the sun shines down on you, and God can see you better, and singing comes easier to you. You see a herb growing; you mark it, and pick it. There may be water flowing – for instance, spring water, from the source, holy water; you drink your fill – you mark it, too. The birds of the heaven sing ... And then, beyond Kursk, come the steppes, the steppe-country, the surprise of it, the joy to your heart, the spaciousness of it, the blessing of God! Why, the steppes run, so they say, right to the warm seas, where lives the Gamayun bird with the sweet voice, and the leaves never fall from the trees in winter, nor in autumn, and golden apples grow on silver branches, and all men live in joy and righteousness ... and that's where I'd be fain to go ... I have done my fair share of travelling! I've been to Romyon, and to Simbirsk, the noble city, and right to Moscow of the golden domes; I've been to Oka the life-giver, to the kindly Tsna, and to mother Volga; I've seen many good Christian folk and I've been in fine cities... Well, I'd be fain to go there... so I would... and I, poor sinner that I am, I'm not the only one. There are plenty of Christian folk going round in rope shoes, wandering the face of the earth, seeking the truth... yes!... What is there to stay at home for, eh? There is no righteousness inside man's heart – and that's the truth...'

These last words Kasyan pronounced rapidly, almost inaudibly: then he said something more which I couldn't distinguish at all, and his face took on such a strange expression that I couldn't help remembering his nickname, 'the crank'. He lowered his head, cleared his throat and seemed to come to himself again.

'Look at the sun!' he said in an undertone. 'Look at the Lord's blessing! Look at the warmth inside the forest!'

He moved his shoulders, fell silent, looked vaguely round and began to sing quietly. I could not catch all the words of his long drawn-out song; I made out the following:

> *Kasyan is my name,*
> *My nickname is the Flea ...*

'Aha!' I thought, 'so he makes verses...'

Suddenly he started and fell silent, looking fixedly into the undergrowth of the forest. I turned and saw a little peasant-girl of about eight, in a blue dress, with a check handkerchief over her head and a wicker basket over her bare sunburnt arm. She had probably never expected to meet us; she had stumbled on top of us and stood motionless in a green hazel-thicket on a shady patch of grass, looking timorously at me with her black eyes. I had hardly caught sight of her when she darted behind a tree.

'Annushka, come here, don't be afraid,' called the old man tenderly.

'I *am* afraid,' came her thin little voice.

'Don't be afraid, don't be afraid, come to me.'

Annushka slowly abandoned her hiding-place, walked quietly round, her little feet hardly rustling in the thick grass, and came out of the bushes beside the old man. This was no girl of eight, as I had thought at first, judging by her small size, but one of thirteen or fourteen. Her whole body was small and thin, but trim and graceful, and her pretty little face was strikingly like Kasyan's own, although Kasyan himself was no beauty. She had the same sharp features, the same strange expression, at once cunning and trustful, reflective and penetrating, and the same movements . . . Kasyan looked her over; she was standing beside him.

'Well, have you got some mushrooms?' he asked.

'Yes, some mushrooms,' she answered, with a timid smile.

'Have you found plenty of them?'

'Yes, plenty.' She looked quickly at me and smiled again.

'Some white ones, too?'

'Yes, white ones, too.'

'Show me, do . . .'

She lowered the basket from her arm and half-lifted a broad burdock leaf which covered the mushrooms.

'Oh,' said Kasyan, stooping over the basket, 'what fine ones! Well done, Annushka!'

'Is she your daughter, Kasyan, eh?' I asked. Annushka's face showed a slight blush.

'She's a sort of relation,' said Kasyan, with assumed care-lessness.

'Well, Annushka, off you go,' he added at once; 'off you go, and good luck to you. And be careful . . .'

'But why should she walk?' I interrupted him. 'We could give her a lift . . .'

Annushka flushed the colour of a poppy, clutched with both hands at the string handle of her basket and looked anxiously at the old man.

'No, she'll get there all right,' he rejoined in the same indifferent, casual voice. 'Why should we? . . . She'll get there all right . . . Be off with you.'

Annushka went nimbly off into the forest. Kasyan looked after her, then lowered his gaze and smiled. In this long smile, in the few words which he had said to Annushka, in the very tone of his voice when he spoke to her, there was more passionate love and tenderness than language can express. He looked again in the direction in which she had vanished, smiled again, wiped his face, and nodded his head several times.

'Why did you send her off so quickly?' I asked him. 'I should like to have bought some of her mushrooms...'

'Why, it does not matter to you, you can buy them at home whenever you like,' he answered me, using the formal 'you' for the first time.

'Well, you've got a pretty one there.'

'No... well... there it is...' he answered, as if reluctantly, and from that moment he relapsed into his earlier mood of silence. Seeing that all my efforts to engage him again in conversation were proving vain, I went off to the clearing. Meanwhile it had grown slightly less hot; but my ill-success continued, and I returned to the hamlet with only one corn-crake besides my new axle. As we were driving up to his yard, Kasyan suddenly turned to me: 'Master, I say, Master,' he began. 'I'm sorry for what I did to you; you see, it was I who called all the birds away from you.'

'What do you mean?'

'It's my trick. That's a clever dog you have, and a good one, but all the same there was nothing he could do... When you come to think of it, what are men? Here's an animal, too, and what have they made of him?'

It would have been futile to try to convince Kasyan of the impossibility of 'putting spells' on game, and therefore I gave him no answer. Meanwhile we had turned through the gates.

Annushka was not in the cabin; she had already been there and left the mushrooms. Erofei fixed the new axle, after first submitting it to a harsh and unjust appraisal; within an hour I drove off, leaving some money with Kasyan, who at first refused to take it, but then, after thinking and holding it in the palm of his hand, put it into his bosom. During this hour he had uttered hardly so much as a word. As before, he stood leaning against the gates, without answering the reproaches of my coachman. He took leave of me very coldly.

As soon as I had returned, I had at once observed that my Erofei was again in a gloomy mood ... In fact he had found nothing to eat in the village and the water for the horses was brackish. We drove off. With dissatisfaction expressed even at the back of his head, he sat on the box, wanting desperately to talk to me; but while awaiting my first question he limited himself to faint grumblings under his breath and to words of instruction addressed to the horses, but sometimes venomously expressed. 'Village!' he muttered. 'Village, indeed! Why, I tried asking for kvass and they haven't even got that ... Good Lord! and as for the water, it's just filth!' He spat loudly. 'No cucumber, no kvass, nothing. Well, you,' he added loudly, turning to the right side-horse, 'I know you, you fraud, you! You like pretending, to be sure ...' He struck the horse with the whip. 'He's become an utter rascal, and yet he used to be such an obedient beast ... Well, just you look out!'

'Tell me, Erofei,' I began, 'what sort of fellow is this Kasyan?'

Erofei didn't answer at once: he was always a man of reflection and deliberation; but I guessed at once that my question had pleased and calmed him.

'The Flea?' he said at length, changing his grip on the reins. 'A queer fellow: a regular crank, a queer fellow whose like you wouldn't find in a hurry. You see, he's exactly like this horse of ours; he has become quite unmanageable, too ... so far as making him work goes. Well, of course, he's no use as a worker – he's hardly got any body for his soul to hang on to – well, anyway ... You see, he's been the same ever since he was a boy. First of all, he went into the driving business with his uncles; they drove in troikas; then, of course, he got bored and chucked it. He started living at home, but even at home he couldn't sit still, such a restless chap he is – a proper Flea. Luckily he happened to have a good master who didn't make him do anything, and since then he has done nothing but wander about like a stray sheep. And such a strange fellow he is, God knows. Sometimes still as a stock, then suddenly he starts talking – and what it's all about, God knows. What sort of manners is that? No sort of manners at all. He makes no sense, and that's the truth. He sings well, though, solemn and well.'

'Is it true that he is a healer?'

'Healer, indeed! . . . Whatever next? A fellow like him! All the same he did cure me of jaundice . . . A stupid fellow if ever there was one,' he added, after a silence.

'Have you known him for long?'

'Yes. We were neighbours at Sychovka, near Fair Springs.'

'But this girl who met us in the forest – Annushka – is she anything to do with him?'

Erofei looked at me over his shoulder and smiled all over his face. 'Ho . . . yes, they're related. She's an orphan: no mother, no one knows who her mother was. But she must be a relation of his: she's so like him . . . Anyway, she lives with him. She's a smart girl; she's a good girl. And you won't believe this, but, if you please, he's had the idea of teaching his Annushka to read and write. That's just like him. He's such an extraordinary fellow. Such a flighty chap, with such big ideas, too . . . eh, eh, eh!'

My coachman suddenly interrupted himself and, holding the horses, bent over sideways and started sniffing the air. 'Isn't there a smell of burning? I thought so! Oh, these new axles! . . . I was right to give it a good greasing . . . I must get some water: luckily, here's a pond.'

Erofei slowly dismounted from the box, untied the bucket, went to the pond, and, returning, listened, not without enjoyment, to the hissing of the wheel-hub under the sudden shock of water . . .

Six times in some ten versts he had to drench the overheated axle. The evening was already far advanced when we returned home.

The Bailiff

FIFTEEN VERSTS away from my property there lives an acquaintance of mine, a young landowner, a retired Guards officer, by name Arkady Pavlich Penochkin. There is plenty of game on his land, his house is built to the plans of a French architect, his servants are dressed in the English manner, he gives excellent dinners, receives his guests amiably, yet all the same one goes to his house with reluctance. He is a judicious, steady fellow, he had what is considered an excellent education, served in the army, moved in the best society, and now devotes himself to agriculture with a great deal of success. Arkady Pavlich, to use his own words, is strict but just, has the good of his serfs at heart, and punishes them – for their good. 'One must treat them like children,' he says on such occasions. 'Illiteracy, *mon cher, il faut prendre cela en considération*.' He himself, when 'the painful duty' impels him, avoids sharp or abrupt movements, dislikes raising his voice, and prefers to slide his hand out, adding calmly: 'But I asked you to, my good fellow,' or 'What is the matter with you, my friend? Wake up,' and this with only a slight clenching of the teeth and a twist of the mouth to one side. He is of small stature, neat of build, not at all bad-looking, with carefully-kept hands and nails; his red lips and cheeks fairly breathe good health. He has a ringing, carefree laugh, accompanied by an attractive narrowing of his clear brown eyes. He dresses excellently and with taste. He gets French books, illustrations and papers sent to him, but he is not a great reader. It was all he could do to plough through 'The Wandering Jew'. At cards, he plays a masterly game. All in all, Arkady Pavlich is considered one of the most cultured gentlemen and eligible bachelors of our province; the ladies are mad about him, and particularly admire his manners. He conducts himself extremely well, is as careful as a cat, and has never in all his life been mixed up in any trouble; although,

on occasion, he likes to throw his weight about and to embarrass and snub the timid. He resolutely spurns low company –
from fear of compromising himself; all the same, in his
moments of high spirits, he declares himself for a devotee of
Epicurus, though his general opinion of philosophy is poor,
and he describes it as the 'cloudy sustenance of the Teutonic
mind', or sometimes, simply, as 'twaddle'. He loves music; at
cards, he sings through his teeth, but with feeling; he remembers a few airs from *Lucia di Lammermoor* and *Somnambula*, but
sings them all slightly sharp. In the winter he goes to Petersburg. His house is remarkably well-ordered; even the coachmen have felt his influence and not only clean the harness and
their own coats every day, but wash their own faces. Arkady
Pavlich's house-serfs have, it is true, a somewhat sidelong look
– but in Russia it is never possible to distinguish the surly from
the merely sleepy. Arkady Pavlich speaks in a soft and pleasant
voice, with deliberation, as if it gave him pleasure to pass his
words one by one through his handsome, scented moustache.
He also uses plenty of French expressions like: '*Mais c'est
impayable! Mais comment donc!*' and so on. With it all, I, for
one, am never over-keen to visit him, and if it weren't for the
blackcock and the partridge I should probably have lost sight of
him altogether. A strange uneasiness takes hold of you in his
house; even the comfort gives you no pleasure, and every time,
in the evening, when a footman with curled hair, in a blue
livery with heraldic buttons, appears before you and begins
obsequiously pulling your boots off, you feel that if, instead of
his pale, lean figure, there could suddenly bob up in front
of you the enormous wide cheek-bones, the improbable snub
nose, of a sturdy young peasant-lad, only just taken by his
master from the plough, but already successful in having burst
at a dozen places the seams of his new nankeen coat, you would
be quite overjoyed, and would eagerly submit yourself to the
danger of having your leg pulled right off from the hip-bone
with the boot.

Notwithstanding my aversion for Arkady Pavlich, I once
stayed the night in his house. Early the following morning

I ordered my carriage to be harnessed, but he refused to let me go without taking breakfast in the English manner, and led me into his study. We were served with tea, cutlets, soft-boiled eggs, butter, honey, cheese and so forth. Two footmen in clean white gloves swiftly and silently forestalled our slightest wish. We were sitting on a Persian divan. Arkady Pavlich was wearing wide silk trousers, a black velvet jacket, a handsome fez with a blue tassel, and yellow heelless Chinese slippers. He drank tea, laughed, inspected his nails, smoked, tucked cushions under his side, and in short was in an excellent humour. After breakfasting amply and with evident satisfaction, Arkady Pavlich poured himself out a glass of red wine, lifted it to his lips and suddenly frowned.

'Why is the wine not warmed?' he asked one of the footmen, in a fairly sharp voice.

The man became confused, halted as if rooted to the ground, and turned pale.

'I am asking you a question, my good fellow,' continued Arkady Pavlich calmly, without shifting his gaze from him.

The unhappy footman fidgeted where he stood, twisted his napkin, and said not a word. Arkady Pavlich lowered his head and looked thoughtfully at him from under his eyebrows.

'*Pardon, mon cher*,' he said with an agreeable smile and a friendly touch of his hand on my knee, and stared again at the footman. 'Well, you can go,' he added, after a short silence, lifted his eyebrows, and rang.

A man came in, a stout, swarthy fellow with black hair and a low forehead and eyes completely buried in fat.

'About Fyodor ... the necessary steps,' said Arkady Pavlich, in a low voice and with complete self-possession.

'Very good, sir,' answered the fat one and went out.

'*Voilà, mon cher, les désagréments de la campagne*,' remarked Arkady Pavlich gaily. 'But where are you off to? Wait, sit down again for a bit longer.'

'No,' I answered. 'It is time for me to go.'

'Always shooting! Oh, you shooting men! But where are you going now?'

'To Ryabovo. Forty versts away.'

'Ryabovo? Goodness me, why in that case I'll come with you. Ryabovo is at most five versts from my place at Shipilovka, and it is ages since I was last there: I could never find a moment to go. This is a piece of luck: you shoot at Ryabovo today, and in the evening you come to my place. *Ce sera charmant*. We will dine together – we will take the cook with us, and you will stay the night with me. Splendid!' he added, without waiting for me to answer. '*C'est arrangé*. Hey there! Tell them to harness the carriage for us, and be quick about it. You've never been to Shipilovka? I would have been ashamed to suggest that you should spend the night in my bailiff's cabin, but I know you're not fussy and wouldn't have minded spending the night at Ryabovo in a hay-shed . . . Let's go, let's go!'

And Arkady Pavlich began to sing a French love-song.

'You may not know,' he continued, swaying from one leg to the other, 'that my peasants there are rent-paying. It's that Constitution – and there's nothing one can do about it. All the same, they pay their rent regularly, or of course I would have transferred them to labour-duty long ago, but there is so little land! Even as it is, I am surprised at the way they make both ends meet. Anyhow, *c'est leur affaire*. The bailiff I have there is a stout fellow, *une forte tête*, a born administrator! You'll see . . . Well, what a piece of luck this is!'

There was nothing for it. Instead of leaving at nine o'clock in the morning, we left at two. Sportsmen will imagine my impatience. Arkady Pavlich loved, as he put it, to make a fuss of himself when he got the chance, and took with him an immense supply of linen, victuals, liquor, perfumes, pillows and dressing-cases of all sorts, such as would have lasted a careful, self-denying German for a whole year. Every time we went downhill Arkady Pavlich treated the coachman to a short but vehement lecture, from which I was able to conclude that my acquaintance was a thorough poltroon. Our journey went off without a hitch; except that on a recently-mended bridge the cook's cart broke down and the cook's belly got bruised by the back wheel.

Seeing the mishap to his home-trained Karem, Arkady Pavlich got a bad fright and at once sent to ask if his hands were all right. Receiving an affirmative answer, he calmed down at once. What with all this, we had spent a long time under way; I sat in the carriage with Arkady Pavlich and towards the end of the journey I became bored to death, the more so because, as the hours went by, he talked himself out and even got round to liberalism. At last we came, not to Ryabovo, but straight to Shipilovka; it just happened that way. In any case, it would have been too late for me to go shooting that day, so I contained myself and submitted to my fate.

The cook had arrived a few minutes before us and evidently had already managed to take the necessary steps and warn those concerned, for at the very moment when we crossed the village boundary we were met by the headman (the son of the bailiff), a sturdy, red-headed peasant, seven feet high, on horse-back, capless, and wearing a new overcoat, unbuttoned. 'But where is Sofron?' Arkady Pavlich asked him. The headman first jumped nimbly from his horse, bowed deeply to his master, and said: 'Good day, father Arkady Pavlich,' then raised his head, pulled himself together, and announced that Sofron had gone to Perov, but that they had already sent to fetch him. 'Well, come along after us,' said Arkady Pavlich. The headman led his horse respectfully to one side, clambered on to it and trotted after the carriage, holding his cap in his hand. We drove through the village. A few peasants in empty carts were driving towards us; they were coming from the threshing-floor and singing songs, beating time with their bodies and waving their legs in the air; but, when they saw our carriage and the headman, they suddenly fell silent, took off their winter caps (it was in fact summer) and sat up as if expecting orders. Arkady Pavlich gave them a gracious bow. A mood of anxious excitement spread visibly through the village. Peasant-women in check skirts threw bits of wood at dogs who were slow in the uptake or over-zealous; a lame old man, with a beard which began immediately under his eyes, snatched a horse which had not finished drinking away from the well, struck it on the side for no apparent reason, and only then made his bow. Little boys in long blouses ran wailing to the cabins, lay on their stomachs on the high thresholds, hung down their heads, threw their legs in the air, and thus disappeared with great agility behind doors into dark passages from which they did not reappear. Even the chickens made off under the gates at a rapid trot; one bold cock, with a black chest like a satin waistcoat and a red tail which came curling right up to his crest, made as if to stay in the road and was just preparing to crow, but suddenly became self-conscious and ran off too. The bailiff's cabin stood away from the others in the middle of a thick green hemp-yard. We halted in front of the gates. Mr. Penochkin got up, threw off his cloak with a picturesque gesture and alighted from the carriage, casting a friendly glance around. The bailiff's wife welcomed us with low curt-sies, then came up and kissed her master's hand. Arkady Pavlich let her kiss away to her heart's content and then went up to the porch. Inside the passage, in a dark corner, stood the headman's wife and she curtsied too, but didn't dare kiss hands. In the so-called 'cold room' – to the right of the passage – two other women were already busy; they were carrying out all kinds of junk, empty jugs, sheepskin coats that had gone stiff, greasy pots, and a cradle containing a heap of rags and a mottle-faced baby, and were sweeping up the dust with bath-brooms. Arkady Pavlich sent them packing and installed himself on the bench under the icons. His coach-men began to carry in trunks, chests and other accessories, while doing everything possible to deaden the sound of their heavy boots.

Meanwhile, Arkady Pavlich was questioning the headman about the harvest, the sowing, and other farm topics. The headman answered adequately, but with a certain dull awk-wardness, like a man buttoning up a coat with frozen fingers. He was standing in the doorway, constantly looking over his shoulder and making way for the swift-footed valet. Behind his powerful frame I managed to get a glimpse of the bailiff's wife quietly beating another woman in the passage. All at once a cart rattled up and halted in front of the porch, and the bailiff came in.

This 'born administrator', to quote Arkady Pavlich, was a short, broad-shouldered, squat, grey-haired man with a red nose, little blue eyes and a fan-shaped beard. Let us remark in passing that in all her history Mother Russia has never known a man make good and grow rich without a substantial beard; a man may have worn a meagre goatee all his days, then suddenly you see him enveloped on all sides in a kind of halo – wherever can all the hair come from! The bailiff must have taken a drop in Perov: his face was quite bloated, and he smelt of drink, too.

'Oh, sir, father, benefactor,' he began in a sing-song voice, and with such emotion in his face that you expected the tears to start at any moment. 'At last you have done us the honour!... Your hand, sir, your hand,' he added, sticking out his lips in anticipation.

Arkady Pavlich satisfied his wish.

'Well, Sofron, my friend, how are things with you?' he asked in a kind voice.

'Oh, father!' exclaimed Sofron. 'How could they be but well? For you, our father, sir, our benefactor, have done us the honour of brightening our village with your presence, and have made us happy to the end of our days! Praise be to the Lord, Arkady Pavlich, praise be to the Lord! All is well, thanks to your goodness.'

Here Sofron fell silent, looked at his master, and, as if carried away again by a wave of emotion (added to which the drink inside him was claiming its due), begged leave to kiss his hand for a second time and began again with a more pronounced sing-song than before.

'Oh, sir, father, benefactor... and what besides! Goodness me, I've gone quite off my head from joy... Goodness me, I can't believe my eyes... Oh, father!...'

Arkady Pavlich looked at me, laughed, and asked: '*N'est-ce pas que c'est touchant?*'

'But, sir, Arkady Pavlich,' continued the irrepressible bailiff, 'how comes it? You have quite distressed me, sir; you never warned me of your visit. Where will you spend the night? Look at all the dirt and dust here...'

'Never mind, Sofron, never mind,' answered Arkady Pavlich with a smile. 'It's all right here.'

'But, father – all right for who? All right for peasants like me; but for you, you... Oh, father, benefactor, oh, father mine!... Forgive me, I'm a fool, I've gone off my head; goodness me, I have gone all silly.'

Meanwhile supper was served and Arkady Pavlich fell to. The old man dismissed his son. 'You're spoiling the air,' he said.

'Well, have you got the boundaries settled, gaffer?' asked Mr. Penochkin, in an evident attempt at a peasant's way of talking, and with a wink at me.

'Yes, sir – all thanks to your goodness. The day before yesterday they signed the whole story. To begin with, the Khlynovo folk made difficulties... they did, father, they did indeed. They asked... and asked... God knows what they didn't ask; they're such fools, sir, such a stupid lot. But we, sir, thanks to your goodness, we offered a little something to Nikolai Nikolaich, who was the arbitrator, and satisfied him; we followed your instructions closely, sir; we did exactly what you were good enough to tell us, and Egor Dmitrich knows just what we did.'

'Egor reported to me fully,' observed Arkady Pavlich pompously.

'Of course, sir, of course he did.'

'Well, I suppose you're satisfied now?'

Sofron was waiting just for this. 'Oh, father, oh, benefactor!' he began to intone again. 'Forgive me... you see, we pray to the Lord God day and night for you, father... Of course we've so little land...'

Penochkin interrupted him. 'Well, all right, all right, Sofron, I know what a faithful servant you are. But tell me, how is the yield?'

Sofron sighed.

'Well, the yield is not too good, sir. Let me tell you, Arkady Pavlich, sir, about something that has happened.' Here he spread out his arms, came closer to Mr. Penochkin, bent down and narrowed one eye. 'A dead body was found on our land.'

'How so?'

'I can't make head or tail of it, sir, father: an enemy must have had a hand in it. Yes, luckily it was found near the boundary; but on our land, all the same – it's no good denying it. I at once gave orders for it to be dragged off to the neighbour's bit of land while that was still possible, and posted a sentry on it and told my people to hold their tongues. But, to take no risks, I reported it to the district police officer. "This is the way things are," I told him; and I gave him a cup of tea and a little something besides... Well, sir, what do you think? It's ended up round somebody else's neck: a dead body is just a matter of two hundred roubles – and that's all there is to it.'

Mr. Penochkin laughed heartily at his bailiff's ruse, and said to me several times, pointing at him with his head: '*Quel gaillard, ah?*'

Meanwhile it had grown quite dark out-of-doors; Arkady Pavlich ordered the table to be cleared and straw to be brought. The valet made our beds and arranged the pillows; we lay down. Sofron retired, after receiving his orders for the following day. Arkady Pavlich, while dropping off to sleep, still had quite a lot to say about the excellent qualities of the Russian peasant, and at the same time observed to me that, since Sofron had been in charge, the peasants of Shipilovo had not been a farthing in arrears... The watchman hammered on his board; a child, who had evidently not yet succeeded in acquiring a fitting sense of self-abnegation, cried somewhere in the cabin... We fell asleep.

Next day we rose fairly early. I was preparing to leave for Ryabovo, but Arkady Pavlich wanted to show me his estate and induced me to stay. I was in fact not reluctant to verify in practice the excellent qualities of that born administrator,

Sofron. The bailiff appeared. He wore a blue overcoat girt with a red belt. He had much less to say than the day before, he met his master's gaze with a sharply attentive stare and answered him coherently and to the point. We set off with him for the threshing-floor. Sofron's son, the seven-foot headman, who showed every sign of extreme stupidity, followed us as well, and we were also joined by the village constable Fedoseich, an ex-soldier with huge moustaches and the peculiar expression of a man who very long ago had been extremely surprised at something and had never recovered since. We inspected the threshing-floor, the threshing-barn, the drying-barns, the cart-shed, the windmill, the cow-byre, the winter-fields, the hemp-yards; everything was in fact extremely well-kept: only the sad faces of the peasants caused me a certain perplexity. Sofron's care was not purely utilitarian but covered the amenities as well: he had planted willows round all the ditches, he had made paths between the ricks leading to the threshing-floor and sprinkled sand on them; on the windmill he had fixed a weather-vane in the shape of a bear with open jaws and a red tongue; he had adorned the brick cow-byre with something in the nature of a Grecian pediment and under the pediment he had written in white letters: BILT IN THE VILLEGE OF SHIPILOVO IN THE YEAR ONE THOWSEND AIT HUNDRID FORTY. THIS COW-BIRE. Arkady Pavlich grew quite sentimental and let himself go in an explanation to me in French of the advantages of the rent-system, observing that labour-duty was the more advantageous system for the landowner – but that that wasn't everything ... He began to give his bailiff advice on how to plant potatoes, how to prepare fodder for cattle, and so on. Sofron listened to his master's dissertation attentively, gave him an occasional rejoinder, but no longer dignified Arkady Pavlich with the title of father or benefactor, and kept on stressing that they had so little land and that there was no reason against some more.

'Why, buy away,' said Arkady Pavlich. 'Buy in my name. I don't mind.'

Sofron gave no answer to this but simply stroked his beard.

'But now it wouldn't do us any harm to ride to the forest,' observed Mr. Penochkin. Horses were immediately brought for us to ride, and we proceeded to the forest. Here we found dense undergrowth and lots of game, for which Arkady Pavlich praised Sofron and patted him on the shoulder. Mr. Penochkin adhered to the Russian school of forestry, and took the opportunity of telling me what he called a very amusing instance of how a practical joker of a landowner had made his forester see the light by pulling out about half his beard to prove that cutting timber down doesn't make it grow any thicker. In other respects, however, neither Sofron nor Arkady Pavlich was afraid of innovation. When we returned to the village, the bailiff led us to inspect the winnowing-machine which he had recently ordered from Moscow. The machine certainly functioned well, but, if Sofron had known what an unpleasant incident awaited him and his master on this last bit of their tour, he would probably have stopped with us at his home.

This is what happened. As we came out of the shed, we saw the following spectacle. A few paces away from the door, beside a muddy pond, in which three ducks were splashing about without a care in the world, two peasants were kneeling. One was an old man of about sixty, the other a youth of about twenty. Both wore patched and crumpled shirts, with bare legs and belts of cord. The constable Fedoseich was fussing busily around them and would probably have induced them to go away if we had stayed longer in the shed, but, seeing us, he went all taut and remained rooted to the spot. Near him stood the headman with open mouth and fists hanging down undecidedly. Arkady Pavlich frowned, bit his lip, and went up to the petitioners. They both bowed at his feet in silence.

'What do you want? What is your request?' he asked, in a strict, slightly nasal voice. The peasants exchanged glances and said not a word, but only narrowed their eyes as if against the sun, and began to breathe more quickly.

'Well, what is it?' continued Arkady Pavlich, and immediately turned to Sofron. 'From what family?'

'From the Toboleyev family,' answered the bailiff slowly.

'Well, what is it?' began Mr. Penochkin again. 'Have you no tongues, or what? Tell me, you, what d'you want?' he added, motioning his head towards the old man. 'Don't be afraid, you fool.'

The old man stuck out his dark-brown, wrinkled neck, opened his bluish lips crookedly and pronounced hoarsely: 'Defend us, my lord!' And he again struck his forehead on the earth. The young peasant bowed too. Arkady Pavlich gazed with dignity at the backs of their necks, threw his head back and planted his legs farther apart.

'What is it all about? Of whom are you complaining?'

'Have mercy on us, my lord! Give us a chance to breathe . . . We're being plagued to death.' The old man spoke with difficulty.

'Who has been plaguing you?'

'Why, Sofron Yakovlich, sir.'

Arkady Pavlich was silent.

'What is your name?'

'Antip, sir.'

'And who is this?'

'My son, sir.'

Arkady Pavlich was silent again and worked his moustaches.

'Well, in what way has he been plaguing you?' he began, looking at the old man through his moustaches.

'Sir, he's utterly ruined us. He's sent two of my sons out of their turn to join the army, and now he is taking the third one away too. Yesterday, sir, he took my last cow out of my yard and he beat my old woman – that was *his* kind work.' He pointed at the headman.

'H'm,' said Arkady Pavlich.

'Don't let him finish us right off, kind sir.'

Mr. Penochkin frowned.

'What is the meaning of all this?' he asked the bailiff, in a low voice and with an expression of displeasure.

'He's a drunkard, sir,' answered the bailiff, using the respectful form for the first time. 'He won't work. He's not been out of arrears for the last five years, sir.'

'Sofron Yakovlich paid the arrears for me, sir,' continued the old man. 'It's five years now since he paid them – and ever since then he's made a slave of me, sir, that's what he's done . . .'

'But how comes it that you have been in arrears?' asked Mr. Penochkin threateningly. The old man hung his head. 'I suppose you like getting drunk, hanging around the pot-houses?'

The old man began to open his mouth.

'I know you,' continued Arkady Pavlich, his temper flaring up. 'All you think of is drinking and lying over the stove, and then the good peasant has to answer for you.'

'He's a rude fellow, too,' the bailiff interjected while his master was still speaking.

'Well, that goes without saying. It's always the same way; I've noticed it more than once. He spends the whole year in debauchery and impertinence and now he throws himself at my feet!'

'Arkady Pavlich, sir,' began the old man desperately. 'Have mercy on me, protect me – how have I been rude? The Lord be my witness, it's more than I can bear. Sofron Yakovlich doesn't like me, for some reason or other – the Lord be his judge! he's ruining me for good, sir . . . this is the last of my sons . . . and him too . . .' In the old man's yellow, puckered eyes a teardrop twinkled. 'Have mercy, my lord, protect me . . .'

'And we aren't the only ones,' the young peasant was beginning.

Arkady Pavlich suddenly burst out: 'And who is asking you, eh? No one, so you keep quiet . . . What sort of behaviour is this? Keep quiet, I tell you, keep quiet! . . . My goodness! this is sheer sedition. No, my friend, I don't advise sedition on my land, on my land . . .' Arkady Pavlich stepped forward, then probably remembered my presence, turned away and put his hands in his pockets . . . '*Je vous demande bien pardon, mon cher*,' he said with a forced smile and a significant lowering of his voice. '*C'est le mauvais côté de la médaille* . . . Well, all right, all right,' he continued, without looking at the peasants. 'I shall give suitable orders. All right, you may go.' The peasants remained kneeling. 'All right, I tell you . . . You can go. I shall give suitable orders, I tell you.'

Arkady Pavlich turned his back on them. 'Perpetual discontent,' he said through his teeth, and returned home with long strides. Sofron followed behind him. The constable opened his eyes wide, as if he was preparing for a very long jump. The headman chased the ducks away from the puddle. The petitioners stayed where they were, looked at each other and then trudged away without looking round.

Two hours later I was at Ryabovo and prepared to go out shooting with Ampadist, a peasant of my acquaintance. Right up to the moment of my departure, Penochkin had kept Sofron in disgrace. I started a conversation with Ampadist about the peasants of Shipilovo and about Mr. Penochkin and asked whether he knew the bailiff there.

'Sofron Yakovlich? . . . I should think I do!'

'What sort of a man is he?'

'A dog, not a man: a dog such as you won't find between here and Kursk.'

'But how so?'

'Why, Shipilovo is supposed to belong to, what's his name, Penkin; but he's not the master: Sofron's the master.'

'Really?'

'He's the master, and treats it like his own property. The peasants all round are in his debt, they work for him as if they were his own labourers; some he sends off with the waggons, some he sends off somewhere else. He chases them about properly.'

'They haven't got much land, I think?'

'Not much? Why, in Khlynovo alone he farms two hundred acres, and three hundred in our village – five hundred acres in all. And land is not his only interest: he trades in horses, cattle, tar, pitch, oil, hemp, and all the rest of it . . . He's clever, damned clever, and rich, too, the beast! The worst thing is the way he knocks them about. He's an animal, not a man. It's well-known: a dog; a dirty dog, if ever there was one.'

'But why don't they complain about him?'

'Ho! What does it matter to the master? There are no arrears, so what does he care? If you go and complain,' he added, after a short pause, 'he'll, he'll . . . treat you like he did that other fellow . . .'

I remembered about Antip and told him what I had seen.

'Well,' said Ampadist, 'he'll be eating him up now, eating the fellow alive. The headman will be giving him such a beating now. Poor, unlucky wretch, just fancy! And what's he suffering for? Because he quarrelled with him at a meeting, with this bailiff-fellow, probably he couldn't put up with it any longer . . . A fine thing! That's how he got his knife into Antip. Now he'll finish the job off. He's such a dog, such a dirty dog – may God forgive my sins – he knows who to fasten on. He doesn't touch any of the older people who have got a bit of family or money, he doesn't touch them, the crafty devil, but with that Antip he's really let himself go. You see, he's sent Antip's sons to the army out of their turn, the wicked rogue, the dog – may God forgive me my sins.'

We set off to shoot.

The Estate Office

IT WAS autumn. I had spent several hours roaming the fields with my gun, and would probably not have returned before evening to the inn on the Kursk highway where my troika was awaiting me, if the remarkably fine, cold rain which had been chasing me around since early morning, like a tireless and determined spinster, had not finally forced me to seek at any rate a temporary shelter somewhere close at hand. While I was still considering which way to go, my gaze lighted unexpectedly on a low hut beside a field of peas. I went up to the hut, peered under the thatched eaves, and saw an old man in an advanced state of decrepitude which at once reminded me of the dying goat found by Robinson Crusoe in a cave on his island. The old man was squatting down, with his dim little eyes screwed up, and, busily but carefully, like a hare (the poor fellow had not a tooth in his head), was chewing a hard, dry pea and constantly shifting it from one side of the mouth to the other. He was so absorbed in this occupation that he didn't notice my arrival.

'Grandfather, I say, grandfather!' I exclaimed.

He stopped chewing, arched his brows and with an effort opened his eyes.

'What?' he mumbled in a husky voice.

'Where is the nearest village?' I asked.

The old man resumed his chewing. He hadn't heard what I said. I repeated my question louder than before.

'Village? ... Why, what do you want?'

'I want to shelter from the rain.'

'What?'

'To shelter from the rain.'

'Oh!' He scratched the nape of his sunburnt neck. 'Well, there, that's the way to go,' he said suddenly, with a confused wave of his hands. 'Then, when you've passed the wood –

149

that's how you go – you'll see a track; you leave it, the track, and all the time keep to the right, keep to the right, keep to the right . . . well, there you'll find Ananyevo. Or else you'd be at Sitovka.'

I had difficulty in following the old man. His moustache got in the way, and his tongue did its duty badly.

'Where are you from?' I asked him.

'What?'

'Where are you from?'

'From Ananyevo.'

'What do you do here?'

'What?'

'What do you do here?'

'I sit and keep watch.'

'What do you watch?'

'The peas.'

I could not help laughing.

'But for goodness' sake, how old are you?'

'God knows.'

'I suppose you don't see so well?'

'What?'

'You don't see so well, I suppose?'

'No. And sometimes I don't hear anything either.'

'Then how can you keep watch, for goodness' sake?'

'Ask my elders and betters.'

Elders and betters! I thought, and looked with pity at the poor old man. Fumbling, he took from inside his coat a piece of dry bread and began to suck it like a child, laboriously drawing in his cheeks, which were anyway sunken enough.

I went off in the direction of the wood, turned to the right, kept on bearing to the right as the old man had directed me, and finally reached a big village with a stone church in the new taste, that's to say with columns, and a big manor house, also with columns. From some way off, through the fine net of the rain, I noticed a cabin with a wooden roof and two chimneys, larger than the others, probably the home of the headman of the village. I went towards it, in the hope of finding there a samovar

with tea, sugar and some not completely sour cream. Accompanied by my shivering dog, I went up to the porch and into the
passage, opened a door, but saw, instead of the usual appoint-
ments of a cabin, tables piled with papers, two red cupboards,
bespattered ink-wells, heavyweight pewter sandboxes, the
longest possible quills, and so on. At one of the tables sat a
youth of about twenty, with a puffy, unhealthy face, tiny little
eyes, a greasy forehead, and side-locks of unconscionable
length. He was decently dressed in a grey nankeen coat which
had worn shiny round the collar and over the stomach.

'What can I do for you?' he asked me, with a jerk of the head,
like a horse which never expected to be taken hold of by
the mouth.

'Does the factor live here . . . or? . . .'

'This is the head office of the estate,' he interrupted me.
'I am the clerk on duty . . . Did you not see the notice outside?
That's what it's put there for.'

'Where can one dry oneself here? Has anyone in the village
got a samovar?'

'Of course there are samovars,' replied the youth in the grey
coat, with dignity. 'You can go to Father Timofei or failing that
to the servants' cabin, or failing that to Nazar Tarasich, or
failing that to Agrafena the hen-woman.'

'Who are you talking to, you blockhead? You're spoiling my
sleep!' came a voice from the next room.

'Here's a gentleman has come and is asking where he can
dry himself.'

'What gentleman?'

'I don't know. He's got a dog and a gun.'

A bed creaked in the next room. The door opened and in
came a man of about fifty, stout, short, bull-necked, pop-eyed,
very round-cheeked and with a face that shone all over.

'What do you require?' he asked me.

'I want to dry myself.'

'This isn't the place for it.'

'I didn't know that this was an office; but, by the way, I'm
ready to pay . . .'

'I suppose it *could* be done here,' rejoined the stout one. 'Won't you come this way?'

He led me into another room, which was not the one from which he had come himself.

'Will you be all right here?'

'Yes... You couldn't get me some tea with cream?'

'Certainly, at once. If you'll take your things off and rest yourself, tea will be ready in a moment.'

'Whose estate is this?'

'It belongs to Elena Nikolaevna Losnyakova.'

He went out. I looked round: along the partition dividing my room from the office stood a huge leather sofa, and two chairs, also of leather and with extremely high backs, were planted on both sides of the only window, which looked out on the village street. On the walls, which were papered in green with a pink design, hung three huge pictures painted in oils. One of them depicted a spaniel with a blue collar, on which was written: 'This is my Joy.' At the dog's feet was a river, and on the opposite bank, underneath a pine-tree, sat a hare of disproportionate size with one ear pricked. The second picture showed two old men eating a water-melon: behind the water-melon could be seen in the distance a Grecian portico with the inscription: *The Temple of Content*. The third picture represented a half-nude woman in a recumbent attitude, foreshortened, with red knees and enormous heels. My dog, without an instant's delay, got himself under the sofa, by supernatural exertions, and there apparently found a lot of dust, because he began to sneeze his head off. I went to the window. Boards had been laid obliquely across the street from the manor house to the office: a very useful precaution, since all round, thanks to our black soil and the prolonged rain, the mud was terrible. Outside the manor house, which stood with its back to the street, was a scene typical enough in such a setting: maids in faded print dresses were darting backwards and forwards; house-servants were strolling about in the mud, halting and reflectively scratching their backs; the constable's tethered horse was slowly swishing its tail and tossing its head and gnawing at the fence; hens were clucking, consumptive-looking turkeys gobbling away at each other. On the porch of a dark, decrepit building, probably a bath-house, sat a sturdy lad with a guitar singing, not without gusto, the well-known ditty:

> *Away to the desert I'm bound to go,*
> *From this enchanted spot.*

The fat fellow came into the room.

'Your tea's just coming,' he told me with an agreeable smile.

The young man in the grey coat, the duty-clerk, set out, on an old card-table, a samovar, a tea-pot, a glass with a broken saucer, a bowl of cream, and a string of Bolkhovo biscuits, which were hard as flint. The fat fellow went out.

'Who is that?' I asked the duty-clerk. 'The factor?'

'No, sir: he used to be the head cashier, but now he has been promoted head clerk.'

'Haven't you got a factor?'

'No, sir, we have a bailiff, Mikhailo Bikulov, but no factor.'

'D'you have an agent?'

'Certainly, a German, Lindamandol, Karlo Karlich; only it's not he who gives the orders.'

'Who does, then?'

'The lady herself.'

'So that's how it is? ... Well, have you got many people working in the office?'

The young man reflected.

'Six altogether.'

'Who are they all?' I asked.

'Well, first there is Vasily Nikolaich, the head cashier; then, Pyotr the clerk; Pyotr's brother Ivan, also a clerk; another Ivan who is a clerk, too; Koskenkin Narkizov, also a clerk; and me – there's no end of us.'

'I suppose your lady has a lot of house-servants?'

'Not so many as all that.'

'Well, how many?'

'I dare say there are a hundred and fifty or so.'

We were both silent.

'Well, are you a good handwriter?' I began again.

The lad smiled proudly, nodded, went into the office and brought back a sheet of paper covered with writing.

'This is my hand,' he said, still smiling.

I looked; on the quarto sheet of greyish paper, in a fine large hand, was written the following:

ORDER

From the Head Office of the Ananyevo Estate
to the Bailiff Mikhailo Bikulov. No. 209.

Immediately on receipt of this present, you are hereby instructed to ascertain who it was that last night went past the English garden in a state of intoxication, singing indecent songs, awakening and alarming the French governess Madame Enzhenie, what the nightwatchmen were up to, and which of them was on duty in the garden and permitted such dastardly behaviour. You are instructed to inquire into all particulars of the foregoing and to report to the office forthwith.

NIKOLAI KHVOSTOV,
Head Clerk.

Affixed to the order was an enormous armorial seal with the legend, 'Seal of the Head Office of the Ananyevo Estate', and below it was added a minute: 'To be carried out to the letter. Elena Losnyakova.'

'The lady wrote that herself, did she?' I asked.

'Certainly she did, sir: she always does it herself. Otherwise the order can't take effect.'

'Well, so you'll send the bailiff this order?'

'No, sir, he'll come himself and read it – that's to say, it will be read to him; you see, he can't read.'

The duty-clerk paused again. 'Well, sir,' he added, smiling, 'd'you like my writing?'

'I do.'

'I admit it wasn't I who drafted it. Koskenkin is the master-hand at that.'

'What? . . . Do you actually have your orders drafted first?'

'Of course, sir. It would never do to go straight to the fair copy.'

'What salary d'you get?' I asked.

'Thirty-five roubles, and five roubles shoe-money.'

'And you're satisfied?'

'Yes, certainly. It's not everyone who can get into the office. In my case, of course, it was the hand of God; my uncle's the butler.'

'And you're all right?'

'Yes, sir. To tell the truth,' he continued with a sigh, 'working for merchants, for instance, we clerks are better off. Working for merchants, we clerks do very very well. Why, last night we had a visit from a merchant from Venyovo – so his man told me ... Well-off, there are no two ways about it.'

'You mean that a merchant pays a higher salary?'

'Good Lord, no! He'd chuck you out if you asked him for a salary. No, if you work for a merchant, you live on faith and fear. He gives you food and drink and clothes and so on. If you serve him well, he'll give you even more ... Salary! you don't need one at all ... and a merchant will live simply, in the good old Russian way: you take the road with him – he drinks tea and so do you; what he eats, you eat too. The merchant ... is a happy-go-lucky fellow; it's not like working for a gentleman. There are no fads about your merchant; if he's angry with you, he beats you and the thing's done with. None of your nagging, none of your sly digs ... But working for a gentleman is dreadful! Nothing's ever right: this is badly done, that's all wrong. You give him a glass of water or some food – "Ah, the water stinks! Ah, the food stinks!" You take it away; you wait behind the door, bring it back again, "Well, now it's all right, now it doesn't stink any more." And as for ladies, well, as for ladies! ... And as for young ladies, what's more! ...'

'Fedyushka!' came the voice of the fat man from the office. The duty-clerk hurried out. I drank my glass of tea, lay down on the sofa and went to sleep. I slept for two hours. Wakening, I meant to get up, but laziness won the day; I shut my eyes, but didn't fall asleep again. Behind the partition, in the office, a discreet conversation was in progress. Involuntarily I began to listen.

'Just so, just so, Nikolai Eremeich,' said one voice. 'Just so. We have got to take that into account; certainly we have got to . . . H'mm!'

The speaker coughed.

'You can take my word for it, Gavrila Antonich,' rejoined the voice of the fat man. 'You can judge for yourself whether or not I know the way things are here.'

'Of course you do, Nikolai Eremeich. One might say that you are the top man here. Well, how shall it be?' continued the voice that was unknown to me. 'What shall we decide on, Nikolai Eremeich, if you don't mind my being curious?'

'Yes, what shall we decide on, Gavrila Antonich? It depends on you, so to speak; you don't seem very keen.'

'Good heavens, Nikolai Eremeich, whatever d'you mean? It's our job to trade and do business; it's our job to buy. That's the very ground we stand on, Nikolai Eremeich, as you might say.'

'Eight roubles,' said the fat one with deliberation.

I could hear a sigh.

'Nikolai Eremeich, it's an awful lot that you're asking.'

'Gavrila Antonich, I swear before God that it's the only course I can take.'

Silence reigned.

I raised myself softly and looked through a crack in the partition. The fat fellow was sitting with his back to me. Opposite him sat a merchant, a man of about forty, thin and pale, looking as if he had been anointed with Lenten oil. He kept wagging his beard and blinking away busily and twitching his lips.

'The winter-fields this year are tip-top, as you might say,' he began again. 'I have been admiring them as I drove along. Tip-top, they were, all the way from Voronezh – first-class, one might say.'

'They're certainly not bad,' answered the head clerk. 'But as you know, Gavrila Antonich, autumn proposes and spring disposes.'

'Just so, Nikolai Eremeich: everything is as God wills it; it's absolutely true, what you've just said . . . Your guest won't have woken up?'

The fat one turned round . . . listened . . .

'No, he's asleep. All the same, maybe that . . .'

He went to the door.

'No, he's asleep,' he repeated, and returned to his place.

'Well, how shall it be, Nikolai Eremeich?' began the merchant again: 'We must conclude our business. Let's have it like this, Nikolai Eremeich. Let's have it like this,' he continued, blinking away the whole time. 'Two grey notes and a white one for your good self and six and a half roubles for over there.' He nodded towards the manor house. 'Shall we shake hands on it?'

'Four grey ones,' answered the clerk.

'Three, then.'

'Four grey ones and no white ones.'

'Three, Nikolai Eremeich.'

'Three and a half and not a farthing less.'

'Three, Nikolai Eremeich.'

'Don't waste your breath, Gavrila Antonich.'

'What a stubborn fellow,' muttered the merchant. 'Why, I could get a better deal direct with the lady.'

'As you like,' answered the fat one. 'You could have done that long ago. I really don't know what all the fuss is about . . . You'd get a much better deal.'

'Oh, all right, Nikolai Eremeich, all right. How you flew into a rage! Why, I was just talking, like that.'

'No, I really don't know . . .'

'It's all right, I tell you. . . . I tell you, I was joking . . . Well, take your three and a half, there's nothing else to be done with you.'

'I ought to have taken four, but, like a fool, I was in too much of a hurry,' grumbled the fat one.

'So it's six and a half over there, at the house, Nikolai Eremeich – the price of the corn is six and a half.'

'Six and a half was what we said.'

'Well, then, let's shake hands on it, Nikolai Eremeich.' The merchant spread out his fingers and struck them against the clerk's palm. 'And now with God's speed!' The merchant rose. 'Now, sir, Nikolai Eremeich, I will go to the lady, and send my name in, and say to her: "Nikolai Eremeich has agreed to sell for six and a half, madam."'

'That's right.'

'And now please take this.'

The merchant handed the clerk a small wad of notes, bowed, shook his head, took his hat in two fingers, twitched his shoulders, and, with a rippling movement of his person, went out, his shoes squeaking decorously. Nikolai Eremeich crossed to the wall, and, as far as I could observe, began to sort the notes which the merchant had handed to him. Round the door appeared a red head with thick side-whiskers.

'Well?' asked the head, 'everything in order?'

'Everything in order.'

'How much?'

The fat fellow waved a hand irritably and pointed towards my room.

'Oh, all right,' rejoined the head, and disappeared.

The fat fellow went to the table, sat down, opened a book, took up an abacus and began to sling the beads backwards and forwards, using not the fore-finger but the third finger of his right hand: it looks more decorous.

The duty-clerk came in.

'What do you want?'

'Sidor has come, from Golopleky.'

'Oh! well, bring him in. No, wait ... first go and look whether the strange gentleman there is still asleep or whether he's woken up.'

The duty-clerk came cautiously into my room. I had put my head on the game-bag which served me as a pillow and closed my eyes.

'He's asleep,' whispered the duty-clerk, returning to the office.

The fat fellow mumbled something through his teeth.

'Well, call Sidor,' he said finally.

I sat up again. A peasant came in, an enormous fellow of about thirty, hale, red-cheeked, fair-haired, with a smooth, curling beard. He prayed before the icon, bowed to the head clerk, took his hat in both hands and straightened himself out again.

'Good day to you, Sidor,' said the fat one, rattling the abacus.

'Good day, Nikolai Eremeich.'

'Well, how's the road?'

'All right, Nikolai Eremeich. A bit muddy.' The peasant spoke slowly and softly.

'Is your wife well?'

'Well enough.'

The peasant sighed and put one foot forward. Nikolai Eremeich set his pen behind his ear and blew his nose.

'Well, what have you come for?' he continued, putting his check handkerchief away in his pocket.

'It's like this, Nikolai Eremeich, they want carpenters from us.'

'Well, haven't you got any, or what?'

'Of course we have, Nikolai Eremeich: we are right in the forest, no question of that. But it's the working-time, Nikolai Eremeich.'

'The working-time! Tck, tck, you're dead keen to work for anyone else, but when it comes to working for your own master, you don't like it ... It's all the same work.'

'The same work, certainly, Nikolai Eremeich ... but ...'

'Well?'

'The pay is very ... that is ...'

'I never did! You're thoroughly spoilt. Get along with you!'

'Well, there's more to it, Nikolai Eremeich. The work is supposed to be for a week, all told, but it takes a month to get through. Either the materials aren't there, or else they send us into the garden to sweep the paths.'

'I never did! It's orders from the lady herself, so there's nothing for you and me to say about it.'

Sidor said nothing and began shifting his weight from one leg to the other. Nikolai Eremeich twisted his head to one side and rattled away busily at his beads.

'Our ... peasants ... Nikolai Eremeich,' began Sidor finally, hesitating over every word, 'have sent me to present ... here ... there's ...' and he thrust his enormous hand inside his overcoat and began to pull out a rolled-up towel with a red pattern on it.

'What's the matter, you fool, have you gone off your head, or what?' the fat one interrupted him suddenly. 'Get along to my cabin,' he continued, practically pushing out the astonished peasant. 'Ask the wife ... she will give you tea, and I'll be over straight away, so be off with you. Get along with you, I say.'

Sidor went out.

'You ... bear!' muttered the head clerk after him, and he shook his head and applied himself again to his abacus.

Suddenly there were cries of 'Kuprya, Kuprya! You can't do down Kuprya!' coming from the street and from the porch, and a few moments later there came into the office a short, consumptive-looking man with an extremely long nose, great, immobile eyes and a very arrogant manner. He wore an old, tattered coat of the colour known as Adelaide (or, in our part of the world, 'odelloid'), with a velveteen collar and tiny buttons. He was carrying a bundle of faggots on his shoulder. Around him jostled five house-servants, shouting: 'Kuprya! You can't do down Kuprya! Kuprya's the new boiler-man, boiler-man!' But the man in the coat with the velveteen collar paid not the slightest attention to the uproar of his companions and kept an absolutely straight face. With measured steps he crossed to the stove, threw down his burden, straightened himself, brought a snuff-box out of his back pocket, opened his eyes wide and took a large pinch of grated trefoil mixed with ashes.

At the entry of this noisy mob, the fat fellow had begun by frowning and rising from his seat; but, on seeing the cause of the commotion, he smiled and merely told them not to shout, as there was a sportsman asleep in the next room.

'What sportsman?' asked two people at once.

'A gentleman.'

'Oh!'

'Let them shout their heads off,' said the man in the velvet collar, spreading out his hands. 'What do I care, so long as they keep their hands off me? I'm the new boiler-man.'

'Boiler-man! Boiler-man!' the mob repeated joyously.

'It was the lady's orders,' he continued, shrugging his shoulders. 'But just you wait . . . you'll be swineherds yet. But the fact that I'm a tailor, a good one, apprenticed to the best master-tailors in Moscow, and that I've made uniforms for generals – *that* no one can take away from me. What are *you* so proud of, anyway? . . . Eh? You're just so many drones, so many sluggards, that's all you are. If I get my freedom, I shan't die of hunger, I shan't fall by the wayside. If I get my passport, I shall pay in a good rent and satisfy my masters. But what will happen to you? You'll fall by the wayside, you'll just die like flies, and that's the truth!'

'That's a fine story,' interrupted a pock-marked, white-lashed youth with a red cravat and tattered elbows. 'You've been out on a passport, but the masters have never seen a copeck of rent from you and you've never earned so much as half a copeck for yourself: it was all you could do to drag yourself back home, and you've worn the same little coat ever since.'

'Well, what of it, Konstantin Narkizich?' rejoined Kupryan. 'A man falls in love and then he's dead and done for. You just live as long as I have before you judge me.'

'And what have you chosen to fall in love with? A proper monster!'

'No, don't say that, Konstantin Narkizich.'

'Who are you talking to, anyway? Why, I saw her; last year, in Moscow, I saw her with my own eyes.'

'Last year she was a bit under the weather, and that's a fact,' observed Kupryan.

'No, gentlemen, listen,' said, in an offhand casual voice, a
tall, thin man with a pimply face and curled, oiled hair, doubtless a valet. 'Just let Kupryan Afanasich sing us his song. Now,
Kupryan Afanasich, begin away!'

'Yes, yes!' took up the others. 'Quite right, Alexandra! –
That's finished Kuprya off, hasn't it just? ... Sing, Kuprya! ...
Good for Alexandra!' (Serving-folk often use feminine
forms in an endearing sense when talking about a man.) 'Sing!'

'This is no place for singing,' rejoined Kupryan firmly, 'this
is the Estate Office.'

'What has that to do with you? Are you aiming at becoming
a clerk yourself?' answered Konstantin roughly, with a laugh.
'That must be it.'

'Everything depends on the masters' pleasure,' observed
the poor fellow.

'You see, you see what he'd like to become, you see the sort
of chap he is! Ooh! ooh! ah!'

They all burst out laughing and some of them started jumping about. The one who roared loudest of all was a lad of about
fifteen, probably the son of some aristocrat of the servant world:
he wore a waistcoat with bronze buttons and a lilac-coloured
cravat and had already managed to grow a pot-belly.

'But listen, tell us, Kuprya,' began Nikolai Eremeich complacently; he was evidently amused and mollified: 'It's no fun
to be boiler-man? It isn't, eh?'

'Well, Nikolai Eremeich,' said Kupryan, 'you're now head
clerk, certainly; there's no question about that, admittedly; but
even *you* have been in disgrace in your time and lived in a
peasant's cabin.'

'You be careful and don't forget yourself in front of me,' the
fat man interrupted him irritably. 'They're laughing at you for
the fool that you are; a fool like you ought to appreciate it, and
be thankful, when anyone takes notice of – a fool like you.'

'The words just slipped off my tongue, Nikolai Eremeich.
I'm sorry ...'

'Even if they did ...'

The door opened and a page ran in.

'Nikolai Eremeich, the lady wants to see you.'

'Who is with the lady?' he asked the page.

'Axinya Nikitishna and a merchant from Venyovo.'

'I shall come at once. But you, my friends,' he continued in a voice that carried conviction, 'you'd better go somewhere else with your newly-promoted boiler-man, otherwise the German might turn up and he'd complain at once.'

The fat fellow straightened the hair on his head, coughed in his hand, which was almost completely hidden by the sleeve of his coat, buttoned up his coat and set off to see the lady, straddling his legs widely as he walked. After waiting a moment, the whole throng moved away after him, Kupryan with them. Only my old acquaintance the duty-clerk remained behind. He made as if to trim some pens, but dropped off to sleep where he sat. Some flies immediately took advantage of the opportunity and crawled over his mouth. A mosquito sat on his forehead, spread out its legs methodically, and slowly plunged the whole length of its sting into the soft flesh. The same red-whiskered head as before again appeared round the door, stared hard, then entered the office, with a tolerably hideous body attached to it.

'Fedyushka! always asleep!' said the head.

The duty-clerk opened his eyes and got up from his chair.

'Has Nikolai Eremeich gone to see the lady?'

'Yes, Vasily Nikolaich, he has.'

Oho! I thought, here he is, the head cashier.

The head cashier began to pace up and down the room, in fact he prowled rather than paced, and his whole demeanour resembled a cat's. From his shoulders hung an old black frock-coat, with very narrow tails; he kept one hand at his breast, but with the other he fidgeted away at his high, tight horsehair cravat, and turned his head intently from side to side. He wore goatskin shoes without a squeak in them and stepped out very softly.

'Yagushkin the landowner was asking after you to-day,' added the duty-clerk.

'H'm, he was, was he? What did he say, exactly?'

'He said that he was coming to Tyutyurev this evening and would wait for you there. He said he wanted to talk with Vasily Nikolaich on business, but on what business he didn't say. Vasily Nikolaich will know, he said.'

'H'm!' rejoined the head cashier, and went over to the window.

'Hey, is Nikolai Eremeich in the office?' said a loud voice in the passage, and a tall man, evidently angry, with irregular but expressive, bold features, and reasonably tidily dressed, strode across the threshold.

'Isn't he here?' he asked with a quick look round.

'Nikolai Eremeich is with the lady,' answered the cashier. 'Tell me what I can do for you, Pavel Andreich; you can tell me . . . What do you want?'

'What do I want? You want to know what I want?' The cashier gave a nervous nod.

'I want to teach him a lesson, the worthless pot-belly, the low tale-bearer that he is . . . I'll teach him to tell tales!'

Pavel threw himself down in a chair.

'What on earth is the matter, Pavel Andreich? Calm your-self . . . Aren't you ashamed? Don't forget who you are speak-ing about!' whispered the cashier.

'Who, indeed? What do I care if they have made him head clerk? A fine fellow, indeed, they've found for the job! They've let the goat loose among the cabbages, with a vengeance!'

'That'll do, Pavel, that'll do! Enough of that . . . what non-sense are you talking?'

'So Foxy Sly-Boots is wagging his tail, is he! . . . I'll wait for him,' said Pavel with feeling, and he thumped his hand on the table. 'Ah, here comes his worship,' he added, looking out of the windows. 'Talk of the devil. And welcome back!' He got up.

Nikolai Eremeich came into the office. His face radiated satisfaction, but at the sight of Pavel he showed a certain confusion.

'Good day, Nikolai Eremeich,' said Pavel significantly, moving slowly to meet him. 'Good day.'

The head clerk made no answer. In the doorway appeared the face of the merchant.

'Why don't you do me the favour of answering?' continued Pavel. 'Anyway, no . . . no . . .' he added. 'That's not the way; you'll gain nothing by shouting and cursing. You'd do much better to tell me civilly, Nikolai Eremeich, what you're chasing me around for, and why you're out to ruin me. Well, speak, man, speak out.'

'This is not the place for an explanation between us,' rejoined the head clerk, not without agitation. 'Nor the time either. But I'm certainly surprised at one thing: what has given you the idea that I am out to ruin you or that I am chasing you round? And anyway, how could I do so? You don't work with me in the office.'

'No, indeed,' answered Pavel. 'That would be the last straw. But what's the point of pretending, Nikolai Eremeich? You understand what I mean.'

'No, I don't.'

'You do.'

'Before God, I don't.'

'Taking God's name in vain into the bargain. If it comes to that, tell me: have you no fear of God? Then, why don't you let the poor girl alone? What d'you want from her?'

'Who are you talking about, Pavel Andreich?' asked the fat one in feigned astonishment.

'Oho, he doesn't know, eh? I'm talking about Tatyana. You should fear God – and not seek revenge. You ought to be ashamed of yourself – you, a married man with children of my own size, whereas I am not after anything else . . . I want to get married: I am going about it the honourable way.'

'But how am I to blame, Pavel Andreich? The lady doesn't allow you to get married; she is our mistress, and that's her will! How do I come into it?'

'How do you come into it? I suppose you have never come to any agreement with that old witch of a housekeeper? I suppose you have never told her any tales, eh? You've not brought up every kind of trumped-up story against a defenceless girl?

I suppose it had nothing to do with your kind help that she was moved from the laundry to the scullery? That she was beaten, and punished by being made to wear slops? ... You ought to be ashamed of yourself, an old man like you! Why, a palsy might take you at any moment ... You'll have to answer for it to God.'

'That's right, Pavel Andreich, roar your head off ... Are you going to go on roaring like that for much longer, do you think?'

Pavel exploded.

'What? you dare to threaten me?' he said furiously. 'You think I am afraid of you? No, my friend, you're not dealing with anyone like that! What have I got to be afraid of? ... I can earn my bread anywhere. But it's a different story with you! All you can do is live here and tell tales and steal ...'

'He's got a fine idea of himself,' interrupted the clerk, who was also beginning to lose patience. 'A plain hospital orderly, a wretched little medico; but to listen to him – phew! what an important person he must be!'

'Yes, a hospital orderly, but without him your worship would now be rotting in the graveyard ... And an evil spirit it was that made me cure him,' he added, through his teeth.

'So you cured me? No, you wanted to poison me, you made me drink aloes,' asserted the clerk.

'What of it, if aloes were the only thing which could have an effect on you?'

'Aloes are forbidden by the Board of Health,' continued Nikolai. 'I'll lodge a complaint against you yet ... You wanted to do me in, and that's the truth! But the Lord didn't let you.'

'That'll do, gentlemen, that'll do,' began the cashier.

'Hold your tongue!' shouted the clerk. 'He wanted to poison me! D'you understand what I say?'

'As if I needed to ... Listen, Nikolai Eremeich,' began Pavel desperately. 'I'm asking you for the last time ... you've driven me further than I can bear. Leave us alone, d'you hear? or else, by God, no good will come of it to one or the other of us, I can promise you that.'

The fat one lost all control. 'I'm not afraid of you,' he shouted: 'Do you hear, you milk-sop! I've settled accounts with your father in my time; I broke his horns too – let that be an example to you, and look out for yourself!'

'Don't you start on my father, Nikolai Eremeich, don't you start on that!'

'Get out! Who are you to lay down the law to me?'

'I tell you, don't you start on that!'

'But I tell you, don't you forget yourself... However necessary you may think you are to the lady, if she has got to choose between us two – it won't be you that keeps his place, my little dove! No one has got the right to sedition, so look out!'

Pavel was trembling with fury. 'And as for the girl Tatyana, it serves her right... You wait, there's more trouble coming to her yet!'

Pavel threw himself forward with fists raised, and the clerk fell heavily to the floor.

'Put him in irons, put him in irons,' groaned Nikolai Eremeich...

I will not take it upon myself to describe the end of this scene. Even as it is, I am afraid I may have offended the reader's feelings.

The same day I returned home. A week later, I learnt that Mrs. Loznyakova had kept both Pavel and Nikolai on in her service, but sent away the girl Tatyana: it seemed that her services were not required.

The Bear

ONE EVENING I was returning alone from shooting in my racing drozhky. I was still eight versts from home; my good trotting-mare was going smartly along the dusty road, snorting and fidgeting her ears from time to time; my tired dog maintained a position within a pace of the rear wheels, as if fastened to them. A thunderstorm was approaching. Ahead of me a huge lilac-coloured storm-cloud slowly rose from behind a forest; long grey clouds floated above me and towards me; there was an anxious stir and murmur among the willows. The stifling heat suddenly gave way to a moist chill; swiftly the shadows gathered. I flicked the horse with the reins, went down into a ravine, crossed a dry stream-bed, completely overgrown with willow-bushes, climbed a hill and entered a forest. Ahead of me the road wound between thick clumps of hazel, already plunged in darkness; I made progress with difficulty. The drozhky jolted over the hard roots of hundred-year-old oaks and limes, which kept on intersecting the deep ruts left by cartwheels; my mare began to stumble. All of a sudden, high above me, a strong wind whistled, the trees swayed violently, heavy raindrops splashed and smacked sharply on the leaves, lightning flashed, and the storm burst. Rain fell in rivers. I drove on at a walk, and was soon compelled to stop: my mare was stuck, and I could see not an inch ahead of me. Somehow or other I found shelter under a spreading bush. Huddled together, with my face covered, I was patiently awaiting the end of the downpour, when, suddenly, in a flash of lightning, I thought I saw a tall figure on the road. I began staring that way – and the figure started right up out of the ground beside my drozhky.

'Who's there?' asked a resonant voice.

'Who are *you*?'

'I'm the forester here.'

I told him my name.

'Oh, I know! Are you on the way home?'

'Yes. But what a storm! . . .'

'A storm, certainly,' answered the voice.

A white lightning-flash lit up the forester from head to foot; a short, crackling thunderclap followed immediately after. The rain came sluicing down with redoubled force.

'It'll be some time passing,' continued the forester.

'What can I do about it?'

'If you like, I'll show you the way to my cabin,' he said abruptly.

'I'd be much obliged.'

'If you'll keep your seat . . .' He went to the mare's head, took hold of the bridle and pulled. We began to move. I held on to the cushion of the drozhky, which was tossing like a coracle on the high seas, and called my dog. The poor mare splashed heavily about in the mud, slithered and stumbled; in front of the shafts, the forester swayed about to right and to left like a spectre. We drove on for some way; at length my guide halted. 'Here we are, sir, we're home,' he said calmly. A gate squeaked, and several puppies set up a friendly barking. I lifted my head, and saw, illuminated by the lightning, a small cabin in the middle of a spacious yard surrounded by a fence. From the one little window a light glowed faintly. The forester led the mare up to the porch and knocked on the door. 'Coming, coming!' said a faint little voice; there was a patter of bare feet, a bolt screamed, and a girl of about twelve, in a little shift tied together with list, appeared on the threshold with a lantern in her hand.

'Light the way for the gentleman,' he said to her, 'and I will put the drozhky into the shed.'

The girl glanced at me and went into the cabin. I followed her in.

The forester's cabin consisted of a single room, soot-blackened, low and empty, without any smaller chambers or partitions. A tattered sheepskin coat hung on the wall. On a bench lay a single-barrelled gun, in a corner was an untidy pile of rags; two big pots stood beside the stove. A splinter of wood burnt on the table, flaring and dying lugubriously. Right in the middle of the cabin hung a cradle attached to the end of a long pole. The girl put out the lantern, sat down on a tiny stool and began with her right hand to swing the cradle and with her left to trim the splinter. I looked round and my heart sank within me: visiting a peasant's cabin at night is cheerless indeed. The child in the cradle was breathing heavily and fast.

'Are you alone here?' I asked the girl.

'Yes, alone,' she pronounced, in a hardly audible voice.

'Are you the forester's daughter?'

'Yes, the forester's,' she murmured.

The door squeaked, and the forester, stooping his head, strode across the threshold. He lifted the lantern from the floor, went to the table and lighted the wick. 'I dare say you're not used to a splinter-light?' he said with a shake of his curly head.

I looked at him. Rarely have I seen such a sturdy fellow. He was tall, broad-shouldered and admirably built. Through his wet shirt his powerful muscles stood out in relief. A black, curly beard half-covered his stern, masculine face; from under his wide brows, which met in the middle, small, brown eyes looked boldly out. He rested his hands lightly on his sides and came to a halt in front of me. I thanked him and asked him his name.

'My name is Foma,' he answered. 'But they call me the Bear.'

'Oh! *you're* the Bear!'

I looked at him with redoubled curiosity. From my friend Ermolai, and from others, I had often heard stories about the Bear, whom all the peasants of the neighbourhood feared like death. According to them, there had never been in the world such a master of his craft. 'He won't let you take away so much as a faggot; whatever the time may be, even if it's midnight, he'll swoop down on you, like snow on your head. And there's no hope of resisting – he's as strong and neat-handed as the devil himself . . . And there's no way of getting at him: neither drink, nor money; there's no bait at all to catch him. There's good folk have tried to do him in, more than once, but no – there's no catching him.' Such were the terms in which the peasants of the neighbourhood spoke of the Bear.

'So you're the Bear,' I repeated. 'I've heard of you, my friend, they say you let no one get past you.'

'I do my duty,' he answered solemnly. 'It isn't right to eat the master's bread without earning it.'

He took a hatchet from his belt, sat down on the floor and began to cleave a splinter.

'You have no wife?' I asked him.

'No,' he answered, with a mighty blow of the hatchet.

'Is she dead, then?'

'No . . . yes . . . she's dead,' he added, and turned away.

I was silent. He raised his eyes and looked at me.

'She ran off with a fellow from the town who happened to be passing,' he pronounced with a savage smile. The girl lowered her head; the baby woke up and began to cry; the girl went to the cradle. 'Well, feed him,' said the Bear, pushing into her hand a dirty feeding-bottle. 'She chucked *him*, too,' he continued in a low voice, pointing at the baby. He went to the door, halted and turned round. 'I suppose that you, sir,' he began, 'wouldn't want to eat our bread, but bread is all that I . . .'

'I'm not hungry.'

'Well, as you like. I would have got the samovar going for you, but I have no tea. I'll go and see how your mare is.'

He went out and slammed the door. I looked round again. The cabin seemed to me even sorrier than before. The sharp smell of stale smoke oppressed my lungs. The girl never stirred from where she sat or lifted her eyes; from time to time she gave the cradle a push, or shyly pulled the shift on to her shoulder when it had slipped. Her bare legs hung motionless.

'What's your name?' I asked.

'Ulita,' she said, holding her sad little face even lower than before.

The forester came in and sat on the bench.

'The storm is passing,' he observed, after a short silence: 'If you wish, I'll see you out of the forest.'

I got up. The Bear took his gun and examined the trigger.

'What's that for?' I asked.

'They're up to their tricks in the forest. They're cutting down a tree in Mare's Valley,' he added, in answer to my inquiring glance.

'Can you hear it from here?'

'You can hear it from the yard.'

We went out together. The rain had stopped. In the distance, heavy cloud masses were still banking up, and long lightning flashes burst out from time to time. But, over our heads, here and there we could already see the dark-blue heaven, and stars twinkled through thin, scurrying clouds. The outlines of trees, rain-drenched and wind-stirred, were beginning to loom up out of the darkness. We listened. The forester took off his cap and lowered his head. 'Th – there,' he said suddenly, and stretched out a hand. 'You see what a night he's chosen.' I heard nothing except the rustling of leaves. The Bear led the horse out of the shed. 'Like this, maybe,' he added aloud, 'I won't catch him.'

'I could come with you . . . if you like?'

'All right,' he answered, and backed the horse in. 'We'll catch him in no time, and then I'll see you on your way. Let's go.'

We set off, the Bear in front and I behind him. God knows how he found the road, but he only halted occasionally, and then just to listen for the sound of the axe.

'There,' he murmured through his teeth. 'D'you hear? D'you hear?'

'But where?'

The Bear shrugged his shoulders. We went down into a ravine, the wind dropped for a moment – and the sound of measured blows fell clearly on my ears. The Bear looked at me and motioned with his head. We went on through wet bracken and nettles. There was a dull, prolonged crashing . . .

'He's felled it . . .' murmured the Bear.

Meanwhile the sky continued to clear. In the forest it was just light. We made our way at last out of the ravine. 'Wait here,' the forester whispered to me; he bent down, and, holding up his gun, vanished among the bushes. I listened intently. Through the continuous noise of the wind I thought I could catch faint sounds from not far off; cautious blows of an axe on branches, the squeaking of wheels, the snorting of a horse . . . 'Where are you going? Stop!' roared the Bear's iron voice all of a sudden. Another voice called plaintively, like a hare's . . . A fight began. 'Oh, no, you don't,' insisted the Bear breathlessly. 'You're not going to get away . . .' I dashed in the direction of the noise and arrived, stumbling with every step, at the scene of battle. On the ground, beside a felled tree, the forester was busily engaged. He held the thief under him and was twisting his arms behind his back with a belt. I went up to them. The Bear rose and set him on his feet. I saw a peasant, dripping wet, in rags, with a long dishevelled beard. A wretched nag, half-covered under a sheet of matting, stood close by, together with a rudimentary sort of cart. The forester uttered not a word; the peasant also kept silence, and simply shook his head.

'Let him go,' I whispered in the Bear's ear. 'I'll pay for the tree.'

The Bear silently took the horse by the forelock in his left hand: with his right he held the thief by the belt. 'Well, look sharp, you scoundrel,' he said sternly.

'Take the axe, over there,' murmured the peasant.

'Yes, why leave it behind?' said the forester, and picked up the axe. We set off. I walked behind . . . Rain began spitting again and was soon falling in torrents. With difficulty we got back to the cabin. The Bear left the captured nag in the middle of the yard, led the peasant into the room, loosened the knot in the belt, and made him sit down in a corner. The girl, who had gone to sleep beside the stove, jumped up and looked at us in silent terror. I sat down on the bench.

'Look at it, how it's pouring,' remarked the forester. 'We'll have to wait till it's over. Wouldn't you like to lie down for a while?'

'No, thank you.'

'I'd have shut him up in the closet for your honour,' he continued, indicating the peasant, 'but, you see, the bolt...'

'Leave him where he is, don't touch him,' I interrupted the Bear.

The peasant gave me a sidelong look. I promised myself that, whatever happened, I would set the poor wretch free. He sat motionless on the bench. In the light of the lantern I could make out his lean, wrinkled face, his overhanging, yellow eyebrows, his restless eyes, his thin limbs... The girl lay down on the floor right at his feet and went to sleep again. The Bear sat at the table, his head propped on his hand. A cricket chirruped in the corner... the rain rattled on the roof and slid down the windows; we were all silent.

'Foma Kuzmich,' began the peasant suddenly, in a dull broken voice. 'Foma Kuzmich.'

'What d'you want?'

'Let me off.'

The Bear didn't answer.

'Let me off... It's hunger that... let me off.'

'I know you,' rejoined the forester morosely. 'Your village are all the same – one thief on top of another.'

'Let me off,' repeated the peasant. 'The agent... ruined ... that's what we are... let me off!'

'Ruined!... No one has the right to steal.'

'Let me off, Foma Kuzmich... That chap of yours will gobble me up, you know he will, and that's the truth.'

The Bear turned away. The peasant was twitching as if at the onset of fever. He kept shaking his head, he breathed irregularly.

'Let me off,' he repeated with mournful desperation. 'Let me off, for God's sake do! I'll pay, really I will, by God. By God, it was hunger that... with children to feed, you know what it is. It's hard, and that's the truth.'

'All the same, you shouldn't go out stealing.'

'My horse,' continued the peasant; 'let the horse go, if only that... that's the only animal I've got...'

'I tell you, I can't. I'm not my own master, either; they'll make me pay. It's not for me to spoil you, anyway.'

'Let me off! It's want, Foma Kuzmich. It's want that does it . . . let me off!'

'I know you.'

'But let me off.'

'Oh, what's the use of arguing with you; sit quiet, d'you hear, or else . . . Can't you see the gentleman, eh?'

The poor wretch sank his head. The Bear yawned and put his head down on the table. The rain still went on. I waited to see what would happen next.

The peasant suddenly sat up. His eyes began to blaze and a flush spread over his face.

'Well, then, eat away, and choke yourself,' he began, screwing up his eyes and dropping the corners of his mouth. 'You damned murderer, drink the blood of Christian folk, drink away.'

The forester turned round.

'I'm talking to you . . . you bloodsucking Tartar, you!'

'Are you drunk, to start swearing like this?' said the forester in astonishment. 'Have you gone off your head, eh?'

'Drunk! On your money, I suppose, you damned murderer, you brute, you!'

'You . . . I'll give it you!'

'What do I care? I'm done for anyway; where can I go without my horse? Kill me – it's one way of finishing; whether it's hunger, or that – it's all the same. Do them all in: wife, children – let the whole lot die like animals . . . but we'll get you, just you wait!'

The Bear half-rose.

'Beat away,' repeated the peasant savagely. 'Beat away.'

The girl hurriedly got up from the floor and stared at him.

'Beat away.'

'Be quiet!' roared the forester, and took two steps forward.

'That'll do, Foma,' I exclaimed. 'Leave him alone . . . the poor devil.'

'I won't be quiet,' continued the unfortunate. 'It's always the same – dying like animals. You murderer, you brute, there's no end to the harm you do . . . but wait, your reign won't be for long! They'll get you by the throat, just you wait!'

The Bear seized him by the shoulder . . . I dashed to the peasant's rescue.

'You keep out, sir,' the forester shouted at me.

I would not have feared his threats and had already put out my hand, when, to my astonishment, he jerked the belt from the peasant's elbows in a single turn, seized him by the scruff of the neck, rammed his cap down over his eyes, opened the door and threw him out.

'Go to the devil, and your horse, too!' he shouted after him. 'But look, the next time I catch you . . .'

He came back into the cabin and started rummaging in a corner.

'Well, Bear,' I said at last, 'you surprise me; I see you're a good sort.'

'Oh, no more of that, sir,' he interrupted me crossly; 'not a word about it, please. And now I'd better see you on your way,' he added. 'I don't suppose you'll be waiting till the rain is over.'

In the yard the wheels of the peasant's cart rattled. 'There he goes, sneaking off,' he muttered. 'I'll give it him! . . .'

Within half an hour he parted from me at the forest's edge.

Two Landowners

I HAVE already had the honour to present to you, indulgent readers, some of the gentlemen of my neighbourhood; allow me now, in passing (for us writers, everything is 'in passing'), to acquaint you with two more landowners on whose land I have often shot; highly-respected, well-intentioned gentlemen, enjoying the universal esteem of several districts.

First I shall describe for you Major-General (retired) Vyacheslav Ilarionovich Khvalinsky. Imagine a tall man, once well-built, now a bit run to fat, but far from decrepit, indeed not even touched by age, a man of mature years, right in his prime. True, his once regular and still agreeable features have somewhat changed, his cheeks hang, crowded wrinkles have taken up a position radiating out from his eyes, some of his teeth are no longer with him (such was Sadi's phrase, if Pushkin is to be believed); his fair hair, or at least that part of it that remains intact, has turned to a lilac colour, thanks to a compound bought at Romyon horse-fair from a Jew professing to be an Armenian; but Vyacheslav Ilarionovich steps out briskly, laughs resonantly, jingles his spurs, twirls his moustaches, and sooner or later refers to himself as an old cavalryman, whereas it is well-known that really old men never refer to themselves as old at all. He is usually dressed in a coat buttoned right up, a high cravat with a starched collar, and pepper-and-salt trousers of military cut; he wears his hat down over his eyes, leaving the whole of the back of his head uncovered. He is a capital fellow, but has somewhat strange principles and habits. For example, he can never treat gentlemen who are poor, or have no official position, as his own equals. In conversation with them, he generally looks at them sideways, leaning his cheek heavily on his stiff white collar, or suddenly goes and flashes at them a bright, unblinking stare, but says nothing, and moves the whole skin of his head underneath the hair; he even pronounces words differently and, for instance, instead of saying, 'Thanks, Pavel Vasilich', or 'Come along, Mikhail Ivanich', addresses them as, 'ks,Pall'Asilich', or 'C'long,Mikhall'Vanich'. With people lower down the social scale he behaves even more strangely: he never looks at them at all, and, before explaining to them his wishes or giving them orders, he repeats several times over, with a preoccupied, dreamy look: 'What's your name?... What's your name?' emphasizing heavily the first word '*what*', but pronouncing the rest very fast, so that the whole phrase acquires a resemblance to the call of the cock-quail. He is fussy, terribly mean, does badly out of his land: he employs as steward a retired sergeant-major, a Little-Russian, a man of unusual stupidity. Incidentally, in agricultural matters none of us has yet outdone an important official from Petersburg who, seeing from his agent's reports that the barns for drying crops on his land were subject to frequent fires, which caused the loss of a great deal of grain, gave the strictest instructions that in future no sheaves were to be put into the drying-barn until the fire had been completely extinguished. The same dignitary had the idea of sowing all his fields with poppies, in view of what appeared a very simple calculation: poppies are dearer than rye, therefore it's better business to sow poppies. He it was, too, who told his women-serfs to wear *kokoshniks* on a pattern sent from Petersburg; and indeed, to this day, the peasant-women on his lands wear this head-dress ... only on top of their own ... But let us return to Vyacheslav Ilarionovich. He is a great fancier of the ladies, and has only to see a pretty face in the main street of the local market-town, to dash off after her at once, at the same time – and that is the remarkable circumstance – starting to limp. He likes playing cards, but only with people of lower station; they call him 'Your Excellency', and he blows them up and ticks them off to his heart's content. When he happens to be playing with the Governor or with some official personage, an extraordinary transformation takes place in him: he smiles, he nods, he looks them in the eye – honey fairly flows from him ... He even loses without complaining. He reads little and, while doing so, keeps up a constant working of his moustaches and eyebrows, as if from the upward passage of a wave across his face. This wave-like movement on the face of Vyacheslav Ilarionovich is especially noticeable when he happens (in the presence of guests, of course) to be running through the columns of the *Journal des Débats*. At election-time he plays a fairly important rôle but refuses, from meanness, the honourable estate of Marshal of the Nobility. 'Gentlemen,' he will say to noblemen who may approach him on the subject, speaking in a voice of patronage and heavy self-sufficiency, 'I am greatly obliged for the honour; but I am resolved to devote my leisure to retirement,' and, having said these words, he moves his head several times to right and left, and then with a dignified movement presses his chin and his cheeks against his cravat. In his youth he served as adjutant to some important Personage, whom he never refers to except by his Christian name and patronymic; the story goes that he discharged not only the functions of adjutant, but that, for example, having donned full parade-dress, having even done up the hooks, he had been wont to give his chief a good steam-bath – but one can't believe all the rumours that one hears. General Khvalinsky himself doesn't like to speak of his military career, which on the whole is somewhat strange; it seems moreover that he never saw active service. General Khvalinsky lives alone in a small house. He has had no experience of married bliss, and therefore still considers himself marriageable, and highly eligible too. As to his housekeeper, a woman of about thirty-five, black-eyed, black-browed, plump, fresh and moustached, she goes about on weekdays in starched dresses, and on Sundays adds a pair of muslin sleeves. Vyacheslav Ilarionovich is a good man at the big dinner-parties given by landowners in honour of Governors and other potentates; there he is, you might say, absolutely in his element. On such occasions he usually sits, if not on the Governor's right, at any rate not far from him; at the beginning of dinner he is very conscious of his own importance and, throwing himself back, but without turning his head, sweeps a sidelong glance down the round pates and stand-up collars of the guests; however, towards the end of the meal, he becomes gayer, begins to smile in all directions (in the Governor's direction he has been smiling since dinner started), and sometimes even proposes a toast to the honour of the fair sex – the adornment of our planet, to use his own words. General Khvalinsky is not bad, either, on solemn and public occasions, examinations and church functions; he is also a master-hand at receiving ceremonial benedictions. At cross-roads, ferries and other such places, the servants of Vyacheslav Ilarionovich never shout or bawl; on the contrary, in making people give way for him or in calling forward his carriage, they say in a pleasant, throaty baritone: 'Make way, please, make way, please and let General Khvalinsky pass'; or, 'General Khvalinsky's carriage'...True, Khvalinsky's carriage is of fairly antiquated type; the lackeys and footmen wear fairly shabby livery (it's of course hardly necessary to mention that it is grey with red facings); the horses, too, are getting on and have seen service in their time, but Vyacheslav Ilarionovich has no pretensions to foppishness and, indeed, doesn't think it suitable to his station to throw dust in people's eyes. Khvalinsky has no special command of language, or, perhaps, has no occasion to show his eloquence, because he tolerates no argument, no objection even, and studiously avoids all long conversations, especially with the young. That's certainly the safer course; indeed the pity is that people nowadays are losing the habit of obedience and forgetting all respect. In the presence of his superiors, Khvalinsky is silent most of the time, but with his inferiors, whom he seems to despise but who are nevertheless his only familiars, he holds forth abruptly and to the point, caustically using expressions like the following: 'What you say is absolutely non-sens-ical!' or, 'I find myself at last obliged, m'dear sir, to make it clear to you,' or, 'All the same, you ought to know to whom you are speaking,' and so on. He is the special terror of postmasters, permanent delegates, and station-inspectors. At home he never entertains, and lives, so one hears, the life of a miser. With it all, he is a splendid type of landowner. 'An old campaigner, an irreproachable character, a man of principles, a *vieux grognard*,' so his neighbours describe him. Only the Public Prosecutor of the province allows himself to smile, when mention is made in his presence of Khvalinsky's capital, solid qualities – but there are no lengths to which envy will not go! . . .

Now let us pass on to another landowner.

Mardary Appollonich Stegunov is not in the least like Khvalinsky; he can hardly have seen service and has never passed as handsome. He is an old man, short, podgy, bald, with a double chin, soft hands and a fair-sized belly. He is a famous host and joker; he lives for his pleasure, as the saying goes; goes about winter and summer in a striped, quilted dressing-gown. In one respect only he resembles General Khvalinsky: he too is a bachelor. He has five hundred serfs. Mardary Apollonich occupies himself rather superficially with his estate; ten years or so ago, in order to keep in the swim, he bought a threshing-machine at Butenop's in Moscow, locked it up in a barn, and worried no more. On a fine summer's day he will even order his racing drozhky to be harnessed and drive into the fields to have a look at the crops and pick cornflowers. He lives entirely in the good old style. His house is of old-fashioned construction: in the hall there is the proper smell of kvass, tallow candles and leather. On the right is a sideboard with pipes and towels; in the dining-room are family portraits, flies, a big pot of geraniums and an ill-tuned piano; in the drawing-room, three sofas, three tables, two looking-glasses and a wheezing clock, with blackened enamel and hands in carved bronze; in the study, a table covered with papers, bluish screens stuck with pictures cut out of various works of the last century, cupboards full of musty books, spiders and black dust, a bulging armchair, an Italian window, and a firmly nailed-up door to the garden . . . In a word, everything is as it should be. Mardary Apollonich has crowds of serving-folk, all dressed in the old-fashioned style: long blue coats with high collars, drab-coloured pantaloons and short yellowish waistcoats. They address guests as 'father' . . . The management of his land is in charge of a bailiff, one of his own peasants, with a beard that quite covers his sheepskin coat. His house is run by a wrinkled, mean old woman with a brown kerchief over her head. Mardary Apollonich has in his stables thirty horses of miscellaneous calibre; he drives out in a heavyweight home-made carriage. He loves receiving guests and entertains them lavishly, that's to say, thanks to the stupefying qualities of Russian cooking, he deprives them, right up to nightfall, of any capacity to attend to anything but Preference. He himself has no occupations and has even stopped reading 'The Dream Book'. But in Russia there are still fairly many landowners of this type; it will be asked, why, and with what object, I have started to speak of him. Well, allow me, instead of answering, to tell you about one of my visits to Mardary Apollonich.

I arrived at his house at about seven o'clock on a summer evening. The evening service was just over and the priest, a young man who was evidently very timid and just out of the seminary, was sitting in the drawing-room near the door on the very edge of his chair. As was his custom, Mardary Apollonich gave me the warmest of welcomes; he was unfeignedly glad to see any guest, and he was anyway the kindest of men. The priest got up and took his hat.

'Wait, Father, wait,' said Mardary Apollonich, without letting go of my hand. 'Don't go away . . . I've ordered some vodka for you.'

'I don't drink, sir,' murmured the priest, with embarrassment, and he blushed to the ears.

'What nonsense! Not drinking, in your profession!' answered Mardary Apollonich. 'Mishka! Yushka! Vodka for the Father!'

Yushka, a tall, lean old man of about seventy, came in with a glass of vodka on a black-painted tray with flesh-coloured spots on it.

The priest began by refusing.

'Drink, Father, drink; don't make such a fuss, it isn't right,' observed the landowner in a tone of reproach.

The poor young man obeyed.

'Well now, Father, you may go.'

The priest started bowing.

'Well, all right, all right, off you go ... A capital fellow,' continued Mardary Apollonich, looking after him. 'I'm very pleased with him, but the only thing is that he's a bit young. Preaches sermons all the time and then doesn't drink. But how are you, my dear friend? How *are* you? Let's go on to the balcony – it's such a glorious evening.'

We went out on to the balcony, sat down and began to talk. Mardary Apollonich looked down and suddenly became terribly agitated.

'Whose are those hens? Whose are those hens?' he shouted. 'Whose are those hens in the garden? ... Yushka, Yushka! Go and find out at once whose they are; how many times have I forbidden it, how many times have I told them!'

Yushka ran off.

'That's a fine state of things!' declared Mardary Apollonich. 'It's frightful!'

The unfortunate hens – I remember them still, two speckled ones and a white one with a crest – were continuing to walk about under the apple-trees with the utmost calmness, from time to time expressing their feelings by a prolonged clucking, when suddenly Yushka, capless and with a stick in his hand, and three other serving-folk, all of whom had reached the years of discretion, darted at them simultaneously. Then the fun started. The hens squawked, flapped their wings, jumped, and clucked fit to deafen you; the servants ran, stumbled, fell; the master shouted from the balcony like a madman: 'Catch them! catch them! catch them! ... Whose are they, whose are they?' Finally one of the servants succeeded in seizing the crested hen, catching it between his chest and the ground, when at the same moment, through the garden fence from the road, jumped a girl of about eleven, dishevelled and with a long switch in her hand.

'Oh, that's whose they are!' exclaimed the landowner triumphantly. 'Ermil, the coachman's! He sent his Natalka to chase them ... of course he hasn't sent Parasha,' added the landowner in a low voice, and with a significant grin. 'Hey, Yushka! Leave the chickens. Catch Natalka for me.'

But before the breathless Yushka could reach the terrified girl, the housekeeper, arriving from nowhere, caught her by the hand and slapped the poor girl several times on the back . . .

'That's the way, that's the way,' asserted the landowner. 'There, there, there! . . . Take the chickens away from her, Avdotya,' he added loudly, and turned to me with a radiant face: 'What a chase, eh? Why, look, I'm all of a sweat.'

And Mardary Apollonich burst out laughing.

We stayed on the balcony. It was indeed an unusually fine evening.

We were served with tea.

'Tell me,' I began, 'Mardary Apollonich, are those outlying farm-buildings yours, over there on the road beyond the ravine?'

'Yes . . . what of it?'

'But how can you allow it, Mardary Apollonich? Why, it's shameful. The huts assigned to the peasants are mean and cramped; there's not a tree to be seen around, not even a pond either, there's one well, but even that is no use at all. Couldn't you really find another site? . . . And they say that you've even taken away the old hemp-yards that were there?'

'But what can you do, when your boundary is fixed by agreement?' answered Mardary Apollonich: 'I'm fed right up to here with the whole business.' He pointed to the back of his neck. 'And I foresee no good from it, either. But as for my taking away their hemp-yard, and not digging the pond for them there – well, my friend, I know all about that. I'm a simple chap and I go about things in the old-fashioned way. As I see it, the master is the master, and the peasant is the peasant . . . and that's all there is to it.'

There was of course nothing to be said in answer to such a clear and convincing argument.

'And anyway,' he continued, 'they're a bad lot of peasants, they're in disgrace. There are two families there in particular; even my late father, God rest his soul in peace, couldn't stand them at any price. But I tell you, I believe in the saying that if the father's a thief, the son's a thief too; you can say what you like . . . it's blood that counts. I tell you frankly, from those two families, I have sent men to the army out of turn and I have scattered them about all over the place. But they don't change, and what can you do about it? They are great breeders, too, curse them.'

Meanwhile the air had grown completely still. Only occasionally a breeze rippled past and, finally dying away around the house, brought to our ears the sound of measured blows, sounding from the direction of the stable. Mardary Apollonich had just lifted to his lips a full saucer and was already dilating his nostrils, without which, as is well-known, no true Russian can imbibe tea, but he stopped, listened, nodded, gulped and, putting the saucer down on the table, pronounced, with the kindest of smiles, as if involuntarily echoing the blows: 'Chooky-chooky-chook! Chooky-chooky-chook!'

'What's that?' I asked in amazement.

'That's a naughty boy being punished on my instructions. D'you know my butler Vasily?'

'Which is he?'

'The one who served us at dinner the other day. He goes about with big side-whiskers like this.'

The fiercest indignation could not have resisted the clear and gentle gaze of Mardary Apollonich.

'What's the matter, young man, what's the matter?' he said, shaking his head. 'D'you think I'm a brute, eh, that you are staring at me like that? Whom he loveth, he chasteneth – *you* know.'

A quarter of an hour later I took my leave of Mardary Apollonich. Driving through the village, I saw Vasily the butler. He was walking along the road munching nuts. I told my driver to stop the horses and called to him. 'Well, my lad, so you were punished to-day?' I asked him.

'How d'you know?' rejoined Vasily.

'Your master told me.'

'The master himself?'

'Why did he have you punished?'

'It was quite right, sir, quite right. We don't get punished for nothing; there's none of that sort of thing with us – no, certainly not. Our master is not that sort, our master . . . you won't find another master like him in the whole province.'

'Go on!' I said to the driver. There's the old Mother Russia for you, I thought on my way home.

Lebedyan

ONE of the chief advantages of shooting, my dear readers, is that it involves you in a constant change of scene, which, for an idle fellow, is a most agreeable condition. True, sometimes (particularly in rainy weather) there's not much fun in roaming the by-ways, 'keeping right on', stopping every peasant you meet with the question: 'Hey, my friend, what's the best way to Mordovka?' then in Mordovka cross-examining some dull-witted peasant-woman (the men all being away working in the fields) about how far it is to the inn on the high road, and how to get there – and, after covering ten versts, instead of the inn, finding oneself in the ruined manor-village of Khudobubnov, to the extreme amazement of a whole herd of pigs who are up to their ears in dark-brown mud right in the middle of the road and very far indeed from expecting any such interruption. It is no fun, either, to cross breath-takingly insecure foot-bridges, to clamber down into ravines, to ford marshy streamlets; it's no fun driving for twenty-four hours on end over the greenish waves of the high road or – heaven protect us from it – bogging down for several hours in front of a gaily-coloured mile-post with the figure 22 on one side and the figure 23 on the other; it's no fun living for weeks on eggs, milk and the much-vaunted rye bread. But all these discomforts and setbacks are redeemed by advantages and satisfactions of another order. Anyway, let us get on to our story.

After the above remarks I need not explain to the reader how it was that, five years ago, I chanced to arrive in Lebedyan when the horse-fair was in full swing. We sportsmen can easily drive out from our more or less ancestral homes on a fine morning with every intention of returning in the evening of the following day, and then, by easy stages, without ceasing to shoot snipe, finish up on the blessed banks of the Pechora; moreover, every sportsman of the gun-and-dog variety is a passionate admirer of the noblest animal in the world – the horse. So it was that I arrived in Lebedyan, put up at the inn, changed my clothes and went out to the fair. (The waiter, a tall gaunt youth of twenty or so, who spoke in a sweet nasal tenor, had already had time to inform me that his Highness Prince N——, Remount Officer of the—— Regiment, was staying in the inn, that many other gentlemen had arrived, that in the evenings the gypsies were singing and there were performances of *Pan Tvardovsky* in the theatre, that horses were fetching a decent price and that anyway there were some good ones to be seen.) On the fair-ground stood endless rows of carts and, behind them, horses of every possible kind: trotters, stallions, cart-horses, draught-horses, coach-horses, and plain peasant-nags. Some, well-fed and sleek, of matched colours, covered with blankets of various hues, tethered short to tall racks, gave anxious sidelong glances at the too familiar whips of their lords the dealers; gentlemen's horses, sent by steppe-landowners from a couple of hundred versts away under the supervision of some decrepit coachman and two or three thick-skulled grooms, waved their long necks, stamped their hooves, and gnawed the fences out of sheer boredom; two little roan mongrel horses jostled each other closely; majestically immobile, like lions, the broad-cruppered trotters stood, with wavy tails and shaggy fetlocks, grey-roan, black and bay. Fanciers paused respectfully in front of them. In the lanes between the carts people of every class, age and appearance were jostling each other; horse-copers in blue coats and tall caps looked out knowingly as they waited for buyers; pop-eyed, curly-headed gypsies dashed backwards and forwards like a house on fire, looking horses in the teeth, lifting their hooves and tails, shouting, quarrelling, acting as go-betweens, drawing lots, or pressing round some remount officer in his forage-cap and beaver-trimmed military overcoat. A huge cossack sat on a lean gelding with a deer-like neck and offered to sell him 'all-in', that's to say, with saddle and bridle. Peasants in sheepskin coats torn under the arms pressed their way desperately through the crowd and swarmed in their dozens into a cart

harnessed to a horse which needed 'trying out' or, away to
one side, with the help of a shifty gypsy, bargained themselves
silly, struck each other's hands a hundred times, each insisting
on his price, while the subject of their dispute, a wretched
little nag covered with a piece of warped matting, just blinked
as if it had nothing to do with him . . . and indeed it made no
difference to the horse who was going to beat him! Landowners
with wide foreheads, dyed moustaches and pompous expressions, wearing confederate caps and camlet coats put on by
one sleeve only, chatted condescendingly with fat-bellied
merchants in pot-hats and green gloves. The place was alive
with officers of different regiments; a long cuirassier of German extraction coolly asked a lame dealer 'how much he
wished to receive for that sorrel horse'. A little fair-haired
hussar of about nineteen was trying to find a side-horse to
match a lean pacer; a postilion, wearing a low hat with a
peacock's feather wound round it and a brown coat with
leather gauntlets thrust under his narrow green belt, was
looking for a shaft-horse. Coachmen plaited their horses'
tails, wetted their manes and gave gentlemen respectful pieces
of advice. Those who had completed a deal hurried off to the
inn or the pot-house, according to their condition . . . And the
whole crowd – hustling, shouting, fussing, quarrelling and
making it up again, cursing and laughing, were up to their
knees in mud.

I wanted to buy three passable horses for my britzka: my
own were getting past their work. I found two, but couldn't see
a third to match them. After a dinner which I will not under-
take to describe (did not Æneas know how disagreeable it is to
recall past griefs?), I made my way into the so-called coffee-
house, which was a meeting-place every evening for remount
officers, horse-breeders and other visitors. In the billiard-
room, flooded with leaden waves of tobacco smoke, were a
score or so of people. There were dandified young landowners
in Hungarian jackets and grey trousers, with long side-
whiskers and oiled moustaches, looking proudly and gallantly
around them; other gentlemen in frock-coats, with extremely

short necks and eyes sunk in fat, wheezed painfully; merchants sat about in corners, so to say, on edge; officers conversed easily among themselves. At the billiard-table was Prince N——, a young man of about twenty-two, with a gay, somewhat contemptuous face, wearing his coat unbuttoned, a red silk shirt and baggy velvet trousers. He was playing with Ensign (retired) Viktor Khlopakov.

Viktor Khlopakov, a lean, swarthy little fellow of about thirty, with black hair, brown eyes and blunt, upturned nose, is an untiring visitor to elections and fairs. He walks with a hop, throws his elbows out in a swaggering gesture, wears his hat at an angle and turns up the sleeves of his military coat, which is lined with dove-coloured calico. Mr. Khlopakov has a talent for making up to well-to-do young bucks from Petersburg, smokes, drinks and plays cards with them, and addresses them in the second person singular. Why they accept him is hard enough to understand. He is not clever, he is not funny: even his jokes are no good. True, they treat him with friendly indifference, like a good-hearted but insignificant fellow; they hobnob with him for two or three weeks, then suddenly cut him, and he starts cutting them, too. Ensign Khlopakov specializes in employing continuously for a whole year, sometimes for two, a single expression, which is not always to the point, and is in no way amusing, but which, goodness knows why, makes everyone laugh. Eight years ago, he used to say at every step: 'My respects to you and humblest thanks' – and every time his current protectors died of laughter and made him repeat 'my respects'. Then he began to use a tolerably complicated expression: 'Cross my heart, *kesskersay*, that's a bit of all right' – and with the same brilliant success. Two years later he thought out a new pleasantry: '*Ne voo fuss-ay pas*, you jolly good chap, in your sheepskin wrap' – and so forth. Well, these phrases, simple though they may be, are his meat, drink and raiment. (He long ago ran through his own fortune and lives entirely at his friends' expense.) Observe that he has absolutely no other agreeable qualities; true, he smokes a hundred pipes of Beetle mixture a day, lifts his right foot above his head at the billiard-table and, when taking aim, rubs his cue furiously with his hand – but it is not everybody who appreciates these accomplishments. He is a fair drinker, too ... but in Mother Russia it is hard to achieve distinction on that score ... In short, I find his success a complete enigma ... There is one thing about him, though: he is cautious, never lets a quarrel go further, or says a bad word about anyone.

Well, I thought when I saw Khlopakov, what is his present catchword?

The prince hit the white.

'Thirty-love,' sang out the marker, a consumptive-looking fellow with a dark face and leaden rings below the eyes.

The prince put the yellow ball into the end pocket with a bang.

'Ho!' came an approving, full-bellied wheeze from a fat merchant sitting in a corner at a rickety one-legged table – a wheeze that dwindled into a fit of shyness. But luckily no one had noticed him. He sighed and stroked his beard.

'Thirty-six to a duck's egg!' called the marker through his nose.

'Well, what about it, my friend?' the prince asked Khlopakov.

'What about it? Why, it is a rrrrapssscallion, of course, a real rrrrapsscallion.'

The prince burst out laughing.

'What, what? Say it again?'

'A rrapssscallion!' repeated the retired ensign complacently.

So that's the new slogan, I thought.

The prince put the red into the pocket.

'Hey! don't do that, prince, don't do that,' came a sudden murmur from a little blond officer with bloodshot eyes, a tiny nose and the face of a sleepy child. 'Don't play it like that ... you ought to have ... not like that!'

'How then?' asked the prince over his shoulder.

'You ought to have ... gone for a triplet.'

'Indeed?' muttered the prince through his teeth.

'I say, prince, are you going to the gypsies this evening?' continued the young man hastily, in some embarrassment. 'Steshka is going to sing . . . and Ilyushka.'

The prince didn't even answer him.

'Rrrrapscallion, old boy,' said Khlopakov, with a sly wink of his left eye.

The prince burst out laughing.

'Thirty-nine love,' intoned the marker.

'Love, love . . . just look what I'm going to do to the yellow . . .'

Khlopakov jiggled the cue on his hand, took aim and missed.

'Oh, rrapscallion,' he exclaimed in disgust.

The prince laughed again.

'What? What?'

But Khlopakov refused to repeat his slogan; a little coquetry never does any harm.

'You missed it, sir,' observed the marker. 'Kindly put some chalk on . . . Forty to a duck's egg!'

'Gentlemen,' began the prince, turning to the company in general, but looking at no one in particular, 'you know, in the theatre this evening we must call for Verzhembitskaya.'

'Certainly, certainly, of course,' shouted several gentlemen in emulation, remarkably flattered by this opportunity of answering the princely remark: 'Verzhembitskaya.'

'Verzhembitskaya is a first-rate actress, much better than Sopnyakova,' squeaked from the corner a seedy little fellow with side-whiskers and glasses. Poor wretch! he was secretly head-over-heels in love with Sopnyakova, but the prince didn't think him worth so much as a glance.

'Waiter, hey, get me a pipe!' shouted, through his cravat, a tall gentleman with regular features and a noble bearing – and all the characteristics of a sharper.

The waiter ran for a pipe and, returning, announced to his Highness that the coachman Baklaga was asking for him.

'Oh! tell, tell him to wait, and give him some vodka.'

'Very good, sir.'

Baklaga, as I learnt afterwards, was a young, good-looking, extremely spoilt coachman; the prince loved him, gave him horses, rushed round with him, spent whole nights in his company... To-day you would never recognize this same prince for the gay spendthrift that he was... What scented, corseted haughtiness! What preoccupation with official duties – and, above all, what sagacity!

The tobacco smoke was beginning to eat my eyes out. After listening once more to Khlopakov's exclamation and the prince's laugh, I went to my room, where my man had already made my bed on the narrow broken-down horsehair sofa with its tall, curving back.

The following day I went to look at the horses in the various yards and began with the well-known dealer Sitnikov. I passed through the gate into the sand-sprinkled yard. In front of the wide-open door of the stable stood the master himself, a tall, stout, middle-aged man in a hareskin coat with its collar turned up and tucked inwards. When he saw me, he moved slowly over to meet me, held his cap above his head in both hands and said in a sing-song voice: 'My compliments to you. Would you like to see some horses?'

'Yes, that's what I have come for.'

'What sort exactly, if I may ask?'

'Show me what you've got.'

'With pleasure.'

We went into the stable. Several white mongrels rose from the straw and ran up to us, wagging their tails; an old goat with a long beard went away to one side in displeasure; three grooms in stout but greasy sheepskins bowed to us in silence. To right and left, in specially-constructed stalls, stood some thirty horses, groomed and combed to perfection. Above the joists, pigeons fluttered and cooed.

'What d'you want the horse for: driving, or stud?' Sitnikov asked me.

'Both.'

'I see, sir, I see,' pronounced the dealer with deliberation. 'Petya, show the gentleman Ermine.'

We went out into the yard.

'Wouldn't you like a seat brought out from inside? ... No? ... As you please.'

There was a clatter of hooves on boards, the crack of a whip, and Petya, a fellow of about forty, pock-marked and swarthy, sprang out from the stable with a grey, rather imposing stallion, made him rear, ran with him twice round the yard and mounted him neatly at the best place for showing him off. Ermine stretched himself, gave a whistling snort, threw up his tail, tossed his head and squinted at us.

You're a wily bird! I thought.

'Give him his head, give him his head,' said Sitnikov and stared at me. 'What d'you think of him, sir?' he asked at length.

'Not a bad horse; the fore-legs aren't all one could wish.'

'They're capital legs!' rejoined Sitnikov with conviction. 'But his quarters ... have a look, sir ... they are broad as a stove, you could fairly sleep on them.'

'He's long in the pasterns.'

'Long, indeed – have a heart! Run him round, Petya, let him trot, let him trot ... don't let him gallop.'

Petya went round the yard again on Ermine. We were all silent.

'Well, take him back,' said Sitnikov, 'and let's see Falcon.'

Falcon, a lean, beetle-black, Dutch-bred stallion with drooping quarters, proved rather better than Ermine. He was the type of horse known to the fancier as 'bumpers and borers', that is, with an action which throws the fore-legs out in all directions, but does not make much direct headway. Middle-aged merchants have a weakness for horses of this type: their action resembles the swaggering gait of a smart waiter; they are all right on their own, for an after-dinner drive: prancing and caracoling, they will eagerly pull a lumbering drozhky, loaded high with a coachman who has gorged himself stupid, an over-fed merchant who is having twinges of heartburn, and his puffy wife in a blue silk mantle with a lilac kerchief over her head. I turned Falcon down too. Sitnikov showed me several more horses.... One, at last, a grey roan stallion of military antecedents, took my fancy. I could not refrain from giving him an appreciative pat on the withers. Sitnikov at once feigned indifference.

'Well, does he go all right?' I asked. (You say 'go' when speaking of a trotter.)

'He does,' answered the dealer calmly.

'Can I see?...'

'Of course you can, sir. Hey, Kuzya, harness Dogonyai to the drozhky.'

Kuzya, the jockey, who was a master of his craft, drove past us three times along the road. The horse went well, without stumbling, or throwing up his quarters; he had a free action, carried his tail well up.

'What are you asking for him?'

Sitnikov opened with an unheard-of price. We were starting to bargain where we stood in the road, when suddenly, from round the corner, thundered a team of three magnificently matched horses which halted smartly in front of the gates of Sitnikov's house. In this rakish, fancier's equipage sat Prince N——, with Khlopakov beside him. Baklaga was driving, and how he drove! The rascal could have driven through an ear-ring. The side-horses were lively little bays with black eyes and black legs, keen as mustard; you had only to whistle and they were gone. The shaft-horse, a dark bay, stood throwing his neck back, like a swan, chest well forward, legs like arrows, head tossing, eyes arrogantly narrowed.... Fine! A turn-out fit for Tsar Ivan on Easter Day!

'Your Highness! Welcome!' shouted Sitnikov.

The prince jumped down. Khlopakov climbed slowly out on the other side.

'Good day to you, my friend. Got any horses?'

'I have always got horses for your Highness. Please come in ...Petya, let's see Peacock! and tell them to get Superb ready. As for you, sir,' he continued, turning to me, 'we will finish our business another time.... Fomka, bring a seat for his Highness.'

They brought Peacock out from a separate stable which I had not noticed at first. The powerful dark bay flew right up into the air with all his legs. Sitnikov looked away and screwed up his eyes.

'Ooh rrrrapscallion!' pronounced Khlopakov. '*Zhemsa!*'

The prince burst out laughing.

They had some difficulty in holding Peacock; he fairly pulled the groom round the yard; finally they got him up against the wall. He snorted, shivered, collected himself, and Sitnikov teased him with a wave of his whip.

'What are you gaping at? Wait till I show you! ooh!' said the dealer, with fond menace, admiring the horse in spite of himself.

'How much?' asked the prince.

'For your Highness, five thousand.'

'Three.'

'Impossible, your Highness, upon my word! . . .'

'Three, did you hear? Rrrrapscallion,' repeated Khlopakov.

I went off without awaiting the end of the deal. At the furthest corner of the road I noticed a big sheet of paper stuck to the gates of a little grey house. At the head of it was an ink drawing of a horse with a trumpet-shaped tail and an interminable neck, and under the horse's hooves were the following words, written in an old-fashioned hand:

'For sale, horses of various breeds, brought to Lebedyan fair from the well-known steppe-country stud of Anastasei Ivanich Chornobai, landowner of Tambov. Horses of excellent antecedents, fully broken and nice-mannered. Purchasers kindly ask for Anastasei Ivanich himself, or, in his absence, for his coachman Nazar Kubyshkin. Gentlemen customers, pray do an old man the honour of a visit!'

I halted. I thought I would have a look at the horses of the well-known steppe-country breeder, Mr. Chornobai. I tried to go through the gate, but, contrary to usual practice, found it locked. I knocked.

'Who's there? . . . A customer?' squealed a woman's voice.

'Yes.'

'Coming, sir, coming.'

The gate opened. I saw a peasant-woman of about fifty, bareheaded, in shoes and with a sheepskin thrown loosely on.

'Please, kind sir, come in, and I'll go and tell Anastasei Ivanich at once . . . Nazar, hey, Nazar.'

'What?' muttered a septuagenarian voice from the stable.

'Get the horses ready; a customer has come.'

The old woman ran into the house.

'A customer, a customer,' muttered Nazar, by way of answer to her. 'I haven't washed all their tails yet.'

Oh, Arcadia! I thought.

'Good day, sir, and welcome,' said a pleasant, slow, fruity voice behind my back. I looked round; in front of me, in a long-skirted blue overcoat, stood an old man of middle height, with white hair, a friendly smile and beautiful blue eyes.

'Horses? Please, sir, please . . . But wouldn't you like to come and take tea with me first?'

I thanked him and declined.

'Well, as you please. You must forgive me, sir: you see, I am old-fashioned.' Mr. Chornobai spoke unhurriedly and with a broad country accent. 'Everything is simple and straight-forward with me. Nazar, hey, Nazar,' he added, drawlingly, and without raising his voice.

Nazar, a little, wrinkled old chap with the nose of a hawk and a triangular beard, appeared on the stable threshold.

'What sort of horses do you want, sir?' continued Mr. Chornobai.

'Not too dear, well-broken, for carriage-work.'

'Certainly, I have some like that, certainly . . . Nazar, show the gentleman the grey gelding, you know, the one at the end, and the bay with the bald spot – no, the other bay, the one by Krasotka, you know?'

Nazar returned into the stable.

'Just bring them out on the halter,' Mr. Chernobai shouted after him. 'My ways, sir,' he continued, looking straight at me with his clear, mild eyes, 'are not those of the dealers – devil take them! They go in for all sorts of ginger, salt, bran.[1] God forgive them, anyway!... But with me, be pleased to note, everything is open-handed and above board.'

The horses were brought out. I didn't like them.

'Well, take them back,' said Anastasei Ivanich. 'Show us some more.'

They showed us some more. Eventually I chose one of the cheaper ones. We began to bargain. Mr. Chornobai remained cool, spoke so judiciously, with such dignity, that I could not fail to 'honour the old man': I paid a deposit.

'Well now,' said Anastasei Ivanich, 'allow me, in the old-fashioned way, to hand the horse over to you from coat-tail to coat-tail... You'll be grateful to me... He's as fresh as a nut... unspoiled. Straight from the steppes! He'll go in every kind of harness.'

He crossed himself, took his coat-skirt in his hand, grasped the halter, and handed the horse over to me.

'He's yours now, and good luck to you. You still won't take tea?'

'No, thank you very much indeed: I must go home.'

'As you please... Shall my coachman lead the horse after you now?'

'Yes, now, if he will.'

'Certainly, my dear sir, certainly... Vasily, hey, Vasily, go with the gentleman; lead the horse and take the money. Well, good-bye, sir, and God bless you.'

'Good-bye, Anastasei Ivanich.'

The horse was led home for me. The very next day he proved broken-winded and lame. I tried putting him in harness: he backed away, and when I struck him with the whip, he balked, bucked and lay down. I at once set off to see Mr. Chornobai. I asked if he was at home.

'Yes.'

'How is this!' I said. 'Why, you've sold me a broken-winded horse.'

---

1 Horses grow fat quickly on bran and salt. – *Author*.

'Broken-winded? . . . Heaven preserve us.'

'And lame into the bargain, and a jibber as well.'

'Lame? I don't know, your coachman must certainly have hurt him somehow . . . but I, before God . . .'

'Really, Anastasei Ivanich, you ought to take him back.'

'No, sir, no, I'm sorry; once he's out of my yard, the deal is done. You should have been good enough to look at him first.'

I understood what I was up against, submitted to my fate, laughed and went off. Luckily I hadn't paid too dear for my lesson.

Two days later I departed, but returned to Lebedyan a week afterwards on the way back. In the coffee-house I found almost the same faces and caught Prince N—— at billiards again. But Mr. Khlopakov's fortunes had already suffered one of their usual vicissitudes. The little fair-haired officer had replaced him in the prince's favours. The poor Ensign (retired) tried once more in my presence to put in his catchword – surely, he thought, it will work as it did before – but the prince not only failed to smile, he actually frowned and shrugged a shoulder. Mr. Khlopakov looked down, shrank into himself, crept away into a corner and began quietly filling his pipe . . .

Tatyana Borisovna and her Nephew

GIVE me your hand, dear reader, and come with me. The weather is glorious; the May sky is a tender blue; the smooth young willow-leaves shine as if they had been washed; the wide, even highway is all covered with that fine, red-stemmed grass which sheep crop with such enjoyment; to right and left, on the long slopes of the gentle hills, a peaceful ripple passes over the green rye; over it glide in faint outline the shadows of small clouds. In the distance are green forests, glittering pools, yellow villages; larks rise in their hundreds, sing, drop like plummets, and sit with necks outstretched on tussocks; rooks halt on the road, look at you, bow down to the earth, let you drive by and, after a couple of hops, fly ponderously away; on the hill across the ravine there is a peasant ploughing; a roan foal, dock-tailed and wild-maned, runs on unsteady legs after his mother; you can hear his faint whinnying. We drive into a birch-wood; the strong, cool smell holds you breathless with delight. We have come to a village-boundary. The coachman gets down, the horses snort, the side-horses look round, the shaft-horse flicks his tail and leans his head against the shaft-bow ... the gate opens with a squeak. The coachman takes his seat ... Off we go! In front of us is the village. After passing five back-yards, we turn to the right, go down into a hollow and drive out over a dam. Beyond a small pond, behind round-topped apple-trees and lilacs, we can see a wooden roof that was once red, and two chimneys; the coachman turns to the left along the fence and, to the whining, throaty barking of three aged mongrels, drives through open gates, wheels smartly round a wide courtyard, past a stable and a barn, bows gallantly to an old housekeeper who has just stepped sideways over the high threshold into the open larder-door, and stops at last before the porch of a dark little house with gleaming windows ... We are at Tatyana

Borisovna's. And here she is herself, opening a casement and nodding her head at us...

Good day to you, madam!

Tatyana Borisovna is a woman of about fifty, with large, protruding grey eyes, a bluntish nose, red cheeks and a double chin. Her face radiates warm-heartedness and affection. Once upon a time she was married, but she early became a widow. Tatyana Borisovna is a very remarkable woman. She never leaves her little estate, hardly knows her neighbours, entertains and loves young people only. She was born of a family of very poor landowners and never received any education, that's to say, she doesn't speak French; she has never been to Moscow – and, notwithstanding all these deficiencies, she is so simple and good, so free in feeling and thought, so little infected with the usual ailments of the ladies of the smaller gentry, that it is really impossible not to admire her... And, indeed, a woman who lives the whole year round in the country, at the back of beyond – and neither gossips, nor squeaks, nor drops curtsies, nor has fits of agitation or choking, nor gets the shivers from curiosity – such a woman is a regular portent! She usually wears a grey taffeta dress and a white bonnet with lilac-coloured ribbons hanging from it; she likes food, but there is no gluttony about her; she leaves jam-making, drying and pickling to her house-keeper. Then what does she do all day? you will ask. Read? – no, she doesn't read; to tell the truth, books are not printed for the likes of her... If she has no company, my friend Tatyana Borisovna sits alone at the window and knits a stocking – in winter, that is; in summer she walks in the garden, plants and waters her flowers, plays for whole hours with her kittens, feeds her pigeons... She has little to do with the management of her land. But if someone calls, some young neighbour, whom she likes, Tatyana Borisovna becomes quite animated; she makes him sit down, serves him with tea, listens to his stories, laughs, sometimes pats his cheek, but speaks little herself; in misfortune or grief she will have comfort and good advice to give. How many people have confided in her the secrets of their homes and hearts, how many have wept on her shoulder! Sometimes she sits opposite her visitor, leans quietly on one elbow and looks him in the eyes with such sympathy, smiles with such affection, that the visitor thinks in spite of himself: You're a wonderful woman, Tatyana Borisovna! let me tell you all that's in my heart. In her small, cosy rooms it is comfortable and warm; the weather in her house is always fine, if I may so express it. Tatyana Borisovna is a marvellous woman, and yet no one marvels at her: her common sense, her firmness and frankness, her burning sympathy in the joys and sorrows of others, all her good qualities, in a word, seem to have been born with her and to have cost her no pain or trouble... It would be impossible to imagine her otherwise; therefore there can be nothing to thank her for. She particularly likes looking on at the pranks and games of the young; she folds her arms below her breasts, throws back her head, screws up her eyes and sits there smiling, then suddenly sighs and says: 'Oh, you children, my children!'... So, at times, you want to go up to her, take her by the hand and say to her: 'Listen, Tatyana Borisovna, you don't know your own worth; with all your simplicity and lack of book-learning, you're a remarkable being.' Her very name has something familiar and welcoming about it, one likes pronouncing it, it excites an affectionate smile. Often, for instance, I have chanced to ask a passing peasant how to get, say, to Grachevka. 'Ah, sir, you go first to Vyazovoye, and from there to Tatyana Borisovna's, and from Tatyana Borisovna's anyone will be able to show you the way.' And at the name Tatyana Borisovna the peasant has a special shake of the head. In keeping with her means, she has few servants. Her house, laundry, larder and kitchen are under the charge of Agafya the housekeeper, her old nurse, an excellent, tearful, toothless creature; two hale and hearty girls, with firm, dove-coloured cheeks like Antonov apples, serve under her direction. The functions of footman, major-domo and butler are discharged by a seventy-year-old man-servant named Polikarp, a freak if ever there was one – a well-read fellow, a retired violinist and devotee of Viotti, a personal enemy of Napoleon, or, as he calls him, 'Bonapartishka', and a passionate trapper of nightingales. He always has five or six of them in his room. In early spring he sits for whole days beside the cages, waiting for the first 'roll' and, when his vigil is over, covers his face with his hands and groans, 'Oh, dear, dear me!' and bursts into floods of tears. Polikarp is assisted by his grandson Vasya, a curly-headed, quick-eyed lad of twelve; Polikarp loves him to distraction and grumbles at him from morning to night. He also occupies himself with his education. 'Vasya,' he says, 'say "Bonapartishka is a rascal".' 'And what will you give me, grandfather?' 'What will I give you? . . . I'll give you nothing . . . Look here, what are you? Are you a Russian?' 'I'm an Amchanian, grandpa: I was born in Amchensk.'[1] 'You stupid! and where is Amchensk?' 'And how should I know?' 'Amchensk is in Russia, stupid!' 'What if it is in Russia?' 'What if it is? Why, Bonapartishka was driven off Russian soil by his Grace the late prince Mikhailo Ilarionovich Kutuzov of Smolensk, with the help of God. That's when they made up the song:

> *Bonaparte's forgot his paces*
> *Since he went and lost his braces . . .*

D'you understand: he liberated your native land.' 'But what's that got to do with me?' 'Oh, you stupid, stupid boy. Look, if his Grace Prince Mikhailo Ilarionovich had not driven Bonapartishka out, some *Moussieu* would be hitting you on the noddle with a stick. He would come up to you, see, and say to you: "*Coman voo portay voo?*" – and then, rap-rap.' 'But I'd punch him in the pot.' 'And he'd say to you: "*Bonzhur, bonzhur, venay ici*" – and he'd pull you by the hair.' 'But I'd get him by the legs – by the spring-onions.' 'Quite right, their legs *are* like spring-onions . . . But supposing he began to tie your hands?' 'I wouldn't let him; I'd call Mikhei the coachman to help me.' 'Why, yes, Vasya, the Frenchman wouldn't be able to stand up against Mikhei, would he?' 'Stand up against him,

---

1 Dialect version of 'Mtsensk', the name of a town in Orel province. – *Translators.*

indeed! Why, Mikhei's as strong as a horse.' 'Well, and what would you do to him?' 'We'd give it to him on the back, we would . . .' 'But he would shout: "*Pardon, pardon, sivooplay!*"' 'And we would answer him: "None of your *sivooplay*, you Frenchman, you!"' 'Well done, Vasya! . . . Well, shout it out, then: "Bonapartishka is a rascal!"' 'And you give me some sugar!' 'There's a lad for you!'

Tatyana Borisovna has few dealings with the ladies of the neighbourhood; they are not fond of visiting her and she is unskilful at entertaining them, drops off to sleep to the murmur of their conversation, then starts up, struggles to open her eyes, and drops off to sleep again. On the whole, Tatyana Borisovna doesn't like women. One of her friends, an excellent and quite young man, had a sister, an old maid of thirty-eight and a half, a very good creature, but warped, overstrung and given to enthusiasms. Her brother used often to tell her about their neighbour. One fine morning my old maid – just like that, out of the blue – ordered her horse to be saddled and set off to Tatyana Borisovna's. In her long dress, with a hat on, a green veil and straying curls, she entered the hall and, passing the astonished Vasya, who took her for a fairy, rushed into the drawing-room. Tatyana Borisovna, startled, tried to get up, but her legs gave way. 'Tatyana Borisovna,' began the visitor, in a voice of entreaty, 'forgive my boldness. I am the sister of your friend Alexei Nikolaevich K——, and I've heard so much about you from him, that I've decided to make your acquaintance.' 'Very much honoured,' murmured her stupefied hostess. The visitor threw off her hat, shook her curls, sat down beside Tatyana Borisovna, took her by the hand . . . 'So this is she,' she began thoughtfully, with a catch in her voice. 'This is that good, serene, noble, holy being! This is she, that woman so simple and at the same time so profound! What a joy, what a joy! What friends we are going to be! I can breathe at last! . . . Just as I imagined her,' she added in a whisper, gazing into the eyes of Tatyana Borisovna. 'You're not angry with me, you good kind soul?' 'Not at all, I am very pleased . . . won't you have some tea?' The visitor smiled condescendingly. '*Wie wahr, wie unreflectirt*,' she murmured, as if to herself. 'Let me kiss you, you dear creature!'

The old maid sat on at Tatyana Borisovna's for three hours, without even a moment of silence. She tried to explain to her new acquaintance just what her significance was. As soon as the unexpected guest had left, the poor lady took a bath, had a good drink of lime tea and went to bed. But the next day the old maid returned, sat for four hours and left with a promise to visit Tatyana Borisovna every day. She had determined to put the finishing touches to the evolution and development of what she described as such a richly-endowed nature. And indeed she would probably have finished her off completely if, in the first place, she hadn't been thoroughly disillusioned about her brother's friend before two weeks were up, and secondly, if she hadn't fallen in love with a young student who was passing by and with whom she at once embarked on an energetic correspondence; in her epistles, she sent him the customary blessings for the holiness and beauty of his life, offered 'to sacrifice her whole being', asked him just to call her sister, went off into descriptions of nature, referred to Goethe, Schiller, Bettin and German philosophy, and ended by landing the poor young man into a state of black despair. But youth claimed its own: one fine morning he woke up in such a frenzy of hatred for his 'sister and best friend' that he almost killed his servant in the heat of the moment, and for a long time afterwards he practically snapped at the slightest allusion to pure and exalted love ... But from that time on Tatyana Borisovna began to avoid contacts with the ladies of the neighbourhood even more decidedly than before.

Alas! There is nothing durable on earth. All that I have told you about the good lady's way of life is a thing of the past; the peace that reigned in her house is broken for ever. For more than a year she has had living with her a nephew, an artist from Petersburg.

Eight years ago there lived at Tatyana Borisovna's a lad of twelve, an orphan, little Andrei, the son of her late brother.

Little Andrei had big, bright, dewy eyes, a tiny little mouth, a straight nose and a fine high forehead. He spoke in a sweet, gentle voice, conducted himself in a neat and orderly fashion, was charming and attentive with guests, and kissed his aunt's hand with all the sensibility of an orphan. You had hardly time to appear before, lo and behold, he would be bringing you a chair. He never got into any sort of mischief: he never made a noise; he would sit by himself in a corner with a book, and so quietly and modestly, he wouldn't even lean against the back of the chair. A visitor would come in – and up Andrei would get, with a respectful smile and a blush; the visitor would leave – down he would sit again, bring out of his pocket a little brush and looking-glass, and tidy his hair. From his earliest years he had been fond of drawing. If a scrap of paper came his way, he would at once ask Agafya the housekeeper for a pair of scissors, carefully cut out of the paper an exact square, put a border round it and get to work: he would draw an eye with an enormous pupil, or a Grecian nose, or a house with a chimney and a spiral of smoke, a dog '*en face*' looking like a bench, or a tree with two pigeons, and underneath he would write: 'Drawn by Andrei Belovzorov, on such and such a date in such and such a year, in the village of Malye Bryki.' For the two weeks before Tatyana Borisovna's name-day he was at work with a special zeal: he was the first to appear with good wishes, and brought a little scroll tied up in pink ribbon. Tatyana Borisovna kissed her nephew on his forehead and undid the knot. The scroll opened and the curious gaze of the beholder fell on a round frame in bold shading, with pillars and an altar in the middle; on the altar was a burning heart and a wreath and above, on a twisted banderole, was written in bold letters: 'To his aunt and benefactress Tatyana Borisovna Bogdanova from her respectful and loving nephew, as an expression of his deepest affection.' Tatyana Borisovna kissed him again and gave him a silver rouble. All the same, she felt no great attachment towards him: little Andrei's obsequiousness did not altogether please her. Meanwhile Andrei was growing up; Tatyana Borisovna began to feel anxious about his future.

An unexpected development delivered her from her perplexity...

This is what happened: one day, eight years ago, she received a visit from a certain Mr. Pyotr Mikhailich Benevolensky, a Collegiate Councillor and Cavalier of an Order. Mr. Benevolensky had once held a Government appointment in the nearest provincial town and had been assiduous in his visits to Tatyana Borisovna; then he had been transferred to Petersburg, entered a Ministry, reached a fairly important position, and on one of his frequent tours on official business had remembered his old acquaintance and turned up to see her, with the intention of resting for two days from the cares of office in the bosom of the peaceful countryside. Tatyana Borisovna received him with her usual cordiality, and Mr. Benevolensky... but before we proceed with our story, allow me, amiable reader, to acquaint you with this new character. Mr. Benevolensky was a stoutish, soft-looking man of medium build, with short legs and podgy little hands. He wore a voluminous and extremely neat frock-coat, a high, wide cravat, snow-white linen, a gold chain on his silk waistcoat, a ring with a stone in it on his index finger, and a blond wig; he spoke quietly and with authority, walked noiselessly, had a pleasant smile, a pleasantly roving eye and a pleasant way of sinking his chin in his cravat: he was an altogether pleasant person. He had also been endowed by the Lord with an excellent heart: he was easily moved to tears or enthusiasm; in addition to which he burnt with a disinterested passion for the arts, a really disinterested one, because the truth was that in matters of art Mr. Benevolensky understood not the first thing. It is a mystery, from what quarter, in virtue of what secret and incomprehensible laws, this passion had gained its hold on him. He gave the impression of being a matter-of-fact, indeed a humdrum sort of man... in fact his type is fairly well represented in Mother Russia...

Their love for art and artists gives these people an indescribable, cloying sweetness; acquaintance or conversation with them is excruciating: they are bores of a honeyed variety. For instance, they never call Raphael Raphael, or Correggio

Correggio. 'The Divine Sanzio, the inimitable de Allegris,' they say, in a voice which is invariably affected. Every home-bred, self-satisfied, over-subtilized, mediocre talent becomes a genius for them: the blue sky of Italy, the lemons of the south, the scented mists of Brenta's banks never leave their tongue. 'Ah, Vanya, Vanya,' or: 'Ah, Sasha, Sasha,' they say to each other with emotion: 'We ought to be off to the South, to the South ... you and I are Greeks at heart, ancient Greeks.' They are to be observed at exhibitions, before certain works of certain Russian painters. (It must be remembered that for the most part these gentlemen are impassioned patriots.) Now they take two steps back and put their heads to one side, now they go up to the picture again; their eyes are veiled in oily moisture ... 'Phew, my goodness me,' they say at last, in a voice broken with emotion, 'what soul, what soul! ... look, what heart, what heart! He's put his soul into it! – his very soul! ... And the composition! The masterly composition!' And the pictures that hang in their own drawing-rooms! The artists that go to their evening parties, drink their tea, listen to their discourses! The offerings they receive, the perspectives of their own rooms with a brush in the right foreground, a pile of dirt on a glossy floor, a yellow samovar on a table by the window and the master himself in a dressing-gown and skull-cap, with a sharp highlight on his cheek! What long-haired nurselings of the Muses visit them, and with what feverishly superior smiles! What pale-green young ladies whine at their pianos! For such is the custom in Mother Russia: a man cannot devote himself to a single art, – he must take on the whole lot. So it is not at all surprising that these gentlemen-amateurs also extend their vigorous protection to Russian literature and in particular to the drama ... It is for them that works like *Jacob Sanazar* are written. The thousand-times depicted struggle of unrecognized talent against society, against the whole world, shakes them to the bottom of their soul ...

The day after Mr. Benevolensky's arrival, at tea, Tatyana Borisovna told her nephew to show the visitor his drawings. 'So he draws, does he?' said Mr. Benevolensky in some surprise, and he turned to little Andrei with interest. 'Certainly, he does,' rejoined Tatyana Borisovna. 'He's so keen! and all on his own too, without any teacher.' 'Oh, show me, show me,' repeated Mr. Benevolensky. Blushing and smiling, Andrei produced his sketch-book for the visitor. Mr. Benevolensky began to turn over the pages with the air of a connoisseur. 'Well done, young man,' he pronounced at last. 'Very well done,' and he stroked Andrei's head. Andrei kissed his hand in mid-air. 'There's talent for you! I congratulate you, Tatyana Borisovna, I do indeed.' 'You know, Pyotr Mikhailich, I can't find him a teacher here. To get one from the town is expensive, my neighbours the Artamonovs have a painter, an excellent one, I understand, but the lady of the house forbids him to give lessons outside, she says it will spoil his taste.' 'Hmm, hmm,' pronounced Mr. Benevolensky; he reflected, and gave a sidelong look at Andrei. 'Well, we'll talk it over,' he added suddenly, and rubbed his hands. The same day he asked Tatyana Borisovna if he could speak with her alone. They were closeted together. Half an hour later they called for little Andrei. Little Andrei went in. Mr. Benevolensky was standing in the window, slightly flushed, and radiant-eyed. Tatyana Borisovna was sitting in a corner drying her tears. 'Well, little Andrei,' she began at length, 'say thank you to Pyotr Mikhailich: he is going to take you under his guardianship and carry you off to Petersburg.' Andrei was fairly rooted to the spot. 'Tell me honestly,' began Mr. Benevolensky in a voice of dignity and condescension. 'Do you want to be an artist, young man, do you feel a holy vocation to art?' 'Yes, I want to be an artist, Pyotr Mikhailich,' rejoined little Andrei tremulously. 'Well then, I am very glad. You will, of course,' continued Mr. Benevolensky, 'find it painful to leave your revered aunt; you should feel the liveliest gratitude towards her.' 'I adore my aunt,' Andrei interrupted him, and began to blink. 'Of course, of course, that's very understandable and does you much credit; all the same, imagine what joy when you succeed . . .' 'Kiss me, Andrei,' whispered the good lady. Little Andrei threw himself on her neck. 'Well, now say thank you to your benefactor...' Little Andrei put his arms round Mr. Benevolensky's stomach, stood up on tiptoe and managed to reach his hand, which the benefactor permitted, certainly, but without any undue enthusiasm... After all, he must console and gratify the child, well, yes, and also pander to his own vanity a bit. Two days later Mr. Benevolensky departed, taking with him his new charge.

During the first three years of his absence, little Andrei wrote fairly often and sometimes appended drawings to his letters. Occasionally Mr. Benevolensky added a few words from himself, approbatory for the most part; then the letters got fewer, and finally broke off altogether. For a whole year there was no word from the nephew; Tatyana Borisovna was beginning to grow anxious, when suddenly she received a note of the following tenor: 'Dear Aunt, three days ago my protector, Pyotr Mikhailich, passed away. A cruel paralytic stroke bereft me of this last support. Of course, I am already nineteen; in the last seven years I have made considerable progress; I have great hope of my talent, and can live by it; I am not despondent, but all the same, if you can, send me by the first opportunity 250 roubles in notes. I kiss your hand and remain, etc.'

Tatyana Borisovna sent off the 250 roubles to her nephew. Two months later he asked for more; she collected what she could and sent it off. Six weeks after this second despatch, he asked for money a third time, saying that it was for paints for a portrait ordered from him by Princess Tertereshneva. Tatyana Borisovna refused. In that case, he wrote to her, he intended to come and stay with her in the country in order to restore his health. And so indeed, in May of the same year, little Andrei returned to Malye Bryki.

At first Tatyana Borisovna did not recognize him. Judging by his letter, she expected a thin, sickly fellow, but what she saw was a sturdy-shouldered lad with a broad, red face and curled, oily hair. Thin, pale little Andrei had turned into a stalwart Andrei Ivanich Belovzorov. It was not only his appearance which had altered. The punctilious timidity, precision and neatness of previous years had given place to a careless joviality and an unbearable slovenliness; he had a rolling gait, threw himself into armchairs, collapsed over the table, sprawled about, yawned his head off; he was rude to his aunt and to the servants. I, he seemed to say, am an artist, a free Cossack! This is how we are! Sometimes he would not take a brush in his hand for days on end; but when the so-called inspiration overcame him, he would strut about like a man in a daze, heavy-footed, awkward, noisy; his cheeks would blaze with a coarse flush, his eyes would be bleary; he would go off into discourses about his talent, his successes, his development, his progress . . . It appeared in fact that his skill hardly ran to passable portrait-sketches. He was an utter dunce, read nothing, indeed what has an artist to gain by reading! Nature, freedom, poetry – these are his element. All he need do is shake his curls, sing like a nightingale and smoke himself silly with Beetle mixture! The devil-may-care Russian touch is all very well, but it only suits a few; untalented, second-rate exponents of it are unbearable. Our friend Andrei Ivanich settled in at his aunt's: free food evidently suited his palate. On visitors he inflicted mortal boredom. He would sit down at the piano (for Tatyana Borisovna actually had one) and begin strumming 'The Dashing Troika' with one finger; he would strike a chord, hammer away at the keys; for whole hours he would painfully howl his way through Varlamov's songs: 'The Lonely Pine-tree' or 'No, Doctor, come not', and all this with his eyes sunk in fat and his cheeks as shiny as a drum . . . Then suddenly he would roar out: '*Die away, ye Throbs of Passion*' . . . Tatyana Borisovna would fairly jump out of her skin.

'It's a strange thing,' she remarked to me one day, 'how all the songs written to-day are sort of desperate; in my time they used to write them differently: there were sad songs too, but all the same they were pleasant to listen to . . . For instance:

> *Come, come to me in the meadow;*
> *Where I wait for you in vain;*
> *Come, come to me in the meadow*
> *Where I shed tears like the rain.*

Alas, when you come to me, I fear
That all too late 'twill be, my dear.'

Tatyana Borisovna smiled slyly.

'I su-u-ffer, I su-u-ffer,' bawled her nephew in the next room.

'That's enough, Andrei.'

'Parting makes the soul despo-o-ond,' continued the ir-repressible singer.

Tatyana Borisovna shook her head. 'Oh, these artists!'

A year has passed since then. Belovzorov is still living with his aunt and still preparing to move to Petersburg. In the country he has grown as fat as he is tall. His aunt – would you believe it? – dotes on him, and girls of the neighbourhood fall in love with him . . .

Many of her former acquaintances have stopped visiting Tatyana Borisovna.

Death

I HAVE a young neighbour, a farmer and a sportsman. One
fine July morning I rode over to see him with the suggestion that we should go out together after blackcock. He agreed.
'Only,' he said, 'let's go to my bit of brushwood at Zusha; on
the way I'll have a look at Chapligino; my oak-wood, d'you
know? It's being felled.' 'Let's do that,' I said. He ordered his
horse to be saddled, put on a green coat with brass buttons
shaped like a boar's head, a game-bag with a woolwork pattern,
and a silver flask, shouldered a new French gun, took a self-
satisfied turn in front of the looking-glass and called to his dog
Esperance, which had been given to him by a cousin, an old
maid with an excellent heart but without a hair on her head.
We set out. My neighbour took with him his constable Arkhip,
a stout, thick-set peasant with a square face and the
pronounced cheek-bones of prehistoric man, also his
newly-appointed agent, a youth of nineteen from the Baltic
provinces, thin, fair, short-sighted, with sloping shoulders, by
name Mr. Gottlieb von der Kock. My neighbour himself had
only recently come into possession of his property. He had
inherited it from an aunt, Mrs. State-Councillor Kardon-
Kataeva, an extremely fat woman with a habit of groaning
long and plaintively even when in bed. We reached the 'brushwood'. 'Wait for me here in the clearing,' said Ardalion
Mikhailich (my neighbour) to his companions. The German
bowed, dismounted, took a book from his pocket, probably a
novel by Johanna Schopenhauer, and sat down beneath a bush;
Arkhip halted in the sun and never stirred for a whole hour.
We made a circle in the bushes without putting anything up.
Ardalion informed me that he meant to go on into the wood.
Somehow or other, that day, I had no confidence in our luck:
I trailed after him. We went back to the clearing. The German
marked his page, got up, put his book in his pocket and, with

some difficulty, mounted his sorry, dock-tailed hack, which whined and kicked at the slightest touch; Arkhip gave a start, pulled both reins at the same time, clattered his feet and finally set his dazed, downtrodden little nag in motion. Off we went.

I had known Ardalion's wood since my childhood. In company with my French tutor, Monsieur Désiré Fleury, the best-hearted of men (who, incidentally, all but ruined my health by making me drink Leroy's mixture every night), I often used to go to Chapligino. The whole wood consisted of some two or three hundred huge oaks and ash-trees. Their majestic and mighty trunks stood out superbly in black against the translucent, golden green of the hazels and mountain ashes; higher up, they silhouetted themselves gracefully against the clear blue sky and threw out their spreading, knotty branches to make a tent; hawks, merlins and kestrels came whistling past below the motionless tree-tops; spotted woodpeckers tapped sharply on the thick bark; the ringing song of the black thrush came suddenly through the thick foliage, following close on the staccato cry of the oriole; below, in the bushes, robins, siskins and chiff-chaffs chirruped and sang. Chaffinches hopped nimbly about the paths; a white hare stole along the edge of the wood, hopping cautiously, as if on crutches; a red-brown squirrel jumped now and then from tree to tree and sat still all of a sudden, with its tail raised above its head. In the grass beside the tall ant-hills, in the faint shade of the finely-carved bracken leaves, violets and lilies-of-the-valley blossomed, and mushrooms of all kinds – yellow and brown, oak-mushrooms and scarlet fly-agaric – grew there; on the turf, between the spreading bushes, was the bright red of the wild strawberry ... And the shade there was inside the wood! In the sultriest heat, at noon, it was absolute night: stillness, perfume, freshness ... The times I had spent at Chapligino had been happy, and consequently it was with a sad heart, I confess, that I went into this wood I had known so well. The disastrous snowless winter of 1840 had not spared my old friends, the oaks and ashes; parched, stripped, just covered here and there with unhealthy verdure, they towered sadly up above the young trees, which had been planted instead but would never fill their place . . . [1] Some of them, still overgrown with leafage at their base, raised dead shattered branches aloft, as if in protest or despair; on others, from foliage that was still fairly thick, though not so abundant or luxuriant as before, protruded stout, dried-up dead boughs; some had already lost all their bark; others had finally fallen right over and lay rotting on the ground like corpses. Who could have foreseen it – that at Chapligino there would be no shade to be found! Well, I thought, as I looked at the dying trees, I suppose it must be shameful for you and bitter? . . . I remembered the lines of Koltsov:

> *What is there left*
> *Of your lofty eloquence,*
> *Your proud strength,*
> *Your imperial brilliance?*
> *Where is it now,*
> *Your green majesty? . . .*

'How comes it, Ardalion,' I began, 'that these trees weren't felled the year after? Why, they won't fetch a tenth now of what they would have before.'

He merely shrugged his shoulders. 'Ask my aunt; the merchants came, brought the money and pestered her to sell.'

'Mein Gott! Mein Gott!' exclaimed von der Kock at every step. 'Petty! Petty!'

'How d'you mean, petty?' remarked my neighbour with a smile.

'That's to say, vot a petty, vot a shame, that's vot I meant.'

---

1 In 1840, in spite of the severest frost, no snow fell until the very end of December; vegetation froze to death, and many fine oak-woods were ruined, in this pitiless winter. It is difficult to replace them: the productive power of the earth is visibly failing; on the plots of ground that have been 'lustrated' (walked round with icons), instead of the noble trees that stood there before, birches and aspens are growing like weeds; we have not yet learnt how to plant trees scientifically. – *Author*.

His compassion was especially aroused by the oaks that lay on the ground – and he was right: any miller would have paid a good price for them. Meanwhile the constable Arkhip preserved an imperturbable calm and showed no sign of grief. On the contrary, it was even with a certain satisfaction that he jumped over them and flicked them with his whip.

We were emerging on to the scene of the felling, when suddenly, immediately after the crash of a falling tree, there was a cry and the sound of voices, and a few minutes later a young peasant, pale and shock-headed, came dashing out of the thicket towards us.

'What's the matter? Where are you off to?' Ardalion asked him.

He stopped at once.

'Oh, Ardalion Mikhailich, sir, something terrible!'

'What?'

'Maxim's been caught under a tree.'

'How so? . . . D'you mean Maxim the contractor?'

'Yes, sir. We were felling an ash and he was standing watching . . . He stood and stood, then off he went to the well to get some water; you see, he was thirsty. Then suddenly the ash comes toppling down just where he is. We shout to him, "Run, run, run." He ought to have dodged to one side, but he went and ran straight ahead . . . he must have been scared. The ash fairly hid him under its top branches. Why it fell so soon, the Lord alone knows. Maybe its heart was rotten.'

'And it hit Maxim?'

'Yes, sir.'

'Killed him?'

'No, sir, he's still alive – but then his legs and arms are crushed. I was running to Seliverstich to get a doctor.'

Ardalion ordered the constable to gallop to Seliverstich village, and set off himself at a vigorous trot towards the clearing . . . I followed him.

We found poor Maxim on the ground. Some half a dozen peasants were standing round him. We dismounted. There was scarcely a groan from him; now and then he opened his eyes

wide, looked round as if in astonishment, and bit a bloodless lip
... His chin trembled, his hair was plastered to his brow, his
chest rose irregularly: he was dying. The gentle shade of a
young lime-tree fell peacefully across his face.

We bent over him. He recognized Ardalion.

'Sir,' he began indistinctly, 'tell them ... priest ... to
send ... the Lord ... punished me ... my legs and arms, all
broken ... to-day ... Sunday ... and I ... and I ... you see ... I
didn't give the lads the day off.'

He was silent. His breath came with difficulty. 'My
money ... give it ... my wife ... when my debts are paid ...
Onisim knows what I owe ... and who to ...'

'We have sent for the doctor, Maxim,' said my neighbour.
'You may live yet.'

He tried to open his eyes, and raised his eyebrows and
eyelids with an effort.

'No, I'm dying ... Here ... here it comes, here it is,
here ... Forgive me, lads, for anything ...'

'God will forgive you, Maxim Andreich,' said the peasants
in gruff unison, and they took off their caps. 'You forgive us.'

All of a sudden he gave a desperate jerk of his head, and a
mournful heave of his chest, then sank back again.

'But it isn't right for him to die here,' exclaimed Ardalion.
'Get the mat out of the cart, lads, and let's carry him to the
infirmary.'

Two men ran off to the cart.

'From Efim ... at Sychovo ...' whispered the dying man.
'I bought a horse yesterday ... I paid a deposit ... so the horse
is mine ... my wife to have it too ...'

They began to move him on to the mat ... he shuddered all
over, like a shot bird, then straightened himself out ...

'He's dead,' murmured the peasants.

We mounted our horses in silence and rode away.

Poor Maxim's death plunged me in reflection. Strange how
death takes the Russian peasant! His state of mind at his last hour
cannot be called indifference or dull-wittedness; he dies as if he
were going through a ceremony: coldly, and with simplicity.

Some years ago, on the land of another neighbour of mine, a peasant was badly burnt in a drying-shed. (Indeed he might have been left there, if a passing townsman hadn't pulled him out, more dead than alive: he had plunged into a cask of water, then taken a run at the door and broken it in with the roof above it ablaze.) I visited the peasant in his cabin. Inside it was dark, stuffy. I asked where the patient was. 'There he is, sir, on the stove-bench,' answered a dejected-looking woman, in a sing-song voice. I went across, and found the peasant lying covered with a sheepskin and breathing heavily. 'Well, how do you feel?' The sick man fidgeted above the stove, tried to rise, all injured as he was and at the point of death. 'Lie down, lie down . . . Well, how are you?' 'Pretty bad,' he said. 'D'you feel pain?' Silence. 'Is there anything you want?' Silence. 'Shall I send you some tea, eh?' 'I don't want it.' I left him and sat down on a bench. I sat for a quarter of an hour, half an hour – and, in the cabin, the silence of the tomb. In a corner, at a table under the icons, a little girl of five was hiding and munching bread. Now and then her mother would scold her. In the passage there were comings and goings, knockings, voices: a brother's wife was chopping a cabbage. 'Hey, Axinya!' said the patient at last. 'What?' 'Give me some kvass.' Axinya gave him some kvass. More silence. I asked in a whisper if he had had communion. 'Yes.' Well, then, everything was in order: he was waiting for death and that was all there was to it. I could bear it no longer and left . . .

Another time, I remember, I looked in at the village infirmary of Krasnogore to see my friend Kapiton, the medical orderly, who was a keen sportsman.

The infirmary consisted of what had been an outlying wing of the manor house; the lady herself had arranged it, that's to say, she had ordered that upon the door should be stuck up a blue board with the inscription in white letters 'Infirmary of Krasnogore', and had herself given Kapiton a handsome album to record the names of his patients. On the first page of this album, one of the good lady's spongers and toadies had written the following lines:

Dans ces beaux lieux, où règne l'allégresse,
Ce temple fut ouvert par la Beauté;
De vos seigneurs admirez la tendresse,
Bons habitants de Krasnogorié!

and another gentleman had added below:

Et moi aussi j'aime la nature!
JEAN KOBYLIATNIKOFF.

The orderly had bought six beds at his own expense and, wishing himself luck, had launched out on his career of healing. Besides himself, the hospital staff consisted of two: Pavel the wood-carver, who was subject to fits of madness, and a peasant-woman named Melikitrisa, who had a shrivelled arm and occupied the position of cook. Both of them prepared medicines and dried herbs and made infusions from them; they also calmed patients with the fever; the mad wood-carver had a surly appearance and was sparing of words; at night he sang a song about 'Beauteous Venus', and approached every passer-by with the request that he should be allowed to marry a girl named Malanya, who had been dead for some time. The woman with the shrivelled arm used to beat him and make him take care of the turkeys. Well, one day I was sitting with Kapiton, the orderly. We had started talking about our last shoot, when suddenly a cart drove into the yard, harnessed to an unusually stout grey horse of the sort that only millers possess. In the cart sat a sturdy peasant in a new overcoat, with a pepper-and-salt beard. 'Hey, Vasily Dmitrich,' called Kapiton from the window, 'welcome to you ... It's the miller from Lyubovshin,' he whispered to me. With a groan, the peasant climbed down from the cart, came into the orderly's room, looked for the icon and crossed himself. 'Well, Vasily Dmitrich, what's the news? Why, you must be poorly: your face is off-colour.' 'Yes, Kapiton Timofeich, I've got something wrong.' 'What's the matter?' 'Here's the matter, Kapiton Timofeich. The other day I bought some grindstones in the town; well, I brought them home, and, as I was getting them out of the cart, I must have strained myself or something, there was a sort of "plonk" in my innards as if something had torn... And, ever since, I've been poorly all the time. To-day it's pretty bad.' 'H'm,' said Kapiton, and took a pinch of snuff. 'It must be rupture. Is it long since it took you that way?' 'Ten days.' 'Ten?' The orderly drew in a long breath through his teeth and shook his head. 'Let me feel you... Well, Vasily Dmitrich,' he said at last, 'I'm sorry for you with all my heart, but you're in a bad way; you're ill, beyond a joke; you'd better stay here. I'll do my best for you, but I don't promise anything.' 'Is it as bad as that?' murmured the miller in astonishment. 'Yes, Vasily Dmitrich, it's bad; if you'd come to me two days earlier, it would have been nothing at all, just a hand's turn; but now you've got inflammation, that's the trouble; before you've time to look, it'll have turned to gangrene.' 'But it can't be, Kapiton Timofeich!' 'But I tell you it is.' 'But how can it be?' The orderly shrugged his shoulders. 'And am I going to die from this sort of nonsense?' 'That, I didn't say... but just you stay here.' The peasant thought and thought, looked at the floor, then glanced at us, scratched the back of his head and reached for his cap. 'Where are you off to, Vasily Dmitrich?' 'Where to? Why, home of course, if I'm as bad as that. I must put things in order, if that's how it is.' 'But you'll bring on the worst, Vasily Dmitrich, for goodness' sake; why, even as it is, I can't think how you got here. Stay.' 'No, Kapiton Timofeich, my friend, if I've got to die, I'll die at home; if I die here, God knows what will happen at home.' 'It's too early yet to say how it will go, Vasily Dmitrich... Of course there's danger, great danger, and no denying it, but that's all the more reason for your staying.' The peasant shook his head. 'No, Kapiton Timofeich, I won't stay... just you prescribe me a little medicine.' 'Medicine alone won't help you.' 'I'm not staying, I tell you.' 'Well, do as you like, only don't blame me afterwards!'

The orderly tore a page from the album and, after writing out a prescription, gave certain further instructions. The peasant took the paper, gave Kapiton half a rouble, left the room and took his place in the cart. 'Well, good-bye, Kapiton Timo-feich, don't hold it against me, and don't forget the orphans, if anything...' 'Hey, Vasily, stay here!' The peasant simply jerked his head, flicked his horses with the reins and drove out of the yard. I went into the road and looked after him. The road was muddy and full of pot-holes; the miller was driving carefully, unhurriedly, guiding his horse with skill, exchanging greetings with passers-by. Three days later he was dead.

Yes, people die strangely in Russia. I can call many such cases to mind. I remember my old friend Avenir Sorokoümov, the student who never finished his studies – the best and noblest of men. I can see again his greenish, consumptive face, his thin blond hair, his gentle smile, his look of enthu-siasm, his long limbs; I can hear his soft sweet voice. He lived with a landowner in Great Russia named Gur Krupyanikov, taught his children, Fofa and Zyozya, reading and writing in Russian, geography and history, patiently bore the heavy jokes of Gur Krupyanikov himself and the coarse familiarities of the butler and the vulgar pranks of the naughty little boys; with a bitter smile, but without a murmur, he carried out the capri-cious demands of his bored lady; then the relief, the sheer bliss, when, after dinner, finished at last with all duties and occupa-tions, he could sit down before the window and reflectively smoke a pipe, or dip avidly into some mutilated, greasy copy of a bulky journal, brought from town by the surveyor, another homeless wretch like himself! How he loved all kinds of poems and stories; how easily tears started in his eyes; how gaily he laughed; how sincerely he loved his fellows; how penetrated with noble sympathy for everything good and beautiful was that pure and youthful soul! The truth must out: no special brilliance was his; nature had endowed him with neither memory nor concentration; at the University he passed for one of the worst students; at lectures he slept, at examinations he preserved a solemn silence; but whose were the eyes that shone with joy, whose the breath that had a catch in it, at the success or triumph of a comrade? Avenir's ... Who believed blindly in the high calling of his friends? Who would extol them with pride and defend them with ferocity? Who knew no envy, no self-love? Who would sacrifice himself without a thought of his own interests? Who would eagerly take second place after people unworthy to undo the latchet of his shoes? ... Always our good Avenir! I remember how broken-heartedly he took leave of his friends as he drove away on his 'contract'; what evil forebodings beset him ... And with reason: in the country he fared ill; in the country there was no one for him to listen to with reverence, no one to admire, no one to love ... The gentry, boors and cultivated ones alike, treated him as a tutor, some roughly, others with indifference. Indeed he was not an impressive figure; shy, blushing, sweating, stammering ... Even his health got no benefit from the country air; the poor fellow wasted away like a candle. True, his little room opened on to the garden; cherries, apple-trees and limes scattered over his table, his ink-pot, his books, their light blossoms; on the wall hung a little blue silk cushion for his watch, given to him at the moment of parting by a kind and sensitive German governess with fair hair and blue eyes; now and then an old friend came out to see him from Moscow and delighted him with verses composed by others or even by himself; but the loneliness, the intolerable slavery of the tutor's condition, the impossibility of freeing himself from it, the endless autumns and winters, the persistent malady ... Poor, poor Avenir!

I visited Sorokoúmov not long before his death. He was already practically unable to walk. The landowner Gur Krupyanikov did not turn him out of his house, but stopped paying his wages, and Zyozya was given another tutor. Fofa had been sent off to the Corps of Cadets. Avenir was sitting by the window in an old armchair of Voltairean design. It was a wonderful day. The bright autumn sky was gay and blue above a dark-brown wall of bare lime-trees, on which, here and there, the last bright-gold leaves stirred and fluttered. The frost-pierced earth was sweating and thawing in the sun; its slanting, ruddy rays fell lightly on the pale grass; a faint crackling could be heard in the air; workers' voices came loud and

clear from the garden. Avenir wore an old Bokhara robe; a
green neckerchief threw a corpse-like tinge over his terribly
emaciated face. He was very glad to see me, held out his hand,
talked and coughed. I made him collect himself and sat down
beside him ... On Avenir's knees lay a notebook containing
Koltsov's poems, carefully written out; he tapped it, with a
smile. 'There's a poet for you!' he murmured, smothering
a cough with an effort and beginning to recite in a scarcely
audible voice:

> *Is the falcon's*
> *Pinion bound?*
> *Or his journeying*
> *Hedged around?*

I stopped him: it was against doctor's orders for him to talk
too long. I knew how to please him. Sorokoúmov had never
'kept up', as they say, with science, but he liked hearing, as he
put it, 'how far our great minds have got'. He would take a
friend aside into a corner and begin cross-examining him: he
would listen, he would be astonished, he would believe every
word, and repeat it all after his friend. German philosophy
interested him especially. I began talking to him about Hegel.
(It is a story of days long since, as you can see.) Avenir nodded
his head approvingly, raised his eyebrows, smiled, whispered:
'I see, I see! ... Oh, good, good!' I confess that the child-like
curiosity of this poor wretch, dying homeless and abandoned,
touched me to tears. I should observe that Avenir, unlike
consumptives in general, had no sort of illusions about his
illness ... and yet he never sighed, showed no sign of distress,
never even alluded to his condition ...

After mustering his strength, he began to talk of Moscow,
his friends, Pushkin, the theatre, Russian literature; he mentioned our carouses, the heated discussions of our circle, and
pronounced with regret the names of two or three of our
friends who had died.

'D'you remember Dasha?' he added at last. 'There was a
heart of solid gold! and how she loved me! ... What's

become of her now? I suppose the poor girl has faded and pined away?'

I had not the heart to disillusion the sick man – and indeed, why should he know that his Dasha was now broader than she was long, went around with merchants, with the brothers Kondrachkov, that she powdered and rouged herself and had become a squeaking scold. And yet, I thought, looking at his exhausted face, is it impossible to get him out of here? It may be that there is still a chance of moving him ... But Avenir didn't allow me to finish my suggestion.

'No, thank you, my friend,' he said. 'It's all the same to me where I die. I shan't see the winter ... Why upset people to no purpose? I've got used to this house! It's true that the family here ...'

'Nasty, eh?' I took him up.

'No, not nasty; just wooden. But I can't complain about them. There are neighbours: the landowner Kasatkin has a daughter, a cultivated, charming, delightful girl ... not proud ...'

Sorokoümov had another coughing fit.

'I shouldn't mind at all,' he went on, when he had got his breath, 'if only they allowed me to smoke my pipe ... But I won't die without managing to smoke one first,' he added with a cunning wink. 'Praise be to God, I've lived my time, I've known some good people ...'

'You might write to your family,' I interrupted him.

'What for? Help – they won't give it; if I die – they'll find out. So there's nothing more to be said about it. No, tell me what you saw when you were abroad.'

I began to tell him. He fairly drank my words in. Towards evening I left, and ten days later I got the following letter from Mr. Krupyanikov.

'I have the honour, my dear Sir, to advise you hereby that your friend, the student who lived in my house, Mr. Avenir Sorokoümov, passed away three days ago at 3 o'clock in the afternoon and that to-day he was buried at my expense in my parish church. He asked me to forward to you the enclosed books and notebooks. He left 22½ roubles, which, with his other effects, are being duly transmitted to his relatives. Your friend was fully conscious when he passed away and, I may also say, fully insensible, for he showed no signs of regret, even when my whole family said good-bye to him. My wife Kleopatra Alexandrovna sends you her regards. The death of your friend could not fail to have its effect on her nerves; for my own part, I am, thank God, in good health, and have the honour to remain,

Your most humble Servant,

G. KRUPYANIKOV.'

Many more instances still come to mind, but I cannot relate them all. I will confine myself to one.

I was present at the death of an old lady, the wife of a landowner. The priest had begun to read the last rites over her, when suddenly he noticed that the sick woman was really expiring and hurriedly gave her the cross. The lady moved back in displeasure. 'Why so quick, Father?' she said, with faltering tongue. 'There's plenty of time...' She kissed the cross, put her hand under the pillow, and – drew her last breath. Under the pillow lay a silver rouble: she had wanted to pay the priest for her own last rites...

Yes, death takes the Russian strangely!

The Singers

THE small village of Kolotovka, which once belonged to a lady known in the neighbourhood as Fidget from her bold and spirited ways (her real name is not recorded) but is now owned by some German or other from Petersburg, lies on the slope of a bare hill, cleft from top to bottom by a fearsome ravine, which, yawning like an abyss, winds its hollow, eroded way along the very middle of the village street and, worse than any river (for a river could at least be bridged), divides the unfortunate hamlet into two. A few lean willows droop timidly along its sandy sides; at the bottom, which is dry and copper-yellow, lie huge flagstones of shale. A cheerless sight, there's no denying – but nevertheless the road to Kolotovka is well-known to all the people of the neighbourhood: they use it frequently and as a matter of course.

Right at the top of the ravine, a few paces off the spot where it begins as a narrow crevice, stands a small square cabin, on its own, apart from the others. It is thatched with straw and has a chimney; a single window, like a watchful eye, looks towards the ravine, and on winter evenings, lit up from within, can be seen from afar through the dull frost-haze and, for many a peasant on his way, shines out like a guiding star. Over the door of the cabin is nailed a little blue board; the cabin is a pot-house, and goes by the name of the 'Snug Nook'. It is a pot-house where in all probability drinks are sold no cheaper than the fixed price, but it is much better attended than any other establishment of the same sort in the neighbourhood. The reason for this is the tapster, Nikolai Ivanich.

Nikolai Ivanich was once a lithe, curly-headed, ruddy peasant lad, but is now an extremely stout, already grizzled man, with a face deep in fat, eyes of a sly benevolence, and a greasy forehead criss-crossed with a web of wrinkles. He has lived at Kolotovka for more than twenty years. Nikolai is a man of sagacity and resource, as most tapsters are. Without any special amiability or talkativeness, he has the knack of attracting and holding customers, who somehow find it entertaining to sit in front of his counter, under the calm, hospitable, but watchful eye of their phlegmatic host. He has plenty of common sense; he is well-acquainted with the ways of landowner, peasant and townsman; in difficult situations he can give shrewd advice, but, like the cautious egoist that he is, he prefers to stay on the sideline and goes no further than a vague hint, uttered as if without the least purpose, to guide his clients – and then only his favourite clients – in the way of truth. He knows what he is talking about on every subject of importance or interest to the Russian male: horses and cattle, timber, bricks, crockery, textiles and leather, singing and dancing. When he has no custom, he is in the habit of sitting like a sack on the ground in front of the door of his cabin, his thin legs tucked up beneath him, swapping pleasantries with every passer-by. He has seen plenty in his time, has outlived more than a dozen of the lesser gentry who used to look in on him for a drop of 'distilled', knows everything that happens for a hundred versts around, never lets on, never shows so much as in his look that he knows what even the most penetrating police officer fails to suspect. He simply keeps mum, chuckles, and busies himself with the glasses. The neighbours respect him deeply: His Excellency Mr. Shcherepetenko, the leading magnate of the district, bows to him affably every time he passes his abode. Nikolai Ivanich is a man of influence: he forced a well-known horse-thief to return a horse stolen from someone of his acquaintance; he made the peasants of a neighbouring village listen to reason when they had refused to accept a new factor, and so on. Incidentally, it mustn't be supposed that he did this from love of fair play, from any zeal for his neighbours' interest; no, he is simply at pains to avert anything that might in any way disturb his own peace. Nikolai Ivanich is married and has children. His wife, a brisk, sharp-nosed, quick-eyed townswoman, has lately put on a good deal of weight, just like her husband. He relies on her absolutely, and the money is locked up in her charge. The noisily-drunk hold her in awe; she dislikes them; there is no profit from them, only a lot of noise; the silent and sullen ones are closer to her heart. Nikolai's children are still small. The first ones all died, but the survivors resemble their parents; it is a pleasure to look at these healthy children with their clever little faces.

It was an unbearably sultry July day, when I trudged slowly, accompanied by my dog, up the Kolotovka ravine in the direction of the 'Snug Nook' pot-house. The sun was blazing away in the sky with a kind of fury; it was mercilessly, bakingly hot; the air was absolutely saturated with choking dust. Glossy rooks and crows, with gaping beaks, looked piteously at the passer-by, as if to beg his sympathy; only the sparrows were undistressed and, fluffing out their feathers, twittered and scuffled about the fences even more actively than usual, or flew up from the dusty road in a flock, or hovered in grey clouds over the green hemp-yards. I was tortured by thirst. There was no water at hand: at Kolotovka, as in many other steppe-villages, in the absence of springs and wells, the peasants drink a sort of liquid filth from a pond . . . But who would give the name of water to this repulsive draught? I had it in mind to ask Nikolai Ivanich for a glass of beer or kvass.

It has to be admitted that at no season of the year does Kolotovka present a cheering spectacle; but it arouses a particularly mournful emotion when the blazing sun of July rains its pitiless rays on the tumbledown brown roofs, the deep ravine, the parched, dusty common-land, on which some thin, long-legged chickens are roaming despondently, and the shack of grey aspenwood with holes for windows, a remnant of the former manor house, grown over with nettles, weeds and wormwood, and the pond, covered with goose-feathers, black, molten-looking, fringed with half-dried mud, and the sideways listing dam, near which, on the fine-ground, cinder-like earth, sheep, breathless and sneezing from the heat, crowd lugubriously together and with a dismal patience hang their heads as low as can be, as if waiting for the moment when the unbearable sultriness will finally pass. With exhausted steps I was at last nearing Nikolai Ivanich's place, exciting in children the usual amazement, expressed in intense and inane stares, and in dogs the usual indignation, voiced in such hoarse and savage barking that all their insides seemed to be torn loose, afterwards subsiding into a fit of coughing and choking, when suddenly, on the threshold of the pot-house, there appeared a tall man, capless, in a frieze overcoat held below the waist with a blue belt. He had the look of a house-serf; thick grey hair burst out untidily above his dry wrinkled face. He was calling somebody and making vigorous gestures with his arms, which were clearly swinging out much farther than he intended. It was evident that he had already had a drop.

'Come on, come *on*!' he stuttered, raising his thick eyebrows with an effort. 'Come on, Blinker, come on! Why, man, you're simply crawling. It isn't right, man. They're waiting for you, and you're just crawling . . . Come on!'

'All right, all right,' came a jarring voice, and, from behind the cabin to the right, a short, stout, lame fellow appeared. He wore quite a neat cloth coat, with only one sleeve on; a high, pointed hat, rammed straight down over his brows, gave his podgy, round face a sly, mocking look. His little yellow eyes fairly darted around; a contained, forced smile never left his thin lips, and his long sharp nose stuck jauntily out ahead like a rudder. 'I'm coming, my friend,' he went on, limping in the direction of the drinking establishment. 'What are you calling me for? . . . Who's waiting for me?'

'What am I calling you for?' rejoined the man in the frieze coat, reproachfully. 'You're a strange one, Blinker: you're called to the pot-house, and yet you ask: what for? There's all kind of good folk waiting for you: Yasha the Turk, and Wild Master, and the huckster from Zhizdra. Yasha and the huckster have made a bet: they've wagered a quart of beer to see which wins, that is, sings best . . . d'you see?'

'Yasha's going to sing?' said the man nicknamed Blinker, with animation. 'You're not lying, Muddlehead?'

'I'm not,' answered Muddlehead with dignity. 'It's you that's the liar. Of course he's going to sing, if he's made a bet, you ladybird, you twister, you, Blinker!'

'Well, let's go, you ninny,' rejoined Blinker.

'Well, kiss me at least, joy of my heart,' stammered Muddlehead, flinging his arms out wide.

'You great milk-sop,' replied Blinker, contemptuously elbowing him aside, and they both stooped and went in through the low doorway. The conversation I'd heard excited my keen curiosity. More than once rumours had reached me of Yasha the Turk, as being the best singer in the neighbourhood, and now an opportunity had suddenly presented itself to hear him in competition with another master. I quickened my pace and entered the establishment.

Probably not many of my readers have had occasion to look inside a country pot-house – but we sportsmen, there's nowhere we don't go. The arrangement of these pot-houses is remarkably simple. They usually consist of a dark entrance-passage and a room divided in two by a partition, behind which none of the customers has the right to go. Cut in the partition, above a broad oak table, is a large longitudinal aperture. On this table or counter the drink is sold. Sealed flasks of different measures stand in a row on shelves immediately opposite the aperture. In the front part of the cabin, the part at the disposal of customers, are benches, two or three empty barrels, and a corner table. Country pot-houses are for the most part pretty dark and you hardly ever see on their log walls any of those brightly-coloured popular prints without which the ordinary peasant's cabin is seldom complete.

When I went into the 'Snug Nook' pot-house a fairly numerous company was already assembled there.

Behind the counter, suitably enough, and filling almost the whole width of the aperture, stood Nikolai Ivanich. In a gay cotton shirt, with an indolent smile on his chubby cheeks, he was pouring out two glasses of spirits with his podgy white hand for the two friends, Blinker and Muddlehead, who had just come in; behind him, in the corner near the window, could be seen his sharp-eyed wife. In the middle of the room stood Yasha the Turk, a lean, well-built man of twenty-three, dressed in a long-skirted blue nankeen coat. He had the appearance of a dashing young mechanic and looked as if his health was nothing to boast about. His sunken cheeks, great, restless grey eyes, straight nose with its fine, mobile nostrils, his wide-domed forehead with the pale blond curls thrust back from it, his bold but handsome and expressive lips – his whole face revealed an impressionable, passionate nature. He was in great excitement, blinking, breathing irregularly, his hands trembling as if with the fever – and indeed he had a fever, that sudden trembling fever which is so familiar to all who speak or sing in public. Beside him stood a man of about forty, broad-shouldered, with broad cheek-bones, and a low forehead, narrow Tartar eyes, a short flat nose, a square chin, and black, shiny, bristle-like hair. The expression of his face, which was swarthy with a leaden undertone, and especially of his full lips, might almost have been called ferocious if it had not been so calmly reflective. He hardly stirred, just looked slowly around like an ox from below the yoke. He wore a sort of shabby frock-coat with smooth copper buttons; an old black silk handkerchief swathed his massive neck. He was nicknamed 'Wild Master'. Right in front of him, on the bench below the icons, sat Yasha's competitor, the huckster from Zhizdra: a short, sturdy man of about thirty, pock-marked and curly-headed, with a blunt, upturned nose, lively brown eyes and a sparse beard. He was looking briskly round, with his hands tucked up beneath him, carelessly swinging and stamping his feet, which were clad in dandified boots with trimmings. He wore a thin new overcoat of grey cloth with a velvet collar, against which a strip of scarlet shirt, buttoned up tightly round his throat, stood out sharply. At a table in the opposite corner, to the right of the door, sat a peasant in a threadbare, greyish coat with an enormous hole at the shoulder. The sunlight fell in a fine, yellowish stream through the dusty panes of the two small windows and seemed unable to dispel the normal darkness of the room: every object was sparsely and patchily illuminated. Nevertheless, it was almost cool in the room and the feeling of stuffiness and sultriness fell from my shoulders like a burden the moment I crossed the threshold.

My arrival, I could see, at first rather confused Nikolai Ivanich's guests; but, observing that he bowed to me as to an acquaintance, they set their minds at rest and paid me no more attention. I ordered some beer and sat down in the corner next to the peasant in the torn coat.

'Well, then,' sang out Muddlehead all of a sudden, after drinking a glass at one gulp, and accompanying his exclamation with those strange gestures of the arms without which he evidently never uttered a word. 'What are we waiting for? It's time to begin, eh, Yasha?'

'Time to begin,' repeated Nikolai Ivanich with approbation.

'Let's begin, if you like,' said the huckster coolly, with a self-confident smile. 'I'm ready.'

'So am I,' pronounced Yasha excitedly.

'Well, begin, lads, begin,' squeaked Blinker.

But notwithstanding this unanimously-expressed wish, neither of them did begin; the huckster did not even rise from his bench – it was as if everyone was waiting for something to happen.

'Begin,' said Wild Master sharply and with displeasure.

Yasha shivered. The huckster got up, tightened his belt and cleared his throat.

'Who's to begin?' he asked, with a slight change of voice, addressing himself to Wild Master, who was still standing motionless in the middle of the room, his thick legs widely planted, his powerful arms thrust almost to the elbow into the pockets of his trousers.

'You, huckster, you,' murmured Muddlehead; 'you, lad.'

Wild Master gave him a sidelong look. Muddlehead squeaked faintly, faltered, looked away at the ceiling, wriggled his shoulders and fell silent.

'Draw for it,' pronounced Wild Master with deliberation, 'and set the quart out on the counter.'

Nikolai stooped, groaned, fetched up a quart jug from the floor and set it on the table.

Wild Master looked at Yasha and said: 'Well!'

Yasha rummaged in his pockets, found a two-copeck piece and marked it with his teeth. The huckster brought a new leather purse out from the skirt of his coat, slowly undid the strings, poured out a lot of small change into his hand and chose a new two-copeck piece. Muddlehead held out his battered hat with its loose and crumpled peak: Yasha and the huckster threw their coins into it.

'You choose,' said Wild Master to Blinker.

Blinker grinned with self-satisfaction, took the hat in both hands and began to shake it up.

For a moment deep silence reigned; the coins chinked faintly against each other. I looked round attentively: every face expressed strained anticipation; even Wild Master had screwed up his eyes; even my neighbour, the peasant in the torn coat, had stuck out his head inquisitively. Blinker put his hand into the hat and drew out the huckster's coin: there was a general sigh. Yasha flushed, and the huckster passed his hand through his hair.

'I *said* it was you,' exclaimed Muddlehead, 'I said so.'

'Now, now, don't get all of a flutter,' observed Wild Master contemptuously. 'Begin,' he continued, nodding to the huckster.

'What shall I sing?' asked the huckster, with rising excitement.

'Whatever you like, of course,' rejoined Nikolai Ivanich, slowly folding his arms on his chest. 'We can't tell you what to choose. Sing what you like; only sing it well; and then we'll judge as our conscience tells us.'

'That's right – as our conscience tells us,' repeated Muddlehead, and he licked the rim of his empty glass.

'Just let me clear my throat,' said the huckster, fingering the collar of his coat.

'Now, don't waste time – begin!' said Wild Master decisively, and he looked down.

The huckster thought for a moment, shook his head and set off. Yasha stared at him with all his eyes...

But before I proceed to describe the contest itself, it may be as well to say a few words about each of the personages in my story. The ways of some of them were already known to me when I met them in the 'Snug Nook' pot-house; I found out about the rest subsequently.

To begin with Muddlehead. His real name was Evgraf Ivanov; but no one in the neighbourhood ever called him anything but Muddlehead, and he used the nickname in speaking of himself, so well did it fit him. And indeed it could not have been better suited to his insignificant, perpetually-worried expression. He was an unmarried, drunken house-serf, whose master had long since despaired of him and who, having no duties and receiving not a farthing's wages, nevertheless found means of making merry every day at someone else's expense. He had many acquaintances who treated him to drinks and to tea, though they couldn't have said why, because, so far from being amusing in company, he fairly disgusted everyone with his witless chatter, his unbearable importunity, his feverish movements and his ceaseless unnatural laughter. He could neither sing nor dance; from birth he had never made a clever remark nor even a sensible one; he just muddled along and told any fib that came into his head – a regular Muddle-head! And, with it all, there wasn't a single drinking party for forty versts around at which his spindle-shanked figure failed to turn up among the guests, so used to him had people become, and so tolerant of his presence, as of an unavoidable mishap. True, they treated him contemptuously, but it was Wild Master alone who could put a curb on his crazy moods.

Blinker never left Muddlehead's side. He too was well-served by his nickname, although he didn't blink more than anyone else; but it is a plain truth that the Russians are past-masters at giving nicknames. In spite of my efforts to trace his past in every detail, I found – and so, probably, did many others – that there were dark passages in his career, places which, to use a bookish expression, were veiled in a thick mist of obscurity. I discovered only that he had once been coachman to an old, childless lady, had run away with the troika entrusted to his care, disappeared for a whole year, then, doubtless convinced by experience of the drawbacks and miseries of the vagrant's life, returned, now lame, thrown himself at his mistress's feet and, having expiated his offence by several years of exemplary conduct, had gradually won his way back into her favour, had eventually earned her full confidence and been promoted to the post of clerk; that on the lady's death he had somehow or other acquired his freedom, registered as a burgess, begun leasing melon-gardens from the neighbours, grown rich and now lived in clover. He was a man of experience, with his head well screwed on, neither bad nor good, but calculating, rather; a sly dog who understood people and knew how to make use of them. He was cautious and enterprising at the same time, like a fox; chattered like an old crone, never gave himself away, made everybody else speak their mind. What is more, he never posed as a simpleton, as some of the sly ones of his kind do; indeed, pretence could not have come easily to him. I have never seen more penetrating, shrewder eyes than his tiny, cunning 'peepers'.[1] They never simply looked, they were always searching and spying. Sometimes Blinker would spend whole weeks reflecting on some apparently simple enterprise, then suddenly resolve on a desperately daring course, and you would think he'd break his neck over it . . . you would look again – and it would have come off perfectly, smooth as a knife through butter. He was lucky, believed in his luck and in omens. In general, he was highly superstitious. He was not liked, because he was not in the least interested in others, but he was respected. His family consisted of one small son, whom he fairly adored, and who, brought up by such a father, would probably go far. 'Little Blinker's the spit of his father,' the old men were already saying of him in low voices, as they sat on the

---

1 The people of Orel call eyes 'peepers' in the same way as they call a mouth a 'gobbler'. – *Author*.

mounds of earth outside their cabins and gossiped on summer evenings; and they all understood what that meant, and didn't need to say more.

Of Yasha the Turk and the huckster there is not much to be said. Yasha, nicknamed the Turk, because he was indeed the offspring of a captured Turkish woman, was at heart an artist in all senses of the word, but by vocation a dipper in a merchant's paper-mill. As for the huckster, whose lot, I confess, remains unknown to me, he struck me as a smart, resourceful townsman. Of Wild Master, however, it is worth speaking in rather greater detail.

The first impression his appearance gave was one of rude, ponderous, irresistible force. He was clumsily built, 'piled-on', as we say in our part of the country, but he fairly radiated irrepressible vitality, and, strangely enough, his bearish figure was not without a certain individual grace, which proceeded perhaps from a completely serene confidence in his own strength. It was difficult to determine at first glance to what condition of life this Hercules belonged. He resembled neither servant nor townsman, neither the impoverished scrivener living in retirement nor the ruined, horse-fancying, quarrel-picking member of the smaller landowning gentry. He was something absolutely special. No one knew whence he had descended on our district; it was said that he came of free-holding stock and had previously been in Government service somewhere or other, but nothing certain was known of this; and indeed there was no one to learn it from – certainly not from him himself: a more taciturn, surly fellow never existed. No one could say for sure, either, what he lived on; he plied no trade, visited no one, hardly knew anyone, and yet he had money; not much, it is true, but money, all the same. He conducted himself, not indeed with modesty – there was absolutely nothing modest about him – but quietly; he lived as if he noticed no one around him and definitely wanted nothing from anyone. Wild Master (such was his nickname; his real name was Perevlesov) enjoyed an enormous influence in the whole neighbourhood; he was obeyed instantly and eagerly, although, so far from having any right to give anyone orders, he never made the slightest claim on the obedience of people with whom he came in contact. He spoke – and was obeyed: power always claims its due. He hardly drank, had no dealings with women, and was a passionate lover of singing. There was much that was puzzling about him; it was as if some immense forces were lying, sullenly inactive, within him, as if they knew that, once aroused, once let loose, they must destroy themselves and everything they touched; and I am sadly mistaken if some such explosion had not already occurred in the man's life, so that, taught by experience, and having just escaped destruction, he was now holding himself under an inexorable, iron control. What specially struck me about him was the mixture of a certain inborn, natural ferocity with an equally inborn nobility – a mixture such as I have met in no one else.

So the huckster stepped forward, half-closed his eyes, and began to sing in a very high falsetto. His voice was quite sweet and agreeable, though somewhat husky; he played with it, twirled it about like a toy, with constant downward trills and modulations and constant returns to the top notes, which he held and prolonged with a special effort; he stopped, then suddenly took up his previous tune again with a certain rollicking, arrogant boldness. His transitions were sometimes daring, sometimes rather comical. They would have given a connoisseur great pleasure; they would have shocked a German deeply. He was a Russian *tenore di grazia* or *ténor léger*. He sang a gay dance-tune, whose words, so far as I could catch them among the endless embellishments, extra harmonies and exclamations, were as follows:

> *I'll plough a little ground, my lass,*
> *And sow it with scarlet flowers.*

He sang, and we all listened to him with close attention. He clearly felt that he had to do with experts, and so he fairly climbed out of his skin, as the saying goes. Indeed in our country we are connoisseurs of song, and it is not for nothing that the village of Sergievsk, on the Orel highway, is renowned throughout all Russia for its specially sweet and harmonious singing. The huckster sang on for quite a while, without arousing any marked sympathy in his hearers: he missed the support of a choir. At length, after one particularly successful transition, which made even Wild Master smile, Muddlehead could not contain himself and shouted out his satisfaction. Everybody jumped. Muddlehead and Blinker began taking up the tune, joining in and calling: 'Smartly does it! ... Strike it, rascal! ... Strike it, hold it, you snake! Hold it, go on! Hotter still, you dog, you Herod's son!' and so on. Nikolai Ivanich, behind the counter, waved his head approvingly to right and left. At length Muddlehead began to stamp and scrape his feet and twitch his shoulder, – Yasha's eyes blazed like coals, he trembled all over like a leaf and smiled confusedly. Only Wild Master kept the same countenance and remained motionless as before; but his gaze, fixed on the huckster, softened a little, though his lips kept their contemptuous expression. Encouraged by the signs of general satisfaction, the huckster fairly whirled along and went off into such flourishes, such tongue-clickings and drummings, such wild throat-play, that at length, exhausted, pale, bathed in hot sweat, he threw himself back, let out a last dying note – and his wild outburst was answered in unison by the company. Muddlehead threw himself on his neck and began smothering him with his long bony hands; a flush came over Nikolai's greasy face, and he seemed to have grown younger; Yasha shouted like a madman, 'Bravo, bravo!' – and even my neighbour, the peasant in the torn coat, could bear it no longer and, striking his fist on the table, exclaimed: 'A-ha! good, devil take it – good!' and he spat to one side with determination.

'Well, lad, you've given us a treat!' cried Muddlehead, not letting the fainting huckster out of his embrace. 'A treat, and that's the truth! You've won, lad, you've won! Congratulations – the quart is yours! Yasha can't touch you ... Not by a long chalk, I tell you ... Believe me!' And he again pressed the huckster to his bosom.

'Let him go: let him go, you leech...' said Blinker crossly. 'Let him sit down on the bench here; he's tired, see... You're a fool, lad, a real fool! Why stick to him like a fly-paper?'

'Why, then, let him sit, and I'll drink his health,' rejoined Muddlehead, going to the counter; 'you're paying, lad,' he added, turning to the huckster.

The huckster nodded, sat down on the bench, drew a towel out of his cap and began to wipe his face. Muddlehead drank a glass in thirsty haste, groaned, and took on the sad, pre-occupied look of the serious drinker.

'You sing well, lad, so you do,' observed Nikolai Ivanich amiably. 'Now it's your turn, Yasha: don't be nervous, mind. We'll see who's best, we will... But the huckster sings well, by God he does.'

'Very well, so he does,' observed Nikolai's wife, smiling at Yasha.

'So he does, too!' said my neighbour in a low voice.

'Eh, you Polesyan Thomas!'[1] sang out Muddlehead suddenly and, coming over to the peasant with the hole in the shoulder of his coat, pointed a finger at him, began to jump, and burst into a jarring laugh. 'You Polesyan! What are you doing here? Come on! you doubting Thomas!' he shouted through his laughter.

The poor peasant grew embarrassed and was just about to rise and depart hurriedly, when all of a sudden came the metallic voice of Wild Master:

'What's that unbearable animal up to now?' he said, grinding his teeth.

'Nothing,' muttered Muddlehead, 'nothing... I just...'

'All right then, shut up!' rejoined Wild Master. 'Yasha, begin!'

Yasha took his throat in his hand.

'Why, lad, there's something... why... H'm... I don't rightly know...'

---

[1] The inhabitants of Polesya have a name for incredulity and suspicion. – *Author.*

'Now, that'll do, don't be shy. Shame on you! ... What's the fuss? ... Sing, as God tells you to.'

And Wild Master looked down and waited.

Yasha said nothing, but glanced round and covered his face with his hand. The whole company stared at him with all their eyes, especially the huckster, whose face showed, through its usual self-confidence and the triumph of his success, a faint, involuntary anxiety. He leant against the wall, again tucked his hands in beneath him, but no longer swung his legs. When at last Yasha uncovered his face, it was as pale as a corpse's; his gleaming eyes hardly showed through their lowered lashes. He breathed deeply and began to sing ... His first note was faint and uneven, and came, it seemed, not from his chest, but from somewhere far away, as if it had chanced to fly into the room. This trembling, ringing note had a strange effect on us all; we looked at one another, and Nikolai's wife stood bolt upright. This first note was followed by another, firmer and more prolonged, but still perceptibly trembling, like a string, when, after the sudden pluck of a strong finger, it wavers with a last, quickly-dying thrill: after the second came a third, and, gradually taking on warmth and breadth, the mournful song flowed on its way. '*The paths that lay across the field*,' he sang, and we all had the feeling of something sweet and unearthly. Seldom, I confess, have I heard such a voice: it was somewhat worn and had a sort of cracked ring; at first it had even a certain suggestion of the morbid; but it also held a deep, unsimulated passion, and youth, and strength, and sweetness, and a deliciously-detached note of melancholy. The truthful, fervent Russian soul rang and breathed in it and fairly caught at your heart, caught straight at your Russian heartstrings. The song developed, went flowing on. Yasha was clearly overcome by ecstasy: his shyness had left him, he had surrendered completely to his happiness; his voice trembled no longer – it quivered, but with the scarcely perceptible inner quivering of passion, which pierces like an arrow into the hearer's soul. His voice grew steadily in strength, firmness and breadth. One evening, I remember, at low tide, on the flat sandy shore of the sea, which was roaring away menacingly and dully in the distance, I saw a great white gull: it was sitting, motionless, its silky breast turned towards the scarlet radiance of sunset, now and then slowly stretching its long wings towards the familiar sea, towards the low, blood-red sun; I remembered it as I listened to Yasha. He sang, completely oblivious of his rival and of us all, but clearly sustained, as waves lift a strong swimmer, by our silent passionate attention. He sang, and with every note there floated out something noble and immeasurably large, like familiar steppe-country unfolding before you, stretching away into the boundless distance. I could feel tears swelling up in my heart and rising into my eyes; dull, muffled sobs suddenly fell on my ears . . . I looked round – the tapster's wife was weeping as she leant her breast against the window. Yasha threw her a quick glance and his song flowed on still more sonorously and sweetly than before. Nikolai Ivanich looked down, Blinker turned away; Muddlehead, quite overcome by emotion, stood with his mouth stupidly gaping; the little grey peasant was quietly whimpering in his corner and shaking his head and muttering away bitterly to himself; down the iron face of Wild Master, from under his deep overhanging brows, slowly rolled a heavy tear; the huckster had raised a clenched fist to his brow and never stirred . . . I cannot imagine how this general state of heartfelt rapture would have been dispelled if Yasha had not suddenly ended on a high, extremely thin note – as if his voice had broken. No one shouted, no one even stirred; everyone seemed to be waiting in case he would sing on; but he opened his eyes, as if surprised at our silence, cast a questioning glance round at us all, and saw that victory was his . . .

'Yasha,' said Wild Master, putting a hand on his shoulder, and – said nothing more.

We all sat as though benumbed. The huckster got up quietly and went across to Yasha. 'You . . . it's yours . . . you've won,' he brought out at last with difficulty and dashed from the room . . .

His swift decisive movement seemed to break the spell: everyone suddenly started talking loudly, joyfully. Muddle-head sprang up in the air and began to splutter and wave his arms like the sails of a windmill; Blinker stumbled over to Yasha and they began to kiss each other; Nikolai Ivanich stood up and solemnly announced that he would add another quart of beer on his own account; Wild Master laughed a good-natured laugh, such as I had certainly not expected to hear from him; the little grey peasant kept on repeating in his corner, wiping his eyes, cheeks, nose and beard on both sleeves: 'Good, by God, it's good, why, take me for a son of a bitch, it's good!' and Nikolai's wife, deeply flushed, stood up quickly and went away. Yasha enjoyed his victory like a child; his whole face was transfigured; in particular his eyes simply radiated happiness. He was dragged across to the counter; he summoned over to it the little grey peasant, who had burst into tears, he sent the host's boy after the huckster, whom, how-ever, he failed to find, and the party began. 'You'll sing to us again, you'll sing to us until evening,' repeated Muddlehead, raising his arms aloft.

I looked once more at Yasha and went out. I did not want to stay – for fear of spoiling my impression. But the heat was still as unbearable as before. It was as if it hung right over the earth in a thick, heavy film; in the dark-blue sky, little flashing lights seemed to be astir behind the fine, almost black dust. Every-thing was still; there was something hopeless, something oppressive about this deep stillness of enfeebled nature. I made my way to a hayloft and lay down on the newly-mown but already almost dried-up grass. For a while I could not drowse off; for a while Yasha's irresistible voice rang in my ears ... but, at length, heat and exhaustion claimed their due, and I fell into a death-like sleep. When I awoke, it was dark all around; the litter of grass smelt strongly and there was a touch of dampness about it; between the thin rafters of the half-open roof, pale stars flickered faintly. I went out. The sunset glow had died away long ago, and had left behind only the faintest pallor on the horizon; in the air, so glowing-hot not long before, there was still a sense of heat underneath the freshness of night, and the lungs still thirsted for a breath of cold. There was no wind, no cloud; the sky stood round, clear, darkly translucent, quietly shimmering with countless hardly visible stars. In the village, lights twinkled; from the brightly-lit pot-house near by came a discordant and confused hubbub, in the midst of which I thought I recognized Yasha's voice. At times there were bursts of wild laughter. I went across to the window and pressed my face against the pane. I saw a sad, though lively and animated scene: everyone was drunk – everyone, starting with Yasha. He was sitting, bare-chested, on a bench, singing in the huskiest voice some dance song of the streets, and lazily plucking and pinching the strings of a guitar. Clusters of wet hair hung above his livid face. In the middle of the pot-house, Muddlehead, coatless and completely 'unscrewed', was dancing and hopping away in front of the little peasant in the grey coat; the peasant, in turn, was laboriously stamping and scraping with his exhausted feet, smiling witlessly through his dishevelled beard, and occasionally waving a hand, as if to say: 'Let it rip!' Nothing could have been more ludicrous than his face; however high he lifted his brows, his heavy lids refused to stay up and drooped right down over his hardly visible, bleary eyes, which were nevertheless brimming with sweetness. He was in the endearing condition of the completely tipsy, when every passer-by who looks him in the face is absolutely bound to say: 'A fine state, a fine state!' Blinker, red as a lobster, nostrils blown out wide, was laughing sardonically from a corner; only Nikolai Ivanich, as befits a good tapster, had kept his imperturbable sang-froid. Many new faces had collected in the room, but there was no sign of Wild Master.

I turned away and struck off quickly down the hill on which Kolotovka stands. A broad plain spreads out at the foot of this hill; swamped as it was with the misty waves of evening haze, it seemed vaster than ever, and as if merged with the darkened sky. I was walking with great strides along the track beside the ravine, when suddenly, from far away on the plain, came a boy's ringing voice. 'Antropka! Antropka-a-a! . . .' it called, in stubborn, tearful desperation, with a long dragging-out of the last syllable.

For a few moments it was silent, then began to call again. The voice carried clearly in the unmoving, lightly-sleeping air. Thirty times at least it had called Antropka's name, when suddenly, from the opposite end of the meadow, as if from a different world, came a scarcely audible reply:

'What-a-a-a-at?'

The boy's voice called at once, glad but indignant:

'Come here, you devil!'

'What fo-o-o-r?' answered the other, after a pause.

'Because father wants to be-ee-ee-eat you,' called the first voice promptly.

The second voice made no further reply, and the boy again started calling 'Antropka'. I could still hear his cries, growing rarer and fainter, when it had become completely dark and I was passing the bend in the wood that surrounds my village, four versts away from Kolotovka.

'Antropka-a-a,' I still seemed to hear in the air, which was full of the shadows of night.

Pyotr Petrovich Karataev

FIVE years ago, in the autumn, on the road from Moscow to Tula, I happened to spend the best part of a day sitting at the post station, as there were no horses for me. I was on my way back from shooting and had been unwise enough to have sent my troika on ahead. The postmaster, an old surly fellow, with his hair hanging down over his nose and little sleepy eyes, answered all my complaints and requests with an abrupt growl, slammed the door in a fury, as if by way of cursing his own duty – and, going out into the porch, scolded the drivers, who were slowly wandering about in the mud with heavy shaft-bows in their hands, or sitting on a bench yawning and scratching and paying no special attention to the wrathful exclamations of their chief. I had already managed to drink tea three times, had several times tried vainly to sleep, had read all the inscriptions on the windows and the walls: a terrible boredom oppressed me. With numb, hopeless despair, I was looking at the uplifted shafts of my travelling-carriage, when suddenly I heard the jingling of bells, and a small cart harnessed to three exhausted horses came to a halt in front of the porch. The new arrival jumped from the cart and with a cry of 'Horses – and be quick about it!' came into the room. While he listened, with the usual bewildered surprise, to the postmaster explaining that there was not a horse to be had, I contrived to scrutinize my new companion from head to foot with all the greedy curiosity of the bored. He looked about thirty. Smallpox had left its indelible traces on his dry, sallow face, which had a disagreeable coppery gleam to it; long bluish-black hair hung in ringlets over the back of his collar and twisted itself up in front into rakish side-whiskers; his puffy little eyes stared and stared. A few hairs sprouted from his upper lip. He wore the clothes of a gentleman-rake and frequenter of horse-fairs, namely, a gaily-coloured, rather greasy Caucasian overcoat, a cravat of faded mauve silk, a waistcoat with copper buttons, and grey trousers with enormous bell-bottoms, beneath which the tips of his uncleaned boots were scarcely visible. He smelt strongly of snuff and vodka; on his thick red fingers, practically hidden by his coat sleeves, could be seen rings of silver and of Tula work. Such creatures are to be met in Mother Russia, not by the dozen, but by the hundred; their acquaintance, it must be confessed, affords no sort of pleasure; yet in spite of the prejudice with which I looked at the new arrival, I could not help remarking the carefree good-nature, and the passion, expressed on his face.

'Why, this gentleman here has been waiting more than an hour,' said the postmaster, indicating me.

More than an hour! The scoundrel was laughing at me.

'It may not matter so much to him,' answered the new arrival.

'Well, that I couldn't say,' said the postmaster sullenly.

'So you really can't do it? Positively no horses?'

'Nothing to be done. Not a single horse.'

'Well, tell them to bring me a samovar. I'll wait, there's nothing else for it.'

The new arrival sat down on a bench, threw his cap on the table and passed his hand over his hair.

'Have you had tea?' he asked me.

'Yes.'

'Won't you have some more, to keep me company?'

I consented. The fat, reddish samovar appeared for the fourth time on the table. I got out a bottle of rum. I had not been wrong in taking my interlocutor for one of the smaller landowning gentry. His name was Pyotr Petrovich Karataev.

We fell into conversation. Not more than half an hour after his arrival he had, with all the good nature and outspokenness in the world, told me the story of his life.

'Now, I'm on my way to Moscow,' he informed me, as he finished his fourth glass of tea. 'There's nothing more I can do in the country.'

'How so?'

'There just isn't. The land's been ruined by mismanage-
ment, let's admit it. I've played havoc with the peasants; we've
had some bad years: poor crops, and one thing and another,
you know . . . Yes, and anyway,' he added, with a rueful sideways smile, 'I'm a fine one for looking after land!'

'Why?'

'No,' he broke in. 'To be quite honest, you can't manage
land the way I do. You see,' he went on, screwing his head to
one side and sucking away hard at his pipe, 'you here, looking
at me, might think that I'm . . . well, I must confess, I had a
middling sort of education; we weren't well off. You'll forgive
me, I'm an outspoken chap, and on the whole . . .'

He left the sentence unfinished and waved a hand. I began
to assure him that he was mistaken, that I was very glad to meet
him, and so forth, and then I remarked that the running of an
estate didn't seem to me to call for any excessive degree of
education.

'Agreed,' he answered. 'I quite agree with you. But you
need a special sort of disposition. Some fellows play hell with it
all, and no harm's done, but I . . . Tell me, sir, are you from
"Peter" or from Moscow?'

'From Petersburg.'

He blew a long stream of smoke from his nostrils.

'I'm going to Moscow to join the Government service.'

'Which branch d'you think of joining?'

'I don't know; it depends how things go there. I don't
mind telling you, I'm scared of the Government service;
you get landed with responsibilities at once. I've always
lived in the country; I've grown used to it, you know . . . but
it can't be helped . . . needs must! Oh, how I hate that "needs
must"!'

'But you'll be living in the capital.'

'Yes . . . well, I don't know what's so good about that. I'll
see, perhaps it *will* be good. But as for a home in the country,
I don't think there's anything can be better than that.'

'But can't you go on living there any longer?'

He sighed.

'No. It seems that it doesn't belong to me any more.'

'What's happened, then?'

'There's a good man there, a neighbour...a bill of exchange...'

Poor Pyotr Petrovich passed a hand over his face, thought, and shook his head.

'Well, there it is!...And to tell the truth,' he added after a slight pause, 'I can't blame a soul – it's my own fault. I liked cutting a dash!...I still do, damn it!'

'You had a gay time of it at home?' I asked him.

'Sir,' he answered with deliberation, looking me straight in the eyes, 'I kept twelve couple of hounds, such hounds as you'll seldom see, I can tell you.' He pronounced the word 'seldom' in a sing-song tone. 'They'd only to put up a hare or a deer – and they'd be off like snakes, regular snakes. And my horses were something to boast about, too. Now it's all past history, there's no point in telling lies. I used to go out shooting. I had a dog called Kontesska, a wonderful pointer, she had a sublime nose and never missed. I'd go up to a bog and say, seek! and if she wouldn't start seeking, then you could take a dozen dogs, but you'd be wasting your time, you wouldn't find a thing. But when she did start – why, she'd be ready to die on the spot!... And indoors she had such good manners. You'd give her a bit of bread in your left hand, and say, "A Jew ate it," and she wouldn't take it, but give it to her in your right hand, and say, "A lady ate it" – she'd take it and eat it up at once. I had a puppy from her too, a capital puppy, I even wanted to take him to Moscow, but a friend of mine asked me for him and for my gun too. He said: "In Moscow, my friend, you won't have time for this sort of thing; it's all quite different there." I gave him the puppy, and the gun too; so, you see, I left everything behind.'

'But even in Moscow you could get some shooting.'

'No, what's the use? I couldn't control myself before, and now I've got to pay for it. I'd rather you told me, if you will, what it's like living in Moscow – expensive?'

'No, not too bad.'

'Not too bad? . . . But, tell me, it's true that gypsies live in Moscow?'

'What gypsies?'

'The ones that go the rounds of the fairs?'

'Yes, in Moscow . . .'

'Well, that's good. I love the gypsies, damn it, so I do . . .' and Pyotr Petrovich's eyes sparkled with rakish merriment. But suddenly he began to fidget on his bench, then grew thoughtful, looked down, and held out to me his empty glass.

'Give me some of your rum,' he said.

'But your tea is all finished.'

'Never mind, I'll have it like that, without tea . . . Ugh!'

Karataev put his head in his hands and leant on the table. I looked at him in silence, anticipating those emotional exclamations, nay, those tears even, which come so easily to the man who has had a drop; but, when he raised his head, I confess I was struck by the expression of deep sorrow on his face.

'What's the matter?'

'Nothing. I'd remembered the old times. It's quite a story . . . I'd tell you, only I don't want to bore you . . .'

'Please!'

'Yes,' he continued with a sigh. 'The things that happen . . . even in my case, for example. Why, if you like, I'll tell you about it. I don't know, though . . .'

'Tell me the story, my dear Pyotr Petrovich.'

'Very well, although it's rather . . . Well, you see,' he began, 'but I really don't know . . .'

'Oh, that's quite enough, my dear Pyotr Petrovich.'

'Very well then. This is roughly my story. I lived in the country . . . Suddenly a girl caught my fancy, oh, and what a girl she was . . . Beautiful, clever, and so good-hearted too! Her name was Matrona. She was a simple girl, that's to say a serf, you understand, just a serf-girl. And she was not mine, but someone else's – that was the whole devil of it. So I fell in love with her – quite a story you see – well, and so did she. So Matrona started to ask me to buy her from her mistress, and I'd had the same idea myself . . . Her mistress was rich, a terrible

old hag; she lived about fifteen versts away from me. Well, one
fine day, as the expression is, I ordered my three-horse
drozhky to be harnessed – my shaft-horse was a trotter, a
regular rascal, he was called Lampurdos, too – I put on my
best clothes and drove off to see Matrona's mistress. I arrived
there; a big house with wings and a garden . . . Matrona was
waiting for me at the turning, she seemed to want to talk to me,
but she only kissed my hand and went away. So I went to the
front hall and asked "At home?" and a great tall footman says
to me: "Whom shall I announce?" I say: "Announce, my
friend, that the landowner Karataev has come to discuss business." The footman went off, and I waited by myself and
wondered what would happen. Supposing the beastly woman
put a frightful price on her, in spite of being so rich. Suppose
she asked five hundred roubles. Well, at last the footman
comes back and says, "This way, please." I go after him into
the drawing-room. In an armchair sits a little yellowish old
woman and blinks her eyes and says, "What can I do for you?"
First of all, you know, I thought I ought to say that I was glad to
make her acquaintance. "You're mistaken, I'm not the lady of
the house, I am a relation of hers. What can I do for you?" I told
her on the spot that I had something to discuss with the lady of
the house. "Marya Ilyinichna is not receiving to-day: she is
indisposed . . . What can I do for you?" There was nothing for
it, I thought to myself, but to explain my position to her. The
old woman heard me out. "Matrona? which Matrona?"
"Matrona Fyodorova, Kulik's daughter."

' "Fyodor Kulik's daughter . . . and how do you know her?"
"Just by chance." "Is she aware of your intention?" "Yes."
The old woman paused. "Why, I'll give it her, the good-for-
nothing hussy!" I confess I was surprised. "Whatever for, for
goodness' sake! . . . I'm ready to pay cash for her, if you'll
kindly just name a sum." The old sour-puss fairly began to
hiss. "That's a fine surprise you've planned: your money
means such a lot to us! But I'll just show her. I'll give it
her . . . I'll knock the nonsense out of her . . ." The old woman
had a coughing-fit from sheer spite. "Doesn't she like it here

with us, or what?... Oh, she's a little devil, may the Lord forgive me my trespasses!" Here I confess that I exploded. "What are you threatening the poor girl for, what is *she* to blame for?" The old woman crossed herself. "Oh, Lord Jesus Christ! Can't I do what I like, even with my own serfs?"

' "But she's not yours!"

' "Well, that's Marya Ilyinichna's affair, it's nothing to do with you, sir; but I'll show that little Matrona whose serf she is." I confess that I nearly went for the wretched hag, but I remembered Matrona and lowered my hands. I was so scared, I just can't tell you; I started begging the old woman to take whatever she liked. "But what is she to you?" "I like her, madam; put yourself in my situation... Allow me to kiss your hand." And so I kissed the old villain's hand. "Well," muttered the old woman. "I'll tell Marya Ilyinichna; it will be for her to decide; you come back in two days' time." I drove home in great anxiety. I began to suspect that I had handled the affair clumsily, that I had been wrong to give my situation away, but I had spotted it too late. Two days later I went to see the lady. I was shown into the study. Masses of flowers, wonderful ornaments, and the lady herself, sitting in one of those funny armchairs, with her head thrown back on a pillow, and her relative, who had been there before, sitting there too, and also another lady with pale hair and a green dress and a crooked mouth – a companion, she must have been. The old lady bowed: "Please be seated." I sat down. She began asking me how old I was, where I had served, what my plans were, the whole thing very lofty and dignified. I answered her fully. The old lady took a handkerchief from the table and waved it and waved it towards herself... "I –" she said, "I have learnt from Katerina Karpovna of your intention. I have learnt," she said, "but I have made it my rule," she said, "never to release my serfs for service elsewhere. It is not proper, it is not worthy of a well-ordered household: it is not in order. I have already taken the necessary steps," she said. "You have no further cause for concern." "How do you mean, please – concern?... But perhaps you need Matrona Fyodorova?"

"No," she said, "I don't need her." "Well, why ever don't you want to hand her over to me?" "Because it doesn't suit me; it doesn't suit me, and that's the end of it. I have already told you that I have taken the necessary measures: she has been sent to my property in the steppes." It hit me like a thunderclap. The old woman said a couple of words in French to the lady in green, who went out. "And I," she said, "am a woman of strict principles, and my health is poor, I can't stand worry. You're still a young man: I'm an old woman and in a position to give you advice. Would it not be better for you to settle down, marry, look for a good *parti*; heiresses are scarce, but you ought to be able to find some poor girl of good character." I looked at the old woman without understanding at all what she was driving at; I heard her speaking about marriage, but "my property in the steppes" kept ringing in my ears. Marriage! . . . Damnation take it . . .'

Here the narrator suddenly stopped and looked at me.

'I say, you're not married?'

'No.'

'Well, of course, you know how it is. I couldn't stand it any longer: "For heaven's sake, madam, what nonsense is this, what has marriage got to do with it? I simply wish to learn from you whether you will hand over to me your girl Matrona or not." The old woman groaned: "Oh, he's upset me! Oh, tell him to go away! Oh! . . ." Her kinswoman darted up to her and started screaming at me and the old woman kept on groaning: "What have I done to deserve this? Am I not mistress in my own house? Oh, oh!" I snatched up my hat and ran away like a madman.

'Perhaps,' continued the narrator, 'you will blame me for having formed such a strong attachment for a girl of low estate; indeed I have no intention of defending myself . . . It just happened like that! . . . Believe me, I had no peace, day or night . . . I was in torment! Why, I thought, I had ruined the poor girl! Then all of a sudden I would think of how she would be chasing geese, wearing a peasant's coat, and kept in disgrace by her mistress's orders, and how the overseer, a peasant in high boots, would be roaring loudly at her – and cold sweat would fairly roll off me. Well, I couldn't stand it; I found out what estate she had been sent to, saddled my horse and rode over. It wasn't until nearly evening on the second day that I arrived. Evidently they had never expected me to make such a stroke, and no instructions had been given about me. I went straight to the overseer, as if I had been a neighbour; I went into his yard, and what did I see but Matrona, sitting on the porch with her head in her hands. She was just going to cry out, but I shook my finger at her and pointed towards the back-yard and the fields. I went into the cabin; I had a chat with the overseer, spun him the devil of a yarn, waited for my moment and went out to Matrona. Poor thing, she fairly hung on my neck. She had got pale and thin, my darling had. Then, you know, I told her: "Never mind, Matrona, never mind, don't cry," but the tears were simply streaming down my own cheeks. Then, at last, I grew ashamed. I said to her: "Matrona, tears won't put things right, what we must do is this: we must take what they call decisive measures; you must run away with me, that's what we must do." Matrona practically fainted. "How can I! I'd be done for, they'd eat me right up!" "You silly, who's going to find you?" "They'll find me all right. Thank you, Pyotr Petrovich – I'll never forget your kindness, but you must leave me now; it's just the hand of fate." "Why, Matrona, and I took you for a girl of character." And so she was, she had lots of character. She was gold, pure gold! "Why on earth should I leave you here! Whatever happens, it can't be worse than this. Tell me: you've had a taste of the overseer's fists?" Matrona flared up and her lips began to tremble. "But my family won't be given any peace, all on my account." "Well, what will they do to your family? . . . Send them away, will they?" "Yes, they'll send my brother away, for sure." "And your father?" "They won't send my father away, he's the only good tailor in the place." "Well, there you are, you see; and it won't mean the end of your brother." I can tell you, I had a job to talk her round; she had the idea of arguing some more, about how I would have to answer for it . . . "But that isn't your affair," I told her ... Anyway I just carried her off ... Not that time, but another time: it was at night, I came with a cart – and carried her off.'

'You carried her off?'

'Yes ... So she settled down at my place. I had a small house and not many servants. My people adored me, I'll make no bones about it; they wouldn't have given me away for anything in the world. I was in clover. Matrona had a good rest and got better; I grew fonder and fonder of her ... What a girl she was! Where had she got it all from? She could sing, dance, play the guitar ... I didn't show her to the neighbours, they'd only have talked. But I had a friend, a bosom friend, Pantelei Gornostaev – you may know him? He simply worshipped her; he kissed her hand as if she had been a lady, really he did, and I can tell you, Gornostaev is not my sort: he's an educated man, he's read the whole of Pushkin; he would get talking to Matrona and me, and we'd be all ears. He taught her to write, amazing fellow! And then the clothes I gave her – better than the governor's wife's, absolutely they were; I had a coat made for her of raspberry-coloured velvet with trimmings of fur ... and how that coat suited her! It had been made by one of those Madams in Moscow, in the new style, with a tight waist. Oh, she was a marvellous girl, Matrona! She would start thinking and sit for hours on end, looking at the floor, not moving an eyebrow; and I would sit too, and look at her, and I just couldn't look at her enough, it was as if I'd never seen her in my life. She would smile, and my heart would give a sort of shiver, as if somebody was tickling it. Then suddenly she'd be in the mood to laugh and joke and dance, she'd embrace me so warmly, and hold me so tight, that my head would be in a whirl. From morning to night all I'd think about was how I could make her happy. And I tell you, I'd give her presents, just to see how pleased she'd be, the darling, how she'd go all red from joy, how she'd try my present on, how she'd come up to me in her new clothes and give me a kiss. I can't think how her father, Kulik, smelt the story out, but the old man came to have a look at us and fairly burst into tears ... Tears of joy, of course, what did you think?

We gave him presents. As he was leaving, she gave him a five-rouble note, the darling – and he plumped down at her feet – it was so funny! We lived for five months in this way; and I wouldn't have minded living like that with her for ever. But I reckoned without my cursed bad luck.'

He paused.

'What happened, then?' I asked sympathetically.

He waved his hand.

'It all ended devilish badly. I was the ruin of her, too. My little Matrona was mad keen on sledge rides, and used to drive herself; she'd put on her fur coat and her embroidered gloves, and simply shout for joy. We always went for our drives in the evening, so as not to meet anybody. Then there came one really glorious day: frosty, clear, not a breath of wind. We set out. Matrona took the reins. Suddenly I looked and saw where she was making for. Could she really be making for Kukuevka, for her mistress's estate? Yes, Kukuevka it was. I said to her: "Are you crazy? Where are you going?" She gave me a look over her shoulder and grinned. "Let's cut a dash," she said. Oho, I thought, let's … it's a good idea to drive right past the mistress's house – don't you think? On we drove. My trotter fairly swam along; as for the side-horses, I can tell you, they absolutely whirled – already we could see the church at Kukuevka; and then, creeping along the road, comes an old green winter-carriage with a footman sticking up on the boot … It was the mistress, so it was, driving towards us! I was getting scared, but Matrona flicked the horses with the reins and darted straight at the carriage! The coachman saw us flying towards him – tried to get out of the way, turned too sharply and tipped the carriage up into a snowdrift. The window broke – the lady screamed, "Ai-ai-ai! ai-ai-ai!" – the companion squeaked, "Hold on! Hold on!" and we – God give us legs to run with – got past. We galloped off, and I thought to myself: it will be a bad business, I was wrong to let her drive to Kukuevka. Well, what d'you expect? The old lady had recognized Matrona and myself, and she started proceedings against me: "A runaway girl of mine is living at Mr. Karataev's," she said; and she produced something suitable in the way of a sweetener. The next thing I knew, I got a visit from the district police inspector; he was an acquaintance of mine, Stepan Sergeich Kuzovkin, a good man, or rather, not really a good man. Well, he arrives and says: "It's like this and like that, Pyotr Petrovich – what's this that you've been up to? . . . It's a serious responsibility, the law is quite clear on the point." I say to him: "Well, of course, we must have a chat about that, but won't you have a bite after your journey?" He agreed to have a bite, but he said: "The law must take its course, Pyotr Petrovich, you can see for yourself that it must." "Yes, of course, the law," I said; "of course . . . By the way, I believe you've got a black horse, you wouldn't like to change it for my Lampurdos? . . . But there's no such girl as Matrona Fyodorova here!" "Well," he said, "Pyotr Petrovich, the girl's here, we don't live in Switzerland . . . but as for Lampurdos, I could certainly change my horse for him; or, if you liked, I could just take him." Well, on that occasion, somehow or other, I got him out of the house. But the old lady made a worse fuss than ever: "I shan't mind if it costs me ten thousand," she said. You see, when she first saw me, she had suddenly taken it into her head to marry me off to her green companion – so I found out afterwards: that's why she took it all so much to heart. What ideas these ladies get! It must be the boredom, I suppose. Things went badly for me. I didn't spare money, and I kept Matrona hidden – but no! They harried me like a driven hare. I got into debt, my health failed, and, well, one night I was lying in bed thinking: Oh Lord, what am I suffering for? What am I going to do, if I can't stop loving her? . . . and I just can't and that's all there is to it! – when suddenly Matrona came into my room. At that time I'd been hiding her in one of my farms, two versts away from the house. I had quite a shock. "What? Have they been bothering you, even there?" "No, Pyotr Petrovich," she said. "No one disturbs me at Bubnov; but this can't go on any longer. It tears my heart," she said; "I'm so sorry for you, my darling; I'll never, never forget your kindness, Pyotr Petrovich, but now I've come to say good-bye." "What d'you mean? Are you crazy? . . . What d'you mean, to say good-bye?" "Just like that . . . I'm going to give myself up." "You're crazy, I'll lock you up in the attic . . . D'you want to be the death of me, d'you mean to kill me, or what?" But the girl said nothing, and looked at the floor. "Well, go on, say something!" "I don't want to cause you any more trouble, Pyotr Petrovich!" Well, go on, argue with her . . . "But you see, you fool, you see, you crazy girl . . ." '

And Pyotr Petrovich began to sob bitterly.

'Well, what d'you think?' he continued, striking his fist on the table and trying to frown, with the tears still running down his burning cheeks: 'The girl gave herself up – she went and gave herself up . . .'

'The horses are ready, sir,' exclaimed the inspector solemnly, coming into the room.

We both stood up.

'And what became of Matrona?' I asked.

Karataev waved his hand.

A year after my encounter with Karataev I happened to go to Moscow. One day, before dinner, I dropped in to the coffee-house in Huntsman's Row – that singular Moscow coffee-house. In the billiard-room, through clouds of smoke, loomed crimson faces, moustaches, tufts of hair, old-fashioned Hungarian jackets, and coats of the latest cut. Thin old men in modest frock-coats were reading the Russian papers. Servants were flashing past briskly with trays, stepping softly over the green carpet. Merchants were drinking tea with agonized intensity. Suddenly, from inside the billiard-room, came a man – somewhat dishevelled and not altogether steady on his legs. He put his hands in his pockets, let his head fall forward and looked heedlessly around.

'Hey, hey! Pyotr Petrovich . . . How are you?'

Pyotr Petrovich practically threw himself on my neck and with a slight stagger dragged me into the little private room.

'Here,' he said, carefully seating me in an armchair, 'here you'll be comfortable. Waiter, beer! No, I mean champagne!

Well, I must say I never, never expected ... Been here long?
Staying long? Why, heaven must have sent you, so to speak,
I mean ...'

'Yes, d'you remember ...'

'Of course I do, of course I do,' he interrupted me hurriedly.
'That old story ... that old story ...'

'Well, what are you doing here, my dear Pyotr Petrovich?'

'Just living, sir – as you may perhaps have observed. It's a
good life here, they're a jolly lot. I've found peace here.'

He sighed and raised his eyes to heaven.

'Are you in the Government service?'

'No, not yet, but I hope to fix up something soon. What's a
job, anyway? ... People, that's the main thing. The people I've
got to know here! ...'

The boy came in with a bottle of champagne on a black tray.

'Here's a good fellow, too ... aren't you a good fellow,
Vasily? Your health!'

The boy stood, shook his head respectfully, smiled and
went out.

'Yes, they're good people here,' continued Pyotr. 'They've
got feelings, they've got souls ... Would you like me to introduce you? Such splendid chaps ... They'll all be glad to know
you. I'll tell them ... Bobrov's dead, that's the pity of it.'

'Who is Bobrov?'

'Sergei Bobrov. He was a splendid fellow; he took me
under his wing when I was just an ignorant bumpkin from
the steppes. Pantelei Gornostaev's dead too. Everybody's
dead!'

'Have you been in Moscow all the time? Haven't you been
away to the country?'

'Country ... my place in the country has been sold.'

'Sold?'

'By auction ... It's a shame you didn't buy it!'

'What are you going to live on, Pyotr Petrovich?'

'With God's help, I won't die of hunger! I may not have
money, but I'll have my friends. What's money anyway? Dirt!
Gold is just dirt!'

He screwed his eyes up, rummaged with his hand in his pocket and offered me in his palm two pieces of fifteen copecks and one of ten.

'What is it? Just dirt!' The money went flying to the floor. 'But, tell me, have you read Polezhaev?'

'Yes.'

'Have you seen Mochalov in *Hamlet*?'

'No, I haven't.'

'You haven't, you haven't...' And Karataev's face went pale, his eyes began roaming restlessly; he turned away; faint spasms passed across his lips. 'Oh, Mochalov, Mochalov! To die, to sleep,' he said dully.

> *No more; and by a sleep to say we end*
> *The heart-ache, and the thousand natural shocks*
> *That flesh is heir to, 'tis a consummation*
> *Devoutly to be wished. To die, to sleep!...*

'To sleep, to sleep!' he whispered several times.

'Tell me,' I began; but he continued fervently:

> *For who would bear the whips and scorns of time,*
> *The oppressor's wrong, the proud man's contumely,*
> *The pangs of despised love, the law's delays,*
> *The insolence of office, and the spurns*
> *That patient merit of the unworthy takes,*
> *When he himself might his quietus make*
> *With a bare bodkin... Nymph, in thy orisons*
> *Be all my sins remembered.*

He dropped his head on the table. He began to stammer and drivel.

'A little month,' he pronounced with renewed strength:

> *A little month, or ere those shoes were old*
> *With which she followed my poor father's body,*
> *Like Niobe, all tears: – why she, even she –*
> *O God! a beast that wants discourse of reason*
> *Would have mourn'd longer...*

He lifted a glass of champagne to his lips but, without drinking, continued:

> *For Hecuba!*
> *What's Hecuba to him, or he to Hecuba,*
> *That he should weep for her?...*
> *Yet I... a dull and muddy-mettled rascal...*
> *Am I a coward?*
> *Who calls me villain?... gives me the lie in the throat?*
> *'Swounds, I should take it: for it cannot be.*
> *But I am pigeon-liver'd and lack gall*
> *To make oppression bitter...*

Karataev dropped the glass and held his head in his hands. I had an idea that I understood him.

'Well, anyway,' he said at last. 'When sorrow sleeps, wake it not... Isn't that right?'

He laughed. 'Your health!'

'Are you staying on in Moscow?' I asked him.

'I shall die in Moscow.'

'Karataev!' came a voice from the next room. 'Karataev, where are you? Come here, there's a good fellow!'

'They're calling me,' he said, rising heavily from his chair. 'Good-bye, come and see me if you can. I live at—— '

But on the following day unforeseen circumstances obliged me to leave Moscow and I never saw Pyotr Petrovich Karataev again.

The Rendezvous

I WAS sitting in a birch-wood one autumn, about the middle of September. Ever since morning a fine drizzle had been falling, giving way now and again to warm sunshine: it was fluky weather. One moment the sky would be all overcast with puffy white clouds, at another it would suddenly clear in places for a moment, and, through the rift, the azure would appear, clear and smiling, like the glance of a brilliant eye. I sat and looked about me and listened. The leaves were whispering faintly over my head: you could have told the time of year from their whisper alone. It was not the gay, laughing shiver of spring, nor the soft murmur, the long discourse of summer, nor the cold, frightened rustling of late autumn, but a scarcely perceptible, drowsy converse. A little breeze was just stirring among the tree-tops. The interior of the wood, drenched with rain, kept changing its appearance as the sun shone out or went in behind the clouds: sometimes it was all ablaze, as if everything there was smiling: the slender boles of the scattered birches suddenly took on the fresh brilliance of white silk, the tiny leaves on the ground gleamed and blazed with purple and gold, and the handsome stems of the tall, curly bracken, already tinged with their autumn hue, the hue of overripe grapes, stood out luminously before me in an infinite, criss-crossed maze; then suddenly the whole scene took on a faint shade of blue: in an instant, the bright colours went out, the birches stood blankly white as new-fallen snow, not yet touched by the cold light of the winter sun; and furtively, slyly, the finest of drizzles began to spray and whisper through the wood. The leaves of the birches were almost all of them still green, though of a marked pallor; only here and there stood a single young one, quite red or quite gold, and it was a sight to see how brightly it flared up when the sun's rays suddenly found their way to it, slipping and dappling through the thick net of fine branches, all newly washed in sparkling rain. There was not a sound from the birds: they were all snuggled down and keeping quiet; just occasionally the laughing voice of the tit-mouse rang out like a tiny steel bell. Before coming to a halt in this birch-wood, my dog and I had passed through a tall spinney of poplars. I confess that I am not over-fond of this tree – the poplar – with its pale lilac-coloured trunk and the grey-green, metallic foliage which it lifts up as high as it can and throws out in a trembling fan into the air; I dislike the perpetual shaking of its untidy round leaves, fixed so awkwardly on their long stems. The poplar is good only on certain summer evenings when, standing out sharply from amidst the low brushwood, it faces straight into the glowing rays of the setting sun, and blazes and shines, suffused from root to summit with an even, yellowish purple – or on a clear windy day, when the whole tree ripples and murmurs under the blue sky, and every leaf is as if seized with a longing to break loose and fly off far away into the distance. But for the most part I am no lover of this tree, and so I didn't pause for rest in the poplar-spinney, but went on to the birch-wood, curled myself under a tree whose branches began close to the ground and so could give me shelter from the rain, and, after admiring the scene around me, fell into the unbroken and tranquil sleep which is known only to the hunter.

I cannot say for how long I slept, but, when I opened my eyes, the whole inside of the wood was filled with sunlight, and in all directions, through joyfully murmuring foliage, the sky appeared, bright blue and sparkling; the clouds had vanished, chased by a newly-risen breeze; the weather had cleared, and you could feel in the air that special dry freshness which, filling the heart with a sense of well-being, nearly always presages a calm bright evening after a day of rain. I was preparing to get up and try my luck again, when suddenly my eyes came to rest on a motionless human figure. I peered at it: it was a young peasant-girl. She was sitting twenty yards away from me, her head sunk in reflection, and both hands dropped on her knees; in one hand, which was half-open, a thick bunch of wild flowers lay, and every-time she breathed it slipped quietly farther down on to her check skirt. A clean white blouse, buttoned at the front and wrists, lay in short, soft folds around her body; two rows of thick yellow beads fell from her neck on to her breast. She was quite pretty. Dense fair hair, of a fine ash colour, emerged in two carefully-brushed half-circles from beneath a narrow head-band, worn right down on her forehead, which was white as ivory; the rest of her face was faintly sunburnt, with that golden tan which comes only to a fine skin. I couldn't see her eyes – she did not raise them; but I saw clearly her fine, arched brows, her long eyelashes: they were wet, and, on one of her cheeks, the sun caught the drying streak of a tear that had stopped just at the side of her palish lips. It was a charming head; even a somewhat thick round nose didn't spoil it. I liked especially the expression of her face. It was so simple and gentle, so sad, so full of a child-like bewilderment in the presence of a private sorrow. Evidently she was waiting for someone; there was a faint crackling in the wood; she lifted her head at once and looked around; in the translucent shadow I could see the swift flash of her eyes, large, bright and timid, like a doe's. For a few moments she listened, without moving her wide-open eyes from the place whence the faint sound had come, sighed, quietly turned her head, bent down even lower and began slowly to arrange her flowers. Her eyelids reddened, her lips trembled with grief, and a fresh tear rolled out from beneath her thick lashes, halting and sparkling brilliantly on her cheek. Quite a while passed like this. The poor girl never stirred – only now and then a cheerless gesture of her hands – and listened and listened . . . Again there was a noise in the wood – she started. The noise continued, grew clearer, approached, and at last swift decisive steps could be heard. She sat up and seemed to be afraid; her attentive gaze wavered, kindled with anticipation. Soon a man's figure appeared through the undergrowth. She stared, blushed suddenly, burst into a joyous, blissful smile, made as if to get up, and at once sank back again, turned pale, became embarrassed, and only raised her trembling, almost imploring look to the new arrival when he had already come to a halt beside her.

I looked at him curiously from my hiding-place. I confess that the impression he made on me was disagreeable. By all appearances he must have been the spoiled valet of a rich young master. His clothes displayed a pretension to good taste and a dandyish negligence; he wore a short, bronze-coloured over-coat, probably off his master's shoulders, buttoned right up, a pink cravat with lilac ends, and a black gold-laced velvet cap rammed right down on his forehead. The rounded collar of his white shirt pushed up mercilessly against his ears and cut into his cheeks, and starched cuffs covered his whole hand down to his curving red fingers, which were adorned with silver and gold rings with forget-me-nots in turquoise. His face, ruddy, fresh, cheeky, was one of those which, so far as my observation goes, exasperate men and, unfortunately, very often appeal to women. He was clearly trying to give his coarse features an expression of contempt and boredom; he kept narrowing his milky-grey eyes, which were anyway tiny enough, making wry faces, dropping the corners of his lips, yawning constrainedly and with a careless, but not quite easy nonchalance, adjusting his reddish, nattily-brushed temples, or fingering the yellow hairs which bristled from his thick upper lip – in a word, he was intolerably affected. His affectation began from the moment he caught sight of the young peasant-girl waiting for him; he came up to her slowly, with a lounging gait, halted, worked his shoulders, plunged both hands into the pockets of his overcoat, and, hardly bestowing on the poor girl so much as a cursory, indifferent glance, sank down on the grass.

'Why,' he began, still looking far away into the distance, fidgeting his leg and yawning, 'been here long?'

The girl could not answer him immediately.

'Yes, Viktor Alexandrich,' she said at last, in a hardly audible voice.

'Oh!' He took off his cap, passed his hand majestically over his thick, tightly-curled hair, which began practically at his eyebrows, and, looking round with dignity, scrupulously covered his precious head again. 'I nearly forgot altogether. Besides, there was the rain, you see!' He yawned again. 'Lots of work: you can't keep your eye on everything, with him scolding you into the bargain. We leave to-morrow . . .'

'To-morrow?' the girl brought out, turning a frightened gaze upon him.

'To-morrow . . . There, there, there, for goodness' sake!' he interjected hurriedly and with irritation, seeing that she had started to tremble all over and had quietly dropped her head. 'For goodness' sake, Akulina, don't cry. You know I can't bear it.' And he wrinkled his snub nose. 'Or else I'll go away at once. It's too stupid – grizzling!'

'No, no, I won't,' said Akulina hurriedly, swallowing her tears with an effort. 'So you're leaving to-morrow?' she added after a short silence. 'When will God grant us to see each other again, Viktor Alexandrich?'

'We'll see each other again all right. If not next year – then later. I think the master wants to go to Petersburg and get a Government job,' he went on, pronouncing the words negligently and slightly through his nose, 'but it's possible that we shall go abroad.'

'You'll forget me, Viktor Alexandrich,' said Akulina sorrowfully.

'No, why should I? I won't forget you: but just you be sensible; don't do silly things, do what your father tells you . . . I won't forget you – no-o.' And he stretched calmly and yawned again.

'Don't forget me, Viktor Alexandrich,' she went on, in an imploring voice. 'I do love you so much, there's nothing I wouldn't do for you . . . You tell me to obey my father . . . But how can I obey him? . . .'

'Well?' He pronounced the word as if from his stomach, lying on his back, with his hands folded beneath his head.

'But how can I, Viktor Alexandrich – you know very well . . .' She paused. Viktor played with his steel watch-chain.

'You're no fool, Akulina,' he began at length, 'so you mustn't talk nonsense. I've got your interests at heart, d'you

see? Of course, you're no fool, you're not just an ordinary
peasant-girl, as it were; your mother wasn't always a peasant,
either. All the same, you've got no education – so you ought to
do as you're told.'

'But I'm scared, Viktor Alexandrich.'

'Pooh, what nonsense, my dear; what is there to be scared
about? What have you got there?' he added, moving closer to
her. 'Flowers?'

'Yes,' answered Akulina sadly. 'This I picked from a wild
costmary,' she went on, with somewhat more animation, 'it's
good for calves. This one's marigold – good against the scro-
fula. Then look at this wonderful flower; such a wonderful
flower as I've never seen in all my days. These are forget-
me-nots, and this one's called mother's darling. And these are
for you,' she added, taking out, from below the yellow costmary, a small bunch of blue cornflowers bound with a slender
grass. 'Would you like them?'

Viktor lazily stretched out a hand, took the flowers, smelt
them indifferently, and began to turn them over between his
fingers, looking up meanwhile, meditative and aloof. Akulina
gazed at him ... In her sad glance there was so much tender
devotion, reverent submissiveness and love. She was afraid of
him, she didn't dare cry, she was saying good-bye to him,
admiring him for the last time: while he lay, sprawling like a
sultan, and suffered her adoration with magnanimous patience
and condescension. I confess that I looked indignantly at his
red face, in which, through the pretence of contemptuous
indifference, a contented, surfeited egoism peeped out. Akulina was so lovely at that moment: her whole soul bared itself
trustfully, passionately, to him, and strove in all humility to
approach him, while he ... he dropped the cornflowers in the
grass, brought out from the side pocket of his coat a little round
glass in a bronze frame and proceeded to squeeze it into his eye;
but, try as he might to hold it in, with screwed-up brow, raised
cheek, even with his nose – the glass kept falling out and
dropping into his hand.

'What's that?' asked Akulina at length, in astonishment.

'A lorgnette,' he answered, with dignity.

'What for?'

'To see better with.'

'Let me look.'

Viktor scowled, but gave her the glass.

'Look out, don't break it.'

'Don't worry, I won't break it.' She put it shyly up to her eye. 'I can't see anything,' she observed innocently.

'But your eye – you must screw up your eye,' he rejoined in the voice of a dissatisfied instructor. She screwed up the eye in front of which she was holding the glass. 'Not that one, not that one, stupid! The other one!' exclaimed Viktor and, without allowing her to correct her mistake, took the lorgnette away from her.

Akulina flushed, laughed faintly and turned away.

'It's not meant for the likes of us, I can see,' she said.

'It certainly isn't!'

The poor girl was silent and sighed deeply.

'Oh, Viktor Alexandrich, it'll be so hard for us, without you,' she said suddenly.

Viktor wiped the lorgnette with his coat-tail and put it back in his pocket.

'Yes, yes,' he said at length; 'it'll be hard for you at first, certainly.' He patted her condescendingly on the shoulder; she gently took his hand from her shoulder and shyly kissed it. 'Well, yes, you're certainly a good girl,' he went on, smiling complacently; 'but there's nothing for it, is there now? The master and I can't stay here; it'll soon be winter now, and winter in the country – you know it yourself – is sheer misery. While, in Petersburg! There are such marvellous sights there, such as you could never imagine, you stupid, not even in a dream. The houses, the streets, the society, the education – simply amazing! . . .' Akulina listened to him with consuming attention, her lips slightly parted, like a child's. 'But anyway,' he added, turning over on the ground, 'what's the good of my telling you all this? It's something that you can never understand.'

'Why not, Viktor Alexandrich? I've understood; I've understood it all.'

'There you go!'

Akulina lowered her head.

'There was a time once when you didn't talk to me like this, Viktor Alexandrich,' she said, without looking up.

'Once? . . . once! There you are! . . . Once!' he observed, with a hint of indignation.

They were both silent.

'Well, it's time I was going,' said Viktor, who had already propped himself up on his elbow . . .

'Wait a little longer,' said Akulina imploringly.

'What for? . . . I've already said good-bye to you.'

'Wait,' repeated Akulina.

Viktor lay back again and started to whistle. Akulina still kept her eyes fixed on him. I could see that she was growing more and more agitated: her lips twitched, her pale cheeks were faintly flushed.

'Viktor Alexandrich,' she began, at length, chokingly. 'It's wrong of you . . . it's wrong, before God, it is.'

'What's wrong?' he rejoined, scowling, and he lifted himself slightly and turned his head towards her.

'It's wrong, Viktor Alexandrich. You might at least have had a kind word for me when you're saying good-bye; you might have had a word for me, poor little orphan that I am . . .'

'What can I say to you?'

'I don't know; it's you who should know, Viktor Alexandrich. Here you are, leaving, and not so much as a word . . . What have I done to deserve it?'

'What a funny girl you are! What else can I do?'

'Only a word . . .'

'Always the same thing,' he said crossly, and got up.

'Don't be angry, Viktor Alexandrich,' she added hastily, hardly holding in her tears.

'I'm not angry, you're just such a fool . . . What d'you want? I can't marry you – can I now? So what else d'you want? What is it?' He looked blank, as if waiting for an answer, and spread out his fingers.

'Nothing . . . I want nothing,' she answered, stammering, and only just daring to stretch her trembling hands out towards him: 'Just a word, to say good-bye . . .'

And her tears started streaming down.

'There it is, she's started to cry,' said Viktor coldly, tilting his cap forward over his eyes.

'I want nothing,' she went on, gulping and covering her face with both hands; 'but what will it be like for me at home now, what'll it be like? What will become of me, poor wretch that I am? They'll marry me off to someone I don't love . . . poor, wretched me.'

'Sing away, sing away,' muttered Viktor in a low voice, shifting his position.

'He might have said a word, just one even . . . "Akulina," he might have said, "I . . ." '

Sudden heart-rending sobs prevented her from finishing – she buried her face in the grass and burst into bitter, bitter tears . . . Her whole body shook spasmodically, she raised her head . . . Her long pent-up grief had at last found a way out. Viktor stood over her, stood, shrugged his shoulders, turned and strode away.

A few moments passed . . . She grew quiet, lifted her head, jumped up, looked round, and threw up her arms: she made as if to run after him, but her legs failed her, and she fell on her knees . . . I could stand it no longer and rushed towards her – but the moment she saw me, goodness knows where she got the strength from, she rose with a faint cry and vanished behind the trees, leaving the flowers scattered on the ground.

I stopped, picked up the bunch of cornflowers and walked out of the wood into the field. The sun stood low in the pale, clear sky, and its rays seemed to have faded and grown cold: they had no radiance; it was an even, almost watery light they distilled. There was only half an hour to nightfall, but the sunset had hardly begun to glow. A gusty wind blew headlong towards me over the parched yellow stubble; tiny, shrivelled leaves, whirling swiftly up before it, flew past across the road, along the edge of the wood; the side of it that abutted like a wall on the field was all shivering and sparkling with a fine glitter that had clarity but no brilliance; on the reddish grass, on blades and straws, everywhere, in glittering festoons, lay countless autumn spiders' webs. I stopped ... sadness overcame me; behind the crisp yet cheerless smile of languishing nature, I thought I sensed the gloom and dread of approaching winter. High above me, cutting the air with sharp, heavy wing-strokes, flew a cautious raven: he looked at me with a sideways turn of his head, shot upwards and disappeared, croaking abruptly, behind the wood; a big flock of pigeons, flying gaily from the threshing-floor, suddenly formed up into a pillar and settled swiftly on the field – sure sign of autumn! On the other side of the bare hill, someone was driving by in a loud-rattling, empty cart.

I returned home; but it was some time before poor Akulina's image went out of my head, and I still have her cornflowers, faded long since.

Prince Hamlet of Shchigrovo

O N one of my travels I received an invitation to dine with a rich landowner and sportsman named Alexander Mikhailich G———. His village lay about five versts away from a small one where I was staying at the time. I put on a tail-coat, without which I advise nobody to travel, even on a shooting trip, and set out for Alexander Mikhailich's. Dinner was at six o'clock. I arrived at five and found a large number of gentlemen already there in uniform, civilian dress, and other less distinct-ive attire. My host received me amiably but then ran away at once to the pantry. He was expecting a great Personage and was a prey to a certain agitation, which suited oddly with his wealth and independent situation in the world.

Alexander Mikhailich had never married and disliked women; his parties were of the bachelor type. He lived in great style, had improved and decorated his ancestral halls with magnificence, ordered about 15,000 roubles' worth of wine from Moscow every year, and in general stood in the highest esteem. He had been in retirement for some consider-able time and was not interested in acquiring distinctions. What was it then that impelled him to force his invitation upon this Personage and to spend the day of the great dinner, from dawn onwards, in trepidation? That must remain shrouded in deepest mystery, as a pettifogging lawyer of my acquaintance used to say when asked whether he accepted bribes offered him by voluntary contributors.

After parting from my host, I began to stroll through the rooms. Almost all the guests were complete strangers to me; a score or so were already sitting round the card-tables. Among these amateurs of Preference were two military gentlemen with noble but somewhat worn features, a number of civilian char-acters with high, tight cravats and those pendulous dyed whiskers which are found only on men of determination but also of the best intentions (these well-intentioned ones picked up their cards with dignity and threw sidelong glances at the passers-by without turning their heads); five or six district functionaries with pot-bellies, chubby, sweating hands and modest, stuffed demeanours (these gentlemen spoke in soft voices, smiled timidly in all directions, held their cards right up against their shirt-fronts and, when trumping, did not thump the table, but allowed their card to fall with a wavering motion on the green cloth, and collected the trick to the accompaniment of a faint, a very polite and respectful scraping sound). Other gentlemen were sitting on sofas, standing in groups in doorways and beside windows; one landowner, no longer young, but of feminine appearance, was standing in a corner, wincing, blushing and awkwardly twisting his watch-fob on his stomach, although nobody was paying him any attention; some gentlemen in tail-coats of rounded cut and check trousers, from the hand of the Moscow tailor and master craftsman Firs Klyukhin, were conversing with remarkable briskness and abandon, freely turning the bare and fleshy napes of their necks this way and that; a blond, short-sighted young man of about twenty, in black from head to foot, was smiling sardonically despite his obvious shyness . . .

I was beginning to get rather bored, when all of a sudden I was joined by one Voinitzin, a student who had never finished his studies and was living in the house of Alexander Mikhailich as . . . it is hard to say exactly what. He was a capital shot and knew how to train a dog. I had known him in Moscow. He was one of those young fellows who at every examination 'get lockjaw', that is, never answer a word when questioned by the indignant professors. Such gentlemen, from their elegance of style, were also known as 'whisker-fanciers'. (It is a story of days long passed, as you may have been pleased to observe.) This is what would happen: they would call out, for instance, Voinitzin – Voinitzin, who up till then had been sitting motionless and upright on his bench, bathed from head to foot in warm sweat, and looking slowly but blankly around, would rise hurriedly, button up his tunic, and make his way sideways to the examiners' table. 'Please to take a ticket,' the professor would say to him agreeably. Voinitzin would stretch out a hand and touch the piles of tickets with trembling fingers. 'Kindly do not choose,' would say the jarring voice of some strange but irritable old gentleman, a professor from another faculty who had taken a strong dislike to the unhappy whisker-fancier. Voinitzin would submit to his fate, take a ticket, show the number and go and sit in the window while his predecessor answered his question. In the window Voinitzin would never take his eyes off the ticket, except just to look round slowly as before, but without the slightest movement of any other part of his body. Then they would finish with his predecessor and would be saying to him, 'Very well, you can go,' or perhaps, 'Good, very good,' according to his abilities. Now they are calling Voinitzin – Voinitzin stands up, and walks across to the table with a firm tread. 'Read the ticket,' they tell him. Voinitzin takes the ticket in both hands, lifts it right up to his nose, slowly reads it, slowly lowers his hand. 'Well, your answer, please,' pronounces the same professor lazily, folding his arms across his chest. A silence of the grave ensues. 'Well?' Voinitzin says nothing. The old visiting professor begins to twitch. 'Well, say something!' My friend Voinitzin preserves a frozen silence. The close-cropped back of his head sticks up, steep and motionless, under the curious gaze of all his comrades. The eyes of the old visiting professor are ready to pop out of his head: he loathes Voinitzin for good and all. 'It's strange, though,' observes another examiner. 'Why stand there as if you were dumb? You don't know, I suppose? Well say so, then.' 'Let me take another ticket,' the poor wretch brings out dully. The professors exchange glances. 'Very well,' answers the head examiner, with a movement of his hand. Again Voinitzin takes a ticket, again he goes over to the window, again he returns to the table, and is again smitten with the same silence. The old visiting gentleman is quite ready to eat him up alive. Finally they dismiss him and give him nought. You may think that now at last he will go away? What else could he do? No, he returns to his place, sits motionless until the end of the examination and, as he leaves, exclaims: 'Phew! *What* a question!' And he walks about Moscow for a whole day, now and then putting his hands to his head and railing bitterly against his ill-starred fate. Needless to say he doesn't touch a book, and the next morning the same story happens all over again.

This was the Voinitzin who joined me. We talked about Moscow, about shooting.

'Wouldn't you like me,' he whispered to me suddenly, 'to introduce you to our leading local wit?'

'Yes, it would be a pleasure.'

Voinitzin led me up to a short man with a tall tuft of hair and side-whiskers, a brown tail-coat and a gay cravat. His mobile, bilious-coloured features certainly radiated wit and malice. A passing, mordant smile kept twisting his lips; his black, narrowed eyes looked insolently out from beneath straggling lashes. Beside him stood a broad, soft, sugary gentleman – a real Sakhar Medovich[1] – and one-eyed as well. He was laughing at the little fellow's sallies in advance and fairly melting with delight. Voinitzin introduced me to the wit, whose name was Pyotr Petrovich Lupikhin. We made each other's acquaintance and exchanged the opening civilities.

'But let me introduce my best friend,' began Lupikhin suddenly, in a sharp voice, seizing the sugary gentleman by the arm. 'Don't resist, Kiril Selifanich,' he added. 'We're not going to eat you. Yes,' he continued, while the embarrassed Kiril bowed as awkwardly as if his stomach was falling off, 'let me introduce this remarkable gentleman. He enjoyed excellent health until the age of fifty, then suddenly had the idea of treating his eyes, as a result of which he lost one of them. Since then he has been treating his peasants – with the same fortunate results. And they of course are more devoted to him than ever.'

'There he goes,' murmured Kiril Selifanich, and burst out laughing.

---

1 Sakhar Medovich – 'Sugar son of Honey'. – *Translators*.

'Carry on, my friend, just carry on,' repeated Lupikhin. 'I'm awfully afraid you may be appointed a justice – you certainly will be, just you see. Well, of course, all the thinking will be done for you by the jurymen; but, even so, one's got to be able to express a thought, even when it *is* someone else's. Suppose the Governor calls – and asks why the judge is stammering; well, suppose they say, "It's a case of paralysis." "Well, bleed him, then," the Governor will say. But in your position it is unseemly, you're bound to agree.'

The sweet-looking gentleman was simply rocking.

'Just look at him laughing,' Lupikhin continued, with a vindictive glance at the quivering belly of Kiril Selifanich. 'And why shouldn't he,' he added, turning to me; 'he's well-fed, healthy, no children, peasants unmortgaged – under treatment from him, what's more – and a wife who's half-cracked.' Kiril turned slightly away as though he hadn't quite heard, and went on guffawing away as before. 'I'm laughing too, although *my* wife ran away with a surveyor.' He showed his teeth. 'Didn't you know? Of course, of course. She just went and ran off and left me a letter saying: "Dear Pyotr Petrovich, Forgive me; carried away by passion, I am departing with the friend of my heart." And the surveyor only got her by not cutting his nails and wearing tight-fitting trousers. You're surprised? There's an outspoken fellow, you're thinking. Good heavens, yes! We steppe-folk always tell God's own truth. But let's go away over here... Why should we stand beside this judge-to-be?'

He took my arm and we went over to a window.

'I pass hereabouts as a wit,' he told me in the course of conversation, 'but don't you believe it, I'm just an ill-natured fellow roaring aloud; that's why I'm so free and easy about it. And why should I stand on ceremony, if it comes to that? I don't care a farthing for anyone's opinion; I've no axe to grind; I'm an ill-natured fellow – and what of it? At least an ill-natured fellow stands in no need of wit. But you'll never believe how refreshing it is... Well, for instance, take our host! What makes him run, I ask you – and keep on glancing at the time, smiling, sweating, looking important and starving us to death? What is there so wonderful about a Personage? Look, he's started running again – tripped up, too, just look.'

And Lupikhin laughed wheezily.

'The only pity of it is, there are no ladies,' he continued with a deep sigh. 'It's a bachelor dinner – but it's the other sort that does good to fellows like us. Look, look,' he exclaimed suddenly, 'here comes Prince Kozelsky – that tall man there, with a beard and yellow gloves. You can see at once that he's lived abroad . . . he always arrives late like this. I can tell you, he's stupid enough for a pair of merchant's horses; but you may have noticed how condescendingly he talks to the rest of us, how magnanimously he deigns to smile at the civilities of our famished mothers and daughters! . . . And at times he tries to be witty, too, though he only comes here on visits – and how witty! It's exactly like sawing with a blunt knife at a piece of twine. He can't stand me . . . I shall go and say how do you do to him.'

And Lupikhin ran off to meet the prince.

'Here comes my special enemy,' he said, suddenly returning to me: 'you see that fat fellow, with a brown face and a bristly head – the one who's squeezing his cap, and creeping along the wall, and looking out in all directions like a wolf? I sold him, for four hundred roubles, a horse that was worth a thousand, and that dumb animal now has every right to despise me; and yet he's so bereft of all power of thought, especially in the morning, until he's had his tea, or immediately after dinner, that you could say to him "Good day" and he'll answer "What for?" And here comes the Excellency,' continued Lupikhin: 'the retired, ruined Excellency. He's got a sugar-beet daughter and a scrofulous factory . . . I'm sorry, I got it wrong . . . well, anyway, you understand. Oh! The architect's turned up, too! He's a German, but he's got whiskers and doesn't know his job. Very unusual! . . . But indeed, what's the use of his knowing his job? All he needs do is take bribes, and run up more columns and pillars for the pillars of our nobility!'

Lupikhin chuckled again . . . But suddenly a tremulous excitement spread through the whole house. The great Personage had arrived. Our host fairly rushed into the hall. After him pressed a few faithful domestics and some assiduous guests. The roar of talk turned to a soft, pleasant buzz, like the springtime humming of bees in their native hives. Only that irrepressible wasp, Lupikhin, and that magnificent drone, Kozelsky, failed to lower their voices . . . And now, at last, the queen bee, the great Personage, came in. Hearts went out to meet him, seated bodies arose; even the gentleman who had bought Lupikhin's horse cheap, even he pressed his chin into his breast. The Personage kept his dignity admirably; with a backward movement of his head, as if bowing, he pronounced a few words of approbation, each one of which began with the letter 'a' pronounced drawlingly through the nose; he looked at Prince Kozelsky's beard as angrily as if he wanted to eat him, and gave the ruined Excellency with the factory and the daughter the index finger of his left hand. After a few minutes, during which the Personage managed to observe twice that he was very glad not to be late for dinner, the whole company made its way to the dining-room, the bigwigs leading.

Need I tell the reader how the great Personage was given the place of honour between the Excellency and the Marshal of Nobility of the Province, a man with a frank, dignified expression, completely in keeping with his starched shirt-front, immense waistcoat, and round snuff-box full of French snuff; how the host fussed, ran about, worried, pressed his guests to fall to, smiled at the great Personage's back as he passed, and, standing in a corner like a schoolboy, hurriedly gulped down a plate of soup or a morsel of beef; how the butler handed round a fish a yard long with a bouquet in its mouth; how liveried, severe-looking footmen gloomily plied each gentleman, now with Malaga, now with dry Madeira; how almost all the gentlemen, especially those of a certain age, as if in reluctant obedience to a sense of duty, drank down glass after glass, and how at last the champagne bottles popped and the toasts began coming out: this is probably all too familiar to the reader. But I was especially struck with a story told by the great Personage himself in the midst of a general, joyful silence. Someone, acquainted with modern literature, I think it was the ruined Excellency, had referred to the influence of women in general and in particular their influence on young men. 'Yes, yes,' rejoined the Personage. 'That's true; young men must be kept under strict obedience to orders, or else they go off their heads at the sight of a skirt.' A smile of childish hilarity darted over the faces of all the guests; one gentleman even had a look of gratitude in his eye. 'Because young men are fools.' Probably to sound important, the great Personage now and then altered the normal accentuation of his syllables. 'Take my own son Ivan,' he continued; 'the fool's only just twenty, and suddenly he says to me: "Please, father, I want to get married!" I tell him he's a fool, he must see some service first . . . Well, there were tears of despair . . . But I made him . . .' These last words the Personage pronounced with his stomach rather than with his lips; he paused, and looked majestically at his neighbour, the Excellency, meanwhile raising his brows far higher than one could have thought possible. His Excellency leant his head amiably to one side and blinked with extraordinary speed, while still gazing at the Personage. 'So now,' began the Personage again, 'he writes to me saying, "Thank you, father, for teaching me such a good lesson." . . . That's how one ought to treat them.' All the guests, needless to say, were in full agreement with the narrator, and seemed to gain in animation from the pleasure and instruction they had received . . . After dinner the whole company rose and moved to the drawing-room with a noise that was loud, but all the same correct, and seemingly designed expressly for this particular occasion . . . They sat down to cards.

Somehow or other I got through the evening and, after telling my coachman to harness my carriage at five o'clock the next morning, I retired to sleep. But I was fated that day to make a most remarkable new acquaintance.

Owing to the number of guests who had turned up, no one was able to sleep alone. In the small, greenish, dampish room to which Alexander Mikhailich's butler conducted me, I found another guest, already fully undressed. At the sight of me he darted nimbly under the blanket, covered himself with it right up to his nose, fidgeted a bit on the yielding feather-bed, and lay still, looking sharply out from below the round brim of a paper night-cap. I went over to the other bed (there were only two of them in the room), undressed, and lay down between the damp sheets. My neighbour turned over in bed . . . I wished him good night.

Half an hour went by. Try as I might, I could not get to sleep . . . One vague, useless thought after another went past in endless file, with the stubborn monotony of buckets on a dredging-machine.

'Can't you sleep?' said my neighbour.

'I can't, as you see,' I answered. 'Nor you either?'

'I never feel sleepy.'

'How so?'

'It's like this. I fall asleep without knowing how; I lie and lie, and then I go to sleep.'

'Then why d'you go to bed before you feel sleepy?'

'What else d'you expect me to do?'

I didn't answer my neighbour's question.

'I'm surprised,' he went on, after a slight pause, 'that there are no fleas here. Wherever d'you think they've got to?'

'You speak as if you missed them,' I remarked.

'No, I don't miss them, but I like due sequence in all things.'

I say, I thought to myself, what words he uses! My neighbour was silent again.

'Would you like to have a bet with me?' he said suddenly, in a rather loud voice.

'About what?'

My neighbour was beginning to entertain me.

'H'm, about what? I'll tell you about what. I'll bet that you take me for a fool.'

'For goodness' sake,' I murmured in amazement.

'For a boor, a wild man from the steppes . . . Admit it . . .'

'I haven't the pleasure of knowing you,' I rejoined . . . 'How you can have concluded . . .'

'How! Why, by the very sound of your voice: you answer me so casually . . . But I'm not at all what you think . . .'

'If you please . . .'

'No, if *you* please. In the first place, I speak French no worse than you, and German even better than you; secondly, I have lived abroad for three years; in Berlin alone I spent eight months. I have made a thorough study of Hegel, my dear sir, and I know Goethe by heart; and into the bargain I was for a long time in love with the daughter of a German professor, and got married, at home, to a consumptive young lady, a bald but very remarkable person. So I'm a bird of the same feather as yourself; I'm no bumpkin from the steppes, as you suppose . . . I too am a prey to reflection, and there's nothing spontaneous about me at all.'

I raised my head and gazed at the strange fellow with redoubled attention. In the dim glow of the night-light I could hardly make out his features.

'You see, now you're looking at me,' he continued, straightening his night-cap, 'and you're probably wondering how it was that you never noticed me this evening. I'll tell you why not; because I never raise my voice; because I hide behind other people, stand behind doors, speak to nobody; because a butler with a tray, going past me, raises his elbow beforehand to the level of my chest. And why does all this happen? For two reasons: first, I'm poor, and secondly . . . I've resigned myself . . . Tell me the truth, you *didn't* notice me.'

'I certainly had not the pleasure . . .'

'There you are, there you are,' he interrupted me. 'I knew it.' He lifted himself slightly and folded his arms; the long shadow of his night-cap twisted its way from the wall up to the ceiling.

'But admit it,' he added, with a sudden sidelong look at me. 'I must strike you as a very odd fellow, as what they call an original, or perhaps, if you like, something even worse: perhaps you think that I'm just pretending to be odd?'

'I must repeat to you again, that I don't know you ...'

He looked down for a moment.

'Why I've so unexpectedly got into conversation with a complete stranger like yourself – the Lord alone knows!' He sighed. 'Not because of any affinity between our souls! You and I are both decent people, that's to say, egoists: you haven't the slightest concern with me, nor I with you; isn't that so? But we can neither of us get to sleep ... so why not talk? I'm in good form, too, which seldom happens to me. I'm shy, you see, not shy in the sense of being an insignificant wretch of a provincial, but in the sense of being a man of intense self-esteem. But sometimes, under the influence of favourable circumstances, of events which I'm not in a position to determine or foresee, my shyness vanishes completely, as now for instance. Now you could put me face to face with the Dalai Lama – and I would just ask him for a pinch of snuff. But perhaps you want to go to sleep?'

'On the contrary,' I rejoined hurriedly, 'I'm enjoying our conversation very much.'

'That is, I am amusing you, you mean ... So much the better ... And so, I must inform you, I'm described hereabouts as an original, described, that is, by those who happen, in the midst of other trifles, to mention my name: "For no one feels greatly concerned with my estate." They want to hurt me ... Oh, my God, if they only knew ... Why, in fact, I'm dying just because there's absolutely nothing original about me, nothing but such pranks as, for example, my present conversation with you; pranks that are not worth a brass farthing. It's the cheapest and basest form of originality.'

He turned his face towards me and threw up his hands.

'My dear sir,' he exclaimed, 'my opinion is that only originals are fit to live on earth: only they have the right to live. *Mon verre n'est pas grand, mais je bois dans mon verre*, as someone said. You see,' he added in a low voice, 'how pure my French pronunciation is. What does it matter to me that someone has a high, capacious brow, understands everything, knows a lot, keeps up with the times – if he's got absolutely nothing individual and peculiar to himself? If there's one more storage-place for platitudes in the world – who gets any satisfaction out of that? No, be as stupid as you like, but in your own way! Have your own smell, your individual smell, that's the answer! And don't think that I expect a great deal from this smell . . . Quite the contrary! There are any number of such originals; look where you will, you'll see one; every man alive is an original, and yet I don't happen to be one of them!

'But all the same,' he continued after a pause, 'in my young days, what expectations I aroused! What a high opinion I cherished of myself, before I left to go abroad, and immediately after my return! Well, abroad I kept my ears pricked, I went my own way, as befits those of us who know a thing or two, but finally realize that they don't even know as far as the letter "A".

'Original, original!' he repeated, reproachfully shaking his head. 'They call me an original . . . but in practice it seems that in the whole world there's no man less original than your very humble servant. I must have been born imitating someone else . . . My God! I even live in imitation of various favourite authors of mine. I live by the sweat of my brow. I studied, fell in love, eventually got married, all as it were against my own will, but carrying out a duty or a lesson – goodness knows what!'

He tore his night-cap from his head and threw it down on the bed.

'Would you like me to tell you about my life?' he asked me abruptly. 'Or rather certain features of my life?'

'Please do.'

'Or no; I'd do better to tell you how I got married. You see, marriage is the principal thing, the touchstone of the whole man; it reflects like a mirror . . . No, that comparison is too hackneyed . . . Forgive me, I must take a pinch of snuff.'

He took out a snuff-box from under his pillow, opened it, and began speaking again, waving the open snuff-box.

'Now, my dear sir, put yourself in my shoes. Just tell me, I ask you, what good could I have derived from Hegel's *Encyclopædia*? Just tell me, what is there in common between this *Encyclopædia* and life in Russia? How can one be expected to apply it to our existence, not the *Encyclopædia* only, but German philosophy in general, or rather German science?'

He started up in bed and began muttering under his breath, his teeth fiercely clenched.

'So that's how it is, is it? ... Then why did you go trailing off abroad, why didn't you stay at home and study the life of your environment on the spot? You would have learnt to know its needs and its future, and you would also have seen more clearly what your own calling was to be ... But, for goodness' sake,' he went on, with another change of tone, as if in timid self-justification, 'how can the likes of us be expected to learn what no genius has yet written in any book! I should have been delighted to take lessons from the Russian way of life – but it keeps mum, the old dear, "Just take me as I am," it says; but I can't manage that; I need the upshot of it, the conclusion ... "Conclusion!" it says. "Here's the conclusion for you: listen to our learned Muscovites – aren't they 'nightingales'?" Yes, there's the trouble, that they sing like nightingales from Kursk and don't talk as the people do ... So I thought to myself: after all, science is the same everywhere and truth's the same too – and so I went off with God's blessing and landed in a strange country, among the heretics ... What can you expect? I was carried away by youth and pride. I didn't want to run to fat before my time, although it's supposed to be quite healthy to do so. And anyway, if nature gave you no flesh, how can you expect your body to run to fat?

'However,' he added, after reflecting a while, 'I think I promised to tell you how I came to get married. So listen. First of all, I must tell you that my wife is no longer in the world of the living; secondly ... but, secondly, I see that I will have to tell you the story of my youth, otherwise you won't understand anything about it ... But don't you want to go to sleep?'

'No, I don't.'

'Splendid! Listen ... There is Mr. Kantagryukhin in the next room, snoring away – so commonly! I was born of poor parents – I say parents, because tradition has it that as well as a mother I had a father! I don't remember him; they say he was not too clever, had a big nose, freckles, and red hair and took snuff up one nostril; his picture hung in my mother's bedroom, in a red tunic with a black collar up to his ears, as ugly as can be. I used to be taken past him to be whipped and on such occasions my mother used to always point to him and say: "*He* would *really* give it to you." You can imagine how that encouraged me. I had no brothers or sisters; or rather, to be quite accurate, I had a poor devil of a little brother with the English disease[1] at the back of his neck, but somehow or other he died very quickly... And what business had the English disease to come all the way to the Government of Kursk and the District of Shchigrovo, you might ask? But that's by the way. My mother took my education in hand with all the impetuous earnestness of the steppe-landowner's lady: she took it in hand from the red-letter day of my birth until the advent of my sixteenth year... You follow the thread of my discourse?'

'Of course I do, please go on.'

'Very well. On the advent of my sixteenth year, my mother, without an instant's delay, went and dismissed my French tutor, who was a German called Philippovich, from the Ukrainian Greeks. She took me to Moscow, entered me at the University, and yielded up her soul to the Almighty, leaving me in the charge of my uncle, Koltun-Babur, the lawyer, a bird whose fame had spread even outside the district of Shchigrovo. My uncle Koltun-Babur, the lawyer, fleeced me good and proper... But that again is by the way. When I entered the University – I must give my mother all credit for it – I was pretty well-prepared; but, even then, a lack of originality could be detected in me. My childhood had been in no way different from the childhood of quantities of other young gentlemen. I grew up in the same stupid, sluggish way, as if underneath a feather-bed. I began repeating verses by heart at the same early age, and languishing under the pretext of a dreamy predilec-

1 Rickets. – *Translators*.

tion . . . for what? – Oh, for the beautiful of course . . . and so on. At the University I didn't strike out a new course; I immediately got into a set. Times were different then . . . but perhaps you don't know what these sets are? I remember Schiller said somewhere:

> Gefährlich ist's den Leu zu wecken
> Und schrecklich ist des Tigers Zahn,
> Doch das schrecklichste der Schrecken
> Das ist der Mensch in seinem Wahn!

'I assure you he didn't mean to say that: he meant to say: "*Das ist ein* 'set' *in der Stadt Moskau.*" '

'What do you see that's so awful about a set?' I asked.

My neighbour seized hold of his night-cap and pushed it forward over his nose.

'What do I see that's so awful?' he exclaimed. 'I'll tell you: a set is the destruction of all individual development; a set is a hideous substitute for society, for women, for life; a set . . . Oh, just wait; I'll tell you what a set is like! It's a lazy, sluggish way of living together, and as such has significance and an appearance of reason; it replaces conversation by argument, induces a habit of fruitless chatter, distracts you from solitary and useful work, gives you a literary itch, and finally deprives you of all freshness and integrity of soul. A set is just triviality and boredom masquerading as brotherliness and friendship, a combination of misunderstandings and pretensions under the guise of frankness and sympathy. In a set, thanks to the right all your friends have, at every hour and every minute, to put their unwashed fingers right into your heart, no one has any clean, untouched place left in his soul; in a set every empty rhetorician, every conceited genius, every premature old man, is received with reverence, every talentless versifier with esoteric ideas is carried shoulder-high; in a set, young lads of seventeen talk slyly and sagely of women and love, but with women they are silent or else they talk the language of books to them – and what they talk about! A set is the forcing-house for a subtilized eloquence; in a set, everyone watches his neighbour as sharply as so many police officials . . . Oh, a set! It's not a set at all: it's a vicious circle which has been the undoing of more than one decent man.'

'No, that's exaggerated, if I may say so,' I interrupted him.

My neighbour looked at me in silence.

'It may be, the Lord knows, it may be. You see, people like myself have only one pleasure left – exaggeration. Anyway, that's how I spent four years in Moscow. I cannot describe to you, my dear sir, how quickly, how terribly quickly, that time passed; besides, it saddens and mortifies me to remember. You would get up in the morning and it would be like going downhill on a sledge . . . You look, and you're already at the end of the run; already it's evening, and a sleepy servant is helping you on with your frock-coat – you dress and wander round to see a friend, you smoke a pipe, you drink weak tea by the glassful and talk about German philosophy, love, the eternal sunshine of the spirit, and other abstruse topics. But even there I met original, individual people: with some people, force themselves as they might, struggle as they might to accustom themselves to the yoke, nature nevertheless prevailed. I alone was unlucky enough to let myself be moulded like soft wax, and my wretched nature put up not the slightest resistance! Meanwhile I had reached the age of twenty-one. I became master of my inheritance, or, more accurately, of that part of my inheritance which my guardian had thought fit to let me have. I gave full powers for the administration of all my estates to a freed serf in my employment named Vasily Kudryashov and went abroad, to Berlin. I lived abroad, as I have already had the pleasure of telling you, for three years. And what of it? Even there, even abroad, I remained the same unoriginal creature. First of all, I need not tell you that I did not learn the slightest thing about Europe or the European way of life; I listened to German professors and read German books, on their native soil . . . That was the only difference. I lived a solitary, monastic sort of life. I made the acquaintance of retired Russian lieutenants, stricken, as I was, with a thirst for knowledge, and incidentally very slow in the uptake and with no gift of self-expression; I hobnobbed with dull-witted families from Penza and other corn-growing provinces; I crawled round the coffee-houses, read the papers, went to the theatre in the evening. I had but a slight acquaintance with the natives, talked to them with a sense of strain, and entertained none of them except two or three importunate youths of Jewish origin who constantly came running to me and borrowed money from me – since *der Russe* is a gullible creature. A strange trick of fate eventually brought me to the house of one of my professors. This is how it was: I asked to see him to enter my name for a course, and he suddenly went and asked me to his house one evening. This professor had two daughters, about twenty-seven, strapping girls, good luck to them – magnificent noses, ringlet-curls, pale-blue eyes, red hands with white nails. One was called Linchen, the other Minchen. I began to go often to the professor's house. I must explain that this professor was, not exactly stupid, but a bit cracked; when he was lecturing, he spoke quite consecutively; but at home he lisped and kept his spectacles up on his forehead; incidentally he was an extremely learned man . . . And what next? Suddenly I thought I was in love with Linchen – and I thought so for a whole six months. It's true that I spoke to her little – I just looked at her, rather; but I used to read aloud to her various touching compositions, and squeeze her hands furtively, and in the evening I used to dream beside her, staring at the moon, or else simply looking up. Besides, she made such excellent coffee! . . . What else could I want, I thought. One thing confused me: even in the so-called moments of indescribable bliss, somehow or other I felt queer in the pit of my stomach, and a depressing, cold shudder ran over my belly. Eventually I could bear my happiness no longer and ran away. After this I spent two more whole years abroad: I was in Italy. In Rome I stood in front of the Transfiguration, in Florence, in front of the Venus; I would suddenly plunge into an extravagant rapture, as if a violent fit had come over me; in the evenings I wrote verses, began a diary; in a word, there too I behaved the same as everybody else. Meanwhile, how easy it would have been to be original. For instance, I don't understand the first thing about painting and sculpture ... Why not say so aloud? ... No, quite impossible! Off I went to take a Cicerone and run around looking at frescoes ...'

He lowered his gaze again, and again took off his night-cap.

'So, at last, I returned to my native land,' he continued in a tired voice. 'I came to Moscow. In Moscow I underwent a surprising change. Abroad I had been rather silent, but there I suddenly began to talk with unexpected briskness and at the same time I put on goodness knows what airs. There were amiable people who thought I was practically a genius; ladies listened sympathetically to my spoutings, but I did not manage to stay at the height of my glory. One fine morning a story about me began to circulate (I don't know who brought it to the light of day: it must have been one of those old maids of the male sex who swarm in Moscow), but it started, and began putting out shoots and tendrils, like a strawberry-plant. I got entangled, tried to jump clear, to burst the clinging threads – I couldn't do it ... I went away. Even in that, I showed my absurdity. I had only to wait quietly for the end of the trouble, like waiting for the end of a nettle-rash, and the same amiable people would again have opened their doors to me, the same ladies would again have smiled at my remarks. But that's the whole trouble: I'm not an original man. It was conscience, I beg you to remark, which suddenly awoke in me: I felt somehow ashamed of chattering, chattering without pause, chattering away – yesterday in Arbat, to-day in Truba, to-morrow in Sivtsev Vrazhok, and always on the same themes ... But if they asked for it? Look at the real champions in this line of business: they find no difficulty about it; on the contrary, it's exactly what they need; some of them will work away with their tongues for twenty years, and all the time in the same direc-tion ... What self-confidence and conceit can do to you! I had it too, conceit, and even now it's not completely dead. But the trouble is, I'll say it again, that I'm not an original man, I have got caught between two stools: nature should either have vouchsafed me much more conceit, or should have given me none at all. But I had a really hard time in my early days; on top of it, my journey abroad had finally ruined my fortune, and I didn't want to marry some merchant's widow with a young body, but already flabby as a jelly – so I went home to the country. I think,' added my neighbour, with another sidelong look at me, 'that I can pass over in silence the first impressions of country life, allusions to the beauty of nature, the quiet charm of solitude and so on!'

'You can indeed,' I rejoined.

'The more so,' continued the narrator, 'that it is all non-sense, at least so far as I am concerned. In the country I was as bored as a locked-up puppy. Although I must admit that on the way home – it was spring – when for the first time I drove past the familiar birch-wood, my head began to spin and my heart to beat with a vague, sweet feeling of anticipation. But those vague feelings of anticipation, as you know, are never realized; on the contrary, other things are realized instead which you don't at all expect, like cattle diseases, arrears of rent, sales by public auction and so on and so forth. Existing from hand to mouth, from one day to another, with the help of my bailiff Yakov, who had superseded my previous agent, and who in the course of time proved to be just as much of a swindler, if not more, and on top of that poisoned my existence with the smell of his tarred boots, I remembered one day about a family I knew in the neighbourhood, consisting of a retired colonel's widow and two daughters, ordered my drozhky to be harnessed and drove over to see them. For me that day must remain for ever memorable: six months later I married the colonel's widow's second daughter!'

The narrator lowered his head and raised his hands to heaven.

'And incidentally,' he added with some warmth, 'I wouldn't wish you to have a bad opinion of the dead lady. Heaven forbid! She was the noblest, best-hearted of creatures, a creature full of affection and of infinite capacity for self-sacrifice, though, it must be admitted, between ourselves, that if I had not had the misfortune to lose her, I would probably have been in no position to converse with you to-day, because in my shed the beam is still extant from which on more than one occasion I planned to hang myself! . . .

'There are certain pears,' he began again, after a short pause, 'which need to lie for some time underground in a cellar, in order to find their true flavour; my late wife was evidently another of nature's works with the same quality. It is only now that I do her full justice. It is only now, for instance, that the memory of certain evenings which I spent with her before our marriage has ceased to awake the slightest bitterness in me, but on the contrary moves me almost to tears. They were people of no fortune; their house, which was very old, wooden but comfortable, stood on a hill between a garden that had run riot and an overgrown courtyard. At the foot of the hill a river flowed by, hardly visible through thick foliage. A big terrace led from the house to the garden, and in front of the terrace lay an oblong bed which was a mass of roses; at each end of the bed grew two acacias, which the late master had trained to the shape of a screw while they were still young. A little farther on, in the very heart of a raspberry-thicket which had been let go and had run wild, stood a summer-house, elaborately painted inside, but so old and decrepit outside that it gave one an eerie feeling to look at it. From the terrace a glass door led into the drawing-room; and in the drawing-room this is what met the curious eye of the spectator: tiled stoves in the corners, on the right a broken-down piano, littered with manuscript music, a sofa covered in a faded blue stuff with a whitish design, a round table, two cabinets with nicknacks in porcelain and beads from the time of Catherine the Great, on the wall the well-known portrait of the blonde girl with the little dove in her bosom and the upturned eyes, on the table a vase of fresh roses. You see how exactly I describe it. In that drawing-room, on that terrace, was played out the whole tragi-comedy of my love. My neighbour was an ill-natured woman with a permanent ill-natured wheeze in her throat, a nagging cantankerous creature; one of her daughters, Vera, was in no way different from the ordinary run of young country ladies; the other, Sofya

– with Sofya I fell in love. The two sisters had another room, a bedroom, which they shared, with two pure little wooden beds, little yellowish albums, mignonette, and portraits of their friends, rather badly done in pencil (outstanding among them was a gentleman with an unusually energetic expression and an even more energetic signature, who in his youth had aroused unlimited expectations, but who ended, as we all do, nowhere at all); busts of Goethe and Schiller, German books, withered wreaths and other objects kept for memory's sake. Into this room I went but rarely and reluctantly; I found something stifling about it. Besides, it is an extraordinary thing, but I liked Sofya best when I was sitting with my back to her, or perhaps even when I was thinking or rather dreaming about her, especially in the evening, on the terrace. Then I would look at the sunset, at the trees, at the slender green leaves, already growing dark, but still sharply defined against the rosy sky; Sofya would be sitting in the drawing-room at the piano, constantly playing over some favourite, passionately brooding phrase of Beethoven's; the ill-natured old woman would be snoring peacefully as she sat on the sofa; in the dining-room, in a flood of warm light, Vera would be bustling about preparing tea; the samovar would be whistling fancifully, as if it was pleased about something; there would be the cheerful crackle of breaking pretzels, the musical chime of spoons on cups; the canary, which had trilled away unmercifully all day, had suddenly fallen silent, with only an occasional chirrup, as if asking about something; a small, transparent cloud went by and a few raindrops fell . . . And I sat, and sat, and listened, and listened, and looked, and my heart expanded, and I thought again that I must be in love. So, under the influence of such an evening, I asked the old woman one day for her daughter's hand, and two months later I got married. I thought I was in love with her . . . Even now, though it's high time I did, I still don't know whether I was in love with Sofya. She was a good-natured, intelligent, silent creature, with a warm heart, but, goodness knows why, whether it was from having lived so long in the country, or from some other cause, she had at the bottom of her soul (if the soul has such a thing as a bottom) a secret wound, or, to put it better, a running sore, which nothing could heal, and neither she nor I could even put a name to it. Of course, I didn't guess the existence of this wound until after our marriage. Worry myself about it as I might, nothing helped. When I was a child, I had a pet siskin, which a cat had once caught in its claws; though he had been saved and healed, my poor siskin never recovered; he pouted, he languished, he stopped singing... The end of the story was that one night a rat found its way into his open cage and bit his beak off, as a result of which he finally made up his mind to die. I don't know what cat had held my wife between its paws, but anyway she too pouted and languished like my poor siskin. Sometimes she plainly wanted to shake it off, to leap for joy in the fresh air, in the sunshine, in complete freedom; she would try to – and then roll herself up into a ball again. And yet she loved me; how many times did she assure me that she had nothing more to wish for – and then, devil take it, her eyes would go all dull. I wondered if there wasn't some story in her past life. I made inquiries; I could find nothing. Well, now, you can form your own opinion: an original man would have shrugged his shoulders, perhaps heaved a couple of sighs, and then set about leading his own life; but I, like the unoriginal creature I am, began casting an eye up at the beams. My wife had so far succumbed to the habits of an old maid – Beethoven, walks at night, mignonette, correspondence with friends, albums – that she was quite unable to accustom herself to any new way of life, particularly to that of mistress of a house; and you must admit it was ridiculous for a married woman to languish under a nameless regret and sing, of an evening: "*Awake her not at dawn.*"

'Well, we enjoyed this sort of bliss for three years; in the fourth year Sofya died, of her first child, and – a strange thing – I had had a kind of premonition beforehand that she would not be able to present me with a daughter or a son, or the earth with a new inhabitant. I remember her funeral. It was in the spring. We have a little old parish church, with a blackened iconostasis, bare walls and a dilapidated tiled floor; in the choir, on either side, there is a huge old icon. They carried in the coffin, put it down right in the middle, in front of the main doors of the iconostasis, covered it with a faded cloth, and set three candlesticks round it. The service started. A little doddering clerk, with a little pigtail behind, and a green belt below his waist, was mumbling lugubriously in front of the lectern; the priest, who was old too, with a good-natured, short-sighted face, in a purple vestment with a yellow pattern, was conducting the service and acting as deacon as well. Across the open windows the fresh young leaves of the weeping birch-trees murmured and stirred; from outside came the smell of grass; the red flame of the wax candles paled in the gay light of the spring day; the twittering of the sparrows filled the whole church, and now and then, from under the dome, came a cheerful exclamation from a swallow which had flown in. In the golden dust of the sunlight, the fair heads of a few peasants, zealously praying for the dead lady, rose and fell busily; in a fine, bluish wisp, smoke rose from the mouth of the censer. I looked on the dead face of my wife . . . God! Even death, death itself, had not freed her, had not healed her wound: the same ailing, frightened, dull expression – as if she was ill at ease even in her coffin . . . I felt the ache of the blood stirring within me. She had been such a good creature, but she had done well for herself to die!'

The narrator's cheeks were flushed and his eyes were dimmed.

'Finally,' he began again, 'when I had got over the deep depression which seized me after the death of my wife, I thought I would set my hand to the plough, as the saying goes. I took up official duties in the provincial capital, but in the big rooms of the Government building my head would begin to ache and my eyes to do their job badly; there were other reasons as well . . . and I retired from my appointment. I wanted to visit Moscow, but, first of all, I hadn't enough money, and secondly, I've already told you of my mood of resignation. It had come over me suddenly, and yet not so suddenly after all. In spirit I had resigned myself long ago, but my head still refused to be bowed. I attributed the placid state of my emotions and thoughts to the influence of country life, to my unhappiness ... On the other hand, I had long since observed that almost all my neighbours, young or old, who had at first been stunned by my erudition, my travels abroad, and the other advantages of my education, had not only managed to get completely accustomed to me, but had even begun to treat me in an offhand manner, didn't wait for the end of my stories, and, when they talked to me, no longer used polite forms of speech. I have also forgotten to tell you that, during the first year after my marriage, out of boredom, I had tried to go in for literature, and had even sent in a contribution to a paper – a story, if I am not mistaken – but some little time later I received from the editor a polite letter saying, amongst other things, that though he could not deny me intelligence, he had to deny me talent, and that in literature only talent was required. On top of that, the news got round to me that a visitor from Moscow, incidentally a very good-natured young fellow, had made a passing reference to me at a party of the Governor's as being someone who was finished and played out. But my half-deliberate blindness continued. You see, I didn't want to give myself a smack in the face: but at last, one fine morning, my eyes were opened. This is how it happened. The police inspector had called on me with the object of drawing my attention to a broken-down bridge on my estate, which I was unable to repair for lack of funds. After chasing down a glass of vodka with a piece of smoked sturgeon, this affable guardian of the public peace reproached me in a fatherly way for my lack of circumspection, but put himself in my position and advised me just to tell my peasants to put on more manure, lit a pipe and began talking about the elections which were shortly to take place. The high estate of Marshal of Nobility of the Province was at that time coveted by one Orbassanov, an empty wind-bag, and a taker of bribes into the bargain. Besides, he had neither wealth nor fame to distinguish him. I spoke my mind on this score with some degree of superiority: I must admit that I looked down on Mr. Orbassanov from somewhere far above. The inspector glanced at me, clapped my shoulder in a friendly way, and said good-naturedly: "Hey, Vasily Vasilyich, it's not for the likes of you and me to judge such folk – who are we to do so? . . . The cricket must know his own hearth." "But, for goodness' sake," I rejoined indignantly, "what is the difference between me and Mr. Orbassanov?" The inspector took his pipe out of his mouth, opened his eyes wide – and fairly spluttered with laughter. "You are a one," he brought out at length, through tears. "That's a good one . . . eh?" and from then on until he took his departure he kept making fun of me, giving me an occasional dig in the ribs with his elbow and addressing me in the second person singular. Finally he left. It was the last drop needed; the cup brimmed over. I paced several times up and down the room, halted in front of the looking-glass, gazed and gazed at my embarrassed countenance, slowly put out my tongue and shook my head in bitter mockery. The veil had fallen from my eyes; I could see clearly, more clearly than my own face in the looking-glass, what an empty, insignificant, useless, unoriginal fellow I was!'

The narrator paused.

'In one of Voltaire's tragedies,' he went on sadly, 'there is a gentleman who rejoices in having reached the extreme limit of misfortune. Although there is nothing tragic about my fate, I must confess that I have experienced something of the same sort. I have known the poisonous delights of cold despair; I have learnt how sweet it is to spend a whole morning lying motionless in bed and cursing the day and hour of my birth; – I could not resign myself straight away. And I had some reason, you know: my straitened circumstances chained me to my detested country home; agriculture, state service, literature, nothing had suited me. I shunned my neighbours; books had become repugnant to me. Your insipidly plump, morbidly sensitive young ladies, who shake their curls and feverishly repeat the word "freedom", found me uninteresting, since I had stopped chattering and waxing enthusiastic. A life of complete seclusion was beyond my abilities and my powers.

I began ... what d'you suppose? I began dragging myself round to visit my neighbours. As if drunk with self-contempt, I deliberately submitted to every trivial humiliation. I was left out when the dishes came round, greeted coldly and haughtily, finally not even noticed; I was not even allowed to join in a general conversation, and I would purposely sit in a corner agreeing with some perfectly stupid chatterbox who in the old days, in Moscow, would have been enraptured to lick the dust off my feet or the hem of my coat. I didn't even allow myself to believe that I was enjoying the bitter-sweets of irony ... What's the good of irony in solitude! So that, sir, is how I continued for several years on end, and how I am still continuing to-day ...'

'But I've never heard of such a thing,' grumbled the sleepy voice of Mr. Kantagryukhin from the next room. 'Who's the fool there who's taken it into his head to talk all night?'

The narrator darted swiftly under his blanket and, looking timidly forth, shook his finger at me.

'Sh ... sh ...' he whispered and, as if with an apologetic bow in the direction of Kantagryukhin's voice, he said respectfully: 'Yes, very good, very good, I'm sorry, sir ... He's got every right to sleep, he ought to sleep,' he went on again in a whisper; 'he must get new strength, well, even if only to be able to eat to-morrow with the same satisfaction. We have no right to disturb him. Anyway, I think I have told you all I want; probably you too would like to sleep. I wish you good night.'

The narrator turned away with feverish haste and buried his head in his pillows.

'At least let me know,' I asked, 'with whom I have had the pleasure ...'

He lifted his head briskly.

'No, for heaven's sake,' he interrupted me, 'don't ask me or anyone else my name. Let me remain for you an unknown creature, the ill-starred Vasily Vasilyich. Besides, an unoriginal fellow like myself doesn't even deserve a name of his own ... But if you positively wish to call me something, then call me ... call me the Hamlet of Shchigrovo district. There are numbers of such Hamlets in every district, but it may be that you have not come across the others. Therewith, I wish you farewell.'

He buried himself again in his quilt, and next morning when they came to call me he was no longer in the room. He had gone away before daybreak.

Chertopkhanov and Nedopyuskin

O NE hot summer's day I was returning in the cart from shooting; Ermolai sat dozing and nodding beside me. The dogs twitched as they lay at our feet in a dead sleep. Now and again the coachman flicked the gad-flies off the horses with his whip. A faint cloud of white dust floated after the cart. We drove into the brushwood. The road grew worse and our wheels began catching on roots. Ermolai started up, looked around . . . 'Hey!' he said. 'There ought to be blackcock here. Let's get out.' We halted and went into the undergrowth. My dog put up a covey. I fired, and was beginning to reload my gun, when suddenly, from behind me, I heard a loud crackling and, parting the bushes with his hands, a man on horse-back came riding up to me. 'But kindly inform me,' he began in a haughty voice, 'by what right you are shooting here, my dear sir?' The stranger spoke extremely quickly, jerkily, and through his nose. I looked him in the face: never in all my life have I seen anything like him. Imagine, dear reader, a small, fair-haired man with a little red turned-up nose and interminable ginger side-whiskers. A pointed Persian cap with a top made of raspberry-coloured cloth covered his forehead right down to the eyebrows. He wore a shabby yellow coat with black cartridge-pleats at the chest and faded silver braid at all the seams; from his shoulders hung a horn, out of his belt stuck a dagger. His scraggy, hook-nosed, sorrel horse fidgeted under him like one possessed; two thin crooked-legged borzoi dogs kept circling close beneath it. The stranger's face, his look, his voice, all his movements, his whole being, breathed a crazy bravado and a limitless, unheard-of arrogance; his pale-blue, glassy eyes rolled and squinted like a drunkard's; he threw his head back, puffed out his cheeks, whinnied and twitched all over, as though from a surfeit of dignity – a regular turkey-cock of a man. He repeated his question.

'I didn't know it was forbidden to shoot here,' I answered.

'My dear sir,' he went on, 'you are on my land.'

'Very well, I'll go away.'

'But kindly inform me,' he rejoined, 'have I the honour to address a nobleman?'

I told him my name.

'In that case, please go on shooting. I am a nobleman myself, and very glad to oblige one of my peers... My name is Pantelei Chertopkhanov!'

He leant forward, whooped, and gave the horse its head; the horse started, reared up, bucked to one side and trod on the paw of one of the dogs. The dog gave a piercing yelp. Chertopkhanov boiled, hissed, punched the horse on the head between the ears, jumped down quicker than lightning, looked at the dog's paw, spat on the wound, gave the dog a push in the side with his foot to stop it whining; took hold of the horse's withers and put his foot in the stirrup. The horse threw up his head, lifted his tail and bucked sideways into the bushes; Chertopkhanov went after him hopping on one leg, managed at last to scramble into the saddle, whirled his whip like a raving madman, blew his horn and galloped off. I had not had time to recover my senses after Chertopkhanov's unexpected apparition, when suddenly, almost noiselessly, there rolled out of the bushes, on a smallish, blackish horse, a fat little man of about forty. He stopped, took off his green leather cap and asked me in a faint soft voice if I hadn't seen a man on a sorrel horse. I answered that I had.

'Which way would he have gone?' he continued, in the same voice, and without replacing his cap.

'That way.'

'Thank you very much indeed, sir.'

He smacked his lips, swung his legs against his horse's sides, and jogged away – trit-trot, trit-trot – in the direction indicated. I looked after him until his horned cap disappeared behind the branches. This new stranger in no way resembled his predecessor in appearance. His face, which was chubby and round as a ball, wore an expression of embarrassment, good nature and timid resignation; his nose, which was also chubby and round and mottled with blue veins, indicated the good liver. There was not a single hair left on the front of his head, but at the back there were some sparse blond tufts sticking up; his little eyes, which were like slits made with a reed, twinkled amiability; there was a pleasant smile on his red, puffy lips. He wore a coat with a stand-up collar and copper buttons, very worn, but clean; his little cloth breeches were rucked up high; a pair of fat little calves showed above the yellow turnovers of his boots.

'Who is that?' I asked Ermolai.

'That? Tikhon Ivanich Nedopyuskin. He lives at Chertop-khanov's.'

'What, is he badly off?'

'Not well off; and Chertopkhanov has not got a brass farthing either.'

'Then why has he gone to live with him?'

'Well, you see, they became friends, they're always together... thick as the horse and his hoof, or the crab and his shell, as the saying goes.'

We walked out of the brushwood; suddenly two beagles gave tongue near at hand, and a big white hare came darting through the oats, which were already standing fairly high. Close on his heels there burst from the trees a pack of beagles and borzois, and close on their heels Chertopkhanov himself came flying out. There were no shouts from him, no cries of 'go on' or 'seek': he was puffing and choking; from his half-open mouth burst now and again an abrupt inarticulate sound; he flashed past, eyes bursting out of his head, flogging his unlucky horse furiously with his whip. The borzois were gaining ground, when the hare crouched down, doubled sharply back and bolted past Ermolai into the bushes. The borzois streamed past. 'Go *on*, go *on*!' the fainting huntsman whispered laboriously, as if tongue-tied. 'Good boy, you take care of him!' Ermolai fired... The wounded hare spun round like a top on the smooth, dry grass, sprang up into the air and screamed between the teeth of a hound that was worrying him furiously. The pack had swooped on him at once.

Chertopkhanov threw himself from his horse like a whirlwind, snatched out his dagger, ran straddle-legged over to the pack, tore the mangled hare away from them with furious oaths, and, with his whole face distorted, plunged his dagger into its throat right up to the hilt . . . plunged it in, and began to roar with laughter. Tikhon Ivanich appeared at the edge of the wood. 'Ho, ho, ho, ho, ho!' bawled Chertopkhanov for the second time. 'Ho, ho, ho, ho, ho,' repeated his companion calmly.

'But it isn't right to hunt in the middle of summer,' I observed, drawing Chertopkhanov's attention to the trampled oats.

'It's my land,' answered Chertopkhanov, hardly breathing. He disembowelled the hare, quartered it and distributed its paws among the dogs.

'I must pay for your shot, my friend, according to the rules of the chase,' he said, addressing Ermolai. 'And as for you, my dear sir,' he added in the same abrupt, sharp voice, 'thank you.'

He mounted his horse.

'Kindly tell me . . . I have forgotten your name.'

I told him again.

'Very glad to make your acquaintance. If opportunity offers, I hope you'll pay me a visit . . . But where's that fellow Fomka?' he went on, with feeling. 'They got the hare without him.'

'His horse fell,' answered Tikhon with a smile.

'Fell? Orbassan fell? Where . . . where is he?'

'Over there, behind the wood.'

Chertopkhanov struck his horse's head with the whip and galloped off helter-skelter. Tikhon bowed to me twice – once for himself, and once for his friend, and again went off at a jog-trot into the bushes.

These two gentlemen stirred my curiosity strangely . . . What was it that could hold two such different creatures together in the bonds of inseparable friendship? I began to make inquiries, and this is what I learnt.

Throughout the district Pantelei Eremeich Chertopkhanov had the reputation of a dangerous, crazy, proud fellow, and a first-class picker of quarrels. He had served for a very short time in the army and had resigned as a result of 'unpleasant-nesses' with the rank that has given rise to the saying that a hen is no bird.[1] He came of an old family which had once been wealthy. His ancestors had lived sumptuously, after the manner of the steppes; that is to say, they received all and sundry, fed them to surfeit, allowed visiting coachmen a quarter of oats for each troika, kept musicians, singers, buffoons and hounds, treated their people to wine and home-brewed beer on feast-days, drove away in the winter to Moscow in heavy travelling-coaches drawn by their own horses, and now and then sat for months on end without a farthing and lived on home-grown poultry. The family fortune was already dissipated when Pan-telei's father succeeded to it; he in his turn enjoyed life heartily, and, when he died, left to his sole heir, Pantelei, the mortgaged village of Bessonovo, with thirty-five serfs and seventy-six women, and thirty-nine acres and one rood of poor land in the wilderness of Kolobrodova, on which, incidentally, there were no serfs entered in the title-deeds of the deceased. The deceased, it must be agreed, had ruined himself in the most remarkable way: 'Cost Accounting' had been his undoing. According to his principles, a gentleman ought not to depend on merchants, townsmen and other such 'pilferers', as he termed them; he imported into his estate every possible trade and skill. 'It looks better and costs less,' he said. 'Cost Account-ing!' This disastrous idea stuck with him to the end of his life; and this it was that ruined him. But he had a good run for his money! There was no whim that he denied himself. Among other inspirations, he rigged up one day, following his own calculations, such a huge family coach, that, notwithstanding the combined efforts of peasants' horses, rounded up from the whole village, and of their owners, it came to grief and disin-

---

1 The lowest rank. 'A hen is no bird, a woman no human being, an ensign no officer.' – *Translators*.

tegrated on the first slope. Eremei Lukich (such was the name
of Pantelei's father) gave orders for a monument to be erected
on the slope, but otherwise was not in the least put out. He also
had the idea of building a church, on his own, of course, and
without the help of an architect. He burnt up a whole forest in
baking the bricks, he laid the foundations – and they were
immense: fit for a cathedral in a provincial capital! He built the
walls, and started putting on the dome: the dome collapsed. He
started again, again the dome fell in; he did it a third time, a
third time the dome crashed. Eremei Lukich took thought:
there must be something a bit wrong . . . he pondered . . . there
must be an evil spell on it . . . so suddenly he gave orders that all
the old women in the village were to be whipped. And whipped
they were – but all the same the dome never went up. He
started rebuilding his peasants' huts on a new plan, all based on
Cost Accounting; he grouped every three back-yards together
in a triangle, and in the middle he put up a pole, with a painted
box full of starlings, and a flag. Every day he would have a new
brain-wave: now it would be making soup out of dock-leaves,
now it would be clipping horses' tails to make caps for the
house-servants, now it would be plans to substitute nettles for
flax or to feed pigs on mushrooms. His brain-waves were not
only financial, either; he also worried his head about the welfare of his servants. One day he read in the *Moscow News* an
article by a landowner from Kharkov, a certain Mr. Khryakà-
Khrupyorski, about the importance of morality in the peasants'
life, and the very next day he gave orders that all his peasants were forthwith to learn the landowner's article by heart –
this is how it began: 'Attained at last, thanks to the redoubled
exertions of a humane administration, the exalted goal dear to
every true scion of the fatherland,' and so on. The peasants
learnt the article; their master asked them if they understood
what it said, and the agent answered that of course they understood! About the same time he ordered that numbers should be
given to all his serfs, in the interests of orderliness and Cost
Accounting, and that each one should have his number sewn
on his collar. On meeting the master, each one of them would

cry: 'Here comes such and such a number!' And the master would answer affably: 'Carry on, bless your heart.'

Nevertheless, in spite of his orderliness and Cost Accounting, Eremei Lukich fell on very hard times: he began by mortgaging his villages, then he went on to sell them; finally the cradle of his ancestors, the village with the unfinished church, was sold by the public exchequer, luckily not in Eremei's lifetime – he could never have withstood the blow – but two weeks after his decease. He managed to die in his own house, in his own bed, surrounded by his own servants and under the care of his own doctor; but all that was left to poor Pantelei was Bessonovo.

When he heard of his father's illness, Pantelei was already on military service, right in the thick of the 'unpleasantness' referred to above. He had just turned nineteen. Since childhood he had never left home, and, under the guidance of his mother, a very kind-hearted but absolutely dull-witted lady named Vasilisa Vasilyevna, he had grown up into a thoroughly spoilt young gentleman. It was she alone who saw to his education; Eremei Lukich, plunged in his economic calculations, had no time for that. It is true that one day he personally gave his son a beating with a whip for saying 'artsy', instead of 'rtsy', but that was a day when Eremei Lukich was suffering from a deep and secret wound: his best dog had run into a tree and killed itself. Anyhow Vasilisa Vasilyevna's exertions in regard to Pantyusha's education were confined to a single painful effort: by the sweat of her brow she managed to give him a tutor, in the shape of a retired Alsatian soldier, one Bierkopf, and to the day of her death she trembled like a leaf before him: if he leaves, she would think – I'm done for! which way shall I turn? wherever shall I find another tutor? Even Bierkopf had only been enticed away from a neighbour with the greatest difficulty! And he, like a man of sagacity, at once exploited his monopoly: he drank himself silly and slept from morning to night. On the conclusion of his 'course of studies' Pantelei went into the army. Vasilisa Vasilyevna was already dead. She passed away six months before this important event

– from shock: in a dream she had seen a man in white riding a bear and, written on his chest, 'Antichrist'. Eremei Lukich soon followed his spouse.

At the first news of his illness, Pantelei galloped off home helter-skelter, but was too late to find his parent alive. What was the astonishment of the dutiful son when he found himself quite unexpectedly transformed from the heir to a fortune into a beggar? There are few who can withstand such a violent change of fortune: Pantelei grew savage and embittered. From a man of honour, sobriety and good nature (though also a flighty and quick-tempered one) he changed into an arrogant picker of quarrels, broke off relations with his neighbours – he was ashamed to meet the rich ones and despised the poor ones – and treated everyone with unheard-of impertinence, including even the powers that be, as much as to say: 'I am a member of the old nobility.' Once he practically shot a police inspector who came into his room without taking his cap off. Of course the powers that be, on their side, did not forgive him, and reminded him of their existence on occasion; but all the same they were afraid of him because he was such a terrible hot-head and after the second word would be ready to fight you with knives. At the slightest rejoinder Chertopkhanov's eyes would begin to rove, his voice would crack... 'Why, why – why,' he would mutter, 'damn my eyes!'... and he would be ready to run up the walls! Yet with all that he was an honest man and never mixed up in any intrigue. Of course no one ever went to see him... And yet he was good-hearted, even greathearted, in his own way: he could not stand the sight of others' suffering, of injustice or oppression; he was a tower of strength to his peasants. 'What?' he would say, furiously beating his own head. 'Interfering with my people, *mine*? As if I was not Chertopkhanov!!!...'

Unlike Pantelei, Tikhon Ivanich Nedopyuskin could not boast of his origins. His father came of freeholder stock and only acquired noble rank after forty years of state service. Mr. Nedopyuskin the father belonged to that class of people whom misfortune dogs with unflagging, inexorable cruelty, with a cruelty like a personal hatred. Throughout his sixty years, from the day of his birth to the day of his death, the poor wretch had wrestled with all the constraints, ailments and miseries which are the lot of small folk; he struggled like a fish on ice, never ate enough, never slept enough, bowed, fussed, brooded and languished, trembled over every copeck, suffered quite unfairly in his official career, and died at last, in a garret or a cellar, without having managed to earn himself or his children their daily bread. Destiny had harried him like a hunted hare. He was a good, honest man, but took bribes – 'according to rank' – from a ten-copeck piece up to two silver roubles inclusive. He had a thin, consumptive wife; there were children too; luckily they all died young, except for Tikhon and one daughter, Mitrodora, nicknamed the 'merchant's glory', who after many sad and laughable adventures married a retired attorney. Mr. Nedopyuskin the father, while still alive, had managed to find Tikhon a place as a minor official in a chancery, but as soon as his father died Tikhon retired. The perpetual anxieties, the anguished struggles with cold and hunger, his mother's brooding depression, the worrying and despair of his father, the bullying rudeness of landlords and shopkeepers, all this daily, continual suffering had engendered an indescribable shyness in Tikhon: the mere sight of his chief made him tremble and swoon like a bird in a snare. He gave up the service. An indifferent and perhaps mocking nature endows people with different capacities and inclinations, without any regard to their means and position in society; with the care and love which are peculiar to her, she had moulded Tikhon, the son of a poor official, into a sensitive, soft, susceptible creature – a creature excessively intent on enjoyment, gifted with an extraordinarily fine sense of smell and taste... She moulded him, carefully put the finishing touches, and – left her product to grow up on sour cabbage and rotten fish. And so this product grew up, and began, as it is called, to 'live'. The fun started. Destiny, which had tormented Nedopyuskin the father unceasingly, now started on the son: she had clearly acquired a taste for it. But with Tikhon she used a different method: instead of tormenting him, she played with him. She never brought him to despair, never forced him to feel the shameful pangs of hunger, but tossed him about, from one end of Russia to another, from Veliky-Ustyug to Tsarevo-Kokshaisk, from one humiliating and ridiculous employment to another. First she would appoint him 'major-domo' to an ill-tempered, bilious lady-bountiful, then she would place him as hanger-on to a rich skinflint of a merchant, then she would make him principal private secretary to a pop-eyed Muscovite prince with his hair cut in the English fashion, then she would promote him to be half-butler, half-buffoon to a steppe landowner, a keeper of hounds and picker of quarrels ... In a word, destiny made poor Tikhon drink, drop by drop and to the last dregs, the bitter, poisonous draught of the underdog's life. He knew what it was to serve the oppressive caprice, the sleepy, ill-natured boredom, of idle masters. How often, alone in his room, released at last with God's blessing by a pack of guests who had had their fill of amusement, fairly bursting with shame, and with cold tears of despair in his eyes, did he swear to run away secretly the next day, to try his luck in the town, to find himself if it were only a job as clerk, or just to die once and for all from hunger in the street. But, first, God had not given him the strength; secondly, his timidity was too much for him, and thirdly and lastly, how was he going to find himself a job, whom was he going to ask? 'They'll never give me one,' the poor wretch would murmur, dozing miserably on his bed, 'they'll never give me one!' And the following day he would return to his tread-mill. The situation was all the more painful in that the same considerate nature had not bothered to endow him with the smallest share of those qualities and talents without which the buffoon's profession is all but impos-sible. For instance, he could neither dance until he fell down, wearing a bearskin inside out, nor crack jokes and exchange pleasantries in the midst of a throng of excited whippers-in; if driven out stark naked into twenty degrees of frost, he some-times caught cold; his stomach could not digest wine mixed with ink and other filth, nor fly-agaric and toad-stool minced in vinegar. Lord knows what would have become of Tikhon if the last of his benefactors, a newly rich tax-farmer, had not had the idea, by way of a joke, of adding to his will: 'To Zyozyo (or Tikhon) Nedopyuskin, I bequeathe, for himself and his descendants in perpetuity, the village of Besselendeyevka, acquired by me, with all the dependencies thereto appertaining.' A few days later, over his sterlet soup, the benefactor died of a stroke. There was a great to-do; the law arrived unexpectedly and put seals on the property in due form. The relations assembled; they opened the will; they read it, they called for Nedopyuskin. Nedopyuskin appeared. The majority of those present knew what had been Tikhon's functions in his benefactor's household. He was met by deafening shouts and jocular congratulations. 'Here he is, the new landowner!' shouted the other heirs. 'Here he is,' repeated one of them, a well-known joker and wit, 'yes, here he is, definitely . . . in actual fact . . . the . . . what d'you call it . . . the heir . . .' and everyone fairly exploded with laughter. For a while Nedopyuskin could not believe his good fortune. They showed him the will – he blushed, screwed up his eyes, and began throwing out his hands, and sobbing, and weeping buckets. The laughter of those present turned into a single sustained roar. The village of Besselendeyevka consisted of only twenty-two peasants; nobody minded much about it, so why not take the opportunity for a good laugh? Only one of the heirs, an official from Petersburg, a striking-looking man with a Greek nose and a noble expression, Rostislav Adamich Stoppel, was unable to restrain himself, and sidled up to Nedopyuskin and looked at him contemptuously over his shoulder. 'As far as I can observe, my dear sir,' he began in a tone of contemptuous indifference, 'you were employed by the respected Fyodor Fyodorich in the capacity of a kind of house-jester?' The official from Petersburg expressed himself in language that was unbearably clear, crisp and precise. In his distraction and excitement, Nedopyuskin did not take in the words of the gentleman, who was a stranger to him, but all the others immediately stopped talking: the wit smiled condescendingly. Mr. Stoppel rubbed his hands

and repeated his question. Nedopyuskin looked up in amazement and opened his mouth. Rostislav Adamich narrowed his
eyes offensively.

'Congratulations, my dear sir, congratulations,' he went
on; 'it's true that not everyone would be prepared to earn
his daily bread in such a fashion, but *de gustibus non est dis-
putandum*, that is to say, we all have our own tastes . . . Haven't
we?'

Someone in the back rows gave a short, discreet whoop of
astonishment and delight.

'Tell me,' went on Mr. Stoppel, much encouraged by the
smiles of the whole company, 'to what talent in particular do
you owe your good fortune? No, don't be shy, tell us; all of us
here are, as it were, *en famille*. Isn't that so, gentlemen, that we
are *en famille* here?'

The gentleman to whom Rostislav Adamich happened to
address this question unfortunately knew no French, and
therefore confined himself to a single faint grunt of approbation. But another beneficiary, a young man with yellowish
blotches on his forehead, asserted hastily: '*Voui, voui*, of
course.'

'Perhaps,' began Mr. Stoppel again, 'you can walk on your
hands, with your legs in the air, as it were?'

Nedopyuskin looked round unhappily – every face wore a
malicious grin, every eye was wet with mirth.

'Or, perhaps, you can crow like a cock?'

There was a burst of laughter all round which died away at
once, stifled by anticipation.

'Or, perhaps, on your nose, you . . .'

'Stop!' A sharp and ringing voice suddenly broke in. 'You
ought to be ashamed to tease the poor fellow like that!'

Everyone looked round. In the doorway stood Chertopkhanov. As a third cousin of the deceased tax-farmer, he too had
received a letter of invitation to the family gathering. While the
will was being read he had, as usual, kept proudly at a distance
from the others.

'Stop,' he repeated, arrogantly throwing back his head.

Mr. Stoppel turned round quickly and, seeing a badly-dressed, insignificant-looking man, asked his neighbour under his breath (for caution never harmed anyone): 'Who's that?'

'Chertopkhanov – a smallish bird,' replied the neighbour in his ear.

Rostislav Adamich assumed an expression of contempt: 'And who are you to give orders?' he said, through his nose, with his eyes screwed up. 'What sort of bird are you?'

Chertopkhanov blew up like powder from a spark. Rage hampered his breathing.

'Dz–dz–dz–dz,' he hissed, as if he was being throttled, then suddenly thundered out: 'Who am I? Who am I? I am Pantelei Chertopkhanov, a man of the oldest nobility, my great-great-great-great-grandfather served the Tsar, and who are you?'

Rostislav Adamich turned pale and took a step back. He had not expected such a repulse.

'A bird, *me*, *me*, a bird . . . Oh, oh, oh!'

Chertopkhanov rushed forward; Stoppel jumped away in great agitation, and the guests dashed in to meet the indignant landowner.

'Shoot it out, shoot it out at once, across a handkerchief!' cried Pantelei in a frenzy. 'Or apologize to me and to him too . . .'

'Apologize, apologize,' whispered the anxious beneficiaries surrounding Stoppel. 'You see what he is; a madman – and a homicidal one, too.'

'Forgive me, forgive me, I didn't know,' began Stoppel in a faltering voice. 'I didn't know.'

'Apologize to him, too!' shouted Pantelei indefatigably.

'*You* forgive me, too,' added Rostislav Adamich, addressing Nedopyuskin, who himself was trembling as if in a fever.

Chertopkhanov calmed down, went over to Tikhon, took his arm, looked arrogantly round, and, not meeting a single glance, solemnly, in the midst of a deep silence, walked from the room accompanied by the new owner of the Besselendeyevka property.

From that day on they were inseparable. (The village of Besselendeyevka was only eight versts away from Bessonovo.) Nedopyuskin's unbounded gratitude soon changed to an obsequious devotion. Weak, soft, and not entirely straight, Tikhon humbled himself to the dust before the fearless, reproachless Pantelei. It's tremendous! he thought to himself from time to time: he talks to the Governor, looks him straight in the eye ... why, you would think he was Christ himself!

He admired him to stupefaction, until his faculties became confused; he thought of him as a man of extraordinary intelligence and learning. And indeed, poor as Chertopkhanov's education was, nevertheless compared with Tikhon's it could be termed brilliant. It is true that Chertopkhanov read little in Russian and understood badly in French, so badly that one day, when a Swiss tutor asked him: '*Vous parlez français, monsieur?*' he answered: '*Je ne* understand,' and after a moment's thought added, '*pas*'; but all the same, he knew that there had once been a very clever writer called Voltaire and that Frederick the Great, King of Prussia, had had a distinguished military career. Among Russian writers he admired Derzhavin, loved Marlinsky and called his best hound Ammalat Bey ...

A few days after my first encounter with the two friends, I went over to Bessonovo to call on Pantelei. His little house could be seen from afar; it stood in a bare patch half a verst away from the village, conspicuous as a hawk above a ploughed field. Chertopkhanov's whole establishment consisted of four old wooden structures of various sizes, namely, the house, the stable, the barn and the bath-house. Each of these structures sat by itself, apart from the others; there was no fence around, no gate to be seen. My coachman stopped in perplexity beside a crumbling, choked-up well. By the barn some thin, dishevelled borzoi puppies were worrying a dead horse, probably Orbassan; one of them lifted a blood-stained muzzle, gave a hasty bark, and again set about gnawing the exposed ribs. Beside the horse stood a lad of about seventeen, with a plump, sallow face, Cossack's dress and bare feet; he looked solemnly at the dogs entrusted to his care, and now and then gave the greediest of them a flick of his whip.

'Is the master at home?' I asked.

'The Lord knows!' answered the lad. 'Knock on the door.'

I jumped down from the drozhky and went up to the porch of the house.

Mr. Chertopkhanov's residence had a very sorry look: the woodwork was blackened and bellying out in front, the chimney had slipped, the corners had been propped up but even so were out of true, and little windows of a dim, dove-grey colour looked out with an indescribably sour expression from beneath the shaggy roof that was jammed down above them: they looked like the eyes of some old prostitute. I knocked; no one answered. But, behind the door, I heard words sharply spoken: 'A, B, V; well, go on, you fool,' said a husky voice. 'A, B, V, G ... no! G, D, E! E! E for Eat! Go on, you fool!'

I knocked again.

The same voice shouted: 'Come in – who is it?'

I went into a little, empty front hall, and through an open door I caught sight of Chertopkhanov himself. He was sitting in a chair, in a greasy Bokhara robe, wide trousers and a red skull-cap; with one hand he was squeezing the muzzle of a young poodle, and with the other he was holding a piece of bread right in front of his nose.

'Ah!' he said with dignity, not stirring from his place. 'Very glad to see you. Kindly be seated. I am having trouble with Venzor here ... Tikhon,' he added, raising his voice, 'come here, will you. We have a visitor.'

'Coming, coming,' answered Tikhon from the next room. 'Masha, give me my cravat.'

Chertopkhanov addressed himself again to Venzor and put the piece of bread on his nose. I looked around. The room had no furniture except a warped folding-table on thirteen uneven legs, and four sagging straw-chairs; the walls, which ages ago had been painted white with blue star-shaped spots, were peeling in many places; between the windows hung a dim, battered little looking-glass in a massive frame of imitation

mahogany. Guns and chibouks stood in the corners; spiders'
webs hung, dense and black, from the ceiling.

'A, B, V, G, D,' said Chertopkhanov slowly, then all of a
sudden he exclaimed furiously: 'E! E! E! for Eat!... what a
stupid creature... E for Eat!'

But the unlucky poodle only shivered and could not make
up his mind to open his mouth; he went on sitting, with his tail
pressed miserably down, his mouth screwed up, humbly blinking and narrowing his eyes, as if to say: 'Of course, you're the
master.'

'Well, eat it, go on! Take it!' repeated the indefatigable landowner.

'You've frightened him,' I observed.

'Well, get away with you, then!' He gave him a push with his
foot. The poor wretch got up, quietly dropped the bread off his
nose and went, as it were on tiptoe, into the front hall, deeply
offended. And with reason: a stranger had come to the house
for the first time, and this was how they treated him.

The door leading from the next room squeaked discreetly
and Mr. Nedopyuskin came in, bowing amiably and smiling.

I got up and bowed.

'Don't move, don't move,' he murmured.

We sat down. Chertopkhanov went out into the next room.

'Have you been long in our part of the world?' began
Nedopyuskin in a soft voice, after coughing carefully into his
hand and holding his fingers in front of his lips for good
manners' sake.

'Nearly two months.'

'Quite so.'

Silence descended.

'Delightful weather now,' continued Nedopyuskin, and he
looked gratefully at me, as though the weather depended on
me. 'We ought to have a fine crop.'

I nodded my head in sign of agreement. There was a silence.

'Yesterday Pantelei Eremeich caught two hares,' began
Nedopyuskin, not without effort, with an obvious wish to
enliven the conversation. 'Yes, sir, very big hares, sir.'

'Has Mr. Chertopkhanov got good hounds?'

'They're remarkable, sir!' rejoined Nedopyuskin with gusto. 'I dare say they are the best in the province.' He drew closer to me. 'Why, Pantelei Eremeich is a wonderful fellow! Anything he wants, any idea he has – you look, and it's all prepared, the whole thing fairly on the boil. I tell you, Pantelei Eremeich...'

Chertopkhanov came into the room. Nedopyuskin chuckled, fell silent, and indicated him to me with his eyes, as much as to say: Just see for yourself. We started to talk about hunting.

'Would you like me to show you my leash of hounds?' Chertopkhanov asked me and, without waiting for an answer, he called: 'Karp!' A sturdy lad came in, wearing a green nankeen coat with a blue collar and livery buttons.

'Tell Fomka,' said Chertopkhanov abruptly, 'to bring round Ammalat and Saiga, and tidily, too, understand?'

Karp smiled with his whole mouth, uttered an indeterminate sound and went out. Fomka appeared, neat-headed, tightly buttoned, wearing shoes and accompanied by his hounds. For politeness' sake I admired these stupid animals (all borzois are extraordinarily stupid). Chertopkhanov spat right into Ammalat's nostrils, which appeared to give the hound not the slightest satisfaction. Nedopyuskin stroked Ammalat on the hind-quarters. We resumed our conversation. By degrees Chertopkhanov softened up completely, and stopped crowing and snorting; the expression on his face changed. He looked at me and Nedopyuskin...

'Hey!' he exclaimed suddenly. 'Why should she sit there all by herself? Masha! I say, Masha! Come here.' Someone moved in the next room, but there was no answer.

'Ma-a-sha,' repeated Chertopkhanov pleadingly. 'Come here. Never mind, you needn't be afraid.'

The door opened quietly and I saw a woman of about twenty, tall and well-built, with a dark, gypsy face and yellowish-brown eyes and pitch-black locks; her big white teeth fairly glittered between full, red lips. She wore a white dress; a blue shawl, fastened at the throat with a gold pin, half-hid her slender thoroughbred arms. She took two steps forward, with the embarrassed clumsiness of a wild thing; then halted and looked down.

'Well, let me introduce you,' said Pantelei. 'Wife or no wife, let her pass for one.'

Masha blushed slightly and smiled from embarrassment. I gave her a specially deep bow. I liked her very much. Her fine aquiline nose, with its arched, transparent-looking nostrils, the bold, high sweep of her eyebrows, her pale, slightly-sunken cheeks – all her features spoke of self-willed passion and reckless daring. From her braided hair down to her sturdy neck ran two lines of tiny gleaming hairs – the sign of blood and vigour.

She went to the window and sat down. I had no wish to add to her confusion, and began talking to Chertopkhanov. Masha turned her head slightly and began to study me with a sidelong, furtive, wild, swift gaze. Her glance flashed like a viper's fang. Nedopyuskin sat down beside her and whispered something in her ear. She smiled again. When she smiled, she slightly wrinkled her nose and raised her upper lip, which gave her face an expression which was half-cat, half-lioness.

Oh, you're an elusive one, I thought, shooting a furtive glance in my turn at her willowy waist, her deep breast and angular, nimble movements.

'Well, Masha,' asked Chertopkhanov, 'we ought to offer something to our guest, eh?'

'We have got some jam,' she answered.

'Well, bring it here, and some vodka, too, and listen, Masha,' he called after her, 'bring your guitar as well.'

'Why the guitar? I'm not going to sing.'

'Why not?'

'I don't want to.'

'Oh, nonsense, you'll want to, if . . .'

'If what?' asked Masha with a swift wrinkling of the brows.

'If you're asked to,' Chertopkhanov concluded with a certain embarrassment.

'Oh!'

She went out, soon returned with the jam and vodka, and sat down again in the window. A little furrow had already appeared on her forehead . . . Her brows kept darting up and down like a wasp's whiskers . . . Have you ever noticed, reader, what a wicked face a wasp has? Well, I thought, there's going to be a storm. The conversation was not going well. Nedopyuskin had dried up completely and wore a constrained smile; Cher-topkhanov puffed and flushed and his eyes were starting out: I began making as if to leave . . . Suddenly Masha rose, and in a flash opened the window, leant her head out and gave a hearty shout of 'Axinya!' after a passing peasant-woman. The woman started, began to turn round, slipped, and fell down heavily on the ground. Masha threw herself back with a ringing laugh; Chertopkhanov chuckled, too, and Nedopyuskin squeaked with delight. We all came to life. The storm had broken with nothing but lightning . . . the air had cleared.

Half an hour later no one would have recognized us: we were talking and laughing away like children. Masha was in higher spirits than anyone. Chertopkhanov fairly devoured her with his eyes. Her face had gone paler, her nostrils had expanded, her glance blazed up and dimmed again all at the same time. The wild creature was well away. Nedopyuskin stumbled after her on his fat little legs, like a drake following a duck. Even Venzor crept out from under the bench in the hall, stood in the doorway, looked at us and suddenly started jump-ing up and barking. Masha fluttered out into the next room, brought her guitar, threw the shawl off her shoulders, sat quickly down, lifted her head and struck up a gypsy song. Her voice rang and thrilled like a cracked glass bell, blazed out, faded away . . . It gave one a pleasant creepy feeling inside. '*Ay, burn and speak!* . . .' Chertopkhanov embarked on a dance. Nedopyuskin stamped and jumped and took little mincing steps. Masha was all a-quiver, like birch-bark on a fire: her slender fingers ran gaily over the guitar, her brown throat rose slowly under her double necklace of amber. One moment she would suddenly be silent, sink into a doze, pluck the strings with seeming reluctance, and Chertopkhanov would halt with only his shoulder twitching and shuffle from one foot to the other where he stood, and Nedopyuskin would shake his head like a porcelain Chinaman; then she would be off again in a frenzy, straighten her back, throw out her breast, and Chertopkhanov would be squatting on the ground again, jumping up to the ceiling, spinning like a top, and shouting 'Bravo!...'

'Bravo, bravo, bravo!' Nedopyuskin gabbled after him.

It was late in the evening when I left Bessonovo...As for Masha's own story, I shall tell it to my forbearing readers some other time.

The End of Chertopkhanov

I

TWO years after my visit, Pantelei's disasters began – 'disasters' is the only word. Disappointments, failures, misfortunes had pursued him even before then; but he paid them no attention and 'reigned' as before. The first disaster which struck him was the most painful one of all: Masha left him.

What induced her to forsake his roof, to which she had seemed so well-accustomed, it would be hard to say. Until his dying day, Chertopkhanov remained convinced that the blame for Masha's treachery lay with a certain young neighbour, a retired captain of Lancers by the name of Yaff, who, in Pantelei's words, got his way just by perpetually twisting his whiskers, thickly oiling his hair and sniffing significantly; but it may be supposed that it was rather the effect of the wandering gypsy blood which flowed in Masha's veins. Anyway, however that may be, one fine summer evening Masha tied a few rags together into a small bundle and walked out of Chertopkhanov's house.

For three days previous to this she had been sitting in a corner writhing and pressing up against the wall like a wounded vixen. If only she had said a word to somebody – but no, she just rolled her eyes the whole time, looked thoughtful, twitched her eyebrows, bared her teeth slightly and fidgeted with her hands, as if to wrap herself up. The same sort of mood had come over her before, but had never lasted long; Chertopkhanov knew this, and consequently was not disturbed himself and didn't disturb her either.

But when returning from the kennels, where, in the words of his whipper-in, the last two hounds had 'gone stiff', he met a maid who announced to him in a trembling voice that Marya

318

Akinfyevna sent her compliments and said that she wished him all the best, but would never return to his house again, Chertopkhanov, after turning round twice where he stood and giving vent to a husky roar, at once dashed after the fugitive – snatching up his pistol on the way.

He found her about two versts from his house, beside a birch-wood, on the high road leading to the nearest town. The sun stood low over the horizon and everything round suddenly turned scarlet: trees, grass and earth.

'To Yaff, to Yaff!' groaned Chertopkhanov as soon as he caught sight of Masha. 'To Yaff,' he repeated, running up to her and almost tripping with every step.

Masha halted and turned to face him. She stood with her back to the light – and looked quite black, as if carved in ebony. Only the whites of her eyes showed up as little silver almonds, but her eyes themselves – the pupils – were darker than ever.

She threw her bundle aside and folded her arms.

'You're on the way to Yaff's, you hussy!' repeated Chertopkhanov, and tried to seize her by the shoulder, but met her gaze, faltered, and fidgeted where he stood.

'I'm not going to Mr. Yaff's, Pantelei Eremeich,' answered Masha calmly and evenly. 'I just can't live with you any more.'

'Why can't you? What for? Have I done anything to offend you?'

Masha shook her head. 'You've done nothing to offend me, Pantelei Eremeich. I have just got bored living with you ... Thanks for times past, but I can't stay on – no!'

Chertopkhanov was dumbfounded; he even slapped his thighs and jumped up into the air.

'How can that be? You've lived, and lived, and known nothing but pleasure and peace – and suddenly: you're bored! So you tell yourself, I'll chuck him! You go and throw a handkerchief over your head and set off. You've been treated with every respect, the same as a lady.'

'Not that I wanted it at all,' interrupted Masha.

'You didn't want it? Turned from a wandering gypsy into a lady – you didn't want it? What d'you mean, you child of Ham?

D'you expect me to believe that? There's treachery behind this, treachery.'

He had begun to hiss with rage again.

'There's no thought of treachery in my mind and never has been,' said Masha in her clear, sing-song voice. 'I've already told you: I got bored.'

'Masha,' exclaimed Chertopkhanov, and punched himself in the chest. 'Stop, that's enough, you've made me suffer quite enough. Good heavens! Just think what Tisha will say; you might have thought about him!'

'Please give my respects to Tikhon Ivanich and tell him . . .'

Chertopkhanov waved his arms.

'Oh, no, you're wrong – you won't get away! Your Yaff can go on waiting for you.'

'Mr. Yaff——' began Masha.

'Mr. Yaff, indeed,' imitated Chertopkhanov. 'He's a twister and a rogue, if ever there was one – and a face like a monkey, too!'

For a whole half-hour Chertopkhanov argued with Masha. Now he would go close up to her, now he would dart away, now he would lift his arm at her, now he would bow to her from the waist and weep and curse.

'I can't,' asserted Masha. 'I'm so sad there . . . so bored and miserable.'

Her face had gradually assumed such an indifferent, almost sleepy expression that Chertopkhanov asked her if she had not taken a nip of thorn-apple spirit.

'Bored,' she said for the tenth time.

'And supposing I were to kill you?' he cried all of a sudden, and pulled the pistol out of his pocket.

Masha smiled; her face became animated. 'Why, kill away, Pantelei Eremeich: I'm at your mercy; but one thing I won't do, and that's come back.'

'You won't come back!' Chertopkhanov pulled back the cock.

'No, my dear . . . Never in my life, and I mean it.'

Chertopkhanov suddenly thrust the pistol into her hand and sat down on the grass.

'Well, then, *you* kill me! I don't want to live without you. If you're tired of me – then I'm tired of everything else.'

Masha bent down, picked up her bundle, put the pistol down in the grass with the muzzle away from Chertopkhanov, and went up to him.

'Why, my dear, what's all the fuss about? Don't you know us gypsy girls? It's our way, it's how we are. Once the longing to be off comes over us, and calls our hearts away to somewhere else far off, how can we stay where we are? Remember your Masha – you won't find another friend like her – and I, too, I won't forget you, my falcon; but our life together is over!'

'I loved you, Masha,' mumbled Chertopkhanov into his fingers, with which he was clutching his face.

'And I loved you, Pantelei Eremeich, my friend.'

'I loved you, I still love you to distraction – and when I think now that here you are, for nothing at all, without rhyme or reason, chucking me, and starting to wander about the world – well, it strikes me that if I wasn't a poor wretch of a beggar you wouldn't leave me.'

At these words Masha simply chuckled.

'And you used to tell me I had no thought for silver,' she said, and with a sweep of her arm she hit Chertopkhanov on the shoulder.

He jumped to his feet.

'Well, at any rate take some money from me – otherwise how will you manage, without a farthing? But, best of all: kill me! I tell you plainly, kill me once and for all!'

Masha again shook her head. 'Kill you? What do they send people to Siberia for, my dear?'

Chertopkhanov shuddered. 'So it's just because of this, for fear of punishment that you . . .'

He collapsed again on the grass. Masha stood over him in silence. 'I'm sorry for you, Pantelei Eremeich,' she said with a sigh; 'you're a good man . . . but there's nothing for it. Good-bye!'

She turned away and took two steps. Darkness had fallen and the shadows of night were welling up on every side. Chertopkhanov got up nimbly and seized Masha from behind by both elbows.

'So you're off, you snake? To Yaff's!'

'Good-bye!' repeated Masha sharply and with emphasis, and she broke loose and went on her way.

Chertopkhanov looked after her, ran over to the spot where the pistol lay, picked it up, aimed, fired . . . but, before pressing the trigger, he raised his hand: the bullet hummed over Masha's head. She looked at him over her shoulder as she went, and continued on her way with a waddling motion, as if to mock him.

He covered his face – and set off at a run . . .

But he had not run as much as fifty paces, when suddenly he stopped as if rooted to the spot. A familiar, a too familiar voice floated to his ears. Masha was singing. '*Days of youth so charming*,' she sang; and every note was magnified in the evening air, in a plaintive, sultry way. Chertopkhanov listened with his head on one side. The voice went farther and farther into the distance; now it faded, now it came floating back again, hardly perceptible, but still burning . . .

She's doing it to spite me, thought Chertopkhanov; but the same moment he groaned: 'Oh, no! She's saying good-bye to me for ever' – and he burst into floods of tears.

The following day he turned up at the residence of Mr. Yaff, who, like a true man of the world, disliked country solitude, and had settled in the nearest town, 'nearer to the ladies', as he expressed it. Chertopkhanov did not find Yaff at home: the footman said that he had left the day before for Moscow.

'That's it!' exclaimed Chertopkhanov furiously. 'They had a plot; she's run off with him . . . but just wait!'

He forced his way into the young captain's study, despite the opposition of the footman. In the study, over the sofa, hung an oil portrait of the master in Lancer uniform. 'So that's

where you are, you monkey without a tail!' thundered Chertopkhanov, jumping on to the sofa – and he struck his fist
against the stretched canvas and burst a great hole in it.

'Tell your good-for-nothing master,' he said to the footman,
'that, failing his own odious face, Mr. Chertopkhanov, gentleman, has disfigured the painted version of it; and that if he
desires satisfaction from me, he knows where to find Mr.
Chertopkhanov, gentleman! Otherwise I'll find him myself!
I'll find the dirty monkey if I have to go to the bottom of the sea!'

With these words, Chertopkhanov jumped off the sofa and
solemnly took his departure.

But Captain Yaff demanded no satisfaction from him – he
never even met him – and Chertopkhanov didn't think it worth
searching for his enemy, so nothing happened between them.
Soon afterwards Masha herself vanished without trace. Chertopkhanov started drinking; but in time he 'came round again'.

Here, however, his second disaster overtook him.

II

That is to say, his bosom friend Tikhon Ivanich Nedopyuskin died. Some two years before his death, his health had
started to fail; he began suffering from asthma, kept dropping
off to sleep and, on waking up, couldn't at once recover his
senses. The local doctor asserted that these attacks of his were
'little strokes'. During the three days preceding Masha's departure, the three days in which she got 'bored', Nedopyuskin had
been lying at home at Besselendeyevka: he had caught a bad
chill. The effect on him of Masha's action was all the more
unexpected: it was almost more profound than on Chertopkhanov himself. In keeping with his gentle, timid disposition, he
showed nothing except the tenderest sympathy with his friend
and a certain painful incomprehension, but something had
burst and sagged inside him. 'She has stolen my soul away,'
he whispered to himself, as he sat on his favourite oilskin
sofa and twined his fingers round each other. Even when

Chertopkhanov recovered, Nedopyuskin didn't – and went on feeling that he was 'empty inside'. 'Just here,' he would say, pointing at the middle of his chest, above the stomach.

In this way he dragged on until winter. At the first frosts, his asthma got better, but, against this, he had what was no longer a little stroke, but a real proper one. He did not lose consciousness at once; he could still recognize Chertopkhanov, and even, in answer to the despairing exclamation of his friend: 'How is this, Tisha, that you're leaving me, without my permission, just as bad as Masha?' he stammered: 'But, Pa...lei E...E...ich, I've al...ays o...eyed you.' Yet this did not prevent him from dying the same day, without waiting for the local doctor, who, at the sight of his cold corpse, had nothing left to do but sadly admit the transitoriness of earthly things and ask for 'a drop of vodka with a piece of smoked sturgeon'. Tikhon Ivanich left his property, as was only to be expected, to his revered benefactor and magnanimous protector, Pantelei Eremeich Chertopkhanov. But his revered benefactor did not derive much advantage from this, since it was quickly sold by auction – chiefly to cover the expenses of his funerary monument, a statue which Chertopkhanov (his father's strain coming out in him!) had the idea of erecting over his friend's ashes. This statue, which was supposed to represent an angel in prayer, he had ordered from Moscow, but the contractor who had been recommended to him, calculating that but few experts on sculpture are to be met in the provinces, sent him, instead of an angel, a goddess Flora which had for many years adorned one of those neglected parks in the neighbourhood of Moscow which date back to the time of Catherine the Great – this statue, which incidentally was very elegant, in the rococo manner, with chubby hands, fluffy curls, a garland of roses hung round its bare breast, and a curved waist, having come into the contractor's possession free of charge. So over Tikhon's grave there stands to this day a mythological goddess, with one foot graciously raised, gazing with a truly Pompadour-like grimace at the calves and sheep which wander around it – those unfailing visitors of our village graveyards.

III

After the loss of his faithful friend, Chertopkhanov began drinking again, this time much more seriously. His affairs went straight downhill. There was nothing to shoot, the last money was spent, the last servants departed. Pantelei Eremeich was left completely alone; there was no one to speak a word to, no one to confide in. Only his pride remained undiminished. Indeed, the worse his affairs became, the more arrogant and overbearing and inaccessible he grew. Finally he went completely wild. One consolation, one joy remained to him: a remarkable saddle-horse, a grey, bred by the Don, named by him Malek Adel, an extraordinary animal indeed.

He had acquired this horse in the following manner.

Riding one day through a neighbouring village, Chertopkhanov heard a babble of peasant voices and the roar of a crowd from the direction of the pot-house. In the middle of this crowd, at one particular spot, sturdy hands were steadily rising and falling.

'What's going on here?' he asked, in the tone of command which was peculiar to him, addressing an old peasant-woman who was standing in the doorway of her cabin.

Leaning against the lintel, as if in a dream, the old woman was looking towards the pot-house. A small white-headed boy in a cotton shirt, with a little crucifix of cypress wood on his bare chest, was sitting, with spread-out legs and clenched fists, between her bast shoes; close by a chick was picking at a crust of rye bread which had gone as hard as wood.

'The Lord knows, sir,' answered the old woman, and, leaning forward, she put her dark wrinkled hand on the boy's head. 'I heard that our lads are beating a Jew.'

'A Jew? What Jew?'

'The Lord knows, sir. A Jew of sorts turned up here, and as for where he came from – who can tell? Vasya, sir, come to mother: tch-tch, you rascal.' She drove off the chick, and Vasya grasped her skirts.

'So now they're beating him, sir.'

'Why? What for?'

'I don't know, sir. It must be for something he has done. Anyway, what should they do but beat him? Wasn't it he that crucified Christ!'

Chertopkhanov gave a whoop, put his horse into a gallop with a blow of the whip, rode straight at the crowd – and, tearing his way into it, began indiscriminately whacking the peasants to right and left with the said whip, saying in a staccato voice: 'Taking . . . the law . . . into . . . your own hands! Punishment is for the law to give – not for pri . . . vate per . . . sons! The law! The law!! The LAW!!'

Inside of two minutes the whole mob had retreated in various directions – and on the ground, in front of the door of the pot-house, appeared a small, thinnish, darkish creature, wearing a nankeen coat, tousled and tattered . . . A pale face, eyes rolled up, mouth open . . . What was it? A terror-stricken faint, or death itself?

'Why have you killed the Jew?' exclaimed Chertopkhanov in a voice of thunder, with a threatening wave of the whip.

There was a faint buzz from the crowd in answer. One peasant was holding his shoulder, a second his side, a third his nose.

'He's asking for a fight!' came a voice from the back rows.

'With his whip! Anyone could do that!' said a second voice.

'Why have you killed the Jew? I'm asking you, you pack of Tartars!' repeated Chertopkhanov.

But the creature who had been lying on the ground now jumped nimbly to his feet and, running up behind Chertopkhanov, took hold convulsively of the edge of his saddle.

There was a general roar of laughter from the crowd.

'He's got nine lives!' came a voice, again from the back rows. 'Just like a cat!'

'Your worship, protect me, save me!' lisped the unhappy Jew meanwhile, pressing his whole chest against Chertopkhanov's leg, 'or they'll kill me, so they will, your worship!'

'Why did they do it to you?' asked Chertopkhanov.

'I swear I don't know! You see, their cattle began to die . . . so they suspected . . . and I . . .'

'Well! We'll go into that later!' interrupted Chertopkhanov. 'But now you hang on to my saddle and follow me. And as for you!' he added, turning to the crowd. 'Do you know me? I am Pantelei Chertopkhanov, landowner, I live in the village of Bessonovo – and, well, I mean, you can put in a complaint against me whenever you like, and against the Jew, too!'

'Why should we complain?' said a staid, grey-bearded peasant, a regular ancient patriarch, bowing low. (Incidentally he had pommelled the Jew as soundly as the best of them.) 'We know your kind heart well, Pantelei Eremeich, sir; we're very grateful to your good self for giving us a lesson!'

'Why should we complain?' repeated the others. 'But as for that infidel, we'll get our way with him! He won't escape us! We'll run him down like a hare in a field . . .'

Chertopkhanov fidgeted his brows, snorted, and set off at a walk to his own village, accompanied by the Jew whom he had delivered from his persecutors in exactly the same way as he had once delivered Tikhon Nedopyuskin.

IV

A few days later, Chertopkhanov's only surviving boy-servant announced to him that a man on horse-back had arrived and wished to speak to him. Chertopkhanov went out into the porch and saw his acquaintance, the Jew, mounted on a magnificent Don horse, which was standing proud and immobile in the middle of the yard. The Jew wore no cap: he was holding it under his arm, his feet were not in the stirrups, but resting against the stirrup-leathers, and his tattered coat-tails hung down on both sides of the saddle. Seeing Chertop-khanov, he smacked his lips, twitched his elbows and swung his legs. But Chertopkhanov, far from acknowledging his greeting, grew furious and suddenly exploded. A dirty Jew, daring to sit on such a splendid horse...it was quite shocking!

'Hey, you black devil!' he shouted. 'Get off at once, if you don't want to be pulled off into the mud!'

The Jew at once obeyed, fell out of the saddle like a sack and, holding the reins in one hand, smiling and bowing, came towards Chertopkhanov.

'What d'you want?' asked Pantelei Eremeich with dignity.

'Your honour, can you see what sort of horse it is?' said the Jew, without ceasing to bow.

'Well...yes...he's a good horse. Where did you get him? Stole him, I suppose?'

'Whatever next, your honour! I'm an honest Jew. I didn't steal him, I got him specially for your honour! I tried and tried! and here he is. On the whole of the Don you won't find another horse like him. – Look, your honour, there's a horse for you! Just come over here! – Go on...go on...turn round, stand sideways on! – We'll just take the saddle off. Do you see what sort of horse he is, your worship?'

'He's a good horse,' repeated Chertopkhanov with feigned indifference, though his heart was fairly hammering away in his breast. He was a passionate fancier of horse-flesh and knew what was what.

'Just stroke him, your worship! Stroke his neck, hee-hee-hee, like this.'

As if against his will, Chertopkhanov put his hand on the horse's neck, patted it twice, then drew his fingers from the withers along the back, and, when he came to the well-known spot above the kidneys, pressed the spot gently like a connoisseur. The horse arched his back, and, giving Chertopkhanov a sidelong look with his insolent black eye, snorted and fidgeted his four legs.

The Jew laughed and gently clapped his hands.

'He knows his master, your worship, so he does.'

'Don't talk nonsense,' Chertopkhanov interrupted angrily. 'I have not the means to buy horses from you, and as for accepting a present, I've never accepted a present from the Lord God himself, let alone from a Jew!'

'And how should I dare to give you a present, for mercy's sake!' exclaimed the Jew. 'Buy him, your worship . . . and as for the money – I'll wait for it.'

Chertopkhanov reflected.

'What will you take for him?' he said at length, through his teeth.

The Jew shrugged his shoulders.

'What I paid for him myself. Two hundred roubles.'

The horse was worth twice – perhaps even three times – that sum.

Chertopkhanov turned away to one side and yawned nervously.

'But when . . . for the money?' he asked, scowling unnaturally and not looking at the Jew.

'When it suits your honour.'

Chertopkhanov threw his head back, but without raising his eyes.

'That's nonsense. Talk sense, you spawn of Herod! – D'you want to put me under an obligation to you, or what?'

'Well, let's say,' replied the Jew hurriedly, 'in six months' time . . . Agreed?'

Chertopkhanov answered nothing.

The Jew made an effort to look him in the eye. 'Agreed? Shall I put him in the stable?'

'I don't want the saddle,' pronounced Chertopkhanov abruptly. 'Take the saddle – d'you hear?'

'Of course, of course, certainly, certainly,' murmured the delighted Jew, and he humped the saddle on his shoulder.

'And the money,' Chertopkhanov went on, 'in six months' time. And not two hundred, but two hundred and fifty. Silence. Two hundred and fifty, I tell you! To my account.'

Chertopkhanov could still not make up his mind to raise his eyes. Never had his pride suffered so severely. It's an obvious present, he was thinking. The wretched fellow's brought it by way of gratitude! He could have embraced the Jew, he could have struck him . . .

'Your honour,' began the Jew, who had grown bolder, and put on a smirk, 'we ought to hand him over in the Russian way, from coat-tail to coat-tail . . .'

'Whatever next? A Jew . . . in the Russian way! – Hey! Who's there? Take the horse and put him in the stable. And give him some oats. I'll come along myself in a moment and have a look. And listen: his name is Malek Adel!'

Chertopkhanov was about to go up to the porch, but he turned sharply on his heels, ran up to the Jew and squeezed his hand hard. The Jew bowed and was already offering his lips, but Chertopkhanov recoiled with a bound and, saying in a low voice, 'Don't tell a soul!', vanished behind the door.

V

From that day forward, the main business, the main pre-occupation and delight in Chertopkhanov's life, was Malek Adel. He loved him even more than Masha, grew more attached to him even than to Nedopyuskin. And what a horse he was! All fire and gunpowder – and yet with the gravity of a Boyar! Untirable, a stayer, ready to go anywhere, mild as a lamb; costing nothing to feed: if he couldn't get anything else, he would eat the ground under his feet.

He walks, and it's as if he's carrying you in his arms; he trots, and it's as if he is rocking you in a cradle; but when he gallops, not even the wind can catch him! He never loses his breath – his windpipe's too sound for that. His hooves are of steel; as for stumbling – there's never been the slightest question of it! Jumping a ditch or a fence means nothing to him; and what a brain he's got! You call him, and he'll come running up, head thrown back; you tell him to stop, and you leave him – he won't stir; as soon as you start coming back he'll whinny faintly: 'Here I am.' He fears nothing: in the darkest night or a snow-storm he'll find the way; and he'll never let a stranger take hold of him, he would tear him with his teeth! And woe betide any dog that bothers him: he'll get a fore-hoof to his skull at once – ponk! and the dog will have had its day. He's a horse with ambitions: you can wave the whip over him, just for show – but God help you if you touch him! Anyway, why make a long story of it: he's not a horse, he's a treasure!

If Chertopkhanov had sat down to describe his Malek Adel – heaven knows where he would have found the words to do so! And how he curried him and cosseted him! Malek Adel's coat was shot with silver – and not old silver, either, but new silver with a dull polish on it; if you stroked him with the flat of your hand, it was absolute velvet! Saddle, saddle-cloth, bridle – every bit of harness was so well-fitted, well-kept, well-scrubbed – you could just take a pencil and draw! It was Chertopkhanov himself – who else? – who with his own hand plaited his darling's forelock, washed his mane and tail in beer, and more than once anointed his hooves with oil.

He would mount Malek Adel and ride out, not exactly to visit his neighbours – he had no more connection with them than before – but over their land, and past their seats . . . as if to say: Admire, you fools, from afar! Then he'd hear of hunting in progress somewhere – some rich landowner visiting his out-lying properties – and at once he'd be off there, and prance about in the distance, on the horizon, amazing all beholders with the beauty and speed of his horse, but letting no one come near him. On one occasion a huntsman set off after him, with all his suite in attendance, saw that Chertopkhanov was walk-ing away from him, and started shouting after him with all his might, while at full gallop: 'Hey, you, listen! Take what you like for your horse! I won't grudge you a thousand! I'll give my wife and children for him! Take my last penny!'

Chertopkhanov suddenly halted Malek Adel. The hunts-man dashed up to him. 'Tell me, sir,' he shouted, 'what d'you want? My own father?'

'If you were the Tsar,' said Chertopkhanov deliberately (and in all his born days he had never heard of Shakespeare), 'you could give me your whole kingdom for my horse, and even so I wouldn't take it!' He spoke, he laughed, he made Malek

Adel rear up, he spun him round in mid-air, standing on nothing but his hind legs, like a top – and gallop! He fairly streaked off across the stubble. And the huntsman (who, so the story goes, was a prince, a man of enormous wealth) threw his cap on the ground – and buried his face in it. He lay like that for a good half-hour.

It was only natural that Chertopkhanov should treasure his horse. Was it not through him that further proof had been given of his own undoubted and final superiority over all his neighbours?

VI

Meanwhile time passed, the date of payment was approaching – and, so far from having two hundred and fifty roubles, Chertopkhanov had not so much as fifty. What could he do, where could he turn for help? Well, he resolved at last, if the Jew wouldn't relent and agree to go on waiting, he'd give him his house and land. 'I'll mount the horse,' he said to himself, 'and ride off wherever the spirit moves me. I'll die of hunger rather than sell Malek Adel!' He was greatly disturbed, and was even reduced to reflection; but here, for the first and last time, fate took pity on him and smiled. A distant aunt, whose very name was unknown to Chertopkhanov, left him in her will a sum which in his eyes was enormous, a whole two thousand roubles! And he received this money in the very nick of time, the day before the Jew's arrival. Chertopkhanov was almost out of his mind with joy. But the thought of vodka never even entered his head: from the day that Malek Adel had come to him, not so much as a drop had passed his lips. He ran to the stable and kissed his friend on both sides of the muzzle, above the nostrils, on the spot where a horse's skin is so delicate. 'No more parting for us now!' he exclaimed, slapping Malek Adel on the neck, below his combed-out mane. Returning to the house, he counted out two hundred and fifty roubles and sealed them up in a packet. Then, lying on his back and smoking his pipe, he dreamt of how he would dispose of the

rest of the money – and in particular what hounds he would
get: the proper Kostroma strain, and they must have red
markings, too! He also spoke to Perfishka, promised him a
new coat with yellow galloons at all the seams – and went to
sleep in a most peaceful frame of mind.

He had a bad dream: he dreamt he was out hunting,
mounted, however, not on Malek Adel, but on some strange
animal like a camel. There came running to meet him a fox
which was absolutely white like snow. He wanted to wave his
whip, to set the hounds on the fox – but instead of a whip he
found a wisp of straw in his hand and the fox ran just in front of
him and put its tongue out at him. He jumped down from his
camel, stumbled, fell . . . and fell straight into the arms of a
gendarme, who was summoning him before the Governor-
General, and whom he recognized as Yaff . . .

Chertopkhanov woke up. It was dark in the room; just after
the second cockcrow . . .

From somewhere far, far away in the distance a horse
neighed.

Chertopkhanov lifted his head. Once more came the faint,
faint neighing.

That's Malek Adel's neigh! he thought. It's his neigh! But
why so far away? My goodness . . . It can't be . . .

Chertopkhanov suddenly went cold all over, sprang from
his bed in the twinkling of an eye, felt for his shoes and clothes,
dressed, and, seizing the stable key from under the pillow,
dashed out into the yard.

VII

The stable lay at the far end of the yard; one of its
walls backed on to the fields. Chertopkhanov did not get the
key into the lock at once – his hands were trembling – nor could
he turn the key at once . . . He stood motionless, holding
his breath: if only something would move behind the
door! 'Maleshka, Malek!' he called in a low voice: but silence!
Without meaning to, Chertopkhanov pulled the key: the

door squeaked and opened ... So it wasn't locked. He strode across the threshold, and again called his horse, this time by its full name: 'Malek Adel!' But there was no answer from his faithful friend, only the rustling of a mouse in the straw. Then Chertopkhanov rushed to the stall – one of three in the stable – in which Malek Adel was kept. He found his way straight to it although the darkness was dense enough to knock your eye out! Empty! Chertopkhanov's head began to reel; a bell seemed to be droning inside his skull. He wanted to say something – but could only wheeze; and, with hands groping, up, and down, and sideways, panting, with faltering knees, he made his way from one stall to another ... In the third stall, which was piled almost to the top with hay, he ran into one wall, then into the other: he fell head over heels, got up, and suddenly ran out helter-skelter through the half-open door into the yard ...

'He's been stolen! Perfishka! Perfishka! He's been stolen!' he roared at the top of his voice.

The boy Perfishka, in nothing but his shirt, flew out like a whirlwind from the garret where he slept.

The two of them, the master and his only servant, collided like drunken men in the middle of the yard; as if possessed, they circled round each other. The master could not explain what was the matter; the servant could not understand what he was called on to do. 'Oh dear, oh dear,' muttered Chertopkhanov. 'Oh dear, oh dear,' repeated the boy after him. 'A lantern, come on, light a lantern, lights, lights!' Chertopkhanov brought out at length, in a fainting voice. Perfishka ran into the house. But it was no easy matter to light a lantern or to get a light. At that time wax matches were a rarity in Russia: the last fires in the kitchen had long been out, tinder and flint took time to find and worked badly. Grinding his teeth, Chertopkhanov snatched them from the hands of the dumbfounded Perfishka to strike a light himself, sparks flew in plenty, curses and even groans in greater plenty still – but the wick either wouldn't catch, or went out, notwithstanding the combined efforts of four concentrated cheeks and lips! At last, after a full five minutes, the greasy candle-end at the bottom of the broken lantern began to glimmer, and Chertopkhanov, accompanied by Perfishka, rushed into the stable, lifted the lantern above his head and looked round . . .

It was absolutely empty!

He darted out into the yard, ran round in all directions – no horse to be found! The fence which had surrounded Pantelei's seat had long ago become dilapidated and at many places had listed over and touched the ground . . . Opposite the stable it was completely down to the width of a whole yard. Perfishka showed Chertopkhanov this spot.

'Master, just look here: it wasn't like this to-day. And here are the stakes, too, sticking out of the ground – someone must have pulled them up.'

Chertopkhanov ran over with the lantern, and moved it close to the ground . . .

'Hooves, hooves, horse's shoe-marks, fresh marks!' he muttered quickly. 'Here's where they took him over, here, here!'

In a flash he had jumped over the fence and, shouting, 'Malek Adel, Malek Adel,' was running straight out into the field.

Perfishka was left standing dumbfounded beside the fence. The circle of light from the lantern soon vanished from his sight, swallowed up in the dense gloom of the starless, moonless night.

Ever fainter and fainter sounded the despairing cries of Chertopkhanov.

VIII

The day was already dawning when he returned home. He looked like nothing human, his clothes were all covered in mud, his face had taken on a wild, terrifying look, his eyes had a dull, morose stare. He chased Perfishka away in a husky whisper and locked himself in his room. He could hardly stand from exhaustion, but, instead of lying down on his bed, he sat on a chair by the door and put his head in his hands.

'Stolen! Stolen!'

But how had the thief been clever enough to steal Malek Adel by night out of a locked stable? Malek Adel, who even by day would let no stranger approach him – to steal him without a knock, without a sound? And how was it to be explained that not one of the dogs had barked? True, there were only two of them, two young puppies, and they had dug themselves into the ground from cold and hunger: but all the same!

What am I going to do now without Malek Adel? thought Chertopkhanov. I've lost my last friend. It's time for me to die. Buy another horse, since I've got the money? But where shall I find another horse like him?

'Pantelei Eremeich! Pantelei Eremeich!' came a timid cry from behind the door.

Chertopkhanov jumped to his feet.

'Who's there?' he shouted in an unnatural voice.

'It's me, your boy Perfishka.'

'Who d'you want? Has he been found? Has he come home?'

'No, no, sir; but the Jew-man, who sold him ...'

'Well?'

'He's come.'

'Ho, ho, ho.' Chertopkhanov roared with laughter – and at once flung the door open. 'Bring him here, come on! Bring him here!'

On the sudden appearance of the tousled, wild-looking figure of his benefactor, the Jew, standing behind Perfishka, tried to slink off, but Chertopkhanov took two bounds forward, caught him, and like a tiger fastened on to him by the throat.

'Ah, come for your money! money!' he wheezed, as if he were being strangled himself, instead of strangling the other. 'Stole him by night, and come by day for your money? Eh?'

'Mercy, your ho ... nour,' the Jew was groaning.

'Tell me, where's my horse? What have you done with him? Who've you sold him to? Tell me, go on, tell me!'

The Jew could no longer even groan; his face had gone blue and had actually lost its expression of terror. His arms hung limply; his whole body, in response to Chertopkhanov's furious shaking, was swaying backwards and forwards like a reed.

'I'll pay you your money. I'll pay you in full, to the last copeck,' shouted Chertopkhanov. 'But I'll wring your neck like a miserable chicken, if you don't tell me at once . . .'

'But you *have* wrung his neck, master,' observed the boy Perfishka humbly.

It was only then that Chertopkhanov came to his senses.

He let go of the Jew's neck; the Jew fairly thumped down on the ground. Chertopkhanov picked him up, sat him on a bench, poured a glass of vodka down his throat and brought him round. And, having done so, began to talk to him.

It appeared that the Jew had not had the faintest inkling of Malek Adel's theft. Indeed, what motive could he have had for stealing the horse which he himself had found for 'his deeply-respected Pantelei Eremeich'?

Then Chertopkhanov led him to the stable. Together they inspected the stalls, the mangers, the lock on the door; they rummaged through the hay and the straw, and then walked round the back-yard; Chertopkhanov showed the Jew the hoof-marks by the fence and suddenly smacked his thighs.

'Wait,' he exclaimed. 'Where did you buy the horse?'

'In the district of Little Arkhangel, at Verkhosensk fair,' answered the Jew.

'Who from?'

'A Cossack.'

'Wait! This Cossack, was he young or old?'

'Middle-aged, a steady sort of fellow.'

'But what was he like? What did he look like? A complete rogue, I suppose?'

'Certainly a rogue, your honour!'

'Well, what did he tell you, this rogue-fellow – had he owned the horse for long?'

'Yes, so I seem to remember, for some time.'

'Well, then, he's the only one that could have stolen the horse! Listen, you, listen here, and tell me what you think . . . what's your name?'

The Jew started and his little black eyes shot a look at Chertopkhanov.

'What is *my* name?'

'Yes: what do they call you?'

'Moshel Leiba.'

'Well, tell me what you think, Leiba, my friend – you're a clever chap. Would Malek Adel have let anyone take him, except his old master? Why, he saddled him, and bridled him, and took the blanket off him – there it is lying on the hay! . . . He simply behaved as if he was at home. Why, if it had been anyone else, who hadn't been his master, Malek Adel would have crushed him under his hooves. He would have made such a din he would have roused the whole village! Do you agree with me?'

'Certainly, of course, your honour.'

'Well, then, it means we must first of all find that Cossack!'

'But how can we find him, your honour? I only saw him just once – I've no idea where he can be now, or what his name is. Ai, vai, vai!' added the Jew, shaking his side-curls sadly.

'Leiba!' shouted Chertopkhanov suddenly, 'Leiba, look at me! I'm out of my own mind, I'm not myself! . . . I'll do myself a mischief, unless you help me!'

'But how can I . . .'

'Let's go together – and start looking for the thief.'

'But where shall we go?'

'Round the fairs, the highways and by-ways, round the horse-thieves, round towns, villages and farms – everywhere, everywhere! And don't worry about money: I've had a legacy! I'll spend my last copeck – but I'll find my friend! And that Cossack won't escape us either, the villain – where he is, we'll be there too! If he's under the ground, so will we be. If he's gone to the devil, we'll go to Satan himself!'

'Oh, why to Satan?' observed the Jew, 'we can manage without him.'

'Leiba!' repeated Chertopkhanov, 'Leiba, although you're a Jew and a heathen, you've got a better heart than many a Christian! Take pity on me! It's no good my going alone; I shan't be able to handle this by myself. I'm too quick-tempered – but *you* have got a head on your shoulders, a head of gold! Your tribe are all the same; get anything you want, without book-learning! You may be doubtful about my money. Come to my room – I'll show you the money too. Take it, take the cross from my neck – only give me back Malek Adel, give him back to me!'

Chertopkhanov was trembling as if from fear: a stream of sweat poured down his face and, mingling with his tears, lost itself in his whiskers. He pressed Leiba's hands, he implored him, he almost kissed him. He began to rave. The Jew tried to raise objections, to assert that it was quite impossible for him to absent himself, that he had business . . . but to no avail! Chertopkhanov would not listen to a word. There was nothing for it; the unhappy Leiba agreed.

The following day Chertopkhanov and Leiba drove away from Bessonovo in a peasant cart. The Jew looked somewhat confused, held on to the rail with one hand, his whole flabby body bouncing about on its shaky perch; he held his other hand pressed to his bosom, where he kept a packet of banknotes wrapped up in newspaper. Chertopkhanov sat like an idol, motionless, except for his roving eyes and deep-chested breathing. There was a dagger stuck in his belt.

'Well, my wicked rival, look out for yourself now,' he muttered as they drove out on to the high road.

He had left his house in the care of the boy Perfishka and of the deaf old peasant-woman who cooked for him and whom he had taken in out of the kindness of his heart.

'I shall come back to you on Malek Adel,' he called to them by way of farewell, 'or not at all!'

'We ought to get married, eh?' laughed Perfishka, digging his elbow into the cook's ribs. 'Why not? – we shall never see the master back, and you'll die of boredom otherwise!'

IX

A year passed, a whole year. There was not a whisper of news about Pantelei Eremeich. The cook died; even Perfishka was preparing to abandon the house and set off for the town, whither he was beckoned by a cousin, apprenticed to a barber – when suddenly it was rumoured abroad that the master was returning. The parish deacon had received a letter from Pantelei Eremeich himself, announcing his intended arrival at Bessonovo, and asking him to warn the servants so that they could make suitable arrangements for his reception. Perfishka understood these words to mean that he must wipe away some of the dust – though he had no great faith in the accuracy of the news; he had, however, to admit that the deacon had spoken the truth, when a few days later Pantelei Eremeich himself, in person, appeared in the courtyard of his house, mounted on Malek Adel.

Perfishka dashed to his master and, taking hold of the stirrup, made as if to help him to dismount; but his master jumped down unaided, and, throwing a triumphant glance around, loudly exclaimed: 'I said that I would find Malek Adel – and find him I did, to the mortification of my enemies and of destiny itself.' Perfishka went and kissed his hand, but Chertopkhanov took no notice of his servant's attentions. Leading Malek Adel after him by the bridle, he strode off to the stable. Perfishka looked closely at his master – and had a shock. He thought: Oh, how thin and old he has got within the year – and how grim and stern his face has grown! You would suppose that Pantelei ought to have been glad he had found his own; and so he was, certainly . . . but all the same Perfishka had a shock: in fact he felt quite creepy. Chertopkhanov put the horse in his old stall, patted him gently on the quarters and said: 'Well, there you are, home again. Just look! . . .' The same day he engaged a reliable watchman – a peasant who had no taxes to pay – installed himself again in his rooms, and resumed his former life . . .

Not quite his former life, however . . . But of this later.

The day after his return, Pantelei sent for Perfishka and, for want of anyone else to talk to, began to tell him, without of course losing the sense of his own dignity, and in a gruff bass voice, how he had managed to find Malek Adel. As he spoke, Chertopkhanov sat facing the window, smoking a long chibouk; Perfishka stood in the doorway, hands clasped behind his back and, looking respectfully at the back of his master's head, heard how, after many vain attempts and excursions, Pantelei at length arrived at Romyon fair, by this time alone, since Leiba the Jew, from weakness of character, had not lasted out and had run away from him; how, on the fifth day, when getting ready to depart, he had taken a last turn along the rows of carts and suddenly, between three other horses tied to a post, he had seen – Malek Adel! How he recognized him at once – and how Malek Adel had recognized him too and started neighing and straining and tearing the ground with his hoof. 'And he wasn't with the Cossack,' continued Chertopkhanov, still without turning his head and in the same bass voice, 'but with a gypsy horse-coper; naturally I at once took hold of my horse and tried to get him back by force; but the beastly gypsy started howling as if he'd been scalded, all over the square, began swearing that he had bought the horse from another gypsy and wanted to produce witnesses . . . I spat and paid him his money: may the devil fly with him! The great thing for me was that I had found my friend and set my soul at rest. Then, in the district of Karachevo, I ran into a Cossack who fitted the Jew's description – I took him for the thief and bashed his face in; but the Cossack turned out to be the son of a priest instead, and he took the skin off my back by way of damages – one hundred and twenty roubles. Well, money can always be made – but the main thing is that I've got Malek Adel back. I'm happy now and I shall be able to enjoy peace and quiet. But for you, Porfiry, I have only one instruction: as soon as you see a Cossack about – which heaven forfend – that very second, without saying a word, run and bring me a gun, and I shall know all right what to do next!'

This was how Pantelei spoke to Perfishka; these were the words he spoke; but his heart was far from being as calm as he declared.

Alas! at the bottom of his heart he was not wholly convinced that the horse he had brought back was really Malek Adel at all!

X

This was the beginning of a difficult time for Pantelei Eremeich. Peace and quiet was precisely what he enjoyed least of all. True, he had his good days, when the doubt which had dawned on him seemed to be nonsensical; he chased the absurd idea away like an importunate fly, he even laughed at himself; but he also had his bad days, when the nagging idea began again to gnaw and scratch at his heart, like a mouse under the floor-boards, and he suffered bitterly from secret pangs. During the memorable day when he found Malek Adel, Chertopkhanov had been conscious only of a blissful happiness. But the following morning when, beneath the low lean-to roof outside the inn, he started saddling up his discovery, after having spent the whole night by its side – for the first time he felt a certain pricking... He merely shook his head – but the seed had been sown. During his journey home (which lasted a week) he had but few doubts; they grew stronger and clearer as soon as he returned to his own Bessonovo, as soon as he found himself on the spot where the earlier, indubitable Malek Adel had lived... On the journey he had walked his horse for most of the way, swaying, looking from side to side, smoking his chibouk and without a thought in the world except occasionally to say to himself with a grin: 'The Chertopkhanovs always get their way! None of your nonsense for them!' But with his arrival home, another chapter began. He kept the whole thing to himself, of course; his pride alone would never have allowed him to speak of his inner anxiety. He would have 'torn in half' anybody who had even remotely hinted that the new Malek Adel was perhaps not the old one. He received congratulations on his 'happy find' from the few persons he happened to meet; but he didn't solicit these congratulations: more than ever he avoided people – a bad sign! He put Malek Adel, if I may so express myself, through an almost continuous examination; he would ride off with him far away over the fields and set him a test; or else he would creep into the stable, lock the door behind him, and, standing right in front of the horse's head, would look him in the eyes and ask him in a whisper: 'Are you Malek Adel? Are you? Are you? . . .' Or else he would gaze at him in silence, with a fixed stare, for whole hours at a time, now joyfully murmuring, 'Yes! Yes! of course he is!' now perplexed and, indeed, troubled in his heart.

What troubled Chertopkhanov was not so much the physical dissimilarities between *this* Malek Adel and the *other* . . . of which, incidentally, there were a few: the *other's* tail and mane seemed to have been thinner, his ears sharper, his pasterns shorter and his eyes brighter – but this may have only seemed to be so; Chertopkhanov was troubled by what might be termed the moral dissimilarities. The *other's* habits were different, his bearing was not the same. For instance: the *other* Malek Adel used to look round and whinny gently every time, the moment Chertopkhanov entered the stable; but *this* one went on munching hay unconcernedly – or else drowsing with lowered head. Neither of them moved when their master was dismounting, but the *other* came at once when called – while *this* one went on standing like a stump. The *other* galloped at the same speed as this one, but jumped higher and farther; *this* one had a freer motion in walking, but a jerkier trot – and was sometimes 'loose' with his hooves – that's to say, he knocked a back hoof on a fore one; the *other* had never shown such a fault – God forbid! *This* one, it seemed to Chertopkhanov, was always pricking his ears, in a stupid sort of way – quite the contrary to the *other*, who would cock one back and keep it there – watching his master! The *other* had only to see dirt around him and he would kick the walls of his box with his rear hoof; but *this* one never cared, you could have poured dung right up to his stomach. You had only to put the *other* one head to wind for him to be breathing at once with all his lungs and wide awake; but *this* one would simply whinny. The *other* was made uneasy by a rainy dampness in the air; *this* one didn't mind it at all. This one was coarser, coarser by far! And he had none of the other's charm and a mouth as hard as – but why go on! The other horse was a dear – but as for this one . . .

These were the thoughts that sometimes passed through Chertopkhanov's mind, and they had a bitter taste. But at other times he would let his horse out at full gallop over a newly-ploughed field, or make him jump down into the bottom of a hollow ravine and out again the steepest way. His heart would faint within him from delight, a loud whoop would burst from his lips and he would know, know for sure, that the horse under him was the real, the indubitable Malek Adel, for what other horse could have done the same?

Even so, however, there were frequent moments of pain and grief. Chertopkhanov's prolonged search for Malek Adel had cost him a lot of money; he no longer even thought of Kostroma hounds, and he rode about the neighbourhood quite alone as before. Well, one morning, five versts away from Bessonovo, Chertopkhanov ran into the same princely hunting party, before which he had cut such a brilliant dash a year and a half before. It was fated to happen that way; as then, so again to-day – a hare jumping up from beneath a boundary fence under the hounds' noses and scuttling away across the slopes. After him, after him! The whole field went off at full tilt, and so did Chertopkhanov – only not with them, but two hundred yards to the side – exactly like the time before. An enormous ravine ran diagonally downhill and, getting deeper and narrower as it went, cut across Chertopkhanov's path. At the point where he would have to jump it, and where he had in fact jumped it a year and a half before, it was still eight yards across and fourteen feet deep. In anticipation of a triumph, so miraculously repeated, Chertopkhanov gave a victorious chuckle, shook his whip – the huntsmen were galloping too, but without taking their eyes off the daring rider – his horse was flying like an arrow, here was the ravine right under his nose – over it, like the time before!...

But Malek Adel jibbed suddenly, wheeled to the left and galloped off *along* the brink, try as Chertopkhanov might to pull his head sideways towards the ravine...

He had refused, or, in other words, he had not been sure of himself!

Then Chertopkhanov, blazing with shame and anger, practically in tears, let out the reins and drove his horse straight ahead and uphill, away, away from the huntsmen, anywhere so as not to hear them mocking him, anywhere so as to escape as soon as possible from their accursed gaze!

With lacerated flanks, and all bathed in soapy foam, Malek Adel galloped home, and Chertopkhanov at once locked himself up in his room.

'No, he's not the same, he's not my friend! The other one would have broken his neck, but he would never have betrayed me!'

XI

What finished Chertopkhanov off for good was the following incident.

One day, mounted on Malek Adel, he was picking his way through the priest's back-yard, adjoining the church of the parish in which Bessonovo lay. With his fur hat rammed down over his eyes, slouching, with both hands dropped on the pommel of his saddle, he was moving slowly ahead; there was gloom and confusion in his heart. Suddenly someone called him.

He stopped his horse, raised his head and saw his correspondent, the deacon. With a brown three-cornered hat on his brown, pigtailed head, dressed in a yellowish nankeen coat, girt well below the waist with a piece of blue stuff, this server at the altar had come out to inspect his plot of ground and, on catching sight of Pantelei Eremeich, thought it his duty to pay him his respects – and incidentally to get something out of him. As is well-known, the clergy do not converse with secular people without some further purpose of this kind.

But Chertopkhanov had no time for the deacon; he hardly acknowledged his bow, and, muttering something between his teeth, was already waving his whip . . .

'But what a wondrous horse you have!' the deacon hastened to add. 'It can indeed be accounted to you for honour. Verily, you are a man of wondrous spirit; a very lion!' The father deacon prided himself on his eloquence – and thus very much irritated the father priest, in whom the gift of words was not inborn and whose tongue even vodka failed to unloose. 'Having lost one beast, through the evil designs of the wicked,' continued the deacon, 'and no whit cast down by this, but trusting all the more in Divine Providence, you have taken unto yourself another, no whit worse than the former one, and perchance even better . . . Therefore . . .'

'What nonsense is this?' interrupted Chertopkhanov darkly. 'What other horse? This is the same one, this is Malek Adel . . . I found him. Rambling talk like that . . .'

'Eh! eh! eh! eh!' said the deacon deliberately, as if wishing to draw the words out, his fingers playing in his beard and his bright, eager eyes watching Chertopkhanov. 'How so, my good sir? Your horse, if God grants me to remember aright, was stolen last year, two weeks after the feast of the Intercession, and it is now the end of November.'

'Well, what of it?'

The deacon went on playing with his fingers in his beard. 'It means that more than a year has passed since then, and yet your horse is now exactly as he was then, a grey roan; indeed he seems even darker in colour. How could that be? Grey horses turn much whiter in the course of a year.'

Chertopkhanov started . . . it was as if a spear had been thrust into his heart. The deacon was right; of course a grey coat changes colour! How was it that such a simple fact had not occurred to him until then?

'You bundle of blasphemy! Leave me alone!' he barked out, his eyes flashing with fury – and vanished in a twinkling out of the astonished deacon's sight.

So it was all finished!

Really finished, broken right up, the last card trumped! Everything had collapsed at once with the single word 'whiter'!

Grey horses turn whiter.

Gallop, gallop, curse you! – but you will never be able to gallop away from that word!

Chertopkhanov rushed home and again locked himself up.

XII

That this wretched nag was not Malek Adel, that between him and Malek Adel there was not the slightest resemblance, that everyone with the slightest sense was bound to see as much at first glance, that he, Pantelei Chertopkhanov, had been most grossly taken in, no! – that he had deliberately, and with premeditation, deceived himself, wrapped himself in this fog – of all that there could not be the slightest doubt! Chertopkhanov paced up and down his room, turning on his heels in the same way every time he came to the wall, like a beast in a cage. His pride suffered unbearably; but it was not only the pain of wounded pride that rent him: despair ruled him, hatred stifled him, the thirst for revenge blazed in him. But on whom? On whom was he to revenge himself? The Jew, Yaff, Masha, the deacon, the Cossack-thief, all the neighbours, the whole world, or, finally, himself? His mind grew confused. His last card had been trumped! (He liked this figure of speech.) And he was again the most insignificant and despised of men, the most generally ridiculous, a tomfool, a blithering idiot, an object for the deacon's mirth! He imagined, he pictured clearly to himself, how that bundle of filth would tell the story of the grey horse and the stupid master. Oh, curse it all! ... In vain Chertopkhanov strove to calm his raging bile, in vain he sought to assure himself that this ... horse, even if not Malek Adel, was nevertheless . . . a good one, and could serve him for many years; simultaneously he would thrust this thought furiously from him, as if it contained a new cause of offence against the *other* Malek Adel, towards whom he already considered himself quite guilty enough . . . Yes, indeed! This jade, this nag, *he* had compared to Malek Adel, stone-blind oaf that he was! And as for the service which this nag could still give him . . . why, would he ever condescend to mount him? Not for anything in the world! Never . . . Sell him to a Tartar, as food for dogs – that was all he deserved . . . Yes! That would be best of all!

For more than two hours Chertopkhanov wandered up and down his room.

'Perfishka!' he ordered suddenly. 'Go at once to the pot-house, fetch a gallon of vodka! D'you hear? A gallon, and be quick about it! I want the vodka standing here on my table this very second.'

The vodka was standing on Pantelei's table without delay, and he began to drink.

XIII

Anyone who had then observed Chertopkhanov, who could have witnessed the sullen fury with which he emptied glass after glass, would certainly have been horror-struck in spite of himself. Night had fallen; a greasy candle burnt faintly on the table. Chertopkhanov had stopped pacing from corner to corner; he sat, all flushed, with glazed eyes which he would now lower to the floor, now turn fixedly towards the window; he would get up, pour out some vodka, drink it down, sit again, again fix his gaze on one spot, and remain stock-still – except that his breath came ever faster and his face grew ever more flushed. It seemed that within him some decision was ripening which troubled him, but to which he was gradually growing accustomed; the same thought came inexorably and incessantly nearer, the same image outlined itself more clearly before him, and in his heart, under the burning pressure of strong liquor, the irritation of wrath had already given way to a mood of brutal cruelty, and a sinister smile had appeared on his lips.

'Well, anyway, it's time to act!' he said, in a business-like, almost bored tone of voice. 'Enough of this dallying!'

He drank down a final glass of vodka, brought out his pistol from under the bed – the same pistol with which he had fired at Masha – loaded it, put a few caps into his pocket 'against emergencies' – and set off for the stable.

The watchman came running up to him as he began to open the door, but he shouted at him: 'It's me, can't you see? Be off with you!' The watchman withdrew a little way. 'Be off to bed!' Chertopkhanov shouted at him again. 'There's nothing for you to guard here! This wonder horse, this treasure!' He went into the stable... Malek Adel, the false Malek Adel, was lying among the litter. Chertopkhanov kicked him and said: 'Get up, you crow!' Then he undid the halter from the manger, took off the blanket and threw it on the ground, and, roughly turning the obedient horse round in the stall, led him out into the yard and from the yard into the fields, to the utter amazement of the watchman, who was quite unable to understand where the master could be off to in the middle of the night leading an unbridled horse. He was naturally too much afraid to ask, but simply followed him with his eyes until he vanished round a turning of the track leading to the nearby forest.

XIV

Chertopkhanov walked with long strides, never halting and never looking back; Malek Adel – for so we will call him until the end – walked submissively after him. The night was fairly light; Chertopkhanov could distinguish the jagged outline of the forest, forming a solid black mass ahead of him. At the touch of the cool night air he would certainly have got drunk from the vodka, if... if it had not been for another, stronger intoxication which mastered his whole being. His head grew heavy, the blood drummed in his throat and ears; but he stepped out firmly and knew where he was going.

He had resolved to kill Malek Adel. He had thought of nothing else the whole day ... Now he was resolved!

He went about his business, not exactly calmly, but confidently, without turning back, like a man obeying a sense of duty. It seemed to him a very simple affair: by doing away with the impostor, he would get even with 'them all', punish himself for his folly, put himself right with his real friend, and show the whole world (Chertopkhanov thought a great deal about 'the whole world') that he was not a man to be trifled with ... But the main thing was that he would do away with himself along with the impostor, for what was there left to live for? How all this fell into place inside his head, and why it seemed to him so simple, would be difficult to explain, though not altogether impossible. Injured, lonely, without a human soul for friend, without a brass farthing, and also with his blood on fire from drink, he was in a condition bordering on madness; and there is no doubt that the most absurd actions of the insane have, in their own eyes, a special kind of logic and rightness. Anyhow Chertopkhanov was fully convinced of his own rightness; he never faltered, he was in a hurry to carry out his sentence on the guilty one, without, however, clearly explaining to himself exactly whom he meant by this term ... The truth was that he had not thought out what it was that he intended to do. 'I must get it over, I must,' he assured himself dully and grimly: 'I must get it over!'

Meanwhile the innocent culprit jogged and ambled submissively behind his back ... In Chertopkhanov's heart, however, there was no pity.

XV

Not far from the edge of the forest to which he had led his horse, ran a small ravine, half-overgrown with oak-bushes. Chertopkhanov went down into it ... Malek Adel stumbled and nearly fell on top of him.

'Do you want to crush me, curse you?' shouted Chertopkhanov – and, as if in self-defence, he snatched the pistol from his pocket. He no longer felt any bitterness, but only the special feeling of woodenness that is supposed to come over a man who is about to commit some terrible crime. His own voice frightened him – so wild was its ring under the dark canopy of the branches, in the damp, rotten-smelling fustiness of the ravine in the forest! And then, in answer to his exclamation, some great bird suddenly began flapping about on the tree-top above his head. Chertopkhanov started. It was as if he had woken up a witness to his deed – even in this dead place, where he should not have come upon a single living thing...

'Be off, you devil – away with you, to all the points of the compass!' he said between his teeth – and, letting go of Malek Adel's halter, struck him a swinging blow on the shoulder with the butt of his pistol. Malek Adel immediately turned back, scrambled out of the ravine...and fled. The sound of his hooves soon died away. A wind had arisen, which choked and hid every sound.

In his turn Chertopkhanov slowly made his way out of the ravine, reached the edge of the forest and trudged off on the road home. He was dissatisfied with himself; the heaviness which he had felt in his head and heart spread through all his limbs; he walked on, angry, morose, discontented, hungry, as if someone had injured him, robbed him of a prize, or of bread itself...

His feelings were those of a suicide who has been prevented from carrying out his design.

Suddenly something touched him behind, between the shoulder-blades. He looked round...Malek Adel was standing in the middle of the road. He had followed his master, had touched him with his muzzle...had reported his presence.

'Ah!' cried Chertopkhanov, 'you've come of your own accord, to meet your death! Very well, then!'

In the twinkling of an eye he had snatched out his pistol, cocked it, put the muzzle against Malek Adel's forehead and fired.

The poor horse shied to one side, reared up, jumped back about ten paces and suddenly crashed heavily down, wheezed, and rolled convulsively on the ground.

Chertopkhanov stopped his ears with his hands and ran off. His knees faltered beneath him. Drunkenness, anger, grim self-confidence – all had vanished in a flash. He was left with nothing but a feeling of shame and ugliness – and the consciousness, sure beyond a doubt, that this time he had made away with himself as well.

XVI

Six weeks later, the boy Perfishka thought it his duty to stop the inspector of police as he drove past Bessonovo.

'What's the matter?' asked the guardian of the law.

'Please, your honour, come in,' answered the boy with a low bow; 'Pantelei Eremeich seems in a fair way to die; that's what I fear.'

'What? Die?' the inspector repeated after him.

'Just so, sir. First of all he'd be taking vodka every day, and now he's gone to bed and got very, very thin. I think that now he doesn't understand anything any more. He's quite lost his tongue.'

The inspector got out of his cart. 'Well, I suppose that at any rate you have been and fetched the priest? Has your master confessed? Has he taken communion?'

'No, sir.'

The inspector frowned. 'But how is that, my friend? Is it possible – eh? Don't you know that for this . . . there's a heavy responsibility – eh?'

'But I asked the master the day before yesterday, and yesterday as well,' protested the intimidated boy, 'wouldn't he like me to go for a priest? "Silence, you fool," he says, "mind your own business." But to-day when I reported to him – he just looked at me and twitched his moustache.'

'Did he drink a lot of vodka?' asked the inspector.

'A terrific lot! But please, your honour, come and see him in his room.'

'Well, lead the way!' grunted the inspector and followed Perfishka.

A strange spectacle awaited him.

In the back room, which was dank and dark, on a miserable bed which was covered with a horse blanket, with a shaggy felt cloak for pillow, lay Chertopkhanov, no longer pale, but yellowish green, the colour of a corpse, his eyes sunk under eyelids with a sheen on them, his nose grown sharper, but still red, above his dishevelled moustache. He lay dressed in his perpetual tunic with the cartridge-pleats round the chest and his blue Circassian trousers. The fur cap with the raspberry-coloured crown covered his forehead right down to the eyebrows. In one hand Chertopkhanov held a hunting whip, in the other an embroidered red tobacco-pouch – Masha's last present to him. On the table beside the bed stood an empty decanter; over the head of the bed, fastened to the wall with pins, hung two water-colours: one, so far as it could be made out, represented a fat man with a guitar in his hands, probably Nedopyuskin; the other depicted a galloping horseman ... The horse was like those galloping animals which children draw on walls and fences; but its carefully-shaded roan markings, and the cartridges round the horseman's chest, the sharp points of his boots and his enormous moustache, left no room for doubt: the picture was meant to represent Pantelei Eremeich mounted on Malek Adel.

The puzzled inspector didn't know what to do next. Deathly silence reigned in the room. He must be dead already, he thought and, raising his voice, said: 'Pantelei Eremeich! I say, Pantelei Eremeich!'

Then something extraordinary happened. Chertopkhanov's eyes slowly opened, his dim pupils moved first from right to left, then from left to right, stopped at the visitor, saw him ... something kindled in their dim whiteness, a semblance of vision appeared in them ... the blue lips gradually parted, and from them came a husky voice, already the voice of the grave:

'Pantelei Chertopkhanov, nobleman of ancient lineage, is dying; who can prevent him? – He owes nothing, he wants nothing... Leave him alone! Go!'

The hand with the whip tried to raise itself... in vain! The lips stuck together again, the eyes closed! – and Chertopkhanov lay as before on his hard bed, stretched out flat as a layer of bricks, the soles of his feet pressed close together.

'Let me know when he dies,' whispered the inspector to Perfishka as he left the room; 'and I think you could still go for the priest. Things must be done properly, he must have the last rites.'

The same day Perfishka went for the priest, and the next morning it was his duty to report to the inspector that Pantelei Eremeich had died during the night.

When they buried him, his coffin was followed by two people: the boy Perfishka and Moshel Leiba. The news of Chertopkhanov's death had somehow or other reached the Jew – and he did not fail to pay the last tribute to his benefactor.

The Live Relic

Motherland of long-suffering –
Land of the Russian people!
F. TYUTCHEV

THE French proverb has it that a dry fisherman and a wet hunter make a sorry sight. Never having been addicted to fishing, I am no judge of a fisherman's feelings in fine clear weather and of the extent to which, in a downpour, the satisfaction afforded him by a good catch offsets the unpleasantness of getting wet. But, for the hunter, rain is a real disaster. A disaster of this kind befell Ermolai and myself on one of our excursions after blackcock in the district of Belevo. From daybreak the rain had not stopped. We had done everything possible to escape it. We had put rubber capes practically over our heads, we had stood under trees to avoid the drops. Our waterproof capes, besides hindering us from shooting, had let the water through in the most shameless manner; and, as for the trees – true, at first there seemed to be no drops, but then the water accumulated in the leaves suddenly burst through; every branch poured down on us like a rain-pipe, a cold stream found its way under the cravat and ran down the spinal column... That was the last straw, as Ermolai put it. 'No, Pyotr Petrovich,' he exclaimed at last, 'we can't go on like this!... We can't shoot to-day. The dogs' noses are washed-out, the guns are misfiring...Phew! It's too much!'

'What shall we do?' I asked.

'I'll tell you what. We'll go to Alexeyevka. You may not know it – it's a little farm, belonging to your mother; eight versts from here. We'll spend the night there, and to-morrow...'

'We'll come back here?'

355

'No, not here...I know some places beyond Alexeyevka much better than here for blackcock.'

I did not think fit to inquire of my trusty companion why he had not conducted me straight to these places, and the same day we reached my mother's farm, the existence of which I confess I had not suspected until then. Beside the farm we found a little pavilion, very decrepit, but uninhabited and therefore clean; in it I passed a fairly peaceful night.

The next day I woke up very early. The sun had just risen; there was not a cloud in the sky; the whole scene sparkled brightly with a double brilliance: the brilliance of the early morning rays, and of the previous day's downpour.

While my dog-cart was being harnessed, I went for a stroll in a small garden, once an orchard, now run wild, which surrounded the pavilion on all sides with its lush, scented growth. Oh, how good it was in the open air, under the clear sky, in which larks were trilling, and from which their sweet voices fell in silver beads! They had certainly carried off dewdrops on their wings, and their songs seemed drenched in dew. I took off my cap and joyously breathed in with all my lungs... On the slope of a shallow ravine, beside a fence, I saw a bee-garden; a narrow path led towards it, winding like a snake between unbroken walls of weed and nettle, above which towered, planted heaven knows how, the pointed stalks of dark-green hemp.

I went along the path, and came to the bee-garden. Beside it stood a little wattle shed, the place where the hives were put in winter. I looked in through the half-open door: it was dark, quite dry; there was a smell of mint and balm. In a corner there was an arrangement of trestles and on them, covered in a blanket, a sort of small figure...I was going away...

'Master, I say, master! Pyotr Petrovich!' came a voice, weak, slow and husky, like the rustling of sedge in a marsh.

I stopped.

'Pyotr Petrovich! Come closer, please!' repeated the voice. It issued from the corner where I had noticed the trestles.

I came closer – and stood stock-still from amazement. Before me lay a live human being, but what on earth...?

A head completely dried up, all one colour, the colour of bronze, nothing more nor less than an ancient icon; a nose as thin as the blade of a knife; lips almost invisible – only the pale glimmer of teeth and eyes, and, winding out from under a handkerchief on the brow, a few thin strands of yellow hair. Beside the chin, on the fold of the blanket, slowly twisting their twig-like fingers, moved two tiny hands of the same bronze colour. I looked closer: the face was far from ugly, it was beautiful even – but strange and frightening. And all the more frightening because on it, on its metallic cheeks, I could see – forcing... forcing its way, but unable to spread across – a smile.

'Don't you know me, master?' whispered the voice again; it seemed an exhalation from the hardly-moving lips. 'But how could you know me! – I'm Lukerya... D'you remember, I used to lead the country dances, at your mother's, at Spass-koye... d'you remember, I used to lead the singing, too?'

'Lukerya!' I exclaimed. 'Is it you? Is it possible?'

'Yes, master, it is. I'm Lukerya.'

I didn't know what to say, and gazed as if dumbfounded at that dark, motionless face, with its bright, death-like eyes fixed upon me! Was it possible? This mummy – Lukerya, the greatest beauty of all our household – tall, plump, pink and white – full of laughter and dancing and song! Lukerya, clever Lukerya, who was courted by all our young swains, for whom I too had sighed in secret, I – a lad of sixteen years!

'For goodness' sake, Lukerya,' I said at last, 'what's happened to you?'

'Oh, I've had terrible trouble! But you mustn't be put off, master, you mustn't look down on me for my bad luck – sit down over there on the cask – nearer, or you won't be able to hear me... you see what a fine voice I've got!... Well, I *am* glad to see you! How did you come to turn up at Alexeyevka like this?'

Lukerya spoke very quietly and faintly, but without faltering.

'Ermolai, the hunter, brought me here. But tell me . . .'

'Tell you about my trouble? – Very well, master. It happened some time ago now, six or seven years back. I had just been betrothed to Vasily Polyakov – d'you remember him, a fine-looking chap, with curly hair – he was serving as butler at your mother's? You had left the country by then and gone to Moscow to study. Vasily and I loved each other very much; he was never out of my thoughts. It was in the spring. Well, one night . . . It was not long before dawn . . . and I couldn't sleep: a nightingale in the garden was singing so wonderfully sweet! . . . I couldn't stay still, I got up and went out to the porch to listen to him. He went flowing, flowing on . . . and suddenly it seemed to me that someone with Vasily's voice was calling me, quietly-like: "Lusha!" I looked round, half-asleep, you know – slipped, fell right off the floor of the porch and went flying down, thump, on the ground! And it didn't seem as though I'd hurt myself badly, because I got up at once and went back to my room. Only it felt as if inside me – in my belly – something had torn . . . Let me get my breath . . . just a minute, master.'

Lukerya paused and I looked at her in bewilderment. What bewildered me particularly was that she told her story almost gaily, without groans or sighs, never complaining or asking for sympathy.

'From then on,' continued Lukerya, 'I started fading and withering away; a blackness came over me, it got hard for me to walk, and then – I couldn't even use my legs; neither stand nor sit: I'd just lie the whole time. And I didn't want to eat or drink; I got thinner and thinner. From the kindness of her heart your mother showed me to the doctors and sent me to hospital. But I got no relief from it. Not a single doctor could even say what my illness was. They did everything they could think of to me: they burnt my back with red-hot iron, they sat me down in broken ice – all no good. At length I grew all stiff, like a board . . . So the mistress decided that there was nothing more to be done to cure me, and as it isn't possible to keep a cripple in the manor house ... well, they sent me over here – because here I have relations. And here I live, as you see.'

Lukerya paused again and again, made an effort to smile.

'But it's a terrible plight to be in!' I exclaimed ... and, not knowing what to add, I asked: 'And what about Vasily Polyakov?'

It was a very stupid question.

Lukerya turned her eyes away.

'What about Polyakov? He moped and moped, and married someone else – a girl from Glinnoye. D'you know Glinnoye? Not far from us. Her name was Agrafena. He loved me very much ... but he was young, you see ... there was no reason why he should stay a bachelor. And what sort of a sweetheart could I be to him now? He found himself a good wife ... they've got children. He lives on a neighbouring estate, in the agent's office; your mother let him go with a passport, and, praise be to God, he's very happy.'

'And so you just lie and lie?' I asked again.

'Yes, master, I have lain like this for more than six years. In summer I lie here in this wattle hut, but when it gets cold they'll move me inside the bath-house. And there I lie.'

'But who looks after you? Who keeps an eye on you?'

'Oh, there are good folk here, too. They don't leave me to myself. And I don't take much looking after. As for food, I don't eat anything, and as for water – here it is in the mug: there's a supply of clear spring water always standing there. I can reach the mug myself: one of my hands still works. There's a girl here, an orphan; now and again she looks in on me, bless her. She was here just now ... didn't you meet her? Pretty, she is, and fair-skinned. She brings me flowers; I'm very fond of them, of flowers. There are no garden flowers here ... there were, but they've died out. But wild flowers are good, too, they smell even better than garden ones. Take the lily of the valley ... What could be sweeter?'

'Aren't you bored, aren't you restless, my poor Lukerya?'

'What can I do? I don't want to lie to you – it was very sad at first; but then I got used to it, I grew patient – I came not to mind; there are some people who are even worse off.'

'In what way?'

'Some people haven't even anywhere to go! And some are blind or deaf! But I, praise be to God, I can see beautifully and I can hear everything, everything. If a mole burrows under-ground – even so, I hear him. And I can smell every smell, even the faintest there are! If buckwheat blossoms in the field, or lime in the garden – you needn't tell me: I'm always the first to know. So long as only a breath of wind comes from there. No, why anger God? – there are many worse off than I. For example, someone who's well can sin very easily; but even sin itself has left me. The other day Father Alexei, the priest, came to give me communion, and said: "I need not confess you: how can you sin in your condition?" And I answered him: "But what about sin in thought, Father?" "Well," he says and laughs, "that's not a big sin." And even in this sin of thought I couldn't be much of a sinner,' continued Lukerya, 'because I've taught myself not to think and, more important still, not to remember. Time passes quicker like that.'

I was, I confess, surprised. 'You're quite alone all the time, Lukerya; then how can you prevent thoughts coming into your head? Or do you sleep all the time?'

'Oh, no, master! I can't always sleep. Although I have no big pains, it nags me here, inside me, and in my bones, too; it doesn't let me sleep as I ought to. No . . . I just lie by myself, I lie and lie – and I don't think; I feel that I'm alive and breathing – and that all of me is here. I look and I listen. The bees in the garden will buzz and bumble away; the pigeon will sit on the roof and start cooing; the mother-hen will look in with her chickens to pick up the crumbs; or else a sparrow will fly in, or a butterfly – I enjoy it so much. The year before last some swallows even built a nest over there in the corner and hatched a family. How funny it was! One of them would fly in, drop into the nest, feed the chicks – and away. You'd look again, and the other would already be there inside. Sometimes they wouldn't fly in, but just swoop past the open door. And at once the chicks – how they'd squeak and open their beaks!...I thought they'd come the next year, too, but they say that some sportsman hereabouts shot them with his gun. What good can it have done him? A whole swallow is no bigger than a beetle. How cruel you are, you sporting gentlemen!'

'I don't shoot swallows,' I hastened to observe.

'Then, once,' began Lukerya again, 'I had a great joke! A hare ran in, really he did! The hounds were after him, but he came lolloping straight in at the door!...He sat right close to me – sat for quite a while – kept moving his nose and twitching his whiskers – a regular officer! And how he looked at me. He must have understood that he'd nothing to fear from me. At last he got up, hop-hop to the door, looked round from the threshold – what a one he was! Such a funny one!'

Lukerya looked up at me...as if to say, isn't it amusing? To please her, I laughed. She bit her dried-up lips.

'Well, in winter, of course, I'm worse off, because it's dark; it would be a pity to light a candle, and what for? Although I know my letters and was always fond of reading, what is there to read? There are no books here at all, and, even if there were, how am I going to hold one? Father Alexei brought me a calendar to occupy my mind; then he saw that it was no good, and he went and took it away again. But even when it's dark, there's always something to hear; a cricket chirrups, or somewhere a mouse starts scratching. Then, too, the best plan is not to think!

'Or else I say prayers,' continued Lukerya after a short rest. 'Only I don't know many of them, these prayers. And why should I go and bother the Lord God? What can I ask Him for? He knows better than I do what I need. He has sent me a cross – it means He must love me. That's how we are told to understand it. I say "Our Father" and "Mother of God" and the prayer for all that suffer – and then I just go on lying again without a thought in my head. And I don't mind!'

Two minutes passed. I didn't break the silence and didn't stir on the narrow little cask which served me for a seat. The cruel, stony immobility of the unfortunate living creature lying before me communicated itself to me, too: I, too, was as if benumbed.

'Listen, Lukerya,' I began at length. 'Listen, I'm going to suggest something to you. Would you like me to arrange for them to take you to hospital, a good hospital in town? Who knows, perhaps they could still cure you? In any case you won't be alone . . .'

Lukerya just moved her eyebrows. 'Oh, no, master,' she said in a worried whisper, 'don't move me to hospital, don't touch me. I'll only get more suffering out of it. What's the use of treating me now! . . . Why, once a doctor came here: he wanted to look at me. I said to him: "Don't bother me, for the Lord Christ's sake." What was the good of asking him! He started turning me over, moved my arms and legs, bent them about; he said: "I'm doing this for science's sake; you see, I'm in the service of science! and you," he said, "can't resist me, because for my troubles I've had an Order given me, and I try my best for fools like you." He pulled me about, and pulled me about, he told me the name of my illness – a learned sort of name – and with that he went away. And for a whole week afterwards all my bones ached. You say I'm alone, always alone. No, not always. I get visitors. I'm quiet – not in anyone's way. Peasant-girls will come to me and gossip: a pilgrim-woman will look in and start telling of Jerusalem and Kiev and the holy cities. And it's not as if I was frightened to be alone. I'm even better off, I promise you . . . Master, don't touch me, don't take me to hospital . . . Thank you, you're kind, but don't touch me, my dear.'

'Well, as you like, Lukerya. I just thought that, for your own good . . .'

'I know, master, that it was for my own good, but, master, dear master, who can help anyone else? Who can get inside someone else's soul? Let everyone help himself! You won't believe me – but sometimes I lie alone like this . . . and it's as if there was no one in the whole world but me. I'm the only one alive! And it seems to me, it sort of dawns on me ... ideas come to me – and such strange ones!'

'What are they about, Lukerya, these ideas of yours?'

'That, master, I can't tell you either: you'd never make it out. And I forget them afterwards. It will come, like a little cloud, it will burst, it will be all fresh and good, but what it was – you'll never understand! Only it seems to me that if there were people near me, none of this would happen, and I'd feel nothing except my own unhappiness.'

Lukerya sighed painfully. Her chest was doing its work no better than the rest of her body.

'I can see by looking at you, master,' she began again, 'that you feel very sorry for me. But don't feel too sorry, don't indeed! Listen, I'll tell you something: even now, sometimes, I ... well, you remember how gay I used to be in my time? Such a lively one! ... Well, do you know what? Even now I sing songs.'

'Songs? ... You?'

'Yes, songs, old songs, round songs, carols, songs of all sorts! You see, I used to know many of them and I've not forgotten. Only I don't sing dance songs. As I am now, there wouldn't be any point.'

'So you sing them ... to yourself?'

'To myself, and aloud. I can't sing loudly, but loud enough to understand. I told you about the girl who comes to see me. An orphan, so she's an understanding sort. Well, I've taught her; she's already caught four songs from me. Don't you believe it? Wait, now I'm going to ...'

Lukerya collected her strength ... The thought that this half-dead creature was getting ready to sing horrified me in spite of myself. But, before I could say a word, there trembled in my ears a drawn-out, scarcely audible, but pure and true note ... and after it followed another, then another. Lukerya was singing 'In the meadows'. She sang with no play of expression on her petrified face; even her eyes were fixed. But so touchingly did her poor, forced little voice sound, wavering like a wisp of smoke; so hard did she strive to pour out her whole soul . . . It was no longer horror that I felt: an indescribable pity gripped my heart.

'Oh, I can't!' she said suddenly. 'I haven't the strength . . . I've been so pleased to see you.'

She closed her eyes.

I put my hand on her tiny, cold fingers . . . She looked up at me – and her dark eyelids, trimmed with golden lashes, like those of an ancient statue, closed again. After a moment they glittered in the twilight . . . A tear had moistened them.

I sat there motionless as before.

'Just look at me!' said Lukerya suddenly, with unexpected force and, opening her eyes wide, tried to wipe the tears from them. 'Oughtn't I to be ashamed? What do I want? This hasn't happened to me for a long time . . . not since the day when Vasily Polyakov was here last spring. As long as he was sitting talking to me – I didn't mind – but when he went away – I fairly cried away to myself! Where did it all come from? . . . But tears cost nothing to girls like us. Master,' added Lukerya, 'I expect you've got a handkerchief . . . Don't be put off, wipe my eyes.'

I hastened to carry out her wish, and left her the handkerchief. At first she refused it . . . 'What do I want with such a present?' she said. The handkerchief was very plain, but clean and white. Then she seized it in her weak fingers and did not loosen them again. I had grown used to the darkness in which we both were, and could make out her features clearly, could even discern a faint ruddiness, showing through the bronze of her face, could descry in that face, or so at least I thought, the traces of her former beauty.

'You asked me, master,' began Lukerya again, 'if I sleep. I certainly don't sleep much, but every time, I dream – good dreams! I never dream about myself as ill: I'm always well and young, in my dreams . . . The only pity is that I wake up – and I want to have a good stretch – but it's as if I was all in chains. Once I had such a marvellous dream! Would you like me to tell you? Well, listen. I was standing in a field and all round was rye, so tall, and ripe like gold! . . . And with me there was a red dog, fierce, very fierce – trying all the time to bite me. And in my hands I had a sickle, not just an ordinary sickle, but absolutely like the moon, when it's like a sickle. And with this moon I had to cut down the rye, every stalk of it. Only I was very tired from the heat, and the moon dazzled me, and laziness came over me; and around me cornflowers were growing, such big ones! and they all had their heads turned towards me, and I thought: I'll pick these cornflowers, Vasya promised to come – so I'll make a garland for myself first . . . I've still got time for reaping. I began to pick the cornflowers, but they melted between my fingers, and melted, and there was nothing I could do! So I couldn't make my garland. But then I heard someone coming towards me, quite near, and calling: "Lusha! . . . Lusha! . . ." Oh, I thought, what a shame – I haven't finished! Never mind, I'll put this moon on my head instead of the cornflowers. I put on the moon, just like a head-dress, and at once I seemed to be all aglow. I lit up the whole field around. I looked, and over the very tops of the ears of rye comes sweeping quickly towards me, not Vasya, but Christ himself! And how I knew that it was Christ, I can't say – He was not as He is in pictures – yet it was Him! Beardless, tall, young and in white, but with a golden belt – and He stretches out His hand to me. "Never fear," He says, "my well-adorned bride, but follow Me; you will lead the dances in My Heavenly Kingdom and play the music of Paradise." And how I clung to His hand! – my dog at once went for my legs . . . But away we whirled! He was ahead . . . His wings spread out over all the sky, long, like a seagull's – and I went after Him! And the dog had to stay behind. It was only then that I understood that this dog was my illness, and that there would be no place for it in the kingdom of heaven.'

Lukerya was silent for a minute.

'And then I had another dream,' she began again – 'or perhaps this one was a vision . . . I don't know. It seemed to me that I was alone in this cabin and that my dead parents came to me – my father and mother – and bowed low to me, but said nothing. And I asked them: "Why are you bowing to me, father and mother?" "Why," they said, "because you're suffering so much in this world that you've not only lightened your own soul's burden, but you've taken a heavy weight off us as well, and it's got much easier for us in the other world. You've already finished with your own sins; now you're overcoming ours." And, so saying, my parents bowed to me again – and I could see them no longer: the walls were all I could see. I wondered very much afterwards what it was that had come over me. I even told the priest in confession. But he thinks that it couldn't have been a vision, because visions come only to those of the priestly calling.

'Then I had another dream,' Lukerya went on. 'I was sitting by a high-road, under a willow-tree, holding a peeled stick, with a bundle on my shoulder and my head wrapped in a kerchief – a regular pilgrim-woman! And I had to go some-where far, far away, on a pilgrimage. And pilgrims kept on going past me; quietly they'd go, as if against their will, always the same way: they had sad faces, all very much like one another. And I saw, winding her way amongst them, a woman a head taller than the others, wearing a strange dress, not like ours in Russia. And her face was strange, too, a stern, fasting sort of face, and all the others seemed to keep away from her; and suddenly she turned – and came straight for me. She stopped and looked at me; her eyes were like a falcon's, yellow, big, and oh, so bright. And I asked her: "Who are you?" and she said to me: "I am your death." I ought to have been afraid, but on the contrary I was glad, so glad, I crossed myself! And this woman, my death, said to me: "I'm sorry for you, Lukerya, but I can't take you with me. – Good-bye!" Lord! how sad I was then! . . . "Take me," I said, "mother, dearest one, take me!" And my death turned round to me, began to talk to me . . . I understood that she was telling me my hour, but darkly, as if in riddles . . . "After St. Peter's," she said . . . With that I woke up . . . That's the sort of strange dreams I have!'

Lukerya looked up . . . reflected . . .

'Only my trouble is this: it happens that a whole week goes by and I don't go to sleep once. Last year a lady drove by, saw me, and gave me a bottle with some medicine against sleeplessness; she told me to take ten drops at a time. It helped me a great deal and I slept. Only now the bottle has been finished long ago...D'you know what medicine that was, and how to get it?'

The passing lady had clearly given Lukerya opium. I promised to get her just such a bottle, and again could not refrain from admiring her patience aloud.

'Eh, master!' she rejoined. 'What are you saying? What is this patience of mine? Simeon on the Pillar really did have great patience: he stood on his pillar for thirty years! And another martyr ordered himself to be buried in the ground up to his chest and the ants ate his face. And once, someone who had read many books told me that there was a certain country, and this country had been conquered by the heathen, and they tortured or put to death all the people in it; and try as the people of the country might, they couldn't free themselves. And then there appeared among those people a saintly virgin: she took a great sword, she put on herself clothes weighing seventy pounds, went out against the heathen and drove them all out beyond the sea. And only after she had driven them out, she said to them: "Now burn me, because such was my promise, to die by fire for my people." And the heathen took her and burnt her, and her people have been free ever since! There was a great deed for you! and what have I done?'

I marvelled to myself at this far-flung version of the Joan of Arc legend, and, after a pause, I asked Lukerya how old she was.

'Twenty-eight...or twenty-nine...less than thirty. But why count them, the years? I'll tell you something more...'

Lukerya suddenly coughed dully and groaned.

'You're talking a great deal,' I remarked to her. 'It can do you harm.'

'True,' she whispered, in a hardly audible voice, 'it's the end of our talk, but no matter. Now, when you go away, I shall have all the silence I want. At least, I have got a lot off my mind...'

I started saying good-bye to her, repeated my promise to send her the medicine, and asked her to think carefully once more and tell me whether there was nothing she needed.

'I need nothing; I'm absolutely content, praise be to God,' she pronounced, with extreme effort, but also with emotion. 'May God grant health to everyone! And you, master, please speak to your mother – the peasants here are poor – if she would only bring down their rent, just a little! They haven't enough land, they make nothing out of it!...They would pray to God for you...but I need nothing, I'm absolutely content.'

I gave Lukerya my word to carry out her request, and was already making for the door when she called me back.

'D'you remember, master,' she said, with a wonderful brightening of her eyes and lips, 'what hair I had? D'you remember – right down to my knees! For a long time I couldn't make up my mind...Such hair it was!...But how could I comb it! In my condition! So I cut it off...yes...Well, good-bye, master! I can't say more...'

The same day, before setting out to shoot, I had a talk about Lukerya with the local constable. I learnt from him that in the village she was called 'the Live Relic', also that she caused no trouble; there was not a grumble to be heard from her, not a complaint. 'She asks nothing for herself, on the contrary she's grateful for everything; she's as quiet as quiet can be, that I must say. She's been smitten by God,' so the constable concluded, 'for her sins, no doubt; but we don't go into that. As for condemning her, for example, no, we certainly don't condemn her. Let her be!'

A few weeks later I heard that Lukerya was dead. Death had come for her after all...and 'after St. Peter's'. The story went that on the day of her death she kept hearing the sound of bells, although it is more than five versts from Alexeyevka to the church, and it was on a weekday. Besides, Lukerya said that the sound came, not from church, but 'from above'. Probably she did not venture to say – from heaven.

The Knocking

'I've got something to tell you,' said Ermolai, coming into the cabin where I was. I had just had dinner and lain down on a camp-bed to rest myself after a fairly successful and exhausting day shooting blackcock. It was in the middle of July and the heat was terrible. 'I've got something to tell you: all our shot's finished.'

I jumped up from the bed.

'Our shot finished! How on earth? Why, we must have taken thirty pounds from home! A whole bagful.'

'Certainly; and a big bag, too: it ought to have been enough for two weeks. But who knows? Perhaps there was a slit in it; anyhow there isn't any shot... just about enough for ten charges.'

'Whatever are we going to do? The best places are ahead of us. They promised us six coveys for to-morrow.'

'Send me into Tula. It's no distance – only forty-five versts. I'll fly like the wind and bring back the shot – forty pounds of it, if you like.'

'But when will you go?'

'I'll go at once. Why waste time? Only there's one thing about it: we shall have to hire horses.'

'Hire horses! What are our own for?'

'We can't use our own. The shaft-horse is lame, dead lame.'

'Since when?'

'Since just lately – when the coachman took him to be shod. Well, they shod him. The smith must have been no good. Now he can't even walk on the hoof – the fore-hoof... So he carries it... like a dog.'

'Well, at least he's been unshod?'

'No, he hasn't, but he'll have to be unshod at once. The nail must have gone right into the flesh.'

369

I sent for the coachman. It appeared that Ermolai had spoken the truth: the shaft-horse was indeed lame in one hoof. I at once gave orders for him to be unshod and stood on wet clay.

'Well? Shall I hire horses and go to Tula?' insisted Ermolai again.

'But can you so much as find horses in this miserable hole?' I exclaimed, annoyed in spite of myself...

The village in which we found ourselves was solitary and out of the way; all its inhabitants seemed to be desperately poor; with difficulty we had found a single cabin that had no chimney, certainly, but was quite roomy.

'Yes,' answered Ermolai, imperturbable as ever. 'You're right about this village, but even here there lived a peasant – very clever... and rich! He had nine horses. He's dead now, and his eldest son manages it all. He's the stupidest man that ever lived, but he hasn't yet managed to run through his father's fortune. We'll get horses from him. If you wish it, I'll fetch him. He's got brothers – bright lads, so I've heard... but all the same he's the head of the family.'

'How is that?'

'Because he is the eldest! That means, the younger ones have got to knuckle under.' – Here Ermolai expressed himself forcibly and unprintably about younger brothers in general. – 'I'll fetch him. He's a simple chap. It won't be difficult to come to terms with him.'

While Ermolai went to fetch the 'simple chap', it occurred to me that it might be better for me to drive into Tula myself. In the first place, taught by experience, I knew I couldn't rely on Ermolai. I had once sent him into a town to make some purchases; he had promised to carry out all my commissions during a single day – and vanished for a whole week, spent all the money on drink, and returned on foot – having set out in a racing drozhky. Secondly, I had an acquaintance in Tula who was a horse-dealer; I could buy a horse from him to replace my lame shaft-horse.

That's decided, I thought. I'll drive in myself; I can sleep on the way, too – luckily my carriage is well-sprung.

'I've brought him!' exclaimed Ermolai a quarter of an hour later, bursting into the cabin. Behind him entered a sturdy peasant, in a white shirt, blue trousers, and shoes, fair-haired, short-sighted, with a little pointed red beard, a long, swollen nose and a wide-open mouth.

He certainly looked a 'simple chap'.

'Here, sir,' said Ermolai, 'he has got horses and it's all settled.'

'That is, that's to say, I . . .' began the peasant in a husky, stammering voice, shaking his sparse hair and fingering the band of the cap which he held in his hands. 'I, that's to say . . .'

'What's your name?' I asked.

The peasant looked down and seemed to reflect. 'What is my name?'

'Yes; what do they call you?'

'They call me Filofei.'

'Well, listen, Filofei, my friend; you have got horses, I hear. Bring three of them here; we'll harness them to my carriage – it's quite a light one – and then you drive me into Tula. There's a moon to-night, it's light, and it will be cool driving. What sort of road have you got here?'

'Road? the road's all right! It's twenty versts at most – to the highway. There's one place . . . a bit awkward, but all right.'

'What's the place that's awkward?'

'You have to cross a river by a ford.'

'So you're going into Tula yourself?' inquired Ermolai.

'Yes, I am.'

'Well!' said my faithful attendant, and shook his head. 'We-ell!' he repeated, spat and went out.

The drive to Tula evidently held no more attraction for him; in his eyes it had become an empty and uninteresting business.

'D'you know the way all right?' I said to Filofei.

'Of course I know the way! Only, I mean, of course, you're the master, but I can't . . . all of a sudden, like this.'

It turned out that Ermolai, in engaging Filofei, had declared that he need have no doubt of being paid, fool that he was ... and that was that! Fool though he was, according to Ermolai, Filofei was not satisfied merely with this declaration. He asked me for fifty roubles in notes – an enormous price. I offered him ten roubles – a low price. We started bargaining. Filofei at first was obstinate, then began to yield ground, though stubbornly. Coming in for a moment, Ermolai began to assure me 'that this fool' ('he must like the word!' observed Filofei under his breath;) 'this fool has no idea of the value of money' – which incidentally reminded me how, twenty years before, a tavern which my mother had established at a busy spot at the crossing of two high-roads had failed completely because the old serving-man, who had been installed there as host, really didn't know the value of money, but paid out by quantity; that is to say, he would change a silver twenty-five copeck piece for six brass pieces of five copecks each, swearing heartily the whole time.

'Oh, you, Filofei, you're a regular Filofei!' exclaimed Ermolai at length, and he went out and slammed the door with feeling.

Filofei answered nothing, as if recognizing that to be called Filofei was indeed not altogether felicitous and that such a name could even be used as a term of reproach, although the whole guilt for it lay with the priest, who had not been suitably remunerated before the christening.

Finally he and I agreed on twenty roubles. He went off for his horses and within an hour brought five of them for me to choose from. They turned out to be decent horses, although their manes and tails were tousled and their bellies were large and taut as drums. With Filofei came two of his brothers, who in no way resembled him. Small, black-eyed, sharp-nosed, they certainly made the impression of 'bright lads' – talked fast and much, 'bubbled', as Ermolai expressed it, but obeyed their elder.

They rolled the carriage out from the shelter, and busied themselves with it and with the horses for an hour and a half; one moment they would be slackening off the string traces, the next, they would be making them fast as hard as they knew how. The two brothers wanted badly to harness the roan horse, because 'he knew how to go downhill', but Filofei decided on the bay, so the bay it was that was harnessed to the shaft.

They piled the carriage up with hay and pushed under the seat the collar belonging to my lame shaft-horse – in case we had occasion to fit it on to a newly-bought horse in Tula. Filofei, who had found time to run home and return in a long white overall inherited from his father, a cone-shaped cake of a hat, and well-greased boots, solemnly mounted on to the box. I took my seat, and looked at the time: it was a quarter past ten. Ermolai didn't even say good-bye to me, he was busy beating his dog Valetka. Filofei twitched the reins, called out in a very faint voice: 'Hey, my tiny ones!' His brothers jumped back on both sides, gave the side-horses a flick under the stomach, the carriage moved off, turned through the gate into the road – the bay tried to dart home to his yard, but Filofei brought him to his senses with a few blows of the whip – and there we were driving out of the village and rolling on over a fairly good road between dense, unbroken hazel-thickets.

It was a glorious, still night, perfect for driving. Now the wind would be rustling in the bushes, swaying the branches, now it would die right away; here and there in the sky you could see motionless, silvery clouds; the moon stood high and lit up the countryside distinctly. I stretched out on the hay and was already dozing off . . . when I remembered the 'awkward place' and started up.

'Hey! Filofei, how far is it to the ford?'

'To the ford? Eight versts or so.'

Eight versts, I thought. We shan't be there in less than an hour. I can sleep until then.

'You know the way well, Filofei?' I asked again.

'Of course, I know the way. It isn't the first time . . .'

He said something more, but I didn't hear the rest . . . I was asleep.

*

I was awakened, not by my own intention to wake after exactly an hour, as is often the case, but by a strange though faint squelching and gurgling right under my ear. I raised my head . . .

What in the world was this? I was lying in my carriage as before, but around the carriage – and a foot away, no more, from its edge – was a watery expanse, moonlit, quivering, and breaking into tiny, precise ripples. I looked forward: on the box, head down, back bent, Filofei was sitting like a statue, and, farther forward still, above the bubbling water, was the curving line of the shaft-bow and the heads and backs of the horses. And everything so motionless, so soundless, as if in an enchanted kingdom, in a dream, a fairy dream . . . What in the world? I looked back over the hood of the carriage . . . Why, we were right in the middle of the river, thirty yards from the bank!

'Filofei!' I exclaimed.

'What?' he rejoined.

'What d'you mean, "what"? For goodness' sake, where *are* we?'

'In the river.'

'I can see we're in the river. And likely to drown at any moment. Is this the way to ford it? Eh? You're asleep, Filofei! Answer me!'

'I made a little bit of a mistake,' said my guide. 'You see, I took the wrong way, too much to one side, and now we've got to wait.'

'What d'you mean, we've got to wait? Wait for what?'

'Why, just to let the shaft-horse take a look round. The way he turns will be the way for us to go.'

I raised myself slightly in the hay. The head of the shaft-horse emerged motionless from the water. But it was possible to see, in the bright moonlight, that one of his ears was just moving – first forward, then back.

'But he's asleep, too, your shaft-horse!'

'No,' answered Filofei, 'he's now sniffing the water.'

And again all was still, except, as before, for the faint
gurgling of the water. I, too, sat still, as if petrified.

The moonlight, the night, the river, and we in it . . .

'What's that hissing noise?' I asked Filofei.

'That? Ducks in the rushes . . . or else snakes.'

Suddenly the shaft-horse's head began to turn from side to
side, his ears pricked, he whinnied and fidgeted. 'Ho-ho-ho-
ho-o!' came a sudden full-throated roar from Filofei, and he sat
up and waved his whip. The carriage at once began to move, it
lurched forward, across-stream, and moved on, jolting and
swaying. At first I thought that we were sinking, going to the
bottom, but, after two or three jolts and dives, the level of the
water seemed suddenly to drop . . . it dropped farther and
farther, the carriage emerged from it, the wheels and the
horses' tails were already visible – and then, throwing up
great, heavy splashes, which burst into sheaves of diamonds
– no – not diamonds – sapphires, in the even brilliance of the
moonlight, and pulling cheerfully together, the horses dragged
us out on to the sandy bank and struck off along a track which
led uphill, stepping out, as if to race each other, with their
glittering wet hooves.

What'll Filofei say now, I wondered: 'You see, I was
right!' or something like that? But he said nothing. So I on
my side didn't think it necessary to reproach him for his
carelessness and, lying down on the hay, tried to go to sleep
again.

But I could not go to sleep; not that I wasn't tired from
shooting – and not that the anxiety which I had felt had driven
away my sleep – but we were passing through a landscape of
great beauty. There were vast, spreading, grassy water-
meadows, with countless smaller meadows, lakelets, brooks,
creeks with banks overgrown with sallow and osier, real
Russian country, such as the Russian people love, the sort of
country into which the heroes of our ancient folk-lore rode out
to shoot white swans and grey duck. The rough track wound in
a yellowish ribbon, the horses went easily, and I couldn't close
my eyes – I was lost in admiration! And the whole scene floated

past so softly and smoothly under the friendly moon. Even Filofei was affected.

'We call these St. Egor's meadows,' he told me. 'And after them come the Grand Duke's meadows; such meadows as you won't find in the whole of Russia . . . They're really beautiful!' The shaft-horse snorted and shook himself . . . 'God bless you!' said Filofei sedately, under his breath. 'Really beautiful!' he repeated, and sighed, and then gave a prolonged grunt. 'It'll soon be mowing-time, and the amount of hay they'll get here – whew! And there are plenty of fish in the creeks. Wonderful bream!' he added in a sing-song voice. 'You just don't want to die, and that's the truth.'

Suddenly he raised his arm.

'Oh – look, just look! Above that lake, is that a heron standing? Can he really be fishing, at night-time, too? Oh, no! it's a stake – not a heron. I was wrong! The moon's always playing tricks!'

So we drove on and on . . . But at last even the meadows came to an end, and woods and ploughed fields appeared. Away to one side was a hamlet with two or three winking lights . . . we were not more than five versts from the high-road. I went to sleep.

Again something woke me. This time it was Filofei's voice.

'Master . . . hey, master!'

I sat up. The carriage was standing on a smooth patch right in the middle of the high-road; looking at me from the box with wide-open eyes (in fact I was amazed, I had no idea that his eyes were so big) Filofei was whispering significantly and mysteriously.

'The knocking! . . . The knocking!'

'What d'you say? . . .'

'I say: the knocking! Just bend down and listen. D'you hear it?'

I put my head out of the carriage and held my breath. Indeed, from somewhere far, far away behind us, I heard a faint, staccato knocking, as if from rolling wheels.

'D'you hear it?' repeated Filofei.

'Well, yes,' I answered. 'There's some sort of carriage coming.'

'But don't you hear it . . . eh? *There* . . . bells, and whistling, too . . . d'you hear it? Take off your cap . . . you'll be able to hear better.'

I didn't take off my cap, but strained my ears. 'Well, perhaps . . . But what of it?'

Filofei turned to face the horses.

'It's a cart coming . . . travelling light, wrought-iron wheels,' he said, and picked up the reins. 'It's bad men coming, master; just here, by Tula, they're up to all sorts of tricks.'

'What nonsense! Why d'you suppose that it must be bad men?'

'I'm sure of it. With bells . . . and in an empty cart . . . Who else could it be?'

'By the way – are we far from Tula?'

'About fifteen versts still, and there is not so much as a house hereabouts.'

'Well, go faster then, there's no point in hanging about like this.'

Filofei waved his whip and the carriage moved on again.

Although I didn't believe Filofei, nevertheless I could no longer go to sleep. Supposing what he said were true! An unpleasant feeling stirred within me. I sat up in the carriage – until then I had been lying down – and began to look out. While I had been asleep, a fine mist had gathered – not on the ground, but in the sky. It stood high up, and inside it the moon hung in a yellowish patch, as if seen through smoke. The whole scene had grown dim and confused, although it was clearer near the ground. Around us lay a flat and cheerless landscape. Fields, more fields, small bushes, ravines – and still more fields, most of them fallow, under a sparse growth of weeds. Deserted . . . dead! Not so much as the cry of a quail.

We drove on for about half an hour. Now and again Filofei waved his whip and clucked with his lips, but neither of us spoke a word. We came out on to a small hill . . . Filofei halted the horses, and said at once:

'The knocking ... The *knocking*, master!'

I leant out of the carriage again; but I could have remained under the shelter of the hood, so clearly, though still far off, could I hear the knocking of iron wheels, the sound of people whistling, the jingling of bells and even the clopping of horses' hooves; even, I thought, the sound of singing and laughter. True, the wind was blowing from that quarter, but there could be no doubt that the unknown travellers had gained on us by a whole verst – perhaps even by two.

Filofei and I exchanged glances. He merely moved his hat from the back of his head on to his forehead, and at once bent over the reins and began whipping up the horses. They set off at a gallop, but could not keep it up for long and fell into a trot. Filofei kept whipping them up. We had to get away!

I could not explain to myself why, when I'd not shared Filofei's suspicions to start with, I had now suddenly become convinced that they were indeed bad men who were on our tracks. I had heard nothing new: the same bells, the same knocking of a cart travelling light, the same whistling, the same vague hubbub. But I no longer had any doubt. Filofei could not be mistaken!

So another twenty minutes went by. During the last of these twenty minutes, above the rattling and rumbling of our own carriage, we could already hear another rattling and rumbling ...

'Stop, Filofei,' I said. 'It doesn't matter – it'll all be the same in the end!'

Filofei clucked apprehensively. The horses stopped, as if delighted at the chance of a rest.

Good heavens! The bells were simply thundering right behind us, the cart was rumbling and jolting, men were whistling and singing, horses were snorting and beating the ground with their hooves ...

They had caught us!

'Oh *dear*,' said Filofei deliberately under his breath, and he clucked irresolutely and began to urge the horses on. But, simultaneously, something suddenly tore up out of the darkness, there was a roaring and a rushing – and an enormous ramshackle cart, harnessed to three lean horses, whirled past us obliquely, galloped ahead and at once fell into a walk, blocking the way.

'A regular cut-throat's trick,' whispered Filofei.

I confess that my heart contracted . . . I stared ahead intently – into the dim mist-veiled moonlight. Sitting or lying in the cart in front of us were half a dozen men in blouses and unbuttoned coats; two of them were capless; their long-booted legs swung and dangled over the edge, their arms rose and fell aimlessly . . . their bodies jolted . . . it was as clear as daylight: they were all drunk. Some were roaring out anything that came into their heads; one was whistling very piercingly and accurately; another was swearing; a giant in a sheepskin jacket was sitting driving on the box. They drove at a walk, as if taking no notice of us.

What could we do? We drove after them, also at a walk . . . willy-nilly.

We went on in this way for about a quarter of a verst. Agonizing apprehension! Salvation, self-defence . . . what a hope! There were six of them and I had not so much as a stick! Turn round the other way? They would catch us at once. I remembered Zhukovsky's line from the passage where he tells of the murder of Field-Marshal Kamensky:

The assassin's axe abhorred . . .

Or, if not that – strangling with a muddy cord . . . and into the ditch . . . croak there, and struggle like a hare in a trap . . .

Oh, it was a black look-out indeed!

The others kept on at a walk and took no notice of us.

'Filofei,' I whispered, 'just try pulling out to the right, as if to go past them.'

Filofei tried and pulled out to the right . . . but they at once pulled out to the right, too . . . it was impossible to get past.

Filofei tried again: he pulled out to the left . . . but they wouldn't let him pass the cart on that side either. What was more, they began to laugh . . . It was clear that they were not going to let us pass.

'Regular cut-throats,' Filofei whispered to me over his shoulder.

'But what are they waiting for?' I asked, also in a whisper.

'Ahead of us – in a hollow – over a stream, there's a bridge... That's where they'll get us! That's always their way... at bridges. Our business is settled, master,' he added with a sigh. 'They aren't likely to let us go alive; so the great thing for them is that no one shall be any the wiser. There's one thing I'm sorry about, master: my three little horses will go – and my brothers won't get them.'

I might have been surprised that at such a moment Filofei should still be able to worry about his horses, but I confess I had no time for such thoughts myself... Will they really kill us? I repeated to myself. What for? Why, I'll give them everything I've got.

But meanwhile the bridge drew nearer and nearer and we could see it more and more clearly.

Suddenly there came a shrill whoop and the horses ahead of us seemed to whirl into the air, dashed away, and, galloping up to the bridge, halted all of a sudden, as if nailed to the spot, a little to one side of the road. My heart fairly sank within me.

'Oh, Filofei, my friend,' I said, 'we're going to our death. Forgive me for having brought this on you.'

'But it isn't your fault, master! There's no escaping your own fate! Well, shaft-horse, my faithful one,' said Filofei, 'go on, boy! Do me your last service! It's all the same thing in the end... God bless us all!'

And he put his horses into a trot.

We began to approach the bridge and the cart, which stood there motionless and threatening... In it, all was still, as if from set purpose. Not a sound! It was the silence of the pike, of the hawk, of every creature of prey, when its victim approaches. So we drew level with the cart. Suddenly the giant in the sheepskin jacket jumped down from it and came straight at us.

He said nothing to Filofei, but Filofei of his own accord at once pulled on the reins and the carriage halted. The giant put both his hands on the doors and, bowing his shaggy head forward and grinning, pronounced, in a quiet even voice, with a mechanic's accent, the following words:

'Honoured sir, we are coming from a party, everything fair and above board, a wedding; we've married off our boy; we've put him to bed, good and proper; our lads are all young and hot-headed – they've had plenty to drink and they've nothing to sober down with; so would you be good enough to give us just a very little money, so that we could get a pint to toast our brother? We'd drink your health, we'd call upon your honour's name; won't you be so good? ... and please don't be angry with me!'

What could this be? ... I thought ... A game? ... A practical joke?

The giant stood there with his head bowed. That moment the moon came out of the mist and lit up his face. It was grinning, this face – grinning with its eyes and with its lips. There was no threat to be seen in it, but it was full of a certain alertness ... and such white teeth, and such big ones, too ...

'With pleasure ... take this,' I said hurriedly, and getting my purse out of my pocket I pulled out two silver roubles from it – it was the time when silver coins were still current in Russia. 'Here, if this is enough.'

'Most grateful!' barked the giant, military-fashion, and his thick fingers snatched from me in a flash, not my whole purse, but just the two roubles. 'Most grateful!' He shook his locks and ran back to the cart.

'Lads!' he cried. 'The gentleman-traveller has given us two roubles!' They all burst out laughing together ... The giant tumbled up on to the box ...

'Good-bye and good luck!'

And that was all we saw of them! The horses darted off, the cart rumbled up the hill, it showed for a flash against the dark line dividing earth from heaven, sank beyond and disappeared.

And soon we couldn't even hear the knocking, the shouting, the bells ...

Dead silence fell.

*

It was some while before Filofei and I recovered ourselves.

'You joker, you!' he said at length – took off his hat, and began crossing himself. 'A proper joker,' he added, and turned to me with a happy face. 'He must be a good man – he must. Go on, my little ones! Get a move on! Your skins are saved! All our skins are saved! D'you remember how he wouldn't let us pass? He was the one that was driving. A regular joker, that lad! Go on! and God bless you!'

I said nothing, but I felt good inside. Our skins are saved, I repeated to myself, and lay down on the hay. We had got off cheap!

I was even slightly ashamed of having remembered that line of Zhukovsky's.

Suddenly a thought occurred to me:

'Filofei!'

'What?'

'Are you married?'

'Yes.'

'With children?'

'Yes.'

'Why didn't you think about them? You were sorry about the horses – but what about your wife and your children?'

'But why be sorry about them? They would not have fallen into the hands of thieves. But I had them in mind the whole time . . . and so I have now . . . and that's the truth.' Filofei paused. 'Perhaps . . . it was on their account that the Lord God spared you and me.'

'But supposing they weren't cut-throats?'

'How can you tell? Can you get inside someone else's soul? Other people's souls – it's a well-known thing – are just so much darkness. But it's always better, with God's help . . . No . . . as for my family, I always . . . Go on, my little ones, God bless you!'

It was almost light when we started to enter Tula. I was lying, half-asleep and oblivious . . .

'Master,' Filofei said to me suddenly, 'just look; there, standing in front of the pot-house, that's their cart.'

I raised my head . . . so it was; their cart and their horses. On the threshold of the drinking establishment there suddenly appeared my friend the giant in the sheepskin jacket.

'Master,' he exclaimed, waving his cap, 'we're having a drink at your expense! Well, coachman,' he added, with a wave of the head at Filofei, 'you *were* scared, weren't you?'

'A very funny fellow,' observed Filofei, when we had driven fifty yards past the pot-house.

And so at last we were in Tula; I bought some shot and incidentally some tea and vodka – and I also got a horse from a dealer. At noon we set off on the return journey. As we passed the spot where we had for the first time heard the cart knocking along behind us, Filofei, who had had a drop in Tula, and turned out a very talkative fellow – he had even been telling me stories – suddenly burst out laughing.

'D'you remember, master, how I kept on saying to you: "The knocking . . . the knocking," I said, "the knocking!"'

He moved his arm several times in a back-handed gesture. By now this expression struck him as very amusing.

The same evening we returned to his home village.

I informed Ermolai of the incident that had befallen us. Being sober, he expressed no sympathy – simply sniffed, approvingly or censoriously – I dare say he didn't himself know which. But two days later he informed me with pleasure that, the very same night on which Filofei and I had driven into Tula, and on the very same road, a merchant had been robbed and murdered. At first I refused to believe this story: but afterwards I had to believe it; its truth was confirmed to me by a police inspector who arrived post-haste to investigate. Was this not the 'wedding' from which our hot-heads were returning, and was this not the 'lad' whom they, to quote the giant-joker, had put to bed? I stayed five days more in Filofei's village. Whenever I met him I would say to him: 'The knocking? Eh?'

'A funny fellow,' he would answer every time, and burst out laughing.

Forest and Steppe

THE reader is perhaps already weary of my notes. I hasten to reassure him with the promise that I will limit myself to the fragments already printed; but, in taking my leave of him, I cannot refrain from saying a word about the pleasures of shooting.

Shooting with gun and dog is a joy in its own right, '*für sich*', as our fathers used to say ... but let's suppose that you are not a born hunter; all the same, you're a lover of nature and freedom; and you cannot therefore help envying the rest of us. Listen to me ...

Do you know, for example, the delight of starting out in spring, before dawn? You walk out on to the porch ... Away in the dark-blue sky the stars are twinkling; from time to time a moist breeze blows gently past: you can hear the discreet, confused murmuring of the night; a faint rustle comes from trees deep in the shadow. Your men are already spreading out the rug in the cart; under your seat they put the case which holds the samovar. The horses shiver, snort and take small prancing steps; a couple of white geese that have just woken up pass silently and slowly across the road. Behind the fence, in the garden, the nightwatchman is snoring peacefully; every sound seems to stand in the cool stillness of the air – to stand, and go no farther. You take your place; the horses set off together, and the cart rattles behind noisily ... Away you go – past the church, down the hill to the right, across the dam ... The mist is just beginning to rise from the pond, you feel the chill, you hide your face in the collar of your coat; you begin to nod. The horses splash their way noisily through the puddles; the coachman whistles softly. By now you have covered about four versts ... Near the horizon the sky is growing scarlet; in the birches, jackdaws are waking up and flapping about awkwardly; sparrows are chirruping round the dark ricks. The air grows lighter, the road begins to glimmer and the sky to clear; the clouds are tinged with white, the fields with green. In the cottages there is a red blaze of firewood, and sleepy voices come from inside the gates. By now the dawn has begun to blaze; the sky is striped with bands of gold; mists curl in the valleys; larks sing noisily, the dawn breeze blows – and the blood-red sun swims quietly up. Light fairly streams forth; the heart starts up inside you like a bird. Freshness, laughter, beauty! The eye ranges for far around. Away there behind the trees is a village; there in the distance is another, with a white church; over there is a birch-wood on a hill; behind it is the marsh for which you are bound . . . Step out, horses, step out! Forward at a fast trot! . . . Only three versts more. The sun is rising quickly into a clear sky . . . It will be a glorious day. A herd of cattle comes winding out of the village towards you. You have reached the top of the hill . . . What a view! The river winds for about ten versts, dimly blue through the mist; behind it, water-green meadows; behind the meadows, sloping hills; in the distance, lapwings are wheeling and calling over the marsh; through the brilliance of the moisture transfusing the air, the distance stands out sharply . . . how different from the summer! How freely you breathe, how briskly you move, what strength courses through all your being, lapped in the fresh breath of spring! . . .

Or take a summer morning – a morning in July. Who but a sportsman knows the joy of wandering through the brakes at sunrise? Your footprints make a green trail across the dew-whitened grass. You part the dripping bushes, and are all but drenched with the concentrated warmth and fragrance of the night; the air is heady with the sharp freshness of wormwood, the honey-sweetness of buckwheat and clover. In the distance an oak-wood stands up like a wall and flashes and blushes in the sun; it is still cool, but you can already feel the sultriness to come. Your head is dizzy and languid, surfeited with scents. The brushwood stretches endlessly away . . . Here and there in the distance is the yellow glow of rye that is almost ready for the harvest; here and there, narrow strips of reddening buckwheat. Then you hear the creaking of a cart; the peasant driver is threading his way forward at a walk; then he stops, and leaves his horse in the shade, before the heat becomes too great; you exchange greetings and pass by. From behind you comes the ringing chime of a scythe. The sun mounts higher and higher. The grass dries quickly. By now it is already hot. An hour passes, then a second one ... The sky grows darker about the horizon; the motionless air exhales a tingling sultriness. 'Where can I get a drink hereabouts, my friend?' you ask a mower. 'There's a well down there in the valley.' Through dense hazel-bushes, tangled with clinging grass, you drop down to the bed of the valley. Sure enough, at the very foot of the slope, there's a hidden spring; an oak-thicket has thirstily spread its splay-fingered boughs above the water; big, silvery bubbles rise, swaying, from the bottom, which is covered with a fine velvety moss. You throw yourself to the ground, you drink your fill, but now you feel too lazy to move. You are in the shade, breathing an air redolent with dampness; you have a sense of perfect well-being – but opposite you the bushes in the sunlight begin to glow an incandescent yellow. What is happening? All of a sudden a wind gets up and blows past you; the air shivers round about; can it be thunder? You come out of the valley ... What is that leaden streak on the skyline? Is the heat growing thicker? Are the clouds piling up? ... Lightning flickers faintly ... Yes, here is the storm! All around, the sun is still shining brightly: it is still possible to shoot. But the cloud is growing. Its forward edge spreads out like a sleeve and forms into a vault above us. Grass, bushes – everything around suddenly darkens ...Hurry! Over there you spy a hay-shed ... hurry! You run to it and take shelter ... what a downpour! What lightning! From somewhere in the straw roof water begins to drip through on to the sweet-smelling hay ... But here once more is the play of sunlight. The storm has passed; you go out again. Heavens above! How gaily it sparkles all around, how fresh and liquid the air, how strong the scent of strawberry and mushroom! ...

But now evening is coming on. The glow of sunset blazes up and suffuses half the sky. The sun is sinking. Near at hand, the air has a special transparent quality, as if made of glass, and the distance is mantled in soft, warm-looking mist. With the falling dew, a crimson splendour drops on forest glades which, a moment before, were drenched in floods of liquid gold; from trees, from bushes and tall haystacks, long shadows run out... The sun has set. A star lights up and trembles in the fiery sea of sunset... Now the fiery sea turns pale; the sky takes on a deeper blue; separate shadows are extinguished and the air is saturated with mist. It is time to go home, to the village, to the cabin where you are spending the night. Throwing your gun over your shoulder, you step out briskly, weary though you are... Meanwhile night comes on; you cannot see twenty paces in front of you; the dogs are white shapes, hardly visible in the darkness. Over there, above those black bushes, there is a dim radiance on the skyline... What is it? A fire?... no, it is the moon rising. But down on the right the village lights are already twinkling... Here, at last, is your cabin. Through the window you see a table spread with a white cloth, a candle burning, and supper laid...

Or else you have the racing drozhky harnessed and drive away to the forest after hazel-hen. It is exhilarating to thread your way along the narrow track, between two walls of tall rye. The rye-ears beat softly in your face, cornflowers cling to your ankles, quails call on all sides, the horse trots lazily on. Here is the forest. Shadow and silence. Stately poplars whisper high above your head; the long, hanging birch-branches hardly stir; the powerful oak stands warrior-like beside the graceful lime. You drive along a green track, chequered with shadow; big yellow flies hover motionless in the golden air and suddenly dart away; a swarm of midges forms a pillar, light in the shadow, dark in the sun; birds sing quietly. The small golden voice of the robin rings out in its innocent, prattling joy: it matches the scent of the lilies of the valley. Farther, farther, ever deeper into the forest... The forest runs wild... An ineffable stillness descends on you; everything around is so drowsy and so still. But soon a breeze passes, and the tree-tops sigh, with the sound of breaking waves. Through the brown mould of last year's leaves, tall grasses grow here and there; mushrooms stand aloof under their little hats. Suddenly a white hare starts up, and with a loud bark the dog dashes after it . . .

And how delicious the same forest is in late autumn, when woodcock are on the wing! They do not lurk in the innermost recesses: you must seek them along the forest skirts. There is no wind, no sun, no light or shade, no movement, no sound; the soft air is drenched with the smell of autumn, redolent as the smell of wine; a fine mist hangs in the distance over the yellow fields. Through the bare brown limbs of the trees you see the mild featureless pallor of the sky; here and there the last golden leaves are still hanging on the lime-trees. The damp earth is springy underfoot; the tall withered blades of grass never stir; long threads glitter on the faded turf. You breathe in peace with every breath, yet a strange unrest comes upon the spirit. You walk along the forest edge, you watch your dog, but all the time images and faces of the beloved, dead or alive, keep coming to mind; impressions that have slumbered for years suddenly spring to life; the imagination hovers and darts hither and thither like a bird, and all the memories it evokes move and stand so vividly before your eyes. At times the heart trembles, beats loudly, and yearns forward passionately; at times it plunges into a world of memory beyond recall. All your life unwinds as smoothly and swiftly as a scroll; all your past, all your emotions, all your faculties, all your soul, are yours to command. There is nothing around to disturb you – no sun, no wind, no sound . . .

Or take the autumn day that is clear and chilly, after a frosty morning, when the birch, all golden like a tree in a fairy-story, stands out delicately against the pale-blue sky; when the low sun has no more warmth in it, but shines out clearer than in summer; when the small poplar-wood sparkles from end to end, as if the trees found relief and exhilaration in standing naked; when there is still the whiteness of hoar-frost in the bottom of the valleys and a cool breeze is stirring faintly and blowing the fallen crumpled leaves; when on the river the blue waves rush joyfully past, gently rocking the geese and duck that float dreamily on them. From the distance comes the hammer of a water-mill, half-hidden among the willows, and above it pigeons wheel swiftly, their colours shifting and changing in the brilliant air...

Delicious too, although not loved by sportsmen, are the misty days of summer. On such days shooting is impossible: the bird that flies up from underfoot vanishes at once in the whitish cloud of stationary mist. But how still, how inexpressibly still a world it is! Everything is awake and silent. You pass a tree – it does not stir: it is just standing at its ease. Through the fine vapour, which is evenly diffused in the air, a long dark stripe looms up before you. You take it for a nearby wood; you approach – and the wood turns into a high ridge of wormwood on a boundary fence. Above you and all round – everywhere there is mist... But now a breeze stirs lightly – a patch of pale-blue sky shows up faintly through the thinning vapour, which seems turned into smoke. Suddenly a golden-yellow ray breaks through, floods down in a long beam, strikes on fields, fixes on a wood – and then the whole scene clouds over again. For a long time this struggle continues; but how unspeakably bright and magnificent is the day, when the light finally triumphs, and the last waves of sun-warmed mist roll down and spread out, flat as linen, or else coil up and vanish in the blue and tender radiance of the heaven...

Or perhaps you have decided to visit an outlying field in the steppes. For about ten versts you have threaded your way along by-roads – and here, at last, is the highway. Past unending processions of country carts, past little inns, each with its wide-open gates and its well and its samovar hissing under the lean-to roof – from one village to another, over limitless fields, past lines of green hemp-bushes, far, far away you drive. Magpies flutter from one willow to the next. Peasant-women with long rakes in their hands plod towards the fields; a man in a threadbare nankeen coat, with a satchel of birch-bark slung over his shoulder, trudges wearily by; a landowner's heavy travelling-coach, drawn by six stalwart, well-broken horses, rolls towards you. Out of the window sticks the corner of a pillow, and behind, holding on by a cord to his perch athwart the foot-board, on a mat-bag, sits a footman in a great-coat, spattered to the eyebrows with mud. Here is the local market-town, with its crooked little houses, its endless fences, its stone mansions untenanted by their merchant owners, its ancient bridge spanning the deep river-bed. On, on!... The steppe-country is approaching. You look round from the hill-top – and what a view meets your eyes! Round, low hills, ploughed and sown to the summit, roll away in sweeping waves; valleys choked with bushes wind between them. Oblong islands of woodland are scattered here and there. Narrow tracks run from village to village; churches gleam whitely; a stream sparkles among willow-bushes, its course broken in four places by dams; a file of bustard stands out far away in the fields; a little old manor house, surrounded by its outbuildings, its orchard and threshing-floor, nestles beside a small pond. Farther and ever farther you drive. The hills grow smaller and smaller – there is hardly a tree in sight. And here, at last, is the interminable, frontierless steppe!

Or on a winter's day, to go out hare-shooting through the deep snowdrifts, to inhale the sharp, frosty air, to screw your eyes unwittingly against the fine, dazzling glare from the soft snow, to revel in the green tinge of the sky above the reddish branches of the forest!...

Or the first days of spring, the glittering, melting time, when through the dense steam that rises from the thawing snow there begins to steal the smell of warm soil; when, on the thawed patches of earth, under the slanting rays of the sun, the larks sing confidently, and with a cheerful, bustling roar the flood-waters roll from gully to gully...

But now it is time to stop. It is fitting that I should have been speaking of spring; in spring, partings are easy – in spring, even the happy feel drawn far away... Reader, farewell! I wish you eternal good-fortune.

ABOUT THE TRANSLATORS

SIR CHARLES HEPBURN JOHNSTON (b. 1912) was a writer and poet as well as a translator. His rendering of Pushkin's *Eugene Onegin* in English verse won him much acclaim, and the translation he made with his wife, formerly Princess Natasha Bagration, of *A Sportsman's Notebook* in 1948 is still widely considered to be the best. He also had a distinguished career as a diplomat, serving as British High Commissioner in Australia from 1965 to 1971. He died in 1986, Natasha in 1984.

ABOUT THE INTRODUCER

MAX EGREMONT is a novelist, biographer and critic. His books include lives of Arthur Balfour and George Wyndham, and his most recent novels are *Painted Lives* and *Second Spring*.

This book is set in EHRHARDT. The precise origin
of the typeface is unclear. Most of the founts were
probably cut by the Hungarian punch-cutter
Nicholas Kis for the Ehrhardt foundry
in Leipzig, where they were left
for sale in 1689. In 1938 the
Monotype foundry pro-
duced the modern
version.